SOUTH-WESTERN
USING VISUAL BASIC®

SECOND EDITION

Michael Spraque

Computer Science and
Programming Instructor

JOIN US ON THE INTERNET
WWW: http://www.thomson.com
EMAIL: findit@kiosk.thomson.com

A service of I(T)P®

South-Western Educational Publishing

an International Thomson Publishing company I(T)P®

Cincinnati • Albany, NY • Belmont, CA • Bonn • Boston
Detroit • Johannesburg • London • Madrid • Melbourne
Mexico City • New York • Paris • Singapore • Tokyo
Toronto • Washington

Managing Editor:	Janie F. Schwark
Developmental Editor:	Angela C. McDonald
Marketing Manager:	John Wills
Cover Designer:	Elaine St. John-Lagenaur
Cover Photographer:	William McElligot, Ottowa, Canada
Text Design & Composition:	Greene Design
Development and Production Services:	Jennings & Keefe

Copyright © 1998
by South-Western Educational Publishing
Cincinnati, Ohio

5 6 7 8 9 10 VH 05 04 03 02 01 00 99 98
Printed in the United States of America

International Thomson Publishing
South-Western Educational Publishing is an ITP Company. The ITP trademark is used under license.

Library of Congress Cataloging-in-Publication Data
Sprague, Michael W., 1954-
    Using Visual Basic / Michael W. Sprague.—2nd ed.
      p. cm.
    Includes Index.
    ISBN 0-538-67886-0
    1. Microsoft Visual BASIC. 2. BASIC (Computer program language)
    I. Title.
    QA76. 73.B3S75   1997
    005.26'8--dc21   96-40490
                                             CIP

Table of Contents

Preface

BASIC (Beginner's All-purpose Symbolic Instruction Code) has a long history as a popular programming language for computer novices, but has suffered from the perception that it isn't suitable for teaching or professional programming. Visual Basic has changed all that. Because of the way it combines a well-known and easily understood syntax with a visual interface and event-driven environment, Visual Basic has become a popular language among both professional programmers and teachers.

Using Visual Basic brings this exciting language to the classroom with an approach that focuses on practical applications over dry programming theory. It addresses Visual Basic programming from the standpoint of the advanced high school or junior college curriculum. The ease with which professional-looking applications are written will impress teachers and excite their students.

Using Visual Basic is divided into fifteen chapters, presented in a sequence and at a pace that makes sense for a beginning programmer. Each chapter uses sample programs to teach the syntax and structure of Visual Basic. Many sections contain a focus program with explanatory text. The student uses the text to work through the focus program. Each focus program covers a new topic, and many are programs students can use in their course work. In addition, focus programs manipulate database information through Visual Basic's ability to interact with other Microsoft applications, including Access and Excel.

Sidebars with additional information, demonstration programs or discussions of programming techniques and syntax are also included. Each chapter concludes with programming problems drawn from the content of high school courses.

A Hands-On Approach

The core of this book's structure is its hands-on approach to teaching programming concepts. The text guides students step-by-step through each sample program. As they build forms and write code, students are given the thought process used to produce each program, to help them learn to think through the development of their own programs. A complete description and explanation of each section of code is included to help the students understand what they're doing.

The benefit of this hands-on approach is that new concepts are reinforced by their context. *Using Visual Basic* introduces new Visual Basic controls just in time for the student to use them in a program. The text explains each new control as it is used, with a complete description of how to use it.

The process comes to fruition when students are asked to write their own programs at the end of each chapter. Each technique needed to solve the problems has already been used by the student while working through the sample programs. For many, the real learning comes when they apply their knowledge to these problems.

Features of the Text

◉ The learning goals are clearly stated at the beginning of each chapter.

◉ Each chapter's overview discusses the topics covered and why they are important.

◉ Each section guides the student through the step-by-step hands-on process of entering, debugging and running a sample program. Each element of the program is explained as it is entered.

◉ Each chapter concludes with a comprehensive summary covering the topics discussed in the chapter.

◉ Questions at the end of each section not only test recall and ask students to analyze material presented, many questions call for the student to modify or enhance the sample program.

◉ Programming problems at the end of the chapter reinforce the concepts presented. The problems are interesting to students and cover a number of topics connected to high school course work or to practical application areas like home finance and management.

◉ Topics are introduced and used immediately in programs.

◉ Highlighted text boxes provide useful additional information about important points in the text and supplement the text about related topics of interest.

◉ Introductions to Windows 3.1 and 95 are included to help students master the Windows environment.

◉ Important data structures and algorithms relating to the Advanced Placement course, such as searching, sorting, and the stack, are covered. This makes the book a good conceptual introduction to the AP course.

◉ Programming in WordBasic and Visual Basic for Applications is covered, allowing students to write applications in Microsoft Office.

◉ Most sections are designed to be used in a lab setting. The material is paced so that one section fills a lab period.

◉ The disk accompanying the book has data files necessary to complete sample programs, as well as the complete code and form definitions for each program.

An Effective Teaching Tool

As a computer science teacher at the high school level for more than ten years, I have taught PDP 11 assembler, BASIC, FORTRAN, Forth, and Pascal. Never have I taught a language that students could do as much with in so short a time. Students love to write programs in Visual Basic. Even when working through a sample program in the text, there is a lot of room for creativity and individualizing programs.

Visual Basic is just plain fun to program. Students who catch on quickly often enhance sample programs far beyond their original form and function. While the book adheres to accepted standards concerning user interface, naming variables and programming techniques, thus providing a good example for students to follow, students are encouraged to find ways to make their programs uniquely their own. Placement and shapes of controls, colors, properties of fonts used, and background images can all be used to individualize a program.

This book's content has been extensively tested in the classroom. Each time students have gone above and beyond the course content, creating programs that meet their special needs. Visual Basic's help system has enabled many students to add features to their programs that quickly engage the interest of others. That interest leads to more students learning more about the language.

Real-World Programming

Another advantage of Visual Basic to students is its ever-increasing professional popularity. Business and industry have adopted Visual Basic as an easy-to-use alternative to C++. Its ability to create Windows applications with such ease and speed has made it a natural for the work environment.

Visual Basic's wide acceptance in the work world means students will be learning a language they will actually use on the job. Whether writing a quick application or interacting with other Windows applications, programmers are making Visual Basic the most popular new language for developing new business programs.

Supplements

Using Visual Basic forms the centerpiece of an integrated system of instruction. The supplements available for this text provide both teachers and students with valuable additional resources for teaching and learning:

- The Teacher's Guide provides teaching tips, class activities, and key words for each chapter; answers to the questions, exercises, and problems in the text and the Study Guide; supplementary lessons in QBasic; and blackline transparency masters.

- The Study Guide includes additional practice exercises and activities to reinforce Visual Basic concepts from the text.

- The Template Disk includes code and form definitions as well as data files for the sample programs developed in the text.

- The Testing Disk includes an electronic test bank containing an extensive database of questions and problems for composing tests and quizzes.

Acknowledgments

If you've ever watched the credits roll by at the end of a movie, you've probably been surprised at just how many people were involved in the project from beginning to end. The production of a textbook is no different.

Thanks must first go to Janie Schwark and Angela McDonald of South-Western, who had the editorial vision to support this project. There would be no book at all if John Thompson and Matt Lusher of Jennings and Keefe had not given an untried author a chance. The developmental editors, Elizabeth Collins and Janet Andrews, and the technical editor, Brian O'Neill, have had a tremendous impact on the finished product. In many ways what you have before you is a joint project of myself, Matt, Elizabeth, and Brian. Thanks for your hard work.

My wife, Bonnie, and children, Joel, Briana, and Erin, were constant sources of encouragement. Thanks for the family time you sacrificed to give me time to work.

Thanks to my computer science students at Libertyville High School, who worked through a great deal of the material. Their comments and corrections helped the work evolve into this final product.

Thanks to the reviewers who gave valuable advice early in the project: Elizabeth Chaskin, Northside Independent School District and San Antonio College, San Antonio, Texas; Lee Reiswig, Nathan Hale High School, Seattle, Washington; Marcie Murphy, Jeb Stuart High School, Falls Church, Virginia; and Paul Davis, Santa Rosa Junior College, Santa Rosa, California.

The production staff at Jennings and Keefe have done a wonderful job producing illustrations and designing an attractive and readable text.

Thanks to Microsoft for writing the most exciting and fun computer language ever.

Finally, thanks to my family and friends, without whose encouragement and prayers, this book would never have been written.

1101

1101 D9

INC

1001

X = X +

x = x1 + 1

D9

Computers, Programming, and Windows

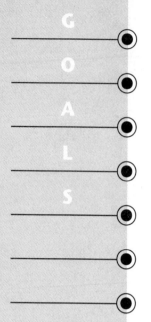

After working through this chapter, you will:

Understand how you can use Visual Basic to solve a wide range of problems.

Be able to identify the hardware components that make up a desktop computer.

Learn how the computer loads and runs programs.

Be able to explain how programming has changed since the 1950s.

Understand the difference between procedural and event-driven programming.

Use Windows commands and applications to manipulate text and files.

O V E R V I E W

You will find Visual Basic to be an excellent tool for solving a variety of problems, such as organizing your CD collection or estimating the number of tadpoles in a pond. You can also use Visual Basic to play with graphics. For example, you could draw a picture freehand, then use Visual Basic to change the color of the drawing from red to green every 60 seconds.

This chapter provides some of the background you may need to review in order to explore Visual Basic. An introduction is provided to computer hardware, and the components of a computer are defined. You will also learn how a computer runs programs by storing, loading, and executing files.

With Visual Basic, you are a programmer. You will create programs that you or your friends can run. This task of programming is much easier with Visual Basic than it used to be. Even one or two decades ago, programmers had to write much more code to run a program than you do now. This chapter describes some of these changes in programming methods and languages.

The programs you will create with Visual Basic are computer files. Before you create a program, you need to know how to create, save, and delete files using Windows. This chapter covers these procedures, as well as how to organize files into directories. Finally, you will have the opportunity to become comfortable with the Windows Program Manager, File Manager, and Notepad.

Visual Basic as a Tool

Professional programmers use Visual Basic every day to meet a range of needs in business, industry, and science. You will use Visual Basic to perform the same kinds of tasks that these programmers tackle. For example, you can use this tool as a simple text editor, as shown in Figure 1-1. The vertical bar at the end of the passage shows that the text can be edited.

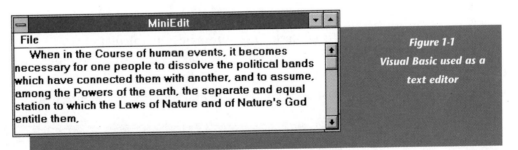

Figure 1-1
Visual Basic used as a
text editor

You can also write programs that read and write files. The program shown in Figure 1-2 reads two files: the first contains a class list; the second, a list of athletes. Both lists are displayed along with a list of students who are both in the class and athletes.

Yet another way to use Visual Basic is to solve mathematical problems. The program shown in Figure 1-3 uses the coordinates of two

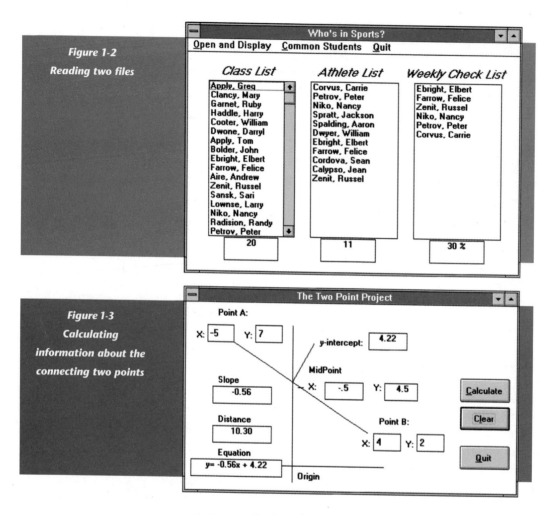

Figure 1-2

Reading two files

Figure 1-3

Calculating information about the connecting two points

points to calculate information about the line connecting the points. Visual Basic fully automates the calculations.

You can write programs for drawing graphics. You can set up this kind of program so that the user can draw freehand or create standard shapes, such as circles and squares. See Figure 1-4.

Figure 1-4

Writing a graphics program

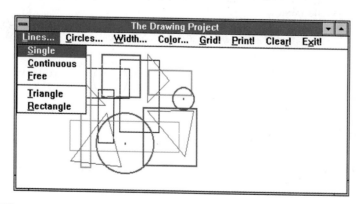

With Visual Basic, you can take advantage of tried-and-true programs such as Microsoft Excel and Word. Why write and debug all the code you would need for a word processing program? Instead, you can open and use Word from within any Visual Basic program. Millions of person-hours have been devoted to creating Microsoft Word. You are unlikely to devote that much time to the task yourself!

These are just some of the challenges and problems you can use Visual Basic to solve. When you are finished with this course, you will be able to write applications for home, school, or any of your outside interests.

Using a Computer

Section

This section introduces the components of a personal computer and outlines their relationship to each other. If you are not already familiar with such concepts as RAM, CPU, and loading a file, you should read this section.

Hardware Components

The physical components of a computer are called hardware. You are used to thinking of a computer as a monitor, a box, and a keyboard. In the paragraphs in this section, you will learn what's inside the box (Figure 1-5).

CPU AND MEMORY

You can think of the central processing unit, or CPU, as the engine of the computer. The CPU does most of the work performed by the computer. It both interprets instructions contained in programs and manipulates data. The CPU can read data from two kinds of computer memory:

- RAM, or random access memory

- ROM, or read-only memory

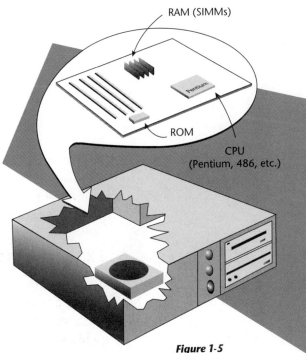

Figure 1-5
Computer hardware

RAM is used to store programs and the information processed by programs on a temporary basis. The CPU can fetch information from any area in RAM, which is why this type of memory is called "random access." When you work in a program such as Word, you are changing information stored in RAM. If your computer loses power suddenly—for example, if you pulled the power cable out of the socket—you would lose the information stored in RAM.

In contrast, ROM is typically used only once in a computer session. The CPU reads the programs and information in ROM when you are booting up the computer, which is the term used for starting the computer. You cannot alter any of the information in ROM; it is permanent.

HOW RAM IS ORGANIZED

RAM is divided into "cells" called bytes. Each byte itself consists of eight "bits." A bit, or binary digit, is a single digit, 0 or 1. The binary number system expresses numbers with just these two digits, 0 and 1. Small numbers fit in a single byte. Large numbers take several. In the following table, you can see how the decimal system converts to binary.

In Decimal	In Binary
1	1
2	10
3	11
4	100
10	1010
500	1 11110100
1000	11 11101000

Just like a house, each cell of memory has a unique address. The CPU identifies memory cells by a numerical address (Figure 1-6). "High-level" programming languages such as Visual Basic let you refer to quantities and objects stored in memory by using meaningful names rather than numerical addresses. GrandTotal, PhoneNumberAtWork, MainWindow, and UserWantsToExit are typical of the names used.

EXTERNAL STORAGE

You keep programs and data for the computer in external storage. RAM is only a temporary storage place, and it is not large enough to hold all the programs you want to run. A personal computer can have three kinds of external storage:

- Hard disk
- Floppy disk
- CD-ROM disk

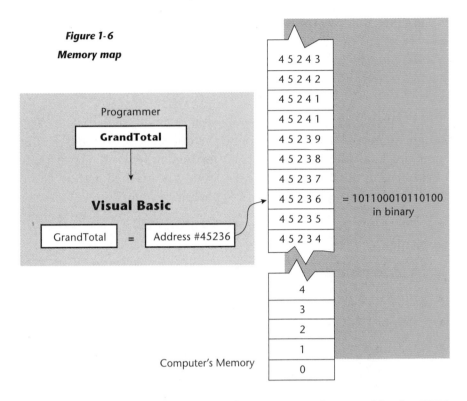

Figure 1-6
Memory map

Programmer

GrandTotal

Visual Basic

GrandTotal = Address #45236

Computer's Memory

45243
45242
45241
45241
45239
45238
45237
45236 = 101100010110100
 in binary
45235
45234

4
3
2
1
0

A hard disk is typically inside the computer (but outside the CPU) (Figure 1-7). You can store 50 to 100 times more information on a hard disk than on a floppy. For example, you probably have seven or more programs such as Microsoft Word stored on your hard drive. You probably cannot fit even one of those programs on a floppy disk.

Floppy disks and CD-ROM disks are easily portable. You can put a floppy disk in a shirt pocket, a CD-ROM disk in your backpack. Depending on the age of your computer, it may not have a drive for CD-ROM disks. Physically, a CD-ROM disk is identical to the CD disks you play in a compact disk player. This newer technology is an excellent way to transport large amounts of information at low cost. A typical CD-ROM can hold as much information as a large encyclopedia. This type of external storage is perfect for holding graphics, music, and animation files.

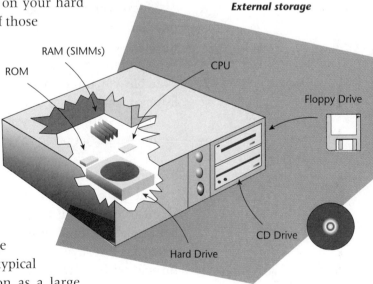

Figure 1-7
External storage

RAM (SIMMs)
ROM
CPU
Floppy Drive
CD Drive
Hard Drive

A CD-ROM drive reads a CD-ROM disk with a laser beam. The laser reflects off pits on the surface of the disk. The presence and absence of pits indicates 0's and 1's. The bitstream is the stream of data read from the disk and transferred to RAM.

PERIPHERALS

Peripheral means "something around the outside." For computers, this term covers all the devices attached to the computer. Some of these devices are in the main case, or box. Some are attached with cables to this box (Figure 1-8). Examples of peripherals include:

- Video cards
- Monitors
- Sound cards
- Printers
- Scanners
- Modems

Video cards are devices that translate computer output so that it can be displayed on a color monitor. How good that display is depends on the quality of the video card and monitor. With more expensive video cards and monitors, for example, you can see more colors on the monitor and images are crisper, with more detail.

Sound cards play a similar role with stereo speakers. They translate, or interface, between the CPU and the speakers. With a sound card installed, you can enjoy an added dimension of programs such as games. When a monster roars or an automobile screeches around a curve, for example, you can hear them. If you have a CD-ROM drive, you can also listen to your favorite music.

Printers provide a physical copy of the output of a computer application. An ink jet printer works by forcing a fine stream of ink onto the paper. A laser printer works by using a laser and a photosensitive drum to transfer toner to paper. The toner is a fine powder that is heated to bond to the paper.

Scanners create machine-readable images of printed material. A light source within the scanner reflects off the surface of the page. The reflection is read as a black-and-white or color image. The reflection is turned into bits and recorded in RAM. These images are stored on disks and can be manipulated by application programs. Fax machines have built-in scanners. The image of the document is transmitted over phone lines to other machines, which then reassemble the image.

Modems give computers the ability to communicate across telephone lines. You can call up another computer, for example, and transfer entire files. If you have the right software, you can send a fax rather than a file. You can also connect to the Internet, which is an international computer network. One of the many ways of using the Internet is to enjoy an online chat with someone. You type the words you want to say instead of speaking them, then they respond.

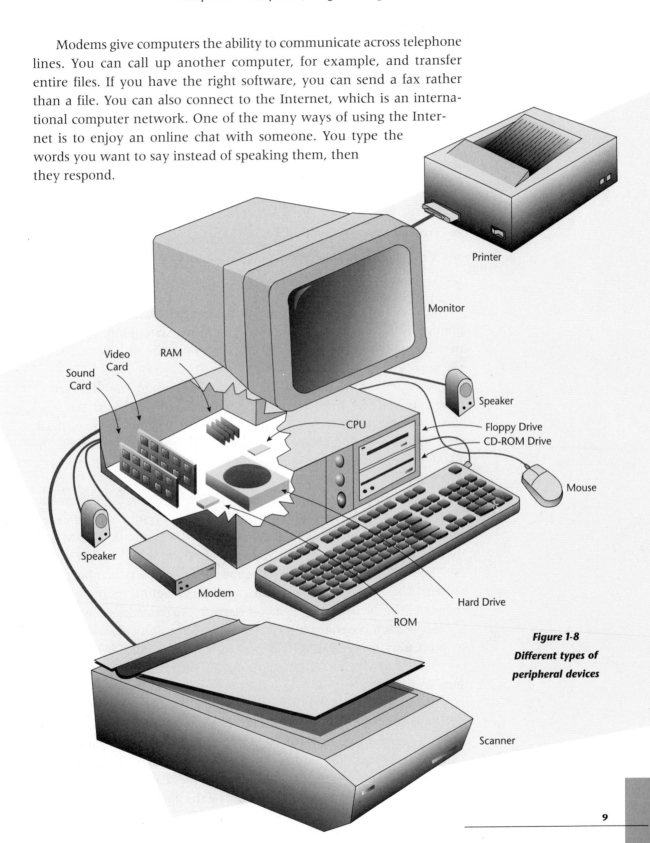

Figure 1-8
Different types of
peripheral devices

9

How a Computer Runs Software

This section introduces computer software. Software includes the programs, both built-in and on disk, that run the computer and turn the personal computer into an information source. Categories of software and the process by which a computer runs a program are discussed.

WHAT IS A PROGRAM?

A program is a sequence of instructions to the computer in a language the computer can understand. Programs fall in three categories:

- Programs used to boot up the computer
- A collection of programs called the operating system
- Application programs

As the name suggests, the operating system is a collection of programs that control the computer. The operating system interprets commands, runs programs, organizes files, operates the disk drives, reads the keyboard, and controls graphics displays.

When you switch on your computer, it boots up by running various programs. Each of these start-up programs accomplishes its task and turns over control of the computer to another program. Some of these start-up programs must be read into RAM from disk; others reside in ROM (read-only memory), so that they can run even if the computer's disk drives are all malfunctioning.

An example of ROM-based start-up code is the self-test that the computer performs when you turn it on. An important task performed by the self-test routines is to check whether the computer's RAM and disk drives are working properly, and to alert you if any appear not to be. The ROM-based routines are not specific to any particular operating system. They obviously must run successfully before any attempt is made to read the operating system's start-up programs from disk.

Application programs are created to perform particular tasks, such as processing text, creating graphics, or communicating between one computer and another. Other applications, such as games, are just for fun. You can use educational software to learn anything from a new language to how to cook the perfect soufflé.

Application programs are usually composed of a large number of files. As you can see in Figure 1-9, programs have many components. Only some of these files are actually programs, which contain instructions for the computer to execute. The other files contain data, and they are usually in a format understood only by the application program.

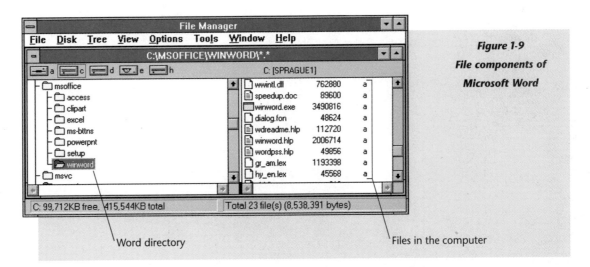

Figure 1-9
File components of
Microsoft Word

For example, a word processing program such as Microsoft Word consists of:

- The executable program **winword.exe**
- Additional program files with the extension **.dll**, containing more instructions that the computer can perform
- Help files, with the extension **.hlp**, containing online help files
- Files with the extension **.lex** that help Word spellcheck and hyphenate your documents
- Style sheets and templates for form letters

LOADING AN APPLICATION PROGRAM

Application programs are kept in external storage. When you or your school buys a program, the files are provided on floppy disk or CD-ROM. Often, you will then transfer the application to your hard drive.

The operating system is responsible for loading a program from external storage (floppy disk, hard disk, or CD-ROM) into RAM. When you choose a program to open, you are sending a message to the operating system to load that program (Figure 1-10). The CPU runs applications from RAM, not from any of the external storage devices.

EXECUTING THE PROGRAM

Once the program's instructions are copied into RAM, the operating system informs the CPU of the location of the program in memory. The CPU fetches each instruction from memory, decodes it, and executes it. While the program runs, it uses RAM to store the data it manipulates, as

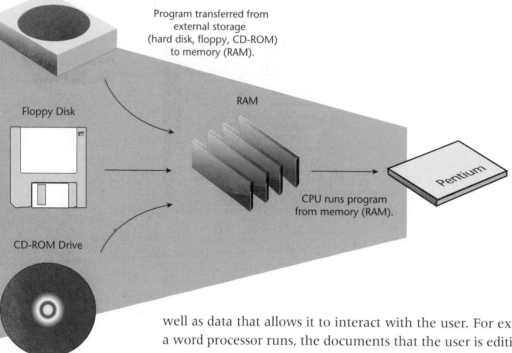

Hard Drive

Program transferred from
external storage
(hard disk, floppy, CD-ROM)
to memory (RAM).

Floppy Disk

RAM

Pentium

CPU runs program
from memory (RAM).

CD-ROM Drive

Figure 1-10
Flow of data
between disk and
RAM

well as data that allows it to interact with the user. For example, when a word processor runs, the documents that the user is editing are stored in RAM, as are collections of information about the windows in which those documents are displayed. Both program instructions and the data with which it works are stored in RAM.

The instructions understood by a CPU from one manufacturer are not necessary understood by a CPU from another manufacturer. A Macintosh program may not be run on an IBM-compatible PC.

QUESTIONS AND ACTIVITIES

1. MS-DOS is the Microsoft disk operating system. If you have MS-DOS installed on your computer, run **msd.com**, usually found in the DOS directory. This is the Microsoft diagnostic program. Run this program and record the following information about your computer:

    CPU type:
    Memory, Base:
        Ext:
        EMS:
        XMS:
    Video:
    Network:
    OS version:
    Mouse:
    Other Adapters:

2. If possible, find an old computer. Take the top off the machine and try to identify the CPU and memory chips. Find the video and disk controllers. Find them by tracing the connections from the montior and the disk drive to the main circuit board. Make a sketch of the inside and label what you can.

3. Using advertisements in computer magazines, or a catalog from a computer hardware vendor, design your ideal computer. List specific boards, their capabilities, and prices. Use this list as a guide.

case	motherboard, CPU
power supply	memory
disk controller	disk drives (floppy, hard)
video controller	video monitor
sound card	CD-ROM
keyboard	tape backup drive
video capture	modem
printer(s)	

4. A keyboard and a mouse are input devices. A monitor and a printer are output devices. Use a computer magazine or catalog to find and describe three input devices and three output devices you don't have on your computer.

5. Find an article about the Internet. Write a one-paragraph summary of the article.

The Basics of Working in Windows

3

Section

Making computers easier to use has been the vision of hardware manufacturers and software companies alike. New hardware has enabled new ways to program: more colorful graphics and faster processors let programmers use video clips; sound cards allow programs to talk or sing. The more power that's available, the more programming options are open.

Software developers have responded with ever more sophisticated ways to use the hardware. Game programmers use graphics displays in ways hardware designers could not have anticipated. The result is before you—the Windows environment. A computer environment is the sum of all the ways the computer interacts with the user. Windows is a step along the evolutionary chain of graphical user interfaces, or GUIs.

This section explains how to start Windows. You need to start Windows to run any Windows applications such as Visual Basic. It also covers how to use icons, move around in individual windows, and work with dialog boxes.

Clicking the mouse means depressing and releasing the mouse button. Double-clicking is pressing the mouse button quickly, twice. Dragging the mouse means depressing and holding the button and moving the mouse.

Starting Windows

Most personal computers start with Windows active on the screen. Sometimes, though, when you turn on a PC you will see:

C:

This means that your computer has started in DOS, the disk operating system. The "C" refers to your hard drive, where Windows is installed. Windows is a set of programs that makes it easy to use the disk operating system. As Windows evolves, it will become an operating system. Type **win** and press Return to start Windows. The Windows Program Manager program is then run, as shown in Figure 1-11.

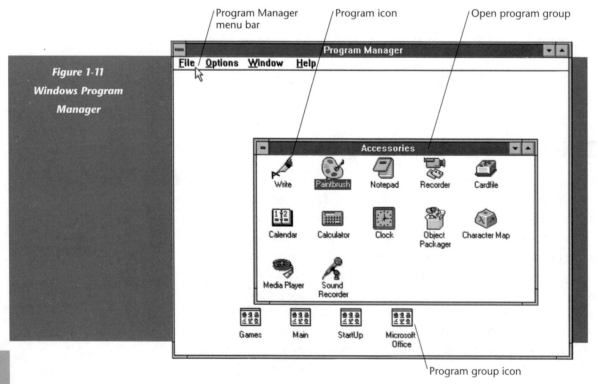

Figure 1-11
Windows Program Manager

Looking at Icons

Windows is a very graphical environment. For example, many of the choices you make in Windows are represented by icons, which are buttons with pictures on them (see Figure 1-11). You can select what you want by clicking on an icon with a mouse, rather than typing or selecting an option from a list. Icons work as shortcuts.

You can use icons to:

◉ Open a program or program group

◉ Perform a task within an application, such as cutting text

Experiment with the first of these in the Program Manager window. There you see icons for different program groups. Program groups are exactly what they sound like: groups of related programs. If you double-click on a program group icon, the program group opens. Try opening the Visual Basic program group (Figure 1-12).

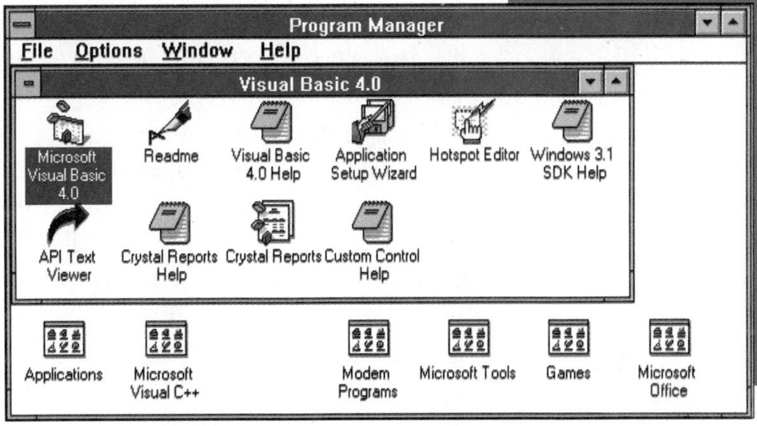

With the program group open, you can see that there are icons for individual programs. To open one of these programs, you double-click on its icon.

Once you are in an application, such as Microsoft Word, you can use icons to perform many tasks. For example, if you select text in Word, then click on the Cut icon, the text is cut. Usually, these icons are grouped together in a toolbar (see Figure 1-13).

Figure 1-12
Open Visual Basic program group

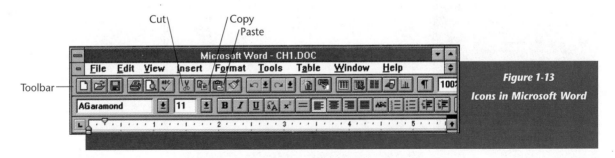

Figure 1-13
Icons in Microsoft Word

Moving Around in Windows

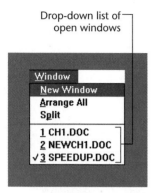

Drop-down list of
open windows

Figure 1-14

**Drop-down list of open
windows in Microsoft Word**

In the Windows environment, you can do more than one thing at once. Each application or file that you open appears in a window. You can have multiple windows open at the same time, moving back and forth between them. You can even move material from one window to the next. Within an application, you can have more than one file open. In Figure 1-14, for example, you can see that there are three Word files open at one time.

You can also open more than one application at the same time. One way to move back and forth between open applications is to press and hold the Alt key, then press Tab.

Windows are not static on your monitor screen. You can close and open them, make them bigger and smaller, and drag them from side to side. You can use the windows in the Program Manager to experiment with the properties of windows. Windows in any Windows application work in the same way.

Double-click on an icon for a program group. The window that opens contains the icons of individual programs in the group (see Figure 1-12). The other program group icons also represent windows. These windows are said to be minimized.

Do you see the two buttons in the upper-right corner of the open program group window? If you click on the button with the down arrow, you will minimize the window. If instead you click on the button with the up arrow, the window is maximized. When a window is maximized, it takes all available space in the Program Manager window (Figure 1-15).

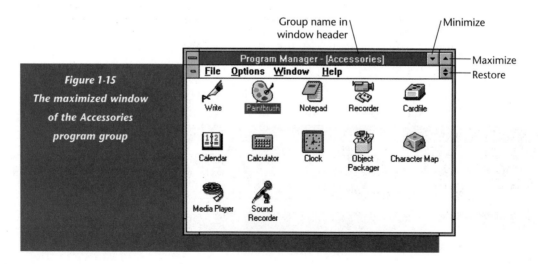

Group name in
window header

Minimize

Maximize

Restore

Figure 1-15
**The maximized window
of the Accessories
program group**

The Program Manager is still running, as you can see by the caption above the menu bar. In addition, a new button with both an up and a down arrow has appeared in the upper-right corner of the window. Clicking this button restores the window to its original size. Experiment with the minimize, restore, and maximize buttons for different program groups in the Program Manager (Figure 1-16).

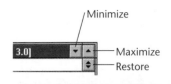

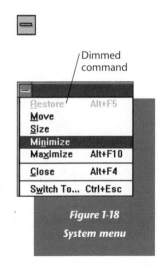

Figure 1-16
The minimize, maximize,
and restore buttons

Now try resizing and moving windows by dragging the mouse. With the mouse cursor above the menu bar, on the colored caption of the window, drag the open Visual Basic window to a new position on the screen.

Now position the mouse cursor along any of the boundaries of any open window. It transforms into a double arrow, indicating you can resize the window (see Figure 1-17). If you drag on a corner of the form, you can change both the horizontal and vertical size of the window.

Figure 1-17
The mouse cursor as a
double arrow

Notice that, in the upper-left corner of the window, there is a button with a horizontal bar in it. When you click on this button, the system menu opens (Figure 1-18). The button's icon resembles the space bar, as a reminder that you can open this menu by pressing the space bar while holding down the Alt key. You can choose to minimize, maximize, restore, resize, or move the window from this menu. Windows programs typically let you perform tasks in several different ways. As you just saw, for example, you can minimize the window by clicking on a button. You could also open this menu and select the minimize command.

If you cannot select a command from a menu, that command is dimmed, or grayed. For instance, if you have already maximized a window before you opened this menu, the maximize command will appear dimmed. Experiment with using different commands in the system menu.

Figure 1-18
System menu

Looking at Menu Bars and Drop-Down Menus

Besides clicking on icons in a Windows application, you can also select a command from a menu. Top-level menu choices appear in a menu bar across the top of the window (see Figure 1-19). If you click on one of these, a drop-down list of commands is displayed. Clicking on a command executes it.

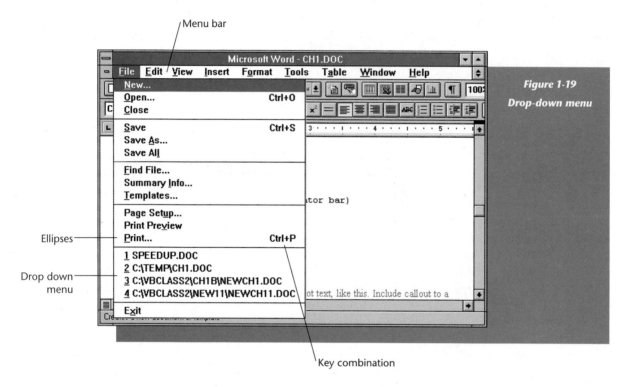

Menu bar

Figure 1-19

Drop-down menu

Ellipses

Drop down menu

Key combination

Often, a drop-down menu contains more than just the names of the commands. You may see:

◉ Ellipses after a command

◉ Names of keys (such as Ctrl+Z)

◉ Small triangle after a command

◉ Check mark

An ellipsis indicates that if you select that command, a dialog box will open. You use this dialog box to make choices about the command you are executing. See the next section for more detail on dialog boxes.

As always with Windows programs, you are given several ways to perform a task. The key combinations listed after the commands remind you that you can execute commands from the keyboard. You do not have to go through the steps of pulling down the menu and selecting a command. The plus sign indicates that you press the two keys at the same time (the keys starting with "F" refer to the function keys along the top row of the keyboard.) Ctrl+Esc, for example, means to press and hold the Control key while pressing the Escape key.

A small triangle to the right of a command indicates that another menu opens if you select that command. You would then select a command from that menu.

A check mark indicates that a menu option is selected. For example, in Microsoft Word, you can choose to show or hide a ruler. If you have the ruler displayed, the Ruler command in the View menu is shown with a check mark. If you are looking at the list of windows you have open, then the check mark indicates the active window (see Figure 1-14).

Figure 1-20
Open window for the Accessories program group

Running an Application

Running a program from the Program Manager is easy. Find the application's icon and double-click it with the mouse. To experiment, try opening the Notepad application. This program is a simple text editor. Its editing commands are similar to those available when you are editing text in Visual Basic. Programmers use the same editing commands to manipulate the program text code. The program code is the text of the program instructions.

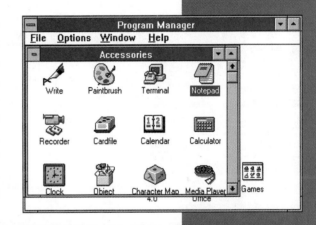

To run Notepad:

1   Open the Accessories program group by double-clicking on its icon (see Figure 1-20).

2   In the Accessories program group, double-click on the Notepad icon. The Notepad window opens (Figure 1-21).

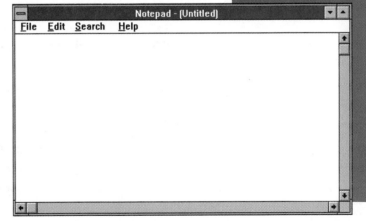

Figure 1-21
Notepad application

NAVIGATING IN A TEXT FILE

Moving around in a text file, or navigating, is easy. You can use either the keypad or the mouse. First, however, you need to enter some text with which to experiment.

1 Begin typing any text you want. Continue until the first words you typed scroll off the page to the right.

As you can see, each line in Notepad is too long to fit in the window. To see all the text you enter, you must select the Word Wrap option.

2 Select Edit from the menu bar, then Word Wrap from the bottom of the drop-down list. What has happened to the text you entered? See Figure 1-22.

Word Wrap is what is known as a toggle. A toggle is a command that is either on or off. When you have Word Wrap on, a check mark appears by the command.

Figure 1-22
Notepad with Word
Wrap selected

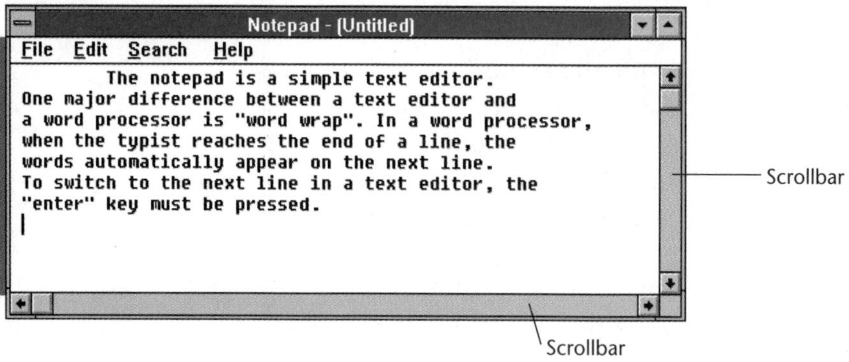

```
Notepad - [Untitled]
File  Edit  Search  Help
        The notepad is a simple text editor.
One major difference between a text editor and
a word processor is "word wrap". In a word processor,
when the typist reaches the end of a line, the
words automatically appear on the next line.
To switch to the next line in a text editor, the
"enter" key must be pressed.
```

Scrollbar

Scrollbar

3 Continue typing until you have five lines of text.

4 Practice moving the text cursor with these keys and key combinations:

To move the cursor:	*Press:*
character to character	left and right arrows
word to word	Ctrl+left, Ctrl+right
line to line	up and down arrows
to top of text	Ctrl+Home
to bottom of text	Ctrl+End

SELECTING TEXT

You select text in Notepad just as you do in other Windows applications. Click at the beginning of the material you want to select and drag the mouse to the end of the last word. The text changes color, showing it is selected.

Another way to select text is to set the cursor to the beginning of the text to be selected, press the Shift key, and move the cursor to the end. While you are holding the Shift key down, you can use any of the cursor movement keys to move the cursor. Now practice selecting different areas of the text you typed in Notepad (Figure 1-23). What happens when you try to select two separate areas of text?

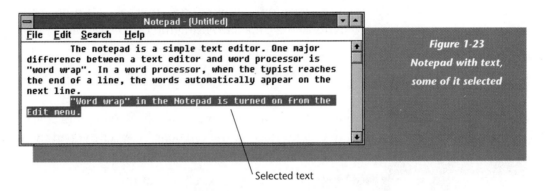

Figure 1-23
Notepad with text,
some of it selected

Selected text

DELETING, PASTING, AND COPYING TEXT

After you have selected text, you can delete or cut it. You should cut, not delete, any text you want to move someplace else.

1   Select a word or two of the text you entered in Notepad.

2   Press the Delete key.
What if you change your mind? Most Windows programs let you "undo" commands such as deleting text.

3   Click on the Edit command in the menu bar, then on Undo.
The text you deleted has been reinserted.

4   Now try cutting some text instead of deleting it. Select some text, then select Edit from the menu bar. Click on Cut, or press the keyboard combination Ctrl+X (press and hold the Control key, then press the letter "x").

5   Paste the text you cut in a different place in the text. Move the text cursor as you want. Select Edit from the menu bar, then Paste. Or, you can use the keyboard shortcut Ctrl+V.

6   You can copy text with a similar set of steps. Select the text first, then select Edit from the menu bar and Copy from the drop-down menu. Move the cursor to the new location and select Paste from the Edit drop-down menu.

Many Windows programs have another kind of shortcut for performing common tasks such as cutting and pasting. The Word icon for pasting is shown to the left. Clicking on the icon has the same effect as selecting the command or using the keyboard combination.

When you cut or copy text, that text is moved into a special area of RAM called the Clipboard, where Windows keeps track of it. You can insert (paste) any text from the Clipboard into other places in the document you're currently working on, or for that matter, any other document in any application you're currently running. You can view the contents of the Clipboard using the Clipboard Viewer.

Now experiment with the Clipboard:

1 Cut some text from your Notepad window.

2 Open the Clipboard Viewer in the Main program group. If you have Windows for Workgroups loaded on your machine, you need to double-click on the Clipboard Viewer to open the Clipboard (Figure 1-24).

3 Check to see that the text you cut appears in the Clipboard (Figure 1-25). Can you edit the text in the Clipboard?

4 To switch back to the Notepad, press and hold the Alt key, then press Tab.
This is a common way of moving between windows you have open.

5 Delete some text from the Notepad using the Delete key.

Figure 1-24
Icon for Clipboard Viewer in program group

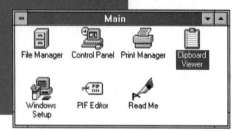

Figure 1-25
Screen shot of Clipboard with text

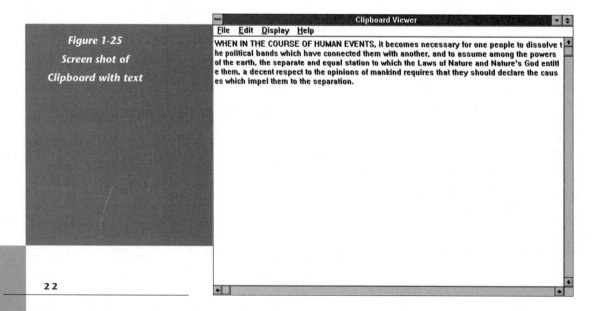

6 Switch back to the Clipboard Viewer. Is the deleted text in the Clipboard?

7 Size and position the windows for the Notepad and the Clipboard so that both are visible. Cut text from the Notepad and watch it appear in the Viewer (Figure 1-26).

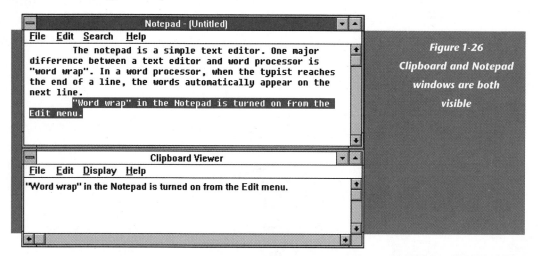

Figure 1-26
Clipboard and Notepad windows are both visible

SAVING A FILE

If you want to keep the text you have typed in the Notepad window, you must save it as a file. To do so, select File from the menu bar. The File drop-down menu is shown in Figure 1-27.

Select Save As from the drop-down menu shown in the figure. The Save As dialog box opens, as shown in Figure 1-28.

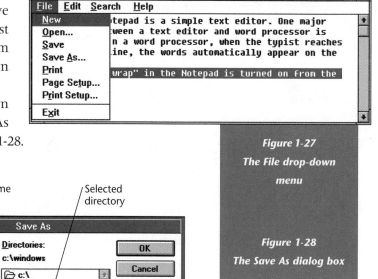

Figure 1-27
The File drop-down menu

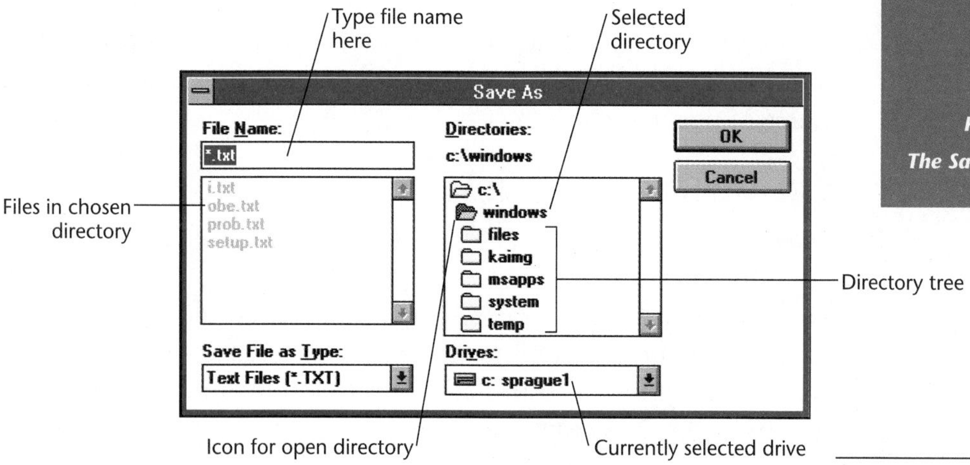

Figure 1-28
The Save As dialog box

When you save a file, you can expect you'll need to find it again later. The computer lets you organize your disk by creating directories, which you can think of as folders for keeping related files together. Within any directory, you can create other directories, called subdirectories, to store more files. Any subdirectory can have its own subdirectories. The directory that contains a particular subdirectory is called the parent directory of that subdirectory. Taken together, the whole structure of parent directories and subdirectories is called the root directory.

Now save your file:

1 Click on the Drives downward arrow. A drop-down list opens, showing the available drives. Keep the default (the C drive, or hard drive).

2 Double-click on a directory or subdirectory in the directory window. You know that you have selected a directory when it appears in the label above the window. Experiment with moving to different points in the directory tree. If you click on **C:**, you will move back up to the top of the tree.

3 Click in the File Name text box and enter a name for the file.

4 Click on the OK button to start the save.

Using the File Manager to Handle Files

Windows provides a File Manager program designed to help you manage files. With the File Manager, for example, you can create and delete directories; copy, move, rename, and delete files; and copy or format disks. You can also compare the directories from two or more disks side by side, then move or copy files between the directories.

To open the File Manager, click on the icon for the Main program group in the Program Manager window. Find the icon for the File Manager in that program group, then double-click on it. The File Manager opens, as shown in Figure 1-29.

Clicking on a directory name in the left window selects that directory. When a directory is selected, the files of that directory appear in the right side of the window.

CREATING DIRECTORIES

To create a directory, use the vertical scrollbar to move up or down the directory tree in the left side of the window. Find the parent for the directory you want to create. For example, if you have a directory named fruit and you want to create a subdirectory named apples, you would click on the fruit directory. If you select the top line of the directory (**C:**), this is the root directory of the drive.

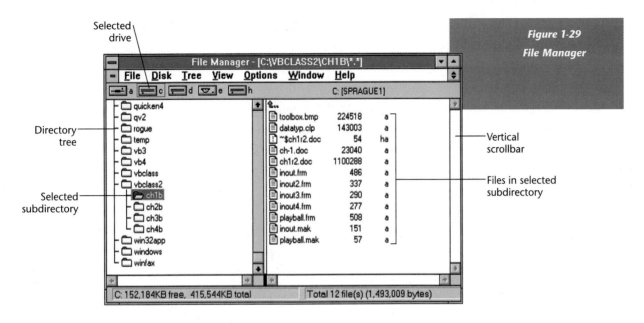

Figure 1-29
File Manager

From the File menu, select Create Directory. A Create Directory dialog box opens, as shown in Figure 1-30.

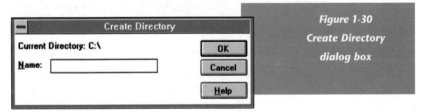

Figure 1-30
Create Directory
dialog box

Enter the name of the directory in the Name text box and click OK. This new directory will appear in the directory window of the File Manager. Now try creating a directory for the Notepad file you created earlier in this chapter. Try to pick a descriptive name, such as Notefile. Windows will cut the extra letters off any name longer than eight characters (Figure 1-31).

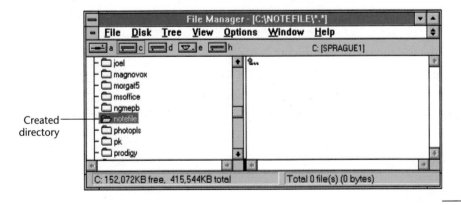

Figure 1-31
Created directory

MOVING FILES BETWEEN DIRECTORIES

After you have created a directory, you can experiment with moving a file or two into it. Select the directory you just created; it is empty of file and directory names, as you can see from the right window. To move the Notepad file into the new directory:

1 Select Window from the File Manager menu bar, then select New Window from the drop-down menu.

2 Select Window again, then click on Tile. You will now see two copies of the file and directory windows of the File Manager (see Figure 1-32).

3 In one of the copies, select the directory in which you originally stored the Notepad file. In the example shown in Figure 1-32, the Notepad file was saved in the Windows directory. In the other copy, select the new directory you just created for the Notepad files.

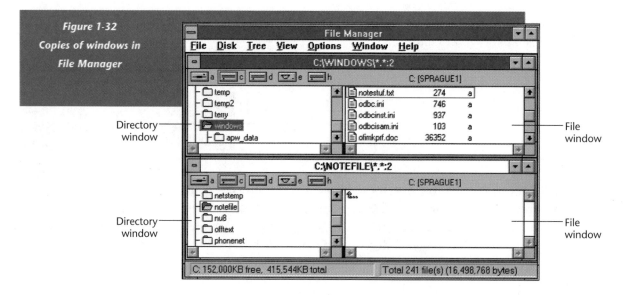

Figure 1-32
Copies of windows in
File Manager

4 Find the Notepad file in its original directory and select it by clicking on its name. In the example shown in the figure, the name of the file is **notestuf.txt**.

5 Drag the file to the window displaying the directory you just created (notefile directory, in this example). Connected to the cursor as you move it will be an icon of a sheet of paper, representing the file (Figure 1-33).

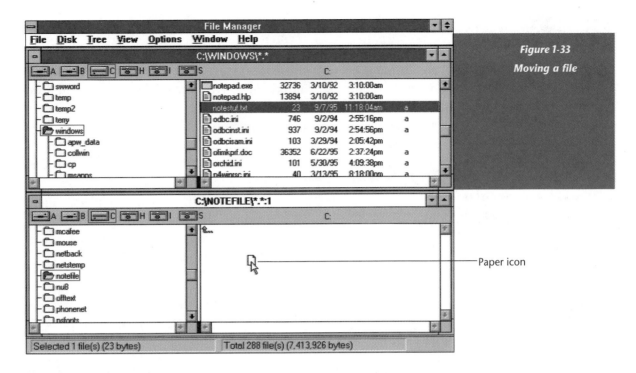

Figure 1-33

Moving a file

6 When a message box appears asking if you are sure you want to move the file, check the file names and then click on Yes.
The File Manager moves the file from one directory to the other (see Figure 1-34).

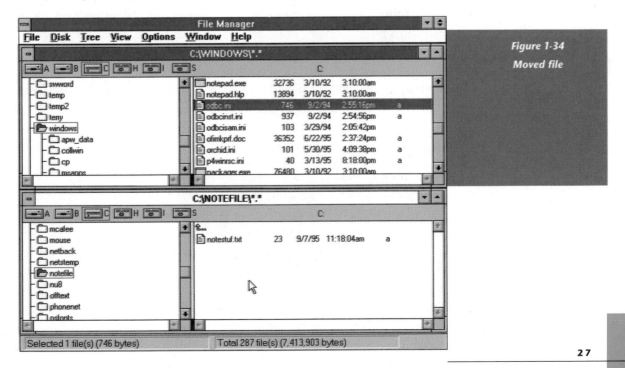

Figure 1-34

Moved file

DELETING FILES AND DIRECTORIES

In some applications, you cannot delete files. In these cases, you need to open File Manager to delete files you no longer need. You have a couple of options for doing so. Find the file, select it with the mouse, and press the Delete key. You can also click on the File Manager's File menu, then select Delete from the drop-down menu.

If you select a directory instead of a file, pressing the Delete key deletes the directory. For both files and directories, Windows prompts you to be sure you want to make the deletion (see Figure 1-35). Because the Notepad directory you created was just an experiment, you should delete it now.

Figure 1-35
Deleting from the
File Manager

4 Section

Writing Programs

Why write computer programs? Programming computers is fun. Writing programs that control expensive hardware, that turn a dumb machine into a homework helper or playmate, is tremendously satisfying. Although learning to program entails a certain amount of work, that work is repaid through a real feeling of accomplishment.

Writing computer programs is good business. Whether you write programs professionally, or occasionally write a program to solve a business or personal management problem, programming means money.

Programming changes as computer hardware and programming techniques evolve. A typical PC today is vastly more powerful than any room-filling computer of 20 years ago and costs dramatically less.

Evolution of Programming

Programming means communicating with a machine. Computer languages define the symbols and structures used to communicate. Computer languages have evolved from 0's and 1's to sophisticated English phrases. This section reviews that evolution.

At the most basic level, the CPU of a computer understands instructions coded in the binary number system. As noted earlier in the chapter, this system uses only the digits 0 and 1 to represent values. These instructions are stored in memory (RAM) and are sequentially fetched, decoded, and executed by the processing unit.

In the earliest computers, these codes were entered with on/off switches on the front panel of the computer. Long rows of switches were used to represent bits. If the switch was in the up position, it represented a 0. If the switch were down, it represented a 1. A pushbutton indicated the number was set. When the pushbutton was pressed, the switches were read and the 0's and 1's were transferred to RAM. Accurately entering the long strings of zeros and ones was very difficult.

Early in the development of these machines, the computer itself was used to help interpret instructions. Instead of simple on/off switches, pushbuttons representing the digits of base 8 or base 16 numbers were used. The computer converted the values represented by the pushbuttons to their binary equivalents.

Programming began evolving when the binary number system was replaced with systems that were easier for people to understand. Imagine trying to read or remember a sequence of 0s and 1s! Binary numbers, still used internally, were replaced externally with numbers based on powers of 8 or 16. These values were shorter and easier to use. Programmers needed a more compact notation in which to work. When these more concise programs were entered into the computer, the computers translated them back into binary and then executed the result. Programs still consisted of numbers, though.

Large computers used more and more sophisticated languages starting in the 1940s. By the time the 1950s were over, a number of easy-to-use computer languages were in use. Small computers didn't arrive on the scene until the first years of the 1970s. The evolution of these small computers was fairly rapid. By the late 1970s, a number of computer languages were available for microcomputers.

The evolution continued toward a computer language that was easier to understand and remember. Numeric codes were replaced with short descriptive syllables called mnemonics. These short syllables were easier to remember (and type) than the longer commands that they represent. Examples include:

```
ADD, ADDC, MOV, SUB, SUBC, ASL, ROT, LDA
```

Each of these instructions is a command that the processor can translate to binary, understand, and execute. By itself, one of these commands can accomplish very little. When joined together, though, these commands can perform any operation of which the computer is capable. For instance, ADDC is the Add with Carry command. This adds two numbers including the carry left over from a previous operation.

The languages that use these short syllables to create code are called assembly languages. Each different processor (such as the one for a PC or a Macintosh) has its own unique assembly language. The languages are different because each kind of processor has a unique architecture that is embodied in its assembly language. A PC CPU cannot understand a program written in the Macintosh assembly language. In hindsight, these assembly languages are called low-level computer languages.

Assembly languages greatly simplified programming, but there was still a long way to go. Computers could understand these languages well enough—much easier than the programmers themselves. Once again, computers were asked to aid in the translation of commands more easily understood by humans, and high-level computer languages were born. Complex computer programs are used to translate the statements of computer languages to the binary commands understood by the processor. The programs are called compilers. The first of these languages, developed in the 1950s, are still in use today.

High-level languages use words similar to English words, and operations similar to familiar math operations to express computer operations. "Visual" Basic advances the evolution of computer languages by introducing a strong graphic element into programming. Programmers work with icons that represent parts of a Visual Basic program.

Machine	Base 16	Assembly	High Level
1101 1001	D9	INC	X = X + 1

INC is the mnemonic for increment.

Models of Programming

As programming languages have evolved, so have methods of programming. This section introduces traditional procedural programming and the newer event-driven programming. The section uses analogies to illustrate the differences.

Imagine that you play in the school band and you are preparing for a concert. That preparation includes learning the music for the pieces to be performed. As you practice each piece, the teacher leads the musicians through section after section, repeating each until it's just right. Finally, the conductor leads the band through an entire performance from beginning to end.

Imagine now that you are a goalie for a soccer team. Your training includes physical conditioning, drills and hours of practice in goal responding to shots. A game consists of reacting, with practiced responses, to the events of the game—the shots on goal.

PROCEDURAL PROGRAMMING

Procedural programming is like playing a piece of music. Each program has a beginning, a middle, and an end, and a particular set of steps to get from one place to another. In procedural programming, the programmer defines the path of the information entered into the program from the beginning of the program, step by step, to the end of the program. Throughout the entire process the program is in control. The program controls the gathering of data from the keyboard or from a file of information, processing the data in some way, and then preparing the information for output or display.

The beginning, middle, and end of a program are not clearly separated, but they can be summarized as shown in the list below.

1. Entering data (beginning)

2. Processing data (middle)

3. Displaying information (end)

For instance, a program to calculate the price of going to a prom, written in the old procedural way, could be summarized as follows:

1. Collect information about prices

2. Calculate totals

3. Display the results

Just like a musician practicing a piece of music, the programmer breaks this program into parts and solves each part, combining the parts into final form when each is mastered.

EVENT-DRIVEN PROGRAMMING

Event-driven programming is like playing goalie in a soccer game. Like a goalie, a program responds to events: a keypress or a mouse click.

A programmer using the event-driven model of programming will use many of the same step-by-step solutions used by a programmer following the procedural model. The techniques are different, though, because the programmer writes programs in which the user is in control. In this model of programming, it is the events generated by the computer user that control the flow of the program.

Visual Basic uses the event-driven model of programming. Programmers in Visual Basic design programs in an environment that responds to user-initiated events.

QUESTIONS AND ACTIVITIES

1. Describe three uses for a computer in the home. Be specific; "Doing your homework" is not a good answer.

2. Give the step-by-step instructions required to open a can of frozen juice and make a pitcher of juice. Is this activity procedural or event-driven?

3. Give three examples of jobs where a day's work cannot be completely planned or anticipated. In such a job, it is important to respond to events as they occur.

4. For one of the jobs listed above describe what events might occur and what a proper response to the events might be.

5. Describe what events might occur when driving a car to school. Describe some possible responses to those events.

Visual Basic is used to provide solutions for the needs of home, business, industry, and the scientific community.

Visual Basic is used to interact and control other applications, like Microsoft Access, Excel, and Word.

The CPU is the central processing unit of the computer. The CPU runs programs and manipulates data.

RAM is random access memory. This memory holds programs as they run and data as it is processed.

ROM, or read-only memory, permanently stores programs that boot up the computer.

Memory records information using the binary number system, a system that uses only 0's and 1's.

Each location in memory has an address, sometimes expressed in binary.

A floppy disk, hard drive, and CD-ROM disk are examples of external storage.

Video and sound cards, printers, scanners, and modems are examples of peripheral devices—devices connected to the computer.

Loading programs means copying programs from external storage to RAM. Running programs means executing a program line by line from memory by the CPU.

Windows can be minimized, maximized, and, once altered, restored.

Windows can be moved and resized with mouse clicks and drags.

Text is manipulated with mouse clicks, menu choices, or keyboard commands. Text can be copied, cut, and pasted.

Files are manipulated with the Program and File Manager programs. Directories can be created and removed. Files can be created, deleted, copied, and moved.

Computer languages have evolved from languages best understood by machines, or low-level languages, to languages easily understood by people, or high-level languages.

Procedural programming assumes every problem can be solved with a predictable step-by-step solution. The solution is always under machine control.

Event-driven programming solves problems by handling events caused by the user and the computer environment. Many events are user-initiated.

txt

txtLastName

txtLastName

CmdDis

UnpaidBalance

lblBirthplace

DisplayPicture

The Grand Tour

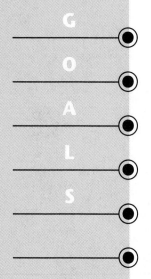
After working through this chapter, you will:

Recognize the components of the Visual Basic programming environment.

Know how to place textboxes, label controls, and command buttons on a Visual Basic form.

Be able to change the properties of controls.

Have explored how Visual Basic responds to the Click and KeyPress events.

Have written a program from beginning to end, including creating, saving, and printing a project as well as creating an EXE file.

O V E R V I E W

Before you can program in Visual Basic, you need to understand the environment in which you are working and the tools at your disposal. It's like walking onto a basketball court for the first time. You have to understand the tools you will have, the process, and the expected end result. For a first basketball game, those would be a basketball (tool), working with teammates to make baskets (process), and having a good time (end result).

After you become comfortable with being in the Visual Basic environment, you will create your first program. You might ask how programming can be that easy. Here you are in the second chapter of the book, and you are programming.

Visual Basic itself is the reason. Not too long ago, you would have had to write a great deal of code to create even the simplest of programs. Now Visual Basic handles much of the code writing for you. You are left with the most challenging part of programming: thinking through programs so that they work well and are appealing to the people who run them.

Touring Visual Basic

This section covers the Visual Basic environment. You will open the application, then take a quick tour through the windows and the Toolbox that you see displayed on the screen.

Section

Using online help is an important aspect of working with any Windows application. Often, you can find an answer to a question much faster by looking in online help than by paging through a user's manual. You need to become comfortable with looking in online help and finding information there.

Start Visual Basic for Windows now. If necessary, double-click on its program group icon in the Program Manager to open the group; then double-click on the Visual Basic icon (Figure 2-1).

Figure 2-1

Selecting the Visual Basic icon

The Opening Screen

On the opening screen of Visual Basic are five elements:

◉ Menu bar and toolbar

◉ Window titled Form1

◉ Project window

◉ Toolbox

◉ Properties window

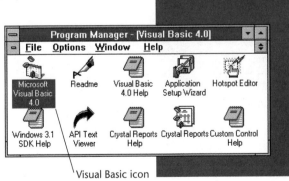

MENU BAR AND TOOLBAR

The menu bar and toolbar appear across the top of the screen (Figure 2-2). As in any Windows program, you use commands from the menu bar to perform tasks, such as opening a file. For some of the more common commands, you can also click on an icon in the toolbar.

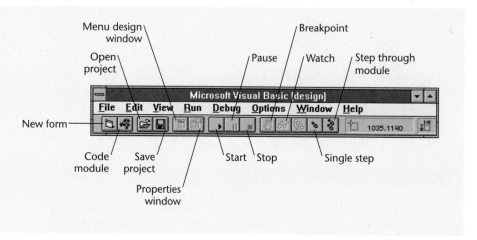

Figure 2-2
Visual Basic menu bar
and toolbar

Menu design window
Breakpoint
Open project
Pause
Watch
Step through module
New form
Code module
Save project
Start
Stop
Single step
Properties window

FORM WINDOW

The form dominates the center of the screen and is empty except for the caption at the top (Figure 2-3). This caption is set to the default form name: Form1. Each additional form you open is numbered sequentially. Try opening another form by clicking on the New Form icon (or selecting New Form from the File menu). Now close it.

The form is a window that contains visual objects (such as a picture box or buttons) and code. You can think of it as the "face" of your program, because it is what people see when they run the program. If you place a picture box in the upper-left corner of the form, for example, the picture will appear in the upper-left corner during run-time.

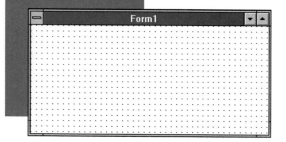

Figure 2-3
Form1

Forms serve a second purpose besides appearance. People interact with your program through the form. For example, someone could enter the name of their favorite country in a box designed for text. Or someone could close the form (and the program) by clicking on an Exit button.

PROJECT WINDOW

Forms are saved in projects. If you need only one form in your program, then that project will contain only a single form. Depending on what you are doing, though, you may need more than one form.

Why more than one? You use forms to organize how people experience your program and how they enter information. For example, imagine that you are developing a program that explains different kinds of musical instruments.

Putting all the information about different instruments on one form would probably be confusing. An alternate approach would be to use an opening form to list the instruments and ask the user to pick one. Then you could create a form for each instrument. If a person picked the guitar, for example, clicking OK on the first form would open a second form about guitars. If someone picked the piano, then the form you created for pianos would open (Figure 2-4).

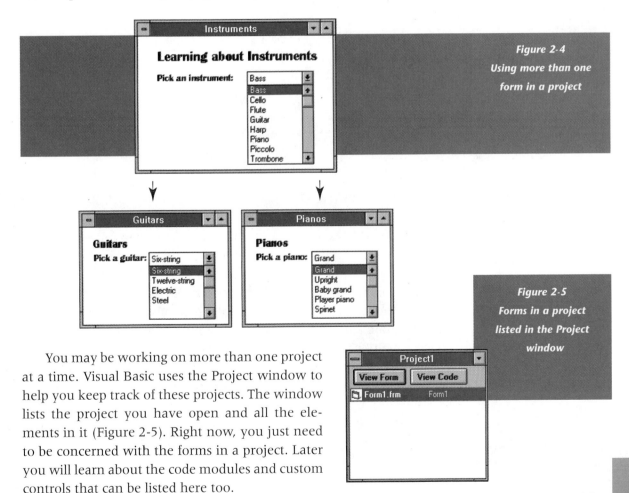

Figure 2-4
Using more than one form in a project

Figure 2-5
Forms in a project listed in the Project window

You may be working on more than one project at a time. Visual Basic uses the Project window to help you keep track of these projects. The window lists the project you have open and all the elements in it (Figure 2-5). Right now, you just need to be concerned with the forms in a project. Later you will learn about the code modules and custom controls that can be listed here too.

The first project you open is called Project1. If you do not specify another project for Visual Basic to open, or when you open a new project, Visual Basic loads a project named **autoload.mak**. This project resides in Visual Basic's own directory and contains a list of controls, the size of the Project window, and some other assumed values.

TOOLBOX

Down the left edge of the screen is the toolbox. This toolbox contains objects for building programs in Visual Basic. Look at the Toolbox now to become familiar with the different kinds of objects (Figure 2-6).

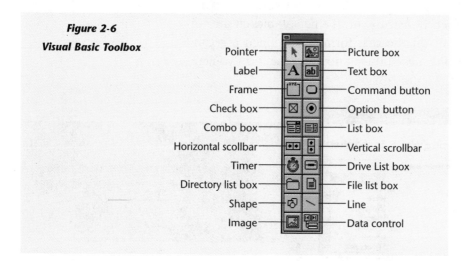

Figure 2-6
Visual Basic Toolbox

Pointer — Picture box
Label — Text box
Frame — Command button
Check box — Option button
Combo box — List box
Horizontal scollbar — Vertical scrollbar
Timer — Drive List box
Directory list box — File list box
Shape — Line
Image — Data control

Find the picture box or image box in the toolbox. Click on it, then move the mouse cursor over Form1. The cursor now looks like two crossed lines. Click and drag to the size you want, then release the button. You have now placed an object on your form. If you imported a picture into the box, then people would see the picture when they run the form. You did not have to write any code to have this happen.

With the toolbox, you can create all the familiar elements in a Windows program. You can create icons, for example, for a toolbar. You can create a menu bar. You can create an Exit button that closes the form. You are not limited to "traditional" approaches, either. For example, you could add a button that, when clicked, covers the form in exploding blue stars.

Now try placing a second object. Find the textbox object in the toolbox. Click on it, then move the mouse cursor into the form. Click and drag to size the textbox, then release (Figure 2-7).

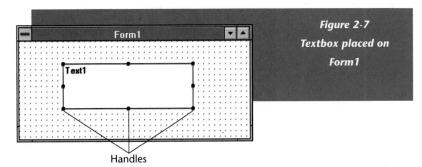

Figure 2-7

Textbox placed on Form1

PROPERTIES WINDOW

One of the characteristics of an object is that it has a "state." This state is made up of a number of properties. To understand this idea, you can think of the state of a common object, such as a glass of water on a desk. The state of that glass includes its position on the desk, its height, its width, whether there is liquid in it, and so forth.

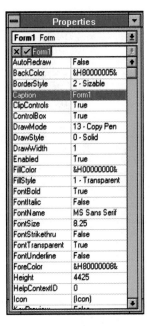

Figure 2-8

Properties of Form1

Visual Basic lists the properties of objects in a Properties window. At any one time, the window shows the properties of only one object. Look in the Properties window to see which properties are displayed. Do the properties there belong to the form or the textbox?

The properties shown in the window belong to the selected object. The black "handle bars" around the textbox you just placed show it is selected. Click anywhere in the form to select the form, which is also an object. Now look in the Properties window. You should see **Form1 Form** at the top of the window. How have the properties changed (see Figure 2-8)?

Just as you can fill an empty glass with water, you can change the properties of Visual Basic objects. To insert text into your textbox, for example, you would change the Text property. You change another property to make the text italic. Figure 2-9 shows a form with six textboxes. In each one, the same text has been inserted, but properties have been set to make the text look very different from box to box. You will experiment with changing the properties of objects in a later section of this chapter.

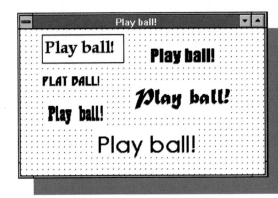

Figure 2-9

Six textboxes

Getting Help

Online help is available through Visual Basic's Help system. Click on Help in the menu bar to open the Help menu. From this menu, select Contents to show the table of contents for the Help system. To find information about a particular word, you would choose Search For Help On, then enter a word. Try the word "menu." Figure 2-10 shows the information on menus that is available. Double-click on the entry you want, then click on Go To.

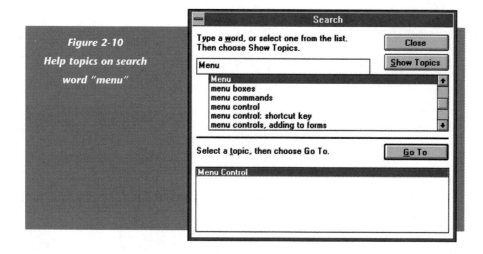

Figure 2-10

Help topics on search word "menu"

Another way to learn is to try working through a tutorial. Tutorials cover common tasks in Visual Basic, such as creating menus or debugging. Select Learning Microsoft Visual Basic from the Help menu to see your choices.

Do not forget to explore the Help system. Once you become familiar with the kinds of information available there, you can find answers to your questions quickly.

QUESTIONS

1. When you open Visual Basic, you see a number of windows. Without looking at the text or your computer, sketch the opening screen with all of the windows. Check your work by opening Visual Basic and comparing. How many did you miss?

2. Where can you find each of the following:
    ◎ A list of an object's properties
    ◎ A list of the forms and code modules of a project
    ◎ A collection of icons representing objects

◎ A collection of buttons representing common tasks

◎ A collection of related objects in a project

3. For each window in the Visual Basic environment, click the arrow boxes in the upper-right corner and observe the effect. Double-click on icons to restore them to their original size. Try minimizing, maximizing, and restoring each window. Try double-clicking on the top-left box of each window to see if you can close it. Re-open any windows you close by selecting Window from the menu bar.

4. Experiment with moving the Visual Basic windows around the screen. Try resizing and rearranging them.

5. Using the Visual Basic Help system, find and read the articles on forms, events, and methods. Use the table of contents to read the article on creating the interface.

Placing Objects

In this section, you will experiment with the steps involved in placing objects. In the process, you will begin to become familiar with working in the Visual Basic environment. Every time you use Visual Basic, you will be repeating these same steps.

2

Section

Starting Out

Open Visual Basic if you do not have it open. Visual Basic automatically opens a form window, as shown in Figure 2-11.

You can see the file name for the form in the Project window (Figure 2-12): **Form1.frm**. The **.frm** extension to the filename identifies the file as a form file. Does the caption at the top of the form match the default form name?

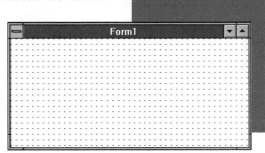

Figure 2-11

Form window

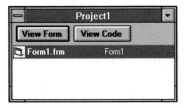

Figure 2-12

Project window

Placing the Objects

Three of the most common and useful objects for Visual Basic programs are the textbox, the label, and the command button. You will be placing these objects on the Form1 open on your screen.

Sometimes you will hear objects called controls. The two terms "object" and "control" are interchangeable. You may also hear the term "control object." All three of these names refer to the contents of the toolbox.

TEXTBOXES

Textboxes are just what they sound like: boxes that contain text. A textbox can display numbers, letters, or a mixture of both (such as "The year is 1995"). You use textboxes to accept input from people running your program. Imagine, for example, that you wanted to include a question with a yes/no answer on a form. You could put the question on the form, then place a textbox at the end of the question. A user of your program could then type yes or no in the textbox.

Create two textboxes on Form1 now (Figure 2-13). Try each of the following:

1   Double-click on the textbox icon in the toolbox. A textbox appears near the center of the form.

2   Click on the textbox icon in the toolbox. Move the mouse cursor into Form1. Click and drag to size the box, then release.

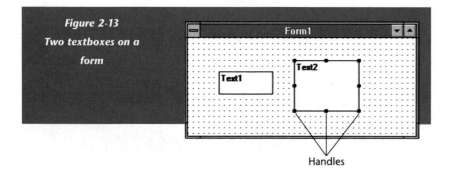

Figure 2-13
Two textboxes on a form

Handles

Now try:

3   Clicking inside one of the boxes and dragging the box to a different place on the form.

4   Dragging a corner handle to resize one of the boxes.

LABELS

You use a label object to tell something to people running your program. Users cannot change the labels you place on a form.

Try using a label as a prompting message for one of your textboxes:

1   Double-click on the label object in the toolbox. The label appears in the form. Now move the label until it is next to, but does not overlap, one of the textboxes (Figure 2-14.)

2   Be sure the label is selected (with handles around the outside edge). In the Properties window, find the Caption property for the label, then select it. What does it say?

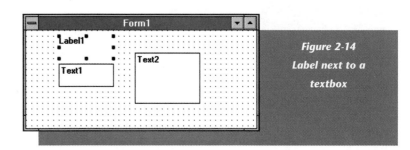

Figure 2-14
Label next to a textbox

3   Type:
   Enter a command:
   Be sure to capitalize the first "E" in "Enter." These words appear in the label box exactly as you typed them. Starting a label with a capital letter looks nicer than using lowercase.

4   See what happens to the label text when you change the size of the label box. Grab the right side of the label object and make the label smaller. Stretch it.

Now, when people run the program, they will be prompted to enter a command in the textbox. They might enter, "eat a tomato" or "put your headphones on."

A second way you can use a label is to display information from your program. For example, you could place a label on a form, then change its caption to read "You have entered the lower catacombs." This would look like the label in Figure 2-15.

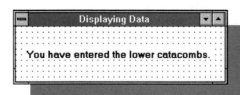

Figure 2-15
Information label

THE COMMAND CONTROL

Command controls are buttons that users click as they are running your program. When a user clicks on one of these buttons, something (an action) happens. The caption of a button, such as "Exit" or "Quit," explains what that action will be.

What makes the program close a form if the user clicks on the Exit button? How does the program know what to do? You assign code to the button, and this code is executed when a user clicks on the button.

The next section explains how to assign program code to a command button. For now, just try placing one of these buttons and changing its caption:

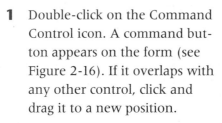

1 Double-click on the Command Control icon. A command button appears on the form (see Figure 2-16). If it overlaps with any other control, click and drag it to a new position.

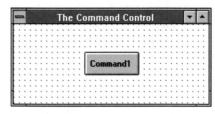

2 With the command control highlighted, look at the Properties window. Be sure that the top of the window shows: Command1 Command button.

3 Find the Caption property. Change the value of this property from **Command1** to **Exit**. As you type, what happens to the command button?

4 Experiment with the size of the command button. Make it longer, then shorter, then taller. Does the caption move as the button is resized?

QUESTIONS AND ACTIVITIES

1. Use the Visual Basic Help system to search for textbox. What are the alternate names for the textbox? Why are they appropriate?

2. Change the caption of the command button to **E&xit**, then note the effect.

3. Add a new form to your project by clicking on the New Form icon on the toolbar. Remove the form by selecting its name from the Project window, then selecting Remove File from the File menu.

4. Using a magazine subscription card from a magazine as a guide, design a form to enter data for a magazine subscription. Use three controls—textbox, label, and command button—in your design.

5. Using the title page of a textbook as a guide, design a form to enter information about books. Use three controls—textbox, label, and command button—in your design.

6. What is the primary purpose of the textbox? Of the label control? Why are they often placed next to each other on a form?

7. Design a form that has the appearance of a four-function calculator. Use command buttons for the keys and a label for the display.
   See Figure 2-17.

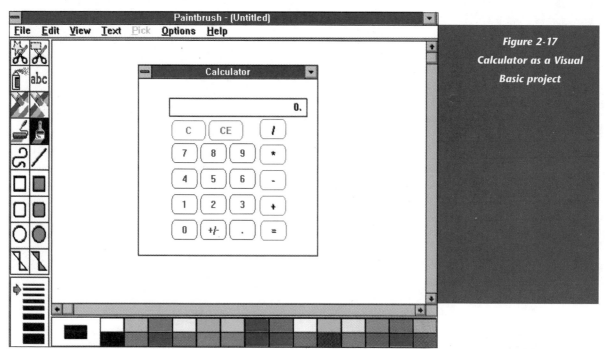

Figure 2-17

Calculator as a Visual

Basic project

Finishing a Program

After you have placed objects on a form, you typically work with their
properties. These properties affect the way objects behave and appear
when the program is run. For example, you may want to move three
text boxes to align with each other. This could change the properties of
each one. You may want to increase the size of an object, or make its
caption larger and italic.

The appearance of your form is called the "look-and-feel" of the
program. Part of the look-and-feel is making your program easy to
understand. You want users to know what to do when they look at a
form. They shouldn't have to study the form to figure it out.

One way to create an understandable form is to follow Windows
conventions. Have you noticed how similar the setup is in Windows
applications? Menu bars are at the top of windows, for example. The
Save command is always found in the File menu. OK and Exit buttons
are typically at the far-right or bottom of a dialog box. When your users

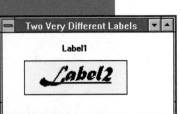

find things where they expect to find them, they can use your program more easily.

Another part of the look-and-feel is how the different elements look. What is different about the two labels in Figure 2-18? Do they create the same tone, or feel?

Defining the look-and-feel of a program before writing any code is a trademark of Visual Basic. In many traditional languages, you write code first, then work with appearance. One reason Visual Basic can reverse the order is because it is a graphical environment. You can place working objects on a form without writing any code.

Generally, though, you do have some code to write or select. You want specific actions to occur when events happen, such as a user clicking on an Exit button. You need to set up the code so that the program closes the form when this event occurs.

The remaining steps in creating a program include saving, printing, and debugging the project. At the very end, you create an "executable". An executable, or **.exe** file, is what people run when they use your program.

More on Properties of Objects

In this section, you will look further at some of the properties of the three most common objects on forms: the textbox, the label, and the command button. You will become more familiar with working in the Properties window.

TEXTBOX

If you do not have a textbox on your form, place one there now. Let's look at two properties of this textbox object:

- Text
- Name

In the previous section, you had the opportunity to change the Text property of a textbox. You saw that the box automatically displays whatever value is in the Text property. The value of the Text property is the contents of the textbox.

You can change the Text property as you design a form. Usually, though, the Text property is changed by:

- A user of your program
- The program itself

For example, a user may be entering information into the program. You may have included a request on a form, such as asking users to enter their names. As the users type their names, this text becomes the new value of the Text property. While the program is running, it can read anything that users type into the Text property of textboxes. Once the names are entered, they can be saved to a file, displayed on the form, or become part of a printed page.

Your program can also use a textbox to display information on a form. As it is running, it can replace the Text property of a textbox on the form. For instance, a name entered by the user may be displayed in a textbox for further editing. In a textbox, the user can change the spelling, or add a middle initial.

An important property of any object is its name. You use the name of an object when you are writing code that uses the object. Every control, when created, has a default name. By default, textboxes are named: Text1, Text2, Text3, ...

You need to be careful not to confuse the Text property with the Name property. When you first place a textbox on a form, both the name and the Text property are the same (such as Text1). To change the contents of the box, you change the Text property. The new contents may be a few words long, such as "This is an apple."

Typically, the new name for an object is only one "word" long. See the textbox for rules on how to name objects. You should use the prefix "txt" when you change the names of textboxes (Figure 2-19):

```
txtLastName
txtBalance
txtHowManyArrows
```

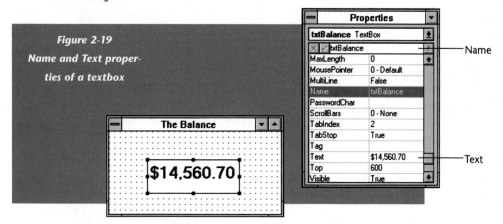

Figure 2-19
Name and Text properties of a textbox

NAMING CONVENTIONS

The way you name the controls placed on a form is important because the names are used to refer to the controls in the program code. Meaningful names make understanding the program code easier.

Textbox names start with the prefix "txt". The prefix for labels is "lbl" and for command buttons is "cmd". The prefix is followed by one or more words describing the function of the control. No spaces are used. Each new word is capitalized. Here are some examples:

```
txtLastName
txtUnpaidBalance
lblBirthplace
cmdDisplayPicture
```

LABELS

Let's look at a few of the properties of the label object:

- Caption
- AutoSize
- BorderStyle

Figure 2-20
Changing the caption
of a label

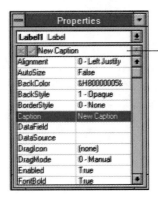

The caption text of a label is displayed on the screen. You experimented with changing caption text in the previous section of this chapter. Try it again now. The text automatically appears in the edit area of the Properties window (see Figure 2-20). The caption also automatically appears in the label.

Now change the AutoSize property of the label. When this property is set to False, the property is turned off. If you turn it on, the label fits itself to the size of the caption. The longer the caption, the longer the label.

Try both ways of changing a property value:

- Select the property and type **True**.
- Double-click on the property.

When you double-click on a property, the Properties window cycles through the different values for that property. Some properties have only two values: False and True. To change the value, then, you only have to double-click. Other properties have more than two possible values. For these properties, you may have to double-click two or more times to find the value you want.

Look at the BorderStyle property. With the default value (0-None), no border appears around the label. Change this value so that a single-line border appears around the label on your form.

Some properties can only be altered at design time; these are listed in the Properties window. Some properties can be altered only when the program is running. Examples include SelLength, SelStart, and SelText, which are properties used to give information about selected text in a textbox. Other run-time properties are listed in the help file for each control. Most properties, though, can be changed at either time.

COMMAND BUTTON

Two important properties of a command button are:

- ◉ Caption
- ◉ Name

The caption of a command button is displayed on its face. Users click on these buttons to perform an action, such as closing a form. You want them to know what the button does, so use captions that are easy to understand. For example, use "Clear" as the caption for a button that clears the text from a textbox.

Just as with textboxes, you use the name of a command button to refer to it in code. Therefore, you need to use names that are easy to remember, such as cmdExit or cmdQuit. A button named cmdQuit should quit the program. Programmers add the "cmd" prefix to these names to indicate that the object is a command button.

Changing an Object's Properties

By this time, you have had a good deal of practice in changing the properties of objects. As a review, the steps you follow to change a property are listed here. Use these steps now to change the properties of objects on your open form.

1 Select an object by clicking on it. The object will visibly change, showing it has been selected. The Form in Figure 2-21 shows two textboxes. The second has been selected.

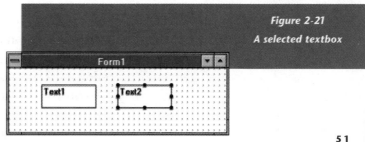

Figure 2-21
A selected textbox

Properties	
Text2 TextBox	
× ✓ Text2	
HelpContextID	0
HideSelection	True
Index	
Left	2400
LinkItem	
LinkMode	0 - None
LinkTimeout	50
LinkTopic	
MaxLength	0
MousePointer	0 - Default
MultiLine	False
Name	Text2
PasswordChar	
ScrollBars	0 - None
TabIndex	1
TabStop	True
Tag	
Text	Text2

Figure 2-22

Properties window for a textbox

2 Look in the Properties window for the properties of that object (Figure 2-22). Use the scrollbar at the right of the Properties window to move up and down the list.

3 Change a property by selecting it, then typing the new value. This new value appears in the edit area at the top of the Properties window (see Figure 2-20). Or, double-click on the property to change the value.

Any change made in the property edit area will take effect immediately.

Attaching Actions to Objects

In Visual Basic, the user controls the action of the program. The user exerts control by causing events to occur. Clicking the mouse is an event. Pressing the Spacebar is an event. Controls from the Toolbox respond to events.

Different events will be introduced throughout this book. One of the most fundamental of Windows events is the Click event. The command button responds to the Click event. When the program is running and a user clicks the command button, an event procedure is executed. The event procedure is the sequence of instructions (code) run when the event occurs.

Visual Basic keeps a list of all the events to which an object responds. Let's look at that list for a command button object:

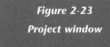

1 Double-click the Command Control icon to place a command button on the form.

2 Find the Project window. If the window is not visible on the screen, select Window from the menu bar, then select Project. The window opens on the screen.

3 In the Project window, select the name of the form.

Figure 2-23

Project window

4 Click on the View Code button (Figure 2-23).

The Code window for the form opens (see Figure 2-24).

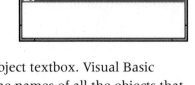

5 In the Code window, click on the downward-pointing arrow by the Object textbox. Visual Basic opens a drop-down list containing the names of all the objects that you have placed on your form (Figure 2-24).

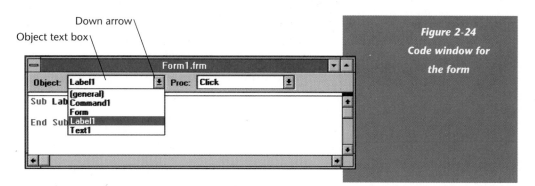

Down arrow

Object text box

Figure 2-24
Code window for
the form

6 Select Command1. This is the default name for the command button, because you have not yet changed it. The Code window displays an empty subroutine for this object. A subroutine is a section of code with one specific purpose. Another word for a subroutine is a procedure. In Visual Basic, code written for events is called an event procedure.

The subroutine is empty because it contains no instructions (statements). The name of the event to which the object responds is shown in the first line (Figure 2-25). By default, this is the Click event.

7 Look at other possible events besides the Click event. Click on the downward-pointing arrow by the Proc textbox. In the drop-down list, Visual Basic displays a list of possible events to which the command button could respond (Figure 2-26). Select one or two, and see how the first line of the subroutine changes.

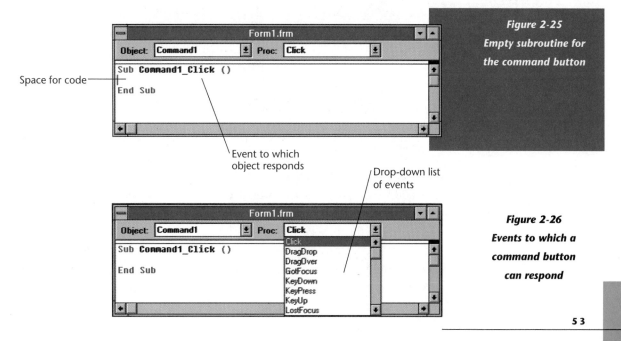

Space for code

Event to which
object responds

Figure 2-25
Empty subroutine for
the command button

Drop-down list
of events

Figure 2-26
Events to which a
command button
can respond

8 Change the event in the Proc textbox back to Click.

The Click event occurs whenever the mouse button is clicked. Whenever the mouse is clicked on the command button, the code in this subroutine will be run. If you do not put any code in the subroutine, no action is taken by the program.

9 Between the lines of the Click Event procedure, insert the line **MsgBox "Hi there!"**

10 Run the program by selecting Start from the Run menu or by pressing the F5 key. Click the command button and note the results.

11 Stop the program by selecting End from the Run menu.

Now experiment with other objects you have placed on your form. In the Code window, open the Object drop-down list and pick a different object.

THE KEYPRESS EVENT

One of the events to which many controls can respond is the KeyPress event. It is often used to process changes in textboxes. It is seldom used with the command button. Select this event from the Proc drop-down list in the Code window. If you look at the KeyPress event procedure, you'll see the parentheses after the name are not empty. The parentheses surround names of values used by the event procedure (Figure 2-27).

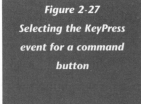

NOTE:

In Visual Basic version 2, the Change event is the default event for the label object; in versions 3 and 4, the default is the Click event.

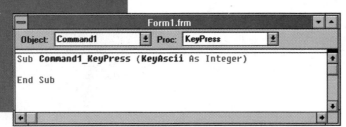

Figure 2-27

Selecting the KeyPress event for a command button

Now, when a user presses a key, the KeyPress event provides the procedure with the ASCII code for the character represented by the key. For instance, if the user presses the "A" key, the KeyPress event passes the code 65, which is the ASCII code for the uppercase A character. Once the value has been passed to the procedure, it can be used to determine what processing takes place (Figure 2-28).

Pressing certain keys on the keyboard does not cause a KeyPress event. The function keys and the arrow keys do not cause the KeyPress event to occur. Only pressing the keys used to enter text initiates the KeyPress event.

ASCII CODES

Early in the history of telecommunications, people realized they needed a standard code to represent characters and commands transmitted over wires. The American Standard Code for Information Interchange is a seven-bit code that is still in use today. These codes let people communicate and exchange information electronically, regardless of the make and model of equipment they are using.

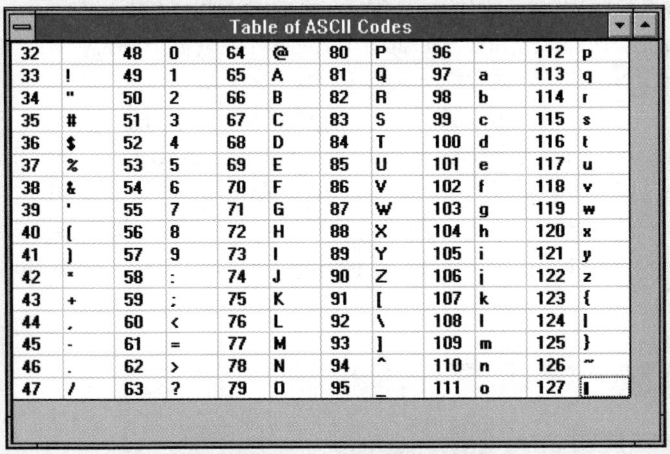

Table of ASCII Codes											
32		48	0	64	@	80	P	96	`	112	p
33	!	49	1	65	A	81	Q	97	a	113	q
34	"	50	2	66	B	82	R	98	b	114	r
35	#	51	3	67	C	83	S	99	c	115	s
36	$	52	4	68	D	84	T	100	d	116	t
37	%	53	5	69	E	85	U	101	e	117	u
38	&	54	6	70	F	86	V	102	f	118	v
39	'	55	7	71	G	87	W	103	g	119	w
40	(	56	8	72	H	88	X	104	h	120	x
41	)	57	9	73	I	89	Y	105	i	121	y
42	*	58	:	74	J	90	Z	106	j	122	z
43	+	59	;	75	K	91	[	107	k	123	{
44	,	60	<	76	L	92	\	108	l	124	l
45	-	61	=	77	M	93	]	109	m	125	}
46	.	62	>	78	N	94	^	110	n	126	~
47	/	63	?	79	O	95	_	111	o	127	

Figure 2-28
ASCII codes

Creating Directories for Your Files

Before saving a project, you need to create a subdirectory to store the Visual Basic files. Create a directory with the File Manager. If you have the File Manager open, you can move from Visual Basic to the File Manager using the System menu. Open the System menu by clicking on the upper-left corner of any window. Select Switch to, then File Manager. If File Manager is closed, you should select Program Manager from the Switch to menu. Alternatively, press Alt+Tab to cycle through the open applications.

Make the new directory in **C:**, the root directory of the disk. Name the new subdirectory **VBFiles**. Return to Visual Basic via the System menu.

A similar box appears to let you save the project file. Giving the same name to the form and to the project is fine, because the two kinds of files have different extensions. In projects with several forms, each form should have a name descriptive of its use.

Saving a Project

Transferring a project from RAM to external storage is called saving. You can reload and run saved projects at any time. Select File from the menu bar. You can see that there are two commands for saving a project:

- ◉ Save Project
- ◉ Save Project As

Save Project saves the project file, the form file(s), and any other optional files comprising your Visual Basic project, with whatever names are currently active. If you have changed the name Form1 to MyForm, for example, the form file will be saved with the name **myform.frm**.

Try saving your project now (Figure 2-29). Select Save Project. The first time you save a project, you are prompted to save the changes to the form or forms first. Then you are prompted to save the files. You may have changed the names of the forms in the Properties window. If you have not, then Visual Basic assumes you want to save these forms as Form1, Form2, and so on.

NOTE:

As with any Windows program, the Save As dialog box opens if you are saving a file for the first time.

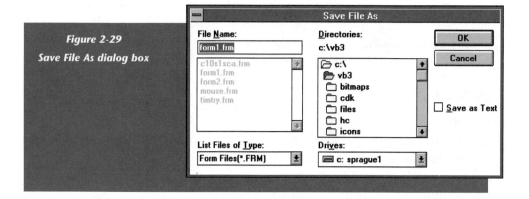

Figure 2-29
Save File As dialog box

After you have saved the forms, you are prompted to save the project itself. The default name for the first project you create is **project1.mak**. You should change this name to something more descriptive. Save all of these files in the directory you created in the File Manager to store Visual Basic programs.

In the directory window, click on **c:** to ascend one branch of the directory tree. Use the scroll bar to find your directory. Move the cursor to the File Name box and type the file name. Click OK or press Enter to save the form.

You use Save Project As if you want to create a copy of a project. Perhaps, for example, you want to experiment with a certain approach, but you don't want to lose the work you've already done. You could save your project as a different name, then experiment. You will be prompted to select different names for the project file as well as any forms or other files contained in the project.

Printing a Project

Printing your project means printing an image of the form, a listing of the code, or a listing of the properties of the controls in the project. Each component is printed on a separate page. There may be more than one form, several event procedures (which form the code), and many controls to print.

To print a component of a project, select Print from the File menu. The Print dialog box shown in Figure 2-30 opens.

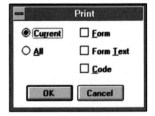

You can print from either a current form or code module, or from all the forms and code modules in a project. The Form option prints a visual representation of the form. The figures shown in this chapter are similar to what you would see. Select Form Text to print text information about the objects included on the form. The result is a list showing the values of properties that have been changed from the default. Select the Code option to list the code for each event procedure.

Figure 2-30
Print dialog box

You can select any or all of the options on the Print dialog box.

Running a Program

Running a program means to give the program control of the computer. Even a form with no controls or code may be run. When it is running other activities of the computer are suspended. The Properties window and the toolbox disappear, emphasizing the differences between run-time and design-time behavior: properties of controls may not be changed through the Properties window when the program is running; the toolbox cannot be used to add controls to a form. Properties can be changed by actions taken in the program code.

There are three ways to run a program:

◉ Select Run from the Visual Basic menu bar, then select Start.

◉ Press the function key, F5.

◉ Click the Start button from the Visual Basic toolbar.

Debugging a Project

Programs have flaws; some large, some small. Occasionally, these flaws, called bugs, keep the program from running. A bug may cause the program to give the wrong answer or perform the wrong action. Finding these problems can be a challenge.

Visual Basic has a number of excellent debugging tools. These tools and common debugging methods will be introduced throughout the text.

Creating an Executable File

Projects, while under development, are usually run from within the Visual Basic environment. The project is opened, loaded into memory, and run by the Visual Basic program. If you need to make additions or corrections, you can do so from within this environment.

Eventually, though, you will finish your project and move on to another one. Finished projects are ready to be run from the Program or File Manager in Windows. Preparing a program to run directly from the Windows environment is called creating an executable file.

To create an executable:

1 From the File menu in Visual Basic, open a project.

2 From the File menu, select Make EXE File.
Visual Basic automatically converts the current project into an executable file. A dialog box prompting you for the location and name of the file appears. The default name of the file is the project name with the file extension **.exe**.

3 To run the file, double-click its name in the File Manager. Or run the file from the Program Manager by selecting Run from the File menu and entering its path and file name.

An executable program created in this way cannot be run from DOS; it must be run in the Windows environment. In addition, the appropriate Dynamic Link Library file (DLL) must be present in the System directory of Windows. For VB version 2, the filename of the DLL is **VBRUN200.DLL**. For version 3 the filename is **VBRUN300.DLL**. These files, which contain procedures necessary for the program to run, may be freely distributed with the programs you write.

QUESTIONS AND ACTIVITIES

1. What is the relationship between objects and properties?

2. What is the relationship between objects and events?

3. Explain the difference between the Name property of a textbox and its Text property.

4. Explain why the AutoSize property of the label control helps the programmer place the label accurately on the form.

5. When you buy gas for a car with a credit card, a great deal of information is recorded on the receipt. Your name, account number, the number of gallons, the price per gallon, and the total cost are all included. Design a form to display this data. Use labels for values that are display-only. Use textboxes for any information entered during the transaction (like number of gallons bought).

6. Open a form. Double-click on the textbox icon in the toolbox. Put the text "Hello, World!" in the Text property and experiment with each of the font properties (including FontName, FontSize, and FontItalic). For the same textbox, experiment with:
   ◎ Different values of the ScrollBars property
   ◎ Color properties

7. Using the Visual Basic Help system, look up and read definitions for the GotFocus, KeyDown, KeyUp, and LostFocus events. Write a few words describing each event.

8. Use the ASCII table in the text to encode your first name.

9. Saving the simplest project involves saving two kinds of files. Describe those files.

10. Using the Visual Basic Help system, search for help on printing code. Read the article and summarize the print choices available.

"Play Ball!"

Now that you have toured through the Visual Basic environment, it is time to create your first real project. Like the classic "Hello, World!" example, used to introduce the C programming language, this section presents a simple project. The program you will create displays "Play Ball!" on a form, along with a button to stop the program (Figure 2-31).

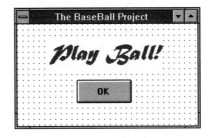

Section

Figure 2-31
The baseball project

Creating the Program

The first steps in creating this project involve putting the necessary objects on the form:

1 Start Visual Basic. If Visual Basic is already running, select New Project from the File menu to create a new project. Save your old project if necessary.

2 Place a label control on the form (Figure 2-32). Double-click the label icon in the toolbox.

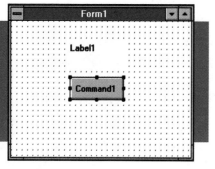

Figure 2-32
Label placed on Form1

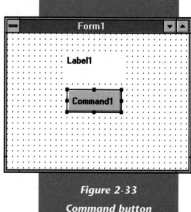

Figure 2-33
Command button placed on Form1

3 Move the label from the middle by dragging it.

4 Place a command button on the form (Figure 2-33). Double-click its icon in the toolbox.

You have now finished putting controls in place. You are ready to move on to the properties of the objects. Start with the form itself.

1 Click on the Properties window. The top line of the window shows the object currently selected. Pull down the menu to select the form (Figure 2-34).

You can also select the form by clicking on the body of the form.

2 Select the Caption property of the form. Change the name of the form to: **The BaseBall Project** (Figure 2-35).

3 Select the label object in the Properties window.

Figure 2-34
Selecting the form

Figure 2-35
Giving the form a new name

4   Change the Caption property to: **Play Ball!** (Figure 2-36).

5   Select the FontName property of the label control. Pull down the font list from the edit area of the Properties window. The fonts listed are determined by the fonts installed in your system. Choose a font that pleases you.

6   Choose other font attributes. FontItalic, FontBold, FontUnderline, and ForeColor are all properties that affect the appearance of the display.

7   FontSize determines the size of the characters. Choose a size larger than the default for impact (Figure 2-37).

8   Once the size takes effect, the caption may no longer be wholly visible (Figure 2-38).

9   Either set the label's AutoSize property to True or resize the label control using the mouse. Once the control is resized, adjust its position on the form (Figure 2-39).

10   Select the command button in the Properties window and change its caption to **OK** (Figure 2-40).

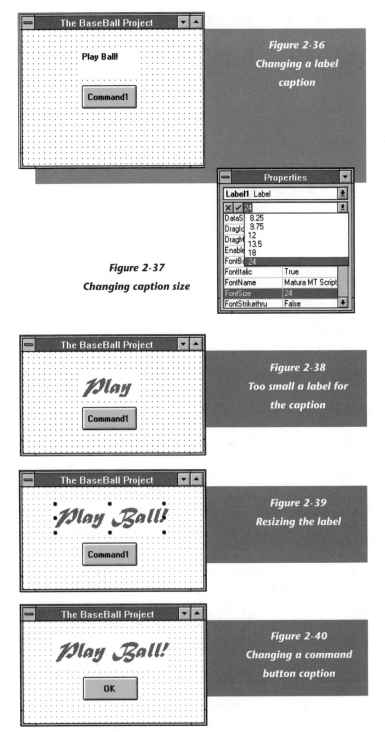

Figure 2-36
Changing a label caption

Figure 2-37
Changing caption size

Figure 2-38
Too small a label for the caption

Figure 2-39
Resizing the label

Figure 2-40
Changing a command button caption

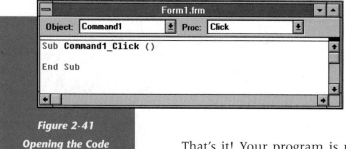

Figure 2-41
Opening the Code
window

11 Double-click on the command button to open the Code window (Figure 2-41).

Between the two lines of the Click event subroutine, type **End**. When executed, this command halts the program.

That's it! Your program is ready to run, save, and print. Print the form, the code, and the form text, the listing of the controls and their properties. You covered all of these tasks in the last section. Do them now for the baseball project. If you need to, refer back to the previous section. Then, create an executable.

Stopping the Program

There are three ways to stop your program:

◉ Select Run from the Visual Basic menu bar, then select End from the menu.

◉ Click the Stop button in the toolbar.

◉ Click the OK button on the program's form.

Once the program is stopped, Visual Basic re-enters design mode. The Properties window and the toolbox reappear.

Loading the Project Again

A project can be reloaded for alterations or just to run it. Most programs are continually modified. Reloading the program returns the project to design mode for changes and enhancements (Figure 2-42).

Start Visual Basic. From the File menu, select Open Project.

Figure 2-42
Reloading a Visual
Basic project

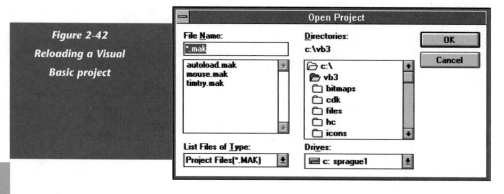

Click your way to the directory you created and double-click the project name of your program. When the program is loaded, the form is not visible. To see the form, select the form's name in the Project window. Click on View Form in the same window to see the original form.

QUESTIONS AND ACTIVITIES

1. Change the BorderStyle property of a label.

2. With a program running, resize the main form.

3. Change a form's BorderStyle. Cycle through the choices, running the program each time and noting the effect. Which do you prefer?

4. Change the MousePointer property of a form. Once again, cycle through the choices, running the program and noting the effect. Which do you prefer?

5. Change the WindowState property of a form, cycling through the choices and running the program each time. Which do you prefer?

6. In a label control, experiment with different foreground and background colors, the ForeColor and BackColor properties.

7. In design mode (program not running), change the shape of the command button. Widen it to touch both of the form's vertical borders.

8. Cycle through the values for the Alignment property of a label. What is the effect of the different values?

The toolbar, across the top of the screen, contains buttons for commonly used Visual Basic operations.

The toolbox, on the left side of the screen, contains objects or controls that are the tools of Visual Basic. Controls are put on forms where they display and accept data and other operations.

The Project window lists the files, forms, and modules that make up a programming project.

The Properties window displays the properties of objects. You can edit these properties in the window.

The Visual Basic Help system is an excellent online resource for the VB programmer.

The form is the "face" of your program. A project may contain many forms.

The textbox control is used to enter text. The text in the box can be edited with all the customary Windows editing commands.

The label control is used to display text. Values are converted to text to display in a label.

The command control responds to a mouse click by executing the code contained in the control.

The Name property of controls allows the control to be referenced in code. The name is used to manipulate the control in Basic statements.

The Text property of a textbox can be read by a program, allowing the user to enter text. The program can also write to the Text property, turning the textbox into a display control.

The Caption property of a label control displays strings written into the property by program statements.

The Caption property of the command button is seldom changed while the program is running. The caption displays the purpose of the button.

The user causes events to which the application is programmed to respond. Each VB control responds to one or more events. Each event is associated with a section of code to handle the event. If the code is not present, the event goes unnoticed by the program.

The Click event responds when the mouse button is clicked on the control. The KeyPress event responds when a text key is pressed.

Saving a project means saving the forms, files, and modules that make up a project. Simple projects have only a single form and the project file to save.

Visual Basic can print the form of a project, just the code, or a text description of the form, called form text.

You can create an executable file from the File menu. The **.exe** file created requires the appropriate copy of **VBRUNxxx.DLL** to run.

To stop a running program, click on the Stop button in the toolbar, select End from the Visual Basic Run menu, or click on a properly coded command button in the program.

1.   Write a program to display "Hello, World!" in a label. Adjust the FontName, FontSize, FontItalic, ForeColor, and BackColor properties to individualize the project. Include an OK button to stop the program. Save and print the project.

```
FallTime = Val (txtTime)

Distance = .5 * Grav *

FallTime ^ 2

lblDistance.Caption =

Distance

cmdClear.SetFocus
```

(txtTime

FallTime

.5

*

Variables, Expressions, and Statements

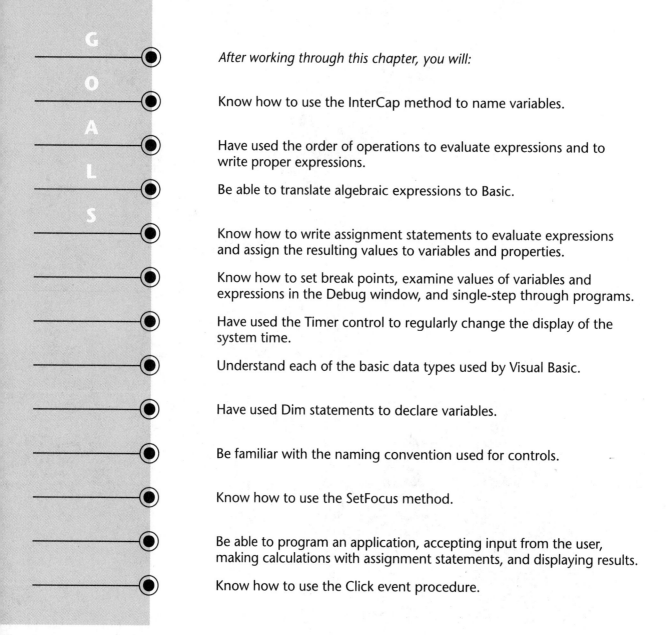

After working through this chapter, you will:

Know how to use the InterCap method to name variables.

Have used the order of operations to evaluate expressions and to write proper expressions.

Be able to translate algebraic expressions to Basic.

Know how to write assignment statements to evaluate expressions and assign the resulting values to variables and properties.

Know how to set break points, examine values of variables and expressions in the Debug window, and single-step through programs.

Have used the Timer control to regularly change the display of the system time.

Understand each of the basic data types used by Visual Basic.

Have used Dim statements to declare variables.

Be familiar with the naming convention used for controls.

Know how to use the SetFocus method.

Be able to program an application, accepting input from the user, making calculations with assignment statements, and displaying results.

Know how to use the Click event procedure.

O V E R V I E W

In Chapter Two, you experimented with the graphical elements in Visual Basic. You placed objects such as textboxes and command buttons on forms. Then you used the Properties window to change properties of these objects, such as the size of the font or the border of a label. These properties determine the look-and-feel of programs.

Now you are ready to work with code. In this chapter, you will learn how to build code by using:

- *Variables, which work on the same principle as variables in algebra*

- *Expressions, which are combinations of variables and operators (for example, a plus sign)*

- *Assignment statements, which are used to give values to variables and properties of objects*

- *Data types, which define the different types of data used by a program (for example, whole numbers or currency)*

- *Methods, which are used to change the state of controls and to make controls perform actions.*

Along the way, you will learn further good programming practices, such as naming conventions for variables and methods for debugging.

Variables, Expressions, and Statements

Section

Look back at the Play Ball program you built in Chapter 2 (see Figure 2-32). Imagine that you wanted to change the color of the text every five seconds. Or you want the text to flash every hour on the hour.

You need variables and expressions to give these types of instructions to the computer. Specifying any calculation for the computer to perform requires using expressions. Unlike the variables of algebra, the values of Visual Basic variables and expressions are not exclusively numeric. You can use them for dates, times, the results of Yes-or-No choices, letters of the alphabet, and chunks of text ranging in length from a single word to an entire term paper.

Variables

Visual Basic programs are designed to deal with a large amount of data stored in the computer. This data is not entered by you the programmer. Instead, it comes from:

- Users entering information

- Data gathered as the program runs

For example, imagine that you set up a label asking "Do you ride mountain bikes? Y/N". Users would enter "Y" or "N" in the textbox you placed next to the label. Now figure that you want to keep a count of all the students who ride mountain bikes. You could have the program add 1 to a counter every time it encounters a "Y" user response. The number of students using bikes is data produced by the program, but it is not data that users (or you) enter.

To access this information after it has been stored, it must be named. You cannot give a computer a request such as, "find all the answers to the question I asked in the second row of Form2."

You don't know what the specific information is. After all, you didn't enter it. You don't know how high the count will be for students using bikes, for example. Or imagine this example: you ask users to type their first names in a textbox labeled "FirstName?" You have no idea, when you create the program, what name any user will enter.

What you do know, though, is the category of information. All answers to the question "FirstName?" are first names. Though you don't know how many students use bikes, you do know that your program produces a bike count. You can, therefore, create names for the categories of information: *FirstName, BikeCount*. These names are called variables (Figure 3-1).

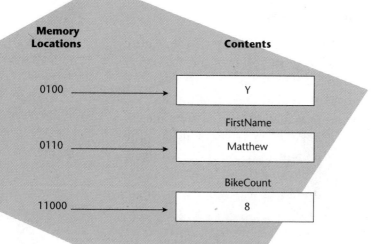

Memory Locations

Contents

0100 ⟶ Y

FirstName

0110 ⟶ Matthew

BikeCount

11000 ⟶ 8

Figure 3-1

Variables as names for categories of information

Using variables, you can refer to the information that is stored as your program runs. And if you can refer to it, you can use it in operations carried out by the program. For example, you may have a variable named Rate. You may want to have the program do something, such as show the user a message on the screen, when the value of Rate reaches a certain number. To build instructions with variables, you use expressions and statements. These are discussed later in this section.

A good variable name should reflect something about the information it represents. If you used the variable name *D* instead of *Rate*, for example, you would forget what it means before the end of the day. What will you do when you look at the program code a week from now?

There are some rules to follow as you create variable names. These names may be up to forty characters (letters or numerals) long. You should also follow the InterCap method to name variables, using capital letters to show how words or portions of words are put together. A variable representing the speed of a train might be *SpeedOfTrain*, using this naming convention.

Expressions

Expressions are used to calculate values. You build expressions from variables and operators. The variables represent data, and the operators represent the actions performed on the data. For example, if you wanted to calculate distance traveled, you would create an expression like the following:

```
AveSpeed * Hours
```

The star is an operator, joining the two variables. It indicates that you want the values of the two variables to be multiplied by each other. You can use any of the five basic math operations to join variables together in this way.

Addition	+
Subtraction	−
Multiplication	*
Division	/
Exponentiation	^

Just as in algebra, you can use more than one operator in a Visual Basic expression. To calculate miles per gallon, for example, you might use:

```
Speed * HoursTraveled/Gallons
```

Which does the program do first, the multiplication or the division? The rules for evaluating Visual Basic expressions are the same as those you use in algebra. You might remember the phrase "Please Excuse My Dear Aunt Sally" from junior high. The letters P, E, M, D, A, and S represent the order of operations:

<u>P</u>arentheses
<u>E</u>xponentiation
<u>M</u>ultiplication and <u>D</u>ivision in order left to right
<u>A</u>ddition and <u>S</u>ubtraction in order left to right

NOTE:

The symbol used in Visual Basic for exponentiation is the caret. You'll find it as a shifted "6" key on the standard keyboard.

Statements

The statements of a program are the instructions you write that the computer executes. Writing a computer program means to write a list of instructions.

One of the most common types of statements you will write is an assignment statement. An assignment statement evaluates an expression and assigns the value to a variable. You use the equal sign to show that an assignment is being made. For example, these are all assignment statements:

```
Rate = 0.035
Interest = Principal * Rate * Time
C = Sqr(a^2 + b^2)
Msg = "Enter a value"
Distance = Velocity * Time
```

Each one of the statements above evaluates the expression to the right of the equal sign and assigns that value to the variable on the left side. Every assignment statement you write must be constructed in exactly this way:

variable = expression

An expression used in an assignment statement may be just a single value.

```
Sum = 0
Years = 30
Message = "Press Enter to continue"
```

The expression may also be a combination of values and variables, such as:

```
Cooktime = Pounds * 17
Layers = 2 * Folds
```

Translating Algebraic Expressions

You will often find yourself using Visual Basic programs to solve mathematical problems. These problems may be simple, such as figuring out the time needed for a train to move from point A to point B. Or they may be complicated, such as figuring out the rate of population growth of tadpoles in a pond in spring.

NOTE:

Visual Basic uses the equal sign as a symbol of comparison as well as for a symbol of assignment. The context in which it is used shows whether an assignment or a comparison is being made.

As you write the code to solve these problems, you will need to translate algebraic expressions into Basic expressions. As you have already learned, the concepts are similar, such as the order in which operations are evaluated. There are some differences, however, in how you write these expressions. The six examples here illustrate this point.

EXAMPLE 1

In algebraic notation:

$I = PRT$

where:

$I = interest$
$P = principal$
$R = interest\ rate$
$T = time$

This simple equation translates easily into Basic.

```
Interest = Principal * Rate * Time
```

EXAMPLE 2

In algebraic notation:

$$F = \frac{9}{5} C + 32$$

where:

$F = degrees\ Fahrenheit$
$C = degrees\ Celsius$

In Basic, this translates to:

```
Fahr = 9 * Cel / 5 + 32
OR
Fahr = 9 / 5 * Cel + 32
```

There are some differences between the two statements in Basic. In the first version, 9 is multiplied first by Cel, then the result is divided by 5 and that result is added to 32. In the second, because Basic strictly adheres to the order of operations, 9 is divided by 5 first, then the result is multiplied by Cel, then that result is added to 32. No parentheses are necessary in the second expression. By the order of operations, multiplication and division are performed in order, left to right.

EXAMPLE 3

In algebraic notation:

$$MPG = \frac{distance}{gallons}$$

This formula calculates the miles per gallon of an automobile by dividing the distance traveled by the number of gallons used. In Basic, you would write:

```
MPG = Distance / Gallons
```

EXAMPLE 4

In algebraic notation:

$$MPG = \frac{speed \times hours}{gallons}$$

The miles per gallon formula from Example 3 has been changed to speed in miles per hour times the number of hours driven in the numerator. The distance traveled by an automobile is the average speed in miles per hour times the number of hours the car travels. In Basic, this translates to:

```
MPG = Speed * HoursTraveled / Gallons
```

EXAMPLE 5

In algebraic notation:

$$P = I^2 R$$

where

$P = power\ in\ watts$
$I = current\ in\ amperes$
$R = resistance\ in\ ohms$

You can express this formula in Basic in two different ways:

```
P = I * I * R
OR
P = I ^ 2 * R
```

The second version uses the symbol for exponentiation.

EXAMPLE 6

In algebraic notation:

$$x = \frac{-b \pm \sqrt{b^2 - 4ac}}{2a}$$

This is the Quadratic Formula, the equation used to find the solutions to quadratic equations:

$ax^2 + bx + c = 0.$

The translation to Basic is a challenge:

```
root1 = (-b + Sqr( b^2 - 4 * a * c )) / ( 2 * a )
root2 = (-b - Sqr( b*b - 4 * a * c )) / ( 2 * a )
```

The minus sign in front of the first b is the "unary minus" sign. It shows that the value of the variable b is negated. **Sqr(x)** is a built-in function that calculates the square root of the number inside the parentheses. The value of the expression inside the parentheses must not be negative. The function, if sent a negative value, will stop the program with an error. An error that occurs while the program is running is called a run-time error.

A common error when translating this equation is to write $4ac$ instead of $4 * a * c.$ In algebraic notation, you do not have to include the multiplication symbol; in Basic, you do.

QUESTIONS AND ACTIVITIES

1. Use the InterCap method of naming variables to name the following:
    a) The height of a building
    b) The length of a hose
    c) The time of day
    d) The number of lives
    e) The distance to Racine

2. In the following expressions, what are the first and second operations performed?
    a) 7 * 8 + 5
    b) 5 + 7 * 8
    c) 5 * 7 / 8 + 5
    d) 5 + 7 / 8 ^ 2
    e) 5 * (7 + 8)
    f) (7 + 8) * (5 − 8)
    g) (7 + 8) ^ (5 − 8)

3. Translate the following equations into their equivalent Basic expressions:

    a) Calories per second = ohms x amperes squared x seconds x 0.24

    b) $H = 0.24 \times I \times R \times T$

4. Translate the following expression to Basic. Use parentheses for both the numerator and the denominator. Don't use H and h for variables. Use *BigH* for H, and *Littleh* for h:

$$F = \frac{H - h}{H' - h'}$$

5. The sine function in Basic is: **Sin(x)**. The value, x, must be expressed in radian form. The cosine function in Basic is **Cos(x)**. Translate the following into Basic:

    a) Take the square root of both sides of the equation, then translate to Basic.

    $$c^2 = a^2 + b^2 - 2ab \text{ cosine } C$$

    b) Solve the equation for a by multiplying both sides by sinA, then translate.

    $$\frac{a}{\sin A} = \frac{b}{\sin B}$$

6. The monthly payment on a mortgage, given the amount borrowed, B, the monthly interest rate, I, and the total number of payments, n:

$$payment = \frac{BI}{1 - (1 + I)^{-n}}$$

    Translate into Basic.

7. Write statements to assign values to these variables: *Weight* is 230 lb., *Strength* is 140, *Health* is 120, *Potions* is 5, *Spells* is 3, *FirstName* is "Doug".

8. A dog's age is expressed in dog years. A single human year is equal to seven dog years. Write an assignment statement that converts a number of dog years, *DogYrs*, to human years. Write a statement that converts a number of human years, *HumanYrs*, to dog years.

9. Every five tardies is counted as a single absence. Write a statement that converts a student's tardies into the equivalent number of absences.

10. A cat has nine lives. Write a statement that will convert a given number of cats into the equivalent number of lives.

11. The interest paid on a loan for a month is the unpaid balance times the monthly interest rate. Write a statement that assigns a value to the interest paid for a month.

12. Robert Boyle was the first person to perform experiments upon what he called the "springiness of the air." Today, Boyle's law is expressed as: The volume of a gas at constant temperature is inversely proportional to the pressure of the gas. In an "inverse proportion," when one value goes up, the other goes down. In this case, when pressure is increased, the volume is decreased, and when the volume is increased the pressure is decreased (Figure 3-2).

    Normally we express this proportion as:

    Volume times Pressure equals a constant

    This expression is not in the form of a Basic assignment statement.
    a) Solve the equation for *Volume*. Write a Basic statement for volume.
    b) Solve the equation for *Pressure*. Write a statement for pressure.
    c) Solve the equation for the constant value, *K*. Write a statement for the constant.

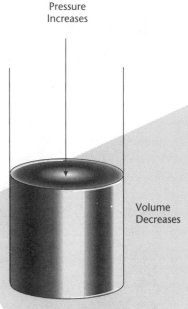

Pressure Increases

Volume Decreases

Figure 3-2
Pressure and volume relationships

13. The following finds the horsepower of a gas engine (Figure 3-3):

$$HP = \frac{D^2 N}{2.5}$$

    where:
    D = diameter of the cylinder in inches
    N = number of cylinders.

    Rewrite the equation as three assignment statements.

    a) Solve for the horsepower. Write an assignment statement.

    b) Solve for the number of cylinders. Write a statement.

    c) Solve for the diameter of the cylinders. Use the **Sqr(x)** function to calculate the square root of the value. Write a statement

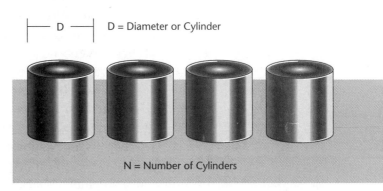

D = Diameter or Cylinder

N = Number of Cylinders

Figure 3-3
Finding the horsepower of an engine

Section

Trying Out Expressions and Statements

This section outlines two simple projects. As you build these projects, you will become used to working with variables, expressions, and statements. At the same time, you will gain experience with the debugging capabilities of Visual Basic.

Variables and Debugging

As opposed to algebraic variables, Visual Basic variables can change values as a program runs. Remember that a variable is a name for a location in which a quantity is stored, and its value is the quantity stored there. In this sense, variables are analogous to phrases such as "the number of oranges in the refrigerator" or "the amount of money in my pocket."

The events of the day can change the amount of money in your pocket. Similarly, the statements of a program can change the contents of a location in which a variable's value is stored. A program is a process that unfolds in time. This dynamic, temporal element is absent from the expressions and equations of algebra, where each variable takes on a value that it retains throughout an entire problem.

A program is a sequence of instructions for the computer to carry out, which programmers specify in its entirety before the program is run. In effect, they build a mental model of how they want and expect the program to behave over time. Then they try to ensure that their sequence of instructions specifies the behavior they have in mind.

Programmers, however, do not always succeed. Sometimes the sequence of instructions they create will be performed in an order they didn't anticipate. Or an expression yields a value different from the one they expected. Or the value of a variable is changed to one that they thought was impossible.

A "bug" is a deviation between the way a program is supposed to behave and the way it actually does. Some bugs are obvious to every user of a program. Others will be apparent only to the program's creator.

The process of eliminating deviations is called "debugging." The most common way to debug a program is to look at the values the program assigns to variables as it runs. If the code is set up correctly, these values should be reasonable and as you expect them to be. For example, imagine that you stop a program, then find a value of 400 assigned to the variable *Age*. This would be an unreasonable value if you were storing human ages. It is a reasonable value for tree ages.

How do you stop a program while it is running so that you can look at variable values? You set break points, which means you mark spots where you want the program to stop executing. When the program is run, it pauses before each highlighted line. During the pause, you can display the values of the variables in the Debug window.

To explore this method of debugging, you will create a form with no controls. You will insert code into the form's Form-Load area, then check the values of variables used in that code.

Generally, you use this area to run code that takes care of housekeeping functions when a form is loaded into memory. You do not need any controls to run the code in this area. Each time a form is loaded, the program automatically executes the commands in the Form-Load section of the form.

Setting Up the Project

Follow these steps to create the project, insert the code, and mark breakpoints:

1 Start Visual Basic. If Visual Basic is already running, select New Project from the File menu. A form opens by default.

2 Select Environment from the Options menu. The Environment Options dialog box opens (Figure 3-4).

3 In the dialog box, set the item Require Variable Declaration to Yes. This means each program will require the declaration of variables. The advantages of this option will be discussed later in the chapter.

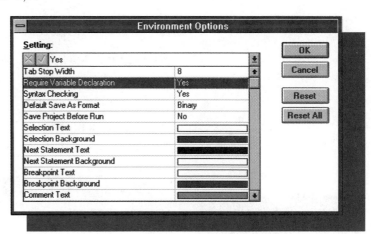

Figure 3-4
The Environment
Options dialog box

4 Click OK.

5 Double-click somewhere on the body of the default form. Visual Basic switches to the Code window for the form. The empty Form-Load subroutine is displayed.

6 In the subroutine, insert the declaration and assignment statements shown in Figure 3-5. Declarations will be described further in the next project.

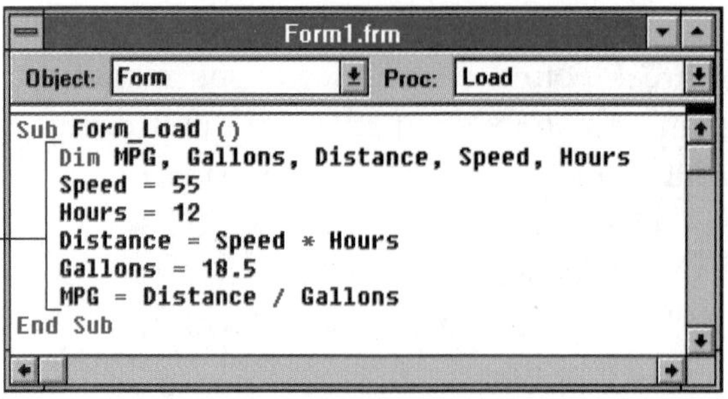

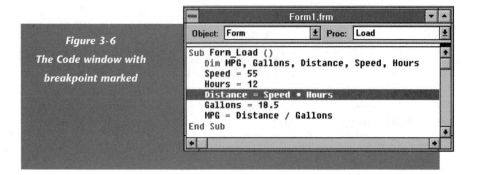

Figure 3-5
The Code window

Code to select

---

 7 Click on the line **Distance = Speed * Hours**. Then click on the Break point tool in the Visual Basic toolbar (Figure 3-6).

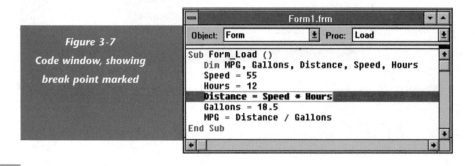

Figure 3-6
The Code window with breakpoint marked

Running the Program

Now run the program:

1 Select Start from the Run menu or click on the Run button on the toolbar to run the program.

The program pauses at the line you marked. The Code window opens again, along with the Debug window (Figure 3-7).

Figure 3-7
Code window, showing break point marked

The break point is now framed. The frame shows the next
statement to be executed, which is the break point line of code.

2 Click on the Debug window. If you cannot see the window, select
Debug from the Window menu.

3 Use the **Print** statement to check the current value of the variables
you added to the Form-Load subroutine. Type into the Debug window (Figure 3-8):

```
Print Speed
Print Hours
Print Distance
```

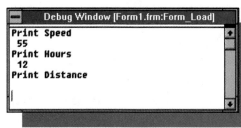

Figure 3-8

Using the Print

statement

The caption bar of the
Debug window shows
the procedure of the form
in which the program is

halted. The values currently assigned to the variables are also
shown. There is no value for *Distance* yet, because the line calculating the distance has not been executed.

Figure 3-9

The Debug Window

4 Type in the Debug window (Figure 3-9):

```
Print Speed * Hours
```

The Debug window allows calculations within
the **Print** statement. Still, although the value
has been calculated in the **Print** statement
entered into the Debug window, the value has
not been assigned to *Distance*.

5 Execute the next line of the program by
clicking on the Single-Step button in the
toolbar (Figure 3-10).

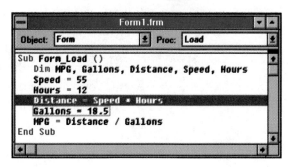

Notice that the frame marking the next
statement to be executed has moved
down. The line above has now been
executed.

6 In the Debug window, type:

```
Print Distance
```

7 Step through the rest of the program.
After each step, print each of the variables
in the Debug window.

Figure 3-10

Executing the next line

of code

In this exercise you will enter the lines of a program to calculate the simple interest earned by $2300 on deposit for two years. Once the program is finished, you set a break point and use the Debug window to examine intermediate values of variables.

To complete the exercise:

1 Select New Project from the File menu.

2 Enter these statements in the Form-Load procedure:

```
Dim Principal, Interest, IntRate, Duration
Duration = 2
Principal = 2300
IntRate = .045
Interest = Principal * IntRate * Duration
```

3 Set a break point on the last line.

4 Run the program.

5 Print the values of the four variables in the Debug window.

6 Single-step one line.

7 Print the value of *Interest*.

Programming a Digital Clock

This project gives you more experience with assignment statements and introduces you to the Timer control. The Timer control lets you perform actions at regular intervals.

If you were writing a game, for example, you could use the Timer to be sure that your animation ran at the same speed on all computers. You would not want the animation to run as fast as possible on all machines. If it did, it would run unplayably fast on powerful machines.

The Timer has only one significant property, the Interval property. This property is loaded with an integer. The Timer counts down from this integer. When the count reaches 0, the control generates a Timer event. You will use this event to set the caption of the digital clock.

You will use an assignment statement to display the current time in the caption of a label. The program takes the current time from a Visual Basic function called **Time**. The value of the Time function is the time of the system clock.

The controls you place on the form will include:

⦿ Command button

⦿ Label

⦿ Timer

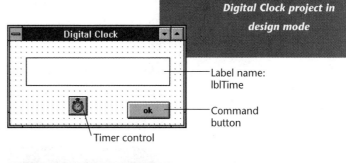

Figure 3-11
Digital Clock project in
design mode

Label name:
lblTime

Command
button

Timer control

You will size the form to fit these three controls.

Figure 3-11 shows the final appearance of the form during the design phase.

Figure 3-12 shows the form's appearance while the program is running.

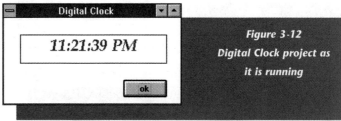

Figure 3-12
Digital Clock project as
it is running

PLACING THE OBJECTS

Follow these steps to create the project:

1 Start Visual Basic. If the application is already running, select New Project from the File menu.

2 Double-click on the label icon in the toolbox. Move the label near the top of the form.

3 Put a command button on the form. Double-click on its icon in the toolbox. Move this button to the bottom-right corner of the form.

4 Put a Timer control on the form. Double-click on its icon in the toolbox. Move this button to the bottom of the form.

ALTERING THE PROPERTIES OF OBJECTS

Now you are ready to change the properties of the objects you've placed:

1 Click the label on the form to select it. In the Properties window:

a) Change the Name to **lblTime**.

b) Change the caption by deleting the characters.

c) Change the BorderStyle to 1.

d) Change the Alignment property to Center. This will center any display within the label.

e) Change the FontName and the FontSize to something pleasing to your eye.

2 Click on the command button to select it. In the Properties window, change the caption to OK.

3 Click on the Timer control to select it. Set the Interval property to 1000.

4 Click on the body of the form to select it.

   a) Change the Caption property to "Digital Clock" (Figure 3-13).

   b) Change the BorderStyle to Single-Fixed.

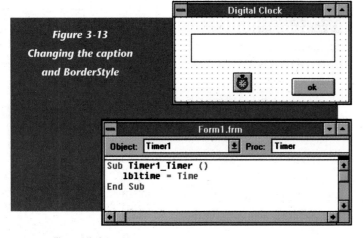

Figure 3-13
Changing the caption and BorderStyle

5 The clock requires only one line of code. Double-click on the Timer control to open its Code window (Figure 3-14).

6 Enter the assignment statement shown in Figure 3-14. The function **Time** is the system clock time, and you are using it to update the caption of lblTime.

7 Open the Code window for the command button. In the Click routine, enter the statement: **End**.

8 Run the program.

9 Save the program. Save both the form and the project files.

Figure 3-14
Code window for Timer control

Data Types

Section

Data types are what they sound like: types of data. Think of the different types of data users could enter as they run a program. They could enter a string of text, for example, a percentage, or an amount of money. Visual Basic defines eight different types of data that a user could enter or a program could produce.

Why do you need to know about data types? Defining data types for variables gives you a way to control what a user can enter into a textbox. Imagine, for example, that you want a user to enter a dollar amount in a textbox labeled "Cost of bike?" You do not want the program to accept other types of data, such as text.

First you create a variable to store the data the user enters into this textbox. Then, you can declare the data type of the variable as Currency and you can write some code that displays an error message if the user enters the wrong data type in the textbox.

Looking at the Different Types

The eight different data types include:

- Integer
- Long
- Single
- Double
- Currency
- String
- Variant
- User defined

Some of these data types are briefly introduced in this section. You will use others of these data types in later chapters.

> **NOTE:**
>
> **Visual Basic version 4 adds several data types: Byte, Boolean, Date, Object, and an additional Variant type.**

INTEGER TYPE

Integers are whole numbers, such as 9 or 100. Many game programs use this data type to represent values such as health points or strength.

You can use this type for whole numbers in the range between -32,768 and +32,767. The difference in the positive and negative limits is due to the way the numbers are represented in memory. Most computers use a scheme called "two's complement binary representation," and because of the way negative numbers are stored, the positive and negative ranges are different.

LONG TYPE

The Long data type is very similar to the Integer type. You use it to represent whole numbers in the range from -2,147,483,648 to +2,147,483,647. Each number of this data type requires twice as much memory to store as a number of the Integer type.

When using long integers, you might be tempted to put in a comma every three digits. While you can format numbers to be displayed with commas, Visual Basic does not recognize numbers with commas in expressions.

SINGLE TYPE

You use the Single data type to represent decimal numbers, which are numbers with a fractional part. Internally, the numbers are stored in something like a binary version of scientific notation.

SCIENTIFIC NOTATION

Scientists and mathematicians represent very small and very large numbers in scientific notation. Like the decimal number system, scientific notation is based on powers of 10. Each positive number is expressed as a decimal number between 0 and 10 times a power of 10.

23,500,000 becomes 2.35 x 10^7

10^7, ten to the seventh power, is 1 followed by 7 zeros: 10,000,000. Thus 2.35 x 10^7 is 2.35 x 10,000,000, or 23,500,000.

Variables of the Single type can represent negative numbers in the range from -3.402823E38 to -1.401298E-45, and positive numbers in the range from 1.401298E-45 to 3.402823E38. The E stands for exponent ,and it means the number that follows is used as a power of ten. The number 3.402823E38 means 3.402823 times 10 raised to the 38th power—1 followed by 38 zeros! Raising 10 to the negative 45 power, as in E-45, means one divided by 10 raised to the 45th power, or 1 over 1 followed by 45 zeros.

1/1,000,000,000,000,000,000,000,000,000,000,000,000,000,000,000

CURRENCY TYPE

You use the Currency data type to represent dollar amounts. A variable of Single type may also be used, but in the conversion from decimal to binary and back, round-off error can occur. This error makes the Single type unsuitable for representation of dollar amounts. The Currency data type avoids round-off errors and maintains values to an accuracy of one hundredth of a cent.

STRING TYPE

The String type is used to represent characters, including:

● Text

◉ Special characters such as the pound sign (#), the underscore (_), and the tilde (~)

◉ Digits, 0 through 9

A set of characters contained in double quotes is called a string literal, or string for short. Visual Basic includes two types of variables to hold strings: fixed-length string variables and variable-length string variables. Variable-length string variables can hold strings up to about 65,000 characters long; fixed-length string variables hold only the number of characters you specify when you declare the variable.

Only strings whose length does not exceed that fixed length can be stored in a fixed-length string variable. Though variable-length strings are more common, fixed-length strings are sometimes more appropriate. For example, you may want to gather a user's first and last name for printing on a form with a box for each letter.

VARIANT TYPE

This special type can represent numbers, or strings of any type, as well as times and dates. In exchange for the versatility of using a single type for almost any kind of data, you give up memory space. A variable of the Variant type takes a lot more memory than a variable of the Integer type.

Data type	Suffix	Size	Range
Integer	%	2 bytes	-32,768 to 32,767
Long	&	4 bytes	+/– about 2 billion
Single	!	4 bytes	-3.4E38 to -1.4E-45 for negative values
			1.4E-45 to 3.4E38 for positive values
Double	#	8 bytes	-1.8E308 to -4.9E-324 for negative values
			4.9E-324 to 1.8E308 for positive values
Currency	@	8 bytes	+/– 922 trillion to 4 decimal places
String	$	variable	0 to about 65,000 bytes
Variant	none	variable	variable

Declaring Variables

Declaring a variable means writing a statement that associates a data type with a variable name. This statement announces the existence of the variable and allocates storage for it.

Once the association is made, any value of the variable will be of the declared data type. To declare a variable in Visual Basic, you use a **Dim** statement:

```
Dim DogYrs As Integer, HumanYears As Integer
Dim a As Integer, b As Integer, c As Integer
Dim chirps As Long
Dim Avogadro As Single
Dim Balance As Currency
Dim LastName As String
Dim Payment As String * 17  (fixed-length string)
```

The Variant data type is the default type for Visual Basic. If you do not declare the type of a variable, Visual Basic declares the variable to be a Variant data type by default.

```
Dim a,b,c
Dim sum, rate, lives
Dim storms, tornadoes
```

Once you have declared a variable as being a specific type, you can use it in an assignment statement. If you place this variable on the left side of an equal sign, it will be assigned the value of the expression on the right. For example:

```
Sum = 34 + 55 + 23
DogYears = 7 * HumanYears
Avogadro = 6.03E23
pi = 3.1415926
rate = 0.08
```

Initializing Variables

You initialize a variable by assigning it a starting value. Before you use a variable in the right side of an assignment statement, you need to initialize it. For example, consider the following:

```
Dim Y As Integer, Z As Integer
Y = 24 + Z
```

Because you haven't assigned a value to Z before using it in an assignment statement, Visual Basic gives the variable a value of 0. This may seem convenient but it can lead to trouble, as you can see here:

```
Dim Y As Integer, Zed As Integer
Zed = 48
Y = 24 + Zd
```

You may have hoped the code above would add 48 to 24 and assign the value to Y. Since Zed is misspelled as Zd in the second statement, Zd is given the default value of 0. Y is assigned the result of 24 + 0, or 24.

OPTION EXPLICIT

Visual Basic gives you a way to avoid this problem that is called Option Explicit. This statement requires that every variable name be declared before it is used. If a variable appears that hasn't been declared, as will be the case if a variable name is misspelled, Visual Basic will flag the use of the undeclared variable as a mistake. Figure 3-15 shows a Code window with the previous lines of sample code, the Option Explicit statement, and the error message that results when the program is run.

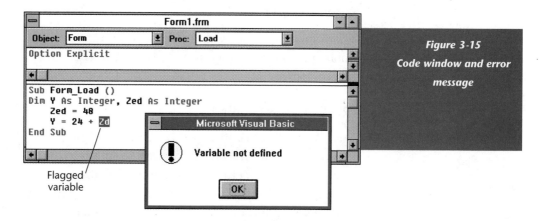

Figure 3-15
Code window and error
message

VARIABLES AND THE VENUS SPACE PROBE

Failing to declare variables can have expensive implications. A NASA Venus space probe was lost due to a bug in a FORTRAN program. The bug was ultimately traced to a variable that the programmer thought was an integer. FORTRAN, though, treated it as a floating-point number. FORTRAN lacks mandatory variable declarations and has a default typing scheme whereby a variable's type is determined by the first letter of its name.

USING SUFFIXES TO INDICATE DATA TYPE

In days of yore, Basic variable names often bore suffixes indicating the data type of the variable. The percent sign showed a variable to be of the integer type, Seconds%. Visual Basic allows the same use of suffixes, with additions to cover some new data types. Generally, these suffixes do not make a program easier to read. They are included in the summary only so you may recognize them if you encounter them in code listings.

Section

The Freefall Program

The Freefall program will give you practice working with three commonly used controls: the label, the textbox, and the command button. The user will use the textbox to enter a value into the program. The program uses labels to display a calculated value and to label the display. The command buttons control making the calculation, clearing the form, and quitting the program.

Starting Out

When you start out working on a program, you figure out what the problem is that the program will solve. You then create a plan to solve the problem.

PROBLEM STATEMENT

What is the distance in feet traveled by an object, calculated from the time the object falls? You can create a program to calculate this distance for whatever time period a user enters. The distance can be displayed in either feet or meters. To display in feet, use 32.2 feet per second squared as the acceleration of gravity. To display in meters, use 9.80 meters per second squared for that acceleration.

To calculate distance, the program needs to solve the following equation:

```
Distance = 0.5 x Grav x Time²
```

This equation calculates the distance traveled by an object falling freely with no initial velocity (no starting speed). The variables represent the following (Figure 3-16):

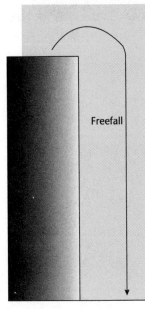

Figure 3-16

A freefalling object

- *Grav* = acceleration of gravity

- *Time* = time the object is falling

- *Distance* = distance that object falls from its starting point

THE PLAN

To solve the problem, you sketch out the form shown in Figure 3-17. You decide to use a textbox for the time, a label for the distance, and three command buttons. The command buttons execute the following actions:

- One button calculates and displays the distance.

- A second clears the textbox and the Distance label. In addition, clicking on this button selects the textbox used for entering the time.

◉ Clicking on the third command
button ends the program.

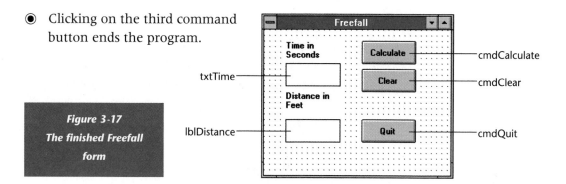

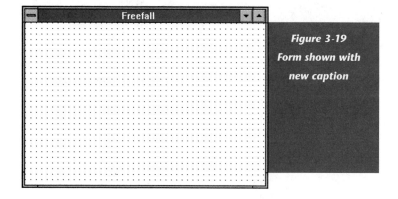

Figure 3-17
The finished Freefall
form

Opening a Form and Changing Its Caption

You use the caption at the top of a form to indicate the form's purpose.
Each form should have a descriptive name. Start this program by changing the default form's caption to "Freefall".

1 Start Visual Basic.

2 Click on the top line of the form and look at the Properties
window. This window lists the properties of the selected object.

3 Select the Caption property and type the word **Freefall** (Figure 3-18).

This word automatically appears in the edit area near the top of
the Properties window. It also appears at the top of the form
window (Figure 3-19).

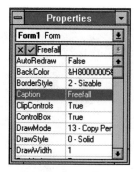

Figure 3-18
New caption for
the form

Figure 3-19
Form shown with
new caption

Placing Objects

In these steps, you are placing the same types of objects you added to a
form in Chapter 2. The form is not only the basis for the program's interaction with the user, it is the container for the program code. The textbox
and the command buttons respond to events initiated by the user. These
events execute the code that does the work of the program.

NOTE:

**The name of the form
has not been altered
even though the Cap-
tion property has been
changed. Don't con-
fuse the name and
the caption.**

TEXTBOX

You need user input in this event-driven program. The user enters a length of time, and the program uses this number to calculate how far the object could fall in that time period. As discussed in Chapter 2, you need to place one or more textboxes on a form if you expect user input. In this case, you need a single textbox.

To add a textbox:

1 Double-click on the textbox icon in the toolbox.

2 Position the box by dragging it to wherever you want it (Figure 3-20).

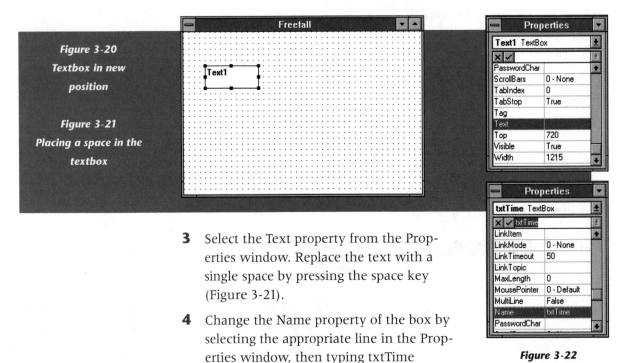

Figure 3-20
Textbox in new position

Figure 3-21
Placing a space in the textbox

3 Select the Text property from the Properties window. Replace the text with a single space by pressing the space key (Figure 3-21).

4 Change the Name property of the box by selecting the appropriate line in the Properties window, then typing txtTime (Figure 3-22).

Figure 3-22
Changing the Name property

LABELS

You need two different kinds of labels for the form. One kind of label is a descriptive caption, an explanation of what the user sees on the form. The program uses the other kind of label to display calculated values. In total, you will place three labels on the form.

To add labels:

1 Double-click on the Label icon in the toolbox.

2 In the Properties window, select the Caption property for this first label. Then type a descriptive label for the Time textbox (Figure 3-23).

Change fonts, font sizes, as well as background and foreground colors to suit your fancy.

3 Position this first label by dragging it above the textbox (Figure 3-24).

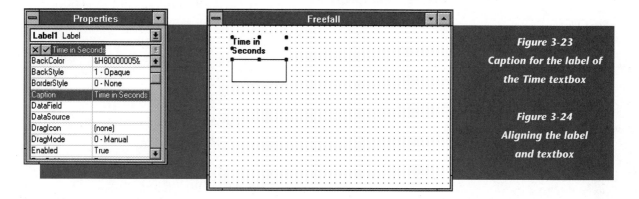

Figure 3-23
Caption for the label of the Time textbox

Figure 3-24
Aligning the label and textbox

4 Now create two more labels. Create one to display the calculated distance and another to be its caption. Change the caption of one label to be a description of the label showing the distance. Change the font, font sizes, as well as the colors to match the descriptive label created in step 2 (Figure 3-25).

5 Delete the text in the caption of the third label by pressing Backspace, then Enter. The caption will change under Program control displaying the distance fallen. Change the BorderStyle property to 1 - Fixed Single (Figure 3-26). The values of this property are available in a list. Double-clicking on the property cycles through the values.

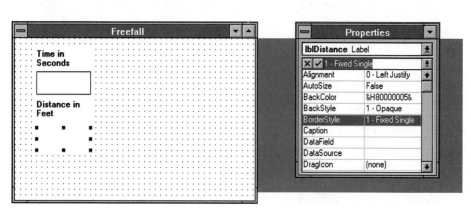

Figure 3-25
Adding more labels

Figure 3-26
Changing the Border Style property

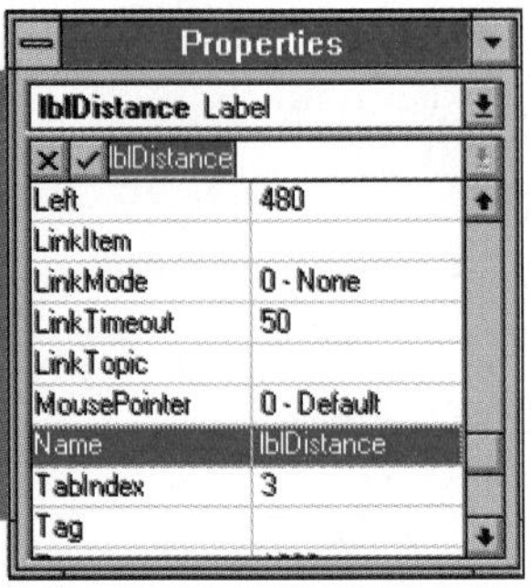

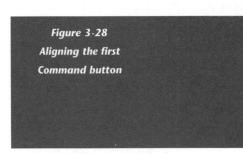

Figure 3-27
Changing the name of
the third label

6 Change the name of the third label to **lblDistance** (Figure 3-27).

COMMAND BUTTONS

Adding command buttons to a form allows the user to initiate program actions. As noted in the program plan, you are adding three to the Freefall form.

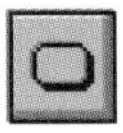

You can create these buttons one at a time, as noted in the steps below. Or you can try the approach explained in the note.

1 Double-click on the Command Control icon in the toolbox.

2 Drag the first button to the top-right corner of the form (Figure 3-28).

NOTE:

You can speed up these repetitive tasks by creating all three command buttons at once, then changing each property for all three buttons at the same time. To change the captions in all three, select the caption in the first button. Type the desired caption. Select the next button. Visual Basic automatically selects the same property for the new command button. Type your change and select the third button.

Figure 3-28
Aligning the first
Command button

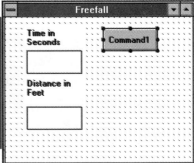

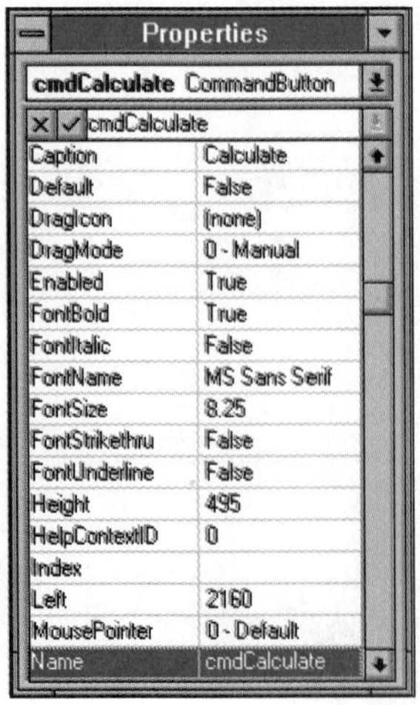

3 Change the Caption property of the button to **Calculate**, then change the Name property of the button to **cmdCalculate** (Figure 3-29).

Figure 3-29
Changing properties
for the first
command button

Here's the form once the changes take effect (Figure 3-30).

4   Create a second command button and drag it below the Calculate button (Figure 3-31). In the Properties window, change the value of the Name property to **cmdClear**, then the value of the Caption property to **Clear**.

5   Create a third command button and drag it below the Clear button. In the Properties window, change the value of the Name property to **cmdQuit**, then the value of the Caption property to **Quit**. Leave some white space between the top two command buttons and the Quit button (Figure 3-32).

The form is designed. It's time to start thinking about the code that will tie everything together.

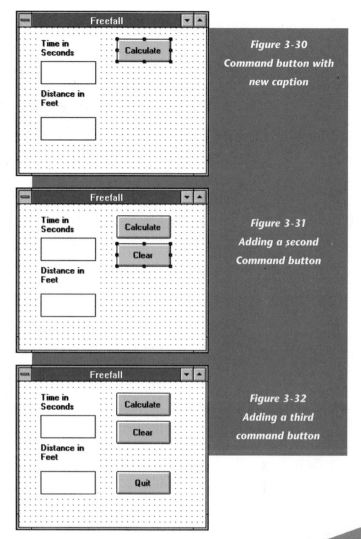

Figure 3-30
Command button with new caption

Figure 3-31
Adding a second Command button

Figure 3-32
Adding a third command button

Writing Command Button Subroutines

The default event procedure for any command button is the Click event. This means that, when a user clicks on the button, the program responds to this event and executes an action. You determine what that action is by writing code in a subroutine. In this program, you want a different action to occur, depending on which button is clicked. When one of the buttons is clicked, for example, distance is calculated. The same event (a user clicking) causes a totally different action to occur with either of the other buttons.

To insert code into the Click subroutine for any of these buttons, you double-click on the button. The Code window for that button opens.

NOTE:

The name of the subroutine is the name of the object with the name of the event appended as a suffix. The empty parentheses after the name of the subroutine indicate that no information is sent into the subroutine by the event.

Visual Basic has already started the code for the routine by providing the top and bottom lines (Figure 3-33).

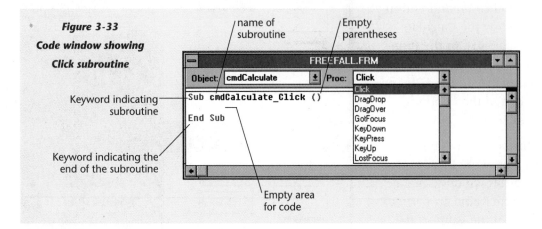

Figure 3-33

Code window showing

Click subroutine

Keyword indicating subroutine

Keyword indicating the end of the subroutine

name of subroutine

Empty parentheses

Empty area for code

CODE FOR THE CALCULATE BUTTON

To write the code for the Calculate button:

1 Double-click on the command button, cmdCalculate, on the form. Pull down the Proc menu on the right. The Procedure menu shows the events to which a command button can respond. You'll be using the default event, Click. Insert the following code between the first and last lines of the Click subroutine:

```
Dim FallTime As Single, Distance As Single
Dim Grav As Single
Grav = 32.2
FallTime = Val(txtTime)
Distance = .5 * Grav * FallTime ^ 2
lblDistance.Caption = Distance
cmdClear.SetFocus
```

The first two of these lines declare the variables. All three variables are declared to be of the Single data type, a type used to represent decimal numbers. The third line assigns the value of 32.2, the acceleration of gravity, to the variable *Grav*.

```
FallTime = Val(txtTime)
```

This line reads the text contained in the box and assigns its value to the variable *FallTime*. However, before the assignment is made, the time, which is entered as a string, is converted to a value. Data entered into a textbox is text data. It is of the String data type. The **Val(x)** command, which is called a function, takes the value of the string, *txtTime*, and converts it to a number. When a textbox name is used and no property is stated, the Text property is assumed.

This line of code is equivalent to:

```
FallTime = Val(txtTime.text)
```

This second version shows how to refer to the properties of objects: state the name of the object, put in a period and follow it with the name of the property. This method is used in programs to change properties of a textbox while the program is running.

The conversion from string to number will fail if the text in the box doesn't represent a number. If **4.5s** is entered, the program will attempt to convert this string to a number, but will fail because of the presence of the letter "s" in the string. The program will halt with a run-time error.

If the program is running within the Visual Basic environment, Visual Basic will pause the program, tell you the error, and highlight the line of code where the problem was encountered. You can fix the problem and either resume or restart the program.

If the text is a proper representation of a number, the conversion will be successful.

```
Distance = .5 * Grav * FallTime ^ 2
lblDistance.Caption = Distance
```

The first of these two lines does the calculation and assigns the value to *Distance*. The second converts the numerical value *Distance* into a string and puts that string into the Caption property of lblDistance. The Caption property is automatically displayed by the label object and the answer appears on the screen. An equivalent statement that doesn't depend on defaults is:

```
lblDistance.Caption = Str$(Distance)
```

In this statement, the **Str$(x)** function converts a number to a string. The string is assigned to *lblDistance.Caption,* which itself represents a string.

The last line of the code uses something not yet mentioned: a method. Once the value for *Distance* has been displayed, the next action is to clear the Input and Output controls (the textbox and the distance label) and select the txtTime box for the next value to be entered. The cmdClear button is intended for this purpose. This line highlights the cmdClear button so that a simple press of the Enter key will execute the cmdClear routine.

METHODS

A method is a built-in subroutine that can be applied to a particular kind of control. The **SetFocus** method is preprogrammed to shift the focus to the object to which it is appended. When a control or textbox has the focus, it receives the user's keyboard input. In fact, the control or window with the focus is, by definition, the one that is the recipient of keyboard input. When a textbox control has the focus, its visual state changes to indicate that it is ready to receive keyboard input.

CODE FOR THE CLEAR BUTTON

The code for the Clear button clears the textbox and the Display Label to prepare for more entries. To create this code:

1 Double-click on the Clear button to open the Code window (Figure 3-34).

Figure 3-34
Code window for the
Clear button

2 Enter the following code between the first and last lines of the Click subroutine:

```
txtTime = ""
lblDistance = ""
txtTime.SetFocus
```

The first two lines again depend on Visual Basic's default to the Text property of a textbox and the Caption property of a label when just their names are used. The Text and Caption properties of the controls are blanked by setting them equal to a string with no characters. The final line highlights the txtTime box so that a user can enter another value, if desired.

CODE FOR THE QUIT BUTTON

When the user clicks on the Quit button, the form closes. To create this code:

1 Double-click on the Quit button to open the Code window.

2 Enter **End** between the first and last lines of the cmdQuit_Click subroutine

GETTING AROUND IN THE CODE WINDOW

After the code is entered, you may want to review or revise it. You can double-click controls to enter the Code window; but once the Code window is open, it is easier to use the Object menu to move from one subroutine to another. Figure 3-35 shows the Code window with the Object drop-down list displayed.

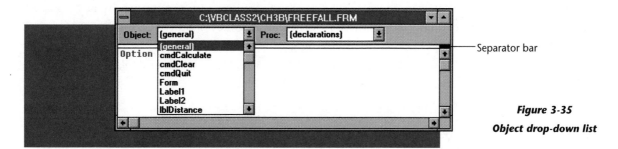

Separator bar

Figure 3-35

Object drop-down list

The Object drop-down list shows the names of each of the objects present on the form, including ones that currently have no code associated with them. The default names of the two descriptive labels appear in the menu.

Selecting the name of an object from the list displays the subroutine for that object. If there is code connected with more than one event procedure, you can display that code by choosing the procedure name from the Proc drop-down list.

When you want to move code from one procedure to another or just compare the code of two procedures, you can display both procedures in the Code window. As you can see in Figure 3-35, there is a narrow bar at the top of the Code window. Use the mouse to drag the bar to the middle of the window. Click in the bottom window and choose the cmdCalculate routine from the Object menu. Figure 3-36 shows the mouse cursor while the separator bar is being dragged.

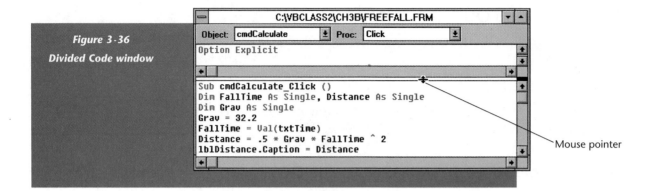

Figure 3-36
Divided Code window

SHIFTING FOCUS

In Windows, clicking an object selects it. Usually, some change in the appearance of the object shows that it has been selected. When an object is selected while the program is running, it is said to "have the focus." You can control the focus of a Windows program both by adding code and by setting the properties of the objects. Start by looking at the properties that control the focus.

The Properties window for a textbox, label control, or a command button contains the following properties:

◉ TabIndex

◉ TabStop

The focus is shifted from one object to another when the Tab button is pressed. The order in which the objects are highlighted is determined by the object's TabIndex. The indexes start at 0. The object with TabIndex 0 will receive the focus first when the program is run. By changing the TabIndex value you can change the order in which objects will receive the focus in response to the Tab key (Figure 3-37).

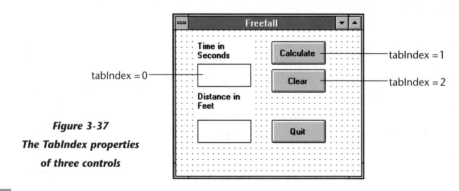

Figure 3-37
The TabIndex properties of three controls

The TabStop value, which can have the values True or False, determines whether or not the focus will stop at an object at all when the Tab button is pressed.

If the tab order is changed by changing the value of the TabIndex, the other objects are automatically adjusted to make room for the reordered values. In our program, it would make sense to set the TabIndex of txtTime to 0, the TabIndex of cmdCalculate to 1, and the TabIndex of cmcClear to 2. After a user enters a value for the time in the txtTime box, pressing the Tab key will shift the focus to the cmdCalculate button. The TabStop property for the other form controls should be set to False.

Finishing the Program

Now you are ready to finish the program:

1   Run the program by pressing F5 or by clicking on the Run button in the toolbar. The Run, Pause, and Stop buttons are designed to resemble buttons on CD players and cassette tape recorders.

2   Stop the program by clicking on the Quit button on the Freefall form or on the Stop button on the Visual Basic toolbar.

3   Save the program by selecting Save Project As from the Visual Basic File menu. Save both the form file and the project file.

QUESTIONS AND ACTIVITIES

1.   Change the caption of the Freefall program form to "The Distance Fallen Program".

2.   The Click event of a textbox is executed whenever the box is clicked. Run the Freefall program and click the textbox. Nothing happens because there is no code in the Click event handler. Add this line to the txtTime_Click () event handler:

```
txtTime.FontItalic = Not (txtTime.FontItalic)
```

Run the program, enter a value in the textbox, and click the box.

3.   When you use the name of a textbox without a property, what property is referenced by default?

4.   Use **Val( )** and **Str$( )** to convert *sPrice* to the value *nPrice* and *nQuantity* to the string *sQuantity*.

5. How is the TabIndex property used to control the movement of the cursor?

6. Describe what focus means.

7. What is a method and what does the SetFocus method do?

Summary

Variables are names of values contained in memory locations. Variables are named with the InterCap method. You build variable names by joining words or portions of words. Capitalize the first letter of each word or word portion.

You can use these arithmetic operations in Visual Basic: exponentiation (^), multiplication (*), division (/), addition (+), and subtraction (−). You can remember the order in which these operations are executed with "Please Excuse My Dear Aunt Sally:"

- Parentheses
- Exponentiation
- Multiplication and division in order, left to right
- Addition and subtraction in order, left to right

The assignment statement evaluates an expression on the right side of the equal sign and assigns that value to the variable on the left side.

variable = expression

The assignment statement is also used to assign values to properties of objects.

object.property = expression

For instance,

```
txtLastName.FontSize = 24
```

Program break points are set from the toolbar. A break point stops program execution at a particular line. While the program is halted, you can print or change the values of variables from the Debug window.

The Single-Step button in the toolbar executes one line of code with each click. After a line is executed, the program halts, allowing you to check and alter values in the Debug window.

The various data types in Visual Basic are:

- Integer (%)
- Long (&)
- Single (!)
- Double (#)

- Currency (@)
- String ($)
- Variant
- User-defined

The Variant type is capable of representing any of the other types.

The **SetFocus** method, a built-in subroutine, shifts the focus from control to control. **txtTime.SetFocus** shifts the focus to the object named txtTime.

The TabIndex property present in most objects lets you set the order in which the focus will shift from object to object when the Tab key is pressed.

The **Str$(n)** function turns a value into a string.

The **Val(s)** function turns a string into a value.

Problems

1. **The Material Problem**

Write a program to calculate the cost of buying material for a dress. Use a textbox to enter the number of yards of material. Use a label to display the final cost. Use $8.50 as cost per yard of the material. The final cost is the cost per yard times the number of yards. Don't include the dollar sign in the cost per yard.

2. **The Material Problem (Part II)**

Modify the program above by adding another textbox for the cost per yard. In this program, the user enters both the number of yards and the cost per yard. The final cost is calculated and displayed as above.

3. **The Pet Problem**

Write a program to calculate and display the cost of buying a pet. Use textboxes to enter values for the following:
   a) Purchase price of pet
   b) Veterinary fee for checking pet
   c) Accessories

Calculate and display the sum in a label as the total cost.

4. **The Prom Problem**

Write a program to calculate and display the cost of going to the prom. Use textboxes to enter values for the following:
   a) Clothing   d) Dinner
   b) Transportation   e) Tickets
   c) Flowers

Calculate and display the sum in a label as the total cost.

5. The Test Average Problem
Write a program to calculate and display the average of three test scores. Use text boxes to enter values for the three test scores. Calculate the sum of the scores and divide by three to calculate the average. Display the average in a Label.

6. The Semester Average Problem
The semester average is a combination of the two quarter averages and the final exam score. One way to calculate this average is to multiply each quarter average by 2 and find the sum of the three values:
   a) quarter 1 x 2
   b) quarter 2 x 2
   c) final exam

   Use text boxes to enter the two quarter averages and the final exam score expressed as a percentage. Divide this result by 5 and display as the Semester average.

7. The Cost-Per-Disk Problem
Write a program to calculate the cost per disk when disks are bought in packages of 12. Use a textbox to enter the price per box. A label displays the cost per box divided by 12.

8. The Universal Gravitation Problem
The force of gravity f generated by two objects of masses m_1 and m_2 is given by the equation:

$$f = G\,\frac{m_1 m_2}{r^2}$$

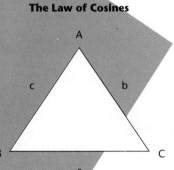

Figure 3-38

The Law of Cosines

where r is the distance between the two masses and G is the universal gravitational constant. The two masses m_1 and m_2 are measured in kilograms (kg) and r is measured in meters (m); G has the value $6.672 \times 10^{-11}\mathrm{N}{\cdot}\mathrm{kg}^2/\mathrm{m}^2$. The force of gravity, f, is measured in Newtons (N). Write a program using textboxes to enter the two masses and the distance between them, then calculate and display the resulting force of gravity. Make sure your textboxes are labeled properly and the force is displayed in a label.

9. Law of Cosines
The law of cosines lets us calculate the side of a triangle. It states:
$$c^2 = a^2 + b^2 - 2ab\cos C$$

where a,b, and c are the sides of a triangle and C is the angle opposite side c. If we know the lengths of two sides a and b of a triangle, and the measure of the angle C between them, we can calculate the length of the third side c by using the law of cosines and taking the square root of each side of the equation.

Write a program using textboxes to enter values for a, b, and C; the program should calculate c and display its value in a label. Arrange the boxes on the form to suggest their relationship to the parts of the triangle they represent. Use the drawing tool to draw the triangle between them.

10. The Drag Race Problem

The distance a race car undergoing a constant acceleration travels over a given period of time is given by the formula:

$$s = \tfrac{1}{2}at^2$$

where s is the distance traveled, a is the acceleration, and t is the elapsed time. Write a program that prompts the user to enter the elapsed time in seconds. Assuming the distance traveled is one-quarter mile (1320 feet), calculate and display the acceleration in feet per second squared. Start by solving the equation for a.

11. Concrete

Write a program to calculate the cost of concrete for a sidewalk. Use textboxes to enter the length and width of the sidewalk in feet. Assume the concrete is poured 4 inches thick. Calculate the volume of the sidewalk by multiplying the length times the width times the depth. Make sure the units agree. Display the volume in both cubic feet and cubic yards. Assume the cost of concrete is 60 dollars per cubic yard. Display the cost of the concrete.

12. The Interest Rate Problem

Calculate the interest rate being charged for a loan if the following information is known:

a)   Amount borrowed
b)   Amount of the monthly payment
c)   Number of years of the loan

Assume for this problem that the number of payments per year is 12.

The calculation is done in three parts. Use textboxes to enter the principal, P; the number of years, Y; and the monthly payment, M. Calculate and display the total payments, TP:

$$TP = 12 \times Y \times M$$

Calculate and display the finance charge, F:

$$F = TP - P$$

Finally, calculate and display the effective interest rate, R:

$$R = \frac{2 \times 12 \times F}{P(Y \times 12 - 1)}$$

End if

If x1 - x2 ""

If x1 - x2 = 0

End if

If X1 - X2 = Then

If X1 - X2 Then

Then

Else

For x = 1 to 10

Print xi ") My

ame is Joclyn"

Decision Making and Looping

After working through this chapter, you will be able to:

Use **If-Then** to ensure that a sequence of statements will be executed only when a given condition applies.

Use **If-Then-Else** to select which of two sequences of statements will be executed, depending on whether a given condition is true or false.

Write Basic expressions to form "Boolean conditions," which are expressions whose possible values are the constants True and False.

Use each of the three forms of **If-Then** appropriately.

Apply the triangle inequality in an application program.

Explain events, parameters, and properties in more detail than previously.

Use compound Boolean expressions, with And and Or.

Use the **Mod** operator to test divisibility.

Keep running totals and count sequences of statements.

Apply concepts of divisibility and running totals to the Prime Number application.

Apply the concept of running totals to join strings together.

Build strings for display in multiline textboxes.

O V E R V I E W

*In this chapter, you will see how to use the three forms of the **If-Then** state-ment, how to test divisibility, how to keep a running total, and how to count the occurrences of a particular statement. You will also be introduced to the fundamental looping statement, the **For-Next** statement.*

These constructs allow more complex "flow of control" within a program than the simple straight-line flow that you have used in programs so far.

Flow of control refers to the order in which statements are executed. In straight-line code, the flow of control is obvious, even trivial: the next statement to be executed is the statement immediately following the current one.

*The **If-Then** statement makes it possible to execute other statements conditionally—for example, only when the value of a given variable exceeds 10. The **For-Next** statement causes the statements it encloses to be executed repeatedly a specified number of times. The computer, in other words, does more work in response to less code (and less typing).*

If-Then Statements

Section

You use **If-Then** statements to make choices in a Visual Basic program. You make the same kind of choices every day. Should I go to a movie or go rollerblading? Should I read a book or write a short story? More decisions follow from whatever choice you make. For example, if you decide to go to a movie, then you need to decide which movie and find a way to get there. If you choose to go rollerblading instead, you need to pick up your rollerblades and kneepads and decide where to go.

Visual Basic uses the same kind of logic to control the flow of a program from one section to another. You express choices in the form of an **If-Then** statement. Then, depending on the choice made, Visual Basic executes different sections of code. A "section of code" may mean a single line. An **If-Then** statement allows you to conditionally insert a line or many lines into the straight-line flow of a program, or run one section instead of another.

For example:

If *the unpaid balance is not zero* **Then**
    Continue to make payments,
Else
    Stop making payments
End If

If *the player's health points are zero* **Then**
    The game is over, so end the game
Else
    Continue play
End If

If *the pathway is blocked* **Then**
    Choose an alternate path
Else
    Proceed along pathway
End If

If *the last name is "McRae"* **Then**
    Display full name
    Display address
    Display phone number
Else
    Continue name search
End If

If *the time is 7am* **Then**
    Ring the alarm
End If

You can see that all of these statements are set up in the same way. The statements have the same general structure:

- The first line starts with **If**.

- The first line ends with **Then**.

- One or more statements follow the **If-Then** line. They will be executed provided that the expression after the word **If** is true.

- The word **Else**, if it is included, begins a new line.

- One or more statements follow the **Else**. They will be executed provided that the expression after the word **If** is false.

- The end of the statements following the **If-Then** or the **Else** is signaled by the words **End If**.

KEYWORDS

The words **If**, **Else**, and **End If** are keywords, also known as reserved words. Basic sets these words aside and gives them special meaning that you cannot override. You cannot name a variable *If*, for example. Visual Basic recognizes its keywords when you type them, and it saves you effort by capitalizing them correctly. Thus, you can simply type *if*; Visual Basic will recognize its keyword, then substitute **If** as soon as you move the cursor onto another line. In fact, Visual Basic even recognizes *endif* as a shorthand for the keyword combination **End If**, and will expand it properly.

This structure is called the syntax of the **If-Then** statement. This section introduces three variations in the syntax of this type of statement. Each variation is appropriate for a specific range of situations that arise in programming.

Writing an If-Then Statement

The simplest version of the **If-Then** statement uses this syntax (see Figure 4-1):

> **If** *condition* **Then**
>
>   *one or more statements, to be executed only if condition is True*
>
> **End If**

The condition is typically an expression that gives a **True** or **False** result when the program evaluates it. Comparisons are the most common examples of such expressions. **True** and **False** are Basic keywords. **False** has the value of 0, while **True** has a nonzero value (specifically, -1). Consider the following three examples of conditions:

a) $2 * x = y$

b) HealthPoints > 0

c) Payments < Years * 12

In a), the value of **2 * x** either is or is not equal to y. If it is, the condition is true, and the comparison expression has the value **True**; otherwise, the condition is false, and the expression has the value **False**. In b), the condition is true, and has the value **True**, if the value of Health-Points is greater than 0. The expression is false, and has the value **False**, if the value of HealthPoints is less than or equal to zero. In c), the expression is true if the value of Payments is less than the number of Years times 12; otherwise, it is false.

Assignment statements, as you may remember, are limited to a single variable on the left-hand side (see Chapter 2). You are not limited in this way with the conditions in an **If-Then** statement. Visual Basic evaluates the left and right sides of the condition, then compares them. The comparison results in a **True** or **False** value.

```
If  x - y = 0 Then
    lblResult.Caption = "x and y are equal"
End If
If x2 - x1 <> 0 Then
    lblSlope.Caption = "The slope exists."
    m = (y2 - y1) / ( x2 - x1)
End If
```

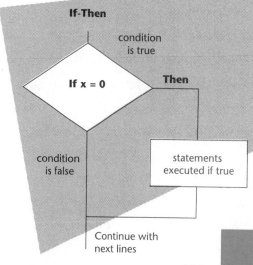

Figure 4-1

The If-Then statement

This form of the **If-Then** statement executes instructions *only if* the condition is true (has a nonzero value). If the condition is false, the program jumps to the first statement following the **End If** keywords, which marks the end of the entire **If-Then** statement. The **End If** signals the end of the **If-Then** section of code.

After the **If-Then** line, you need to provide instructions for the program to follow if the condition is true. What is the code that the program should execute? As you can see in the last example, you can include more than one line of instructions to be executed.

Writing an If-Then-Else Statement

Here is another useful variation on the **If-Then** statement (see Figure 4-2):

If *condition* **Then**
> *statements to be executed if condition is true*

Else
> *statements to be executed if condition is false*

End If

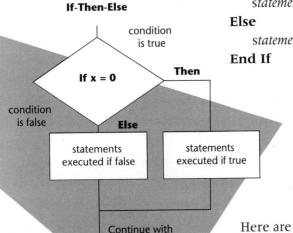

If-Then-Else

Figure 4-2
The If-Then-Else
statement

In this variation, the program executes the first list of statements if the condition is true. So far, this is exactly like a simple **If-Then** statement. Now, though, you add a second list of statements after the **Else**. The program executes *this* list if the condition is false. If the first list executes, the second list does not. If the second list executes, the first does not.

Here are some examples:

```
If Raining = True Then
    lblActivity.Caption = "Go to the movie."
Else
    lblActivity.Caption = "Go to the beach."
End If
If x2 - x1 = 0 Then
    lblSlope.Caption = "No slope"
Else
    lblSlope.Caption = "Slope exists"
    Slope = (y2 - y1) / (x2 - x1)
End If
```

Indentation makes code easier to read by outlining its structure. You should indent the statements that the program executes in the True and

False branches. Visual Basic will not alter "whitespace" at the beginning of the line. Whitespace includes the spaces that indent the line, which you produce by pressing the Space bar or the Tab key.

However, Visual Basic also ignores whitespace and does not use it to determine how statements should be grouped. That is why the **End If** keywords are required to mark the end of the statements comprising the **If** or the **Else** sections of code.

JUST SO YOU KNOW

In the original version of Basic, the **If-Then** statement was restricted to a single line. The syntax of this statement was:

> **If** *condition* **Then** *one or more statements separated by colons (:)*

Visual Basic lets you use this form of the **If-Then** statement, but you will seldom have a good reason to do so. Using separate lines makes the code much easier to read and debug.

Nesting Statements

Some decisions require complicated reasoning to choose the proper path through the program's statements. And, as you've seen, some decisions just lead to more decisions. For example:

> **If** you go to a movie **Then**
>   **If** you choose a romance **Then**
>   **If** you forget your tissues **Then**
>   wipe your tears on your sleeve
>   **Else**
>   blot your tears with tissues
>   **End If**
>   **End If**
> **End If**

When one **If-Then** statement is contained in another, the statements are *nested*.

Another kind of nesting occurs when an **If** statement is contained in the **Else** branch of an **If-Then** statement. For example:

> **If** you choose to rollerblade **Then**
>   Put on rollerblades and pads
> **Else**
>   **If** you choose to bowl **Then**
>   Take bowling ball and shoes to bowling alley
>   **Else**

(continued)

>>**If** you choose to ride a bike **Then**
>>>Get bike out of garage
>>**End If**
>**End If**
End If

Nesting **If** statements can make the logical structure of the program difficult to understand, due to repeated indentation and a forest of **If**'s, **Then**'s, and **Else**'s. To reduce the confusion, Visual Basic uses the **ElseIf** statement.

USING ELSEIF

If you nest **If-Then** statements, the indentation levels of the code can become very confusing. Visual Basic lets you use **ElseIf** as a way to prevent this problem.

For example, you could write:

```
If x = 0 Then
    do something
Else
    If x = 1 Then
        do something different
    Else
        do the default action
    End If
End If
```

VB lets you write a shorter form instead:

```
If x = 0 Then
    do something
ElseIf  x = 1 Then
    do something different
Else
    do the default action
End If
```

Souped-Up Digital Clock

To experiment with the **If-Then-Else** statement, revisit the Digital Clock program and make it more eye-catching (perhaps even annoying). You will modify the Timer event handler so that the displayed time grows and shrinks continually, repeating a cycle every 10 seconds.

The code for the Timer event follows, and it provides a good example of why **ElseIf** is convenient (imagine what the code would look like if it used nested **If-Then-Else**'s) :

INCLUDING COMMENTS

Programming statements can be self-explanatory, but more often they require some explanation. Programmers build explanations into their code by including comments. Comments are brief descriptive sentences or phrases that explain what's going on in the program. Comments can be included anywhere in a line. Start a comment with a single quote. When the default colors are active, Visual Basic will change the text of a comment to green.

Add this code for the Timer event, then run the program:

```
'_A modification to Digital Clock:
Sub Timer1_Timer ()
Dim nHeight As Integer
Dim n As Integer
'_Now is a function that returns the system date and
time in a single value.
'_Second gives a value between 0-59 equal to number
of seconds of current time.
n = Second(Now) Mod 10
If n = 0 Then
    nHeight = 8.25
ElseIf n = 1 Or n = 9 Then
    nHeight = 9.75
ElseIf n = 2 Or n = 8 Then
    nHeight = 12
ElseIf n = 3 Or n = 7 Then
    nHeight = 13.5
ElseIf n = 4 Or n = 6 Then
    nHeight = 18
Else       'n = 5
    nHeight = 24
End If
lblTime.FontSize = nHeight
lblTime.Caption = Time$              ' as before
End Sub
```

All but the last line are new. The label control (as well as the form) must be resized to accommodate 24-point text (the largest size that the displayed time achieves), and its Alignment should be set to Centered so that the horizontal expansion and contraction are more pleasant.

Every 10 seconds "on the 10 seconds," the time is displayed in 8.25 type. On each of the next 5 seconds, the size increases through 9.75, 12, 13.5, 18, and ultimately 24. On each of the next 4 seconds, it decreases, running down through the same sequence of point sizes before starting the cycle again.

ACTIVITIES

1. Write **If-Then** statements for the following.
    a) If the value of the variable x is 2, then set y to 0.
    b) If the value of *LastName* is "McRae", then set the Caption property of label1 to the string "Found".
    c) If the value of *Month* is greater than 48, then set the Caption property of label2 to "The payments are over".

2. The Freefall program will give a run-time error if the user enters a non-numeric value into the time textbox and then clicks on the Calculate button. You can test for this, and take appropriate measures. Change the Click handler of the Calculate button to contain the following code:

    ```
    If IsNumeric(txtTime) Then
        same statements as before
    Else
        lblDistance = "?"
    End If
    ```

3. Convert the following to the **If-Then-Else** syntax (the **mod** operator divides two whole numbers and returns the remainder):
    a) If $x = y$, then set z to 34; otherwise set z to 12 and x to $x + 1$.
    b) If *Month* mod 12 = 0, then set *NewYear* to *NewYear* + 1 and *Month* to *Month* + 1.
    c) If *Prime* mod 2 = 0, then set lblPrime to " not "; otherwise, set *Divisor* to 3.
    d) If *LastName* is "Hanratty", then set *LastPlayer* to True.

4. Convert the following English sentences to Basic statements. Make up variable names where appropriate:
    a) If the year is 1994, then the balance is twelve thousand.
    b) If the computer is a "386", then the label lblWindowsCanRun is "OK"; otherwise, Windows is "no go".

   c) If the bike is a "mountain" bike, then it will go off-road. If it isn't, it won't.

5. Make up three **If-Then** problems of your own. Follow the patterns used in Exercise 2 above.

6. Write nested **If-Then** statements for the following. Make up variable names where appropriate:

   a) If a player's name is "Decker", then the team playing is the "Marlins". Otherwise, if a player's name is "Sosa", then the team playing is the "Cubs".

   b) If a person's age is greater than 12, then if a person's age is less than 18, then *StudentAge* is true.

The Cereal Program

Section

The Cereal project gives you another opportunity to experiment with **If-Then** statements. You will use an **If-Then** statement to choose between two messages the program could display. In the process, you will work with different methods of changing focus within a program. Whatever object has the focus is the active object, the one where keyboard input goes. One of the methods you will use to change focus requires an **If-Then** statement.

Starting Out

No one likes to run out of their favorite cereal. To prevent this from happening, you need to know how much cereal you have in your kitchen and the rate at which you are eating the cereal. With that information, you can predict when you need to add cereal to the grocery list.

You can set up a program to perform the necessary calculations. The program should prompt the user to enter:

⦿ The number of boxes of cereal on hand

⦿ The number of bowls of cereal eaten in a week

On the basis of this input, the program will calculate the cereal available. Depending on that calculation, the program then displays one of two messages:

⦿ "Buy more cereal"

   OR

⦿ "Cereal supply is OK".

You need a single form for this program. Think through the program, then see if your list of objects matches the list below. If not, why not?

- Two textboxes, one to enter the number of boxes of cereal on hand and another to enter the number of bowls eaten each week

- Two labels prompting the user to enter values

- Two labels displaying alternative messages about buying cereal

- Three command buttons to do the following:
  - Perform the calculation and display the result
  - Clear the textboxes
  - Quit the program

The form you are going to create is shown in Figure 4-3.

Figure 4-3

The Cereal program

Now that you are ready to begin:

1 Start Visual Basic. If it is already running, select New Project from the File menu.

2 Change the caption of the form to "Cereal Project".

Placing Labels and Textboxes

Your first step is to place the labels and textboxes, then change their properties.

1 Place two labels for user prompts on the form. Double-click on the Label icon in the toolbox. Position the labels near the top of the form.

2 Place two textboxes. You will use one for the user to enter the number of boxes of cereal and the other for the number of bowls of cereal eaten. Double-click on the textbox icon in the toolbar. Position the textboxes below the labels (Figure 4-4).

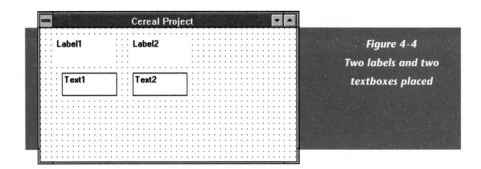

Figure 4-4
Two labels and two
textboxes placed

3   Select the first label. In the Properties window for this object, change the Caption property to **Number of boxes on hand**.

4   Select the second label. In the Properties window for this object, change the Caption property to **Number of bowls eaten per week**.

5   Click and drag to resize the label, then check the new size in the Properties window. Position the labels to leave room along the right side of the form for the command buttons.

6   Select the first textbox. In the Properties window for this object, change the following properties:
   ◎ Text property: Insert a default value. Replace Text1 with **3**, representing three boxes of cereal.
   ◎ Name property: **txtBoxes**
   ◎ TabIndex: 0

7   Select the second textbox. In the Properties window for this object, change the following properties:
   ◎ Text property: Insert a default value. Replace Text2 with **10**, representing 10 servings.
   ◎ Name property: **txtBowls**
   ◎ TabIndex: 1

Figure 4-5
Textboxes with default
values

The form should look something like that shown in Figure 4-5.

8   Place two more labels. Select each of the labels in turn and change its properties as listed below.
   First label:
   ◎ Caption property: **Buy more cereal**
   ◎ BorderStyle property: 1
   ◎ Name property: **lblBuy**
   ◎ Visible property: False
   ◎ BackColor property: Green

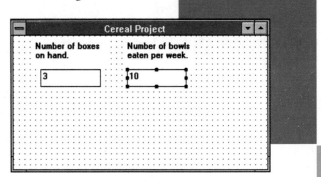

Second label:
- ◎ Caption property: **Cereal supply is OK**
- ◎ BorderStyle property: 1
- ◎ Name property: **lblOK**
- ◎ Visible property: False
- ◎ BackColor property: Red

Although you have set the Visible property to **False** for the last two labels, they will remain visible as you design the form. When the program is running, however, these labels will be invisible until the program sets the Visible property of one of them to **True**. By setting the TabIndex of the two textboxes to 0 and 1, you have established which control will have the focus when the program is started, and which control will gain the focus when the user presses the Tab key.

Setting the TabIndex of the first textbox to 0 ensures that the user can immediately enter the number of boxes on hand as soon as the program is running, without having to move the focus to that textbox by clicking on it or pressing the Tab key one or more times. Once the user has entered the number of boxes on hand, pressing the Tab key moves the focus to the control with the next highest TabIndex—namely, to the second box. Because we read from left to right, we tend to regard that direction as the more natural one for representing operations to be performed in sequence. Although we might not recognize why, the program would seem strange if the TabIndex of the two textboxes were reversed.

The user interface of the Cereal project should now look like the form shown in Figure 4-6.

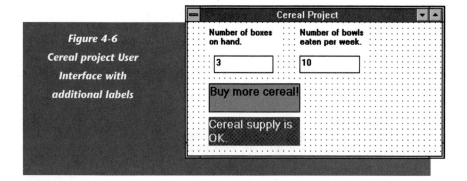

Figure 4-6
Cereal project User
Interface with
additional labels

Adding Command Buttons

You are now ready to set up the three command buttons. As you do so, you should follow the Windows convention for command button captions. Most Windows programs allow users to select a button by pressing a key combination or by clicking on the button. You let users know which key to press by underlining one letter in the button caption.

You can create an underline in a caption by including an ampersand (&) in the caption text. Visual Basic will then underline the character following the ampersand. When the program is run, the user can click on a button to execute an action. The user can also press the Alt key and the underlined character to run the code attached to the button.

To add the buttons:

1 Place the three command buttons. Double-click on the Command button icon in the Toolbox. Then click and drag on the objects to move them into the right positions.

2 Select a command button, then change its properties as shown. Repeat this step for all three buttons.

First command button:
◎ Caption property: **Check &Supply**
◎ Name property: **cmdCheck**
◎ TabIndex property: 2

Second command button:
◎ Caption property: **&Clear**
◎ Name property: **cmdClear**
◎ TabIndex property: 3

Third command button:
◎ Caption property: **&Quit**
◎ Name property: **cmdQuit**
◎ TabIndex property: 4

Writing the Code

If you look at a typical box of cereal, you will see the number of servings listed as 12 per box. The real number is probably lower. You need to write code that will compare the available supply with the user's weekly consumption.

The program must make an evaluation as well. At what point, for example, do you want the program to tell the user to buy more cereal? When the available supply is gone? When there are ten servings left? Twenty?

In the code shown here, the cereal supply is considered to be OK if the supply is at least twice a single week's consumption. In other words, if you run this program every day, it will alert you to replenish the cereal supply beginning two weeks before you run out.

As an additional convenience to the user, you should also handle events associated with keyboard input in the textboxes and in two of the command buttons. When a key representing an alphanumeric character is pressed, the **KeyPress** event is fired, and any handler for that event is executed. If the key pressed is the Enter key, the ASCII code 13 is generated. The Enter key is usually pressed at the end of an entry signifying that the entry is complete.

The **SetFocus** method sets the focus to a specified control. You will use the **SetFocus** method within **KeyPress** event handlers for the textboxes so that pressing the Enter key moves the focus just as the Tab key does. For example, pressing Enter will shift the focus of the program from the txtBoxes control to the txtBowls control. Responding to the Enter key when a button has the focus requires a different approach. A button's Click event is fired when it has the focus and the user presses Enter. Because you will be writing code for each button's Click event anyway, you will only have to add another statement to shift the focus as desired.

To write the code for the Cereal project:

1 Double-click on the Check Supply button to open the Code window. In the Click event for this button, insert the code shown in Figure 4-7.

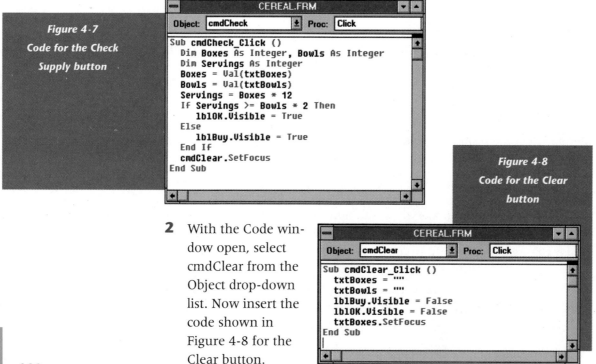

Figure 4-7
Code for the Check Supply button

```
CEREAL.FRM

Object: cmdCheck    Proc: Click

Sub cmdCheck_Click ()
    Dim Boxes As Integer, Bowls As Integer
    Dim Servings As Integer
    Boxes = Val(txtBoxes)
    Bowls = Val(txtBowls)
    Servings = Boxes * 12
    If Servings >= Bowls * 2 Then
        lblOK.Visible = True
    Else
        lblBuy.Visible = True
    End If
    cmdClear.SetFocus
End Sub
```

Figure 4-8
Code for the Clear button

2 With the Code window open, select cmdClear from the Object drop-down list. Now insert the code shown in Figure 4-8 for the Clear button.

```
CEREAL.FRM

Object: cmdClear    Proc: Click

Sub cmdClear_Click ()
    txtBoxes = ""
    txtBowls = ""
    lblBuy.Visible = False
    lblOK.Visible = False
    txtBoxes.SetFocus
End Sub
```

3 With the Code window open, select cmdQuit from the Object drop-down list. Now insert the following line of code for the Quit button:

End

4 With the Code window open, select txtBoxes from the Object drop-down list. Click on the downward-pointing arrow to open the Proc pop-down list. Choose the KeyPress event handler to replace the handler displayed by default (the Change event handler).

5 In the KeyPress subroutine for this textbox, insert the code shown in Figure 4-9.

Figure 4-9

Code for the first textbox

6 Select txtBowls from the Object drop-down list and enter the Key-Press procedure. Enter code similar to figure 4-9, shifting the focus to cmdCheck.

Finishing the Program

Visual Basic programs can be written to solve almost any kind of problem. In the Cereal project, you've used three basic controls and some simple code to solve an important breakfast dilemma. Now you are ready to see how the program runs:

1 Run the program several times; use the Tab key and the Enter key to move from object to object. Be sure to run the program with data that will cause each of the labels to be displayed.

2 Save the program. Save both the form file and the project file. You may give each file the same name; Visual Basic will fill in the **.frm** extension for the form, and **.mak** for the project.

Section 3

The Triangle Inequality Project

Using **If-Then** statements is a powerful way to control the flow of a program. This program is designed to further your understanding of and expertise with this type of control statement in Visual Basic.

You will use the simplest form of the **If-Then** statement:

If *condition* **Then**
    statements to execute if condition is true
End If

You will also use the following variant:

If *condition* **Then**
    statements to execute if condition is true
Else
    statements to execute if condition is false
End If

You insert the first of these **If-Then** statements in the KeyPress event handler. In that subroutine, the statement works to change the focus in the program. You will use the ASCII code generated by pressing the Enter key to control the movement of the cursor by shifting the focus from textbox to textbox and command button.

The second form of the **If-Then** statement is inserted in the cmdCalculate Click event procedure. There, you use it to evaluate whether the three values the user enters could represent the sides of a triangle. You will use the And connective to combine three expressions into a single logical expression.

Starting Out

The triangle inequality is a well-known relationship in mathematics. It states that the sum of the lengths of any two sides of a triangle is greater than the length of the third side. The common sense rendition of this fact says that the shortest distance between two points is a straight line. This relationship is illustrated in Figure 4-10.

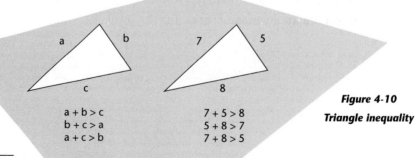

$$a + b > c$$
$$b + c > a$$
$$a + c > b$$

$$7 + 5 > 8$$
$$5 + 8 > 7$$
$$7 + 8 > 5$$

Figure 4-10

Triangle inequality

If the three sides fail to satisfy the triangle inequality, the sides can't be the sides of a triangle. For instance, if the sides measure 3, 2, and 7, the triangle inequality is violated. As you can see, 3 + 2 is not greater than 7 (Figure 4-11).

You are going to create a program to determine if three line segments can be used to form a triangle. The user will enter the lengths of the three segments, then click the Calc button. At that point, the program will test these values to see if they satisfy the triangle inequality. If they do, the program displays the label "It is a triangle!". If they do not, it displays the label "It is not a triangle!". As in the Cereal program, both of these labels are invisible until the program sets the Visible property of one of them to **True**.

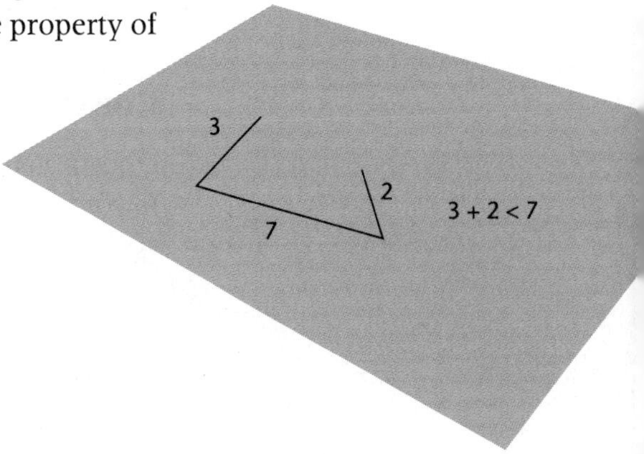

On this form, you will need:

- Three textboxes

- Five labels

- Three command buttons

See Figure 4-12 for a look at the final form.

Figure 4-11

No triangle!

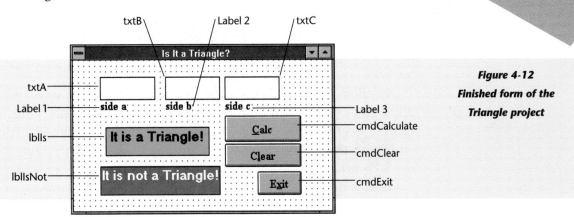

Figure 4-12

Finished form of the Triangle project

As always, start out by opening Visual Basic and changing the name of the default form. In this case, change the caption of the form to **Is It a Triangle?**

Placing Objects on the Form

Follow these steps to place objects on the Triangle form:

1 Place three textboxes across the top of the form. These boxes will receive input from the user.

2 Name the boxes **txtA**, **txtB**, and **txtC**. Delete the text from the boxes.

3 Place labels below the boxes and change the captions of the labels to **side a**, **side b**, and **side c**.

4 Place three command buttons on the form. Change their names to **cmdCalculate**, **cmdClear**, and **cmdExit**. Change their captions to **&Calc**, **C&lear**, and **E&xit**.

5 Place two display labels on the form. Name them **lblIs** and **lblIsNot**. Change the caption of the first to **It is a Triangle!** Change the caption of the second to **It is not a Triangle!** Change the BackColor, ForeColor, and Font properties of the labels to make each distinctive. Change the Visible property of both labels to False.

Controlling Focus

Once a value is entered in the first textbox, a user should be able to move to the next box in any of three ways. These include:

- Pressing the Tab key
- Clicking on the next box
- Pressing the Enter key

To allow users to press the Tab key, you need to change a property in the Properties window. You will change this property for all three textboxes and one command button.

To allow users to click on the next textbox, you do not have to make any changes in the program. Windows automatically shifts the focus to a control that can receive keyboard input when the user clicks on it with the mouse. This way of shifting focus doesn't require any special programming.

To allow users to change focus by pressing the Enter key, you need to make changes to a subroutine in the Code window. You will make changes to accomplish this for all three textboxes and for two command buttons.

WORKING WITH THE TABINDEX PROPERTY

To control the order of the objects that the focus cycles through when the user presses the Tab key, you need to set the tab order for each control. As you saw with the Cereal program, this order is established by setting the TabIndex property of the controls.

To establish the tab order:

1 Select the first textbox (txtA). Set the TabIndex property for that control to 0.

2   Select the second textbox (txtB). Set the TabIndex property for that control to 1.

3   Select the third textbox (txtC). Set the TabIndex property for that control to 2.

4   Select the Calc button. Set the TabIndex property for that control to 3.

When the form opens during run-time, the focus will be on the first textbox. The control with TabIndex 0 automatically has the focus when a program is run.

USING THE KEYPRESS EVENT

You can insert code into event handler subroutines so that users can move the focus by pressing the Enter key. Follow these steps for each of the textboxes:

1   Double-click on the txtA textbox to open the Code window.

2   Click on the downward-pointing arrow to open the Proc drop-down list (Figure 4-13).

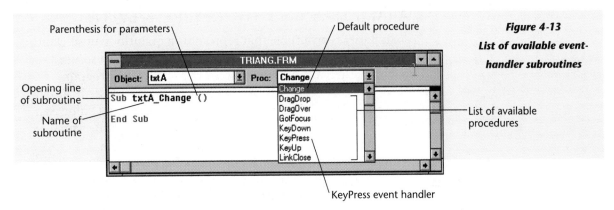

Parenthesis for parameters

Default procedure

Opening line of subroutine

Name of subroutine

KeyPress event handler

List of available procedures

Figure 4-13

List of available event-handler subroutines

3   Change the displayed event handler from Change to KeyPress. To do this, select KeyPress from the Proc drop-down list. As you can see in Figure 4-14, the name of the event now appears as part of the name of the displayed subroutine.

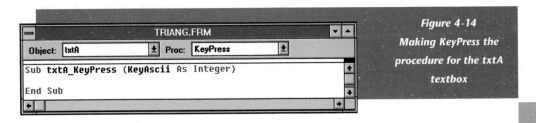

Figure 4-14

Making KeyPress the procedure for the txtA textbox

4   Insert this **If-Then** statement between the Sub line and the End
Sub line:

```
If KeyAscii = 13 Then
    txtB.SetFocus
End If
```

Once you have done so, the name of the event appears in boldface
type in the Proc drop-down list. As a result, you can see at a glance
which event procedures have code in them. This routine shifts the
focus to txtB after the user enters a value in txtA and presses Enter.
See the textbox for more detail on this step.

5   Add similar statements into two more subroutines: txtB_KeyPress
and txtC_KeyPress. Repeat the same steps outlined above for those
two textboxes. The txtB_KeyPress event should shift the focus to
txtC. The txtC_KeyPress event should shift the focus to the command button, cmdCalculate.

PARAMETERS AND THE KEYPRESS EVENT

A parameter is a variable that represents a quantity whose value
comes from outside the procedure. Parameters are also used to
send values from the event procedure to the main program.

In this case, when an alphanumeric key is pressed, Visual
Basic reads the ASCII code of the key, and passes that value as a
parameter to the KeyPress event handler through the variable
KeyAscii (see Figure 4-15).

Whenever the textbox txtA has the focus and the user
presses a key, this procedure is executed. If you did not insert
code into the KeyPress procedure, the program would do

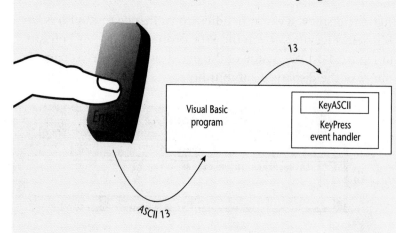

Figure 4-15

Passing a value as a
parameter

nothing in response to the KeyPress event generated in the textbox. However, you are programming the event procedure to react to one key, and one key only. This is the Enter key.

When the Enter key is pressed, the following two ASCII codes are generated: 13 and 10. These codes stand for Carriage Return and Line Feed, respectively. These two actions normally reset the cursor to the beginning of the next line.

The ASCII code 13 is passed to the subroutine through the parameter. At this point, the program will evaluate the condition statement you inserted into the code. Its value is **True**, so the program switches the focus to the second textbox (txtB). If the user pressed any other key, the ASCII code passed to the subroutine would not be 13. Therefore, the program would evaluate the condition statement as **False**, and the focus would not be moved.

Inserting Code

You need to insert code into the Click subroutine for each of the three command buttons. As you do so, you will work with another **If-Then** statement. You will also experiment with using Assignment statements to simplify Condition statements.

Sometimes condition statements can be very long. Long conditions can make it difficult to understand what is being tested. Parts of the condition statement can be assigned to descriptive variables, and those variables are then used in the **If-Then** statements. The shorter condition statements are easier to read and understand.

CALC BUTTON

To write the code for this button:

1   Double-click on the Calc button to open the Code window. If the Code window is already open, select cmdCalculate from the Object drop-down list.

2   Enter this code in the Click subroutine for the button:

```
Dim a As Single, b As Single, c As Single
a = Val(txtA)
b = Val(txtB)
c = Val(txtC)
```

```
If a + b > c And b + c > a And a + c > b Then
    lblIs.Visible = True
Else
    lblIsNot.Visible = True
End If
cmdClear.SetFocus
```

There are no parameters sent to or from this procedure, so the parentheses after the procedure name are empty.

The **Dim** statement reserves memory for the variables *a*, *b*, and *c* and declares them to be of the Single type.

Visual Basic defaults are used in the statements that take care of the conversions. Referring to the textboxes only by name automatically accesses the Text property of each box.

```
a = Val( txtA )
b = Val( txtB )
c = Val( txtC )
```

Whenever you refer to the name of a textbox without a particular property specified, Visual Basic assumes you mean the Text property. The **Val** function ensures a proper conversion from the string type of the textbox's Text property to the appropriate numerical type. To remove any dependence upon defaults, or just to make explicit to a reader of your code that a conversion is being performed, you may use the **Val** function, as shown in the following statements:

```
a = Val( txtA.text )
b = Val( txtB.text )
c = Val( txtC.text )
```

Assigning these values to the three intermediate variables *a*, *b*, and *c* relieves you from forming the condition out of the much lengthier expressions on the right-hand side of the assignments. The resulting code is much more readable. These assignments have another, perhaps less obvious, benefit: the resulting code also runs faster. They perform the conversions of strings to numbers once and once only, for each side of the triangle.

If the condition were written out using the **Val** expressions, then a conversion would be performed as many as three times for each side of the triangle, for a total of nine conversions. With such a simple program, you will probably not notice any difference in speed between the two approaches. Nevertheless, the principle illustrated here—avoiding needless recomputation—is a good one to observe.

The next statement is an **If-Then-Else** with a complicated expression for the *condition* part of the statement. This expression tests all three parts of the triangle inequality at once. It can do so because the three parts are joined together by And connectives. Each of these subexpressions—$a + b > c$, $a + c > b$, and $b + c > a$—can be true or false (and have a **True** or **False** value).

For the expression as a whole to be true, all three subexpressions must be true:

True **And** True **And** True = True

If any one of the subexpressions is false, the entire expression is false.

As you can see in the code, the label "It is a Triangle!" appears if the condition has the value **True**. In other words, the line segments *a*, *b*, and *c* do represent three sides of a triangle. The label "It is not a Triangle!" appears if the condition has the value **False**.

In an **If-Then-Else** statement, only one branch is executed. If the statements after the **Then** branch are executed, the statements after the **Else** branch are skipped. If the statements after the **Then** branch are skipped, the statements after the **Else** branch will be executed (see Figure 4-16).

The final instruction in the code for the Calculate button shifts the focus to the Clear button.

Figure 4-16
Executing a branch of the If-Then-Else statement

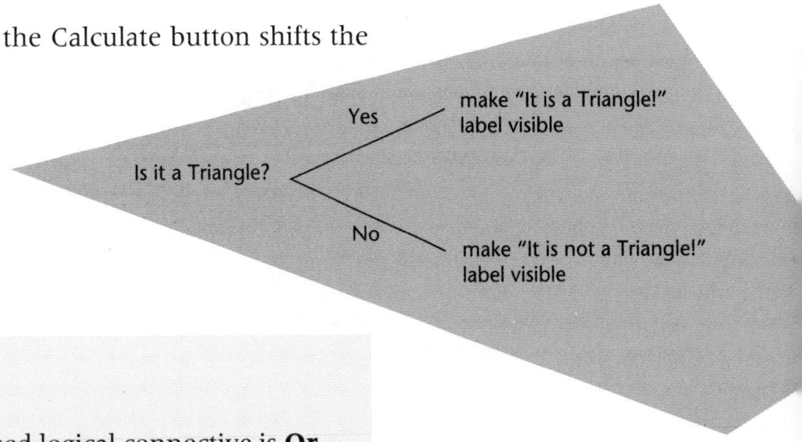

Is it a Triangle?

Yes — make "It is a Triangle!" label visible

No — make "It is not a Triangle!" label visible

OR CONNECTIVES

Besides And, the other commonly used logical connective is **Or**. You have already encountered examples of its use, in the revisited Digital Clock example earlier in this chapter. An **Or** expression has the value **True** if one or the other, or both parts, are true. The only condition under which an **Or** expression is **False** is when both the left- and right-hand expressions are false.

True **Or** True = True
True **Or** False = True
False **Or** True = True
False **Or** False = False

CLEAR BUTTON

To write the code for this button:

1 Double-click on the Clear button to open the Code window. If the Code window is already open, select cmdClear from the Object drop-down list.

2 Enter this code in the Click subroutine for the button:

```
txtA = ""        ' clear the textboxes
txtB = ""
txtC = ""
lblIs.Visible = False  ' make both labels invisible
lblIsNot.Visible = False
txtA.SetFocus    ' shift focus to txtA
```

In this code, the textboxes are cleared by inserting an empty string, represented by the adjacent quotation marks, into the Text property. The empty string is displayed as you would expect: no characters appear in the textboxes, not even spaces. The two boxes indicating "It is a Triangle!" and "It is not a Triangle!" are both made invisible by setting their Visible properties to False. Finally, the focus is set to txtA to prepare for the next round of trial values.

EXIT BUTTON

To code this button:

1 Double-click on the Exit button to open the Code window. If the Code window is already open, select cmdExit from the Object drop-down list.

2 Enter this code in the Click subroutine for the button:

```
End
```

Working with the Finished Program

Try running the program, testing it for several values of *a*, *b*, and *c*. Does the program return the correct result? Is the program right when it says that a triangle can be created from three line segments? Check the math yourself.

Save the project and form files.

QUESTIONS AND ACTIVITIES

1. What are three ways by which focus is changed in a typical Windows program?

2. When you double-click a textbox control to enter its event-handling code, what is the name of the event procedure entered? What causes the code to execute?

3. What is a parameter?

4. In the KeyPress event procedure, what is the purpose of the parameter?

5. Of the three ways for changing the focus in a Visual Basic program, which do you think is the easiest to understand and the most natural to use? Describe how that way operates and justify your opinion.

6. What happens to a textbox when it has the focus and a key is pressed, but there is no code in the KeyPress event? Assume that the KeyPress event handler has been selected for that object in the Code window, but that no code has been added to it.

7. Write the statement that would shift the focus from the txtX1 box to the txtY1 box.

8. Rewrite the following English descriptions in Basic notation:
   a) A number is less than 5 and is not -3
   b) A string is not the empty string
   c) A variable is either 7 or -2
   d) A variable is neither positive nor negative 8

9. Write an **If-Then** statement for each of these situations:
   a) If x is equal to 3, set y to 5
   b) If y is positive, let c equal x plus 9

10. Describe the purpose of the Visible property and how it may be changed.

11. **SetFocus** is a method and Visible is a property. What is the difference?

12. Make up three different English statements that use the word "and".

13. Under what conditions are the following statements True:
   a) Snow is falling or it is cold.
   b) The car is red and the wheels are flat.
   c) The city is near or the bus door is open.
   d) The cupcake is overdone, and the floor has been freshly waxed.
   e) It is your birthday, or it is not your birthday.
   f) It is Friday and the TV is not on.
   g) The statue is not beautiful or the road is torn up.
   h) John is happy but Mary is sad.

14. What is an empty string and can it be used?

15. Write a statement that doesn't depend on any defaults to assign the contents of the textbox txtNumber to the numeric variable *Number*.

16. State the triangle inequality.

Section

Divisibility, Running Totals, and Loops

Repetition is something a computer does very well. A program can repeat a calculation over and over again with complete accuracy and reliability. A program loop is a section of code that repeats again and again. Loops are used in most computer programs. In this section, you will learn to program simple loops that you need for future projects.

Divisibility problems relate to finding whole numbers that divide evenly into other whole numbers. Divisibility comes up in problems ranging from mathematics to graphic displays.

Many programs need to add up long lists of numbers. Repeatedly adding values to a total is called "keeping a running total."

The techniques of determining divisibility and calculating running totals, as well as program loops, are used in the next project (finding prime numbers).

Divisibility

As you write programs, you will often find yourself needing to test for divisibility. This is the process of checking to see whether one number is evenly divisible by another. For example:

15 is evenly divisible by 1, 3, 5, and 15

13 is evenly divisible by 1 and 13

Imagine that you are writing a program that displays a long listing on the screen. This material will scroll too quickly for the user to read it. The solution is to break the information up into chunks that fit on the screen. Because 24 lines of text fit on a screen, you could stop the display at 24, 48, and 72 lines. Setting this up to occur is a divisibility problem. The program will need to count each line as it is displayed. When the number of lines written is divisible by 24 (and is greater than 0), the program must pause the display.

Another way you will use divisibility is to calculate a common factor or divisor. Most programming languages provide an operator to make this easier. The **Mod** operator in Visual Basic divides one number by another and returns just the remainder of that division as its result (Figure 4-17). For example:

5 mod 3 is 2

21 mod 7 is 0

25 mod 2 is 1

24 mod 5 is 4

When the **Mod** operator returns 0, the first number is evenly divisible by the second. In other words, the first number is a *multiple* of the second. The enhanced Digital Clock example earlier in this chapter provides an example of testing for this condition.

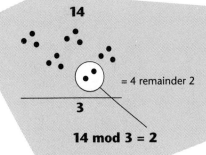

Figure 4-17

Mod operator

14

= 4 remainder 2

3

14 mod 3 = 2

Using Counters and Running Totals

You can use assignment statements to count how often something happens. For example, you could count how often a section of code is executed or how many monsters a user killed in a game. Every time the event happened, the count would increase by 1.

You can also use assignment statements to keep a running total. For example, you could keep a running total of a checking account. Every time you deposit money, the total increases; every time you withdraw, the total decreases.

Assignment statements work for these purposes because they are not algebraic equations. For example, consider the following assignment statement:

```
C = C + 1
```

If you read this as an algebraic equation, you would be able to subtract C from both sides of the statement. This subtraction would leave you with $0 = 1$, which does not make sense.

Now consider the statement as what it is—an assignment statement. This type of statement has the following syntax:

variable = expression

The statement now reads: "1 is added to the old value of C, and the result is assigned back to C. It has become the new value of C." This idea is shown in Figure 4-18.

Here is an example. You have initialized the value of C to 5 ($C = 5$). Initializing the variable means to give it a starting value. You now execute the assignment statement:

```
C = C + 1
```

Figure 4-18

Reading assignment statements

C = C + 1

new
value
of C

old
value
of C

increment

The statement fetches the current (soon to be old) value of C, adds 1 to it, and assigns the result back to C. The "new" value of C is 6.

To use a variable C as a counter, you initialize the value of C. Then you place the statement **C = C + 1** wherever you want to count the number of times an event happens. Every time the statement is executed, the value of the variable is incremented by 1. Incrementing means to add a constant to a value. When the increment is 1, the values increase by one each time through.

To keep a running total instead of a counter, you would use this variation in the assignment statement:

Total = Total + Value

With a running total, for example, you could add up monthly interest on a banking account. You could then choose to display annual interest by printing the total every twelve months.

Keeping a running total is like filling a bucket with values. Start by making sure the bucket is empty (initialize the running total to 0). Keep adding values to the total in the bucket until all the values have been added. The total in the bucket is the running total of the values (see Figure 4-19).

As noted earlier, a checkbook is also a running total. The assignment statement in this case takes the form:

Bal = Bal + Transaction

Any deposit is added to the total and any check is subtracted. Deposits can be represented with positive amounts and checks with negative numbers.

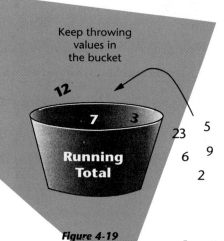

Keep throwing values in the bucket

12

7   3

Running Total

23   5

6   9

2

Figure 4-19

Keeping a running total

Loops

A loop is created by program statements that cause a section of code to be executed over and over again. Because a computer has the speed and accuracy to repeat the same operations quickly and accurately, problems that would defy a solution performed by hand can be solved. A bank processing checks is a good example of a repetitious task that would take too long if done by hand. The volume of checks would keep hundreds of clerks busy around the clock, processing transactions.

Problems involving running totals or counting are obvious candidates for loops. A **For-Next** loop has the following syntax:

For variable = expression **To** expression

the "body" of the loop contains the block of repeated statements

Next variable

Figure 4-20 shows an example of a **For-Next** loop.

Here is an example of such a loop:

```
Dim x As Integer
For x = 1 To 10
    'statements to execute
in the body of the loop
Next x
```

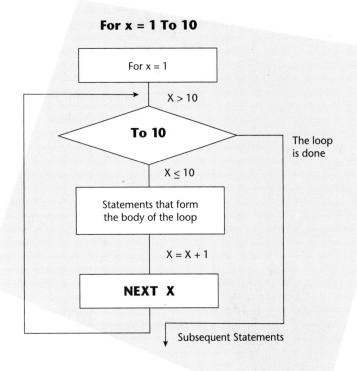

For x = 1 To 10

For x = 1

X > 10

To 10

The loop is done

X ≤ 10

Statements that form the body of the loop

X = X + 1

NEXT X

Subsequent Statements

Figure 4-20

A For-Next loop

The loop starts by setting the value of *x* to 1. One or more statements can be executed in the body of the loop. The statement **Next x** adds 1 to the value of *x* and sends the program back to the top of the loop. The new value of *x* is compared with the limit of the loop, the value 10, following the word **To**. If the value of *x* is greater than 10, the loop ends, jumping to the next statement following **Next x**. The statements that make up the body of the loop can, and generally do, use the loop variable—in this instance, *x*. The actions that they perform can therefore depend on how many times the loop has already been passed through.

The following code uses the **Print** method to display a sentence ten times on the default form. The sentences are numbered, one through ten. To test this code, open a new project and copy the code into the Form_Click procedure. Run the program, then click on the form.

```
Dim x As Integer
For x = 1 To 10
    Print x; "My name is Joclyn"
Next x
```

QUESTIONS AND ACTIVITIES

1. Write an assignment statement that represents the running total of test scores in math class. Use appropriate variable names.

2. You are keeping a running total of monthly interest. You want to print the running total at the end of every twelve months. If the number of months is represented by the variable *Months*, write an expression to test to see if *Months* is divisible by 12.

3. Write an expression to evaluate whether your age is divisible by 3.

4. Write a running total assignment statement that would keep track of a person's parking fines.

Section

Finding Prime Numbers

The Prime Number program is designed to let you experiment with running totals and divisibility. You will also have the opportunity to use multiline textboxes. By changing a default property of a textbox, you can let it display more than one line. In a multiline textbox, text will automatically wrap around to the next line as needed, as in word processing programs. Multiline textboxes can be used to display lengthy passages of text to users while occupying a smaller amount of space on a form. They can also be used to let users enter notes and comments that your program can save and display again when it is next run.

Starting Out

A prime number is an integer that is evenly divisible only by itself or 1. Examples include 3, 5, and 23. If you divide any of these numbers by any number other than the number itself or 1, a remainder results.

This program tests numbers entered by the user to see whether they are prime. The user is prompted to enter a number in a textbox. The program displays the divisors of the number in a multiline textbox. A textbox is set to multiline by selecting the MultiLine property in the box's Properties window. You then type **True** in the edit area of the window. Or, you can toggle from False to True by double-clicking on the property.

One way to display a large amount of data is to put it all into one long string. The string is then written into the textbox. If the MultiLine property is set to True, the contents of the box are displayed on more than one line, if necessary. Note that although the multiline textbox can display several lines of text, it can only display one (possibly long) string at a time. It does not display multiple strings, one on each line.

If the number the user enters is prime, a label with the message "It is prime!" will be displayed. If it is not, the message "It is not prime!" will be displayed. The user can click on a command button to clear the first textbox and enter a second number to be tested. The code also instructs the program to leave the focus on the first textbox and turn off the message labels. To exit the program, the user clicks on a second command button.

You need the following controls for this program (see Figure 4-21):

- Two textboxes, one of which is MultiLine

- Four labels, including:
  - Two prompting labels
  - Two message labels
  - Two command buttons

NOTE:

Multiline textboxes are not typically used for output-only fields. Later, you will learn a more typical way of displaying variable-sized lists.

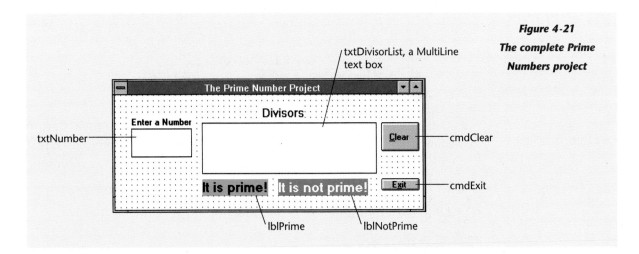

txtDivisorList, a MultiLine text box

Figure 4-21

The complete Prime Numbers project

txtNumber

cmdClear

cmdExit

lblPrime

lblNotPrime

Designing the Form

First, place all the objects on the form and change their properties as necessary. If you need more detail on the steps required, see Chapter 2.

1   Change the caption of the default form to The Prime Number Project.

2   Place the controls shown in the table on the form. Change the properties as listed.

Object	Change object properties to:
Text1	Name = txtNumber
	FontSize = 13.5
	TabIndex = 0
	Text = "" (empty string; clear this property)
Text2	Name = txtDivisorList
	FontSize = 9.75
	MultiLine = True
	Text = "" (empty string; clear this property)
Label1	Caption = "Enter a Number"
Label2	Caption = "Divisors"
Label3	Name = lblPrime
	Caption = "It is prime!"
	AutoSize = True
	Visible = False
Label4	Name = lblNotPrime
	Caption = "It is not prime!"
	AutoSize = True
	Visible = False
Command1	Name = cmdClear
	Caption = "&Clear"
Command2	Name = cmdExit
	Caption = "E&xit"

Coding for the Clear Button

The Clear button should restore the values of controls to their startup values (that is, the values that the controls have when the program is first run). To insert code into the Click event procedure for the Clear button:

1 Double-click on the Clear button to open the Code window.

2 In the subroutine for this button, enter the following code:

```
txtNumber.Text = ""
txtDivisorList.Text = ""
lblPrime.Visible = False
lblNotPrime.Visible = False
txtNumber.SetFocus
```

The first line of this code clears the text from txtNumber. The next line clears the box that contains the divisors (txtDivisorList). Line 3 makes the message label lblPrime invisible. Line 4 makes the message label lblNotPrime invisible. Finally, line 5 uses the SetFocus method to shift the focus back to the first textbox.

Coding for the txtNumber Textbox

The code that does most of the work in this program is attached to the txtNumber textbox. When the user enters a number and presses the Enter key, this code instructs the program to find and display the divisors of that number. For this purpose, you will be using the KeyPress event as you have in earlier programs in this chapter.

To insert code into the event procedure for the txtNumber textbox:

1 Double-click on the txtNumber textbox to open the Code window. If the Code window is already open, select txtNumber from the Object drop-down list.

2 Click on the downward-pointing arrow to open the Proc drop-down list. Select KeyPress. This changes the event selected in the Code window from Change to KeyPress.

3 Now enter the following code in the txtNumber_KeyPress event procedure:

```
Dim Number As Long  ' declare the variables
Dim Sum As Long
Dim Divisor As Long
Dim DivisorList As String
If KeyAscii = 13 Then
   Number = Val(txtNumber)  ' read number
   Sum = 0     ' initialize sum of divisors
   DivisorList = ""  ' initialize list
   For Divisor = 1 To Number   ' loop of divisors
   If Number Mod Divisor = 0 Then    ' test
      Sum = Sum + Divisor      ' running total
      DivisorList = DivisorList & Str$(Divisor) & " "
   End If
   Next Divisor
   txtDivisorList.Text = DivisorList  ' display
   If Sum = Number + 1 Then   ' test if prime
      lblPrime.Visible = True
   Else
      lblNotPrime.Visible = True
   End If
   cmdClear.SetFocus   ' shift focus to Clear
End If
```

The code above makes use of a number of new programming techniques. The first four lines declare variables. The last of these declares a string variable. String variables represent sequences of characters. The program will use this string to assemble a list of divisors for the number entered.

This statement **If KeyAscii = 13 Then** begins the first **If-Then** statement. If the condition is true, the rest of the code will be executed. The code is not executed unless Enter is pressed (KeyAscii = 13).

The statement **Number = Val(txtNumber)** initializes the variable *Number* to the value the user enters in the textbox txtNumber. The program automatically converts the string type of the textbox to the long integer type of the variable.

The next line initializes the variable *Sum* to 0. This variable will be used to count the number of divisors (a running total). **DivisorList = ""** initializes the variable *DivisorList* to an empty string.

The line **For Divisor = 1 To Number** sets up a loop to repeatedly execute a series of statements. The computer can execute these statements far faster than you can. Because the *Divisor* variable has been initialized to 1, the program will test this divisor first. It will then test every number between 1 and the number entered by the user.

The line **If Number Mod Divisor = 0 Then** sets up a branch in the program with a second **If-Then** statement. The **Mod** operator divides *Number* by *Divisor* and returns the remainder of the division. If the remainder is 0, then *Divisor* divides *Number* evenly and the condition is true. In this case, the program takes the old value of *Sum*, adds the current value of *Divisor*, and assigns the result back to *Sum*.

The line **DivisorList = DivisorList & Str$(Divisor) & " "** joins strings together. The **Str$** function converts the integer value of *Divisor* into a string. The old value of the string variable, *DivisorList,* is joined to the string representation of *Divisor,* and the result is assigned back to *DivisorList*. The space within quotes joined to the end of the string inserts space between each number in the list. The ampersand operator(&) is used to join two strings.

The line **Next Divisor** adds 1 to *Divisor* and sends the program back to the top of the loop. The value of Divisor is initially set to 1. The second time through the loop, the value of Divisor will be 2. The program will continue to loop until the value of Divisor exceeds *Number* (which is the number entered by the user). At that point, the loop ends and the program jumps to the next statement outside the loop.

The line **txtDivisorList.Text = DivisorList** transfers the value of the display string to the Text property of the txtDivisorList box. This value will then be displayed.

The next line sets up a branch in the program with a third **If-Then** statement. The condition statement tests to see if the number the user entered was prime. If the number is prime, the sum of the divisors of the number is equal to the number itself plus 1. For any prime number, the loop will have found only two numbers that divide the prime number with a remainder of 0. Those are 1 and the number itself.

The program displays the lblPrime label (It is prime!) if the condition is True. Otherwise (the alternative or False branch of the statement), the program displays the lblNotPrime label (It is not prime!).

Finishing Up

Enter the End statement in cmdExit.

Run the program and test several numbers to see if they are prime. Then save the project and form files.

QUESTIONS AND ACTIVITIES

1. What, typically, is the last job tackled by a Clear command?

2. Describe the use of the MultiLine property of a textbox.

3. Write the statements that make a textbox appear and disappear. The name of the box is txtWarning.

4. Write the statement that will clear the display of the textbox txtNumber.

5. In what event will you find the partial statement:

   ```
   If KeyAscii=13 Then
   ```

6. In you own words, describe what a loop does in a program.

7. Write a statement that will join together these components into a single string and assign the result to the textbox txtEquation.

"y="	a string literal
m	a variable representing a numeric value
"x + "	a string literal
b	a variable representing a numeric value

   The string displayed in the textbox should depend on the values of the variables m and b. For example, when m has the value 17 and b the value 3, the string displayed should be "$y = 17x + 3$".

Summary

The **If-Then** statement has three forms:

1. **If** *condition* **Then** *statements*

2. **If** *condition* **Then**
       statements if true
   End If

3. **If** *condition* **Then**
       statements if true
   Else
       statements if false
   End If

If the condition tested is true, the statements immediately following are executed. If the condition is false, versions 1 and 2 would not execute any statements. Version 3 would execute the statements after **Else**.

The KeyPress event procedure attached to a textbox is executed when the textbox has the focus and a text key on the keyboard is pressed. The ASCII code of the key pressed is passed to the event procedure through the variable (called a parameter) *KeyAscii*.

An And statement is true only if both the left and right expressions are true.

An Or statement is true if either the right expression is true or the left expression is true, or if both are true.

Divisibility of a number by a divisor is tested with the following statement:

If Number mod Divisor = 0 **Then**
    number is divisible by Divisor
End If

The **Mod** operator divides *Number* by *Divisor* and returns the remainder. If the remainder is 0, the *Divisor* divides *Number* evenly.

Running totals are kept with statements like this:

```
total = total + divisor
```

To count the number of times a statement is executed, use a counting statement such as:

```
C = C + 1
```

The basic loop statement, the **For-Next** loop, may look like this:

```
For x = 1 To 100 Step 2
Next x
```

This statement initializes the variable *x* to 1, and increases the value by two's until the limit of 100 is exceeded.

The MultiLine property of a textbox automatically word wraps when the display line exceeds the width of the box.

Problems

1. The Movie Theater Problem

Write a program that uses a textbox to enter a person's age. If the person is 12 or older, they pay the adult fee at the movie theater, $6. If the person is less than 12, the fee is $4.00. Display the label **Adult Fee $6** or **Child Fee $4.00** based on the value entered.

Use the Visible property to turn the labels on and off. Use a button with the caption Test to test the age. Include a Clear button to clear the textbox and turn off the labels.

2. The Floor Problem

The **Rnd** function will return a random numeric value between 0 and 1. Use **Rnd** to make a random branch:

> **If** Rnd < .5 **Then**
>
> > 'value is between 0 and .5'
>
> **Else**
>
> > 'value is between .5 and 1
>
> **End If**

Create a form with two labels and three command buttons. The captions of the two labels are **Fall Through the Floor**, and **The Floor Holds**. Name the labels **lblFall** and **lblHold**. Set the Visible property for both to False. The captions of the command buttons are **Test**, **Reset**, and **Exit**. Name the buttons **cmdTest**, **cmdReset**, and **cmdExit**. The first button, using the **If-Then** statement above, turns on one label or the other. The Reset button makes both labels invisible. The Exit button stops the program. Include a Randomize statement as the first line in cmdTest to generate a different random sequence each time the program is run.

3. The Couch Problem

If-Then statements are used to test strings as well as numbers. For example:

```
If txtName = "Jim" Then ...
```

will compare the contents of the textbox, txtName, with the string "Jim". If they are equal, the True branch of the **If** statement will execute.

Write a program with a textbox named **txtFurniture**. Put a label above the box with the caption **Couch or Chair?**

If the user enters "couch" or "Couch" (use an OR operator), display "The couch is $496" in a separate label. If the user enters "chair" or "Chair", display "The chair is $295".

4. What Kind of Triangle?

Write a program using textboxes to enter three lengths that may represent the sides of a triangle.

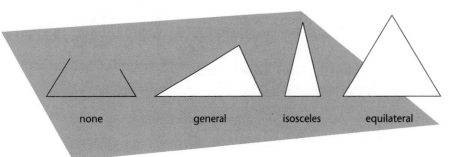

none   general   isosceles   equilateral

Figure 4-22

Use four **If-Then** statements and appropriate And statements to display a label with one of the following responses:

◎ None if it fails the triangle inequality.

◎ General if it is scalene.

◎ Isosceles if two sides are equal.

◎ Equilateral if three sides are equal.

5. Cooking a Turkey

A stuffed turkey should be cooked for 21 minutes per pound. An unstuffed turkey should be cooked for 17 minutes per pound. Display a table that shows:

Column 1: Weight of the turkey in pounds, ranging from 12 to 30

Column 2: The time to cook the unstuffed turkey

Column 3: The time to cook the stuffed turkey

The time should be printed as minutes, or hours and minutes. Use the **Mod** operator to convert the number of minutes to hours and minutes. The backslash operator divides two numbers and gives a whole number result. For instance, 7 \ 2 is 3. Minutes \ 60 is the number of hours. Minutes Mod 60 is the number of left-over minutes.

6.   The Garden Fencing Problem

Write a program to calculate the cost of a rectangular wooden fence. Use two textboxes to enter the dimensions of the garden: the length and width. The amount of fence needed is the perimeter of the garden. Display the cost of fence. Each eight foot section costs $24.95.

7.   The Garden Fencing Problem (Part II)

Add a textbox to the problem above. Label the box so the user will enter a "1" if the fence is rectangular, and a "2" if the fence is circular. If the fence is circular, use the "length" textbox to enter the radius of the garden. Display the cost of the fence and whether the garden is rectangular or circular. Each eight-foot-curved section of fence costs $29.95.

8.   The Paint Problem

Write a program to estimate the quantity of paint needed to paint a room.

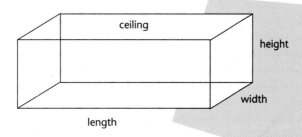

Figure 4-23

Use textboxes to enter the dimensions of the room: length, width, and height. Calculate the area of the four walls and the ceiling.

Assuming a gallon of paint on a smooth surface covers about 400 square feet, display the number of cans of paint needed to cover the walls and the number of cans needed for the ceiling. Display the cost to paint the entire room using $12.95/can as the cost of the paint.

```
Dim strFn As

String

strFn =

UCase$(Trim$(Inp

utBox("Filename"

, "Open File")))

Open strFn For

Output As #1
```

Strings and Table Construction

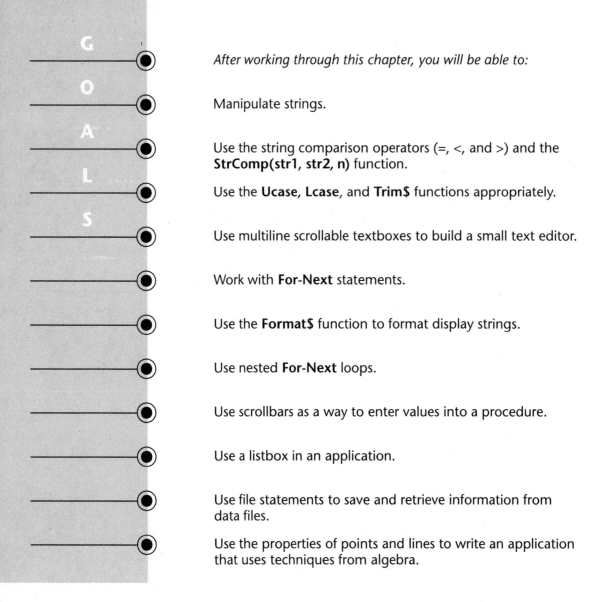

After working through this chapter, you will be able to:

Manipulate strings.

Use the string comparison operators (=, <, and >) and the **StrComp(str1, str2, n)** function.

Use the **Ucase, Lcase**, and **Trim$** functions appropriately.

Use multiline scrollable textboxes to build a small text editor.

Work with **For-Next** statements.

Use the **Format$** function to format display strings.

Use nested **For-Next** loops.

Use scrollbars as a way to enter values into a procedure.

Use a listbox in an application.

Use file statements to save and retrieve information from data files.

Use the properties of points and lines to write an application that uses techniques from algebra.

O V E R V I E W

Visual Basic programs work with strings frequently. Much of the data stored in databases is stored in strings. You can write programs to gather information in the form of strings (such as students' names and favorite occupations). Then you can manipulate these strings, such as by sorting them in a specific order or by selecting only those students who like to hike. You use strings as label captions, to prompt the user for information, or to pass a message.

The second section introduces you to menus, which are a distinctive feature of Windows. With a menu bar, users can quickly see what commands are available in the program. Typically, commands are placed in logical groups so that they are easy to find. For example, you know that the Save command is in the File menu, no matter what Windows application you are using.

In the MiniEdit project, you will create a menu bar with one item (File). You will also create the drop-down menu for that item. Through the program, you will work with opening, saving, and closing files. These are very important tasks for any Visual Basic program.

*Loops are a common way to perform work in a program. Loops let you repeat a series of instructions as many times as you need. When a condition is met (such as all the calculations being complete), the program moves to the next line of code outside the loop. **For-Next** statements are one of the most common types of loops in Visual Basic.*

You can add scrollbars to a textbox on a form through the Properties window or by placing scrollbar objects on the form. In this chapter, you will learn the difference between the two types of scrollbars as well as how to use the scrollbar control.

Section

Strings

Strings are series of characters. These characters may include digits, letters, punctuation, and special characters, including:

Digits = 0,1,2,3,4,5,6,7,8,9
Letters = a,b,...,z, A, B,...,Z
Punctuation = . ? ! ; : , " '
Special characters = ~ @ # $. + | \

When you think of strings, you probably think of text. You may find it surprising that social security numbers, telephone numbers, times, and dates are all usually treated as strings. Can you see the difference between numbers that you multiply, divide, and add, and these "numbers"? Look at the examples below:

331-50-5440, social security number
(708)555-7561, phone number
162-99-2421, driver's license number

These numbers have a specific structure. A social security number, for example, always has three numbers, then two numbers, then four numbers. These numbers also have specific punctuation. The groupings of numbers in social security numbers are always divided by hyphens. The punctuation in phone numbers is admittedly somewhat more variable. Sometimes you see the area code set off by parentheses, but sometimes people just use two hyphens.

Although these numbers consist of digits and (sometimes optional) punctuation, they are best thought of as names—strings that uniquely identify someone or something. Notice that they lack almost all the properties of actual numbers. For example, it makes no sense at all to add two social security numbers. Whose social security number would you have by performing this addition? Furthermore, the result of the addition may simply have too many digits to be a valid social security number. Similarly, it is meaningless to multiply a phone number by 2.

To work with strings, you need to understand their characteristics. Strings:

- Have a length. The number of spaces and characters in a string is its length.

- Can be joined together.

- Can be searched. How often have you searched for a word in a text file, then replaced it with something else?

- Can be displayed on the screen.

- Can be read from controls on the screen. Users enter strings in textboxes. The program can then read the strings from those controls. Figure 5-1 shows a name being entered into a textbox.

Enter a Name: | John Smith |

Figure 5-1
String entered in a textbox

String Literals and String Variables

Some numeric values change often, some change seldom, and some change not at all. In the same way, some string variables change values all the time, some change rarely, and some never change. When an assignment statement is used to give a value to a variable, you're probably looking at a variable whose value changes rarely. The string used in the assignment statement, a series of characters within double quotes, is called a string literal. The variable it is assigned to, used exclusively to represent string values, is called a string variable.

STRING LITERALS

You can dictate a specific string by using a string literal. String literals are series of characters between double quotation marks—for example, "Hello there" or "Please enter a positive number". Placing the period at the end of the sentence outside the closing quotation mark shows that the period is not part of the string.

You can use string literals with the **MsgBox** statement to communicate simple messages to the user, for example, or to ask a simple Yes/No question. You can also assign string literals to string variables. Both of these possibilities are illustrated by the following example:

```
Dim strAskAge As String, strName As String
strAskAge = "How old are you?"
strName = "Wendy"
MsgBox "You are standing on my foot!"
```

STRING VARIABLES

If you want to let the value of a string be determined during run-time, you use a string variable. You also use a string variable if you want to define the value of the variable during design, but let the variable change value as the program runs. The program might then change the value of the string variable by reading a string from a textbox or other control.

For example, look at Figure 5-1. You might define a string variable called *Name*, then have the program insert a text string into that variable during run-time. In this instance, the program would make the value of *Name* equal to "John Smith". Now look back at the Primes program in Chapter 4. The variable *Divisor* is a string variable.

You should declare all string variables with a **Dim** statement. For example:

```
Dim strName As String, strUserPrompt As String
```

Joining Strings Together

Joining strings together is a powerful option you will find yourself using frequently. In Visual Basic, this is called concatenation. For example, consider these two assignment statements:

```
Desire = "I would like to learn to "
ObjectOfDesire = "skydive"
```

You can join these variables together by using the ampersand operator:

```
Desire & ObjectOfDesire
```

The result is a concatenated string: "I would like to learn to skydive".

You need to pay attention to the spaces included within the quotation marks of a string literal. Any character within these marks is part of the string. In this case, the value of *strDesire* ends with a trailing space.

NOTE:

A string can be empty. The empty string is indicated by two double quotes with nothing in between (""). The length of the empty string is 0, because it contains no characters. Just as a numeric variable is sometimes initialized to 0, it is often useful to initialize a string variable to the empty string.

This space provides the proper spacing between the end of this string and the beginning of the string joined to it. Otherwise, in the joined string, the words "to" and "skydive" would run together. A leading space is a space at the beginning of a string.

You also need to pay attention to the order of the string variables in the concatenation. **strDesire & strObjectOfDesire** is not at all the same as **strObjectOfDesire & strDesire**. The latter string has the value: "skydiveI would like to learn to ".

You have already had some experience with joining strings together. In the Primes program (Chapter 4), you joined the divisors of a number to build a list of divisors.

Comparing Strings

Besides joining strings, another common way to work with strings is to compare them. For example, imagine that you want to find a specific word in a file. To do so, you need to have the program compare every word in the file against the search word. If the program finds a match, an action occurs, such as a message being displayed. This is how any program performs a search-and-replace task.

Yet another common reason to compare strings is to sort them. For example, you might have a list of students in your school. To sort these names alphabetically, you would compare them to each other. Using ASCII codes, your program can determine if a name is "less than" another and move it further up the list. One string is "less than" another if it precedes it alphabetically—that is, if it would come first in the dictionary or the phone book.

For these kinds of tasks, you use four different mathematical signs: the equal sign, the greater than (>) sign, the less than (<) sign, and the not equal sign (<>). This section provides a couple of examples showing you how to use these signs to compare strings

The following code uses the equal sign in an **If-Then** statement:

```
Dim Fruit1 As String, Fruit2 As String
Dim Outcome As String
Fruit1 = "Apple"
Fruit2 = "apple"
If Fruit1 = Fruit2
    Outcome = " are equal."
Else
    Outcome = " are not equal."
End If
MsgBox "The strings" & Outcome
```

NOTE:

In older versions of Basic, the string concatenation operator was the plus sign (+). Visual Basic lets you use the plus sign for joining strings, but, because the plus sign is used to add numbers, you should try to use the ampersand.

This code compares the two strings *Fruit1* and *Fruit2*, character by character. It then displays a message informing the user of the result of the comparison. If the words differ in even the slightest way, the strings are not equal. Because "Apple" is not equal to "apple", the message "The strings are not equal" will always be displayed.

This code uses less than and greater than signs to compare strings:

```
Dim Word1 As String, Word2 As String, Msg As String
Word1 = "play"
Word2 = "ball"
If Word1 > Word2 Then
   Msg = "The first word is the greater of the two."
Else If Word1 < Word2 Then
      Msg = "The first word is the lesser of the two."
   Else
      Msg = "The two words are equal."
   End If
```

Because "ball" precedes "play" alphabetically, the condition *Word1 > Word2* is **True**, and *Word1 < Word2* is **False**. Thus, *Msg* will be set to "The first word is the greater of the two."

Visual Basic compares strings by looking at the values, or the ASCII codes, of the characters. The lengths of the strings does not matter. In the example above, "ball" is less than "play". The ASCII code for "b" is 98, and the ASCII code for "p" is 112.

Characters have different ASCII codes, depending on their case. For example, "ball" is greater than "Play". The ASCII code for "P" is 80, compared to 98 for "b". The ASCII codes for uppercase letters range from 65 for "A" to 90 for "Z"; the ASCII codes for lowercase letters range from 97 for "a" to 122 for "z".

Now imagine that you were comparing the strings "play" and "plays". Visual Basic would find a match for the first four characters. The difference lies in the "s" in "plays". The word "play" is what is called a left substring of "plays". As a result, "play" is less than "plays".

Using Functions to Work with Strings

Visual Basic provides some useful tools for working with strings. These tools take the form of string functions (see the text box for a definition of functions). Two of the functions can change the case of the characters in the string. Another function can compare two strings alphabetically. The final function discussed in this section counts the number of characters in a string.

NOTE:

There is a more powerful way to compare strings than using the =, <, >, and <> signs. See the description of the StrComp function in the next section.

UCASE AND LCASE FUNCTIONS

Sometimes, you will want the program to ignore the case of two strings it is comparing. For example, if you are alphabetizing a list of words, you would want "labor" to be listed before "Materials". Or you may want to find *every* instance of the word "text"—including both "text" and "Text". You can use the **UCase** and **LCase** functions for this purpose.

VISUAL BASIC FUNCTIONS

A Visual Basic function is a built-in procedure that performs a specific job and returns a value that can be used in expressions. It is "built-in" in the sense that Visual Basic already contains the code that performs the task in question. These functions are shortcuts that you can use instead of writing code from scratch to perform the same task.

For example, a commonly used numeric function is the square root function, which finds the square root of a positive number. Visual Basic contains the **Sqr** function, which computes square roots so that you do not have to write pages of code to perform that computation. The argument x that you supply to **Sqr** can be any numeric expression with a value that is nonnegative. The following example illustrates the use of the **Sqr** function:

```
Dim dblNumber As Double, dblRoot As Double
dblRoot = Sqr(dblNumber)
```

The **UCase** function works by converting all the characters of a string to uppercase. The **LCase** function converts the characters of a string to lowercase. Here is a sample of code using the **UCase** function:

```
Dim Word1 As String, Word2 As String, Msg As String
Word1 = "hello"
Word2 = "Today"
If UCase(Word1) < UCase(Word2) Then
    Msg = Word1 & " is less than " & Word2
Else
    Msg = Word2 & " is less than " & Word1
End If
```

The **UCase** function converts any lowercase character to its uppercase equivalent. It leaves unchanged any uppercase character or nonletter. Similarly, the **LCase** function converts any uppercase character to lowercase, leaving any other character unchanged.

STRCOMP FUNCTION

You have another, more powerful option for comparing strings than using the =, >, <, and <> signs. You can use the **StrComp** function:

```
Dim Word1 As String, Word2 As String
Dim Result As Integer
'...
Result = StrComp(Word1, Word2, 1)
```

This function uses three parameters. For a review of parameters, see the accompanying textbox. You use the first two parameters to specify the strings that are to be compared. In this sample code, the **StrComp** function compares the values of *Word1* and *Word2*. The third parameter is optional. You can place one of two values in this third parameter:

◉ 1, which makes the comparison case-insensitive. This means that "h" will match with "H".

◉ 0, which makes the comparison case-sensitive. This means that "h" will *not* match with "H".

If *Word1* is less than *Word2*, the value returned by the function and assigned to the variable *Result* is -1. If the strings are equal, the value assigned to *Result* is 0. If the first string is greater than the second, the value assigned to *Result* is 1.

LEN FUNCTION

With the **Len** function, you can count the number of characters in a string. If **Word1 = "hello"**, for example, then **Len(Word1)** is 5, which is the number of characters in the string.

Knowing the length of a string is important when, for example, you need to write code that edits text. Replacing text may require a character count to delete old characters and replace them with new. Searching for an occurrence of a particular string often uses the **Len** function to control the limits of the search.

Exercise

Experiment with the string comparison operators by putting the following statements into the Form_Load procedure of a new project. The **MsgBox** statement displays the string that follows in a message box on the screen. For the program to continue, press the Enter key or click OK.

PARAMETERS

A parameter or argument is a value sent to a procedure or a function. In the KeyPress event procedure, KeyAscii is a parameter. In the square root function, **Sqr(x)**, the value x is a parameter. Many functions take more than one parameter and some have no parameters at all. **Time** is a function with no parameters that returns the current system time.

This exercise demonstrates the string functions and comparison operators discussed above. It works by assigning string literals, such as "apple" and "aple", to string variables and using the comparison operators to compare their values. Each time you run the program, the MessageBox displays the results of the comparison. After each sample, you change the values or the operators and run the program again.

To complete the exercise:

1 Start Visual Basic. If Visual Basic is already running, select New Project from the File menu.

2 Insert the following code into the Form_Load procedure of the default form.

```
Sub Form_Load ()
    Dim Fruit As String, Word As String
    Dim Word1 As String, Word2 As String, Msg As String
    Fruit = "apple"
    Word = "aple"
    If Fruit = Word Then
        Msg = "The strings are equal."
    Else
        Msg = Fruit & " and " & Word & " are not equal "
    End If
    MsgBox Msg
End Sub
```

3 Run the program. Check the output. Was it what you expected?

4 Stop the program and add this code just before the **End Sub** statement:

```
Word1 = "play"
Word2 = "ball"
If Word1 > Word2 Then
    Msg = Word1 & " is greater than " & Word2
Else
    Msg = Word1 & " is less than " & Word2
End If
MsgBox Msg
```

5 Run the program. Check the output. Was it what you expected?

6 Stop the program and add this code just before the **End Sub** statement:

```
Word1 = "Play"
If Word1 > Word2 Then
    Msg = Word1 & " is greater than " & Word2
Else
    Msg = Word1 & " is less than " & Word2
End If
MsgBox Msg
```

7 Run the program. Check the output. Was it what you expected?

8 Stop the program and add this code just before the **End Sub** statement.

```
If UCase(Word1) > UCase(Word2) Then
    Msg = UCase(Word1) & " is greater than " & UCase(Word2)
Else
    Msg = UCase(Word1) & " is less than " & UCase(Word2)
End If
MsgBox Msg
```

9 Run the program. Check the output. Was it what you expected?

10 Stop the program and add this code just before the **End Sub** statement.

```
Dim Result As Integer
Word1 = "play"
Result = StrComp(Word1, Word2, 1)
If Result = 0 Then
    Msg = Word1 & " is equal to " & Word2
ElseIf Result = -1 Then
    Msg = Word1 & " is less than " & Word2
ElseIf Result = 1 Then
    Msg = Word1 & " is greater than " & Word2
End If
MsgBox Msg
```

11 Run the program. Check the output. Was it what you expected?

12 Stop the program and add this code just before the **End Sub** statement:

```
Msg = "The length of " & Word1 & " is " & Str$(Len(Word1))
MsgBox Msg
```

13 Run the program.

14 Stop the program.

QUESTIONS AND ACTIVITIES

In the following questions assume these assignments:

```
a$ = "Hello there "
b$ = "California kid "
```

Write the results of the following operations:

1. Len(a$) + Len(b$)

2. Len(b$) + Len(a$)

3. a$ & b$

4. b$ & a$

5. a$ + b$

Determine for each expression in 6 through 9, whether the expression is true or false.

6. a$ > b$

7. a$ > UCase(b$)

8. a$ = b$

9. UCase(a$) < UCase(b$)

What is the result of each of the following?

10. UCase(a$)

11. LCase(b$)

12. StrComp(a$, b$, 1)

13. StrComp(a$, b$, 0)

2

Section

Menus

In Windows programs, menus are the most common means by which users choose commands. If your program contains many commands, you can see that adding a button for each command would quickly lead to a very cluttered form. In such cases, menus provide an interface that is superior to command buttons.

In other cases, either buttons or a menu bar is an appropriate choice. For example, in the Freefall project (Chapter 3), you could have created a menu to perform the three tasks of calculating, clearing, and quitting. The code you need is not changed; the only question is whether you attach that code to a command button or a menu command.

THE WINDOWS STYLE GUIDELINES
FOR MENUS

The Windows style guidelines are a group of recommendations to software developers that put the user's interests first. These recommendations exist not in order to force a bland uniformity on all application programs, or just to make it more difficult to write a program. The guidelines try to benefit users by encouraging consistency among Windows applications. Users can then learn general principles of how to operate Windows programs, rather than having to start from scratch with each new application.

The great majority of Windows application programs work with files. They allow the user to create files of a particular type, edit these files, save them, and open them again later for further editing or inspection. This type of program organization is so common that Microsoft has defined style guidelines to which programs of this type should adhere. According to these guidelines, a program that opens and saves files that the user can edit should provide a main menu whose first two items are the File and Edit submenus. Each of these menus should contain certain commands, and in a recommended order. Another top-level menu item for which standards exist is Help. To see an example of the standard File, Edit, and Help menus, run Notepad and examine its menu structure.

The style guidelines have a great deal more to say on the topic of how menus should be organized and presented. Here, we'll mention just one more recommendation. A menu item should end in an ellipsis (...) if it does not directly perform an action when chosen but instead presents a dialog box to collect further information. For example, standard File menus always let you save the current file under a different name; the text of the menu item that lets you do this is usually Save As.... When you choose Save As..., a dialog box always opens that lets you specify where and under what name to save the file. You can be sure that when you choose a command that ends in an ellipsis, you won't immediately change the data you're working on.

In the programs you've seen and written so far, you've used command buttons instead of menus to let the user perform actions. Menus are neither "better" nor "worse" than command buttons. They're just a another tool that you can use—one that sometimes is more appropriate. Though menus can give your programs the familiar, uncluttered, and well-organized look-and-feel shared by other Windows programs, keep in mind that it is usually easier and quicker to click a command button than to open a menu and choose a command.

Because users always appreciate programs that let them work rapidly and with a minimum of effort, frequently used commands are excellent candidates for command buttons. When trying to decide whether to use menus or command buttons, keep the user in mind. Put yourself in the position of a user who knows nothing about programming and perhaps not a lot about computers, but who probably knows a great deal about the task that your program is designed to accomplish. Try to create an efficient tool that the user can easily figure out how to operate.

Even after you have created a program, you can change your mind about using command buttons or menus. Simply open the project in design mode and change the interface. In the following steps, you learn how to make that conversion by replacing the three command buttons in the Freefall form with a menu bar containing three commands. You also transfer the code from cmdCalculate to one of these commands.

Like command buttons, menu items have a Click event. When a user clicks on a menu item, the code in the Click event procedure is executed. Just as with objects from the toolbox, you need to name menu commands. For textboxes, you use the "txt" prefix; for labels, the "lbl" prefix; and for command buttons, the "cmd" prefix. For menu commands, you use a "mnu" prefix.

To create a menu bar for the Freefall project, you will add the menu, delete the command buttons, and transfer the code to the menu.

Adding the Menu

You open the Menu Design window by clicking on its button in the toolbar. The button is dimmed unless a form is selected. The menu commands are like the captions of command buttons. Typically, you capitalize the first letter of each caption, and you can designate a character in the caption as a short-cut key by preceding it with the ampersand.

To add the menu:

1 Open the Freefall project by selecting Open Project from the File menu. Click on the View Form button in the Project window to see the form.

2 Select the form, if necessary. In the toolbar, click on the icon for the Menu Design window. This button is dimmed unless the form is selected. The Menu Design window opens.

3 In the Caption textbox, enter the caption of the first menu item, **&Calculate**. Tab to the Name textbox, and enter the name **mnuCalculate** (Figure 5-2).

4 Click on the Next button to enter the next menu command. Enter the caption **C&lear** and the name **mnuClear**.

5 Click on the Next button to enter the next command. Enter the caption **&Quit** and the name **mnuQuit**. The commands appear at the bottom of the window as you enter them.

6 Click OK to close the Menu Design window. The form now has both commands in a new menu bar and the original command buttons (Figure 5-3).

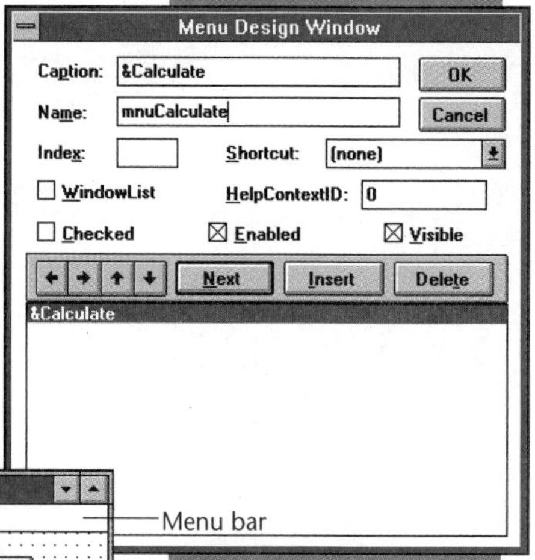

Deleting the Command Buttons

The menu bar is in place, though clicking the menu items still does nothing. Although some programs allow the user to perform actions either by clicking buttons or by clicking menu items, you will remove the command buttons so there is no redundancy.

To delete the buttons:

1 Highlight each button in turn.

2 Press the Delete key.

The code attached to the command buttons is not lost. Visual Basic moves the code, which is now no longer connected with an event procedure of a screen control. The code is placed in the general area of the Code window.

Transferring the Code to the Menu

To work, the menu items need code attached to their event procedures. In this series of steps, you use the code formerly attatched to the command buttons to bring functionality to the menu.

To transfer the code:

1 Open the Code window by clicking on the View Code button in the Project window, or by double-clicking on one of the controls on the screen.

Figure 5-2
Entering information in the Main Design window

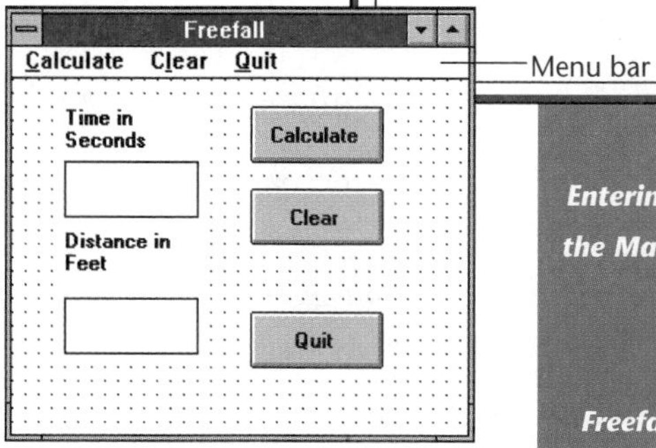

Figure 5-3
Freefall program with both menu bar and command buttons

163

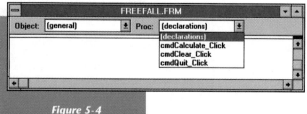

Figure 5-4
Selection of available procedures

2   Open the Object drop-down list by clicking on the downward-pointing arrow. Select the top entry, which is *general*. Open the Proc drop-down list by clicking on the arrow (Figure 5-4). The code of the deleted command buttons is here in the general section.

3   Open an event procedure, such as cmdCalculate_Click. Select and cut the code (not the top or bottom lines).

4   Select the corresponding command from the Object drop-down list, mnuCalculate. Paste the code you just cut into this event procedure (Figure 5-5). Perform this operation for each of the three command buttons you are deleting.

Code from	Move to
cmdCalculate	mnuCalculate
cmdClear	mnuClear
cmdQuit	mnuQuit

After button is deleted, code moves to "general" area

Figure 5-5
Cutting and pasting code

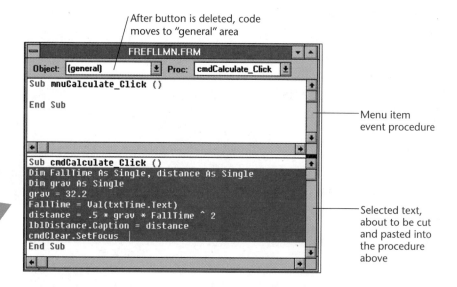

Menu item event procedure

Selected text, about to be cut and pasted into the procedure above

NOTE:

Another approach would be to cut and paste the code first, then delete the buttons.

Finishing Up

Now you are ready to test your changes:

1   Run the program. The program halts before it begins. Can you figure out what the problem is?

2   One line of code from the original cmdCalculate button uses the **SetFocus** method to shift the focus to the Clear button. That button no longer exists. Delete that line of code.

3   Run the program. Test each menu item.

4   Save the project and the file with a new name to preserve the command button version of the program.

QUESTIONS AND ACTIVITIES

1.   Replace the command buttons of the Cereal project with a menu bar.

The MiniEdit Project

Section

The MiniEdit program provides the functions of a text editor. Within the Edit window of the application, the user can create and edit text. With the menu choices you will provide, the user can open, save, and close files.

This project introduces more complicated menus as well as reading and writing files to disk. After working through this project, you will be able to create programs that are similar to professional applications. You want your programs to conform to users' expectations of how a Windows program works. Users will then find your programs easier to understand quickly.

All programs except the simplest utilities save and retrieve information from files. This saving and retrieving is the most common use of computers. Companies, for example, use files to save customer and employee information. All kinds of organizations, from a local karate club to an international wildlife federation, maintain mailing lists in files.

State, local, and federal governments keep files of resident information. Schools keep files of students, classes, teachers, expenditures, and revenues. Word processors use files to store and retrieve documents. If you could not store and open files, you could not start working on a letter or term paper at the beginning of the week, then come back to finish the project several days later.

Game programs save high and low scores as well as complete games on disk. Scientists store files containing information on stars, dinosaurs, and DNA sequences. Communications programs transfer disk files all over the world. These are just a few of the ways we have become dependent on reading and writing computer files.

Starting Out

Each project starts by setting up a directory for the project's files. Once a disk directory has been prepared, you set up the user interface. For

Figure 5-6

The complete MiniEdit project

MiniEdit, you start by defining the menu structure in the Menu Design window. Besides the menu, the multiline text box is the most important feature of the user interface.

One the form has been designed, code is added to provide functionality. You'll start by writing code to resize the edit space to fill the form. Then you'll spend a lot of time working with the code to open, load, and save files. Figure 5-6 shows a shot of the final product.

Creating the Menu and Edit Space

The user interface is one of the most important parts of a program. If the program is not attractive and easy to use, chances are no one will want to use it. This stage of the program development creates a standard-looking user interface. Specifically, you create a File menu.

The body of the form is taken up by a multiline textbox. Remember, a multiline box will automatically wrap text that is too long for the line—just what you want in a text editor. A "form-filling" box just means to size the box to fill the form. Later, in the code, you will adjust the size of the box to fill the form when the program is running and the user resizes the form with the mouse. A vertical scrollbar, provided by the textbox, takes care of scrolling to text that is not visible.

The menu bar contains a separator. Many Windows applications use separators to visually separate related, though distinct, groups of commands. In MiniEdit, the Exit command is set apart from the other file commands with a separator. A single hyphen in the Menu Design window displays a solid bar separating the first three menu items from the last. Although no code is executed by clicking the separator bar on the menu, the bar must have a name. Each item defined in a Menu Design window must have a name and a caption.

Follow these steps to create a menu and edit space.

1 Create a new subdirectory for the MiniEdit project:
   a) Open the File Manager.
   b) Select a directory in which to create the new subdirectory.
   c) Select Create Directory from the File menu and follow the instructions in the window. Create the **Medit** directory.

2 Start Visual Basic. If Visual Basic is already running, select New Project from the File menu.

3 Change the caption of the form to MiniEdit.

4   Click on the Menu Design window button in the toolbar. This
opens the Menu Design window.

5   Create a menu bar with a single item on it
(File). When the user clicks on this menu
item, a drop-down menu opens. See Figure
5-7 for the entries in this menu.

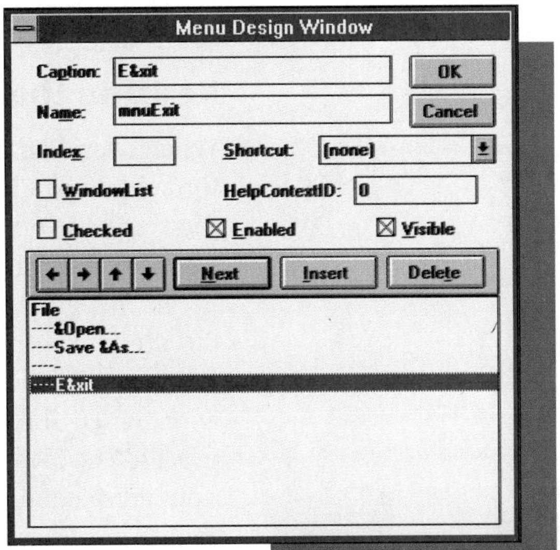

Figure 5-7
*Setting up the last entry
in the subdirectory*

a)   In the Caption textbox, enter **File**. In the
Name textbox, enter **mnuFile**.

b)   Click on the Next button to enter the next
menu item.

c)   Use the right arrow button in the Menu
Design window to create a submenu. The
items in a submenu are indented in the
window. Enter captions and names for
each item in the submenu, as shown
below. After entering this information for
each item, click on the Next button.

Caption	*Name*
&Open...	mnuOpen
Save &As...	mnuSave
-	mnuSeparator
E&xit	mnuExit

6   Create a form-filling multiline textbox. In the Properties window,
be sure that the Top and Left properties of the textbox are both set
to 0. Change the Name property to **txtEdit**. Set the MultiLine
property to True. Change the Scrollbars property to 2-Vertical. Set
the Text property to "". Finally, set the BorderStyle to 0-None (see
Figure 5-8).

7   Run the program.

8   Type some text into the textbox. Type enough text to word wrap to
the next line.

Figure 5-8
Scrollbars property

9   Play with the program. Use the mouse to select text. Press Ctrl+X
and Ctrl+V to cut and paste. Try out the scrollbar. Try out the
menu choices.

10 Stop the program by pressing Alt+F4 or by clicking on the Stop
button on the toolbar.

As you experimented with the program, what did you notice about
it? You cannot save your work, for example, nor can you open an existing file to edit. The menu items do nothing yet. The program does not

execute any action if the user clicks on one of the commands. Also, if you resize the form while the program is running, the textbox does not expand or contract to fill the space.

Resizing the Form

When users run applications, they often want to change the size of the form window. For example, a user may want to fit several windows on the screen at once. This can be done by clicking and dragging on the edge of the form to resize it.

In this project, when the program is started, the multiline textbox fills the available space inside the form. To keep it that way, you need to set up the textbox so that it changes size along with the form. Otherwise, when the form is resized, the textbox no longer fits inside it exactly. The idea behind this form is that the user should have the illusion of typing directly in the window, no matter what its size. The user should not be made aware of a separate entity, the textbox, that limits the available typing area.

When a user resizes a form, a Resize event occurs. This is one of many events attached to the form object. As a result of this change, two of the form's properties change:

- ScaleHeight
- ScaleWidth

You need to insert code into the Resize event procedure so that the height and width of the textbox always match the height and width of the form. Then, when the form is resized during run-time, the textbox will be resized as well. The height and width of the textbox are controlled by two properties: Height and Width. You do not have to create any code to keep setting the Top and Left properties of the textbox to 0 whenever the form is resized. These properties retain their initial 0 values.

To keep the textbox in alignment with a resized form:

1 Click on the body of the form, or click on the View Code button in the Project window.

2 Choose the Form object from the Object drop-down list.

3 Choose the Resize event from the Proc drop-down list.

4 Insert the following code in the event procedure:

```
txtEdit.Width = form1.ScaleWidth
txtEdit.Height = form1.ScaleHeight
```

5 Run the program and enter some text. Resize the form and note the change in the edit box. Figure 5-9 shows the running program with text from the Declaration of Independence.

Figure 5-10 shows how the text is rearranged when the form is resized.

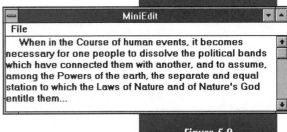

Figure 5-9

Text in the edit box

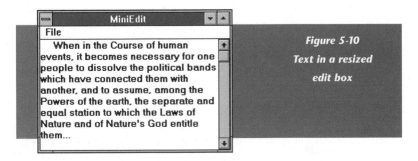

Figure 5-10

Text in a resized edit box

Getting the Exit Command Working

Just like command buttons, menu commands generate a Click event when a user selects them. As a result, you can insert code in the Click event procedure for the menu command. This code will then be executed when a user clicks on the command. You can test this by getting the Exit command working.

To insert code into the mnuExit event procedure:

1 Click on the File menu on the MiniEdit form. This opens the drop-down menu.

2 Double-click on Exit to open the Code window.

3 After the opening line of the mnuExit_Click subroutine, enter **End** (see Figure 5-11).

4 Run the program. Enter text into the textbox. Select Exit. Does anything happen?

Figure 5-11

Setting up the mnuExit event procedure

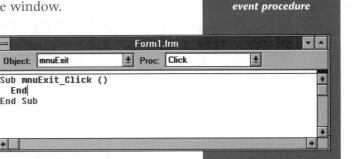

The End command works now, but not quite like a professional program. To see where the difference lies, think about a program like Word for Windows. If you type some text, then select Exit, what happens? The program prompts you to save your work. You cannot expect users to remember to save before they exit your program. You will need to add this functionality to the mnuExit_Click subroutine later.

Implementing the Open Command

Opening text files is a basic operation of MiniEdit. Once a file is opened, the contents are put into the textbox for display and editing. Getting your Open command to work correctly takes a few steps. You must write the code so that the program can:

1. Get a filename from the user.

2. Open the file.

3. Move the contents of the file into the textbox.

4. Change the directory in which the program looks for files.

   Each of these steps is covered separately in this section.

GETTING A FILENAME FROM THE USER

As you write the code necessary for this step, you will use a number of functions:

- **InputBox**

- **Trim$(str)**

- **UCase$(str)**

These functions are covered in the accompanying box. Read this material before you try to perform the following steps.

To get a filename from the user:

1 Select the MiniEdit form and click on the File menu. Double-click on Open. The Code window opens, showing the mnuOpen_Click() event procedure.

2 Insert the following code between the first and last lines of the subroutine.

```
Dim strFn As String
strFn = UCase$(Trim$(InputBox("Filename", "Open File")))
MsgBox strFn
```

3 Run the program.

4 Select Open from the File menu. Enter filenames with and without uppercase characters. Note the resulting filenames in the message box.

The code you just entered declares *strFn* as a string variable to represent the filename. At the core of the following statement is an **Input-Box** statement with two parameters. The first parameter instructs the user to enter the filename. The second is the caption of the input box (Figure 5-12).

Once the entry has been processed, it is assigned to *strFn*. The **Msg-Box** *strFn* statement displays the filename in a message box. You can use this message box to check the program during run-time (Figure 5-13). Later, when you are satisfied that the program is complete, you can remove the statement or comment it out.

Figure 5-12

Open File InputBox

FUNCTIONS

The three functions used in this section are introduced here.

INPUTBOX FUNCTION

The **InputBox** function collects information the user enters from the keyboard and returns the entered string as the value of the function call. This returned string can then be used in an expression, which in practice is usually an assignment to a string variable. The function takes three parameters, the last of which is optional. The syntax of the **InputBox** function is:

variable name = **InputBox** *(prompt string, box title string, default value)*

The **InputBox** function creates a window on the screen. The first parameter is an instruction to the user. The second parameter is the caption of the box created. The third parameter is the string that will initially appear in the box in which the user types. If you don't supply a value for the third parameter, the empty string is used by default. The mnuOpen_Click() event procedure that you created uses this default.

If you want to omit a caption, leave that spot blank in the parameter list. The commas must appear:

Figure 5-13

Filename displayed in a message box

```
x = InputBox("Enter a number",,"345")
```

This statement creates the box and prints the prompting message "Enter a number". In the textbox that the function provides for the user to type in, the default value 345 appears. When a user enters a value and clicks OK, this value is returned by the function. See Figure 5-14.

TRIM$(STR) FUNCTION

The **Trim$(str)** function takes a string as a parameter and returns the string with all leading and trailing spaces removed.

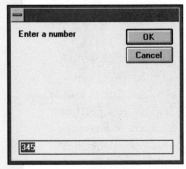

Figure 5-14

Entering a number as prompted

This function can be used to "clean up" strings obtained from the user via the **InputBox** function. You can use **Trim$** on the string returned from **InputBox** to remove any initial or trailing spaces that the user may have accidentally typed.

For example, if you use **InputBox** to obtain a person's name, then it is good practice to use **Trim$** on the returned string, because people's names never begin or end with spaces. Furthermore, if you don't remove accidentally typed spaces at the beginning or end of a name string, the results of comparing that string to other names will not be what you might expect. (The ASCII code for the space character is 32, which is less than the code for every letter.)

UCASE$(STR) FUNCTION

The **UCase$(str)** function was introduced earlier in this chapter, in the discussion of strings. You use it to convert characters of a string to uppercase. One use of **UCase$** is to allow users to easily enter information that should be uppercase, without forcing them to hold down the Shift key or turn on Caps Lock. For example, many product model numbers consist of uppercase letters and digits. After the user fills in a textbox containing a model number, you could use **UCase$** to immediately convert the user's input to the proper form and redisplay the result.

NOTE:

Function names that end in a $ return a string type value. Functions without the $ return values of variant type. Most function names that end in $ can be used without the $ with no change in how the functions work.

OPENING THE FILE

After the program has prompted the user for a filename, it must open the file requested. To make it possible for a user to open a file, you only have to insert a single line of code. In the MiniEdit File menu, double-click on Open. The Code window opens again, showing the mnuOpen_Click() event procedure. Insert this line:

```
Open strFn For Input As #1
```

This statement opens the file whose pathname is in *strFn*. **For Input** tells Visual Basic the file is opened so its contents can be read. The contents of the file are now available to the program. The phrase **As #1** associates the open file with a file number—in this case, the number 1. After the file is opened, you use the file number to refer to the file. When you ask Visual Basic to read from this file and when you tell Visual Basic that you are finished with it, you refer to the file by using #1 rather than the filename itself.

TRANSFERRING FILE INFORMATION TO MINIEDIT

Once the file is open, the contents need to be read into memory. The information from the file must be transferred to the txtEdit box. In order to test the ability of MiniEdit to open files, you have to be sure that a file exists that it can open. Because you have not yet implemented the Save command, you cannot use MiniEdit to create files that it can later open. Fortunately, MiniEdit uses standard text files, which Windows Notepad also creates, reads, and writes. In this section, you will use Notepad to create a text file that you will then open in MiniEdit.

As you write this code, you will become familiar with two new functions:

⦿ **LOF**, which stands for *l*ength *of* *f*ile

⦿ **Input$**

To insert a copy of the file's contents into the textbox:

1   If necessary, reopen the Code window displaying the mnuOpen_Click subroutine. After the last line you entered (Open strFn...), insert:

```
Dim FileSize As Integer
FileSize = LOF(1)
txtEdit = Input$(FileSize, #1)
Close #1
```

For information on **LOF** or **Input$()**, see the accompanying box.

LOF AND INPUT$ FUNCTIONS

The **LOF** function takes a single parameter. You use this parameter to send the file number to the function. The function returns the length in bytes of the file at that file number. You could find out this same information about a file by selecting it in the File Manager. The File Manager displays the file size if the proper options are chosen in the View menu.

The **Input$** function returns a string of *FileSize* length, from the file with file number 1. You want to read the entire file into txtEdit, not just a portion of it. That is why you first used **LOF** to obtain the total size of the file and store that number in the variable *FileSize*. You then tell the **Input$** function to read *File-Size* many characters from the file. As a result, the string returned from the **Input$** function is the entire file. This string is assigned to the txtEdit box.

2 Remove the MsgBox statement. You could also make it a comment by inserting a single quote as the first character of the line.

3 Without exiting Visual Basic, press Alt+Tab to move to the Program Manager. From the Program Manager, run NotePad (usually found in the Accessories program group). In NotePad, type:

```
When in the Course of human events, it becomes nec-
    essary for one people to dissolve the political
    bands which have connected them with another,
    and to assume, among the Powers of earth, the
    separate and equal station to which the Laws of
    Nature and of Nature's God entitle them...
```

4 Save the file as **declare.txt** in a directory you will remember (suggestion: **c:\temp**).

5 Close NotePad and return to Visual Basic.

6 Run MiniEdit.

7 Select Open from the File menu and try to open the file you just created (Figure 5-15). Be sure to enter the complete pathname of the file. If Visual Basic reports *File not found* when you run MiniEdit, try to find the file using the File Manager. If you have left **declare.txt** open in NotePad, the file will not be found.

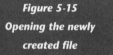

Figure 5-15
Opening the newly created file

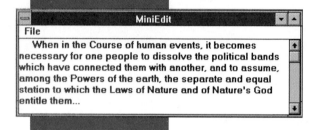

8 Exit MiniEdit.

9 Save the project in the Medit directory.

CHANGING THE DEFAULT DIRECTORY

When a user provides the name of a file to open, Visual Basic looks for it in the default directory. Unless you change the default, this is the Visual Basic directory. To open a file that is not in this directory, a user must provide not only the filename, but also the path. For instance, if you saved the file **declare.txt** in the directory **c:\temp**, you could open the file by entering the complete pathname, **c:\temp\declare. txt**, at the prompt.

The directory that an application resides in should contain the files that it needs to operate. The file **declare.txt** that you create for this project is clearly not one which Visual Basic itself will ever use. It is your data file, and should therefore be stored in a different location than the Visual Basic directory.

Changing the directory only requires a couple of lines of code. However, you will be using a number of statements for the first time:

- The **ChDrive** statement, which changes the current drive to the drive indicated in the string that follows.

- The **ChDir** statement, which changes the current directory to the directory indicated in the string that follows.

- The **App** object, which is the currently running application.

- The Path property of the **App** object, which specifies the complete pathname of the application.

When you include these statements in the Form_Load event procedure, the program changes the current directory and drive to match those of the application being run. In this case, the MiniEdit project is the current application. Unless you saved this project in the Medit directory, then Visual Basic is the current application directory.

To change the directory:

1   Double-click on the MiniEdit form to open the Code window. In the Form_Load event procedure, enter these lines.

```
ChDrive App.Path
ChDir App.Path
```

2   Use the File Manager to move **declare.txt** from **c:\temp** to the MiniEdit application directory, Medit.

3   Run MiniEdit. Open the file named **declare.txt**.

4   Exit MiniEdit.

Inserting Code for the Save As Command

You have a final command to implement: Save As. After a user has opened and worked in a file, the work should be saved.

The original file was opened with the **For Input** clause in the **Open** statement:

```
Open strFn For Input As #1
```

You cannot write to a file opened for input. To save the file, query the user for a filename (it could be the old name), and reopen the file **For Output**. Transfer the text into the file and close the file.

To create this code:

1   With MiniEdit halted, click on the Save As command to open the Code window.

2 In the mnuSave_Click procedure, enter the code:

```
Dim strFn As String
strFn = UCase$(Trim$(InputBox("Filename", "Save As...")))
Open strFn For Output As #1
Print #1, txtEdit
Close #1
```

The **Print #** statement writes an expression to a file at the specified file number. In this case, the expression is the entire text of the file. It is written into the file whose name is entered.

The close statement closes the open file. You can continue editing the contents of the editbox, and save it again under the same name or perhaps a different name.

Summary

While it is certainly possible to further enhance and refine MiniEdit, you have already learned how to harness several powerful capabilities of Visual Basic that you will use again and again. This is a good time to step back and take stock of what you have—and what you have *not*—accomplished in MiniEdit.

WHAT MINIEDIT CAN AND CANNOT DO

With MiniEdit, a user can create a text file and save it to a filename. A user can also open an existing text file, edit, and save the changes.

MiniEdit has a number of shortcomings, however. For example, commands in MiniEdit are always enabled, even when that choice might be inappropriate. In professional Windows programs, a menu command is grayed, or dimmed, whenever it is not meaningful for a user to choose it.

MiniEdit doesn't remember filenames. The user enters a filename to open a file and enters the filename again to save the file. MiniEdit also lets you exit the program without asking you to save your work.

All of these shortcomings could be eliminated if MiniEdit had a way of preserving information from event to event. If the filename entered in the Open event could be saved for use in the Save As event, MiniEdit could include the old filename as a default in the **InputBox** function.

At this point, all variables and their values come into existence when an event occurs. They cease to exist when the program exits the event procedure. As you will see in the next chapter, there is indeed a way to make values persist for longer than the handling of single events.

DEFENSIVE PROGRAMMING

Because MiniEdit does not do any error checking, you can easily make the program terminate with a run-time error. Up to this point, all the programs you have built have functioned in their own little world, not touching data outside themselves. As soon as a program has to interact with the file system, though, you must expect the unexpected.

Think of the problems that could occur. A user may type in a bad filename, for example, or the name of a nonexistent file. The file the user is trying to open cannot be opened, either because someone else on your computer's network has it open exclusively, or because of insufficient memory. The user can't save a file because there is not enough space left on the disk. MiniEdit can detect only some of these errors. You need to learn more about error handling before you can write code to detect all of these errors.

Still, as you build programs, you should anticipate that operations may fail. You should think about ways to have the program recover gracefully if a problem occurs. Instead of terminating with a run-time error, the program should alert the user and then continue. Writing code that guards against errors and prevents them from occurring is called "defensive programming."

The For-Next Statement

Section

As you learned in Chapter 3, you use loops to repeat a section of code again and again. This section focuses on the **For-Next** statement, which is one of the principal looping statements of Basic. As you become more familiar with loops, you will find yourself including them in most of your programs. Using loops is an important way to solve problems.

A **For-Next** loop is called a definite loop. In a definite loop, the number of times the code contained in the loop will repeat is generally known when the loop begins. You should consider using a definite loop whenever you know, or can calculate, the exact number of times you want a section of code to be repeated.

The syntax of the **For-Next** loop is:

For *variable = start* **To** *limit* **Step** *incr*
.....*body of the loop (usually indented for readability)*
Next *variable*   '*–the same variable from first line*

Here, *variable* represents the name of a variable. Also, *start, limit,* and *incr* represent expressions. While an expression is allowed in the places indicated, more often you will be using single variables or literals. The effect of the **For-Next** loop is to execute the body of the loop repeatedly, with the *variable* taking on a different value each time. The variable runs through all the values *start, start + incr, start + incr + incr, ...* that are between *start* and *limit*.

The value of the first expression, *start*, defines the starting point for the loop. The starting point is the initial value of the variable when the loop begins. For example, the starting point of the following **For** loop is 1:

```
For i = 1 To 100 Step 1
.....'—body of the loop
Next i
```

The expression following **Step** defines the increment of the loop. As the loop executes, the value of the variable is changed by the increment. If the increment is 1, as in the above code sample, the value of the variable increases by 1 each time through the loop. If the increment is -2, the value of the variable actually *decreases* by 2 each time through the loop.

The value following **To** defines the limit of the loop. In the code sample above, the limit of the loop is 100. The value of the variable is compared to the limit before the body of the loop is executed. If the comparison succeeds, then the body is performed. If it fails, the loop statement ends.

If the increment of the loop is positive, then the comparison checks that the variable is still less than or equal to the limit. If the increment is negative, the comparison checks that the variable is still greater than or equal to the limit. In the above example, *i* starts at 1 and increases through all values up to 100. The body of the loop is performed each time. Finally, *i* is increased to 101 and compared to 100. Because the increment is positive, and *i* is no longer less than or equal to 100, the loop ends.

When the increment is positive, the starting point must be less than or equal to the loop limit for the body of the loop to be performed at all. When the increment is negative, the starting point must be greater than or equal to the loop limit for the body of the loop to be performed at all.

The default increment is 1, by far the most typical case; if you want the loop variable to increase by 1 each time through the loop, you don't even have to write "Step 1". Therefore, the above code that we have used to illustrate the parts of the **For** loop could more easily be written as follows:

```
For i = 1 To 100
.....'—body of the loop
Next i
```

When the loop ends, the program resumes execution with the statement following the **Next** statement (Figure 5-16).

Working with For-Next Loops

The easiest way to become familiar with **For-Next** loops is to write some yourself.

1 Start Visual Basic. If Visual Basic is already running, select New Project from the File menu.

2 Set the AutoRedraw property of the default form to True.

3 Change the caption of the form to **For-Next Examples**.

4 In the Form_Load event procedure, enter the code shown in Figure 5-17.

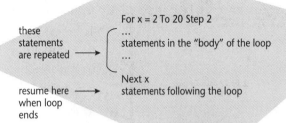

For x = 2 To 20 Step 2

these statements are repeated → ... statements in the "body" of the loop ...

Next x

resume here when loop ends → statements following the loop

Figure 5-16

For-Next loops

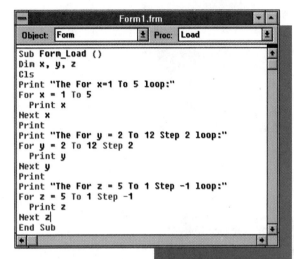

```
Form1.frm
Object: Form      Proc: Load

Sub Form_Load ()
Dim x, y, z
Cls
Print "The For x=1 To 5 loop:"
For x = 1 To 5
  Print x
Next x
Print
Print "The For y = 2 To 12 Step 2 loop:"
For y = 2 To 12 Step 2
  Print y
Next y
Print
Print "The For z = 5 To 1 Step -1 loop:"
For z = 5 To 1 Step -1
  Print z
Next z
End Sub
```

Figure 5-17

Code for the For-Next loop

THE PRINT METHOD

The **Print** method displays expressions on an object, such as a control or a form. The syntax for the **Print** method is:

object.Print expressionlist

If the object name is omitted, expressions are printed on the default form.

Strings and numeric values may be included in the expression list. The **Spc(n)** function may be included to skip *n* spaces in the output. The **Tab(n)** function may be included to skip to print zones in the output. The print zones are equivalent to the tab settings of a text document.

If the **Print** method is used with no *expressionlist*, a blank line is printed.

Do not confuse the **Print** method with the **Print** *statement*. You used the **Print** statement to implement the Save As command in MiniEdit. The **Print** method displays a string in an object; the **Print** statement writes a string to a file.

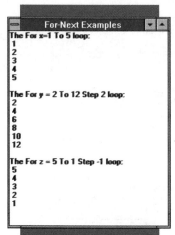

Figure 5-18

Results of running the program

Figure 5-19

Further results from running the program

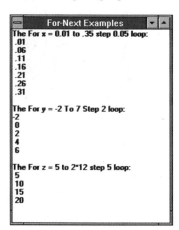

5 Run the program and observe the results (see Figure 5-18).

The *x* loop omits the step value. The variable increments by 1. The *y* loop increments by 2 until the limit is exceeded. The *z* loop steps backwards from 5 to 1, because the increment, defined in the step, is negative.

6 Reenter the Form_Load procedure and replace the **For-Next** statements with these:

```
For x = 0.01 To .35 Step 0.05
For y = -2 To 7 Step 2
For z = 5 To 2*12 Step 5
```

Change the printed labels to match the new **For-Next** statements.

7 Run the program and observe the results (Figure 5-19).

In the first loop, the starting value of *x* is 0.01, one one-hundredth. Each time through the loop, the value is increased by 0.05. The loop ends when the value of *x* exceeds 0.35.

In the second loop, the starting value is a negative number.

In the third loop, the starting value is a calculated value, not a simple constant. The increment is negative. This loop initializes *x* to 2*12 and steps down by 5 each time through. The loop ends when *x* is less than 5.

Try a loop like this: For *w* = 2 To 1. Because the increment is positive, and the starting value is greater than the limit, the body of the loop is never executed.

Nesting Loops

Just as you can write an **If-Then** statement within another **If-Then** statement, you can also write a loop within another loop. When one loop is inside of another, the loops are said to be nested.

Doing homework is like working through nested loops:

For *ChapterNumber* = *1* **To** *15*
   For *ReviewQuestion* = *1* **To** *20*
     Write answer to question
   Next *ReviewQuestion*
Next *ChapterNumber*

In the example above, the outer loop steps through the 15 chapters of a textbook. The inner loop steps through the 20 review questions for each chapter. The answers to 15*20, or 300, questions will be written. If your teacher were to assign only the even questions, for example, you would write the loop like this:

For *ChapterNumber* = *1* **To** *15*
   For *ReviewQuestion* = *2* **To** *20* **Step** *2*
      Write answer to question
   Next *ReviewQuestion*
Next *ChapterNumber*

Nested loops cannot overlap like this:

For *x* = *1* **To** *10*
   For *y* = *1* **To** *10*

     ...

   Next *x*   *'—syntax error!*
Next *y*

The example just given will not run, because the **Next** statements are mismatched. Visual Basic will inform you of the syntax error. The **For** *y* loop begins within the **For** *x* loop, and therefore must be completely enclosed within the outer **For** loop.

Using looping statements, a program can repeatedly execute statements far faster than you could. As a result, the computer can mindlessly crank through complicated procedures that would be far too tedious to work through by hand or even with a calculator.

QUESTIONS AND ACTIVITIES

1. Write **For-Next** statements that accomplish the following:
   a) Generate even numbers from 4 to 140.
   b) Generate odd numbers from 3 to 101.
   c) Count backwards from 89 down to 5 by ones.
   d) Generate multiples of 5 from 25 to 130.
   e) Generate multiples of 3 from 15 backward to -30.
   f) Generate a list of numbers that ranges from 0.45 to 3.50, stepping up by 0.05 each time through the loop.
   g) Generate a list of numbers that ranges from 1.1 to 3.8, stepping up by 0.1 each time through the loop.
   h) Generate a list of numbers from 5.3 down to 1.3, stepping by -0.1 each time through the loop.

2. What do you think happens if the following statements are executed? (hint: this is **not** a syntax error)

```
For y = 1 To 10 Step 0
    y = y + 1
Next y
```

3. What numbers are generated by the following:
    a) For x = 3 To 30 Step 3
    b) For y = 22 To 2 Step -2
    c) For z = 11 To 121 Step 11
    d) For a = 1 To -10 Step -1
    e) For b = 7 To 7*14 Step 2

Section

Scrollbars

In the MiniEdit application, users edit text in a multiline, scrollable textbox. The vertical scrollbar is an integral part of that textbox and not a separate control. The textbox itself manages its scrollbar. You didn't have to write any code to respond to clicks on the scrollbar; nevertheless, it was fully functional.

In this section, you use the scrollbar controls from the Toolbox. Unlike MiniEdit's scrollbar, every aspect of the scrollbar control is programmed either during program design or at run-time. Scrollbar controls can be placed anywhere on a form, not just along the border of the window or of a textbox.

Scrollbars come in two versions: horizontal and vertical. Each has a channel, in which an indicator, called a scroll box, moves. At each end of the channel is an arrow called a scroll arrow. Clicking on this arrow moves the scroll box right or left, up or down (Figure 5-20).

The File Manager uses two vertical scrollbars, one for each window. These scrollbars control the display of directory and file lists. In the File Manager, the scrollbar is used as an input device.

In a word processing program such as MiniEdit, the vertical scrollbar serves two purposes. You can use it as an input control, moving the scroll box up or down. This lets you position the cursor in the text by scrolling (moving) the text up or down within the window.

You can also use a scrollbar as a display indicator. By looking at the position of the scroll box in the scrollbar, you can tell where the cursor is in the document. If the scroll box is halfway down the scrollbar, for example, the cursor is near the middle of the document.

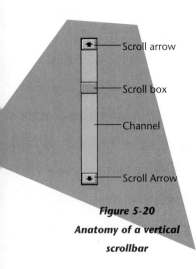

Figure 5-20

Anatomy of a vertical scrollbar

Placing a Scrollbar Control

The Toolbox contains two scrollbar controls: one for a horizontal scrollbar and one for a vertical scrollbar (Figure 5-21). You place a scrollbar control in the exact same way you place any other control.

You can double-click on the control, then click and drag to move the scrollbar to the right place. Or, you can:

1 Click once on the icon, highlighting it.

2 Move the mouse to the form, positioning it where you want the upper-left corner of the scrollbar.

3 Click and drag the mouse to the point at which you want the scrollbar's lower-right corner. Release the mouse. (Figure 5-22).

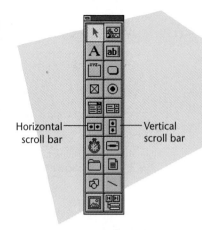

Figure 5-21

Scrollbar controls in the Toolbox

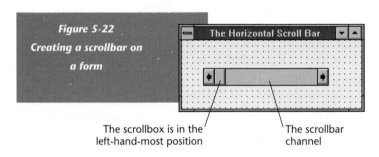

Figure 5-22

Creating a scrollbar on a form

The scrollbox is in the left-hand-most position

The scrollbar channel

Setting the Properties of the Scrollbar

As with any object, you can control the properties of the scrollbar. As the scroll box moves, the Value property of the bar changes. The Value property indicates the current position of the scroll box. The Min property sets the starting value of the Value property. The Max property sets the maximum value of the Value property (Figure 5-23).

As an input device, the scrollbar is used to control displays. The Value property of the scrollbar can be used as a numeric input to a program.

The default settings for a scrollbar control include a minimum value of 0 and a maximum value of 32,767. Before you change these defaults, you should consider the rate at which you want the scroll box to move.

This rate of movement is controlled by the SmallChange property. Clicking either scroll arrow causes a SmallChange. The default value of SmallChange is 1. With Max set to 32,767, each click of a scroll arrow moves the scroll box 1/32,767th of the way from one end of the bar to the other. This is not practical and would be irritating to your users. They would have to click the down scroll arrow 32,767 times to reach the end of a document.

One option is to change the Max property to 10. Then, with every mouse click, the scroll box would move 1/10th of the way from one end

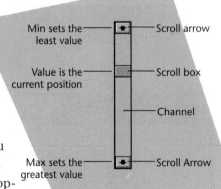

Figure 5-23

Setting different properties for the scrollbar

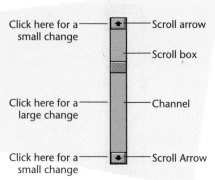

Click here for a — [Scroll arrow]
small change

— Scroll box

Click here for a — [Channel]
large change

Click here for a — [Scroll Arrow]
small change

Figure 5-24

Moving the mouse

scroll box

of the bar to the other. This movement would be far more noticeable.

Another option is to leave the value of the Max property as 32,767. You can still change the effect of a click on the scroll arrow, by changing the value of the SmallChange property to 1000. Each click on the scroll arrow then changes the Value property by 1000, moving the scroll box 1000/32,767ths of the way from one end of the bar to the other.

If the user clicks the mouse in the channel instead of the scroll box or the scroll arrows, a LargeChange occurs. See Figure 5-24.

The default value of LargeChange is 1. Users expect that a click in the channel will move the scroll box further than a click on a scroll arrow. Therefore, you should make this property's value larger than that of SmallChange.

Users also move the scroll box by clicking and dragging the scroll box along the scrollbar. The Value property changes as the scroll box moves.

Using the Scrollbar as a Progress Indicator

Figure 5-25

Placing the scrollbar on

the form

A program can also use a scrollbar to show its progress while performing a lengthy task. It can do this by moving the scroll box from its minimum to its maximum value to indicate the proportion of the task that it has completed. When the program begins its processing, it sets the scroll box to its minimum value. As processing proceeds, the scroll box is set to move toward its maximum value. When the scroll box reaches its maximum, this signals to the user that processing is done.

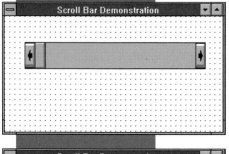

To use a horizontal scrollbar as a progress indicator, follow these steps.

1 Start Visual Basic. If Visual Basic is already running, select New Project from the File menu.

2 Change the caption of the form to **Scrollbar Demonstration**.

3 Place a horizontal scrollbar on the form (Figure 5-25).

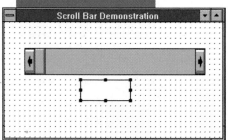

Figure 5-26

Adding a label to

the form

4 Place a label on the form (Figure 5-26). In the Properties window, make the following changes:

◎ Name property: **lblValue**. You will use this label to display the Value property of the scrollbar.

◎ BorderStyle: Fixed Single.

◎ Caption property: delete the default.

◎ Alignment property: Center.

5 Add two command buttons (Figure 5-27). In the Properties window, make these changes:
- ◎ Caption property: &Setup and E&xit.
- ◎ Name property: cmdSetup and cmdExit.

6 In the Code window, add this code to cmdSetup_Click:

```
hscroll1.Min = 1
hscroll1.Max = 100
hscroll1.SmallChange = 1
hscroll1.LargeChange = 10
```

7 Add this code to cmdExit_Click:

```
End
```

8 Run the program. Before clicking on the Setup button, try the scrollbar. Click in the channel, then click on the scroll arrows. Move the scroll box by dragging it along the scrollbar. Click and hold on the scroll arrows. Eventually, enough SmallChanges will occur and you will see the scroll box move.

9 Click on the Setup button. Test the scrollbar as you did in step 8.

10 Click on the Exit button to stop the program.

11 Whenever you click the scrollbar, a Change event occurs. Code in the Change event handler executes each time the scrollbar is clicked. Insert this code in HScroll1_Change():

```
lblValue.caption = hscroll1.value
```

12 Run the program, click on the Setup button, and repeat the tests of step 8.

13 Exit the program

14 Change the Setup code as follows:

```
Dim x As Integer
hscroll1.Min = 1
hscroll1.Max = 1000
hscroll1.SmallChange = 1
hscroll1.LargeChange = 100
For x = 1 To 1000
    hscroll1.Value = x
Next x
```

15 Run the program. This time, the scroll box is moving under program control. The **For-Next** loop in the code for the Setup button

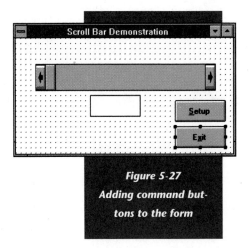

Figure 5-27
Adding command buttons to the form

is changing the value of the scrollbar's Value property. The scroll box moves as the value changes.

16 Exit the program.

QUESTIONS AND ACTIVITIES

1. Describe the significance of the Value property of the scrollbar. Mention both its input role and display functions.

2. How do you set the minimum and maximum values of the Value property?

3. Write the statement needed to use the value of a scrollbar named hscroll1, as the number assigned to the integer variable *Number.*

4. Typically, code attached to a command control is put into its Click event procedure. When attaching code to a scrollbar, you should put it in what event procedure?

5. How would you use the LargeChange event to control the display of a list given that 12 elements of the list fill a full screen?

Section

The Who's in Sports? Project

Photographers for school annuals are often assigned to take pictures of members of a specific class. For this project, the photographers are looking for members of one class who play sports. To figure out which students in the class play, they developed this project.

The Who's in Sports? project opens two files: a class list and a list of athletes. Both lists are displayed. The lists are compared and a third list created. The third list contains the names of the athletes also appearing in the class list. The third list shows the names of students who need their picture taken by the class photographer.

The Who's in Sports? program uses three listboxes to display a:

◉ Class list of student names

◉ List of names of athletes

◉ List of athletes who are students in the class

Listboxes are not only convenient ways to display lists of strings, they also provide easy access to those strings if further processing is needed.

The program introduces the statements and functions needed to open, process, and save the files used to store the lists described above. The program uses a constant to facilitate changes to the program and simplify program testing. Finally, the program uses nested **For** loops to process the names in the lists.

Starting Out

Before you can consider the design of a form, you need to create a class list as well as a list of student athletes. If you were working on this project professionally, you would be given these lists. A class list, for example, normally comes from the school administration. In this case, you need to create the lists along with a new directory for this project.

The class list and the list of athletes are provided in files on the disk that accompanies the text. The class list is in a file named **Clsslist.txt**. The file of athletes is named **Sptslist.txt**. These lists would normally come from the school administration, but you could use MiniEdit or the Notepad to create "custom" lists. The first step in this project is creating a directory to hold the project files and transferring these lists to that directory.

To prepare the lists and create the directory:

1 Open the File Manager.

2 Find a directory to which to attach your new directory.

3 Create a directory named **Athlete**.

4 Transfer the files **Clsslist.txt** and **Sptrlist.txt** from the disk that accompanies this book, or from a disk or network directory prepared by your instructor, to the **Athlete** directory.

5 Close the File Manager.

Designing the Form

You have three lists of students to display:

◉ Class list

◉ Athletes

◉ Members of class who play on a sports team

You can use listboxes to display each of these lists of names. Although textboxes could be used, they do not lend themselves well to the tasks performed by the Who's In Sports? program. It is very easy to loop through the items in a listbox and use each one as a string; it is clumsier to do this with the lines appearing in a textbox.

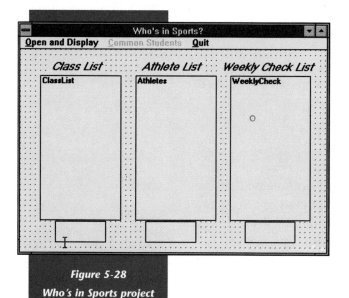

Figure 5-28

Who's in Sports project

To identify the information displayed, you need three labels above the listboxes. In addition, you would like to keep track of the number of student names displayed in each list. For this purpose, you need another three labels. These last labels will display information provided by the program during run-time.

The proposed form is shown in Figure 5-28. As you can see, it also includes a menu bar. With the menu bar, users can display the lists, calculate the overlap between lists, and quit the program.

You are now ready to create the form. To get started:

1 Start Visual Basic, or select New Project from the File menu, if Visual Basic is already running.

2 Change the form's caption to **Who's in Sports?**

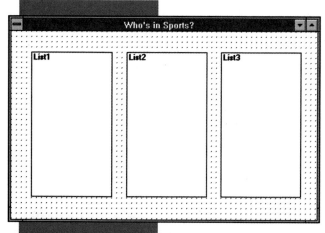

Figure 5-29

Three listboxes on the form

Placing the Objects

To place the objects you need, follow these steps.

1 Place three listboxes, evenly spaced on the form. Leave room above each list for a label (Figure 5-29).

2 Change the names of the lists to:
   a) ClassList
   b) Athletes
   c) WeeklyCheck

3 Place explanatory labels above each list.

4 Below each list, place labels to display the number of people listed. In the Properties window for each control, change these properties:
   ◎ Name property: **lblCLCount**, **lblACount**, and **lblCheckCount**.
   ◎ BorderStyle: Fixed Single.
   ◎ Caption property: Delete default.
   ◎ Alignment: Center.

Sharing Variables and Using Consts

As you will see later, the main work of this program is performed by nested **For** loops. Whenever you want to step through deeply nested code to debug it or verify that it is working properly, your job will be much easier if the loop limits are small. You can achieve this goal in the Who's in Sports? program by imposing an upper bound on the number of names that can appear in the lists. Another way of describing this number is: the number of lines that are read from each file. Clearly, then, this number will be used in more than one procedure of this program.

But what value should be used for the maximum number of names? In order to test the program, you would want this value to be small—for example, 5. Suppose you write the program using the numeric constant 5 everywhere as the maximum number of names. After you test the program and determine that it works as it ought to, you will want it to be able to handle lists of a more realistic size—say, 100. Now you are confronted with an unpleasant task. You have to search for every occurrence of the numeric constant 5 and replace it with the new value.

In this program, doing so would not be hard. But suppose you were working with a program that used 5 in completely unrelated ways. For a concrete example, imagine a program that reads in a list of cities and their temperatures in Farenheit, computes the corresponding Celsius temperatures, and displays a list of the cities and their temperatures expressed in both ways.

The formula to convert from Farenheit to Celsius uses the number 5. In this temperature conversion program, you would not want to change every occurrence of 5 to 100, because doing so would change the conversion formula. To be safe, you would instead have to examine every occurrence of 5, determine whether it means "the maximum number of lines to read," and change it only if it does have that meaning. This process is boring, tedious, and error-prone.

A much better approach is to give a name to the constant value, and use that name in your code. This way, you can use a name like *MAXLINES* wherever you wish to refer to the maximum number of lines to be read. The name tells you its significance immediately; you don't have to guess or hesitate as you do when you see code that contains "magic numbers" like 5 or 100.

Visual Basic lets you declare names for constant values with the **Const** declaration. You declare *MAXLINES* to have the unchanging value 5 by using the following statement:

```
Const MAXLINES = 5
```

To change the value of *MAXLINES*, you only have to edit this statement.

CONSTANTS

A constant names a value that cannot be changed while a program runs. Unlike variables, whose values can be changed, once a constant is set, its value never changes while the program is running. The **Const** statement declares a constant and gives it a value. Here are some examples:

```
Const HousesOfCongress = 2
Const PI = 3.1415927
Const MAXLINES = 5
Const DEFAULT_NAME = "John Doe"
Const ERROR_MESSAGE = "The value that you
enter here must be positive."
```

Constant names are often written in all caps to make them easy to identify. The data type of the constant is the simplest type consistent with the expression used to define the constant. For example, 2 is an integer. Although it *can* be treated as a floating point number, Visual Basic assumes that you intend to define an Integer constant when you initialize a **Const** name with the numeric constant 2.

You can also give names to constants of nonnumeric data types. The last two examples illustrate the declaration of names for string literals.

Using the General Declarations Section of a Form

A final problem remains to be solved: where should the **Const** declaration of *MAXLINES* be put? One option would be to place it in every procedure that used the value. While that would be an improvement over using numeric constants, you would still have to search for all occurrences of **Const MAXLINES** in order to change the value. If you overlook one declaration, different procedures will be using different values of *MAXLINES*—a subtle bug that could be difficult to detect. Ideally, you want to declare *MAXLINES* in one and only one place, and have all procedures use the value it is given there.

If you are going to have only a single declaration of *MAXLINES*, then it cannot be put inside any event procedure. The value of each variable or constant name used in an event procedure is *local* to that procedure. A variable declared in cmdCalculate_Click is not available in cmdCalculate_KeyPress. When the cmdCalculate_Click procedure is over, any values used within the procedure are lost. Constant names declared within one procedure are not visible to other procedures.

To share a name or variable between more than one event procedure, you declare it in the general declarations section of the form. Names and variables declared in this section are available to every event procedure of every object on the form (Figure 5-30).

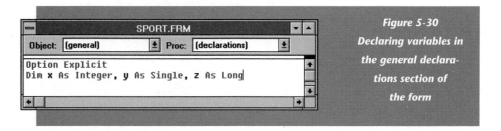

Figure 5-30
Declaring variables in the general declarations section of the form

The values of *x*, *y*, or *z* can be set, accessed, or changed in any event procedure throughout the form.

The Who's in Sports? project uses a constant declaration in the general declarations section of the Code window. Placing the declaration here makes the value of the constant available to every event procedure in the form.

To declare the constant:

1 In the Project window, click on the View Code button to open the Code window.

2 In the Object drop-down list, select the top entry *(general)*. Notice that the Proc drop-down list now displays *(declarations)*.

3 Enter the constant definition shown in Figure 5-31.

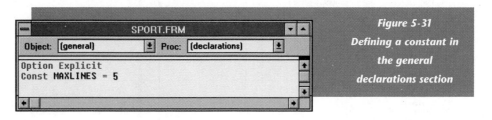

Figure 5-31
Defining a constant in the general declarations section

The **Const** statement defines *MAXLINES* as a constant value. *MAXLINES* is the maximum number of lines that the program will read from each of the two files. The value of 5 makes it easy to test the program; you can increase the value later. *MAXLINES* has the Integer data type.

Designing the Menu

You are going to create a simple menu bar, with three choices and no drop-down menus. You want users to be able to:

◉ Open and display the ClassList and Athletes lists.

◉ Display a list of students who are in both lists.

◉ Quit the program.

Below the first two listboxes are labels. When you click on the Open and Display command, the program should display the lists, then count the number of entries in each list. These counts of students are shown in the labels. The label under the final listbox displays the percentage of athletes in the class.

To create the menu bar:

1 Select the form by clicking on the body of the form.

 2 Click on the Menu Design icon in the toolbar. This opens the Menu Design window.

3 In the Caption textbox, type **&Open and Display**. Then in the Name textbox, type **mnuOpen**.

4 Click on the Next button to clear the entries and repeat step 3 for the other two menu commands.
◎ Caption: **&Common Students**; Name: **mnuCommon**
◎ Caption: **&Quit**; Name: **mnuQuit**

5 Click OK to close the Menu Design window.

Coding the Open and Display Command

You are now ready to write the code for the Open and Display command. You will write the code to display one list, then copy those lines of code for the second list. When you are finished, run the program to test the code (Figure 5-32). Stop the program with the Stop button in the toolbar.

To create the code for the Open and Display command:

Figure 5-32
Who's in sports?
program shown with
data in listboxes

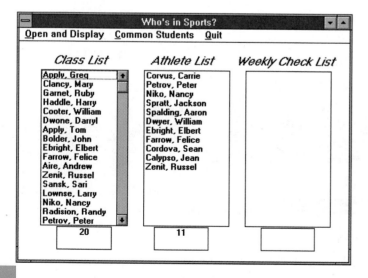

1 Click on the command Open and Display to open the Code window.

2 Enter this code for mnuOpen_Click. This opens a file, reads each line from the file, displays each line in a listbox, and closes the file.

```
'—first part handles clsslist.txt
'—Open file
Open "c:\athlete\clsslist.txt" For Input As #1
'—Read lines
Dim i As Integer
Dim strLine As String
For i = 1 To MAXLINES
    If EOF(1) Then Exit For
    Line Input #1, strLine
    strLine = Trim$(strLine)
    If Len(strLine) <> 0 Then ClassList.AddItem strLine
Next i
'—Close file
Close #1
lblCLCount = ClassList.ListCount
```

3 Select all the lines of code and copy them. Use Ctrl+C or the Edit menu.

4 Paste the lines of code below the existing code. In this new section:
   ◎ Replace references to **clsslist.txt** with **sptslist.txt**.
   ◎ Replace ClassList with Athletes.
   ◎ Replace lblCLCount with lblACount.
   ◎ Delete the duplicate declarations of *i* and *strLine*.

In the code you just entered, the **Open** statement opens the **clsslist.txt** file for input. The file number 1 is assigned to the file. In the **For-Next** loop, the ending value, *MAXLINES*, puts an upper limit on the number of names that may be in a file.

The **EOF(n)** function is true when the end of the file has been reached. It is false otherwise. When the end of file is reached, **Exit For** is executed. This statement halts the **For** loop whether the upper limit has been exceeded or not.

The **Line Input #** statement reads an entire line of text from the text file assigned to the file number. The line is assigned to the string variable *strLine*, then the line is trimmed.

If the length of the line is not 0, it is added to the ClassListbox. The **AddItem** method adds a new entry to a listbox. If the Sorted property is false, a new item is added to the bottom of the list.

The number of items in the list is displayed in the lblCLCount label. The number of items in the list is read from the ListCount property of the listbox.

Coding for the Quit Command

In a number of other projects so far, you have added very simple code for an Exit button or Quit command. This allows the program to end when the command is selected or the button pushed. You will follow the same procedure here:

1 Open the Code window and select the mnuQuit_Click procedure.

2 Enter **End**.

Coding for the Common Students Command

This procedure for this command compares every student name of the class list with every student name of the athlete list. Nested loops control the comparisons. The outer loop reads each name from the class list. The inner loop reads each name from the athlete list. If the names match, the name is put into the common list.

To create this procedure:

1 Click on Common Students to open the Code window.

2 In the mnuCommon_Click procedure, enter this code:

```
'—Compare two lists and write the third
Dim i As Integer, j As Integer
For i = 0 To ClassList.ListCount - 1
    For j = 0 To Athletes.ListCount - 1
    If StrComp(ClassList.List(i), Athletes.List(j)) = 0 Then
        WeeklyCheck.AddItem ClassList.List(i)
    End If
    Next j
Next i
'—Calculate and display Percentage
lblCheckCount = WeeklyCheck.ListCount * 100 / ClassList.ListCount & " %"
```

ADDRESSING THE ITEMS OF A LISTBOX

Each item of a listbox has a number. The first item of the list is number 0. The ListCount property shows the number of items in the list. The last item of the list is number ListCount - 1. The *i*th item of the list can be accessed as ListName.List(*i*). See Figure 5-33. This value is a string and can be used in string comparisons and operations.

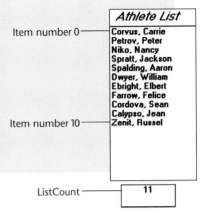

Item number 0

Item number 10

ListCount

Figure 5-33
ListCount property of items in a listbox

Finishing the Project

Running the program and clicking on the Common Students command causes the two files, the class list and the list of athletes files, to be opened, read, and compared. The names that appear on both lists appear in the third list. After you run the program, you will change the lists and run the program again to see the results. Once the program has been tested and *MAXLINES* has been set to a more reasonable upper bound, the program is ready to use.

1 Run the program. Click on Open and Display. Click on Common Students.

2 Exit the program. Click on one of the listboxes. In the Properties window, change the Sorted property to True. Run the program.

3 Exit the program. Save the project in the Athlete subdirectory.

Figure 5-34
Changing the Enabled property to false

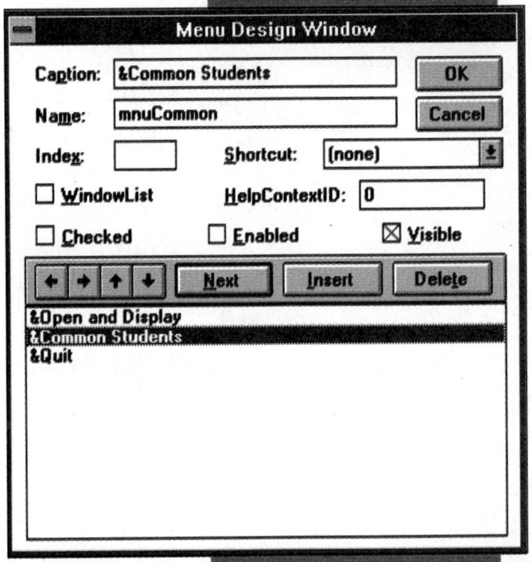

4 Change the *MAXLINES* constant to allow larger files and run the program again. Use NotePad or MiniEdit to add names to either or both files and test the program again.

5 Edit the program and reenter the Menu Design window. The form must be selected to enter this window.

6 Change the Enabled property of Common Students to false (Figure 5-34).
When the program is run, the Common Students menu item is dimmed. It doesn't make sense to pick the common students before the files are read and the lists prepared.

7 Add this line to the end of the mnuOpen_Click procedure.

```
mnuCommon.Enabled = True
```

This statement removes the dimmed **Common Student** command.

8 Run the program. Click on the dimmed **Common Students** command. Click on the Open and Display command. Now that the Common Students command is active, click on it. Exit the program.

Section

The Two-Point Problem

The Two-Point Problem doesn't introduce any new features of Visual Basic. Instead, it shows how Visual Basic can be used to solve a common high school math problem. Any programming language is a tool to be used to solve problems. Visual Basic is an excellent tool to use in almost any class. This problem, finding the properties of a line that passes through two points, with coordinates supplied by the user, can be solved with simple textboxes, command buttons, and labels. The code is no more complicated than an **If-Then-Else** statement. Despite the simplicity of the program (from a programming point of view), it accomplishes a lot.

Starting Out

Computers can calculate far faster than humans. As a result, one of the common uses for computers is to make mathematical calculations. The Two-Point problem illustrates how you can use a Visual Basic program to solve a fairly simple mathematical problem. The user defines the positions of two points. The program then calculates the distance between these two points. As part of that process, it also displays information about the line drawn between the points, including its slope and midpoint.

You may need a refresher on the algebraic concepts used in this program. This information is provided in the following "Background" section. If you are already familiar with concepts such as coordinate systems and the Pythagorean theorem, you can turn immediately to the section titled "Designing the Form."

Background

Understanding the math discussed in this section is necessary to understanding the program you are about to build. Use this section for review of algebraic concepts, if necessary.

COORDINATE SYSTEMS

The Two-Point program graphs a line segment on a coordinate system. The *x* and *y* axes are the number lines that define the plane's coordinate system. These lines are at right angles to each other. The point where the lines cross is called the origin. With the axes in place, you can define the position of any point in the plane with an *x* and *y* coordinate.

For example, look at Figure 5-35.

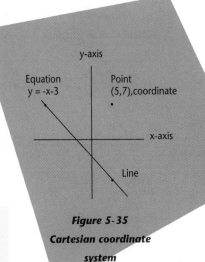

Figure 5-35
Cartesian coordinate system

DEFINITIONS

The point is a fundamental geometric concept. Algebraically, the position of any point on a plane is assigned a unique ordered pair of numbers.

A line is understood to be an infinite collection of points "all in a line."

Two points determine a line. The equation of a line describes the relationship between *x* and *y*, the coordinates of the points of the line.

A line segment is a section of a line with distinct endpoints.

Two intersecting lines determine a plane. A plane is a surface, like a table top.

THE PYTHAGOREAN THEOREM

The Pythagorean theorem is a relationship between the sides of a right triangle. A right triangle contains a right angle, as shown in Figure 5-36.

The Pythagorean theorem states that the length of the hypotenuse—the side opposite the right angle—can be computed from the lengths of the other two sides forming the right angle. The relationship is in fact an identity that is used to compute the length:

$$c = \sqrt{a^2 + b^2}$$

Here, *c* is the length of the side opposite the right angle, and *a* and *b* are the lengths of the sides forming the right angle.

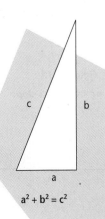

Figure 5-36
Pythagorean theorem

197

This relationship, known for thousands of years, has numerous proofs. It has been used for building and surveying since the time of the ancient Egyptians.

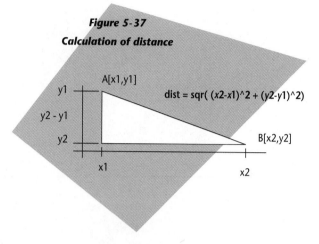

Figure 5-37

Calculation of distance

DISTANCE FORMULA

The distance between two points is calculated using a variation of the Pythagorean theorem, called the Distance formula. If the coordinates of point A are $(x1,y1)$ and the coordinates of point B are $(x2,y2)$, this distance is calculated as shown in Figure 5-37.

The distance between the points A and B is given by the equation (written in BASIC notation):

```
Dist = Sqr ((x2 - x1)^2 + (y2 - y1)^2)
```

where the caret symbol, ^, indicates "raising to a power," and **Sqr(n)** is the square root function. **Sqr(n)** takes a positive number and returns the square root of the number.

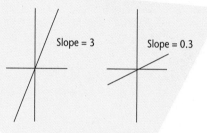

Figure 5-38

Looking at a line's slope

SLOPE

The slope of a line is its slant. If the slope is greater than 1, the slant is steep. If the slope is less than 1, but greater than 0, the slant of the line is "flatter." See Figure 5-38.

The slope is calculated by taking a ratio:

1. Mark two points somewhere along a line.

2. The difference in the heights of the points marked is called the "change in y."

3. The distance between the points in the right to left direction is called the "change in x."

4. The slope of the line is the ratio of the "change in y" to the "change in x." See Figure 5-39.

The slope of a line between the points $A(x1,y1)$ and $B(x2,y2)$ is:

```
slope = ( y2 - y1 ) / ( x2 - x1 )
```

MIDPOINT

A line segment not only has a length, defined by the distance between the two endpoints; it also has a midpoint. The midpoint of a line is the point half way between the endpoints of the line segment. See Figure 5-40.

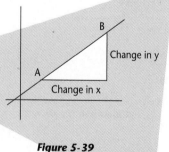

Figure 5-39

Calculating a slope

The coordinates of the midpoint of a line segment with endpoints A($x1,y1$) and B($x2,y2$) are given by:

(($x1+x2$)/2 , ($y1+y2$)/2)

The coordinates of the midpoint are the averages of the coordinates of the two endpoints.

INTERSECTING LINES

Any line that is not parallel to the y-axis intersects it. An intersection is a point where two lines cross. The point at which a line crosses the y-axis is called the y-intercept. The point at which a line crosses the x-axis is the x-intercept.

THE Y-INTERCEPT

The slope-intercept form of a line's equation:

```
y = mx + b
```

shows both the value of the slope of the line and the coordinate of the y-intercept. The m variable represents the slope and b is the y-intercept of the line. You can rearrange the equation to give an expression for the y-intercept:

```
b = y - mx
```

Once the user has provided the coordinates for two points, the program you are building will calculate and display the equation of the line in slope-intercept form ($y = mx+b$).

Designing the Form

On this form, you will need:

◉ Four textboxes for the user to enter x and y coordinates of two points

◉ Twenty labels for the slope, y-intercept, distance, midpoint and equation of the line containing the two points

◉ Three command buttons to make calculations, clear the textboxes and labels, and stop the program
  You should set up the form similarly to that shown in Figure 5-41. To create the form:

1 Open Visual Basic or, if the application is open, select New Project from the File menu.

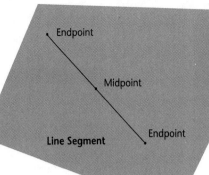

Endpoint

Midpoint

Endpoint

Line Segment

Figure 5-40
Midpoint of a line

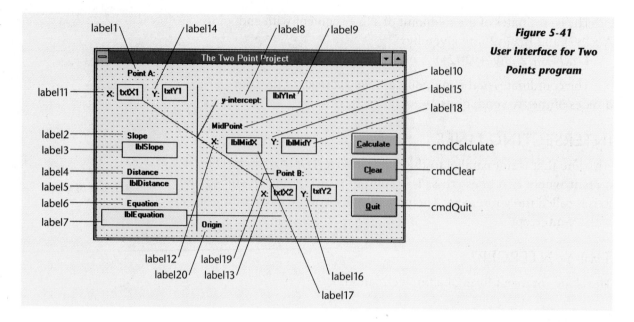

Figure 5-41

User interface for Two

Points program

2 Place the objects on the form, as shown in the previous figure.

3 In the Properties window, make the changes shown in Table 5-1.

Moving Focus Among the Textboxes

Users enter four values in this form: the *x* and *y* coordinates for both endpoints of the line. To enter these values, they need to be able to move from one textbox to the next. For each textbox, then, you need to insert code into the KeyPress event procedure. This code instructs the program to move the focus to the next textbox when the user presses Enter. For an example of the code, see Figure 5-42. How does this code need to change for the other textboxes?

Figure 5-42

Moving focus among

the textboxes

Writing Code for the Calculate Button

To write the code for this button:

1 With the Code window open, select cmdCalculate.

Table 5-1   Properties for Objects

Object	Properties to Change	Object	Properties to Change
Text1	Text: delete text	Label9	Name: lblYInt
	Name: txtX1		Caption: delete caption
	FontSize: 9.75		BorderStyle=1
Text2	Text: delete text		Alignment: Center
	Name: txtY1	Label10	Caption: Midpoint
	FontSize: 9.75		AutoSize: True
Text3	Text: delete text	Label11	Caption: X:
	Name: txtX2		AutoSize: True
	FontSize: 9.75	Label12	Caption: X:
Text4	Text: delete text		AutoSize: True
	Name: txtY2	Label13	Caption: X:
	FontSize: 9.75		AutoSize: True
Label1	Caption: Point A:	Label14	Caption: Y:
	AutoSize:True		AutoSize: True
Label2	Caption: Slope	Label15	Caption: Y:
	AutoSize:True		AutoSize: True
Label3	Name: lblSlope	Label16	Caption: Y:
	Caption: delete caption		AutoSize: True
	BorderStyle=1	Label17	Name: lblMidX
	Alignment:Center		Caption: delete caption
Label4	Caption: Distance		BorderStyle=1
	AutoSize:True		Alignment: Center
Label5	Name: lblDistance	Label18	Name: lblMidY
	Caption: delete caption		Caption: delete caption
	BorderStyle=1		BorderStyle=1
	Alignment: Center		Alignment: Center
Label6	Caption: Equation	Label19	Caption: Point B:
	AutoSize:True		AutoSize: True
Label7	Name: lblEquation	Label20	Caption: Origin
	Caption: delete caption	Command1	Name: cmdCalculate
			Caption: &Calculate
	BorderStyle=1	Command2	Name: cmdClear
			Caption: &Clear
	Alignment: Center	Command3	Name: cmdQuit
			Caption: &Quit
Label8	Caption: y-intercept:		
	AutoSize: True		

2 Insert the following code in the Calculate_Click procedure:

```
Dim x1, x2, y1, y2
Dim Slope, YIntercept, Distance, MidX, MidY
Dim Equation As String
'—transfer text and convert to value
x1 = Val(txtX1)
y1 = Val(txtY1)
x2 = Val(txtX2)
y2 = Val(txtY2)
'—check to see if slope exists
If x2 - x1 <> 0 Then   ' slope exists
    Slope = (y2 - y1) / (x2 - x1)
    lblSlope = Format$(Slope, "fixed")
'—y-intercept
    YIntercept = y1 - Slope * x1
    lblYInt = Format$(YIntercept, "fixed")
'—equation
    Equation = "y = " & Format$(Slope, "fixed") & "x + " & Format$(YIntercept,
"fixed")
    lblEquation = Equation
Else
    lblSlope = "None"
    lblYInt = "None"
    lblEquation = " x = " & Str$(x1)
End If
'—distance
Distance = Sqr((x2 - x1) ^ 2 + (y2 - y1) ^ 2)
lblDistance = Format$(Distance, "fixed")
'—midpoint
MidX = (x1 + x2) / 2
MidY = (y1 + y2) / 2
lblMidX = Str$(MidX)
lblMidY = Str$(MidY)
'—move focus to Clear button
cmdClear.SetFocus
```

Now let's look back at the code we just created. The four lines of code after the variable declarations read entries from textboxes and convert those entries to the values they represent. *x1* and *y1* represent the coordinates of the first point. *x2* and *y2* represent the coordinates of the second point. The two points define a line segment.

Then comes the **If-Then-Else** statement. If the change in the *x* coordinates, from one point to the next, is any number other than 0, the True branch of the statement is executed.

The line:

```
lblSlope = Format$(Slope, "fixed")
```

displays the slope value in the appropriate label object. Values are assigned to labels to display them on the form. The **Str$(n)** function has been used to convert values to strings. In this program, the **Format$(Value, FormatString)** function is used. Values sent to this function are formatted according to the format string. Predefined format strings let you use a variety of formats. **Fixed** converts a number into a string with two decimal places.

The False branch of the **If-Then-Else** statement displays "None" in the appropriate label objects to indicate that the line has no slope and no y-intercept. It also displays the special equation for the line, given that its slope is 0.

The rest of the code calculates the distance between the points as well as the x and y coordinates of the midpoint. These values are displayed, then focus is shifted to the Clear button.

Coding the Clear Button

You need code that clears all the textboxes and labels of their contents if a user clicks on the Clear button. Clicking on this button should also move the focus back to the X1 textbox. A user can then enter another set of coordinates for the two endpoints and recalculate the midpoint, y-intercept, and so forth.

The empty string, "", is used to blank textboxes and labels. Because the Text property is the default property for a textbox, and Caption is the default for the label, just the names of the controls are used in expressions. For example, we use:

```
txtX1 = ""
...
x1 = Val(txtX1)
```

instead of:

```
txtX1.Text = ""
...
x1 = Val(txtX1.Text)
```

Likewise, we use:

```
lblSlope = "None"
```

instead of:

```
lblSlope.Caption = "None"
```

Running the Program

Run the program. Use the sample data provided in the following table:

Trial #	X1	Y1	X2	Y2
1	3	4	2	5
2	3	-4	2	5
3	3	-2	3	5
4	-2	-6	-2	8
5	-2	4	5	4
6	1.2	3.2	-4.1	2.3

Designing good test data is a very important part of program debugging. Your test data should systematically test each part of the program. Every possible outcome of every comparison should be executed by at least one set of input values.

QUESTIONS AND ACTIVITIES

1. Why is it important to use the **Val(str)** function to convert strings to values when assigning those values to a variant-type variable?

2. Why is it a problem to calculate the slope of a line when the "change in y" is 0?

3. Assume a student's average is 72 in the third week of class and 84 in the fifth week. Use the Two-Point program to help you predict the student's average in the seventh week. (Hint: use (3,72) and (5,84) as your points.)

4. In the equation generated from the information in the problem above, what is the significance of the y-intercept?

5. In the third week of track practice, a shot putter tossed the shot put 42 feet. In the fourth week, the shot putter threw 44 feet. Use the Two-Point program to find the equation that describes this situation.

6. How are the **Str$(n)** function and the **Format$(n)** function alike? How are they different?

Summary

Strings are series of characters. The empty string is shown as ""; this represents a string with no characters. Strings can be compared using the following operators: =, <, >, and <>. When you use the less than and greater than operators, the program compares the strings by comparing the ASCII codes of the characters. "A" is less than "Z", but it is also less than "a". Concatenation is the joining together of strings. The concatenation operator is the ampersand (&).

The **UCase$(str)** and **LCase$(str)** functions convert a string to all uppercase or all lowercase characters. Characters that do not represent letters are not affected.

The **StrComp(a$, b$, 1)** function compares the two strings *a$* and *b$* and returns:

a)   -1 if *a$* is less than *b$*
b)   0 if the strings are equal
c)   1 if *a$* is greater than *b$*

The **Len(str)** function takes a string as a parameter and returns a whole number representing the number of characters in the string.

The **Format$(n,format string)** function determines the appearance of values displayed. It displays values with a particular number of decimal places, or a percentage sign or commas are included in the display.

Format$(x, "Fixed") displays the value of *x* with at least one digit to the left of the decimal point and two digits to the right.

The Scrollbars property of a textbox adds a horizontal or a vertical scrollbar to a multiline textbox. You can also choose to add both of these scrollbars. The textbox control itself handles the behavior of the scrollbars; unlike scrollbar controls, you do not have to write code for the textbox scrollbars to work.

The syntax for a **For-Next** statement is:

For *control variable* = *expression* **To** *expression* **Step** *expression*

   ...

Next *control variable*

where *expression* represents a constant, a variable, or an expression (such as T+1).

Loops peform sections of code repeatedly, using a different value of some variable on each repetition. Loops can be nested inside one another.

A scrollbar can be used for output only, to display the value of a variable within the program; or it can be used to let the user input values to the program by moving the graphic scroll box. The Value property provides the connection between a numeric value and the position of the scroll box. The Min and Max properties control the minimum and maximum value the scrollbar can assume.

The SmallChange and LargeChange properties of the scrollbar control what happens when a mouse is clicked on various parts of the scrollbar.

The dimensions of a textbox are determined by the settings in the Height and Width properties of the box. The dimensions of a form are determined by its ScaleHeight and ScaleWidth properties.

When the dimensions of a form are changed, a Resize event occurs. The syntax of the **InputBox** function is:

variable name = InputBox (prompt string, box title string, default value)

Use the **Open** statement to open a file for input or output.

LOF(n) stands for *l*ength *of f*ile. The function returns the length in bytes of the file at that file number, *n*.

The **Input$(FileSize, 1)** function returns a string of *FileSize* length, from the file with file number *1*.

The **Print# n** statement writes a string to the file with file number *n*.

The **ChDrive** statement changes the current drive to the drive indicated in the string that follows.

The **ChDir** statement changes the current directory to the directory indicated in the string that follows.

The **App** object is the currently running application.

The listbox is a control that contains a list, to which items are added using the **AddItem** method. The list can be scrolled, the number of display columns changed, using the control's Columns property. You can maintain the list in sorted order by setting the Sorted property.

Problems

1. Menu Calculator

Write a program with the following menu structure:

    <u>C</u>alculation
    .....<u>A</u>dd
    .....<u>S</u>ubtract
    .....<u>M</u>ultiply
    .....<u>D</u>ivide
    E<u>x</u>it

When an operation is chosen, use the **InputBox** function to collect each of the two numbers from the user, then perform the operation. Display the result of the operation in a textbox on the form.

2. Order Please

Write a program using three textboxes to enter three names of animals. Put the names in alphabetical order using **StrComp** functions in **If-Then** statements. Display ordered names in a textbox.

3. Random Numbers

Use a **For-Next** statement to generate 100 random numbers between 0 and 1. The **Rnd** function generates a random number between 0 and 1. Insert the values in a listbox. Run the program. Change the Sorted property of the listbox to True. Run the program again.

4. Random Number File

Use a **For-Next** statement to generate 100 random numbers between 0 and 1. Write the numbers, converted to strings, into a file named **c:\temp\random.dat**.

5. Pythagorean Triples

Write a program to find and display a table of Pythagorean triples. A Pythagorean triple is a set of three integers that satisfy the Pythagorean theorem. The Pythagorean theorem, which applies only to right triangles, is "The length of the hypotenuse squared is equal to the sum of the squares of the lengths of the other two sides."

Use three nested loops, one for a, one for b, and one for c, where $a^2 + b^2 = c^2$.

Let the value of a range from 1 to 30. Start the b loop at $a+1$ and end it at 30. Start the c loop at $b+1$ and end it at 60.

6. Pythagorean Add-On

Write an addition to the program above to verify that the product of the three numbers forming a Pythagorean triple are divisible by 60. Use the **Mod** operator to test divisibility.

7. The Universal Gravitation Problem

Every mass exerts a gravitational attraction for every other mass. The force of this attraction is given by the formula:

$$F = \frac{Gm_1, \, m_2}{r^2}$$

where F represents the attractive force, G is the Universal Gravitation Constant, m1 and m2 are the two masses, and r is the distance between the masses.

As the masses increase, the force increases. As the distance increases, the force decreases.

The acceleration of gravity at any given elevation can be calculated from this formula. By Newton's law, $F=ma$, "force" equals mass times acceleration. If this expression is substituted for F in the formula above, it becomes:

$$a = \frac{GMe}{r^2}$$

where G is the Universal Gravitation literal, Me is the mass of the earth, and r is the distance from the center of the earth.

Write a program to display the acceleration of gravity for various elevations. Use a **For-Next** statement to generate values for the elevation. Start at 0 and step by 1000-foot increments to a height of 20,000 feet. The value of r is the radius of the earth, plus the elevation.

Display the elevation in feet and the acceleration of gravity in feet per second squared. You may need the following conversion factors:

$G = 1.07 \times 10^{-9} \; ft^3/(lb \; sec^2)$ Gravitation constant

$Me = 1.315 \times 10^{25} \; lb$ Weight of earth in pounds

Radius of the earth = 3955 miles

1 mile = 5280 feet

8. The Factorial Problem

Write a program to calculate and display the factorials of the first 20 numbers in a listbox. N factorial, symbolized as $N!$, is calculated by the following formula:

$N!=N*(N-1)*(N-2)*...*2*1$

9. Drag Race Problem A

The final velocity of an automobile undergoing a literal acceleration of a, is given by the formula:

$v = a \; t$

where t is the time. One of the statistics calculated for a quarter-mile run down the drag strip is the final speed of the vehicle as it passes through the "traps" at the end of the run.

Write a program that prompts the user to enter a value for the desired final velocity expressed in miles per hour. Display a table of accelerations calculated using values of t from 6 seconds to 20 seconds.

$a = v / t$, a is the acceleration, v is velocity, and t is time.

Column one of the table shows the time elapsed, ranging from 6 to 20 seconds. The second column shows the acceleration in feet per second squared. Convert the final velocity from miles per hour to feet per second.

1 mile = 5280 feet

1 hour = 3600 seconds
Use a listbox to show the table.

10. Solving a Pair of Linear Equations
A linear equation in x and y is of the form:

$ax + by = c$

where a,b, and c are real numbers.
Use textboxes to enter the coefficients of two equations:

$ax + by = c$
$dx + ey = f$

The solution to this system of equations includes the values for x and y that satisfy both of the equations.

One way to solve the system of equations mathematically is to use Cramer's rule. Cramer's rule uses discriminants to solve the system.

First calculate the discriminant of the denominator of the x and y values:

$DEN = a*e - b*d$

where a,b,c,d,e, and f are the coefficients of the two linear equations.
If this value is 0, there is no need to proceed. If the value is non-zero, continue with the following calculations:

$x = (c*e-b*f)/DEN$
$y = (a*f-d*c)/DEN$

Display the solution as an ordered pair (x,y)

11. The Distance Between Cities Problem
The distance formula calculates the distance between two points on the x,y plane. If the two points are $(x1,y1)$ and $(x2,y2)$, the distance between the points is given by:

$d = Sqr((x1-x2)^2 + (y1-y2)^2)$

This formula can be applied to find the distance between cities. If the coordinates of the cities are known, the distance between them can be found. The coordinates for the cities are the latitude and longitude for the cities. Find the coordinates for two U.S. cities, then write a program using textboxes to enter the latitude and longitude of the two cities and calculate the distance between the two. To convert the distance from degrees to miles, use the conversion: 1 degree = 69 miles.

```
DispLine =
DispLine & TbCh &
Format$(TotalInt,
     "Currency"

AmortTable(Payment

Number) =

DispLine
```

Formatting and Arrays

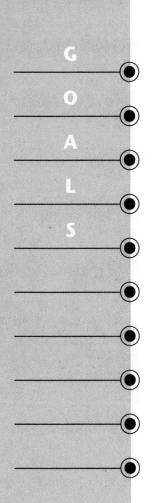
After working through this chapter, you will be able to:

Use the **Format$** string function to format numerical values, dates, and times.

Understand the concept of reusability.

Understand and use the concept of the scope of variables. Both the visibility and the lifetime of variables are discussed.

Use a scrollbar as input to a program. The value of the scrollbar is used to provide a subscript for an array.

Use an array to store information.

Use the **Do-While** loop construct in applications.

Use two drawing methods: Circle and Line.

Use three mouse events: MouseDown, MouseUp, and MouseMove.

Use arrays to store information in a binary file.

O V E R V I E W

Formatting output and using arrays to store lists of values are the two major focus areas of this chapter. The Car Loan project, the Amortization Table project, and the Line Draw project all emphasize the user interface. Two of the three make extensive use of arrays. The third uses graphic methods, mouse events, arrays, and files to create a simple drawing program. You will use the techniques you learn in this chapter repeatedly.

Concepts of code reusability and the scope of variables are very important both in your further study of computer science and in the practical application of programming techniques in the workplace. Reusability implies far more than just saving time and labor by reusing portions of code; it is a programming philosophy that drives the industry.

By understanding the scope of variables used in programs, you will be able to build robust programs—in other words, programs that won't fail when used.

Formatting

Section

This section covers how to format numbers and strings. Formatting is the process of making a number or string appear in a particular way on a form or on a printed page. For example, you could choose to format the number 331455055 in either of these two different ways:

- $3,314,550.55, as currency

- 331-45-5055, as a social security number

The underlying value—the number itself—remains the same, but it is presented differently in these two examples.

Up until this point, you have printed values as either whole numbers or decimals. You are now ready to print currency with dollar signs and two decimal places, percentages with percentage signs, and times and dates with appropriate format.

Why format? First, formatting strings or numbers in different ways changes their meaning. As you can see in the example above, formatting 331455055 as currency is an entirely different way to use the number than formatting it as a social security number. Second, formatting your output makes it easier to read and understand. As soon as users see a dollar sign, for example, they know they are looking at an amount of money.

The Format Function

The **Format$** function in Visual Basic receives values from a procedure. The procedure gets back from the function a formatted string ready for display. This versatile function can format many different kinds of numbers, including integers, decimals, percentages, currency, strings, dates, and times.

You have used the **Format$** function before. Remember the following line of code?

```
Equation = "y = " & Format$(Slope, "Fixed") & " x + " & Format$(YInt, "Fixed")
```

The first usage of the **Format$** function in the line above is passed two values: a numerical value (*Slope*) and a string literal ("Fixed"). The function formats the value of the variable *Slope*. The string constant is an instruction to the **Format$** function describing the way the value should be displayed.

According to this instruction, the value of *Slope* should be displayed with at least one digit to the left of the decimal point and two digits to the right of the decimal point. If the value is 1.234332, for example, the value returned by the **Format$** function is "1.23". If the value sent to the function is 0.0123, the value returned by the function would be "0.01".

You can set up the **Format$** function in two ways to prepare a number for display:

- Using a predefined numerical format, such as "Fixed".

- Using a string that you provide. This string specifies, digit by digit, the way the value should look when displayed.
  This section explores these two options.

Using Predefined Numerical Formats

This table lists the predefined formats for numbers. To use one of the predefined formats with the **Format$** function, you supply the function with the name of the predefined format as a string. We did this in the example above when we used the Fixed predefined format.

Format Name	Effect
General Number	Displays number with no particular modifications
Currency	Commas to show thousands, two digits to the right of the decimal point, negative numbers in parentheses
Fixed	One digit to the left and two digits to the right of the decimal point
Standard	Commas to show thousands, two digits to the right of the decimal point
Percent	Value multiplied by 100, percent sign appended to the right, two digits to the right of the decimal point

Scientific	Shows value as a decimal number between 0 and 10 times the appropriate power of 10
Yes/No	Displays *No* if the value is 0, *Yes* if the value is not 0
True/False	Displays *False* if the value is 0, *True* if the value is not 0
On/Off	Displays *Off* if the value is 0, *On* if the value is not 0

To use the predefined formats in the table, just include them, as shown, between double quotes and send them as parameters along with the values to be formatted to the **Format$** function:

```
txtPrice.Text = Format$( Price, "Currency")
txtMass.Text = Format$( Amount, "Scientific")
txtRate.Text = Format$( IntRate, "Percent")
```

In the first sample, the value of *Price* is formatted as currency. Commas are added to indicate thousands and two digits are included to the right of the decimal point. If the value of *Price* is 13456.9011, the formatted value returned would be "13,456.90".

Similarly, if *Amount* is 0.0000012992, the Scientific format converts the value to the string "1.30E-06". This format shows the number rounded to two decimal places to the right of the decimal point.

In the third example, if the value of *IntRate* is 0.0678, the **Format$** function shown converts the value to the string "6.78%". Once again, this predefined format shows two decimal places to the right of the decimal point.

Experimenting with the Numerical Formats

The instructions that follow take you step-by-step through a program that demonstrates the different built-in formatting strings used with the **Format$** function. To experiment with the formats:

1 Start Visual Basic. If Visual Basic is already running, select New Project from the File menu.

2 Double-click on the body of the form to open the Code window.

3 In the Form_Load procedure, enter the following code:

```
Dim Number As Long
Number = 345811
```

continued

```
Debug.Print Format$(Number, "General Number")
Debug.Print Format$(Number, "Currency")
Debug.Print Format$(Number, "Fixed")
Debug.Print Format$(Number, "Standard")
Debug.Print Format$(Number, "Percent")
Debug.Print Format$(Number, "Scientific")
Debug.Print Format$(Number, "Yes/No")
Debug.Print Format$(Number, "True/False")
Debug.Print Format$(Number, "On/Off")
```

Debug.Print prints results directly in the Debug window.

4 Run the program by clicking on the Single-Step button in the toolbar, the button with the single shoe print. Arrange the Code window and the Debug window so you can see both at once. As you single-step through the program, the next line of code to be executed will be highlighted. The results of the previous line will be visible in the Debug window.

If you instead run the program by pressing F5 or clicking on the Run button in the toolbar, the output appears in the Debug window almost instantaneously. It's hard to tell which line of code produced which line of output.

5 Stop the program by clicking on the Stop button in the toolbar.

Creating Formats Manually

As convenient as the predefined formats are, you may not find one that fits your needs in a specific program. For instance, you may want to include more than two decimal places in a percentage. You can do that by creating a custom format for the percentage. Visual Basic uses symbols to represent the ways digits and other symbols appear when formatted and displayed. Here's an example of a custom format:

```
txtAmount.Text = Format$(Amount, "##0.####%")
```

Each number sign, "#", represents a digit in the final string. With this format, 0.00012933 would be displayed as 0.0129%. The two number signs at the beginning of the format string are unused. They are needed only when the final value has two or three digits to the left of the decimal point.

The "0" immediately to the left of the decimal point also represents a digit. If the value being converted is greater than 1, this 0 is replaced with a digit. If the value is less than 1, Visual Basic places a 0 in the final string. Thus, the "0" is different from the "#", because a digit always appears in this position, to the left of the decimal place.

The number signs to the right of the decimal point indicate how many digits should be displayed on that side. In this case, there are four places to the right of the decimal point. Therefore, the converted value is rounded to the fourth decimal place.

Not only is the percentage sign appended to the final string, the value is also automatically multiplied by 100. This converts 0.05 to 5%, or 1.02 to 102%.

These **Format$** functions will be useful in the next program in the chapter: the Car Loan program.

Using Predefined Time and Date Formats

The table in this section lists the predefined formats for times and dates. The Effect column shows the result of executing:

```
Debug.Print Format$(Now, "xxx")
```

where "xxx" is the Format Name shown in the table. **Now** is the built-in function that reports the system time and date.

Format Name	Effect
General Date	5/19/95 11:15:30 AM
Short Date	5/19/95
Medium Date	19-May-95
Long Date	Friday, May 19, 1995
Short Time	11:15
Medium Time	11:15AM
Long Time	11:15:30 AM

NOTE:
For more about the Format$ function, search for Format in the Visual Basic Help system.

Localizing Format Strings

Microsoft products are sold throughout the world. Many countries use different formats for dates and numbers. Windows is customized to reflect national differences. **Format$** is sensitive to these differences. Strings returned by the **Format$** function match the preferences established when Windows is first installed. You can change these preferences by using the Control Panel. If you do so, you will see the strings returned by the **Format$** function reflect those changes.

Adding the Date to the Digital Clock

Here's a chance for you to go back to an old program and improve it. This is exactly the type of process professional programmers go through all the time. To experiment with the date and time formats discussed above, reopen the Digital Clock program from Chapter 3. In the Timer event handler, you used the following line to copy the system time to **lblTime**:

```
lblTime = Time
```

The system function **Now** returns not only the system time, but the system date. This value can be substituted in the line above with a **Format$** function:

```
lblTime = Format$(Now, "xxxx")
```

Replace "xxxx" with each of the time and date format strings listed above and note the result of each. Before you leave the project, add a second label to display the date in long form. Resave the project and form file.

QUESTIONS AND ACTIVITIES

1. Write a program similar to the one used to test the numerical formats for the date and time formats. Step through the program using the Single-Step button in the tool bar.

2. Write a statement that calls the **Sqr(n)** function. (Calling a function means using it in an expression.)

3. What value is returned when this function is called?

```
Format$(2342.1,"Currency")
```

4. What value is returned when this function is called?

```
Format$(.23421,"Percent")
```

5. Write the statements using the concatenation operator, the ampersand, and the **Format$** function to build the following strings. Use appropriate variable names and the built-in format patterns (such as "Currency" or "Scientific").
   a) "x = 1.456E-03"
   b) "Weekly pay is $145.45"
   c) "Length is 345.22 cm."
   d) "The discount is 4.55%"

6. Given that $x = 234.5567$ and $y = 0.07886$, write the strings that result from the following statements:
   a) Format$(x, "Currency") & " per month"
   b) Format$(x, "Fixed") & " pounds per inch"
   c) "Mark it down " & Format$(y, "Percent")
   d) "It weighs " & Format$(y, "Scientific") & " grams"

7. Build a manual format string for the **Format$** function that returns "00.234" from the value 0.23411.

The Car Loan Program

Section

Buying a car often requires borrowing money. That means that you will be paying for the car in monthly installments rather than all at once. Can you afford the car you want? What terms should you ask for on the loan? You can use a Visual Basic program to answer these questions rather than making the calculations yourself.

This program uses formatted output to show calculated information about getting a car loan. The user enters the loan amount, the length of the loan in years, and the interest rate of the loan. The program calculates and displays the monthly payment, the total interest paid on the loan, and the total amount paid.

You will learn how to use frames on forms to group objects.

Understanding Interest

If you did not have to pay interest, you could determine your monthly payment on a car easily. You would simply take the loan amount and divide by the number of payments.

Banks and other corporations, however, charge interest on loaned money. This interest is charged monthly and added to the loan amount, or principal. As a result, you have to add the interest to the principal each month before dividing by the number of payments.

This program uses a formula that combines these activities into a single expression:

- Calculating monthly interest

- Adding that interest to the loan amount

- Reducing the loan amount by the amount of the monthly payment

- Repeating the process for each monthly payment

The formula for calculating the monthly payment for original loan amount *B* is:

```
p = B*i/(1-(1+i)^(-n))
```

where *p* is the monthly loan payment, *B* is the original loan amount, *i* is the monthly (not the yearly) interest rate, and *n* is the total number of payments.

219

Consider the following example. The original loan amount (*B*) is 10000, the yearly interest rate (*rate*) is 0.05, and the time period for the loan is three years. These calculations are necessary:

- Monthly rate (*i* = *rate*/12 = 0.05/12 = 0.004167)

- Number of payments (*n* = *years* * 12 = 3*12 = 36)
  Using these values, the calculation for the monthly payment becomes:

```
p = $10,000*0.004167 / (1-(1+0.004167)^(-36))
p = $299.71
total payback amount: 299.71 x 36 = 10789.56
total interest: 10,789.56 - 10,000 = 789.56
```

Starting Out

To calculate a car loan, you need the user to enter three values:

- Loan amount

- Yearly interest rate

- Years covered by the loan

As you have often done in other projects, you will use textboxes for user input. You will also try something new: grouping these three textboxes together. To group the textboxes, you use a frame. Frames are captioned boxes containing controls. For a control to be inside a frame, it must be drawn in the frame. You draw the frame first, then place the controls inside it. As always, you will use labels to caption the textboxes.

A frame is a container control. When you move the frame by clicking on it and dragging, the controls that are inside it move with the frame. If you delete the frame, you also delete all the controls that it contains.

In previous projects, you have left input textboxes empty. In this project, though, you will provide initial values in these textboxes. Loading the boxes with sample data accomplishes two goals:

- The user can calculate a sample payment schedule without doing anything other than clicking on a button.

- You provide the user with a guide to the correct format for the values entered. For example, the program will return an error if the user enters commas in the loan amount. Visual Basic cannot convert a string with commas into a value.

Someone trying to decide about a car loan is interested in three pieces of information:

- Expected monthly payment

- Total interest they will pay

- Total amount they will pay over the period of the loan

You use three labels to display this information, as well as another three labels as captions. You will also group these objects in a frame, which you will name "Calculated Values".

To run the program, you need three command buttons (though you could also use a menu bar). These buttons let the user start the calculations, clear the textboxes for new values, and exit the program. The finished form is shown in Figure 6-1.

NOTE:

The program makes some intermediate calculations that are not displayed. You do not have to display all values the program produces.

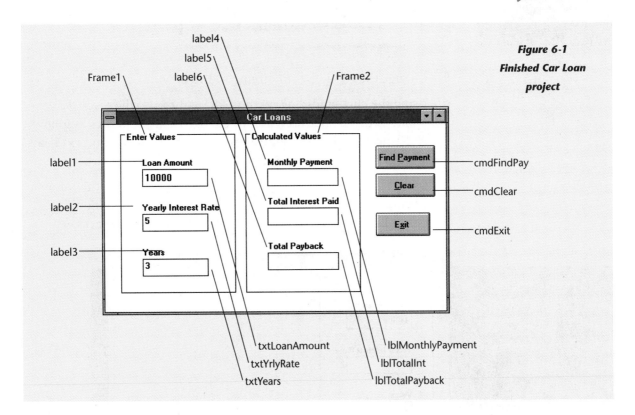

Figure 6-1
Finished Car Loan project

Setting Up the Form

Follow these steps to set up the Car Loan form:

1 Start Visual Basic. If Visual Basic is already running, select New Project from the File menu.

2 Change the caption of the form to **Car Loans**.

3 Click on the Frame icon in the Toolbox.

4 Draw the frame on the form by clicking where you want the left-hand corner of the frame. Drag to the position of the right-hand corner (see Figure 6-2).

Click here —

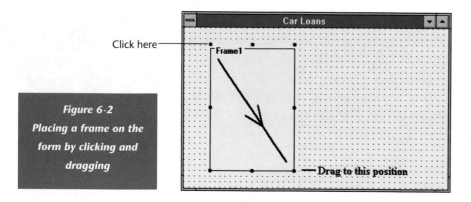

5 Change the caption of the frame to **Enter Values**.

6 Using the click-and-drag method, draw three textboxes *in the frame*. In the Properties window, change their properties as follows:
  ◎ Name property: **txtLoanAmount**, **txtYrlyRate**, and **txtYears**
  ◎ Text property: **10000**, **5**, and **3**

7 Using the click-and-drag method, draw three labels in the frame. Arrange the labels over the textboxes. Change the Caption properties to **Loan Amount**, **Yearly Interest Rate**, and **Years**.

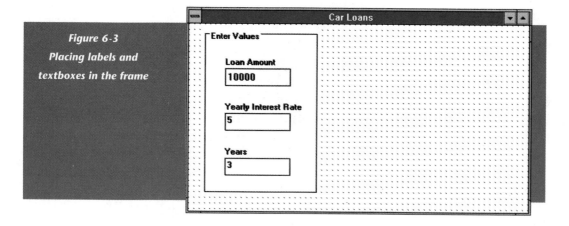

8 Draw a second frame for the calculated values (monthly payment, total interest, and total payback amount). Change the Caption property of the frame to **Calculated Values**.

9 Draw three labels in the frame. Name them **lblMonthlyPayment**,

lblTotalInt, and **lblTotalPayback**. Change their BorderStyle to Single Fixed. Delete their captions.

10 Draw three labels in the frame with the captions **Monthly Payment**, **Total Interest Paid**, and **Total Payback**. Place these over the three labels created in step 9.

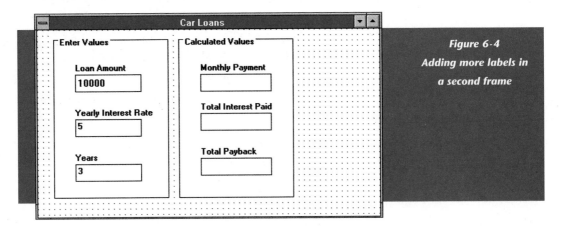

Figure 6-4
Adding more labels in
a second frame

11 Draw three command buttons. Change their names to **cmdFindPay**, **cmdClear**, and **cmdExit**. Change their captions to **Find &Payment**, **&Clear**, and **E&xit**.

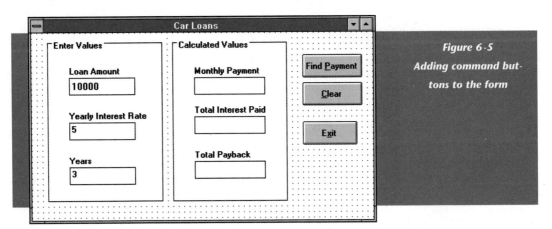

Figure 6-5
Adding command but-
tons to the form

Coding the Command Buttons

The work of this program is performed by the code attached to the Find Payment button. To write this code, you need to understand a few details about interest. Because interest is compounded (calculated) on a monthly basis, the interest rate used in the program is one-twelfth of the yearly interest rate. In addition, the user is expected to enter the yearly interest rate as a percentage—8.5 instead of 0.085, for example.

As a result, you need to have the program divide the interest rate by 100 to convert it to a decimal.

You want the Clear button to work in a slightly different way in this program. What if the user wants to experiment with changing just the yearly interest rate, leaving the other two values the same? The code you will write for this button does not clear the textboxes. Instead, the user can use the Delete key to change a value or two there. The Clear button clears only the labels that display the calculated values.

Follow these steps to write the code for the buttons:

1 Double-click on the cmdFindPay button to open the Code window. In the cmdFindPay_Click() procedure, enter the following code:

```
'—Variable declarations
Dim LoanAmount As Currency, MonthlyPayment As Currency
Dim TotalInt As Currency, TotalPayback As Currency
Dim YrlyRate As Single, MonthlyRate As Single
Dim Years As Integer, Payments As Integer
'—Reading values from the form
LoanAmount = Val(txtLoanAmount)
YrlyRate = Val(txtYrlyRate)
Years = Val(txtYears)
'—Intermediate calculations
MonthlyRate = YrlyRate / 1200
Payments = Years * 12
'—Monthly Payment
MonthlyPayment = LoanAmount * MonthlyRate / (1 - (1 + MonthlyRate) ^ (-Payments))
'—Total Payback
TotalPayback = MonthlyPayment * Payments
'—Total Interest Paid
TotalInt = TotalPayback - LoanAmount
'—Display results
lblMonthlyPayment = Format$(MonthlyPayment, "Currency")
lblTotalInt = Format$(TotalInt, "Currency")
lblTotalPayback = Format$(TotalPayback, "Currency")
```

2 In the cmdClear_Click() procedure, enter the following code.

```
'—Clearing the Display labels
lblMonthlyPayment = ""
lblTotalInt = ""
lblTotalPayback = ""
'—Set focus back to the Loan Amount
txtLoanAmount.SetFocus
```

3   In the cmdExit procedure, enter the instruction **End**.

Finishing Up

Now you are ready to test the program. To do so:

1   Save the project and form files.

2   Run the program and experiment with different values for the loan amount, yearly interest rate, and duration of the loan. Try some of the values in the table below. Note: some of the values below will cause the program to stop with a run-time error. How would you change the program to prevent the errors from occurring?

Loan Amount	Yearly Interest Rate	Duration
30000	8%	4
30000	9%	4
30000	8%	3
30000	8%	5
150000	8%	30
150000	8%	15
30000	-12%	5
30000	8%	-3
10	8%	5

QUESTIONS AND ACTIVITIES

1.   When you are placing objects in a frame, why can't you simply double-click on the objects in the Toolbox? Why do you have to use the click-and-drag method?

2.   Use the Car Loan program to find the approximate loan amounts that satisfy the given situations:
     a)   You can afford $150 a month, the yearly interest rate is 12%, and you want a 3-year loan.
     b)   You can afford $250 a month, the yearly interest rate is 9%, and you want a 4-year loan.
     c)   You can afford $275 a month, the yearly interest rate is 15%, and you want a 5-year loan.

3.   Set up the following default values for the Car Loan program:

```
txtLoanAmount = "15000"
txtYrlyRate = "8.5"
txtYears = "6"
```

Run the program and observe the results.

4. Add the lines and controls to calculate and display the ratio of the total payback amount to the original loan amount.

5. Rewrite the Car Loan program to enter the yearly percentage as 0.07 instead of 7%.

6. An accelerator key is the underlined character in the caption of a command button. Pressing Alt + character executes the command. Change the accelerator key in the Find Payment button caption to the letter "F".

7. Rewrite the code attached to the Clear button to clear the input boxes as well as the display labels.

8. The formula used in the Car Loan project works just as well for home mortgages. Run the program and enter the following data:
Loan amount: 180000
Yearly interest rate: 7.5
Years: 30
Find and record the monthly payment, the total interest paid, and the total payback.

3

Section

Modules and Code Reusability

Every programmer wants to write more code in less time. "Maximum effect, with minimum effort" is an old saying most students would embrace. One of the keys to this kind of productivity is reusing code. Why rewrite code you have already written once?

You ran into this issue in the Who's in Sports? program in Chapter 5. There, you had to copy and paste sections of code twice to finish the subroutine for the Open and Display command. Each time you pasted the section of code, you had to change the names of variables, but you did not have to retype all the code.

In a sense, this is reusing code; but the approach is fairly weak and fragile. There are many opportunities for error. What if you forget to change all the variable names? This approach can also be tedious, depending on how many changes you have to make each time you paste the code.

Reusability is a far more powerful concept than cutting and pasting. The idea is to separate the code that does not change from the code that does. Then, you can reuse these unchanged "modules" of code again and again just by including these modules in your projects.

If you think about it, you'll see that the objects you place on forms are also an example of reusability. They are ready-made components that you can simply "plug in" to your forms in order to obtain predictable and well-tested behavior. Controls let you reuse someone else's work.

Besides saving time, there are other advantages to reusing program components. You can create more consistent forms and programs if you use the same elements as you need them. You can also save yourself debugging time. Once you know a section of code is debugged, for example, you will not need to debug it every time you use it.

Modules

The module is the basic unit of organization in Visual Basic projects. The Project window lists all the modules and controls in the currently open project. Modules come in two types: form modules and code modules. So far, you have only used form modules. A form module contains the form, the controls, the procedures attached to those controls or to the form, and variable declarations. A project can have more than one form module.

A code module contains procedures and declarations in a single file. The procedures and variables declared in the code module are recognized (callable) throughout the project. A code module is not associated with any form—as the name implies, it contains only code. Therefore, the code it contains cannot include event procedures for particular controls (every control that a project uses is placed on some form). However, event procedures can call code in code modules.

FORM MODULES

You have already used the form module. It contains the complete layout of each form, including textboxes, command buttons, labels, menus, and so forth. It also contains the procedures and variable declarations that have been attached to the various controls. The code written for the Click event of a command button, or the code written to shift the focus from one control to another, is included in the form module file.

A project can have more than one form module. While none of your projects has used more than one form, most real-life applications use several. Each one of these forms is saved in its own file. Each one can exist without the others. Each one contains its own layout—the form itself, its controls, their placement, and other initial values of their properties—together with all the code required to make the form functional. The form module completely specifies a form and its behavior.

You can include the same form in more than one project. Of course, it only makes sense to do so with forms that are very general in purpose. For example, suppose you created a form that allowed the user to enter a person's name, address, and phone number, and that performed all necessary error checking on the entered values. You could then easily incorporate this form into other projects. This is a powerful form of code reusability.

There are two ways to add a new form to a project. One way is to select New Form from the File menu. When you do so, a new form opens on the desktop and its name is added to the Project window. Another way to add a form to a project is to click on the New Form button in the toolbar.

When you save your project for the first time, Visual Basic will prompt you to save each form of the project, including any you have added. To specifically save a new form, select its entry in the Project window and choose Save File from the File menu. Each form can be selected from the Project window and saved with a unique name.

CODE MODULES

The code module contains no form definitions at all. It contains procedures and declarations that solve particular problems. These modules are created and added to the list of modules in the Project window by clicking on the Code Module icon in the toolbar. When you do so, the Module window opens (see Figure 6-6):

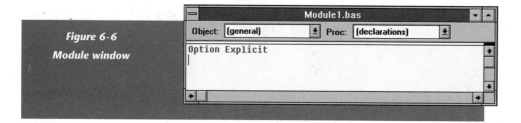

Figure 6-6
Module window

The icon appears as a constellation of forms, and indeed, the code module is used as a common resource for forms. It contains code shared by more than one form and it ensures that the variables declared in the code module are available for use by all other modules, including form modules.

Controls

As mentioned above, controls themselves provide reusability, because they allow you to reuse someone else's work. Visual Basic ships with many useful controls, and the Professional Edition contains still more. But a Visual Basic programmer's choices do not end there. The component-based model of programming that Visual Basic offers has proved so popular that an entire market in Visual Basic controls has sprung up to meet the demand.

Many companies sell controls for use with Visual Basic, generally at attractive prices. Many of these third-party controls are general-purpose, such as full-featured spreadsheet controls that let you enter formulas in cells and that recalculate values automatically. Other controls perform very specific tasks such as voice recognition. The number and variety of available third-party controls is quite large. In fact, after a professional Visual Basic programmer has designed a program, and before writing a single line of code unnecessarily, he or she will routinely investigate whether any third-party controls can be used to create the program.

STANDARD CONTROLS

The Visual Basic toolbox comes with a number of useful tools. You've already used several in your programs: the textbox, the label, the command button. And although it is not properly called a "tool", the Menu Design window is a very powerful part of Visual Basic. In chapters to come, you'll use several more of the standard tools that come with all versions of Visual Basic.

CUSTOM CONTROLS

You can add tools to the Toolbox by placing their files in the System directory of Windows. Visual Basic then automatically adds the new controls to the Toolbox and adds the file containing the controls to the Project window. The Toolbox expands to accommodate the new controls. You can click or double-click to place one of these new controls, just as you do with the standard controls.

For Visual Basic version 3.0 and earlier, files that contain Visual Basic controls have the extension **.vbx**. Visual Basic 4.0 introduces a new, more powerful kind of control; the files containing these controls have an **.ocx** extension. Each such file can contain one or more controls.

QUESTIONS AND ACTIVITIES

1. What is "code reusability"?

2. What is listed in the Project window?

3. How is a code module added to a project? What is the code module used for?

4. Run Visual Basic. Use the buttons in the toolbar to add two forms and two code modules to the default project. Note the appearance

of the Project window. Select Save Project from the File menu. Respond to each prompt with No.

5. Run Visual Basic. Design and print a form to collect a name and address. The form should have labeled textboxes to enter the last name, the first name, the address, the city, the state, and the zip code. Select Save File As from the File menu to save just the form file (not the project).

Section

The Scope of Variables

To use code modules effectively, you need to explore the concept of variables in greater depth. So far, you have only used variables within event procedures in a form module. These variables applied only to the event procedures in which they were located. As you reuse code, though, you will want access to the same variables from different event procedures, and sometimes even from different modules. How widely you can use a variable depends on the variable's scope.

A variable's scope is determined by its:

◉ Visibility

◉ Lifetime

Visibility is a question of the number of procedures, forms, and modules that can use (or "see") the variable. Look at Figure 6-7. If you use the **Dim** keyword to declare a variable in the general declarations area of a module, it is visible to all procedures in that module. If you use the **Global** keyword rather than the **Dim** keyword to declare a variable in the general declarations section of a code module, then that variable will be visible to all modules in the project. If instead, you declare the variable *within* an event procedure, as you have so far, it is visible only to that event procedure.

Figure 6-7

Visibility of a variable

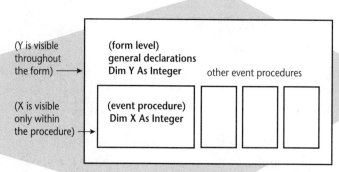

The lifetime of variables is determined by whether their values persist after the associated event ends. See Figure 6-8. In this example, *X* has a limited lifetime. *Y*, on the other hand, is declared in a code module and persists for the life of the program.

Any variable that you declare within a procedure using a typical **Dim** declaration will not be persistent. Sometimes, however, you do want to retain information across events. For example, suppose you wanted to count the number of times that the user clicked a particular button, in order to respond differently after the tenth click. You would need to retain a running count of the number of times the button's Click event occurred, incrementing it each time the procedure was entered.

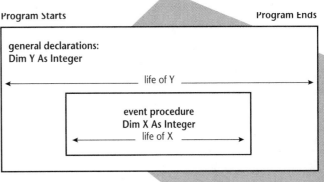

Figure 6-8
Lifetime of a variable

No other procedure needs to see this persistent value holding the click count, so ideally the value should not be stored in a global variable. You want the variable to have local visibility, but you want its lifetime to be the lifetime of the program. Visual Basic lets you declare variables with this kind of scope. They are called static variables.

In terms of scope, then, there are three kinds of variables:

- Local
- Static
- Global

You define the scope of variables by where you place them and the declaration statement you use. All three of these kinds of variables are discussed in this section.

Using Local Variables

By placing variables inside event procedures, you define them as local variables. They can be seen only by the event procedure in which you have placed them. The lifetime of local variables is limited as well. When the procedure is entered, each local variable is assigned a portion of memory where the value of the variable will be stored. As soon as the program executes the **End Sub** statement, the variable "disappears"— the memory that it occupied is reclaimed for use by some other procedure's local variables. The value of the variable, which was stored in that portion of memory, is lost.

Nor can you access the old value when the program once again enters the *same* event procedure. The old value of the variable, established during the previous time through the procedure's code, remains inaccessible. A new value is assigned.

Local variables do have one important advantage: they are safe. If you use local variables, you never have to worry if a change in the variable's value will mess up a calculation in some other procedure. The value of the variable is always completely contained within the procedure.

Using Static Variables

A static variable is a kind of local variable. The scope of a static variable is in between that of a local and a global variable. A static variable can only be seen by a single event or code procedure. However, when the procedure ends, the value of a static variable is not lost. Once a static variable obtains a value within an event procedure, it maintains that value when the event procedure is called again. That means that the lifetime of the variable extends beyond the end of the event procedure.

In Figure 6-9, Y is declared as a static variable in an event procedure and X is declared as a normal local variable in the same procedure. The value of Y persists even thought the particular event procedure may start and stop. The value of X, local to the event procedure, persists only while the procedure is running. Each time the procedure runs, a new value for X is created.

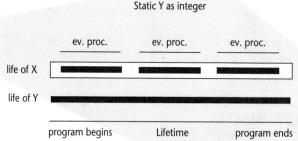

Figure 6-9
Lifetime of a static variable

How do you tell local from static variables? Both are declared in the same place, within an event procedure. However, you identify static variables by using the word **Static** in the place of the word **Dim**:

```
Static Count As Integer
```

Here's a program to illustrate the use of a static variable.

1 Start Visual Basic. If Visual Basic is running, select New Project from the File menu.

2 Change the caption of the form to **Static Variable**.

3   Place a command button on the form. Name the button **cmdCount**. Change the caption to **&Count**.

4   Place a label below the command button. Change the name to **lblHowMany**. Delete the caption.

5   Put a second label above the first, with the caption **How Many?** Change the FontSize to 9.75. See Figure 6-10.

6   Double-click on cmdCount to open the Code window. Insert this code into cmdCount_Click():

```
Static Count As Integer
Count = Count + 1
lblHowMany = Str$(Count)
```

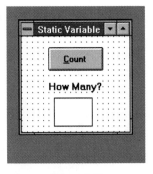

Figure 6-10
Static Variable form with command button and two labels

7   Run the program. Click on the Count button several times and note the result.

The first time the program executes the Click event procedure, *Count* is assigned the value 0. Before *Count* is displayed, its value is increased by 1. This value of *Count* is then displayed in the label, lblHowMany. See Figure 6-11.

Every time you click on the Count button, a new number appears in the label. Each new number is one higher than the old.

Now, make *Count* a local variable and watch the result:

1   Halt the program with the Stop button on the toolbar.

2   Save the project and form files.

3   Replace the **Static** keyword with **Dim**.

4   Run the program. Click on the Count button several times and note the result.

5   Halt the program with the Stop button on the toolbar.

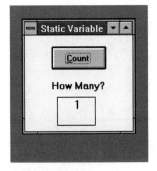

Figure 6-11
*Displaying the value of the **Count** variable*

Just like the **Static** statement, the **Dim** statement declares *Count* to be of Integer type. It is now no longer static, though, so its value will not persist. Each time you (or a user) clicks on the command button, the program creates a new instance of the variable *Count*. Each time, the variable is assigned the value of 0. Then, the code in the Click routine adds 1 and assigns the value to the textbox. Clicking on the command button does not change the value displayed in the label.

One approach that won't work is removing the **Static** or **Dim** statement altogether. *Count* is a property of the form that indicates the number of controls. Removing the declaration, either the **Static** or the **Dim**, lets the value of *Count* default to this other use.

Using Global Variables

To share variables among procedures, you must use global variables. There are two types of global variables. You can create global variables whose values are available to all procedures in:

- A form module
- A code module

Any variable that is global within a form module is available to all procedures in the form. It is not, however, available to procedures in *other* forms in the project. A variable that is global to a code module can have one of two kinds of visibility. It can be available only to the procedures in that module, or it can be made available to all procedures in all forms of the project. (Variables that are visible to all procedures within a single module are sometimes said to have module scope.) You give a code module variable the second, wider kind of scope by using the **Global** keyword instead of the **Dim** keyword when you declare the variable in the general declarations section of the code module.

VISIBILITY IN A FORM MODULE

To make a variable's value accessible to all the procedures of a form module, you need to declare that variable within the general declarations area of the form. If you click on the Code window and scroll to the top of the Object list, you will see the right entry (general). Once you select that entry, Visual Basic displays (declarations) in the Proc drop-down list. See Figure 6-12.

Figure 6-12
Declaring a variable in the general declarations area of the form

```
STCDMO.FRM
Object: (general)    Proc: (declarations)

Option Explicit
```

NOTE:

Notice that you do not use the word "global" when you declare a global variable in a form module. That word is reserved for declaring global variables with project scope in code modules.

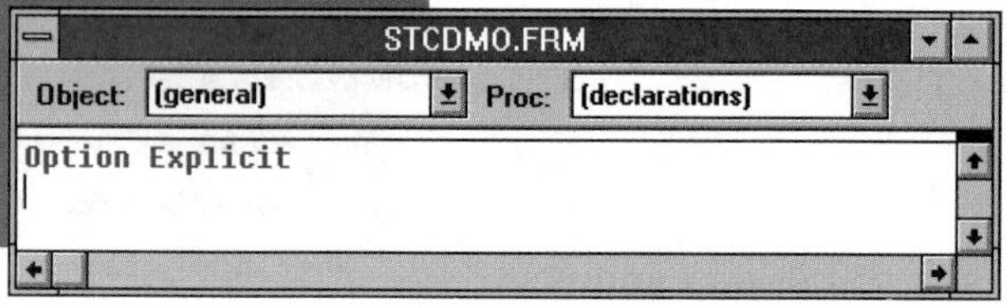

Now that you have the general area open, you are ready to declare variables with global scope within the form module. You cannot define static or local variables here. A static variable declared here would simply be a global variable, so Visual Basic would not let you use the **Static** keyword in this section. Declaring a local variable in the general declarations section makes no sense: what would it be local to? In any case, there is no way to do so, because the syntax you use to declare a local variable within a procedure is the same as the syntax you use to declare a global variable in a form's general declarations section. You can experiment with the Static Variable demonstration program you just created.

Before defining the *Count* variable as global, you need to change its name. Count is a property of the form that indicates the number of controls on it. You cannot place a variable with this name in the general area of the Code window. This was not a problem so long as *Count* was only a local variable.

1 Double-click on the Count button to open the Code window. In the cmdCount_Click() procedure, comment out both the statements that declare the *Count* variable.

2 Change the name of the variable from *Count* to *ClickCount*. The code now reads as shown in Figure 6-13.

3 Select *(general)* from the Object drop-down list. In this section, declare the variable *ClickCount* as an integer (see Figure 6-14).

4 Run the program. Click on the Count button several times and note the results.

5 Halt the program with the Stop button in the toolbar.

The variable *ClickCount* is declared in the general declarations section of the form module. Values assigned to the variable in one procedure are available to any procedure throughout the form module.

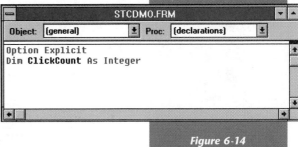

Figure 6-13
Code for cmdCount with the name of the Count variable changed

Figure 6-14
Declaring ClickCount as an integer

VISIBILITY IN A CODE MODULE

Any variables you declare in a code module are visible to all procedures in any form included in the project. So far, you have not used code modules in any of your Visual Basic programs. As an exercise, you'll create a code module for the Static Variable demonstration program.

To work with a code module:

1 Add a code module to the project. Either click on the New Module icon, or select New Module from the File menu. The Code window for the new module appears.
Note that the name of the new code module also appears in the Project window. See Figure 6-15.

2 In the code module, under **Option Explicit**, enter the statement:

```
Dim ClickCount As Integer
```

3 To return to the code for the form module, click on the form's entry in the Project window. Once the form's name is selected, click on the View Code button.

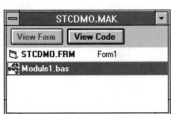

Figure 6-15
Code module in the Project window

4 Remove or comment out the **Dim ClickCount As Integer** statement in the general declarations section of the form.

5 Run the program.
Visual Basic complains that *ClickCount* has not been declared. The **Dim** statement in the code module declares *ClickCount* within that module. To make *ClickCount* available anywhere in the project, change **Dim** to **Global**. You will do so in steps 6 through 9.

6 Halt the program by clicking on the Stop button on the toolbar.

7 Select the code module name in the Project window.

8 Click on the View Code button.

9 In the general declarations section, change **Dim** to **Global**. The line now reads **Global ClickCount As Integer**.

10 Run the program. Click on the Count button several times and note the results.

11 Halt the program.

12 Save the project file, the form file, and the code module file. Code module files are given the extension **.bas**.

QUESTIONS AND ACTIVITIES

1. What is the lifetime of a variable? What is the visibility of a variable?

2. Where are local variables declared?

3. If you change the value of a local variable within an event procedure, what changes occur outside that procedure?

4. If the **Option Explicit** statement is included in the general declarations area of a form, and a variable, declared locally in procedure A is used in procedure B, what happens?

5. What is a static variable? What is the difference between a static variable and a local variable?

6. Where do you put the declarations for a global variable? Where is the value of a global variable available?

7. There are really two kinds of global variables, ones declared with the **Global** keyword and those defined with regular **Dim** statements. What are the similarities and differences between the two? Where are each declared?

The Amortization Table Program

Section

In many ways, the Amortization Table program is exactly like the Car Loan problem earlier in this chapter. You start with the same problem: figuring out whether you can afford a loan at a given interest rate for a given number of years. You use the same approach for prompting users to provide total loan amount, yearly interest rate, and duration of the loan. That is, you place a frame, position three textboxes in the frame, and add labels.

Just like the other program, you use a second frame for the display of calculated values. And you use three command buttons: one for calculating, one for clearing, and one for exiting. When a user clicks on the Calculate button, the program displays the monthly payment in a label within the second frame.

The new functionality in this program lies in the amortization table in the lower third of the form (see Figure 6-16). To create this table, you will use an array for the first time. Arrays are powerful and fundamental data structures that will help you solve a wide variety of problems. Though this will be your first use of arrays, it certainly will not be your last.

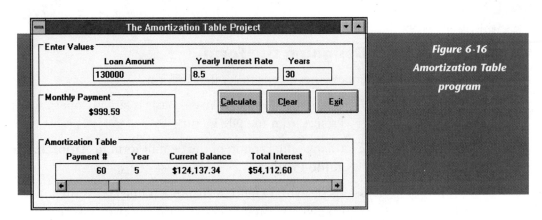

Figure 6-16
Amortization Table
program

The program uses an array to store a table of values calculated as the program runs. For simplicity's sake, this array is displayed in a multiline textbox one line at a time. The user clicks on a horizontal scrollbar to determine which line of the table is displayed in the textbox.

The program is a collection of techniques that you have already learned. Frames group the values entered, textboxes collect values from the user, command buttons control the calculations, and a horizontal scrollbar controls the display of the amortization table. Using the array to store the results of the calculations needed to generate the amortization table and displaying the lines of the table in a label one at a time are new.

ARRAYS

The listboxes that you used in the Who's in Sports? program have many of the features of arrays. However, listboxes have additional features pertaining to their role as displayable interface elements. Unlike listboxes, arrays are not controls. You create them by declaring them in code. See Figure 6-17.

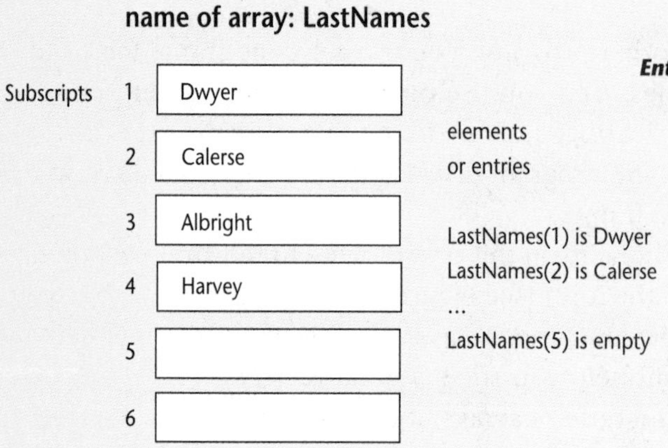

name of array: LastNames

Subscripts

1	Dwyer
2	Calerse
3	Albright
4	Harvey
5	
6	

elements
or entries

LastNames(1) is Dwyer
LastNames(2) is Calerse
…
LastNames(5) is empty

Figure 6-17

Entries in an array

ARRAYS

Arrays are lists of values. The members of the list are called the elements of the array. Arrays have names and subscripts. The name of the array is a variable name that refers to the entire list, not a single value. A subscript of the array is an integer value designating a particular value of the array.

Designing the Form

Follow these steps to set up the form.

1 Open Visual Basic. If Visual Basic is already open, select New Project from the File menu.

2 Change the caption of the default form to **Amortization Table Project**.

3 As shown in Figure 6-16, put a frame across the top of the form. Change the caption of the form to **Enter Values**.

4 Drag and drop three textboxes into the frame. Name the boxes **txtLoanAmount**, **txtYrlyRate**, and **txtYears**. Set the TabIndex properties to 0, 1, and 2, respectively.

5 Drag and drop three labels into the frame. Position them above the textboxes and change the captions to **Loan Amount**, **Yearly Interest Rate**, and **Years**.

6 Draw a second frame. Change the caption to **Monthly Payment**.

7 Draw a label in the second frame. Delete the caption of the label. Change the name to **lblMonthlyPayment**. Because there is no border, the label is invisible within the frame.

8   Draw a third frame across the bottom of the form. Change the caption to **Amortization Table**.

9   Draw a textbox inside the frame. Name the box **txtAmortTable**. Change the MultiLine property to True.

10   Draw a horizontal scrollbar inside the frame, below the textbox. Name the scrollbar **hsbPayment**. Moving the scroll box will change the payment displayed in the textbox.

11   Place three command buttons on the form. Name them **cmdCalculate**, **cmdClear**, and **cmdExit**. Change the captions to **&Calculate**, **C&lear**, and **E&xit**. Set the TabIndex to 3, 4, and 5, respectively.

Enter labels in the amortization table frame, above the textbox: **Payment #**, **Year**, **Current Balance**, and **Total Interest**.

Writing Code for the Command Buttons

This section of the program is much like the simple programs you wrote in Chapter 3: you handle input by reading values from textboxes on the form, calculate the monthly payment, and display the payment in a label on the form. Clicking on the Clear button prepares the form for new data.

1   Double-click on the Calculate button to open the Code window. In the cmdCalculate_Click() procedure, insert the following:

```
'—Variable declarations
Dim LoanAmount As Currency, MonthlyPayment As Currency
Dim YrlyRate As Single, MonthlyRate As Single
Dim Years As Integer, Payments As Integer
'—Reading values from the form
LoanAmount = Val(txtLoanAmount)
YrlyRate = Val(txtYrlyRate)
Years = Val(txtYears)
'—Intermediate calculations
MonthlyRate = YrlyRate / 1200
Payments = Years * 12
'—Monthly payment
MonthlyPayment = LoanAmount * MonthlyRate / (1 - (1 + MonthlyRate) ^ (-Payments))
'—Display results
lblMonthlyPayment = Format$(MonthlyPayment, "Currency")
```

2 Run the program. Enter data for the loan amount, the yearly interest rate, and the duration of the loan in years. Click on the Calculate button. The monthly payment appears in the frame, but the code is not yet complete.

3 Before finishing the code for the Calculate button, enter these lines for the Clear button.

```
'—Clearing the Display labels
lblMonthlyPayment = ""
'—Set focus back to the Loan Amount
txtLoanAmount.SetFocus
```

4 Enter **End** in the subroutine for the Exit button.

5 Save the project and form files.

Implementing the Table

So far, this program is almost identical to the Car Loan program. To create the amortization table, you need to add these additional steps:

1 Declare an array that is visible to the entire form.

2 Add code for the Calculate button that creates the lines of the table, stores the lines in the array, and sets up the horizontal scrollbar.

3 Add code to the horizontal scrollbar Change event to scroll through the lines of the amortization table.
These steps are covered one by one in this section.

DECLARING AN ARRAY

Arrays are declared with **Dim**, **Static**, and **Global** statements. You include the size of the array in parentheses following the name. For example:

```
Dim LastName(20) As String
```

This line declares an array of 20 strings with the name *LastName*. The number in parentheses the name shows that you have just declared an array.

LastName is an array of strings. You can also create an array of numeric values. As with variables, you declare the data type of the array after the word "As". For example:

```
Static PriceList(100) As Currency
```

The array in the amortization program (*AmortTable*) is an array of strings. Each string is made of values joined together. The Tab character, embedded in each string, provides spacing for the display. The Tab character, ASCII code 9, moves the display to the next print zone. These print zones, spaced about 8 characters apart, allow you to arrange display items in columns.

The values joined together in these strings result from calculations performed during run-time. The program performs these calculations whenever a user clicks on the Calculate button. The values are displayed when the Change event of the horizontal scrollbar occurs. You declare the array of strings in the general declarations area of the form to make it visible to all event procedures throughout the form. The maximum size of the table is 360 lines.

To declare the array:

1   Open the project, if it is not already open. To open the Code window, double-click on the body of the form or click on the View Code button in the Project window.

2   In the general declarations area, enter this line:

```
Dim AmortTable(360) As String
```

ADDING CODE FOR THE CALCULATE BUTTON

You are now ready to add more code for the Calculate button. This is the code that sets up the array. It is different from the code in the Car Loan program.

To add the code:

1   With the Code window open, select cmdCalculate from the Object drop-down list.

2   Add this code to the end of the cmdCalculate_Click() procedure:

```
'—Additional local declarations
Dim PaymentNumber As Integer
Dim MonthlyInt As Currency
Dim TotalInt As Currency, CurrentAmt As Currency
Dim YearNumber As Integer, DispLine As String
Const TbCh = Chr$(9) 'the tab character
'—Initialize the TotalInterest and CurrentBalance
TotalInt = 0
CurrentAmt = LoanAmount
'—Set up loop
For PaymentNumber = 1 To Payments
    '—Make calculations
```

continued

```
    MonthlyInt = CurrentAmt * MonthlyRate
    TotalInt = TotalInt + MonthlyInt
    CurrentAmt = CurrentAmt + MonthlyInt - MonthlyPayment
    YearNumber = PaymentNumber \ 12
    '—Build display line
    DispLine = TbCh & Format$(PaymentNumber, "####")
    DispLine = DispLine & TbCh & Format$(YearNumber, "#0")
    DispLine = DispLine & TbCh & Format$(CurrentAmt, "Currency")
    DispLine = DispLine & TbCh & Format$(TotalInt, "Currency")
    '—Transfer display line to array element
    AmortTable(PaymentNumber) = DispLine
Next PaymentNumber      'end of loop
'—Set up scroll bar
hsbPayment.Min = 1
hsbPayment.Max = Payments
hsbPayment.LargeChange = 12  ' one year = 12 payments
hsbPayment.Value = 1
'—Put first line of table into the textbox
txtAmortTable = AmortTable(1)
```

Here is an explanation of these new lines of code. The first five lines of code declare variables. *PaymentNumber* is the number of the payment, *MonthlyInt* is the monthly interest amount, *TotalInt* is the total of interest payments, *CurrentAmt* is the current balance of the loan, *YearNumber* is the current year of the loan, *DispLine* is the string to build output, and *TbCh* is a constant representing the Tab character.

The following lines set total interest (*TotalInt*) to 0, then set current balance (*CurrentAmt*) to the value of LoanAmount. Next comes a **For-Next** loop. The instructions within the loop will be repeated for each payment, with the number of payments setting the upper limit of the loop. More variables are declared, then the code calculates the monthly interest amount for each payment, the running total of the interest payments, the new current balance of the loan for each payment, and the current year number.

The line **DispLine = TbCh & Format$(PaymentNumber, "####")** begins the process of joining the calculated values into a single line of display. This line starts the string with the Tab character and the payment number. The next line takes the string from the previous line and appends a Tab and the year number. Next, a Tab and the current balance are appended to the string, then a Tab and the total interest. At this point, the string is complete.

The line **AmortTable(PaymentNumber) = DispLine** copies

the line into the *AmortTable* array. The subscript of the array is provided by the payment number. Each line goes into a separate position in the array.

The loop ends, and several properties of the scrollbar are initialized. The last of these is the Value property of the scrollbar, which is initialized to 1. This corresponds with the first line of the amortization table. In the last line, the textbox is initialized with the first line of the table.

ADDING CODE TO THE CHANGE EVENT OF THE SCROLLBAR

Some of the last lines of code you inserted into the cmdCalculateClick() subroutine set up the scrollbar. Now, this final line, added to the Change event handler of the horizontal scrollbar, writes a new line of the table to the textbox when the value of the scrollbar changes. The position of the scrollbox is reflected in the value of the Value property of the scrollbar. This value picks the line of the amortization table to display.

To finish the code for the Change event:

1   With the Code window open, select hsbPayment from the Object drop-down list.

2   Enter this line of code in the hsbPayment_Change() event procedure:

```
txtAmortTable = AmortTable(hsbPayment.Value)
```

Finishing the Program

To check your work:

1   Run the program. Enter data for the loan amount, the yearly interest rate and the duration of the loan in years. Click on the Calculate button. The monthly payment appears in the frame. The textbox shows the first line of the amortization table.

2   Click on the right arrow box of the horizontal scroll bar. Click and hold on the right arrow box. Click in the channel to move the display one year at a time.

3   Stop the program.

4   Save the project and form files.

QUESTIONS AND ACTIVITIES

1.   What other applications can you think of, involving tables of values, that could be handled in the same way as the amortization table?

2. In the code for cmdCalculate, change the scroll bar initialization code as follows:

```
hsbPayments.SmallChange = 2
hsbPayments.LargeChange = 24
```

Run the program and observe the results.

3. Remove the declaration for *AmortTable* from the general declarations section of the form. Move the declaration to the Calculate button and run the program. What happens?

4. Add a code module to the project. Move the **Dim** statement for *AmortTable* to the general declarations section of the code module. Run the program. What happens?

5. Change the **Dim** statement in the code module to a global statement. Run the program. What happens?

6. How is a listbox like an array?

7. What is the subscript of an array used for?

8. Write the statement that assigns a string, *Msg*, to the ninth entry of the *AmortTable* array.

9. What symbol forces Visual Basic to perform an integer division?

10. What does the Tab character do in a string being prepared for display?

11. Write a statement that would assign the fourth entry of the *AmortTable* array to the textbox named txtDisplayLine.

Section

Indefinite Loops

The **For-Next** loop construction has served Basic well. For a long time, it was the only built-in looping statement for Basic programs. This loop, however, has a major flaw. To use it, the number of times the loop should be executed must be known before the loop actually begins.

During design time, you may set up the number of times through a **For-Next** loop. Or this number can be determined during run-time but *before* the loop begins. For example, in the Amortization Table program, the number of times the loop executed was determined by the number of payments to be made. You did not know this number when you wrote the program, because it depended on the values entered into the textboxes during run-time. But the number was known before the loop began. The number of payments was the number of years of the loan times 12.

There are situations, however, that require loops, but the number of times the loop is executed is not known before the loop begins. This kind of loop is called an indefinite loop. All modern programming languages provide a way to write these indefinite loops. Visual Basic uses a **Do-Loop** statement.

This program introduces or reviews three topics:

◉ One version of the **Do-Loop** construct

◉ The **InputBox** function

◉ The **MsgBox** statement

The Do-Loop Construct

Look at the loop in Figure 6-18. The two lines following the **Do-While** line will execute so long as *Total* < 1000. While that statement is true, the loop continues. Some calculation or input in the body of the loop signals when this statement becomes false. For an indefinite loop to work, there has to be an action, in the body of the loop, that causes the condition being tested to become false.

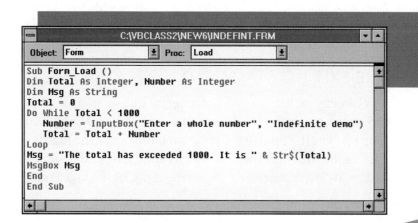

Figure 6-18
Coding an indefinite loop

```
Sub Form_Load ()
Dim Total As Integer, Number As Integer
Dim Msg As String
Total = 0
Do While Total < 1000
    Number = InputBox("Enter a whole number", "Indefinite demo")
    Total = Total + Number
Loop
Msg = "The total has exceeded 1000. It is " & Str$(Total)
MsgBox Msg
End
End Sub
```

As you can see from the figure, the syntax of a **Do-Loop** statement is:
Do While condition
.....Body of the loop (statements to execute as long as condition is true)
Loop

The danger with a **Do-Loop** is never getting out of it. If the condition being tested never becomes false, the loop never ends. For example:

NOTE:

If the condition tested is false, the statements of the loop are not executed even once.

```
Do While 2 < 4
   . . .
Loop
```

The statements represented by the ellipsis (...) can never make 2 > 4. Therefore, the condition is always true. This "runaway loop" condition is known as an infinite loop.

The **Do-Loop** construct is actually more general than the **For-Next** loops that you have already used. The following example shows how to use a **Do-Loop** to achieve the same effect as a **For-Next** loop.

```
x = 1
Do While x <= 100
   . . .
   x = x + 1
Loop
```

The loop above is a replacement for this **For-Next** statement:

```
For x = 1 To 100
   . . .
Next x
```

In this example, the loop starts with $x = 1$ and the condition tests as true. While the loop is executing, the value of x is increased by 1 each time through the loop. Eventually, the value of x is no longer less than or equal to 100 and the condition tests false. When the condition is false, the loop ends.

THE EXIT DO STATEMENT

You can ensure that you do not write infinite loops by including an **Exit Do** statement in the **Do-Loop** construct. This statement interrupts the loop and lets the flow of the program jump out of the loop, even though the condition is still true. To use an **Exit Do** statement, you typically add an **If-Then** statement within the loop. Here's an example:

```
x = 1
Do While 2 < 4
   . . .
   If x > 50 Then Exit Do
x = x + 1
Loop
```

The **If-Then** statement tests the condition **x > 50**. The value of x is incremented within the loop. Even though the condition of the **Do-Loop** is *always* true, when the value of x exceeds 50, the **Exit Do** statement is executed. As a result, the next statement to be executed is the one following the **Loop** statement.

If you have nested **Do-Loop** statements, an **Exit Do** in the inner loop causes the program to jump out of the inner loop to the outer loop. If there are statements following the inner **Loop** statement, those statements are executed.

There are four other significant variations of the **Do-Loop** statement. Future programs use some of these forms. If you can't wait, check the Visual Basic Help system for descriptions of the other forms.

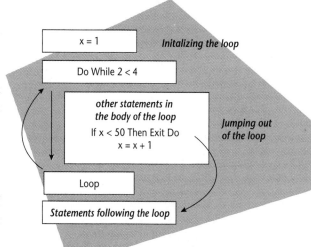

Figure 6-19

Jumping out of an indefinite loop

INDEFINITE LOOPS CONTROLLED BY INPUT

One of the common uses of an indefinite loop is to trigger the end of a series of input operations. When using **InputBox** to collect information from the user, you can designate a special input value with which the user can signal the end of the input process. Such a value, coming at the end of a list of values to signal the end of input, is called a sentinel value.

Here's a sample of code that implements this idea:

```
Msg = "Enter the age <0 to stop>"
Age = InputBox(Msg)
Do While Age<>0
    '—processes data...
    Age = InputBox(Msg)
Loop
```

This loop continues until the value of 0 is entered for the age. This code can be easily adapted for a variety of situations where keyboard data controls the flow of the program.

Sentinel values can also be used to indicate the end data that you read from a file. For example, in a file that contains a list of nonnegative numbers that you read one at a time, you could establish the convention that the value -1 indicates the end of a list.

The InputBox Function

In older versions of Basic, the **Input** statement was the main way to obtain keyboard input from the user. In Visual Basic, textboxes provide the usual means for collecting typed information and displaying it after it has been typed. The **InputBox** function gives an alternative to textboxes.

The syntax of the **InputBox** function is:

variable name = **InputBox** (prompt string, window caption, default value)

The demonstration program shown in Figure 6-22 used an InputBox statement:

```
Sub Form_Load ()
Dim Total As Integer, Number As Integer
Dim Msg As String
Total = 0
Do While Total < 1000
   Number = InputBox("Enter a whole number", "Indefinite demo")
   Total = Total + Number
Loop
Msg = "The total has exceeded 1000. It is " & Str$(Total)
MsgBox Msg
End
End Sub
```

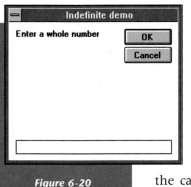

Figure 6-20
InputBox onscreen

Figure 6-21
Inputbox without caption

The **InputBox** function creates a box near the middle of the screen. The caption of the box is given in the second string: "Indefinite demo". The first string is a user prompt: "Enter a whole number". See Figure 6-20 for the result of the **InputBox** statement above.

This example does not make use of the third possible parameter for the function (a default value). If you include a default value, then this value will automatically appear (see Figure 6-21). To accept this value, the user would press the Enter key.

You do not have to include a caption for the box. To omit the caption, leave the spot blank in the parameter list. The commas must appear unless both the caption and the default value are omitted. For example:

```
x = InputBox("Enter a number",,"345")
```

This statement creates the box, displays the prompting message "Enter a number", and provides a default value in the edit space. See Figure 6-21.

The MsgBox Statement

The **MsgBox** statement provides a simple method for displaying information that you do not want the user to overlook. It displays a simple dialog box containing a message that you specify and an OK button. When your program executes a **MsgBox** statement, the user must click the OK button in order to perform any further actions in the program.

Look back at Figure 6-17. According to the code displayed there, a message box will be displayed when *Total* exceeds 1000:

```
Msg = "The total has exceeded 1000. It is " & Str$(Total)
MsgBox Msg
```

The string variable *Msg* is built from a text message and the actual total of the values. It is sent as an argument to the **MsgBox** statement. When this form of the statement is executed, a box appears near the center of the screen displaying the value of *Msg*. (see Figure 6-22). The execution of the program stops until the user clicks OK.

The **MsgBox** statement can take a number of different forms. For more information, take a look at the Msg-Box Function, MsgBox Statement entry in the Visual Basic Help system.

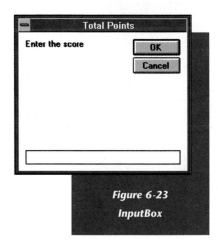

Figure 6-22

Message box on screen, awaiting user response

QUESTIONS AND ACTIVITIES

1. Write the **InputBox** statement that generates the window in Figure 6-22 and assigns the value entered to the variable *Score*.

2. Sketch the **InputBox** window that would result from this statement:

    ```
    Age = InputBox("Enter the age",,"24")
    ```

3. Describe three reasons you might use a message box.

4. What happens if the condition tested in a **Do-While** loop never becomes false?

5. What's wrong with this section of code?

    ```
    index = 0
    Do While index <> 3.7
        ...
        index = index + 0.3
    Loop
    ```

Figure 6-23

InputBox

6. Write **Do-While** loops to replace these **For-Next** loops:

   a)
   ```
   For x = 1 To 25
       . . .
   Next x
   ```

   b)
   ```
   For w = 0.5 To 10 Step 0.1
       . . .
   Next w
   ```

7. Where do you find the **Exit Do** statement, and what does it do?

8. What happens when an **Exit Do** statement is executed from the inner of two nested **Do-While** loops? Draw a diagram to explain your answer.

9. Compare the relative merits of using a textbox or **InputBox** to enter values into a program.

Section 7

The Line Drawing Program

This project uses graphic methods, mouse events, arrays, and binary files to build a simple drawing program. It uses graphics methods and mouse events to build a line drawing program. The coordinates of the endpoints of the lines drawn are stored in arrays. When the drawing is complete, the coordinates are stored in a file. Drawings can be loaded from files.

Starting Out

Before you can build a program that draws circles and lines on a form, you need to explore two methods:

- **Circle** method
- **Line** method

The code for these methods can be placed in several places, including in mouse events. Before you start the Line Drawing program, then, you need to explore the effects of placing the code in different subroutines.

CIRCLE AND LINE METHODS

The **Circle** method is a built-in procedure used to draw circles on an object. The syntax is:

object.**Circle** (x,y),radius

The object, in this case, is the form, a Picture Box control, or the Printer object. The center of the circle is (x,y). X and y are screen coordinates. *Radius* is the radius of the circle. If you omit an object from the syntax, the program draws the circle on the current form.

The **Line** method is a built-in procedure you use to draw lines on an object.

*object.***Line** (x,y)-(x',y')
*object.***Line** -(x,y)

This method draws a line on an object. As is true of the **Circle** method, the object can be a form, a Picture Box control, or the Printer object. If you omit an object, the program draws the line on the current form. The first version of the **Line** method draws a line between (x,y) and (x',y'). The second version draws a line from the last point drawn to (x,y). The coordinates of this last point are saved in the CurrentX and CurrentY properties of the object. When you use the **Circle** method to draw a circle centered at a point (x,y), the last point drawn is set to that point (x,y).

MOUSE EVENTS

A MouseDown event occurs when a user presses a mouse button. A MouseUp event occurs when the user releases a mouse button. The parameters of the event procedure tell you which buttons are pressed or released, as well as the coordinates of the point where the press or release occurred. A MouseMove event occurs when the mouse's position changes. The parameters to the MouseMove event tell you the current coordinates of the mouse cursor.

These three mouse events each have four parameters. In this section, only the last two are important: X As Single, Y As Single. These provide the screen coordinates of the mouse pointer.

The mouse events let you program the mouse with finer control than the Click event gives you. Click events occur after a mouse button is both pressed and released. When the Click event occurs, you are not told the coordinates of the mouse cursor. In the program you are going to write, you will respond to mouse events by saving the mouse cursor coordinates when a mouse button is pressed, saving the coordinates when a button is released, and drawing a straight line between those two points. Clearly, the Click event does not provide enough information to accomplish this.

To experiment with the **Line** and **Circle** methods, follow these steps.

1 Open Visual Basic. If Visual Basic is already open, select New Project from the File menu.

2 Change the caption of the default form to **The Line and Circle Methods**.

3 Double-click on the form to open the Code window.

4 In the Proc drop-down menu, select the MouseDown event.

5 In the Form_MouseDown (...) event procedure, insert the following code. Here, X and Y are parameters of the MouseDown event giving the coordinates of the mouse cursor:

```
Const sglRadius = 50
Circle (X,Y), sglRadius
```

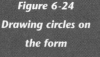

Figure 6-24
Drawing circles on the form

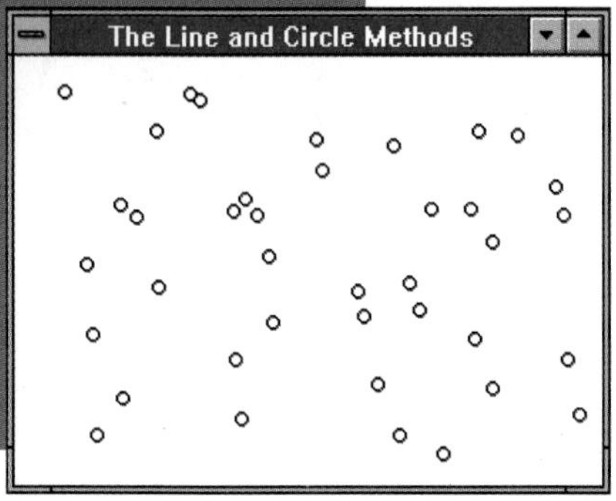

6 Run the program. Move and click the mouse on various spots on the form. Every time you press any mouse button, a small circle appears, centered at the point where you pressed the mouse button (see Figure 6-24). No action is taken in response to releasing mouse buttons or to mouse movement.

7 Stop the program.

Now, you will make the program more general by allowing the user to specify a different radius each time the program is run. The user can enter a new radius, or just accept the default value of 50:

1 Reopen the Code window.

2 Remove **Const sglRadius = 50** from the MouseDown event procedure.

3 Add this line to the MouseDown event:

```
Debug.Print X,Y
```

4 Add this line to the general declarations section of the form:

```
Dim gsglRadius As Single
```

5 Add this code to the Form_Load procedure (select Form from the Object drop-down list and Load from the Proc drop-down list):

```
gsglRadius = Val(InputBox("Enter a value for the radius",,"50"))
```

6 Change the name of the radius variable in the Form_MouseDown event from *sglRadius* to *gsglRadius*, so that the statement that draws the circle looks like this:

```
Circle (X,Y), gsglRadius
```

7 Run the program. An InputBox appears, prompting you to enter a radius. Enter a radius and click OK. Now all the circles that appear will be of that radius.

8 Click on the form in various places. Each time you press a mouse button, a circle appears with the radius you selected.

9 Click on the Debug window. The *X* and *Y* coordinates are displayed of the center of each circle you drew.

10 Stop the program, then run it again. In the InputBox, enter a different radius, and repeat the steps. When you are finished, stop the program.

Now, you will respond to the MouseUp event by using the **Line** method to draw a line between the points at which a mouse button was pressed and released. To do so:

1 Reopen the Code window.

2 Insert this line of code in the MouseUp event procedure:

```
Line -(X,Y)
```

3 Run the program. Enter a radius, as prompted.

4 Press a mouse button. Due to the instructions in the MouseDown event, the **Circle** method draws a circle on the form with the radius you entered, centered at the point where you pressed the button.

5 Now, press a mouse button *and drag* before you release the mouse button. The **Circle** method draws a circle due to the MouseDown event. When you release the mouse button, a MouseUp event occurs. As a result, the instructions in that event procedure are executed and a line appears.

6 Stop the program.

7 Save the project and form files.

If you press and then release a mouse button without moving the mouse, a line is still drawn. However, the beginning and endpoints of the line are identical, so the line is not visible.

Setting Up the Form

Setting up the appearance of this simple drawing program is easy. As you can see in Figure 6-25, you need a menu bar with a single entry (File). This menu opens a drop-down list of four commands. There are no buttons or other objects on the form.

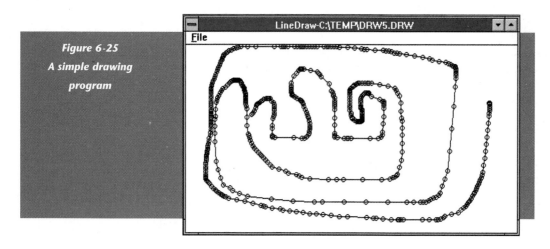

Figure 6-25
A simple drawing program

To set up the form:

1 Create a directory to store the Line Drawing project.

2 Start Visual Basic, or choose New Project from the File menu.

3 Change the caption of the form to **LineDraw**. Change the name of the form to **frmDrawLine**. Change the AutoRedraw property of the form to True. This redraws the contents of the form after a dialog box has appeared and vanished from the form, erasing part of its contents.

Figure 6-26
File menu

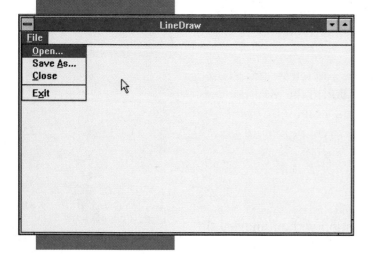

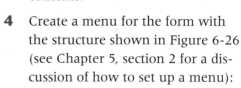

4 Create a menu for the form with the structure shown in Figure 6-26 (see Chapter 5, section 2 for a discussion of how to set up a menu):

Entering Code: Stage 1

Now, add the following code and test the program:

1 In the general declarations section of the form, put the following statements:

```
Option Explicit
Dim gfDrawing As Integer
```

The *gfDrawing* variable is used as a flag. For more detail on flags, see the textbox.

2   Open the form's MouseDown event Code window and enter the code:

```
gfDrawing = True   '—used by MouseMove handler
Circle (X,Y),50
'—Set form's CurrentX, CurrentY properties
CurrentX = X
CurrentY = Y
```

The CurrentX and CurrentY properties provide coordinates used by the next drawing method. The **Line** method uses these coordinates as the first point of a line. True is a constant in Visual Basic equal to -1.

3   Run the program.

4   Press and release a mouse button on the form several times. The **Circle** method draws a circle every time a MouseDown event occurs. That circle has a radius of 50.

5   Stop the program.

6   Save the project and form files in the directory created from the project.

The changes you just made have produced a less complex program than you had before. You have laid the foundation for the next stage, in which you use the flag *gfDrawing* to determine whether or not to draw anything. In the next section, you will clear the *gfDrawing* flag in the MouseUp event. You will also draw in the MouseMove event, only if the flag is set.

Entering Code: Stage 2

This section adds the code that draws the images. You'll find the code surprisingly simple. The **Line** and **Circle** methods are used. Nothing at all is drawn if the flag, *gfDrawing*, is set to **False**.

1   Enter the following code in the MouseMove event procedure:

```
If gfDrawing Then
   Line -(X,Y)
   Circle (X,Y),50
End If
```

FLAGS

A flag is a variable used as a signal in a program. A flag may be True or False, on or off, or yes or no. Flags are set to show conditions. If the flag is set, the condition is True, on, or yes. Flags are used in If-Then statements. They are usually global variables (of Integer type), which are set and cleared in certain procedures to signal that some condition does or does not hold true. The flag is then tested in other procedures, and actions are taken depending on the state of the flag. A common example is the use of a flag to indicate whether a mouse button is down or not.

In this exercise, the variable's prefix, *gf*, indicates that the variable is visible to any procedure in the form. Visual Basic does not automatically make the variable global because of the "g" in the prefix. You made it global by placing it within the general declarations area of the form. When you use the variable in an event procedure, its prefix makes it easy to remember that you are using a global variable. The "f" portion of the prefix indicates that the variable contains a flag.

2   Enter the following code in the MouseUp event procedure:

```
gfDrawing = False
```

3   Enter the following command in the mnuExit_Click() event procedure:

```
End
```

4   Run the program. Press a button, drag, and release the button. Also try pressing and releasing buttons without dragging.

5   Stop the program, then save the project and form files.
The **Circle** method draws a circle whenever either a MouseMove or MouseDown event occurs. You don't, however, get a Mouse-Move event for every point that the mouse moves over. The faster you move the mouse, the more sparse the circles become.

Entering Code: Stage 3

Your next task is to deal with file input/output (i/o). Suppose, for example, that the user of your program has created a drawing and now wants to save it. How do you save a drawing?

Remember the list of x and y coordinates you saw displayed in the Debug window? You can identify lines by the x and y coordinates of their endpoints. You can identify circles by the x and y coordinates of their centers. Therefore, you need to set up two arrays, one to record x coordinates and one to record y coordinates. Procedures can then save the lists of coordinates to a file and read lists of coordinates from files. After reading a list of coordinates from a file, the drawing that those coordinates describe can be recreated.

To set up an array, you need to pick a maximum number of entries. In this program, you use two arrays, both of the same size. An adequate number for the maximum number of entries is 2000.

As you work through these steps, you will also experiment with creating procedures that are not linked to particular events. One of these procedures (Sub DrawCircle) replaces calls to the **Circle** method in the MouseDown event. In addition to drawing circles, this procedure saves coordinates in the arrays.

To create the arrays:

1   Add the following lines to the general declarations section.

```
Const gnMaxPoints = 3000      ' gn = global number
'-gsng = global single
Dim gsngX(1 To gnMaxPoints) As Single
Dim gsngY(1 To gnMaxPoints) As Single
```

```
'—Actual number of points recorded
Dim gnNumPoints As Integer
'—gstr = global string
Const gstrTitle = "LineDraw"
```

2   Create a new procedure by entering the following lines in the general section:

```
Sub DrawCircle (X As Single, Y As Single)
'—Draw the circle
    Circle (X, Y), 50
'—Too many points?
    If gnNumPoints < gnMaxPoints Then
'—Add one more point
        gnNumPoints = gnNumPoints + 1
'—Save X and Y coordinates
        gsngX(gnNumPoints) = X
        gsngY(gnNumPoints) = Y
    End If
End Sub
```

3   In the MouseDown and the MouseMove procedures, replace

```
Circle (X,Y),50
```

with

```
DrawCircle X,Y
```

4   In the Form_Load procedure, enter the following line:

```
gnNumPoints = 0
```

5   Select mnuClose from the **Object** drop-down list in the Code window. In the mnuClose_Click procedure, enter the following code.

```
gnNumPoints = 0
frmDrawLine.Cls
frmDrawLine.Caption = gstrTitle
```

6   Select mnuSaveAs from the Object drop-down list. In the mnuSaveAs_Click procedure, enter the following code.

```
'—Collect filename from user
Dim strFn As String
strFn = UCase$(Trim$(InputBox("Filename", "OpenFile")))
'—Open binary file for output
Open strFn For Binary Access Write As #1
'—Save actual number of points
```

PROCEDURES AND FUNCTIONS

Procedures and functions not linked to particular events can be included in a form module or a code module. To start a new procedure, you can select New Procedure from the View menu. Then, you choose Sub or Function and supply a name.

Another option is to open the general declarations section of a form's code. Under the declarations, enter the top line of the new procedure. As soon as you press Enter at the end of that line, Visual Basic creates the procedure, automatically adding the last line (End Sub). (To see any declarations in the general declarations area, you now have to select declarations from the Proc drop-down list.) Visual Basic will now list this procedure in the Proc list.

continued

```
Put #1, , gnNumPoints
'—Local variable for loop
Dim i As Integer
'—Loop to actual number of points
For i = 1 To gnNumPoints
   '—Save coordinates
   Put #1, , gsngX(i)
   Put #1, , gsngY(i)
Next i
Close #1
'—Reset form caption
frmDrawLine.Caption = gstrTitle & "-" & strFn
```

7 The Open command collects the coordinates of the points and loads those coordinates in two arrays. Once the points are loaded, the DrawLines procedure draws the lines and circles. In the general section of the form, enter the following code.

```
Sub DrawLines ()
   Dim i As Integer
   CurrentX = gsngX(1)
   CurrentY = gsngY(1)
   '—Draw the first circle
   Circle (gsngX(1), gsngY(1)), 50
   '—Plot the rest of the lines and circles
   For i = 2 To gnNumPoints
      Line -(gsngX(i), gsngY(i))
      Circle (gsngX(i), gsngY(i)), 50
   Next i
End Sub
```

8 Select mnuOpen from the Object drop-down list. In the mnuOpen_Click procedure, enter the following code.

```
'—Collect filename from user
Dim strFn As String
strFn = UCase$(Trim$(InputBox("Filename", "OpenFile")))
'—Open binary file for input
Open strFn For Binary Access Read As #1
'—Save actual number of points
Get #1, , gnNumPoints
'—Local variable for loop
Dim i As Integer
'—Loop to actual number of points
```

```
For i = 1 To gnNumPoints
'—Collect coordinates from file
   Get #1, , gsngX(i)
   Get #1, , gsngY(i)
Next i
Close #1
'—Reset form caption
frmDrawLine.Caption = gstrTitle & "-" & strFn
frmDrawLine.Cls
DrawLines
```

9 Run the program. Click and drag, then release.

10 Choose Save As from the File menu. Supply a complete pathname.

11 Choose Close from the File menu.

12 Choose Open from the File menu. Supply the same complete pathname.

The code for Open is almost identical to the code for Save As. Get is substituted for Put. At the end of the routine, the form is cleared and the circles and points are drawn with the DrawLines procedure.

Finishing the Program

Now, use the program:

1 Experiment with drawing, saving, opening, and closing.

2 Stop the program.

3 Save the project and form files.

4 Choose Make EXE File to create a stand-alone application.

QUESTIONS AND ACTIVITIES

1. Comment out the **Circle** statement from MouseDown, DrawCircle, and DrawLines. Run the program and observe the effect. Restore the **Circle** statements.

2. Change the declaration for *strFn* from local to global. Move the **Dim** statement to general declarations. Initialize *strFn* in the Form_Load procedure to "". Rewrite the **InputBox** functions to use *strFn* as a default value.

3. Although drawing starts and stops in response to mouse events, once they are saved and reloaded, the breaks between the connected lines are lost. Currently there is no record of where drawing

stops and starts. Modify the MouseUp event procedure to record coordinates (-1,-1) when the mouse button is released. Modify DrawLines to stop drawing when the (-1,-1) coordinates are encountered.

Summary

The **Format$** function converts values into strings according to certain fixed patterns or according to patterns you provide. The syntax is:

variable = **Format$**(*value, format string*)

Visual Basic shares code through

- Custom controls
- Code modules

To use a custom control, you must place the control's VBX file in the System folder of Windows. Visual Basic will add the filename to the project file list that is displayed in the Project window. You can place procedures you want available to more than one form in a code module.

The scope of a variable is determined by its visibility and lifetime. Visibility is a question of what procedures can use (or "see") a variable. The lifetime of a variable depends on whether the value of the variable is available apart from the limited lifetime of an event procedure. A variable declared and used in one event procedure is not available in another. Variables declared in the form module are available to all event procedures within the form. Variables declared with the **Global** statement in a code module are available to any form in the project and its event procedures.

A static variable, declared within an event procedure, isn't available to other procedures, but its value does persist beyond the end of the procedure in which it is declared. When the procedure is reentered, the static variable is there, with its old value, available for use.

The **Option Explicit** statement is entered in the general declarations section of either a form module or a code module. By using this statement, you require that each variable be declared before use.

You use arrays so that you can save a list of values. The list has a single name. Each element of the list has a unique whole number subscript. For instance, an array of names can be declared as follows:

```
Dim Names(100) As String
```

Another way to declare the same array:

```
Const MaxNames = 100
Dim gstrNames(1 To MaxNames) As String
```

Using 1 To MaxNames lets the programmer specify the starting subscript and use a constant as a maximum subscipt. Using a constant makes it easy to change the references to that value throughout the program with a single change.

The first characters of the name, *gstr*, shows the data type of the variable. The prefix *g* indicates the variable is global; the *str* shows that the variable contains strings.

The backslash (\) operator divides two numbers and gives the whole number result.

Scrollbars can be used to provide a subscript value to access the elements of an array.

The **Do-Loop** statement, one of a number of indefinite loop statements, allows a loop to execute an indefinite number of times. The number of times the loop is executed is controlled by factors within the loop. A sentinel-controlled loop continues until a certain value, called a sentinel, is entered or generated. The syntax of this statement is:

> **Do While** *condition*
>> *statements to execute while condition is true*
>
> **Loop**

The **InputBox** function allows the entry of values without textboxes. The syntax is:

> *variable* = **InputBox** *(Prompt, Caption, Default value)*

Prompt is a string containing the instruction to the user. *Caption* is the caption of the window. *Default value* is a string representing a default value for the variable. If a user presses Enter without changing the default value, this value is assigned to the variable.

Problems

1. The How-Long-in-School Problem

Write a program using textboxes for input, prompting the user to enter the number of hours a day spent in school and the number of daylight hours in a day. Calculate and display the percentage of daylight time spent in school. Use the **Format$** function to display the percentage.

2.   The Sales Tax Problem

Write a program using InputBoxes to enter the amount of a purchase and the percentage sales tax charged. In Illinois the sales tax is 6.25%. You would enter that percentage as 6.25, omitting the percentage sign. Using the Currency and Percent format strings, display the original amount of the purchase (as currency), the sales tax percentage, the sales tax charged (as currency), and the total price including sales tax (as currency).

3. **The Running Total Problem**
Put a textbox on a form. This box is used to enter values. The values are added together. Declare a Single type variable, *RunningTotal*, in the general declarations section of the form. In the KeyPress event of the textbox, when KeyAscii is 13 (the user presses Enter), convert the string in the textbox to a number, and add it to *RunningTotal*. Place a single command button on the form. The button, when pressed, puts a label on the form containing the running total.

4. **The Random Number Program**
Rnd is a built-in function that returns a random single value between 0 and 1. Write a program with an indefinite loop to enter values generated by **Rnd** into a listbox on a form, until a value greater than 0.95 is generated.

5. **The Baby-Sitting Problem**
A season pass to a theme park is $65. Write a program using an Input-Box to enter amounts of money earned baby-sitting. Keep a running total of the amounts entered, and count the number of jobs. When the total amount exceeds $65, display the amount saved and the number of jobs it took.

6. **The Screen Coordinate Problem**
Write a program that will display the values of *x* and *y*, the parameters sent to the MouseDown event, when the mouse is clicked on a form. Use two labels near the bottom of the form to display the values for *x* and *y*.

7. **The Indefinite Average Problem**
Write a program to enter a list of test scores with an InputBox, display them in a listbox, count them, keep a running total (as they are entered), and display the current average as each number is entered. Use these variables: *Total, Cnt, Average, Score,* and *Finish*. The first two are to keep your running total and count the number of entries. *Cnt* should be an Integer, but *Total* could be an Integer, a Single, or left as a Variant type. The *Average* and *Score* should be Single, and *Finish* should be an Integer, which is the type used to represent **True** and **False**. Use *Finish* as a condition to end the loop.

The structure of the loop should be:

```
Finish = False
   ...
Do While Not Finish
   ...
Loop
```

Finish should be set to true when a score of 0 is entered from the InputBox.

When the *Score* entered is not 0, it should be added to the listbox, counted, and added to the running total. The average should be calculated and displayed in a textbox.

8.   The Goldbach Conjecture

Take any positive number. If it is even, divide it by 2. If it is odd, multiply by 3 and add 1. It is conjectured that for any positive number, the sequence of numbers generated by this rule ends in 1. For instance, if the number is 7, we have the following sequence:

7 22 11 34 17 52 26 13 40 20 10 5 16 8 4 2 1

Write a program to use an InputBox to collect a number from the keyboard. Use a multiline textbox or a listbox to display the terms of the sequence. Because the length of the sequence is unknown, use an indefinite loop (a **Do-Loop**) to control the flow of the program.

9.   The Shopping Problem

Write a program to help a shopper know when to stop. Prompt the user for an amount to spend. This is your base amount. Enter the amounts of the shopper's purchases and subtract from the base amount until the amount entered, if subtracted, would cause the base amount to be negative. Display the purchase amount that broke the bank and display the current base amount.

10. The Overloaded Circuit Problem

Most household electrical circuits are designed to handle about 15 amps of current. Write a program to allow the user to enter the amperage requirements of appliances, display the values in a listbox, maintain a running total, and display a warning message if the total exceeds 15 amps.

11. The Length of a Loan Problem

Write a program to enter a loan amount, a yearly interest rate, and a monthly payment. Use a **Do-Loop** to calculate the monthly interest, add that amount to the unpaid balance, and subtract the monthly payment until the unpaid balance is 0. The program should count the number of monthly payments required to pay off the loan and display that result. The monthly interest is the amount of the loan balance times the monthly interest rate. The monthly interest rate is the yearly interest rate divided by 12.

nColor

nColor

ine (nWidth

4 + 3,

or +

(nWidth/2, y +

30),

QBColor(nColor

Mod 16), B

Graphics

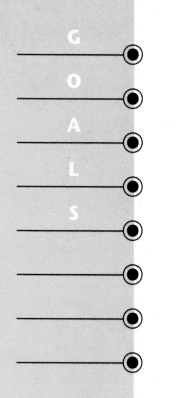

G
O
A
L
S

After working through this chapter, you will be able to:

Understand and use the typesetting and computer display concepts associated with monitor and hardcopy displays.

Describe and use the various built-in coordinate systems provided in the SetMode property of the picture box and the form object.

Initialize and use user-defined coordinate systems appropriate to application programs.

Use the **PSet** method to draw points whose coordinates are stored in an array.

Use the **Line** method to draw lines.

Use the **Circle** method to draw circles and ellipses of various size at various positions.

Use the color functions of Visual Basic.

O V E R V I E W

In this chapter you will see that the "Visual" in "Visual Basic" doesn't just refer to the programming environment. You will use picture boxes and graphics commands to help programs communicate. You will learn about coordinate systems, experiment with color, and draw shapes on forms.

Pixels and Twips

Graphics are images, including everything from line drawings to video clips and animation. Adding graphics to your programs makes them fun to run and visually appealing. People like to see moving objects on the screen, so videos and animation hold a special fascination.

Graphics have an educational purpose as well, because you can use them to convey information quickly. The old adage "a picture is worth a thousand words" is not far from the truth.

To use graphics in Visual Basic, you need to understand pixels and twips. And to understand these terms, you need to look back at how graphic systems have evolved. Graphic systems are the hardware and software used to create and present graphics. Until quite recently, these systems were not powerful enough to display crisp images or videos on screen.

Evolving Graphics Systems

Pixels are the building blocks of everything you see on screen – text as well as graphics. The term "pixel" is short for picture element. It is the smallest graphic element of a display on screen. If you look at your computer's display from a short distance—say, less than 1 foot—you can see individual pixels distinctly. In Figure 7-1, a single pixel has been removed from the dot of the letter i. The pixel is small enough that you would not notice the missing pixel unless the words were magnified.

Figure 7-1
Missing Pixel

The graphical capability of a machine is measured by counting the number, size, and range of colors of the pixels that are displayed on the screen, as well as the speed at which the screen can be redrawn. These capabilities are determined mostly by the video card installed in the machine and the monitor on which the card's output appears. The CPU and the architecture of the machine itself affect only the speed of redrawing. The number of pixels—also called the resolution—determines the amount of detail that that can be shown, and the smoothness of lines.

For example, imagine that only a very small number of pixels could be displayed: not much information could be shown. With such a low resolution, only horizontal and vertical lines would look smooth; all other straight lines, and all curves, would appear jagged. The size of the pixels is determined by the resolution, together with the capabilities of the monitor. If the monitor displays pixels that are too big, they "bleed" into each other and give the image a blurry appearance with inaccurate colors.

The number of possible colors that a pixel can have determines the realism of the displayed images. The greater the possible number of colors, the more photographic are the images that can be displayed. With only 16 colors, photographs cannot be accurately represented. However, 256 colors are sufficient for displaying convincing real-world images. The number of colors offered by current video cards ranges from 16 to 16.7 million. Most cards let you select from among several combinations of resolution and number of colors.

EARLY MACHINES

The earliest computers were primarily "text only," so the number of pixels did not matter so much. People used computers to perform tasks like word processing, writing payroll checks, and deciphering codes. "Graphics" was a term used in art studios, not computer rooms. A few systems tried to use graphic displays for serious work, with poor results.

Yesterday's computers were too slow to manipulate graphic images. The more pixels the system could display, the more work it had to do. You cannot display graphics if the system is so slow that you can type faster than the computer can respond.

As computers have become more powerful, graphical capability has improved. Computers today have more and smaller pixels, more colors, and the ability to move large amounts of graphic information in very short times. The screen on a typical home computer today displays anywhere from 640 by 480 pixels to 1024 by 768 pixels or more. Years ago, 256 by 192 seemed like a lot of pixels.

TODAY, THE TWIP

All graphics systems are based on pixels because the pixel is the smallest hardware element of a display screen. The pixel, then, is still the building block used to create images. Now that computers can handle graphics, however, variations in pixel count and color matter more than before. An image could look great on an artist's computer, for example, with a high-resolution monitor. On a monitor with far fewer pixels, though, that same image could look too small, too large, too blurry, or too plain.

You can also see that this variation presents some difficulty to you as a programmer. Suppose that you write code to draw a 30-pixel line on the screen. This line would appear longer on some screens, shorter on other ones. Without a standard number of pixels per screen, you cannot use the pixel as the basis for a drawing system.

The answer is a "logical" rather than a physical basis for a graphics system. This is the twip. For Visual Basic, the twip is the default standard measure of graphic elements. To a lot of people who have grown up with computers, the term "twip" sounds like a new, made-up word. Twips, however, have been around for a very long time.

When mechanical printing was the norm, type was set using metal blocks, each with a raised letter. The blocks were set in troughs, words separated with spacing blocks, lines separated with long thin spaces called slugs. The trays of letters were inked and pressed against paper.

An extensive vocabulary grew up around the printing presses—a vocabulary still used today, even though most of the old presses are gone. Some of these old words have already been used in the text; font is one of them. Two other words from the old printing press days are points and twips.

Fonts, Points, and Twips

A font is a style of type. When you choose a font, you also choose the size of the font. That size is designated in points. A printer's point, equal to 1/72 of an inch, is the standard of measure for fonts. See Figure 7-2 for an example of fonts and font sizes. A twip is a twentieth of a point. (In fact, "twip" is an abbreviation of the phrase "twentieth of a point.") Thus, there are 1440 twips in one inch. A 12-point font is 12 points x 20 twips/point, or 240 twips high.

When a program draws a straight line of 1440 twips on a printed page, the length of the line is precisely 1 inch. The same line drawn on the screen will typically be longer than 1 inch. The line on the screen measures 1 logical inch. The logical inch is the size of the screen representation of images that occupy 1 inch on a printed page. You may have noticed that programs such as Microsoft Word and Windows Write display a ruler along the top of your documents. These rulers allow you to set margins, columns, and tab stops so that pages will have the appearance you want. However, if you were to measure 1 "inch" as indicated by one of these on-screen rulers, you would find that its length is somewhat longer than 1 inch. (Exactly how long it is depends on the screen resolution you are using.)

The logical inch magnifies physical inches. Without this magnification, point sizes that we commonly use for printing would be unusably

Courier, 10 point

Meridien regular, 11 point

Meridien bold italic, 12 point

Stone sans bold, 16 point

Stone sans regular, 18 point

Industria inline, 24 point

Figure 7-2
Different fonts and
font sizes

small on the screen. Two factors determine the need for on-screen magnification. The first is that we typically view computer monitors from a distance of about 2 feet, whereas we view printed pages at somewhat closer range. The second is that the resolution of the printed page is vastly higher than that of a computer screen. Laser printers print anywhere from 300 to 1200 dpi (dots per inch), and high-quality magazines are printed at resolutions of 2400 dpi and higher. By contrast, there are usually only 96 pixels per logical inch in both the horizontal and vertical dimensions of a screen.

When an image is displayed, Windows still translates twips to pixels. The Screen object in Visual Basic has two read-only properties, TwipsPerPixelX and TwipsPerPixelY, which tell you precisely how the translation is performed. The translation adjusts the final image to maintain the proportions of the original image. The actual adjustment made—the number of pixels per logical inch, in both the vertical and the horizontal dimension—depends on the graphics system. A system with fewer pixels across the screen translates the image differently than a system with more pixels.

In other words, by measuring in twips, you can now instruct a program to draw a line of a specific length. The line will be that length, regardless of the number of pixels displayed on the user's monitor.

QUESTIONS AND ACTIVITIES

1. List some applications that can operate without graphics.

2. List some applications that require graphics.

3. What is a pixel?

4. What is a twip? How big is a twip? Where does the word "twip" come from?

5. What is a font?

6. What is a point? How big is a point? Where does the word point come from?

7. How has the increased speed of computers changed the nature of computer applications over the years?

8. Windows uses two quantities, LOGPIXELSX and LOGPIXELSY, to determine how to scale physical lengths in each dimension for display on the screen. These are the number of pixels per logical inch, in each dimension. Write Visual Basic code that uses **Screen**.TwipsPerPixelX and **Screen**.TwipsPerPixelY to compute these numbers and print them on a form.

Picture Box and Image Box

Section

You have already experimented with drawing freehand in a form. In the previous chapter, you placed circles and lines on a form. You can also import images into a Visual Basic form. These images may have been created in another Windows application. Or you may want to take advantage of images such as clipart that are available publicly.

To import images into a form, you need to place them in a control. Visual Basic provides two controls for this purpose: a picture box and an image box. As you experiment with these two controls in this section, you will see that they have slightly different properties. You can stretch and distort a picture in an image box, for example. You cannot do that with the same picture in a picture box.

Before importing images, you should become familiar with the different types of graphics files. You can tell the type of file from the file extension. Three of the common types of files have these extensions:

- **.bmp** (bitmap)
- **.ico** (icon)
- **.wmf** (Word metafile)

A bitmap is a graphic image stored as a collection of pixels. The pixels are represented in memory as bits or collections of bits. An icon is a small graphic usually used to represent a concept or object. It is limited in size to 32 by 32 pixels. A metafile saves a graphic image as a collection of drawing objects: lines, circles, and colors.

You can find bitmap, icon, and metafiles in the Windows, MSOffice, and VB directories. You should also check your directories for collections of clipart and other graphics.

Importing Images into Visual Basic Controls

Follow these steps to explore the picture box and image box controls.

1   Start Visual Basic. If Visual Basic is running, choose New Project from the File menu.

2   Change the caption of the form to **The Picture and Image Box Demo**.

3   Click on the picture box icon in the Toolbox.

4   Draw the picture box on the form. Click where you want the top-left corner of the box, then drag to the lower-right corner. See Figure 7-3.

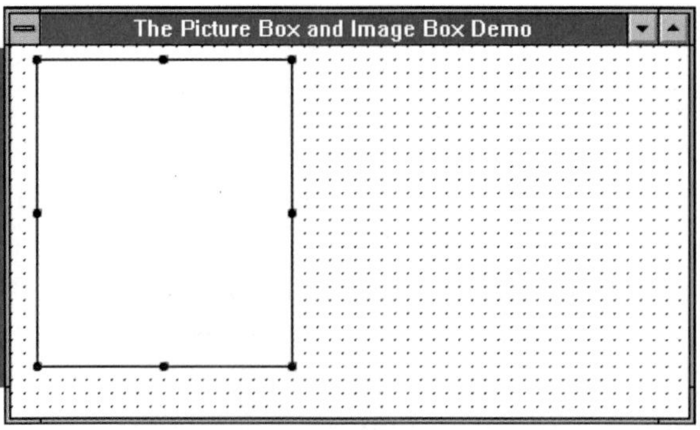

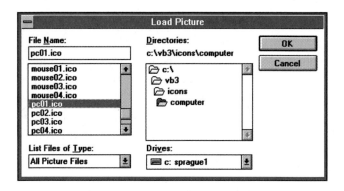

Figure 7-3

Placing a picture box on the form

5 Click on the image box icon in the Toolbox.

6 Draw an image box on the form using the same method as in step 4.

7 To insert an icon or bitmap into a picture box, select the picture box, then bring the Properties window to the front. Double-click on the Picture property of the box. The Load Picture dialog box opens (see Figure 7-4).

This figure shows the computer subdirectory of the icons directory in the Visual Basic directory.

Figure 7-4

Load Picture dialog box, for selecting a graphic to insert in the picture box

8 Select a file. The graphic is then displayed in the picture box. Press Enter or click OK.

In this example, we selected the icon file **pc01.ico**, as shown in Figure 7-4 above. It is shown displayed in Figure 7-5. Feel free to pick a different file, such as

\VB\bitmaps\assorted\happy.bmp.

9 Select the image box, then bring the Properties window to the front. Double-click on the Picture property. Add the same graphic to the image box.

The boundaries of the image box shrink to fit the icon.

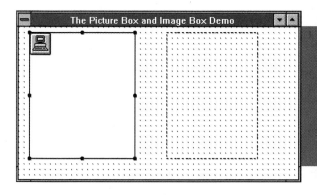

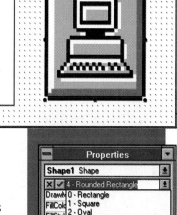

Figure 7-5
Displaying a graphic in
the picture box

Figure 7-6
Stretching a graphic in
an image box

Experimenting with the Images: Stage 1

With the pictures loaded, you are ready to experiment with the properties of the two different controls:

1   Select the image box. Change the Stretch property of the image box to True.

2   Try resizing the image box several times. The icon stretches to fill the box. For an example, see Figure 7-6.

3   Click on the shape control in the Toolbox and draw the shape on the picture box. Click on the upper-left corner and drag to the lower-right corner.
    Shapes and lines can be drawn in a picture box, but not in an image box.

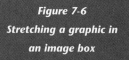

4   With the shape selected, look in the Properties window. The choices for the Shape property of the shape are shown in Figure 7-7.

5   Choose the option called 4-Rounded Rectangle.

6   Move the rounded rectangle so it partially covers the icon in the upper-left corner of the picture box. See Figure 7-8.

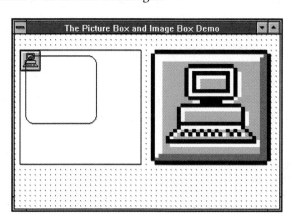

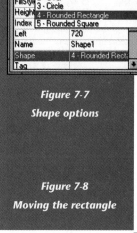

Figure 7-7
Shape options

Figure 7-8
Moving the rectangle

7 Use the shape tool to draw a square within the confines of the image box. Resize the image box. Reposition the image box. Is the square a part of the image box?

8 Select the shape drawn and delete it.

Experimenting with the Images: Stage 2

Now change the images and experiment some more:

1 Select the picture box. Double-click on the Picture property and find the metafile directory in the Visual Basic directory. Select the business subdirectory, then click on a filename and press Enter, or click OK. The image will fill the picture box.

2 Add a different drawing to the image box and note the difference between it and the picture box.

3 Add a drawing to the form itself. The form also has a Picture property. Metafiles are good backgrounds for your forms. See Figure 7-9.

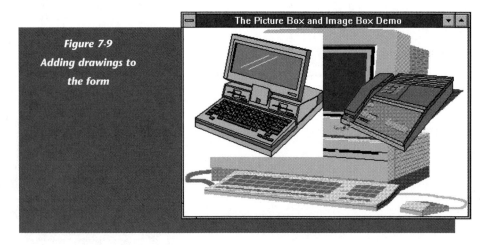

Figure 7-9

Adding drawings to the form

4 Remove the metafile from the form by selecting the Picture property of the form, clicking on the edit area, and pressing the Delete key. The Picture property value changes from (Metafile) to (none).

5 Click on the command button icon in the Toolbox. Click and drag to place the command button in the picture box (see Figure 7-10). (Double-clicking on the command button icon, then moving the button into the picture box will not work.)

6 Select the picture box. Drag the box to a different position within the form. Note the movement of the command button.

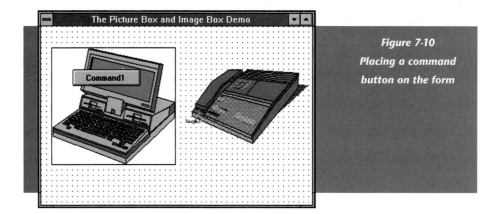

Figure 7-10
Placing a command
button on the form

7 Draw a second command button within the boundary of the image box.

8 Select the image box and move it to a different part of the form. The command button does not move.

Reviewing the Boxes

What have you learned from experimenting with these controls? You can import a bitmap, an icon, or a metafile for display in a picture box. Except for the metafile, you cannot change the size of the imported image by stretching or shrinking it to fit the dimensions of the box. You will display only part of the image if that image is larger than the picture box.

The picture box can act as a container for other controls from the Toolbox. Command buttons, labels, and other controls become part of the picture box when they are drawn within the borders of the box. Text can be printed in the box.

You can use the shape control and line control to draw shapes and lines on a picture box or form. You can combine shapes, colors, patterns, and borders to create many different results.

The image box can display the same kind of graphics files as a picture box: bitmaps, icons, or metafiles. If you set the Stretch property of the image box to True, the image will fill the box, regardless of the box's size or the kind of image. Controls cannot be drawn in the box, nor can text be printed.

Typically, programmers use the picture box for plotting points and as a container for controls, images, and printed text. The image box is used just to hold graphic images, particularly if those images need to be sized. The buttons in a Window's toolbar are image boxes. The container holding the buttons is a picture box.

Coordinate Systems Display Program

Section 3

To draw or position graphics accurately, you need coordinate systems. Coordinate systems let you define each position on a screen with absolute accuracy. You can plot points, for example, by identifying the coordinates for that point. A point's coordinates include the row number and the column number for that point. Often, these row and column numbers are in pixels, but they do not have to be.

Visual Basic provides seven different built-in coordinate systems based on different units. Having this number of coordinate systems gives you a great deal of flexibility in the display of images.

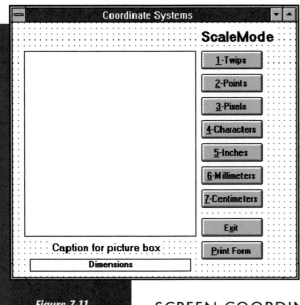

This program uses each of the built-in coordinate systems to draw points in a picture box. The program uses a picture box to display grids of dots, each drawn using a different built-in coordinate system. One command button is used to draw the grid for each coordinate system. The finished form is shown in Figure 7-11.

Starting Out

Before you start building the form, you need to spend some time considering screen coordinate systems. Also, you will need some new methods to build this program.

Figure 7-11
Finished Coordinate
Systems project

SCREEN COORDINATES

Pixels are arranged on the screen in rows and columns. The pixel in the top-left corner of the screen is in the zeroth row and the zeroth column. Rows are counted from top to bottom.

The first number of the screen coordinate is the column number, or *x* value, of the pixel. The second number is its row number, or *y* value. (see Figure 7-12).

Figure 7-12
Screen coordinates

You have already learned why it is awkward to use pixels as the basis for a screen coordinate system. Different screen displays have different numbers of pixels per row or per inch. Programmers now primarily use logical coordinate systems instead.

A logical coordinate system is any system other than pixels. If a coordinate system based on inches designates the length of a line as 1 inch, the line will be 1 logical inch long regardless of the number of pixels per row or per inch. The computer still makes the translation back to pixels, but this is done automatically.

You will be familiar with many of the coordinate systems in Table 7-1. It's not difficult to visualize an *x* and *y* axis marked off at 1-inch intervals or at 10-centimeter intervals. You have used these types of measurement before.

Measurements made using some of these coordinate systems do not provide the same result on different monitors. Forms using a coordinate system based on inches, for example, will be physically smaller on a 14-inch monitor than they are on a 21-inch monitor. Nevertheless, if both monitors are displaying the same resolution, the number of pixels that the form occupies will be the same on each monitor.

Table 7-1. Seven Coordinate Systems

ScaleMode	Coordinate system	Description
1	Twips	1440 per inch
2	Points	72 per inch
3	Pixels	The smallest unit of screen resolution
4	Characters	When printed, a character is $\frac{1}{6}$ of an inch high and $\frac{1}{12}$ of an inch wide.
5	Inches	
6	Millimeters	
7	Centimeters	

The twip coordinate system is the default for all Visual Basic objects. When the form itself is selected (so that its properties appear in the Properties window), the dimensions of the form, expressed in twips, are displayed on the Visual Basic tool bar (see Figure 7-13). If you move the form, or resize the form, the values change.

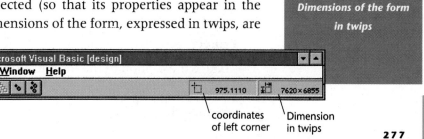

Figure 7-13
Dimensions of the form in twips

coordinates of left corner

Dimension in twips

The coordinates of the left corner of the form are also displayed. The numbers asssume that the upper-left corner of the screen is the coordinate (0,0).

THE SCALEMODE PROPERTY

You can select a coordinate system for a picture box using the box's ScaleMode property. As you can see in Figure 7-14, Visual Basic automatically gives you a choice of all seven coordinate systems. Double-click to cycle through the choices. When you first open the Properties window for the picture box, you will see the twip system selected for this property. Twips are the default coordinate system for Visual Basic.

The code for the command buttons in this project changes the value of the picture box's ScaleMode property. The command buttons are named for the different coordinate systems. The command button for inches, for example, changes the value of the ScaleMode property to 5-Inch.

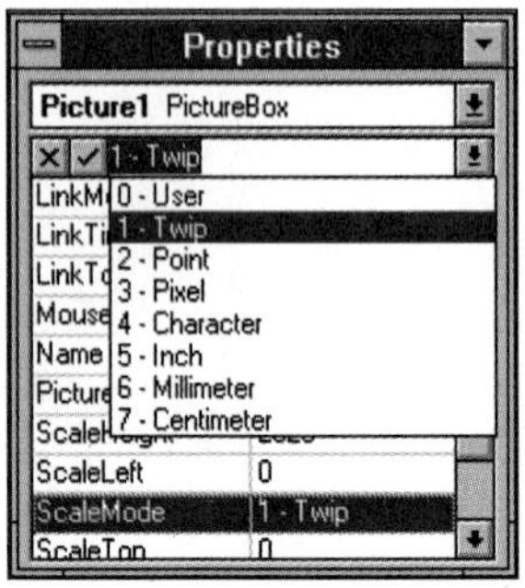

Figure 7-14

Choosing a coordinate system for a picture box

THE PSET METHOD

The program places dots in the picture box to create a grid. The dots are spaced according to which coordinate system you have chosen. Looking at the grid of dots, you can then visualize the differences between the coordinate systems.

To place the dots in the picture box, you need the **PSet** method. This method takes coordinate and color information and places dots on the screen. The simplified syntax for this method is:

object.**PSet** (x,y), *color*

Object is the name of the object, a picture box or a form; (x,y) are the screen coordinates of the point; and color is the color of the point to be plotted. If color is omitted, the point is plotted using the foreground color of the object.

Building the Form

Now that you have the background you need, you are ready to build the form:

1   Start Visual Basic. If Visual Basic is already running, select **New Project** from the **File** menu.

2   Change the caption of the form to **Coordinate Systems**.

3   Draw a picture box in the left two-thirds of the form. Name the box **picGrid**. Set the DrawWidth property to 2. This property determines the size of points and lines drawn on the control.

4 Place eight command buttons in a column down the right side of the form. Change the captions and names to those shown in the following table.

Captions	Names
&1-Twips	cmdTwip
&2-Points	cmdPoint
&3-Pixels	cmdPixel
&4-Character	cmdCharacter
&5-Inch	cmdInch
&6-Millimeter	cmdMillimeter
&7-Centimeter	cmdCentimeter
E&xit	cmdExit

Figure 7-15 shows the form during the design phase of the project.

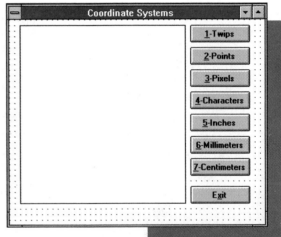

5 Add a label above the command buttons with the caption **ScaleMode.** Add two labels below the picture box. The first provides a caption for the picture box. Change the name of the label to **lblScaleMode.** The label displays the current coordinate system used to draw the grid. The second label gives the dimensions of the box as measured with the current coordinate system. Change the name of the label to **lblDimensions**.

Figure 7-15
Coordinate System
form being built

REARRANGING CONTROLS ON A FORM

Individual controls on a form can be moved by selecting the control with a click of the mouse, then dragging the control to a new position. A control can be resized by dragging a handle of the control. To reposition a group of controls, you use the pointer.

With the pointer, draw a temporary frame around a group of controls you want to move. Start by clicking on the upper-left corner and dragging to the lower-right corner. A gray frame shows the controls have been selected.

Once the controls have been selected, they can be moved as a group.

6 Adjust the size of the form to accommodate the additional controls.

7 Save the form and the project.

Finding the Dimensions of the Picture Box

The lower label displays the dimensions of the picture box in the given coordinate system. The measurements will change for each coordinate system.

The values for these dimensions are available in the properties of the picture box called ScaleWidth and ScaleHeight. When you choose a coordinate system using the ScaleMode property, ScaleWidth and ScaleHeight reflect the measure of the picture box expressed in those terms.

CODING THE TWIP BUTTON

Follow these steps to add code to the 1-Twips button.

1 With the form open, double-click on cmdTwip.

2 Add the following lines to Sub cmdTwip_Click():

```
'—Variable declarations
Dim Row As Integer, Col As Integer
Dim Sizes As String
'—Clear the picture box
picGrid.Cls
'—Choose the Twip coordinate system
picGrid.ScaleMode = 1
'—Set DrawWidth to 1 twip
picGrid.DrawWidth = 1
'—Set ScaleMode and Dimensions labels
lblScaleMode.Caption = "Twips: mark every 100 twips"
Sizes = Str$(picGrid.ScaleWidth) & " by " & Str$(picGrid.ScaleHeight)
lblDimensions.Caption = Sizes
'—Nested loop to plot a grid of dots
For Row = 0 To picGrid.ScaleHeight Step 100
   For Col = 0 To picGrid.ScaleWidth Step 100
       picGrid.PSet (Col, Row)
   Next Col
Next Row
'—Set DrawWidth back to two
picGrid.DrawWidth = 2
```

3 Enter the command **End** in cmdExit_Click().

4 Run the program. Click on the 1-Twips button to test the program (see Figure 7-16).

5 Save the form and project files.

Here is an explanation of the code you have entered, by line:

The first two lines declare *Row*, *Col*, and *Sizes* as variables. You are using the first two of these variables to generate the coordinates of the points plotted. The string variable *Sizes* is used to build a string representing the dimensions of the picture box.

The statement **picGrid.Cls** clears the picture box. The next line sets the grid to the twips coordinate system. The line **pic-Grid.DrawWidth = 1** uses the smallest

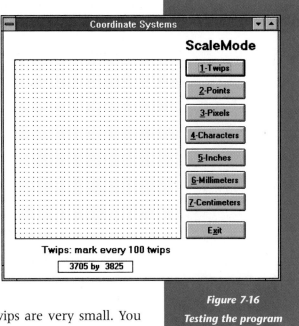

Figure 7-16

Testing the program

DrawWidth possible (1) for the size of dots. Twips are very small. You want to make sure that different dots do not overlap.

The line that starts *Sizes* = joins the width and length of the picture box (contained in ScaleWidth and ScaleHeight properties) into a single string, then assigns that string to the variable *Sizes*. The following line assigns the value of the variable *Sizes* to be displayed in a label.

Next comes a **For-Next** loop. You set up a loop from 0 to the vertical dimension of the picture box. The variable *Row* represents the vertical position of the dot in the box. The value of the variables in the loop increases by 100 each time through, which spaces the dots 100 twips apart.

The second (nested) **For-Next** loop generates values from 0 up to the maximum horizontal dimension of the box. *Col* represents the horizontal position of the dot. The value of the variables also increases by 100 each time through. The line **picGrid.PSet (Col, Row)** plots the dot at the intersection of the coordinates (*Col, Row*).

The last line sets the DrawWidth value back to the design-time setting of 2.

The decision to space the points representing the twip coordinate system 100 units apart was arrived at experimentally. Using a value of 100 seemed to illustrate the relative size of the twip coordinate system well.

CODING THE REST OF THE BUTTONS

You are now ready to code the rest of the buttons. You will be copying the code for the Twips button to the other buttons' subroutines. The

STYLE NOTE

The inner loop, the For Col = loop, is indented. Indentation visually groups statements. The indentation is not a necessary part of the program, but it is certainly a courtesy to anyone reading the program who is unfamiliar with its code. You yourself may fit that description a few months after you have written a program!

spacing of the dots, however, will be different. Instead of 100, use the spacing indicated in the table below.

Coordinate system	Spacing
1:Twips	100
2:Points	20
3:Pixels	20
4:Characters	5
5:Inches	½ inch*
6:Millimeter	10 millimeters
7:Centimeter	1 centimeter

* An additional change must be made for the Inch routine. Declare *Row* and *Col* to be of type Single.

1 Open the Code window and select cmdTwip_Click(). Select all the code except the top and bottom lines. Copy the code with Ctrl+C. Now select the routine cmdPoint_Click() and paste the code you just copied. Use Ctrl+V or select the Paste command from the Edit menu.

2 Change the ScaleMode property to 2.

3 Delete or comment out the statement that changes the DrawWidth to 1.

4 Change every reference to Twip, to Point.

5 Change the label text from:

```
Twips: mark every 100 twips
```

to:

```
Points: mark every 20 points
```

6 Change the step values of 100 in the two **For-Next** loops to 20. Better yet, replace the values with a constant defined as 20.

7 Run the program and test the code.

8 Copy the code into the subroutines for the other command buttons and modify each one. Use the spacing table for suggested loop increments, and Table 7-1 to set the ScaleMode property. Change the declarations for *Row* and *Col* in the code for the Inches button. Change Integer to Single.

9 Run the program. Test each command button. Stop the program. Save the project and form.

QUESTIONS AND ACTIVITIES

1. What are the choices listed for the ScaleMode property? What is the default mode?

2. Change the Coordinate Systems program to use two labels for the dimensions. Instead of joining the width and height in a single string, use two labels, each labeled as the width and height of the picture box.

3. Add a command button to the Coordinate Systems program. The caption is **&Print Form**, the name of the button is **cmdPrintForm**. In the code window of cmdPrintForm_Click(), enter the following line of code:

```
form1.PrintForm
```

   Execute the program, click on the centimeter button, and print the form by clicking on the Print Form button.
   With a ruler, measure the distance between the dots. How close is the distance to 1 centimeter? Measure the dimensions of the box. How close is the printed dimension?

4. What does the **PSet** method do?

5. To what objects can the **PSet** method be applied?

6. What information is needed by the **PSet** method? Which is optional? What happens if the optional information is omitted?

7. Comment out the **picGrid.Cls** statements in at least two command buttons. Run the program and choose those two buttons. Restore the lines and run the program again. Try changing **Cls** to **Clear**. **Clear** works for a listbox or a combobox. **Cls** works for a picture box or a form.
   In the statement:

```
For Row = 0 To picGrid.ScaleHeight Step 100
```

   what does **Step 100** do?

8. Change the DrawWidth property to 5 in for the cmdTwip button. Run the program and note the result.

9. Why is it a good idea to indent the statements making up the body of a loop?

Section

Color, Lines, and Circles

Nowadays, it's hard to think of graphics without thinking of color. This section introduces you to using color in Visual Basic programs. You then experiment with color using the **Line** and **Circle** methods. You first worked with these methods in Chapter 6.

Using Color

You can specify color using either of two functions: **QBColor** or **RGB**. The former maintains a link with older versions of Basic (Quick Basic), providing only sixteen colors. The latter takes advantage of the more flexible and advanced color system of Windows.

THE QBCOLOR FUNCTION

The **QBColor***(n)* function takes one of sixteen values, 0 through 15, as a parameter and returns a color. The first eight colors are the kind of colors you would expect to see in a box of crayons: red, yellow, blue, green. The second eight are lightened versions of the first eight. See Table 7-2.

Table 7-2 Table of QBColor Values

0	Black	8	Gray
1	Blue	9	Light Blue
2	Green	10	Light Green
3	Cyan	11	Light Cyan
4	Red	12	Light Red
5	Magenta	13	Light Magenta
6	Yellow	14	Light Yellow
7	White	15	Bright White

These colors were the ones used by the first color graphics systems for the PC. As you can see, there are not many of these colors. Your color choices for program elements are therefore extremely limited using this function.

The sixteen values of the QBColor function are completely arbitrary.

Today the QBColor function is still used, because sometimes this simple color system is all that's needed to help a program communicate with the user.

THE RGB COLOR SYSTEM

Computer video cards and monitors can now display far more than 16 colors. Each pixel has a "color depth." The color depth is the number of bits used to represent the color of the pixel. Various graphics systems use 2, 4, 8, 16, 24, and 32 bits per pixel. The amount of video memory, the video chips, and the current settings of the operating system determine the number of colors.

The color system of Visual Basic is based on representing colors as a mixture of three primary colors: red, green, and blue. You identify the specific color using the RGB function. The syntax of this function is:

RGB *(red, green, blue)*

For each color—red, green, and blue—you can indicate a value ranging from 0 to 255. These values represent the relative intensity of that color in the resulting color blend. For example, RGB (50, 100, 80) has a larger green component than the color represented by RGB (50, 50, 8). As you might expect, RGB(0, 0, 0) is black, and RGB(255, 255, 255) is white. The numbers you use to represent the red, green, and blue components of a color must be integers.

So how many colors can you create with the RGB function? If you multiply 256 times 256 times 256, you get over 16.7 million different color possibilities. Far more than the 16 possible with QBColor and older machines!

The RGB function returns a long integer representing the color. You may recall from a previous chapter that long integers are whole numbers that range from approximately 0 to 4 billion (if taken as an unsigned integer). You won't see a complete table of color names with their corresponding long integer values because it would be far too long. Many drawing methods, such as **Line** and **Circle**, take an optional color argument. You can use the value returned by RGB to specify that color.

NUMBERS IN THE PROPERTIES WINDOW

An object on a form can have several color properties. For example, place a rectangular shape on a form, then look in the Properties window. You see these color properties:

BackColor
BorderColor
FillColor

The values for these properties represent a color. These values may look strange, because they are expressed in the hexadecimal number system. The hexadecimal number system is based on powers of sixteen: $16^0 = 1$, $16^1=16$, $16^2=256$. The numerals in base 16, which is another name for the hexadecimal number system, are 0 through 9 and A through F. The decimal number 255 is expressed in base 16 as FF.

SEEING COLOR ON SCREEN

The three parameters of the RGB function correspond to the three electron guns in a picture tube that produce color on the screen. Each of the guns shoots electrons, guided by magnetic plates, to one of three color dots on the inside surface of the screen. When a color dot is hit, it glows.

The higher the value of the parameter, the more intense is that component of the color.

When you double-click a color property, such as BackColor, a window appears containing color swatches from which you can select a color by clicking. This window contains a small but very useful subset of the full range of possible colors.

Hexadecimal numbers are expressed in the Properties window with a leading and trailing ampersand (&) and the letter H. The long integer representing a color has the following structure: &H00bbggrr&, where bb is the hexadecimal value of the blue component, gg is the green component, and rr is the red component.

Experimenting with Color: Stage 1

Follow these steps to investigate color numbers. You will choose different colors from the color palette and examine the corresponding color numbers.

1   Start Visual Basic. If Visual Basic is already running, select New Project from the File menu.

2   Change the caption of the default form to **Color Numbers**.

3   Select the BackColor property of the form in the Properties window and note its current value.

4   Double-click on the property to open the color palette. This palette presents only a small fraction of the colors available using the RGB system.

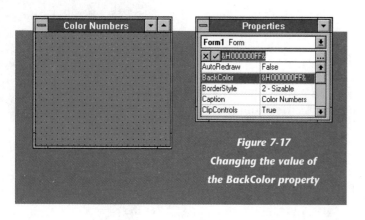

Figure 7-17

Changing the value of the BackColor property

5   Click on a vibrant red. The form changes color. Note the value of the BackColor property. The hexadecimal value, in this case, indicates a strong red component. See Figure 7-17.

6   Double-click on the BackColor property and pick from the palette a bright green. Click on the color and note the value reported in the Properties window.

7   Double-click on the BackColor property and pick a deep blue color. Click on the color and note the value reported in the Properties window.

8   Try other colors from the color palette, noting their color values. Be sure to try black, white, yellow, and magenta.

9   Select the BackColor property and change the value of the color number in the edit area. The blue, green and red components of the color are in the last six digits, two for each component. Change the values two at a time, pressing Enter to make each change. Note the results.

If you do not see much difference in some of the colors you select, the culprit may be your color video hardware. It may not be adequate to show tiny variations in color. Or the screen of your computer may not support the colors you have selected.

Experimenting with Color: Stage 2

You can use scroll bars to change the red, blue, and green parameters in a color. These changed parameters will then be sent to the RGB function.

To automate color changes in this way, follow these steps:

1   Start Visual Basic. If Visual Basic is already running, choose New Project from the File menu.

2   Change the caption of the form to **Red, Green, Blue**.

3   Use the shape control to put a square on the form.

4   Change the name of the shape to **shpColorBox**.

5   Change the BackStyle property to 1-Opaque.

6   Put three horizontal scrollbars on the form below the shape. Name the bars **hsbRed**, **hsbGreen**, and **hsbBlue**.

7   Set the Min and Max properties of each of the bars to 0 and 255, respectively.

8   Label the bars **Red**, **Green**, and **Blue**. See Figure 7-18.

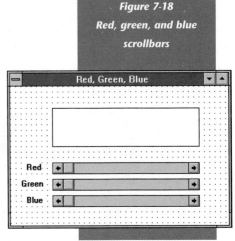

Figure 7-18
Red, green, and blue scrollbars

9   Enter this declaration in the general declarations section of the code. These variables are used in each of the three Change events of the horizontal scroll bars:

```
Dim Red As Integer, Green As Integer, Blue As Integer
```

10   Enter these lines of code in the Change events of each of the three scrollbars:

```
Red = hsbRed.Value
Green = hsbGreen.Value
Blue = hsbBlue.Value
shpColorBox.BackColor = RGB(Red, Green, Blue)
```

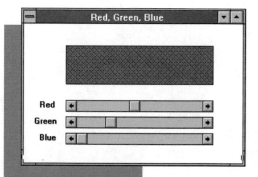

Figure 7-19

Assigning a value to

the BackColor property

through code

11 Run the program. Experiment with moving the scrollbox on each of the scrollbars.

The code reads each of the three scrollbars through the value property. The three values are sent as parameters to the RGB function. The color returned by that function is assigned to the BackColor property of the rectangle on the form. See Figure 7-19.

Using the Line Method

You have already experimented with the **Line** method as a means of drawing lines. You can also draw boxes and filled boxes with this method. Using the method, you can draw on both forms and picture boxes. And, now that you have begun to work with color, you can control the color of the lines.

The **Line** method has the following syntax:

*object.***Line** *(x1,y1)-(x2,y2), color,* BF

In the syntax above, almost everything except the word "Line" is optional. Some valid variations follow:

```
form1.Line (0,1)-(25,40)
Line (0,1)-(25,40)
Line (0,1)-(25,40),QBColor(3)
Line -(25,40), RGB(0, 192, 0)
picture1.Line (0,1)-(25,40), ,B
Line (0,1)-(25,40), ,BF
```

If you leave out the object name, the method draws on the underlying form. You would use this variation to draw graphic images on the form.

The two sets of numbers separated with a dash are coordinates of endpoints. If you include these, the method draws a line between those two points. You can also use the **Line** method to draw a line between points, starting from where the last point was plotted. The coordinates of that last point are stored in the object's CurrentX and CurrentY properties. To do so, you include only the coordinates of the second endpoint, preceded by a minus sign. In other words:

```
Line -(x2,y2)
```

To draw a box using the first coordinate as the top-left corner and the second coordinate as the lower-right corner, include the letter "B" at the end of the statement. To fill that box with color, include the letter "F" immediately after the "B."

If you do not specify any color information, the **Line** method uses the color specified in the ForeColor property of the object. This property is present in most objects, and you may have already experimented with its use. In a textbox, the property controls the color of the displayed text. In objects that have a **Line** method, the property controls the color of the lines drawn.

EXPERIMENTING WITH LINES AND COLOR

To experiment with lines and color, you are going to use four different variants of the **Line** method. The code you will write divides a form into four quarters called quadrants. In one quadrant, the Line method draws lines up and down. In the second quadrant, you will have empty boxes, and in the third, filled boxes. In the final quadrant, the **Line** method draws lines at a zig-zag. Using the **QBColor** function, you will make all of the lines and boxes different colors (see Figure 7-20).

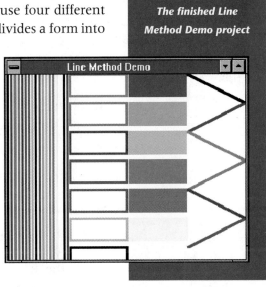

Figure 7-20

The finished Line Method Demo project

To create the program, follow these steps:

1   Start Visual Basic. If Visual Basic is already running, select New Project from the File menu.

2   Change the caption of the form to **Line Method Demo**.

3   Enter the following code in the Form_Click event procedure:

```
Dim nWidth, nHeight, nColor, x, y
ScaleMode = 3
nWidth = ScaleWidth
nHeight = ScaleHeight
DrawWidth = 3
'—First quadrant
nColor = 0
For x = 0 To nWidth/4 Step 5
    Line (x, 0)-(x, nHeight), QBColor(nColor Mod 16)
    nColor = nColor + 1 ' Mod keeps nColor value between 0 and 15
Next x
'—Second quadrant
For y = 0 To nHeight Step 40
    Line (nWidth / 4 + 3, y)-(nWidth/2, y + 30), QBColor(nColor Mod 16), B
```

continued

```
    nColor = nColor + 1
Next y
'—Third quadrant
For y = 0 To nHeight Step 40
    Line (nWidth / 2 + 3, y)-(3 * nWidth/4, y + 30), QBColor(nColor Mod 16), BF
    nColor = nColor + 1
Next y
'—Fourth quadrant
PSet (3 * nWidth/4 + 3, 0)
For y = 40 To nHeight Step 80
    Line -(nWidth, y), QBColor(nColor Mod 16)
    nColor = nColor + 1
    Line -(3 * nWidth / 4 + 3, y + 40), QBColor(nColor Mod 16)
    nColor = nColor + 1
Next y
```

4 Run the program. Place your cursor on the form and move it. Why did the lines appear when you moved the mouse?

5 Save the project and form files.

Here is an explanation of the code:

The first line of the code declares the variables and sets up some preliminary values. *nWidth* and *nHeight* store the dimensions of the form. *nColor* is the parameter sent to QBColor to generate a color for the drawing. *x* and *y* are used as variables to control various loops.

In the second line, you did not specify an object with the ScaleMode property, so the default is Form1. **ScaleMode = 3** indicates the pixel coordinate system. You could use other coordinate systems, but using pixels will give the user an idea of the relative ratio of sizes of the pixel to the screen. The ratio of the width of the lines, set by the DrawWidth property, to the spaces between the lines gives a good sense of the size of the pixels on the screen.

In the line nWidth = ScaleWidth, you assign the value of the ScaleWidth property to the variable *nWidth*. This property is the measure of the width of the form in pixels. The prefix in the variable *nWidth* shows it represents a numeric value. You perform the same step for the height of the form in the following line.

To give the line some thickness, **DrawWidth = 3** sets the DrawWidth property to 3. Thicker lines make the colors of the lines more visible.

In the first line of code for the first quadrant, *nColor* is a variable used to control the color of the lines drawn. It is used in the **QBColor** function mod 16 to provide a value for the parameter of the function. (*nColor* mod 16 is equal to the remainder of *nColor* when it is divided by 16.) Setting *nColor* to 0 guarantees that the colors used to draw lines will start with the QBColor (0), which is black.

The first **For-Next** loop draws vertical lines in the first quadrant. The loop limit, *nWidth/4*, confines drawing to the first quadrant. This section of the program shows what is probably the most common use of the Line method: drawing lines between points (from the top to the bottom of the screen) with a color specified by the QBColor function.

After each line is drawn, the *nColor* variable is incremented. Because that value is taken modulo 16 (divided by 16 and just the remainder returned) inside the function, the result will always be an integer between 0 and 15.

The *x* value in this loop specifies the column number of the display. The loop generates values, stepping up by 5 each time through. The width of the screen, *nWidth*, divided by 4, is the number of columns available in the first quadrant.

The width of the line drawn is set to 3. A new band starts every 5 pixels. This leaves a narrow band of white between each band of color.

The second **For-Next** loop sets up the second quadrant of the form. The variant of the **Line** method you used for this quadrant draws colored boxes (due to the "B" at the end of the line). The coordinates you provided act as two corners of each box.

The loop sets up row values stepping from the top of the form to the bottom, incrementing by 40 pixels each time through the loop. The **Line** method draws a box, 30 pixels high and almost equal to the width of the quadrant.

The column values for the boxes range from *nWidth/4 + 3*, 3 pixels beyond the end of the first quadrant, to *nWidth/2*, the middle of the screen. The row values for each box range from *y* to *y+30*, leaving a 10-pixel space between each box.

The code for the third quadrant is almost identical to that for the second. It draws very similar boxes, from column *nWidth/2 + 3*, to *3*nWidth/4*. The difference is that, in this quadrant, you filled the boxes with color by adding an "F" at the end of the Line statement.

For the final quadrant, you create a zigzag line, moving from the top of the form to the bottom. This last section uses the **Line** method to draw from the last used position on the form to whatever coordinate is specified in the **Line** statement:

The code starts by plotting a single point at the top-left corner of the fourth quadrant. The **For-Next** statement starts *y*, the row value, from a position 40 pixels down from the top. The value is incremented by 80 pixels each time through the loop.

Within the loop, a line is drawn from the original point to the right-hand side of the quadrant, 40 pixels lower than the previous point. From there, a line is drawn back to the left side of the quadrant, also 40 pixels lower than the previous point.

Each time through the loop, you zig from left to right and zag from right to left, each cycle covering 80 pixels top to bottom.

The color variable, *nColor*, is incremented each time. This cycles through each of the 16 possible colors.

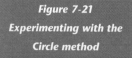

Figure 7-21
Experimenting with the Circle method

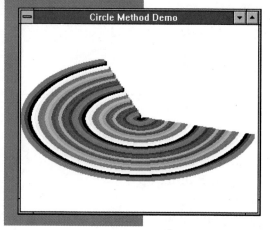

Using the Circle Method

Now that you know more about color, you can also expand your use of the **Circle** method. The **Circle** method can draw ellipses as well as circles, and it can even draw partial ellipses. Like the **Line** method, the **Circle** method also lets you specify the color with which it draws.

See Figure 7-21 for the end result of the code you will write.

Follow these steps to explore the **Circle** method.

1 Start Visual Basic. If Visual Basic is already running, choose New Project from the File menu.

2 Enter the following code in the Form_Click event procedure:

```
Dim x, y, cx, cy, rad, nColor
Dim nWidth, nHeight
Const StartPt = 1.9
Const EndingPt = 6
Const Ellipse = .5
ScaleMode = 3
'—The width of the figure in pixels
nWidth = ScaleWidth
'—The height of the window
nHeight = ScaleHeight
'—The coordinates of the center of the figure
cx = nWidth / 2
cy = nHeight / 2
'—The width of the figure drawn
DrawWidth = 5
'—Color variable
nColor = 0
For rad = 5 To nWidth / 2 Step 5
```

```
Circle (cx, cy), rad, QBColor(nColor Mod 16), StartPt, EndingPt, Ellipse
    nColor = nColor + 1    ' cycle through the colors
Next rad
```

Let's concentrate on the **Circle** statement because most of this code is similar to the code used in the Line Demo program.

Because we are drawing directly on the form, we don't need to specify an object. The Circle method will draw directly on the underlying form. Following the method name, Circle, are the coordinates of the center of the circle. Then comes the radius, expressed in pixels. Scale-Mode is set to 3, the pixel coordinate system. The color of the circle is cycled through the 16 colors possible with the QBColor function, controlled by the value of the variable *nColor.*

The next two values in the Circle statement are interesting. Figure 7-32 shows just a portion of an ellipse. You can select what portion of the ellipse to draw by including a *StartPt* and *EndingPt.* The starting point and the ending point are specified in radians.

In Figure 7-21, an angle in standard position is shown. One side of the angle, the initial side, points due east. The angle is measured counterclockwise from the initial side. The **Circle** method uses measures of angles in the standard position (see Figure 7-22) to give the starting and ending points of the figure drawn.

In the example above, the starting point is 1.9 radians. The ending point is 6 radians, or 6/6.28 (.955) of the circle. If you omit the start and end points, the entire ellipse is drawn.

The last number in the statement, .5, indicates the shape of the figure drawn. If you omit the number, the method draws a circle. If the number is less than 1, a horizontal ellipse is drawn. If the number is greater than 1, a vertical ellipse is drawn. These aren't really different figures at all. A circle is just a special case of the ellipse.

RADIAN ANGLE MEASURE

The measure of an angle is commonly given in degrees. A circle has 360 degrees. Another way of measuring angles is to use radians. There are two times pi, where pi = 3.1415927, radians in a circle. Using the radian measure simplifies the expression of many formulas in physics. The angle measures used by Visual Basic in the Circle method are radian measures.

QUESTIONS AND ACTIVITIES

1. Describe what this statement will do, as well as the location of the resulting graphic:

    ```
    Line (-7,10)-(1,0),  ,B
    ```

2. Place a textbox on a form. Set the Text property to "This tests the ForeColor property". In the Properties window, double-click on the ForeColor property and experiment with different colors. Do the same with the BackColor property.

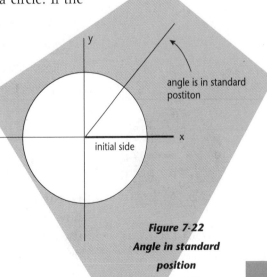

Figure 7-22

Angle in standard position

3. How many colors are theoretically available using the RGB system?

4. In the code for the first quadrant of the Line Method Demo program, change the DrawWidth property to 1 and run the program. Change DrawWidth to 3, 5, 7, and 10. Run the program for each change and note the results.

5. To control the value of the *nColor* variable, the Mod operator is used. This keeps the value of *nColor* between 0 and 15. Add an **If-Then** statement that resets the value of *nColor* to 0 when the current value is 16. After what statement would this statement go?

6. If the width of a picture box were *W*, and you wanted to divide the area into thirds, what expression would you use for the column number of the line dividing the first third from the second? The second from the third?

7. Describe the purpose of each of the expressions in the **Circle** statement.

8. What determines the units of measurement used for the radius of the circle?

9. An angle in standard position may be measured with at least two different units. What are they? How many of each are there in a circle?

10. In the Circle demo program, change the value of the constant *Ellipse*. Try values in the following ranges. After each change, run the program and click the form.

    0 < Ellipse < .5

    .5 < Ellipse < 1

    Ellipse = 1

    1 < Ellipse < 1.5

    1.5 <= Ellipse < 2

5

Section

The Quadratic Formula Program

Quadratic equations pop up pretty often in math and science. Knowing how to solve a quadratic equation is a useful skill. Visual Basic can be used to build a very good quadratic equation solver. Not only will the program calculate and display the solutions to the equation, the program can calculate and display a table of values that satisfy the graph of the equation and draw the graph itself.

The Freefall program from Chapter 3 uses a quadratic equation to calculate the distance an object falls while under the influence of gravity. With a method of solving a quadratic equation, the Freefall program could be turned around to calculate the time it takes to fall a given distance, instead of calculating the distance from the time.

A complete solution to a quadratic equation might include the following:

⦿ The solutions to the equation: the values of x that make the equation true

⦿ A list of ordered pairs that satisfy the graph of the equation

⦿ A graph of the equation

In thinking about how you will solve this problem, do you see the need for the following:

⦿ Textboxes to enter the coefficients of the equations

⦿ Command buttons to execute the calculations, clear the input boxes, and exit the program

⦿ The quadratic formula to calculate the solutions

⦿ A listbox to display the ordered pairs of values that satisfy the graph of the equation

⦿ An array to hold the ordered pairs generated for the listbox and the graph

⦿ A picture box to display the graph of the equation

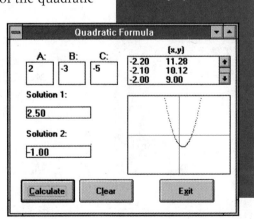

Figure 7-23
The Quadratic Formula project

From the users' point of view, they will see a form similar to the one in Figure 7-23. Users are prompted to enter coefficients of the quadratic equation in three different textboxes. The focus is initially on the box labeled A:. As the user enters values, the focus shifts to each of the next two textboxes. When a user presses Enter from the C textbox, focus shifts to the Calculate button.

At that point, if the user clicks on the Calculate button, the following occurs:

⦿ The roots (which are solutions of the quadratic equation) are calculated and displayed.

⦿ A table of x and y values is displayed.

⦿ A graph of the function is drawn in a picture box.

The x values in the table and the graph range from -10 to 10. The corresponding y values are generated from the quadratic function entered by the user.

Background

The program uses textboxes to enter the coefficients of a quadratic equation in standard form:

$ax^2 + bx + c = 0$

Using the quadratic formula, the solutions are found:

$Discriminant = b^2 - 4ac$
$r1 = (-b + sqr(discriminant)) / (2a)$
$r2 = (-b - sqr(discriminant)) / (2a)$

The discriminant is an important intermediate value that reveals the nature of the solutions to the equation. If the discriminant is negative, there are no "real" roots—that is, the only roots are imaginary numbers. Otherwise, the roots are calculated and displayed.

The program generates and displays a table of *x,y* values for the function. The standard form of the equation, $ax^2 + bx + c = 0$, is turned into a function by replacing 0 with the variable y.

$y = ax^2 + bx + c$

The values used for *x* range from -10 through 10.

An array is used to store the values generated for the table. Those same values are used to plot the graph of the function in a picture box. This graph will be a visual display of the table of values.

Starting Out

Before starting to build the form for this project, you need to learn about the new methods and statements you are going to use. You will learn how to set up a coordinate system with any desired scale and origin.

CUSTOM COORDINATE SYSTEMS

Besides the seven built-in coordinate systems, you can create a custom coordinate system. To do so, you set the SetMode property to 0.

The ScaleHeight and ScaleWidth properties of picture boxes are used to report, or to set, the height and width of the box. The properties ScaleTop and ScaleLeft define the values associated with the top row and first column, respectively. Figure 7-24 shows the default settings.

The default settings for these values are both 0. This indicates the top left corner has the coordinate 0,0. In this program, a coordinate system with *x* values from -10 to 10 and *y* values from -20 to 20 will display graphs nicely. Using the same scale for all the graphs will help give an idea of the relationship between various equations. Some graphs may

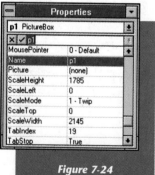

Figure 7-24

Looking at the Scale-Top and ScaleLeft properties of a picture box

not be visible on the given scale at all. Even this is informative, because it shows where the roots are not.

You may want to modify the program to adopt a coordinate system that will always display the graph of the equation in a "nice" way. To do so, you would use high and low values from the list of ordered pairs to calculate scale factors to fit the graph to the screen. Unfortunately, if this scaling is carried out too far, all the graphs will look exactly alike. If this is the case, the graphs are meaningless.

Visual Basic gives us a way to set up these coordinate values, simultaneously setting appropriate values for all the Scale properties. This is the **Scale** method.

The command to set up the coordinate system described above is:

```
pctGraph.Scale (-10,20)-(10, -20)
```

The object to which the method is applied is the picture box named pctGraph. The command **Scale** follows this name after a period. Then comes a space and the coordinates of the upper-left corner of the coordinate system. After a dash, you add the coordinates of the lower-right corner.

Once this statement is executed, the values of all the Scale properties for the picture box are set. In this case, the values are shown in Figure 7-25.

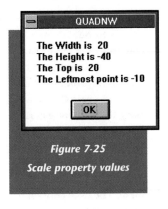

Figure 7-25

Scale property values

DIAGNOSTIC CODE

The message box in Figure 7-25 is one you would use for diagnostic purposes. Programmers often insert diagnostic code into a procedure during the development of a program and then comment the code out by putting in single quotation marks at the beginning of each line.

The diagnostic code can help find a problem when the program doesn't behave the way you expect. Commenting the lines out removes them from the executable program. Later, the lines can be restored to their diagnostic function, should the need arise again because of subsequent modifications.

Using a message box for diagnostic code interrupts the program and requires the user to click OK for the program to continue. Almost the same purpose is accomplished by adding the line:

```
Debug.Print msg
```

This line prints the same information in the Debug window. See Figure 7-26. Unlike **MsgBox**, **Debug.Print** does not pause program execution until the user performs an action.

Figure 7-26

Scale values in Debug window

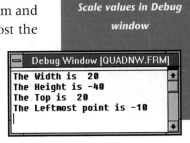

REDIM STATEMENT

An array declaration such as:

```
Dim YValues(1 To 41) As Single
```

fixes the size of the *YValues* array to 41. The size of the array is set when the program is written and may not be changed.

The **ReDim** statement allows the size of an array to be changed while the program is running. For instance, the statement:

```
ReDim YValues(1 To TotalPoints * 2) As Single
```

uses the value of *TotalPoints* in an expression to calculate the size of the array.

The total number of points used depends on the increment between successive points on the graph. The span of *x* values is -10 to 10, or 21 units (remember to count 0). If the increment between successive values is 0.1, the total number of values generated is 21/.1, or 210. The array needs this many spaces to store values.

The increment between successive values is a constant defined in the program. This allows the programmer to change it if more or less resolution is desired. Any change in the increment necessitates a change in the number of values stored in the array. Thus, the array is resized according the number of values needed, as determined by the span of values and the increment between them.

Setting up the Form

The form contains three labeled textboxes in which users enter the coefficients of the equation. It also contains two labels to display the solutions (if they exist), a listbox, a picture box, and command buttons to Calculate, Clear, and Exit.

Follow these steps to set up the form.

1 Start Visual Basic. If Visual Basic is running, choose New Project from the File menu.

2 Change the caption of the form to **Quadratic Formula**.

3 Place three textboxes in the upper-left portion of the form. Name the boxes **txtA**, **txtB**, and **txtC**. Delete the text from each.

4 Over each textbox, place a label. Caption the labels **A:**, **B:**, and **C:**. Set the FontSize to 9.75. Set the AutoSize property to True. See Figure 7-27.

DUPLICATE CONTROLS

You can use edit commands to put identical controls on a form. To experiment, put a textbox on a form. Select the box and press Ctrl+C to copy the control. Press Ctrl+V to paste the control on the form. The new control appears in the upper-left corner of the form. The new control retains all the properties of the original. If you changed the BorderStyle of the control, for example, the copied control retains that changed BorderStyle.

When the duplicate control is created, Visual Basic gives you the option of creating a control array. Creating a control array means creating more than one control with the same name. If you are just trying to duplicate controls, there is no reason to create a control array. Just say No.

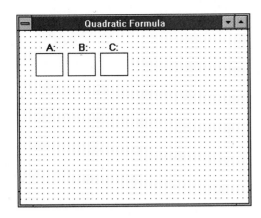

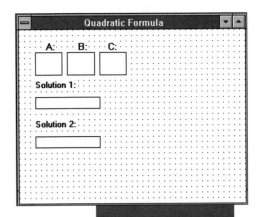

Figure 7-27
Placing textboxes on the Quadratic Formula form

Figure 7-28
Placing labels on the form

5 Place two more labels on the form for the solutions of the equation. Set their BorderStyle to Single. Name the labels **lblSolution1**, **lblSolution2**. Delete the captions. Change the FontSize of the labels to 9.75.

6 Place two more labels on the form to identify the solution labels. Change their captions to **Solution 1** and **Solution 2**. See Figure 7-28.

7 Place a listbox in the upper-right corner of the form. Change the name of the box to **lstTable**.

8 Place a picture box for the graph below the listbox. Change the name of the box to **pctGraph**. The coordinate system for the box will be set in the code. See Figure 7-29.

9 Place three command buttons across the bottom of the form. Change their captions to **&Calculate**, **C&lear**, and **E&xit**. Change the names to **cmdCalculate**, **cmdClear**, and **cmdExit**.

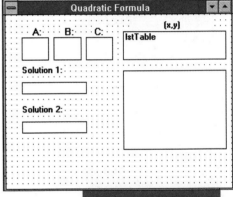

Figure 7-29
Placing a picture box on the form

Writing the Code for the Calculate button

Follow these steps to add code to the quadratic formula project:

1 Double-click on the cmdCalculate button to enter the Code window.

2 Include this code:

```
'—Declarations
Dim a As Single, b As Single, c As Single
Dim Disc As Single
Dim Root1 As Single, Root2 As Single
```

continued

```
'—Collect information from textboxes
a = Val(txtA)
b = Val(txtB)
c = Val(txtC)
'—If a is 0, the equation is not quadratic
If a <> 0 Then
    '—Calculate the Discriminant
    Disc = b * b - 4 * a * c
    '—If the discriminant is less than zero: there are no solutions
    If Disc < 0 Then
        lblSolution1 = "No solution"
        lblSolution2 = ""
    Else
        '—Find the solutions, calculate table, and graph
        Root1 = (-b + Sqr(Disc)) / (2 * a)
        Root2 = (-b - Sqr(Disc)) / (2 * a)
        '—Display solutions
        lblSolution1 = Format(Root1, "Fixed")
        lblSolution2 = Format(Root2, "Fixed")
        '—Generate table
        Dim x As Single, y As Single
        Dim PointNumber As Integer
        Const Increment = .1
        ReDim YValues(1 To 21 / Increment) As Single
        PointNumber = 1
        For x = -10 To 10 Step Increment
            y = a * x * x + b * x + c
            '—Store y value in the array
            YValues(PointNumber) = y
            PointNumber = PointNumber + 1
            lstTable.AddItem Format(x, "Fixed") & Chr(9) & Format$(y, "Fixed")
        Next x
        '—Set up picture box with user defined coordinates
        pctGraph.Scale (-10, 20)-(10, -20)
        '—Diagnostic Code
        Dim nl As String, msg As String
        '—New line character
        nl = Chr$(13) & Chr$(10)
        msg = "The Width is " & Str$(pctGraph.ScaleWidth) & nl
        msg = msg & "The Height is " & Str$(pctGraph.ScaleHeight) & nl
        msg = msg & "The Top is " & Str$(pctGraph.ScaleTop) & nl
        msg = msg & "The Leftmost point is " & Str$(pctGraph.ScaleLeft)
```

```
        MsgBox msg
        Debug.Print msg
        '—Draw the x and y axes
        pctGraph.Line (-10, 0)-(10, 0), QBColor(3)
        pctGraph.Line (0, -20)-(0, 20), QBColor(3)
        PointNumber = 1
        '—Plot the graph
        For x = -10 To 10 Step Increment
            pctGraph.PSet (x, YValues(PointNumber))
            PointNumber = PointNumber + 1
        Next x
    End If
End If
```

Here is an explanation of the code for the Calculate button:

In the first three lines, you declare variables for the coefficients *a*, *b*, and *c*; the discriminant, *Disc*; and the two solutions, *Root1* and *Root2*. Solutions to an equation are often called the roots of the equation.

In the next few lines, you entered the commands to collect the values of the coefficients from the textboxes. If the value of *a* is 0, the equation is not a quadratic equation. The first **If-Then** statement prevents calculations if *a* is 0. The **End If** statement is at the very end of the code.

The value of the discriminant determines whether there are solutions to the equation. The four lines following the **If a<>0** statement calculate the discriminant and test it. If there are no solutions, the label marked Solution 1 is set to "No solution".

If the discriminant is not negative, the equation has solutions that can be calculated. You use the four lines following the **Else** statement to calculate and display the solutions.

In preparation for building the table of *x* and *y* values, you declare variables and constants in the five lines following the **'Generate table** comment. *x* ranges from -10 to 10. *y* is calculated from *x* and the values of *a*, *b*, and *c*. *PointNumber* is a subscript into the *YValues* array. *Increment* is a constant. The value of *x* is increased by this amount each time through the loop. If *Increment* is smaller, more values of *y* are calculated.

The **ReDim** statement reserves space for the *YValues* array. The amount of space is calculated by dividing *Increment* into 21.

You set up the loop for *x* in the line **For x = -10...**, then calculate a value for *y* in the next line. Then you store the *y* value in the *YValues* array. The line **PointNumber = PointNumber + 1** adds 1 to the array subscript, *PointNumber*. The following line joins the values of *x* and *y* together as strings and adds them to the listbox, lstTable.

Then comes a **Scale** statement, which sets up the coordinate system for the picture box. The range of the *x* values matches the range used in the **For-Next** loop.

The eight lines starting with **Dim n1 As String, msg As String** are diagnostic code. This code displays the settings for the Scale properties. These properties are set by the **Scale** method.

The two lines starting with **pctGraph.Line...** draw the *x* and *y* axes in the picture box. The following line sets *PointNumber* to 1. *PointNumber* is the subscript into the *YValues* array. The **For-Next** loop plots the points in the picture box.

The first **End If** statement finishes the **If Disc < 0** statement. The second finishes the **If *a* <> 0** statement.

Entering Code for the Clear and End Buttons

You have much less code to enter for the Clear and Exit buttons:

1 Enter the following code for the Clear command button. The code clears the textboxes for the coefficients, the labels for the solutions, the listbox containing the table, and the picture box displaying the graph.

```
txtA = ""
txtB = ""
txtC = ""
lblSolution1 = ""
lblSolution2 = ""
lstTable.Clear
pctGraph.Cls
txtA.SetFocus
```

2 In the cmdExit_Click() subroutine, enter **End**.

Finishing Up

Now you are ready to try out the program:

1 Save the project and form files.

2 Run the program. Enter the following values and note the results. After a trial or two, stop the program and comment out the code that creates the message box. Run the program and complete the trials.

a	b	c
1	1	1
1	1	-1
1	3	-3
1	-3	-3
-1	5	7
-1	5	-7
1	6	9
0	2	9
25	10	1

QUESTIONS AND ACTIVITIES

The following exercises refer to the program presented in this section.

1. Instead of plotting points, alter the program to connect the dots by using the **Line** method to plot line segments.

2. Alter the program to allow the user to plot more than one graph in the picture box, allowing a comparison of functions.

3. Alter the program to allow the user to set the x and y limits of the graph. Instead of using -10 to 10 for x and -20 to 20 for y, allow the user to enter values for each.

4. Mark the coordinate axes (using the **Circle** method to make a large dot) at each unit.

5. It is often important to know where the graph of a quadratic equation crosses the x axis. How does a table of x and y values help a user discover an approximate range for these points? Run the program and, using just the table of values, estimate the roots of the equation where $a = 2$, $b = 5$, and $c = -8$.

6. Why is it necessary to store only the y values generated from the quadratic equation? Why not store the x values in the array as well?

7. What is the SetMode property value for a user-defined coordinate system?

8. Write the Visual Basic commands that initialize the picture box pct-Graph for the following custom coordinate systems.

Upper left	*Lower Right*
(-5,5)	(5,-5)
(0,50)	(10,0)
(0,10)	(20,-10)

9. Add a statement or two to the program that prints each value of *x* and *y* into the Debug window.

10. Using the Help system as a resource, find and record a brief description of the kinds of message boxes available and the codes needed to create them. Alter the message box code in the program to use a message box with a big exclamation point.

11. Rewrite the code of the Quadratic Formula program to display an error message if the value for the lead coefficient, *a*, is zero.

Summary

A pixel is the smallest graphic element of a display screen. The word is short for "picture element."

Screen dimensions are listed as pixels across by pixels down, for instance, 640x480 is a typical VGA resolution.

A font is a style of type. A printer's point is about 1/72 of an inch. A twip is 1/20 of a point.

Visual Basic provide seven built-in coordinate systems based on twips, points, pixels, characters, inches, millimeters, and centimeters. User-defined coordinate systems are also supported.

The picture box has many uses. It can be:

● Drawn upon with drawing controls like the shape and line controls from the toolbox;

● Drawn upon by graphics methods, like **Line**, **PSet**, and **Circle**;

● A container for labels, textboxes, or other controls from the toolbox;

● A container for an icon, a bitmap, or a metafile.

The image box allows an icon or bitmap to be stretched and distorted.

The value of the ScaleMode property determines the kind of coordinate system used. The ScaleWidth and ScaleHeight properties hold the dimensions of forms and picture boxes. These values depend on the size of the object and the coordinate system chosen in the Scale-Mode property.

The **PSet** method will plot a point of a given color on the screen. It syntax is:

object.**PSet**(*x,y*), *color*

where (*x,y*) is the coordinate of the point, and *color* is the color of the plotted point. The first coordinate is the column number (or horizontal position) and the second is the row number (or vertical position).

The **Cls** method clears the contents of a picture box or a form.

The DrawWidth property sets the size of the dot drawn by any of the drawing methods, like **PSet** and **Line**.

This command:

```
p1.Scale (-10,20)-(10, -20)
```

sets up a user-defined coordinate system with (-10,20) as the coordinate of the upper-left corner of the graph and (10,-20) as the lower-right corner of the graph.

You should insert lines of diagnostic code that help troubleshoot programs. When the code has been debugged, the lines of diagnostics can be commented out.

A variety of different MsgBox boxes are available.

The **QBColor** function generates one of 16 colors. The **RGB** function lets the user specify 256 choices each for the red, green, and blue components of a composite color. The color is represented by a long integer.

The **Line** method draws a line between two points. It can draw a box, using the two coordinates as diagonal corners of the box, or a line from the previously plotted point to a point contained in the **Line** statement. The **Circle** method draws a complete or partial circle or ellipse.

Problems

1.   The Draw a Circle Program
Write a program that allows the user to enter the center and radius of a circle in textboxes. Draw that circle in the default color on a form using (-10,10) as the upper-left corner of the graph and (10,-10) as the lower-right corner of the graph.

2.   The Random Circle Program
Write a program to generate and display 50 random circles on a form. Use the same coordinate system described above. Use the built-in random number generator to generate x and y coordinates for the centers, and the value of r for the radius.

The **Rnd** function will return a random Single between 0 and 1. Multiply by 11 to get a Single between 0 and 11. Assign the result to an integer variable. Use that result for the x value of the coordinate. Repeat for the y value and for the radius of the circle.

Use an InputBox with a default value of 1 to query the user for the shape of the figure to draw. Once that value is entered, use it for each of the 50 random figures.

continued

3. The Skyline Program

Use the Shape and Line controls from the Toolbox to draw a city skyline on a form. Save for use as a background.

4. The Line Graph Program

The data below represents a student's performance on a number of exams. Write a program to enter the pairs of numbers, display them in a listbox, and draw a line graph. Assume there are no more than 10 tests in the list. Use the data and the layout suggested in Figure 7-30.

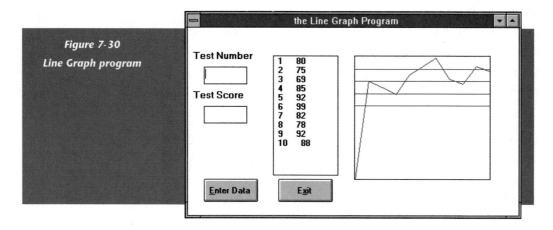

Figure 7-30

Line Graph program

5. The Random Color Program

Draw a picture box on the form. Draw a label on the picture box and change the caption to **Random Color**. Set the Alignment to Center, the FontSize to 13.5, and BackStyle to Transparent.

Declare three integer variables, *Red, Green,* and *Blue*. Give each a random value between 0 and 255 by multiplying *Rnd* by 256.

In the Click event of the picture box, insert code to change the Back-Color of the picture box to a random color using *Red, Green,* and *Blue* in the RGB function. Put the statements in a loop that runs from 1 to 1000.

Run the program, click on the picture box, and note the results.

6. The Crazy Circle Program

In the MouseDown procedure of the default form, declare two Static variables, *Oldx* and *Oldy*. Declare a variable for the radius and calculate using the following formula:

```
Radius = Sqr((oldx - x) ^ 2 + (oldy - y) ^ 2)
```

x and *y* are parameters passed to the procedure. They give the location of the mouse pointer. Set the DrawWidth of the form to 2. Use the **Circle** method to draw a circle with center (*x,y*) and a radius of *Radius*.

Reset *Oldx* to *x*, and *Oldy* to *y*.

Once the program runs, change the **Circle** method to draw the circles with random colors.

7. The Linear Equation Solver

In the last section, the Quadratic Program used the quadratic formula to solve a quadratic equation whose coefficients were entered in text boxes. Write a program to solve and graph a linear equation whose coefficients are entered in text boxes.

The standard form of a linear equation is:

$ax + b = c$

The solution to the equation is $x = (c - b)/a$
The equation to graph is $y = ax + b - c$

8. The Falling How Long Program

The complete equation describing the distance, d_f, an object undergoing a constant acceleration a, moving with an initial velocity of v_o, an initial position of d_i, for time t is:

$d_f = d_i + v_o t + at^2/2$

With a slight rearrangement, this becomes:

$y = (a/2) t^2 + v_o t + d_i - d_f$

You will recognize this as a quadratic equation in standard form where:

$a = a/2$
$b = v_o$
$c = d_i - d_f$

Write a program based on the Quadratic Formula program that accepts the acceleration (set the default to the acceleration of gravity, 32.2 ft/sec²), the initial velocity, the initial and final distance traveled, and calculate the elapsed time using the quadratic formula.

```
Dim Tallies
(1 To 5)
As Integer
For x = 1 To 5
Tallies(x) = 0
Next x
Tallies(x)
Next x
```

Arrays and Chaos

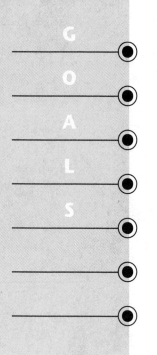

G
O
A
L
S

After working through this chapter, you will be able to:

Use the Checked and Enabled properties in menu designs.

Implement menu control arrays.

Use the **Select Case** statement in programs.

Program with arrays.

Understand the idea of chaos in a dynamic system.

Write programs to illustrate the principles of chaos inherent in the non-linear difference equation: $p_2 = r * p_1 * (1 - p_1)$.

O V E R V I E W

You were introduced to menus in Chapter 5. In this chapter, you will explore some additional features of menus, including the Enabled and Checked properties. These properties let you guide the user who is running your programs. The Enabled property lets you turn menu commands on and off. A disabled, or grayed, menu command is unavailable to the user. A checked menu command indicates that the command has been chosen, or the feature the command selects has already been turned on.

A control array allows you to handle several menu commands with a single event procedure. Regular arrays—arrays that hold numbers or strings—let you process data again and again. Values in arrays persist until the program ends.

Chaos theory is a branch of mathematics that came into being in the mid-1970s. We are just now learning the many areas to which Chaos theory can be applied. The advent of the computer has allowed the discovery and subsequent development of the methodology of Chaos theory. That methodology uses a computer to calculate the hundreds, thousands, or millions of pieces of data required to build a picture of a physical system.

This application of computers has only recently (in the last ten years) come into its own. Scientists have always used computers to analyze data, comparing the results of experiments with the results that their theories predict. Now, however, instead of manually examining large tables of numerical data for patterns, scientists enlist the graphical capabilities of computers in their search for patterns.

The Population Biology program makes predictions about population variations over generations using a simple mathematical relationship.

Menus

Section

This section introduces some new features of menus. The Enabled and Checked properties of menu commands give feedback to users to help them make appropriate menu choices. Menu control arrays are also defined and used.

Both users and programmers benefit if commands are enabled only when it makes sense to choose them. The typical edit commands behave in this way: the Paste command is grayed (disabled) unless something has been cut or copied to the Clipboard. If you leave commands enabled even when it is inappropriate for a user to choose them, users could become confused and you will have more programming to complete. And you have an unpleasant choice to make: do you want your program to do nothing in response to an inappropriate choice, or do you want to inform the user that the choice was inappropriate?

If you decide to have nothing happen when a user clicks on an inappropriate command, a user may think your program is broken, or that a mistake has been made. If you display messages when a choice is inappropriate, then the user will soon feel frustrated and less than happy with your program. Could you defend this choice? Why let users make a choice that they cannot carry out?

Finally, if you enable commands only when appropriate, then you don't have to clutter the code that implements those commands with logic to test whether the program should respond to the user's selection. By isolating the test for appropriateness and performing it separately, the code that implements commands (the command handlers) can always be written with the assumption that the program is going to perform the action associated with that menu command.

On the other hand, a dimmed command could be frustrating if the user doesn't understand why it is dimmed. At times, leaving a menu command enabled and displaying an error message explaining why the command is currently inappropriate is a better choice than disabling the command. As you gain more experience with programming, you will learn when to disable commands and when to display error messages.

Placing checkmarks next to menu commands gives clues to users about their current settings and how to change them. Some commands toggle a condition on and off; placing a checkmark next to such a command indicates that the condition is currently on.

In this section, menu control arrays are also defined and used. Menu control arrays let you write a single command handler for a group of commands. These control arrays benefit you, the programmer, only; they don't offer users any immediate benefit. A running Visual Basic program provides no visual clue that it uses menu control arrays.

Checked and Enabled Properties

When a menu command is enabled, it can be chosen from the menu. If the menu command is disabled, it is dimmed and cannot be clicked.

Professional programmers typically disable commands when users cannot select them. Setting a command's Enabled property to True enables it. Setting the property to False disables it.

Typically, you do not disable a command during project design. If a user can never select the command, why include it in the program? Commands are disabled as the program runs, if a certain condition is not met.

For example, suppose that you open the Edit menu in Microsoft Word. Unless you have placed some material on the Clipboard that could be pasted, the Paste command is dimmed. Dimming the command tells you, the user, that there is no material ready to be pasted. As soon as you cut or copy some text, however, the Paste command is enabled.

To display a check next to a command, set the command's Checked property to True. To remove a check from a command, set the command's Checked property to False.

Suppose that you had a command on a View menu for the Toolbar. This command is a toggle. Choosing it shows or hides the toolbar. When the toolbar is displayed, the menu command appears with a checkmark; choosing it hides the Toolbar and unchecks the menu command. When the toolbar is not shown, the menu command appears unchecked; choosing it shows the toolbar and checks the menu command.

CONTROL ARRAYS

You haven't used control arrays in your programs yet, but this may not be the first time you've seen the term. If you have ever given the same name to more than one control, Visual Basic has prompted you to create a control array. In a control array, more than one control shares the same event procedure. The controls in a control array all have the same name; they are distinguished by a numerical index, much like the elements of a data array declared with the **Dim** statement.

To use a control array, you have to be able to distinguish among the elements of the array. The solution is to give each control in a control array a different number, or index. The Index property serves this purpose. Elements of control arrays have unique index values. Controls in a control array share the same event procedures, which have an extra parameter: the Index of the control in the array that generated the event.

Menu Control Arrays

In a menu control array, you give two or more commands the same name. Commands with the same name share the same Click event handler. Each menu item receives a unique index number, which you assign in the Menu Design window. Commands assigned the same name must be at the same level (such as in the same submenu) and next to each other. The captions of the menu commands—the names by which the user knows the commands—can be whatever you want them to be. Only the Name property of the commands—the means by which you refer to the items in code—must be the same.

When the program is running and a user clicks on a menu command in a control array, the index number is passed to the subroutine as an index parameter. This number is used to determine the program's action.

What Shall I Wear?

This program answers that tough morning question: What shall I wear?

A menu displays a selection of bottoms: three shorts and two pants. When a user clicks on a command, a list of appropriate shirts is displayed. The program makes the assumption that the clothes are dirty after a person has worn them. As each menu item is clicked, it is both checked and disabled.

Figure 8-1
The What Shall I Wear?
form

When the laundry is done, the menu lets the user reset all the choices, enabling and unchecking each item. Figure 8-1 shows the completed form for the project.

DESIGNING THE MENU

Follow these steps to create the menu.

1 Start Visual Basic. If Visual Basic is running, select New Project from the File menu.

2 Change the caption of the default form to **What Shall I Wear?**

3 Select the form. Click on the Menu Design button to open the Menu Design window.

4 For the first menu command, enter the caption **&Clothing** and the name **mnuClothing**.

5 Click Next and the right arrow to create a submenu.

Figure 8-2
Beginning the menu
design

6 Enter the caption **&Blue Shorts** and the name **mnuBottoms**. For the Index entry, enter 0. Note the Checked and Enabled properties. These will be set while the program is running. See Figure 8-2.

7 Click Next and enter the caption **B&lack Shorts** and the name **mnuBottoms**. Enter an Index value of 1.

8 Click Next and enter the caption **&Plaid Shorts** and the name **mnuBottoms**. Enter an Index value of 2.

9 Click Next and enter the separator, a single hyphen. Though this is not a real menu item, it must have the same name as the other menu items. It must also have an index number. Enter **mnuBottoms** for a name and 3 for the Index value. See Figure 8-3.

10 Click Next and enter the caption **B&rown Pants** and the name **mnuBottoms**. Enter an Index value of 4.

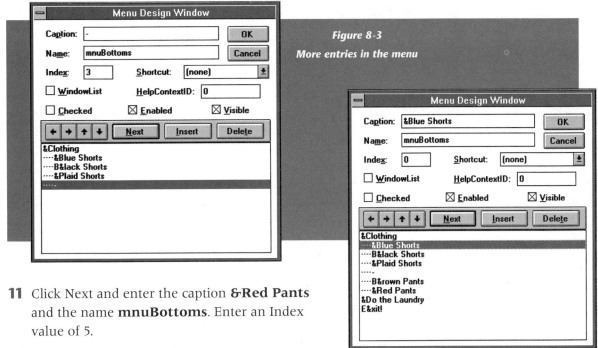

Figure 8-3
More entries in the menu

Figure 8-4
Completed menu

11 Click Next and enter the caption **&Red Pants** and the name **mnuBottoms**. Enter an Index value of 5.

12 Click Next and the left arrow. Enter the caption **&Do the Laundry** and the name **mnuLaundry**.

13 Click Next. Enter the caption **E&xit!** and the name **mnuExit**. An exclamation point is added to menu bar commands that perform tasks, rather than displaying a submenu. Figure 8-4 shows the completed menu.

ENTERING THE CODE

The following steps create a fully functioning menu. By the end of the steps, the program will still not prompt the user regarding what shirt to wear with the selected bottom. You will finish the program in the exercises at the end of this section.

Follow these steps to enter the code.

1 Click Clothing in the main menu bar.

2 Click any of the entries shown in the submenu. The items share the same event procedure, the Click event.

3 The top line of the form shows one of the effects of creating a menu control array. *Index* is passed as a parameter to the event handler. The value of *Index* corresponds to the numbers assigned in the Menu Design window.

```
Sub mnuBottoms_Click (Index As Integer)
```

4 Enter lines to mark the item clicked with a check and disable it:

```
'—Mark clicked item as checked, and disable
mnuBottoms(Index).Checked = True
mnuBottoms(Index).Enabled = False
```

5 Enter lines to handle the only choice appropriate when all the clothes have been worn: Do the Laundry. Each of the menu items is unchecked and enabled:

```
'—Do the laundry
Dim x As Integer
For x = 0 To 5
    '—Get rid of check marks and enable each item
    mnuBottoms(x).Checked = False
    mnuBottoms(x).Enabled = True
Next x
```

6 In the mnuExit command handler, enter the command **End**.

7 Run the program. Click on Plaid Shorts. Click on Clothing. Note the item Plaid Shorts is dimmed and checked.

8 Try to click on Plaid Shorts again.

9 Click on each of the other menu items.

10 Click on Do the Laundry. Note the results.

11 Try to click on the separator.

12 Save the project and form files.

QUESTIONS AND ACTIVITIES

1. Use an **If-Then** statement in the **mnuBottoms** menu handler of the form:

   ```
   If Index = 0 Then ...
   ```

   to display at least one appropriately colored shirt for each bottom in the menu. Use a message box to display the color of the shirt to wear with each bottom.

2. Add a submenu to the Blue Shorts command:
   a) Select the form.
   b) Open the Menu Design window.
   c) Select the command below Blue Shorts.
   d) Click on the Insert button, then click on the right arrow.
   e) Enter the caption **White Shirt**, the name **mnuShirt**, and an Index of 0.

f) Click on the Insert button, then click on the right arrow (if necessary) to put this entry in the same submenu as White Shirt.

g) Enter the caption **Blue Shirt**, the name **mnuShirt**, and an Index of 1.

h) Without running the program, click on Clothing. Click on Blue Shorts. Click on White Shirt.

i) Run the program. Click on Clothing. A run-time error is generated: a command with a submenu cannot display a checkmark.

j) Delete the submenu of Blue Shorts.

3. Rename the Clothing menu to Bottoms. Create a new menu called Tops. In the Tops menu, create a submenu with the following entries:

    White Shirt
    Blue Shirt
    Black Shirt
    Green Shirt
    Reset

Give each of the first four commands in the submenu the same name and index values 0 through 3. As each command is clicked, disable it until the Reset item enables all of the commands again. Give Reset its own name and event procedure.

The Planet Demo Program

Section

The Planet Demo Program calculates what a person's weight would be if measured on another planet of the solar system. The program uses a menu control array to choose a particular planet. In the Click event procedure, you will use a **Select Case** statement to identify which planet was chosen. The person's name and weight are entered through a dialog box, which is another form that you will design and display. This project is the first in which you will use more than one form.

The main form of the program has a very simple appearance (see Figure 8-5).

The menu bar shows three commands: Person, Planet, and Exit. When a user clicks on Person, a dialog box opens, prompting the user to enter the name and weight of a person. The user can enter their own weight, or that of someone else.

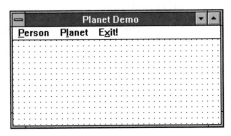

Figure 8-5
Finished Planet Demo
program

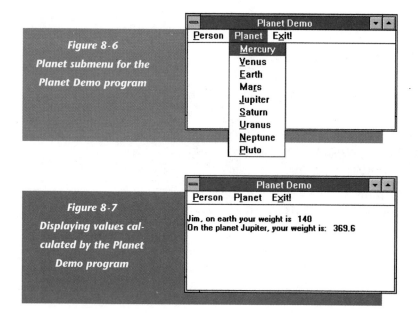

Figure 8-6
Planet submenu for the Planet Demo program

Figure 8-7
Displaying values calculated by the Planet Demo program

Next the user clicks on Planet. A submenu listing nine planets opens (see Figure 8-6).

Once the planet has been picked, the program multiples the person's earthly weight by a factor that adjusts the weight for the chosen planet. The two values are displayed on the main form, as shown in Figure 8-7.

Starting Out

Before you build the simple form for this project, you should focus on the Visual Basic features you will use. These include the **Select Case** statement, dialog boxes, showing and hiding forms, and the **Print** method.

SELECT CASE STATEMENT

This program has nine possible branches, one corresponding to each planet. One way to handle this is with a series of **If-Then** statements, one for each planet. You might write one of the statements this way:

```
If Index = 1 Then
    '—Mercury
    W = Weight * .27
End If
```

Another way to handle this is to use a **Select Case** statement. This statement evaluates an expression and, based on the calculated value, branches to a particular set of statements. The basic syntax for the **Select Case** statement is:

Select Case *expression*
    Case *value1*
        statements executed if value1 matches expression
    Case *value2*
        statements
    ....
    Case Else
        statements executed if the expression doesn't match any of the Values
End Select

In the Planet program, the *expression* is the value of the index parameter. Each valuelist is of the simplest form—a single integer constant giving the index for a planet. The case statements perform the conversion from earth weight to weight on that planet.

The **Select Case** statement permits even greater flexibility than the above syntax indicates. For example, any *value* can be an expression taking either of these forms:

> *expression1* **To** *expression2*   *‘ (for example,* 17 To 25*)*
> *comparison-operator expression1*   *‘ (for example,* > *“John”)*

You may also use a list of values after the **Case** keyword, as an alternative to using multiple **Case** groups with identical statements. Finally, the **Case Else** part is optional. For the details of the **Select Case** statement, consult the Visual Basic Help system.

The **Select Case** statement doesn't let you express anything that you could not already express using only **If-Then-Else**. However, **If-Then-Else** is a very general tool, whereas **Select Case** is tailored for choosing among a range of alternative actions based on the current value of a single expression. In such situations, the **Select Case** statement lets you write more concise code that is easier to read.

DIALOG BOXES

A dialog box is a kind of window that is typically used to collect a specific kind of information from the user, or to perform a specific function. Unlike the main window of a program, dialog boxes appear only when needed, and are closed when they have fulfilled their limited purpose. When you save a program, for example, a dialog box appears (see Figure 8-8). Dialog boxes such as this one contain labels, command buttons, textboxes, and comboboxes.

Figure 8-8

The Save As dialog box

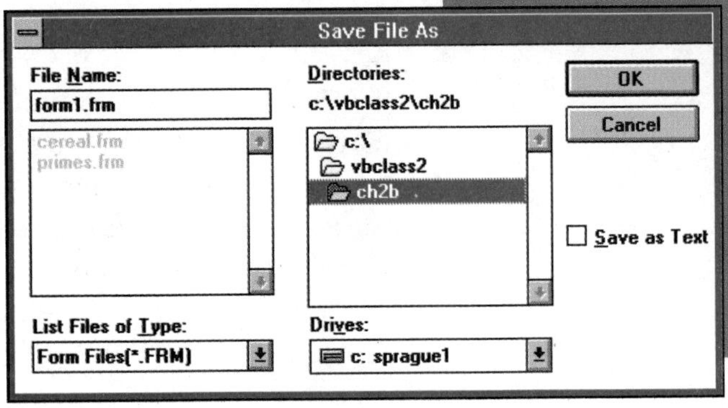

While this dialog box is open, you cannot use any other window of Visual Basic; you must first click OK or Cancel to close this dialog box before you can resume work. A dialog box that requires you to complete your interaction with it before you can resume working with a program is called a modal dialog box. Not all dialog boxes are modal. Those that are not are called modeless dialog boxes. For example, when you choose the Find command in Microsoft Word or Windows Write to search for text, the Find dialog box lets you work in the application while it is open. You close the dialog box when you are finished searching.

The InputBox and MessageBox functions create dialog boxes that you can display in Visual Basic. These dialog boxes are not forms; you do not design their layout, which is very general but also very simple. Often, however, your programs will need to collect from the user more than one piece of information before they can perform a task. Displaying a large number of InputBoxes in succession would annoy the user. To address this need, Visual Basic lets you design and use forms that behave like either modal or modeless dialog boxes. The Planet program uses a form as a modal dialog box to collect the person's name and weight.

SHOWING AND HIDING FORMS

The form that is displayed first and automatically when a Visual Basic program is executed is called the start-up form. If your project contains more than one form, the start-up form is by default the first form added to the project.

You can change the default start-up form if necessary. To do so, select Project from the Options menu. For example, in Figure 8-9, the form frmPlanet is identified as the start-up form. This is the first form a user will see when the program is run.

Figure 8-9
Identifying the start-up form

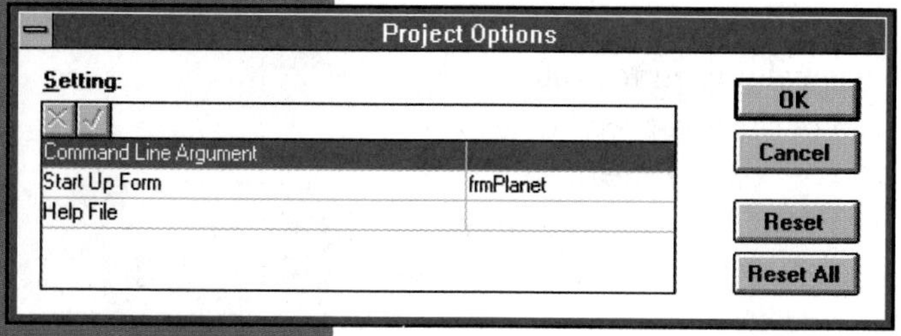

To make any other form appear while the program runs, it must be loaded and displayed. Both are accomplished by the **Show** method. In the Planet program, you want the dialog box frmPerson, which is a form, to appear first. Therefore, you enter this line of code:

```
frmPerson.Show 1
```

The argument 1 indicates that the form frmPerson should be displayed in a modal way: the main form of the Planet program cannot be accessed until the frmPerson form is closed. (If you do not know what the word "modal" means, read the previous section about dialog boxes.) Using an argument of 0 instead of 1 would tell Visual Basic to show the frmPerson form in a modeless way: Visual Basic would make frmPerson visible and active, but the user would be able to switch back to the main form while frmPerson was still open.

To close the frmPerson dialog box and return to the original form, you execute this command:

```
frmPerson.Hide
```

The **Hide** method removes the form from the screen, but does not remove it from memory. The next time your program executes the **Show** method of the frmPerson form, the dialog box will appear on the screen more rapidly, because it does not have to be loaded from disk and constructed in memory by Visual Basic. If your program had many different dialog boxes, most of which were not often used, it would be wasteful for them to occupy memory just because they had been used once. To remove the frmPerson from memory, you would use this statement:

```
Unload frmPerson
```

This statement causes the form's QueryUnload event and then the Unload event to be generated before the form is removed from memory. For more information about the Unload event, consult the Visual Basic Help system.

THE PRINT METHOD

The output for the procedure is displayed directly on the default form using the **Print** method. A statement that uses this method has the syntax:

object.**Print** *string or value*

If you do not specify an object, the **Print** method prints on the default form. You can use the **Print** method to print on forms and picture boxes, as well as in the Debug window. The **Print** method uses the current color and font for the object, and writes its output at the coordinates given by the object's CurrentX and CurrentY properties.

The **Print** method is used to display successive lines of text. It is in many ways a throwback to the era of character mode programs. After the above statement using the **Print** method is executed, CurrentY will be increased by the value of *object*.TextHeight so that a new line can be written beneath the one just printed.

Creating the Menu

The key parts of this program are the menu bar and the dialog box. Let's start with the menu:

1   Start Visual Basic. If Visual Basic is running, choose New Project from the File menu.

2   Change the caption of the form to **Planet Demo**. Change the name of the form to **frmPlanet**.

3   Select the form and open the Menu Design window.

4 For the first command, enter the caption **&Person** and the name **mnuPerson**. This command calls the dialog box, which is then used to collect the name and the weight of the person.

5 Click Next and enter the caption **P&lanet** with the name **mnuPlanet**. This command displays a submenu of the nine planets.

6 Click Next, then the right arrow to create a submenu. Enter the caption **&Mercury** and the name **mnuPlanets**. Set the Index to 0. Note the plural form of Planet.

7 Click Next and enter the following captions, names, and Index values. Because all the entries in the submenu have the same name, you have created a menu control array.

Caption	Name	Index
&Venus	mnuPlanets	1
&Earth	mnuPlanets	2
Ma&rs	mnuPlanets	3
&Jupiter	mnuPlanets	4
&Saturn	mnuPlanets	5
&Uranus	mnuPlanets	6
&Neptune	mnuPlanets	7
&Pluto	mnuPlanets	8

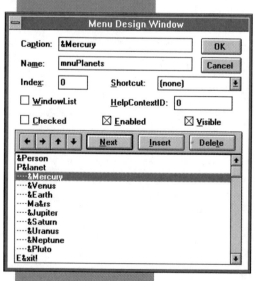

Figure 8-10
Completed menu for the Planet Demo program

8 Click Next, then the left arrow. Enter the caption **E&xit!** and the name **mnuExit**. See Figure 8-10 for the complete menu.

9 Save the project and form files.

Menu control arrays, just like all other arrays, have subscripts in parentheses. Although the parentheses don't appear in the name box of Figure 8-10, they do appear in the listing of objects in the Code window (see Figure 8-11).

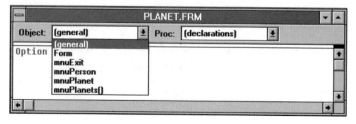

Figure 8-11
Identifying menu control arrays in the Code window

Creating a Code Module

To build a dialog box for the Planet program, first determine what information is to be collected, then determine how that information is to be communicated to the rest of the program.

The dialog box collects a person's name and weight. The name is a string, and the weight is an integer. To communicate between the dialog box and the Planet form, the variables are declared in a code module. A global declaration in a code module makes the value of a variable available to all forms in a project.

Create the code module by following these steps.

1   Select New Module from the File menu.

2   Enter the lines to declare the two global variables (the *g* prefix indicates a global variable):

```
Global gstrName As String
Global gWeight As Integer
```

3   When the project is saved, the module will be saved separately with a name you pick. Before it is saved, the module window uses its default name for a caption. See Figure 8-12.

4   Save the code module.

Figure 8-12

Caption of the module window is the name of the module file

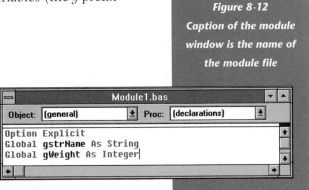

Setting Up the Dialog Box

To create the dialog box form, start by adding a form to the project. The dialog box requires two textboxes, two labels, and a command button.

1   Select New Form from the File menu.

2   Change the caption of the form to **Person's Name and Weight**. Change the name of the form to **frmPerson**.

3   Add two textboxes, **txtName** and **txtWeight**. Clear their text.

4   Add two labels with the captions **Enter the name:** and **Enter the weight:**. Set the FontSize to 9.75. See Figure 8-13.

Figure 8-13

Adding labels to the dialog box

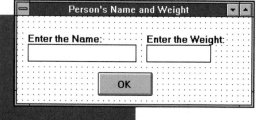

Figure 8-14
The completed form

5 Add a command button. Change the name of the button to **cmdOK** and the caption to **OK**. See the complete form in Figure 8-14.

6 Save this form.

Adding Code to the Dialog Box

The code in the command button reads the textboxes and assigns their values to the global variables. It also manages shifting focus back to the start-up form and enabling the Planet menu command. Follow these steps to add code to the command button:

1 Double-click on the command button cmdOK.

2 Enter these lines to read the values of the textboxes:

```
'—Read the name and weight boxes
gstrName = txtName
gWeight = Val(txtWeight)
```

3 If either the name or weight is blank, the dialog box hasn't done its job. Focus is returned to txtName. Enter these lines:

```
'—If the name is blank or the weight is blank
'set the focus back to txtName
If gstrName = "" Or gWeight = 0 Then
    txtName.SetFocus
    txtWeight = ""
```

4 If a user provides values for both name and weight, the program hides the dialog box and focus returns to the main form. In addition, the Planet command on frmPlanet, the start-up form, is enabled.

```
Else
    frmPerson.Hide
    frmPlanet.mnuPlanet.Enabled = True
End If
```

5 Save the form.

The code in the fourth step can access a menu command from the other form by including the form name in the statement. The syntax of the statement is:

FormName.MenuItem.Enabled = True

Writing the Code for Form Planet

The code in this form has four jobs.

- Declare an array for the planet names. These names are used in the display.

- Initialize the elements of the planet array to the names of the planets.

- Manage the appearance and disappearance of forms and menu items.

- Calculate and display the person's weight on the planet clicked. Follow these steps to write the code for frmPlanet:

1 Select frmPlanet in the Project window. Click on the View Code button.

2 In the general declarations section, add this line to declare an array for the planet names:

```
Dim PlanetName(0 To 8) As String
```

The subscripts match the index numbers assigned in the menu control array. Index 0 corresponds to subscript 0, Mercury.

3 Open the Form_Load procedure for frmPlanet and enter these lines to initialize the PlanetName array:

```
'—Initialize planet names
PlanetName(0) = "Mercury"
PlanetName(1) = "Venus"
PlanetName(2) = "Earth"
PlanetName(3) = "Mars"
PlanetName(4) = "Jupiter"
PlanetName(5) = "Saturn"
PlanetName(6) = "Uranus"
PlanetName(7) = "Neptune"
PlanetName(8) = "Pluto"
```

4 You don't want users choosing a planet before they enter a name and weight. That means you need to enter a final line in the Form_Load procedure that disables the Planet command in the menu bar:

```
mnuPlanet.Enabled = False
```

5 The menu command mnuPerson displays the dialog box. You display the box and shift focus to it by using the **Show** method. Enter this line in the mnuPerson_Click() procedure:

```
frmPerson.Show 1
```

6 Clicking on the **Exit!** command should stop the program. To have this happen, insert **End** in the mnuExit_Click() procedure.

7   Open the Code window and select mnuPlanets() from the Object drop-down list. The parentheses at the end of the name indicate a menu control array. Enter the line declaring a variable for the adjusted weight:

```
'—Declare variable for adjusted weight
Dim AdjWeight As Single
```

8   Add the **Select Case** statement in the same subroutine. The value of *index* corresponds to a menu item. Each menu item is a planet name. Each branch in the **Select Case** statement calculates an adjusted weight for one planet:

```
'—Select Case statement to pick out planet
Select Case index
'—For each planet, calculate weight and
'check the menu item.
  '—Mercury
  Case 0
     AdjWeight = gWeight * .27
  '—Venus
  Case 1
     AdjWeight = gWeight * .86
  '—Earth
  Case 2
     AdjWeight = gWeight
  '—Mars
  Case 3
     AdjWeight = gWeight * .37
  '—Jupiter
  Case 4
     AdjWeight = gWeight * 2.64
  '—Saturn
  Case 5
     AdjWeight = gWeight * 1.17
  '—Uranus
  Case 6
     AdjWeight = gWeight * .92
  '—Neptune
  Case 7
     AdjWeight = gWeight * 1.44
  '—Pluto
  Case 8
     AdjWeight = gWeight * .33
End Select
```

9 Once the calculation is made, you want the planet name checked on the menu. Enter this line to check the planet name:

```
'—Check the planet selected
mnuPlanets(index).Checked = True
```

10 The results are displayed directly on the form. You use the **Print** method to print the person's name, earth weight, clicked planet, and equivalent weight on that planet. Enter these lines to display the results:

```
'—Display results on form
Cls
Print
Print Trim$(gstrName);
Print ", on earth your weight is "; gWeight
Print "On the planet " & PlanetName(index) & ", your weight is: "; AdjWeight
```

The form is cleared, a line is skipped and the person's name is printed. The **Trim$** function deletes any extra spaces around the name, and the **Print** method prints the result on the form. The semicolon means the display stays on the same line. Normally, it would automatically shift to the next line. The earth weight is printed. On the next line, the planet name is printed from the *PlanetName* array, initialized in the Form_Load procedure. Finally, the adjusted weight is printed.

11 Run the program. Click on Person. Enter a name and a weight. Click OK.

12 Click on the Planet menu. Click on a planet. Click on each of the planets to check your program.

13 Save the project file, the form files, and the code module file.

QUESTIONS AND ACTIVITIES

1. Explain some of the important properties of a menu item.

2. How is a menu command like a command button? To what events does a menu command respond?

3. How are the different menu commands differentiated from each other in a menu control array?

4. People between the ages of 0 and 15 cannot receive a license to drive in the state of Illinois. People ages 16 and 17 can receive an Illinois license with their parent's permission. People above the age

of 18 can apply for a license without parental consent. If the age of an applicant is represented by the variable *Age,* write the **Select Case** statement that displays an appropriate message box for each of the three possibilities. Are there other possibilities? If so, make sure your program segment handles those.

5. Rewrite the code for mnuPlanets to eliminate the **Select Case** statement and replace it with nine **If-Then** statements.

6. Rewrite the code for mnuPlanets to eliminate the **Select Case** statement and replace it with a single assignment statement. Declare an array of Single to hold the multipliers for each planet. Initialize the array in the Form_Load procedure, just like the *PlanetName* array.

 In the mnuPlanet*s* code, multiply the person's weight by the multiplier in the multiplier array and assign it to *AdjWeight.*

7. Remove the **Trim$** function from the mnuPlanets code and run the program. Note the change in the display.

8. Enlarge the frmPlanet and add a listbox. Rewrite the mnuPlanets code to display the results in a listbox instead of on the form. Don't clear the listbox between each choice.

9. Change the mnuPlanets code to disable each planet in the menu when it is clicked.

Arrays

Section

One of the data structures implemented on the earliest computers was the list. Lists are everywhere. A computer is dependent on lists. There are lists of files in a computer's directories, lists of commands in programs, lists of data in memory cells. Many processors have special commands that facilitate working with lists. Programming languages have special list-handling capabilities.

A phone book is a list. A file of recipe cards is a list. An individual recipe is a list of ingredients and cooking instructions. It's easy to turn real-life lists into computer lists.

Sometimes a distinction is made between internal lists and external lists. An external list is a list maintained in a file on a disk. An internal list is a list maintained in random access memory. An internal list is called an array. Arrays have already used in previous programs: most often they have been referred to as tables.

Here is a typical statement declaring an array:

```
Dim List(100) As String
```

In this statement, the variable *List* represents 100 string values (the array). This array can store 100 items, which are called elements or members. The elements in this example are of the String data type.

To access a specific element in an array, you need to be able to refer to it. To do so, you use a subscript, which is the number in parentheses. The subscript is a whole number that indicates the position of the element in the array.

The first element of the array is referred to as List(0). If an array is declared (or dimensioned, Dim for short) with a single value, the starting subscript is 0. The eleventh element of the array (starting from 0) is List(10).

Another way to declare an array is to specify the first and last subscript:

```
Dim List(51 To 100) As Single
```

In this example, the array holds 50 elements. The valid subscripts range from 51 to 100. You can also specify subscripts that are negative:

```
Dim List2(-5 To 5) As Integer
Dim List3(-10 To -1) As Single
```

To place a string into the forty-third element of an array, you would use the statement:

```
List(43) = "Here is a sample string."
```

To put the twenty-first element of an array into a textbox named txtDogName, you would use the following statement:

```
txtDogName = List(21)
```

QUESTIONS AND ACTIVITIES

1. Name five household management projects that could be handled with an array.

2. Write the statements to declare the following arrays of values:
   a) 30 whole numbers
   b) 31 whole numbers starting with a subscript of -15
   c) 20 strings starting with a subscript of 21
   d) 5 currency amounts starting with a subscript of 10

3. Describe the following arrays in words:
   a) Dim Shoes(1 To 50) As String
   b) Dim Names(20) As String
   c) Dim Fees(1 To 5) As Currency
   d) Dim Adjustments(10 To 20) As Single

Section 4

The School Cafeteria Project

This program features arrays. Thirty students have been polled about the quality of cafeteria food. They have ranked the food 1 for *horrific* to 5 for *excellent*. Their rankings are stored in an array. The program reads the array and tallies the rankings. The tallies are kept in an array.

The program illustrates the counting principle ($C = C + 1$) described in Chapter 4 in the context of arrays.

Planning the Program

To plan the project, break it down into its component parts. You need to:

⦿ Initialize the array of student rankings. Typically, this information would be read from a file. In this program the array is initialized in the Form_Load procedure.

⦿ Display student rankings in a listbox.

⦿ Tally the results.

⦿ Display the results. The results are displayed in a bar graph, drawn in a picture box. The **Line** method draws the rectangles needed to build the graph.

Figure 8-15 displays the completed program.

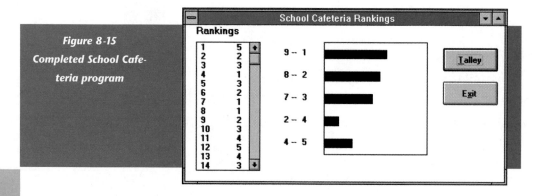

Figure 8-15
Completed School Cafeteria program

Setting Up the Form

Follow these steps to set up the form.

1   Start Visual Basic. If Visual Basic is running, choose New Project from the File menu.

2   Change the name of the form to **frmCafeteria**. Change the caption to **School Cafeteria Rankings**.

3   Place a List box on the form. Change the name to **lstRankings**. This box displays the student responses to the poll.

4   Put a Picture box on the form. Change the name to **pctGraph**. This box displays a bar graph of the tallies.

5   Put two command buttons on the form. Change the captions to **&Tally** and **E&xit**. Change the names to **cmdTally** and **cmdExit**. See Figure 8-16.

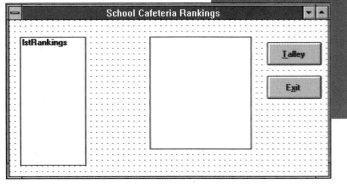

Figure 8-16

The form in progress

6   In the space between the List box and the Picture box, create a control array of labels. Draw a single label, set AutoSize to True, and position it between the boxes in the upper fifth of the space. Change the name to **lblTally**.

7   Select the label and copy with Ctrl+C. Paste with Ctrl+V. When Visual Basic prompts you about control arrays, click on Yes.

8   Paste again and again until there are five evenly distributed labels. These labels will display the ranking, 1 to 5, and the number of responses in each. See Figure 8-17.

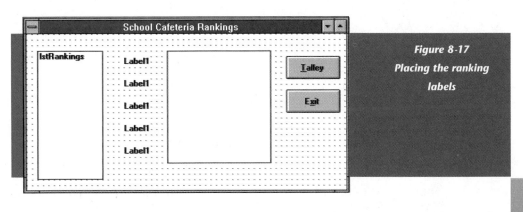

Figure 8-17

Placing the ranking labels

9 Finish the form by putting a label above the List box. The caption should read **Rankings**.

10 Save the project and form files.

Entering the Code

As you write the code, start with the smaller routines:

1 Click on the View Code button in the Project window.

2 In the general declarations section, enter the following declarations:

```
Dim Ranking(1 To 30) As Integer
Dim Tallies(1 To 5) As Integer
```

3 In the Form_Load procedure, enter these lines to initialize the Tallies arrays declared above.

```
Dim x As Integer
'—Initialize the tallies
For x = 1 To 5
    Tallies(x) = 0
Next x
```

4 To initialize the Ranking array, enter a single line:

```
Ranking(1) = 5
```

5 Select the line. Press Ctrl+C to copy the line. Press Ctrl+V 29 times to paste the line into the routine. Move the cursor to each line in the routine and change the subscripts and the values assigned to each array element. The subscripts should range from 1 to 30. The rankings should be random whole numbers between 1 and 5.

```
'—Initialize the 30 student responses
Ranking(1) = 5
Ranking(2) = 2
Ranking(3) = 3
Ranking(4) = 1
. . .
Ranking(28) = 1
Ranking(29) = 2
Ranking(30) = 2
```

The middle lines have been omitted.

6 Enter the **End** statement in the code for cmdExit.

7 Open the cmdTally_Click procedure. Enter the lines to declare a local variable for the loop and clear the listbox for the rankings:

```
Dim x As Integer
lstRankings.Clear
```

8 The next section of code does two jobs. It displays the rankings in the List box. It tallies the rankings using a special counting statement. Each ranking, a whole number between 1 and 5, becomes the subscript to the Tallies array. The ranking is used to determine which tally to add one to. Enter these lines:

```
For x = 1 To 30
    lstRankings.AddItem Str(x) & Chr(9) & Str(Ranking(x))
    Tallies(Ranking(x)) = Tallies(Ranking(x)) + 1
Next x
```

9 Set up the Picture box with a user-defined coordinate system for the graph. A sketch of the coordinate system used is shown in Figure 8-18.
Enter the line to set up the coordinate system:

```
pctGraph.Scale (0, 0)-(15, 5)
```

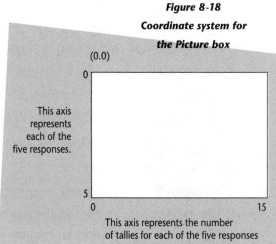

Figure 8-18
Coordinate system for the Picture box

10 The second loop uses the value of each ranking to draw a filled rectangle on the graph. The value is also displayed in the label control array:

```
Dim y As Integer
Const TopEdge = .7
Const BottomEdge = .3
For y = 1 To 5
    pctGraph.Line (0, y - TopEdge)-(Tallies(y), y - BottomEdge), , BF
    lblTally(y - 1) = Str$(Tallies(y)) & " — " & Str$(y)
Next y
```

The length of the bar is given by *Tallies(y)*. The top edge of the bar is *y - TopEdge*. The bottom edge of the bar is given by *y - BottomEdge*.

The actual tally along with the ranking number, 1 through 5, is assigned to the label control array. The control array starts with subscript 0. The value of *y* is decreased by 1 to give the subscript of the label control array, whose elements have indexes ranging from 0 to 4.

Try running the program, then save the project and form files.

QUESTIONS AND ACTIVITIES

1. Experiment with the values of the constants *TopEdge* and *BottomEdge*. Change the values by tenths and run the program with each change.

2. Alter the **Line** statement to change the color of the bars. Look up where to put the color in the Help system.

3. Alter the **Line** statement to draw empty rectangles, not filled rectangles.

4. Use the Notepad to create a file with 30 random entries between 1 and 5. Save the program in the Temp directory with the name **C:\Temp\Response.txt**. Put one value per line. Replace the 30 assignment statements in the Form_Load procedure with code to open the file for input, read the 30 values from the file, and initialize the array.

5. Change the coordinate system of the picture box and the **Line** commands to draw a vertical, not horizontal, graph.

Section

The Population Biology Program

There is an underlying order to nature and the events of nature. Observation of the natural world reveals relationships and patterns that beg for further research and explanation. One way to explain and to study these natural relationships is to create mathematical models.

The program you will build in this section is designed to model the fluctuations in the population of fish in a lake. The application of mathematics to the study of biological populations is called population biology.

Biological systems are enormously complex. The interaction of every part of a system on every other part is very difficult to model. Our ability to do such modeling has been enhanced enormously by using computers. As you will see with this program, the application of simple mathematical models to complex biological systems can sometimes have surprising results.

Background

In order to find a pattern in the fish populations of Butler Lake, you will need a simple mathematical model. This background section introduces both linear and nonlinear models. As you will see in this section, a nonlinear model fits your purposes better than a linear model.

LINEAR MODELS

Many events in life seem to conform to a linear model. A linear model assumes that a change in one event causes a proportional change in an associated event. For instance, if a 10-pound turkey should be cooked for 170 minutes, then it is logical that you would need to cook a 20-pound turkey for (2 x 170) or 340 minutes. See Figure 8-19.

If an investment of $100 earns $5, you might think that an investment of $200 will earn $10. Should studying for one hour a night lead to a grade increase of 10%, if studying for half that time leads to a grade increase of 5%?

Actually, beyond a certain ratio of study time to class time, studies have shown that grades *don't* improve. And there is no guarantee that investing $200 will earn $20 dollars or even $10. These events do not conform to a linear model.

Now, try to figure out whether the populations of fish in a lake would conform to a linear model. How many fish there are depends on how much food is available. If the fish population reaches a stable level, neither increasing or decreasing significantly, an increase in food ought to lead to an increase in the population. More food means more fish. Does it?

To test this question, start with a simple linear model:

$$p_2 = r * p_1$$

Instead of using actual figures for populations, which would make the model specific to a particular pond, in this model p_1 is the level of fish population at time 1 expressed as a number between 0 and 1. p_2 is the level of fish population at time 2. The growth factor that transforms one population number into the next is represented as r.

By this equation, the population grows each year if the growth factor is greater than 1. If the growth factor is less than 1, the population decreases each year.

Growth factors are based on past data and predictions about the future. If the population two years ago was 1000 and the population last year was 1500, the growth factor is 1500/1000 or 1.5. It might be reasonable to assume a population of 1500*1.5 or 2250 for this year.

Often, you compare populations from one year to the next because many animals in the wild have young once a year. You might not use years if the population you are examining reproduces every few days or months. Predicting the growth of a population entails finding a good value for the growth factor. If conditions for growth are right, pick a high value (1 or more) for the growth factor. If food is scarce and predators are many, pick a low value (less than 1).

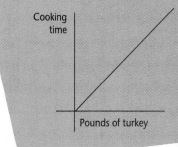

Figure 8-19
A linear model for turkey cooking

Cooking time

Pounds of turkey

APPLYING A LINEAR EQUATION

To experiment with this linear equation for the fish population of a lake, start with a population of 0.5 and a growth factor, r, of 1.1. These numbers represent the current fish population and the conditions for growth. To find the population for the next year, p_2, multiply 1.1 times 0.5. The result, 0.55, is the prediction for next year's population. To continue the predictions, use 0.55 as p_1 and multiply again by 1.1 to predict the next year's population.

An equation applied in this manner is called a difference equation. It calculates the difference between one year and the next. The value it predicts becomes the input used to predict the value of the population for the year after that, and so on, as shown in Table 8-1.

Table 8-1   Fish Population Year to Year

year 1	p_1	p_2
2	0.5	0.55
3	0.55	0.605
4	0.605	0.6655
5	0.6655	0.73205
6	0.73205	0.805255
7	0.805255	0.8857805
8	0.8857805	0.97435855
9	0.97435855	1.071794405
10	1.071794405	1.1789738455

Figure 8-20
Predicting the size of populations

In Figure 8-20, you can see the effect of unrestrained growth on the population. Our artificial limit of 1 on the population is exceeded in the ninth year. In the representation of population figures as values between 0 and 1, 1 represents the theoretical maximum population. This allows you to represent the extremes of population figures without actual numbers.

A very similar process goes on when school districts try to predict enrollments. In a growing community with reasonably priced housing, a school administrator would pick a high value for the growth factor, r. If the community is landlocked, prices

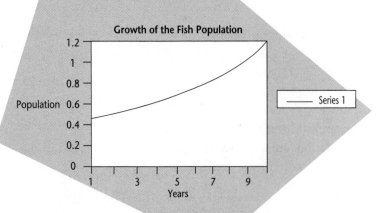

are high, and the population is aging, the administrator would pick a low growth value.

The only problem with this simple model is that it doesn't work. It might work for a year or two, but almost invariably after a few years the model breaks down. One way to explain the breakdown is to say there were factors that weren't taken into account, or new factors that couldn't have been anticipated. But maybe there is a need to modify the model.

THE NONLINEAR MODIFICATION

Even with virtually unlimited resources, the fish population in Butler Lake cannot grow without limit. There is no straight-line relationship that can explain how many fish will be in the lake five years from now. Eventually, the number of fish is just too large for the lake. When the food runs out, the fish start to die.

You need to add a nonlinear modification to your linear model, then see if that works for the fish in the lake. A nonlinear system doesn't assume a straight-line relationship between events. Try changing the linear equation like this:

$$p_2 = r * p_1 * (1 - p_1)$$

Remember, the population is expressed as a number between 0 and 1. The added factor, $(1 - p_1)$, is large, near 1, when the value of p_1 is small. Because it is nearly 1, it affects the product on the right side of the equation very little. As p_1 gets larger (as the fish population grows), the factor $1 - p_1$ starts to shrink. As it shrinks, it affects the growth rate. It acts as an inhibiting factor to unrestrained growth. As p_1 approaches 1, the factor $1 - p_1$ approaches 0. The resulting population in the subsequent year, p_2, is quite small.

If you use a growth value of 1.1 with the nonlinear equation, you will find that the population seems to level off after many years, not growing or shrinking by very much. The size of the population when it levels off is called an equilibrium point. In this case, the equilibrium is 0.090909. See Figure 8-21. Scientists have observed such equilibrium points in natural populations.

What's interesting about this model is what happens when the growth factor, r, is increased. For many values of r, the population

Figure 8-21
Equilibrium points for
fish populations

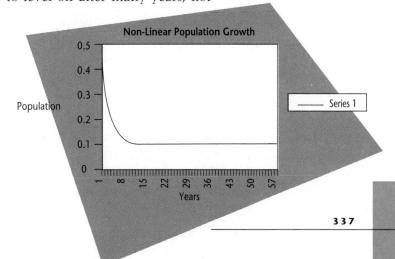

337

reaches an equilibrium point. As r increases, the equilibrium point increases. At a certain point, when the value of r increases, a single equilibrium point is not reached. The population fluctuates year after year, first up, then down. If you continue to increase r, strange things start to happen. The population predictions don't reach equilibrium and they don't bounce back and forth between two or even four values; they become chaotic. The population for each successive year is unpredictable.

When chaotic values were first noticed, scientists assumed that the model had been strained beyond its limits and the results were rejected. Now, a new way of explaining these results, called Chaos theory, explains why the results happen. The next section discusses Chaos theory in more detail.

Starting Out

This program illustrates what happens when a nonlinear model is used to simulate the population growth of the fish in Butler Lake. The program uses a menu to pick values for r and a graph to plot the growth of the population.

The graph is drawn directly on the form. This eliminates the need to specify an object for the graphics commands. The graphics commands used in this program are **PSet**, **Cls**, and **Scale**.

The program declares one global variable, r, in the general declarations section of the program.

Creating a Menu

Build a menu that allows the user to select a value of the growth factor, r, from a list. The values form a menu control array. Follow these steps:

1 Start Visual Basic. If Visual Basic is running, select New Project from the File menu.

2 Change the caption of the default form to **The Fish Population in Butler Lake**.

3 Select the form and open the Menu Design window.

4 Enter the caption **&r Value**. Enter the name **mnuRValue**.

5 Click on Next. Click on the right arrow to create a submenu. For each entry in the submenu, assign the same name e.g., mnuGrowthFactor. This creates a menu control array. Give successive index values to each entry. Click on Next after each entry.

Growth Factor	Index
1.1	0
2.0	1
2.5	2
3.0	3
3.2	4
3.4	5
3.6	6
3.8	7
&You Choose	8

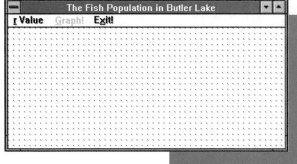

Figure 8-22

Completed menu

6 Click on Next. Click on the left arrow to return to the level of the entries in the main menu bar. Enter the caption **&Graph!** and the name **mnuGraph**. Disable the item by clicking on the Enabled property.

7 Click on Next. Enter the caption **E&xit!** and the name **mnuExit**. See the complete menu design in Figure 8-22.

Adding an Object

The form has a simple appearance, with just the menu bar displayed (see Figure 8-23):
    To finish the form:

1 Draw a label in the center of the bottom of the form.

2 Set the FontSize to 9.75, BorderStyle to 1-Fixed Single. Set the Alignment property to Center. Delete the caption. Name the form lblGrowthFactor.

Figure 8-23

Form with menu bar displayed

Entering the Growth Factor Code

The code for mnuGrowthFactor handles assigning a value to the global variable *r*, the growth factor. To complete this code:

1 In the Project window, click on View Code. Open the general declarations section and enter the following declaration:

```
Dim r As Single
```

2 Open the procedure for mnuGrowthFactor and enter the line declaring a string variable for a message:

```
Dim Msg As String
```

3 Enter the **Select Case** statement that handles the assignment of values to *r*:

```
Select Case index
    Case 0
        r = 1.1
    Case 1
        r = 2.0
    Case 2
        r = 2.5
    Case 3
        r = 3.0
    Case 4
        r = 3.2
    Case 5
        r = 3.4
    Case 6
        r = 3.6
    Case 7
        r = 3.8
    Case 8
        Msg = "Choose a value for r between 1 and 4"
        r = Val(InputBox(Msg))
End Select
'—Check the value
mnuGrowthFactor(index).Checked = True
'—Enable the graph menu item
mnuGraph.Enabled = True
```

Entering the Graph Code

The form itself will display the graph. Follow these steps to enter the code:

1 Click on View Code in the Project window. Open the mnuGraph_Click() procedure.

2 Enter the declarations for the local values:

```
Dim yr As Integer, p1 As Single, p2 As Single
```

3   Clear the form and set the coordinate system. The population values range from 0 to 1. The graph will plot 50 years of population predictions.

```
'—Clear the form
Cls
'—Set the coordinate system
Scale (0, 1)-(50, 0)
```

4   Set the DrawWidth:

```
'—Set the DrawWidth for a thicker point
DrawWidth = 2
```

5   Set the initial population. Set the label to show the current value of *r*.

```
'—Initial population
p1 = .5
'—Set caption
lblGrowthFactor.Caption = "r is " & Str$(r)
```

6   Enter the lines to set up a loop that generate population predictions for 50 years. Generate the new population, plot the point, and update the population variables.

```
'—Fifty years of predictions
For yr = 1 To 50
    p2 = r * p1 * (1 - p1) ' new population, p2
    PSet (yr, p2)
    p1 = p2                ' reset population
Next yr
```

7   Enter the command **End** in the mnuExit procedure.

8   Save the project and form files

9   Run the program. Click values for *r*. Click on Graph!

10 Experiment with values for *r* entered through the Inputbox. Values near 4 give interesting results. See Figure 8-24.

Figure 8-24
Results from the Population Biology program

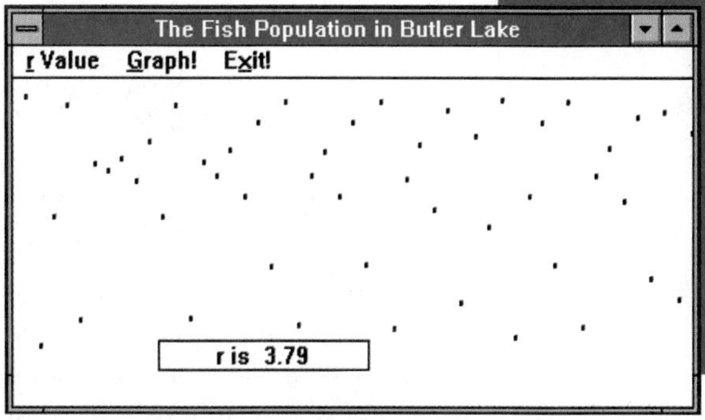

What's Next

Looking at each graph individually is tedious. Imagine the difficulty of producing several graphs without the help of the computer. The computer makes this kind of modeling very easy.

It may have occurred to you to build a program to summarize the data. Imagine a graph that holds data for hundreds of values of r from 1 to 4!

QUESTIONS AND ACTIVITIES

1. What factors would be considered when determining a reasonable growth factor for a wolf population in Yellowstone?

2. During the 1970s, the price of gold was on an upward spiral. One month the price was $200 per ounce, the next it was $250. If this were a linear relationship, what growth factor would you calculate from the data given?

3. Change the initial value of p_1 to various values between 0 and 1. Run the program and note any changes.

4. Alter the program to prompt the user to enter a value for the starting population when the program is run.

5. Modify the graph routine to connect the dots with a **Line** method. Change DrawWidth to 1.

6

Section

Chaos Theory

SCIENTIFIC THEORY

Scientific theories seek to explain and make predictions about events. If a theory is good, its predictions, confirmed by experiments, come true. Over a period of time, theories either evolve or are replaced by new theories. What happens is that, one by one, anomalies in a theory pop up. An anomaly is an unpredicted and, therefore, unexpected event. The anomalies grow in number until they demand explanation. At that point, a whole scientific theory may be scrapped and replaced with another.

The new theory has its own language and its own assumptions about truth. It makes predictions. Although the words used in the new theory may seem familiar, the meanings change so that old words are used in new ways.

In the early 1960s, a mathematician-turned-meteorologist named Edward Lorenz put together a weather simulation on his computer. The machine itself would be unrecognizable today. It had very few of the external parts you think of as belonging to a computer. It did have a processor and memory and could be programmed and display its results. Lorenz used it to put together a weather simulation that did a good job of mimicking real weather patterns.

Lorenz's computer began with a set of initial conditions, which are the conditions that are present at the start of the simulation. From there, he calculated a sequence of weather patterns. One day, he tried to recreate a sequence of weather patterns from the middle of the sequence. He took values from the middle of a run, then entered those values into his program by hand and ran the program again. He expected the second run to match the first. To his astonishment, after a short while, the runs differed dramatically. Soon there was no way to tell the two runs were related at all.

Lorenz entered a value to initialize the system accurate to three significant figures, thinking that weather patterns change in broad strokes, impervious to small changes. That particular number in the original run was calculated to an accuracy of six significant figures. The number Lorenz entered was different by 1 part in 1,000, yet the sequence of weather patterns produced were, after a short while, completely different.

It was then that Lorenz realized that long-range weather prediction would be impossible. The physical systems that govern weather are incredibly sensitive to initial conditions. We cannot know the initial conditions of a physical system well enough to make accurate long-range predictions. This odd result in the weather program was the beginning of a new science. This science finds order behind chaos and is named Chaos theory.

You may have experienced the order behind chaos yourself in your own kitchen. Liquids flow smoothly and predictably until, suddenly, the flow becomes turbulent, like the rapids of a river. Although plumbing systems are designed to prevent this, you may have heard your pipes knocking when water is flowing. Sometimes you can adjust the flow from a kitchen faucet until it starts to knock.

The knocking occurs because even in the midst of chaos (turbulence), order can emerge. The turbulence of the water resolves into a rhythm that becomes knocking.

The water flowing through the pipes of your house, the wind flowing over the wing of an airplane, electrons flowing through conductors and semiconductors—all of these things affect our everyday lives. Understanding the flow of these liquids is necessary for designing systems to handle them.

In the next section, you will be combining the individual graphs of the Population Biology project into a single graph. In that graph, you will see order dissolve to chaos. Order then reemerges, just before chaos takes over again.

QUESTIONS AND ACTIVITIES

1. How do anomalies figure into the development of scientific theories?

2. Give an example of a simple system in which, if you know the initial conditions of the system and the rules that govern the system, you can predict what will happen over a period of time. For instance, a pool table may contain such a system.

3. How did an anomaly occur in Lorenz's experiments?

4. Why is accurate long-range prediction of weather impossible?

5. What does your kitchen faucet have to do with Chaos theory? Try to adjust the water flow in your faucet at home to cause knocking.

6. The swirling of a drop of antifreeze in water is an example of a chaotic system. Write down two examples, not listed in the text, of systems that might be chaotic.

7

Section

The Population Biology Program Revisited

The first population biology program predicted the equilibrium state(s) (if they existed) for populations of fish in Butler Lake. Equilibrium states are population values that keep recurring. If there is one equilibrium point, the same population value recurs each year. In other words, the size of the population is stable.

Intuitively, you would think the fish population ought to be stable. The number of fish that die from old age or lack of resources (like food) should equal the number of fish born. If the conditions are very good in Butler Lake, the equilibrium population should be high. If the conditions are bad, the equilibrium population should be low.

The results from the program, though, did not match that hypothesis. When you tried different values for the growth factor r, you didn't always find a single equilibrium point. Instead, the graph sometimes showed two equilibrium points. In other words, your data identified two different equilibrium values, and these values interchanged each year. One year, the population would reach $p1$; the next year, the value was $p2$; the third year, you were back to $p1$. See Figure 8-25.

Scientists have found the same results in fish population studies. Does this mean our model is wrong? The nonlinear model you have used so far showed that for certain values of r, the growth factor, the population values went wild. See Figure 8-26. Should you throw your results out because they don't square with your intuition? In this second time through the fish population program, you will answer that question.

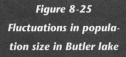

Figure 8-25
Fluctuations in population size in Butler lake

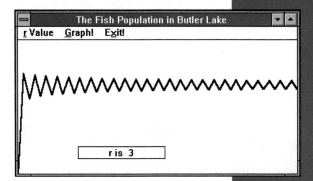

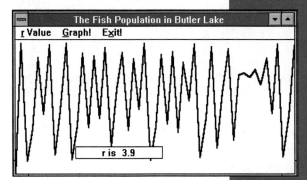

Figure 8-26
Predictions of population size in the lake with a different growth factor than used in Figure 8-25

MISTAKEN PREDICTIONS... OR ARE THEY?

Maybe our model's prediction of unpredictability isn't a mistake or misinterpretation. Maybe the nonlinear model that seems to predict chaos is correct.

This is a significant result. It means that fish populations may be unpredictable. If fish populations are unpredictable, what about school enrollments?

First Program Revisited

Remember, valid values for the population figure are decimal numbers between 0 and 1. Values for the growth factor r run between 1 and 4. A value for r less than 1 results in a population of 0. When the value of r is greater than 4, the population exceeds the upper limit of 1. Assume the population starts at 0.5 and generate each successive population figure from the current one:

```
p2 = r * p1 * ( 1 - p1 )
```

When you applied this equation to successive generations of fish for small values of r, eventually the fish population stopped oscillating and settled down to a single equilibrium value. When you pushed r a little higher, the graph showed two equilibrium points. Then at some point, the steadily increasing value for r caused the resulting graph to bounce all over the place. See Figures 8-26 and Figure 8-27.

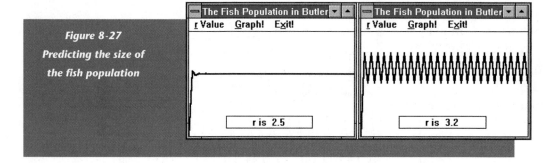

Figure 8-27
Predicting the size of the fish population

The value of the population variable in Figure 8-26 never settles down to a single value, or even two values.

Starting Out

To see patterns in your population data, you need a way to put all the information from the individual graphs you produced in the first population biology program into a single graph.

The Summary Program you are about to build displays this summary graph on the default form. You will use a loop to generate values for r that span the range from 2.5 to 4.

Each column of the graph represents one value of the growth factor, r. For each of these values, the population figures for 150 generations of fish are calculated. You use the **Pset** method to place these population values on the graph in the column for that growth value.

For values of r that produce one equilibrium point, almost all the 150 points representing 150 different population figures will be at about the same place. As the value of r increases, the single equilibrium point will split to two, then to four. Each successive column plots the data for a single value of the growth factor. After several doubling events (a single point, two points, four points), the graph bursts into 150 seemingly random positions all over the column.

The resulting graph shows the equilibrium points for many points in the range from 2.5 to 4.0. See Figure 8-28.

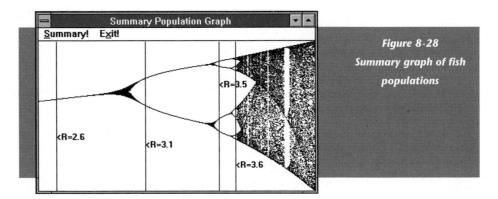

Figure 8-28
Summary graph of fish
populations

Note that the first 20 generations for each value of *r* are not plotted. During the first 10 or so generations, the population figure moves around a lot before settling on its equilibrium point(s). The starting population value is 0.5.

Figure 8-28 can be divided into several regions. In the first region, the population value settles on a single equilibrium point. The column *r = 2.6* is typical of this region. The graph branches to two in the next region. This region shows two equilibrium points. The column *r = 3.06* is typical of the region. The column *r = 3.49* is typical of the region with four equilibrium points. *r = 3.56* is in a region where there are 8 equilibrium points. You can glimpse eight doubling to 16. But then, you find chaos. Finally, the pattern resolves again. From chaos emerges three values. These double and soon dissolve again into chaos.

Building the Menu

In Figure 8-28, you could see the menu bar above the graph. Follow these steps to create that menu.

1   Start Visual Basic. If Visual Basic is running, select New Project from the File menu.

2   Change the caption of the form to **Summary Population Graph**.

3   Select the form and open the Menu Design window.

4   Enter the caption **&Summary!**. Enter the name **mnuSummary**.

5   Click on Next. Enter the caption **E&xit!**. Enter the name **mnuExit**.

6   Save the project and form files.

Planning the Code

Before you start writing the code, you need to think through how to calculate the step, set the scale, and use the MouseDown event.

CALCULATING THE STEP

The values for the growth factor, *r*, are set by a loop. The loop steps up each time through just enough to fill the form with dots. If the step is too broad, there are blank vertical lines between each column. If the step is too small, the same column may be drawn more than once.

To make the step just right, you should first set the ScaleMode to 3. This sets the form to the pixel coordinate system. Save the value of the ScaleWidth property in the variable *WidthInPixels*.

This value is divided into the difference 4.0-2.5 to determine the step for the loop.

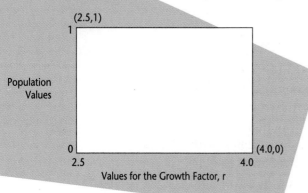

Figure 8-29
Coordinate system for the form

SETTING THE SCALE

The values for the growth factor range from 2.5 to 4.0. The population values range from 0 to 1. The coordinate system for the form is shown in Figure 8-29.

The **Scale (2.5,1)-(4,0)** command sets the coordinate system.

PLANNING THE MOUSEDOWN EVENT

You will use the form's MouseDown event to draw a labeled vertical line on the graph. When the graph is complete and a user clicks on the graph, the program draws a vertical line. Next to the line is the value of *r* for that column. This value comes from the *X* parameter to the Mouse-Down event.

The next place to plot a point or print a message is determined by the CurrentX and CurrentY properties of the MouseDown event. The message displaying the value of *r* is positioned at the mouse click by setting *CurrentX* to x, and *CurrentY* to y.

Entering the Code

Follow these steps to enter the code for the Summary Population Graph program.

1   In the mnuSummary_Click() procedure, enter these lines to declare the local variables.

```
'—Declare variables
Dim Stp As Single, r As Single
Dim Pop As Single, Generation As Integer
Dim WidthInPixels As Integer
Const StartGen = 20
Const StartPop = .5
Const TotalGen = 150
```

Stp is the step value for the loop. *r* is the growth factor. *Pop* is the current population value. *Generation* controls the loop that calculates the successive populations. *WidthInPixels* saves the width of the form in pixels. *StartGen* is a constant. The graph begins for each value of *r* at *StartGen + 1*. *StartPop* is the starting value for the population. *TotalGen* is the total number of generations calculated.

2 Enter the lines to find the width of the form in pixels and set the custom coordinate system.

```
'—Set the coordinate system
ScaleMode = 3
WidthInPixels = ScaleWidth
Scale (2.5, 1)-(4, 0)
```

3 Enter the lines to clear the form and calculate the step value:

```
'—Clear the form
Cls
'—Process step from menu
Stp = (4 - 2.5) / WidthInPixels
```

4 Enter the lines to set up the outer loop and initialize the value of *Pop*:

```
For r = 2.5 To 4 Step Stp
    Pop = StartPop
```

5 Enter the lines to set up the inner loop and calculate and display the population values:

```
For Generation = 1 To TotalGen
    Pop = r * Pop * (1 - Pop)
    If Generation > StartGen Then
        PSet (r, Pop)
    End If
Next Generation
Next r
```

6 Enter **End** in the procedure for mnuExit.

7 Save the project and form files.

8 Run the program. Click on **Summary!**

9 Enter these lines in the MouseDown event procedure of the form:

```
Line (x, 0)-(x, 1)
CurrentX = x
CurrentY = y
Print "<R=" & Format$(x, "#.0")
```

10 Run the program. Click on **Summary!**. When the graph is finished, click on key points of the graph to display the r value.

11 Save the project and form files.

The computer is a science laboratory. It is a place to run experiments and test predictions. The computational and graphic power of the computer make it an indispensable tool for doing science.

The Population Biology programs reveal patterns that can be examined and explored in minutes. By hand, such work would take years. Use problem 8 in the Problems section as a guide to perform real explorations of the information created by the Summary Population Graph program.

QUESTIONS AND ACTIVITIES

1. For a less dramatic graph, but faster execution, experiment with smaller values for *Stp*. Alter the program by changing the statement calculating *Stp*.

   ```
   Stp = 2 * (4 - 2.5) / WidthInPixels
   ```

2. Change the value of *TotalGen* to 50 and *StartGen* to 0. Run the program and observe the results.

3. Change the value of *StartPop* to 0.1, then to 0.9. Run the program. With *StartGen* = 20, what effect does *StartPop* have? Set *StartGen* to 0. Alter the value of *StartPop*. What changes do you observe?

4. A difference equation is an equation used to calculate a prediction from a known value. In the fish problem, you used an equation to calculate next year's fish population from this year's population. Describe two other situations (don't worry about the actual equations) in which you could use a difference equation to predict future values.

5. In the fish population problem, some values for the growth factor r resulted in two equilibrium points. Describe in words why that

might happen. What conditions of the system would cause the succeeding year's population to decrease one year and increase the next?

We say the difference equation:

```
p2 = r * p1 * (1 - p1)
```

is a nonlinear equation. What makes this equation nonlinear? *(hint: multiply out the right side)*

A menu command that is checked shows a check mark at the beginning of the item. A menu item that is enabled can be clicked to generate a Click event. A menu command whose Enabled property is set to **False** is dimmed and does not generate a Click event when clicked.

Giving two or more menu items the same name creates a menu control array in which all items execute the same event procedures. The items are differentiated within the procedure by the value of the index parameter sent to the procedure.

The **Print** method is used for displaying text and values directly on a form.

The **Select Case** statement replaces a series of **If-Then** statements. Its syntax is:

> **Select Case** *expression*
> > **Case** *value1*
> > > *statements if value1 = expression*
> > **Case** *value2*
> > > *statements if value2 = expression*
> >
> > ....
> > **Case Else**
> > > *statements executed if the expression doesn't match any of the Values*
> **End Select**

An array is a list of values in memory. Arrays have a single variable name that refers to the entire list. A subscript is a whole number that selects a single item from the list.

A non-linear difference equation of the form:

```
p2 = r * p1 * (1 - p1)
```

is used as a simple mathematical model for many systems. *p1* is the initial state, *p2* is the final state, and *r* is the growth factor.

Problems

1. **Twenty Random Numbers**
Use the **Rnd** function to generate an array full of 20 random numbers. Print the numbers on the default form.

2. **The Length of a Name Problem**
Use a string array to store 10 names. Use the **Len** function to search the array for the longest name and display the length of the longest name. Use a **For-Next** loop to cycle through the 10 names and a single **If-Then** statement to calculate the length of each string and compare the length with the value of an integer variable. Initialize the integer variable to 0. If the length of a name is larger than the value in the integer variable, replace the integer variable's value with the length of the longer string.

3. **The Licensing Problem**
Write a program using a menu to display information about various licensing fees. This table summarizes the information necessary.

Vehicle licenses		*Pet licenses*	
automobile	$25	neutered dog	$10
motorcycle	15	dog	$25
van	25	neutered cat	$12
commercial	100	cat	$30
airplane	250		

Use two menu control arrays with the items listed above as submenu items. The column headings should appear on the top menu bar. Inside the event procedures, use a **Select Case** statement to choose the correct fee. Once the fee has been determined, use a message box to display the fee.

4. **The Portable Stereo Problem**
Write a program to help diagnose a problem with a portable stereo. The program should allow the user to pick symptoms from a menu and display a message about what to do to solve the problem. Use the information below as a guide.

Stereo won't play	*Tape moves, but no sound*
Are batteries installed?	Do headphones work?
Are batteries charged up?	Are headphones on head?
Is tape jammed?	

5.   The Linear Enrollment Problem

Use a linear difference equation ($p_2 = r * p_1$) to print a table of values based on the following information:

Year	Enrollment
1984	2150
1985	2175

Calculate the growth factor, r, from the information given above. Display a table that predicts the enrollment for the years from 1984 to the year 2000.

6.   Linear Enrollment Revisited

Rewrite the program above but use the non-linear equation, $p_2 = r * p_1 * (1 - p_1/4000)$. Write the program so different values for r, the growth factor, can be entered.

7.   Store Rebate

Write a program using a **Select Case** statement to solve the following problem. A store offers a rebate on a purchase based on the amount of the purchase.

Amount Spent	Rebate
0 - 100 dollars	2%
101 - 1000	3%
1001 - 5000	3.5%
5001 - 10000	4%
10001 and over	5%

Write a program to enter an amount spent, then calculate and display the rebate. Use an integer to represent the amount spent. The **Select Case** statement can designate a range of values with the following syntax:

Case *low* **To** *high*
     statements

8.   More Population Biology

Modify the Summary Population Graph program to allow the user to enter values for the range of r values. Currently, the values 2.5 and 4 are coded directly into the program. Use the MouseDown event to define new values. Replace the old MouseDown code with this new code. The first click should be used as the starting value of r and the second click as the ending value. This allows the user to examine a specific range of values in detail. The automatic scaling done for the *Stp* variable comes in handy here.

```
Open "c:\plist\phone.dat" For Random Access Write As #1 Len = 55
Put #1 PhoneList(x)
```

File Handling

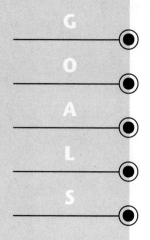

After working through this chapter, you will be able to:

Understand and use the concepts associated with computer databases.

Manipulate random access files.

Program a simple database.

Integrate error-handling routines with programs.

O V E R V I E W

This chapter covers handling data stored in a file. A random access file is used to store names and phone numbers. The information in this chapter is easily adapted to almost any problem involving stored data.

You will also learn in this chapter how to anticipate the possibility of run-time errors when you write code, so that your program can respond to (or "handle") errors that occur when it runs. Programs that can handle run-time errors are more reliable than those that cannot. Each kind of run-time error that a program handles is one fewer source of unexpected crashes.

Review of File Handling

You have already had experience by this point with handling files. In the programs you've built so far, though, you have been focused on finishing the work at hand. You may not have thought about what you were learning about file handling as a way of working. This section reviews what you have learned so far about file handling and brings all the information into one place.

Types of Files

There are three kinds of files that may be opened and accessed in a Visual Basic program: random, sequential, and binary. In a random file, the data is organized into records. A record is a complete set of data for a single entry. Each record uses a predetermined amount of memory declared when the file is opened. For instance, a person's first and last name, social security number, age, and address make up a single record in a file.

A sequential file is used as if it is printed output. The command that prints a line to the printer or to a form can print a line to a sequential file. The same command that collects information from the keyboard is used to collect information from a sequential file. Records in a sequential file are arranged like songs on a cassette tape: one after another.

A binary file is a file arranged to give byte-by-byte access to the user. In a binary file, information is recorded in its most primitive form: the byte.

Open Statement

Before you read from or write to a file, you must open it. You do so with the **Open** statement. This statement tells Visual Basic whether you will use the file as a random, sequential, or binary file. Visual Basic then tells Windows to open the file on behalf of your program. Windows attempts to find or create the file you wish to open. If it succeeds, it sets up internal data structures that record the fact that your program has opened the file, and that keep track of the current position in the file.

Here's an **Open** statement:

```
Open "c:\plist\phone.dat" For Random Access Write As #1 Len = 55
```

After the word "Open," you put the full pathname of the file you want to open. The pathname is listed in the statement or represented by a string variable. After the word "For," you put the mode of file access. This is either one of the keywords (**Random** or **Binary**), indicating the type of file, or it is one of three other options if the file is a sequential file.

Mode	Description
Random	Files organized as records
Binary	Files organized as bytes
Input	For using a sequential file for input operations
Output	For using a sequential file for output operations
Append	For adding information to a sequential file

Next, you indicate the type of access. There are three options:

- ◉ Read: You can open the file but cannot make any changes.

- ◉ Write: You can create the file or modify it if it already exists.

- ◉ Read Write: You can perform either type of operation; this mode applies to random and binary files as well as to sequential files opened for the Append operation.

The **As #** section of the **Open** statement assigns a file number to the file so that other statements may refer to the file by its number rather than its pathname. The **Len = n** section designates the number of characters per record for a file of the random type.

This **Open** statement:

```
Open "c:\plist\phone.dat" For Random Access Write As #1 Len = 55
```

opens the file **c:\plist\phone.dat** as a random access file, opened for writing (the file is created if it does not exist) as file #1, with a record length of 55 characters.

Put Statement

The **Put** statement writes data to a file opened as a **Random** or **Binary** file. Here is an example of the syntax:

```
Put #1, x, PhoneList(x)
```

Following the word "Put" is the file number. Information will be placed into the file associated with the file number 1, an association made with an **Open** statement.

For **Random** files, following the file number is the record number of the data being put into the file. Assuming that #1 is a **Random** file, the variable x indicates that the contents of *PhoneList(x)* are put into the file as record number x. As x changes, each successive piece of data is put into an appropriate spot in the file.

For **Binary** files, the number following the file number is the byte position of the data being put into the file. It is an offset from the beginning of the file, which is byte 1. Assuming that #2 is a **Binary** file, the following statement writes an integer to the file starting at the 100th byte of the file:

```
Dim N
'— ...
Put #2, 100, N
```

If you omit *x* from the **Put** statement, each record is inserted at the current position in the file. The current position is the one immediately following the data written by the last **Put** statement, read by the last **Get** statement, or explicitly set via the **Seek** function. Here's the **Put** statement without the middle value:

```
Put #1, , PhoneList(x)
```

Get Statement

The **Get** statement reads data from an file opened as either a **Random** or **Binary** file. This statement matches the **Put** statement and has a similar syntax:

Get #*file number*, *record number*, *variable*

If #*file number* is a **Random** file, then *record number* refers to the position in the file where the record whose number is *record number* is stored. If #*file number* is a **Binary** file, then *record number* refers to a byte offset from the beginning of the file. The data at this location is read from the file and stored in *variable*.

Here's a typical example of the **Get** statement used with a **Random** file #1:

```
Get #1, x, PhoneList(x)
```

This statement fetches the *x*th entry from the file and assigns it to *PhoneList(x)*. Just as in the **Put** statement, if you leave the middle number out, the records are fetched from the file sequentially.

Close Statement

Without any parameters, the **Close** statement closes all open files. To close a specific open file, use the file's number, as in:

```
Close #1
```

This statement tells Visual Basic that you are done using this file number.

359

Kill Statement

The **Kill** statement deletes a file whose pathname is specified. Here is an example:

```
Kill "c:\plist\phone.dat"
```

If the file doesn't exist, a run-time error occurs. Program execution stops.

EOF Function

EOF stands for End Of File. This function returns the value of **True** when the **Get** command has *failed* to get information from the file because the file is empty. The syntax for this function is:

EOF(*#file number*)

Be sure to notice that **EOF** returns a value of **True** when **Get** has failed. This means that the program makes one attempt to get information from the file beyond the end of the file.

QUESTIONS AND ACTIVITIES

1. What are the three kinds of data files supported by Visual Basic?

2. Write a record that contains eight pieces of information about your school. Include data such as the name and address.

3. Write the **Open** statement that opens the file named **c:\temp\petname.txt** as a sequential file ready to receive information.

4. Write the **Open** statement that opens the file mentioned above to add information to the end of the file.

5. Write the statement that deletes the file created in question 3.

6. What does **EOF** stand for? Describe the purpose of **EOF** in the fragment below.

```
Do While Not EOF(1)
    ...
Loop
```

The Phone List Program

Section

In this section you will write a program to maintain a list of people's names and phone numbers. A List box is used to display the list.

A file is used to store the information. The path and file name is: **c:\plist\phone.dat**.

The program can

◉ Save the current list

◉ Clear an old list

◉ Open an existing list and load it from a file

◉ Add names to the list

◉ Display them sorted by first name, last name, or by phone number

You will use a user-defined variable type to represent the information. The program uses the **Open** statement to open a random access file for reading and writing. The operations it performs on the file's data—saving, clearing, opening, creating, and adding to lists—are representative of what every database program does.

Starting Out

Before you start building the form, you need to learn how to use user-defined data types in Visual Basic. You will learn what user-defined types are, how to declare them, how to declare variables of a user-defined type, and how to use such variables.

A NEW KIND OF DATA TYPE

A record is composed of one or more logically related variables. To relate these variables, you can create a user-defined data type. This type combines one or more variables of various types into a single data type. You specify the name and composition of the data type. After you have defined the data type, you can use it in a program just like one of the predefined types.

Declaring a user-defined type isn't difficult. Here's an example based on the project you are about to create:

```
'—Each record is 55 characters
Type Person
   Last As String * 20
   First As String * 20
   Phone As String * 15
End Type
```

361

The word "Type" is followed by the name of the new data type, Person. The variables and data types that make up the body of the new data type are listed. The Person type is made of three strings, *Last, First,* and *Phone.* Each item in the body of the type definition is a field.

You can define user-defined types only within a code module. Type definitions appear in the general declarations section of a code module. Any variables you declare or types you define within a code module are global. You can use them in any of the event procedures of a form, as well as in any event procedure of any form or code module in the project.

To open the code module's window, double-click on its name in the Project window. The caption of the code module's window reflects the file name of the module. See Figure 9-1.

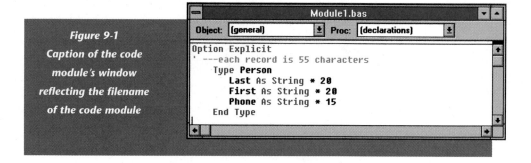

Figure 9-1
Caption of the code module's window reflecting the filename of the code module

ASSIGNING VALUES

You will need to know how to assign values to the fields of a record, and how to use these values in expressions and statements. Assume the following declaration:

```
Dim Aunt As Person
```

To assign the aunt's name and phone number, use the following statements:

```
Aunt.Last = "Johnson"
Aunt.First = "Maudie"
Aunt.Phone = "(708)934-1111"
```

If you declare an array of type Person, you can access the third element of the array using these statements:

```
Dim Relatives(1 To 10) As Person
Relatives(3).Last = "Johnson"
Relatives(3).First = "Tracie"
Relatives(3).Phone = "(708)949-1991"
```

THE WITH STATEMENT – VISUAL BASIC 4

In Version 4 of Visual Basic, the **With** statement simplifies access to the fields of a record. (To check which version you have, select About Microsoft Visual Basic from the Help menu.) For example, assume the following declarations:

```
'—Code module definition of Type
Type Person
    Last As String * 20
    First As String * 20
    Phone As String * 15
End Type
'—Local declaration of variables
Dim Relatives(1 To 10) As Person
Dim PersonNumber As Integer
'—Assign values to the third element as follows
PersonNumber = 3
With Relatives(PersonNumber)
    .Last = "Johnson"
    .First = "Tracie"
    .Phone = "(708)949-1991"
End With
```

Planning the Program

What functions should a phone list program have? The user should be able to record new names and numbers, save the list to permanent storage, recall the list, and list the names and numbers.

One way to bring program development into focus is to plan how the user will interact with the program. You will need a File menu that includes the standard options for handling files:

File
    New...
    Open...
    Save
    Close
    ————
    Exit

To let users add and list names, how about adding another menu:

Names
> **Adding...**
> **Listing...**

When users select Adding from this drop-down menu, you need a way for them to enter new data. The best way is to provide a dialog box for this purpose. The dialog box should open when a user selects the command.

If, instead, the user selects Listing, another menu should open:

> **Listing...**
> > **Last**
> > **First**
> > **Phone**

The commands in this submenu all perform a similar task: each command forms strings from the Person records, then calls a routine that displays that list of strings in a List box. The three menu commands differ only in the order of the record fields that they use to form strings. It's a good idea, then, to make these commands a menu command array. The List box in which the strings are displayed has its Sorted property set to **True**. Different lists are created by rearranging the information displayed. If the first name is first in the display string, the list is ordered by first names.

Creating the Form

The user interface is the menu discussed above. In this section you create a directory for the program files and the data file and set up the form.

Figure 9-2
Creating a directory

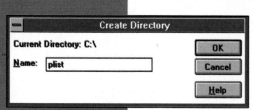

1 Open the Program Manager. Start the File Manager.

2 Create a subdirectory in **c:** named **c:\plist**. See Figure 9-2.

3 Start Visual Basic. If Visual Basic is running, choose New Project from the File menu.

4 Change the caption of the default form to **Phone List**. Change the name of the form to **frmPlist**.

5 Select the form and open the Menu Design window.

6 Enter the caption **&File** and the name **mnuFile**.

7 Click on Next, then the right arrow button to create a submenu item.

8 Enter the captions and names in the table below, clicking on Next between each entry.

Caption	Name	Enabled
&New...	mnuNew	
&Open...	mnuOpen	
&Save	mnuSave	False
&Close	mnuClose	False
-	mnuHyphen	(a separator)
E&xit	mnuExit	

9 Click on Next, then on the left arrow button.

10 Enter the caption **&Names** with the name **mnuNames**.

11 Click on Next, then on the right arrow button to create a submenu of Names. Enter the following captions and names.

Caption	Name	Enabled
Adding...	mnuAdd	False
Listing...	mnuList	False

12 Click on Next, then on the right arrow button to create a submenu of Listing. Enter the following captions. Create a control array for these related commands.

Caption	Name	Index
Last	mnuSort	1
First	mnuSort	2
Phone	mnuSort	3

13 Add a large List box to the form. Change the name of the List box to **lstPhoneNumbers**. Figure 9-3 shows the complete form.

14 Save the project and form files.

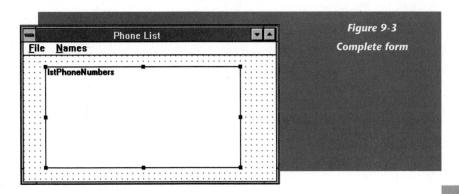

Figure 9-3

Complete form

Creating the Dialog Box

Now create a dialog box to collect a name and phone number.

1   Add a new form to the project. Change the caption of the form to **Name and Phone Number**. Change the name of the form to **frmData.**

2   Add three textboxes to the form. Name the boxes **txtLast**, **txtFirst**, and **txtPhone**. Delete the text from each.

3   Add three labels with captions: **Last Name:**, **First Name:**, and **Phone Number:**.

4   Add a command button with the caption **&OK** and the name **cmdOK**.

5   Add a command button with the caption **&Cancel** and the name **cmdCancel**. The complete dialog box is show in Figure 9-4.

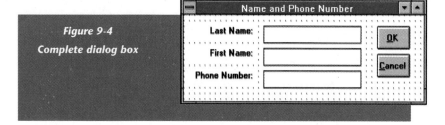

Figure 9-4
Complete dialog box

Declaring Variables

The project has two forms. The two forms communicate with each other through global variables declared in a code module. The variables *Current* and the array *PhoneList,* of type Person, are declared globally. When information is collected from the dialog box, it is put into the array *PhoneList* and *Current* is updated.

The *PhoneList* array, with a capacity of 55 entries, is used to store the information in memory. *Current* indicates the number of entries in the *PhoneList* array. This number is set when information is read from a file, and reset when names are added to the array. The counter is initialized to 0 when the program is executed.

Current is also used to control the display of information in the List box and for writing information into the data file.

To declare the variables:

1   Add a code module to the project.

2   In the general declarations section of the code module, add the following declarations:

```
Type Person
    Last As String * 20
    First As String * 20
    Phone As String * 15
End Type
Global PhoneList(55) As Person
Global Current As Integer
```

3   In the Project window, select frmPlist.

4   In the Form_Load procedure, enter the code to initialize the counter *Current*:

```
Current = 0
```

5   Save the forms, the code module, and the project in **c:\plist**.

Adding Information

Users add information in two steps. First, they click on the Adding command in the start-up form, frmPlist. The code in that procedure tests to see if there is more room in the array and then displays the dialog box, frmData. When all the necessary information has been added to the dialog box, the user clicks OK to transfer the information to the *PhoneList* array.

In the following steps, you create the code that lets the user add data in the way just described:

1   Select frmPlist in the Project window.

2   Click on View Code.

3   Enter the following code in the procedure for mnuAdd:

```
'—Check value of Current to see of array if full
If Current >= 55 Then
    MsgBox "The array is full"
Else
'—Show dialog box to collect data
    frmData.Show
End If
```

The **Show** command makes the dialog box visible.

4   Select frmData in the Project window. Click on View Code.

5 In the cmdOK_Click() procedure, enter the local declarations:

```
'—Declare local variables
Dim Last As String * 20
Dim First As String * 20
Dim Phone As String * 15
```

6 Enter the lines to transfer information from the textboxes to the local variables:

```
'—Read information from textboxes
Last = txtLast
First = txtFirst
Phone = txtPhone
```

7 Test to see if at least the first name and the phone number are not blank. The **Trim$()** function deletes spaces from the strings.

```
'—Must have at least first name and phone number
If Trim$(First) <> "" And Trim$(Phone) <> "" Then
```

8 Enter the lines that increment the counter, *Current*, and add the new information to the array:

```
'—Increment Current and use as a subscript for PhoneList
Current = Current + 1
PhoneList(Current).Last = Last
PhoneList(Current).First = First
PhoneList(Current).Phone = Phone
```

9 Now that information is added to the form, make sure the proper menu commands from frmPlist are enabled. Because the menu commands are defined on the form, the object name, frmPlist, must appear. Enter the lines to turn on menu commands in frmPlist:

```
'—Accessing routines from the frmPlist form.
frmPlist.mnuList.Enabled = True
frmPlist.mnuSave.Enabled = True
frmPlist.mnuClose.Enabled = True
```

10 Enter the lines to blank the textboxes, preparing for the next add operation:

```
'—Blanking textboxes for next add operation.
txtLast = ""
txtFirst = ""
txtPhone = ""
```

11 Enter the lines to hide the dialog box:

```
'—Hide the dialog box
frmData.Hide
```

12 If the user did not enter the minimum data—first name and phone number—set the focus back to the first name:

```
Else
'—Set focus to first name box
   txtFirst.SetFocus
End If
```

13 In the procedure for cmdCancel of frmData enter the following command:

```
frmData.Hide
```

14 This completes the code for frmData.

Saving the Phone List

Assume that names have been added to the *PhoneList*. It's time to create the data file and save the information. To do that, you need to:

- Open the file
- Set up a loop from 1 to *Current*
- Put each record in the file
- Close the file
  Follow these steps to enter the code.

1 Select frmPlist and enter the following lines in the procedure for mnuSave:

```
Dim Entry As Integer
'—Open file for Random Access Write
Open "c:\plist\phone.dat" For Random Access Write As #1 Len = 55
'—Write Current entries of the array into the file
For Entry = 1 To Current
     Put #1, Entry, PhoneList(Entry)
Next Entry
'—Close the file
Close
```

2 Save the forms, code module, and project file.

Opening an Existing File

To open an existing file:

- Check to see if there is an active list
- If not, set subscript variable to one
- Open the file
- Loop while the file is not empty
  - Get information from the file
  - Load information into the *PhoneList* array
  - Increment the subscript
- Close the file
- Set the value of *Current*
- Enable various menu items
  Follow these steps to create the mnuOpen procedure:

1 Select frmPlist and enter the following lines in mnuOpen_Click(). First enter the declaration of a local variable.

```
'—Variable to keep track of entry number
Dim Entry As Integer
```

2 If *Current* is anything but 1, a file has already been loaded or a new one created. Enter the lines that handle this:

```
If Current <> 0 Then
    '—Don't open the file if the list is already loaded.
    MsgBox "There is already a list loaded."
Else
```

3 Enter these lines to open the data file and transfer information into the array:

```
'—Otherwise, set entry to one and collect data.
Entry = 1
Open "c:\plist\phone.dat" For Random Access Read As #1 Len = 55
Do While Not EOF(1)
    Get #1, , PhoneList(Entry)
    Entry = Entry + 1
Loop
Close
```

4   Because **EOF** (End Of File) is true only after **Get** has failed, the value of *Entry* is 2 beyond the end of the list. Enter the code that sets *Current* and enables some menu items:

```
    '—Entry is two beyond the end of the list
    Current = Entry - 2
    '—Enable menu items in frmPlist
    mnuSave.Enabled = True
    mnuClose.Enabled = True
    mnuList.Enabled = True
    mnuAdd.Enabled = True
End If
```

5   Save the forms, code module, and project file.

Coding the New Command

Selecting New closes and deletes any existing file. Before the file is closed, you should prompt the user to be sure that's what the user wants to do. Use an InputBox to get confirmation.

If a file doesn't exist, deleting it causes a run-time error. The **On Error Resume Next** statement will trap the error generated by trying to kill a nonexistent file and resume execution with the statement following the one that caused the error.

Set *Current* to 0, indicating there are no valid entries in the array. The new file is opened and closed, creating a directory entry and a file of length 0.

1   Select frmPlist and enter the following lines for mnuNew_Click(). First enter the declaration of a local variable. Use an InputBox to ask the user to confirm deleting the old list of names. The **Left$(str,number)** function copies the first *number* characters from the left end of the string.

```
'—Check with user to see if this is what they want
Dim answer As String
answer = InputBox("Do you want to clear the file?", "New...", "No")
If Left$(answer, 1) = "Y" Or Left$(answer, 1) = "y" Then
```

If the user enters anything that starts with "y" or "Y", the procedure ends.

2 If the file doesn't exist, the **On Error** statement prevents a runtime error. If the file is found, it is killed and *Current* is reset to 0:

```
'—If file doesn't exit, this will trap the error.
On Error Resume Next
'—Erase file from disk
Kill "c:\plist\phone.dat"
Current = 0   ' Number of elements in list
Open "c:\plist\phone.dat" For Random Access Write As #1 Len = 55
Close
```

3 Enter the code to clear the List box of names and numbers. Enter the lines to enable various menu items:

```
lstPhoneNumbers.Clear
mnuSave.Enabled = True
mnuList.Enabled = True
mnuAdd.Enabled = True
End If
```

4 Save the forms, code module, and project file.

Coding the Close Command

The **Close** procedure clears the List box and sets *Current* to 0, effectively clearing the array of information. A number of menu items are disabled. Once the file is closed, Save, Close, Adding, and Listing become inappropriate actions.

To code the **Close** command, open mnuClose_Click() and enter this code:

```
lstPhoneNumbers.Clear
Current = 0
mnuSave.Enabled = False
mnuClose.Enabled = False
mnuAdd.Enabled = False
mnuList.Enabled = False
```

Writing the Display Routines

The program displays information contained in the *PhoneList* array in the List box lstPhoneNumbers. The Sorted property of the List box is set to **True** at design time. By changing the order of the data within each display line, *DispLine*, the overall ordering of the information is changed.

Display the last name first; the List box sorts using the last name. Display the first name first in each line; the List box sorts using the first name. *Entry* keeps track of the subscripts of the information to display. *DispLine* is a string used to assemble the display line for the List box. *Tb* is the tab character. It is used to display the entries in columns.

MnuSort is a menu control array. When clicked, the three menu commands in the Listing menu (Last, First, and Phone) execute the same event procedure, mnuSort()_Click.

1 Select frmPlist and open the cmdSort() procedure.

2 Enter the lines declaring the local variables and setting up the tab character:

```
'—Declare local variables.
'—used as subscript
Dim Entry As Integer
'—used to build display line
Dim DispLine As String
Dim Tb As String
'—Tab character
Tb = Chr$(9)
```

3 Enter the lines to clear the List box and check to see whether the array is empty:

```
'—Clear the listbox.
lstPhoneNumbers.Clear
'—Display list only if there are elements in the array
If Current <> 0 Then
```

4 If the array is not empty, enter the line to set up the loop. There are *Current* entries in the array.

```
For Entry = 1 To Current
```

5 Enter the lines that pick out what menu command is selected. Arrange the display line according to the kind of list chosen.

```
'—Select statement picks out clicked menu item
Select Case index
'—Arrange by last name
    Case 1
        DispLine = PhoneList(Entry).Last & Tb & PhoneList(Entry).First & Tb &
PhoneList(Entry).Phone
    '—Arrange by first name
    Case 2
        DispLine = PhoneList(Entry).First & Tb & PhoneList(Entry).Last & Tb &
PhoneList(Entry).Phone
    '—Arrange by phone number
    Case 3
        DispLine = PhoneList(Entry).Phone & Tb & PhoneList(Entry).First & Tb &
PhoneList(Entry).Last
End Select
```

6 Enter the line to add the display line to the List box:

```
'—Add line to listbox
lstPhoneNumbers.AddItem DispLine
```

7 Enter the lines to end the loop and handle the **Else** case of the **If** statement from above. These lines execute if the array is empty:

```
    Next Entry
Else
    '—If Current = 0, the array is empty
    MsgBox "The list is empty"
End If
```

8 Run the program. Click on New. Enter names and phone numbers. List the names with each of the three display options. Save the file. Press New. Open the old file. Display the list.

9 Save the form files, the code file, and the project file.

QUESTIONS AND ACTIVITIES

1. Write a definition for a user-defined type to represent the following information:

name of a computer	20 characters
name of processor	10 characters
speed of processor in MHz	integer
megabytes of RAM	integer
megabytes of disk space	integer
cost	currency

2. Declare an array of the computer type declared above. The array should store information for 25 computers.

3. How would you refer to the price of the fourteenth machine in the list created above?

4. Assuming the array above is full, write the code that would display the contents of the array in a List box.

5. What are the three file types?

6. Describe in a few words what each of these statements does: **Open**, **Close**, **Kill**, **Get**, and **Put**.

7. Explain the function of each separate underlined part of the following **Open** statement:

   ```
   Open "c:\vb\phone.dat" For Random Access Write As #1 Len = 55
   ```

8. What are the three parameters of the **Put** statement? Describe each one.

9. In the Phone List program:
   a) Modify to accept a social security number as well as names and phone numbers.
   b) Modify the Listing submenu to include a command to sort the list by social security number. Include the statements necessary in mnuSort().

10. Modify the Phone List program to get a file and pathname from the user.

11. In cmdCancel of frmData, replace frmData. Hide with Unload Me. Run the program and note any differences. Use the Help system to look up Unload and Me.

Section

Error Handling

The Phone List program used a file and pathname permanently written into the code. The MiniEdit program used an InputBox to get the pathname from the user. Programs accessing files should let the user enter file names. Problems arise when the user enters the name of a file that doesn't exist or enters an illegal pathname.

So far, the **On Error Resume Next** statement has been the extent of the error handling. Unfortunately, this allows the program to continue even when a serious error has occurred. The program should not continue without correcting or responding to the error.

Looking at the Options

A run-time error occurs when something interrupts the execution of a program, such as division by 0, an array subscript that is out of bounds, or the use of an illegal pathname. If there is no error trapping, the program stops with an error message. Error trapping means redirecting the flow of execution when errors occur.

The **On Error Resume Next** statement traps an error by executing the statement following the one that caused the error. The action that caused the error is never completed.

The **On Error GoTo** *line* statement redirects the flow of execution to an error-handling routine. An error-handling routine is a piece of code that either resolves the error and lets the program resume its normal course or displays information about the error so that it may be corrected.

Flow is redirected by specifying a line number or a line label. A line label is an identifier, up to 40 characters long, followed by a colon. A line label must be the first entry in a line.

When a run-time error occurs, the **Err** function is set to an error code. You can find a list of error codes in Visual Basic Help, under the heading "Trappable Errors". The **Erl** function, unused in this program, returns the number of the line where the error occurred. Displaying the error code as a part of the error-handling routine helps the user or programmer know how to fix the problem.

The **Exit Sub** statement interrupts the flow of program execution and ends the procedure being executed. An error-handler is a piece of code within the procedure, usually at the end of the procedure. The code should not be run if there are no errors. Placed before the error-handling code, the **Exit Sub** statement leaves the procedure before the error-handling code can execute.

Modifying the Open Routine

Use the **On Error GoTo** statement by modifying the mnuOpen routine of the Phone List program. This modification traps illegal file names. You should also modify the routine in a second way, by adding the **Input-Box** function to collect the name of the file from the user.

To make these changes:

1 Open the event procedure for mnuOpen. You need to keep the following lines; look through the code until you find the end of this section:

```
Sub mnuOpen_Click ()
'—Variable to keep track of entry number
Dim Entry As Integer
If Current <> 0 Then
    '—Don't open the file if the list is already loaded.
    MsgBox "There is already a list loaded."
Else
    '—Otherwise, set entry to one and collect data.
    Entry = 1
```

2 Enter the lines declaring a string variable for the filename and collecting a filename with an **InputBox$**:

```
Dim FName As String
FName = InputBox$("Enter the complete path name", "Open File")
```

3 Enter the next two lines. The second redirects the flow of the procedure to the code marked ErrorHandler at the end of the procedure:

```
'—Declare variable for message.
Dim Msg
'—Set up error handler.
On Error GoTo ErrorHandler
```

4 The next line is modified from the original routine. Change the hard-coded filename **c:\plist\phone.dat**, to the filename **FName**:

```
Open FName For Random Access Read As #1 Len = 55
```

5 The next lines shown are already part of the mnuOpen routine, skip them:

```
Do While Not EOF(1)
    Get #1, , PhoneList(Entry)
    Entry = Entry + 1
Loop
Close
'—Entry is two beyond the end of the list
Current = Entry - 2
mnuSave.Enabled = True
mnuClose.Enabled = True
mnuList.Enabled = True
mnuAdd.Enabled = True
End If
```

6 The ErrorHandler follows. To avoid executing the error-handling code in a normal completion of the procedure, add the **Exit Sub** statement:

```
Exit Sub
```

7 Enter the lines of the ErrorHandler routine. The first line is the line label, ErrorHandler. The **Select Case** statement, using **Err**, prints an appropriate error message. Once the correct message is displayed, the **Exit Sub** statement ends the procedure without any change to the labels:

```
ErrorHandler:
Select Case Err
    Case 53: Msg = "ERROR 53: That file doesn't exist."
    Case 68: Msg = "ERROR 68: Drive " & Drive & ": not available."
    Case 76: Msg = "ERROR 76: That path doesn't exist."
    Case Else: Msg = "ERROR " & Err & " occurred."
End Select
MsgBox Msg      ' Display error message.
Exit Sub
End Sub
```

8 Run the program. Enter an illegal filename. Use a drive letter that doesn't exist or use an illegal character or length. The error handler prints a message and leaves mnuOpen as if nothing has happened.

9 Save the form files, the code module, and the project file.

QUESTIONS AND ACTIVITIES

1. In the Phone List program, change the filename code to collect file-names using the InputBox. Be sure to error trap with **On Error GoTo** *line*.

2. Write an error handler for frmData.cmdOK that displays an error message when the names and phone number are not entered.

3. Assume the array *TrappableErr()* is an array of strings containing the error messages of Visual Basic. The first error message could be displayed with the following code:

    ```
    MsgBox TrappableErr(1)
    ```

    Write an error handler that uses **Err**, and the array described above, to display the error message when a run-time error occurs.

4. Use the Help system to look up the various **Exit xxx** statements, such as **Exit Sub** and **Exit For**. Summarize what each does.

Summary

A database is a file of information. A record is the information about a particular entry. The pieces of information that make up each record are called fields. Three file types can be opened in Visual Basic: the sequential file, the random access file, and the binary file.

The **Get** and **Put** statements fetch and place records in random access files. The **EOF ()** function is **True** when a file is empty. EOF stands for "End Of File".

To keep a program from stopping when a run-time error occurs, special statements trap the error. The **On Error Resume Next** statement allows execution to proceed to the next line. **On Error GoTo** transfers program execution to a line number or line label.

A line label is a name of up to 40 characters followed by a colon. The line label provides a name for a line so that it may be referred to by a **GoTo** statement. The line label must be the first thing on the line.

Problems

1. The Random Number File Program

Write a program to generate 100 random integers in the range from 1 to 100, and put them into an array. Open a random access file named **c:\temp\rand.dat** and put the items of the array into the file. Close the file. Reopen the file, get each item, and display in a two-column List box.

2. The Computer Database Program

Write a program to collect, display, and save information about computers. Each record should contain the following information:

name of a computer	20 characters
name of processor	10 characters
speed in MHz of processor	integer
megabytes of RAM	integer
megabytes of disk space	integer
cost	currency

The internal array used to store the information should have a capacity of 25. Save the information in a file named **c:\vb3\comptrs.dat**. Record the data for each entry either through textboxes on the form or through **InputBox** statements. Display the data in textboxes on the form.

3. The School Assignment Program

Write a program to save and display a database of school assignments and scores. The record for each assignment should include the date of the assignment, a brief description, and a whole number score.

4. The Baseball Card Collection Program

Write a program to collect, save, and display information about baseball cards. Each record should contain information like:
- ◎ Player's last name
- ◎ Player's first name
- ◎ Year of the card
- ◎ Team played on that year
- ◎ Value of the card
- ◎ Location of the card

5.   The Home Inventory Program

Write a program to collect, save, and display information about items in a home. An inventory of home items is important when a fire or theft occurs. A complete inventory helps when making a claim to an insurance company.

Your program should record

◎ Brief description of the item
◎ Date purchased
◎ Purchase price
◎ Appraised value
◎ Current market value

```
= A(j) > A(j + 1 )
                        Then

If    Temp = A(j)

A(j) = A(j + 1)
Then
A(j + 1) = Temp

End if
```

Some Fundamental Algorithms

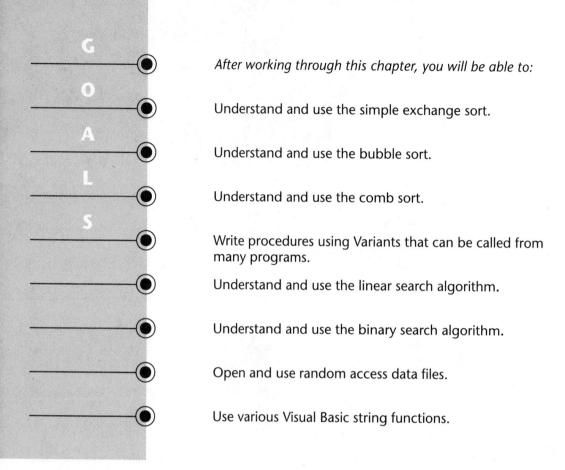

O V E R V I E W

*In this chapter you learn common sorting techniques. These procedures put information in order, either alphabetically or numerically, ascending or descending. Once you can write a sorting program, you are no longer tied to the List box to get a sorted list. In the previous chapter's Phone List program, you sorted an array of Person records by converting their contents to strings, then adding those strings to a List box with the Sorted property set to **True**. The order in which you concatenated the fields of the records determined the sort order. However, often you will want to rearrange the records in the array in some sorted order. It is unneccessary and slow to use a List box to achieve this.*

Sorting is often the first step in searching for information you need. For example, if you are looking for a specific file in the File Directory, one way to find it is to sort the files in a directory by extension or by date. If you sort by date and you know the day you created the file, you should be able to find the file quickly.

This chapter also presents two searching methods: the linear search and the binary search. Searches allow a program to find data in arrays of information. Array subscripts let you obtain the contents of an element once you know its location.

The two topics, sorting and searching, are tied together. Some searches depend on the fact that an array or file is sorted.

Sorting

Section

Sorting means putting data in order. For strings, this usually means alphabetical order. For numeric values, you would place them in ascending or descending order.

Student names would be listed in alphabetical order. Your CD collection, if it is cataloged, is probably in alphabetical order by artist or by album title. How else would you find information, if it were not ordered? If you have very little data, you may not need to sort it. However, as soon as you have gathered a lot of information, such as all the book titles in a library, that information must be ordered in some fashion.

To sort data in a program, you use algorithms. An algorithm is a step-by-step solution to a problem such as sorting. There are many sorting algorithms. Some execute very quickly and some execute slowly. Typically, programmers classify sorting algorithms by how fast they execute.

Different situations call for different sorting algorithms. The perfect algorithm for one sorting problem may not be the best for another. As a result, you need to know several of these algorithms. This chapter introduces three different sorting algorithms: simple exchange sort, the bubble sort, and the comb sort.

The Simple Exchange Sort

If you play cards, you may have used the simple exchange sort. Imagine that you are dealt 13 cards. To keep the example simple, assume all the

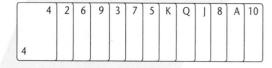

Figure 10-1

Fanning 13 cards

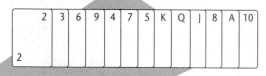

Figure 10-2

The first exchange

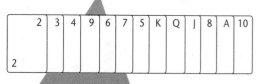

Figure 10-3

Another switch

cards are of the same suit. Pick up all 13 cards and fan them out on the table, as in Figure 10-1.

The goal of the sort is to put all the cards in order from left to right. The sorting algorithm executes the sort by a series of exchanges. It compares two cards to each other, starting from the left. If the card to the right is smaller than the card on the left, they are switched with each other. Look at Figure 10-1. Immediately you notice the 2 is smaller than the 4. The first step of the exchange sort would be to rearrange them, as in Figure 10-2.

Now, the exchange sort compares each of the remaining cards with the current left-most card (2). None of the remaining cards is smaller than 2, so that card is in the correct position.

The next step is to compare the 4 with each card to the right of it. Compare the 4 with 6, with 9, with 3. The exchange sort would *switch* the 4 and the 3, as shown in Figure 10-3.

As you can see, the switch has moved the 4 further out of order than it was. Still, the first two cards are in the correct order because no other card is smaller than 3. Next, you would start with the 6. As soon as you reach 4, you would switch the two cards, and 4 would now be in the correct position. The first three cards are now in order, as shown in Figure 10-4. You would continue until all the cards were in order from left to right, smallest to largest.

This sort algorithm is very slow. Sorting a large list with this algorithm could take hours. It has an advantage, however. The exchange sort is easy to program. To complete the algorithm, you need two **For-Next** statements, an **If-Then** statement, and some assignment statements. You may want to consider using this sort for small jobs. If your list holds fewer than a hundred items, the speed of your computer will make up for the inefficiency of the algorithm.

CODING FOR AN EXCHANGE SORT

Try experimenting with an exchange sort, so you can become comfortable with the code. In this sample, you are sorting a list of random numbers from smallest to largest.

To code the sort:

1 Start Visual Basic. If Visual Basic is running, choose New Project from the File menu.

Figure 10-4

The first three cards in position

2 Change the caption of the default form to **Simple Exchange Sort**.

3 Place two List Boxes on the form. Name the first **lstUnSorted** and the second, **lstSorted**.

4 Place three command buttons on the form. Change their captions to **&Generate**, **&Sort**, and **E&xit**. Change their names to **cmdGenerate**, **cmdSort**, and **cmdExit**. See Figure 10-5 for the completed form.

5 In the Code window, enter the **End** statement in the procedure for **cmdExit**.

6 Enter the following lines in the general declarations section of the form:

```
Const MAXITEM = 200
Dim A(MAXITEM) As Single
```

7 Enter these lines in the cmdGenerate procedure:

```
Dim x As Integer
For x = 1 To MAXITEM
    '—Generate random Single and assign to the array
    A(x) = Rnd
    '—Display unsorted numbers in listbox
    lstUnSorted.AddItem Str$(A(x))
Next x
```

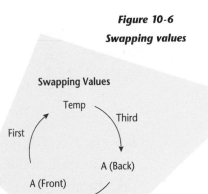

Figure 10-5
Completed simple exchange sort form

8 Enter these lines, clearing the List Boxes and declaring local variables, in the cmdSort procedure:

```
lstUnSorted.Clear
lstSorted.Clear
'—Declare pointers into the array
Dim Front As Integer
Dim Back As Integer
```

9 Enter the line to declare a variable to hold a swapping value. When two values are out of order, one is put into *Temp* temporarily. The second value is put into the first, and the old first value, stored in *Temp*, is put into the second. See Figure 10-6.

```
'—Declare temporary space to swap values
Dim Temp As Single
```

Figure 10-6
Swapping values

Swapping Values

Temp

First   Third

A (Back)

A (Front)

Second

10 Enter the line to set up the outer loop:

```
'—Outer loop goes from front to back of list
For Front = 1 To MAXITEM - 1
```

11 Enter the line to set up the inner loop. The outer loop starts at *Front*. The inner loop starts one position to the right:

```
'—Inner loop starts one after the front and goes to the back
For Back = Front + 1 To MAXITEM
```

12 Enter the lines to compare the values and swap if necessary:

```
If A(Front) > A(Back) Then
        '—Values are out of order, swap
        Temp = A(Front)
        A(Front) = A(Back)
        A(Back) = Temp
    End If
Next Back
Next Front
```

13 The array of values is sorted by this point in the code. Enter these lines to display the array in the second List Box:

```
'—Put sorted values into listbox
Dim x As Integer
For x = 1 To MAXITEM
    lstSorted.AddItem Str$(A(x))
Next x
```

14 Save the form and project files.

15 Run the program. Click on Generate to generate 200 random numbers and display in the first List Box. Click on Sort to sort the array and display in the second List Box. Give the sorting algorithm a minute to work.

NOT VERY SMART

This routine is not very smart. Even if there is a very small value in *Front*, when the program finds a smaller value to the right, the values in those places are swapped, leaving the very small value that used to be in *Front* somewhere to the right.

If the routine is asked to sort an already sorted list, it happily compares each value with every other value, taking a lot of time and accomplishing nothing.

The Bubble Sort

The bubble sort is a more complicated version of the simple exchange sort. It also finds pairs of values that are out of order and swaps them. The bubble sort, however can stop itself when the list is sorted. It stops by noticing that no swaps have occurred during an entire sweep of the list.

If a list is almost sorted and has just a few items out of order, the bubble sort may only run through the list a couple of times before it stops. The simple exchange sort keeps comparing items until all the items have been compared, whether or not the list is in order.

The bubble sort is really no faster than the simple exchange sort in the worst case. That is, there are unsorted arrays that will make the bubble sort compare every two elements. For example, arrays that are sorted in descending order will cause the bubble sort to make the maximum number of comparisons and swaps. On average, however, the bubble sort is more efficient. The best reason for learning this sort is because you will use it to build a much better sort, the comb sort.

HOW THE BUBBLE SORT WORKS

The bubble sort compares elements in the list that are next to each other. The sort sweeps through the list over and over again, swapping elements when appropriate, little by little moving each element closer to its final sorted position.

The bubble sort uses a **True/False** variable that keeps track of whether values have been swapped. If the bubble sort sweeps through the entire array, comparing every pair of adjacent values, and there are no swapped values, the list must be in order.

To compare the bubble sort to the exchange sort, look at the card example again. See Figure 10-7.

Starting from the left and moving to the right, the bubble sort would compare two cards at a time. If those two cards are out of order, they are swapped. Here, then, you compare 4 with 2, then swap those cards. The exchange sort would now compare the 2 with the 6. The bubble sort instead compares the 4 with the 6. No swap occurs. Then, 6 is compared with 9, with no change. A swap is made when 9 is compared with 3, and so forth. When the first sweep is through, the cards appear as shown in Figure 10-8.

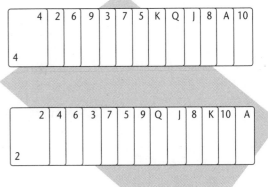

Figure 10-7

13 unsorted cards

Figure 10-8

After the first bubble sort sweep

The largest element, the ace, has traveled to the back of the list. On the next sweep, because the ace is already in position, the comparisons

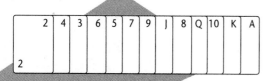

Figure 10-9

After the second bubble sort sweep

stop one short of the end. When the second sweep is complete, the king will be in position next to the ace. See Figure 10-9.

At the beginning of every sweep, a **True/False** variable called *Swapped* is set to **False**. If the sort finds values out of order, *Swapped* is set to **True**. At the end of the sweep, *Swapped* is tested. If there were no swaps, the sort is finished.

CODING FOR A BUBBLE SORT

Try coding the bubble sort so that you will remember it. You will use the same form you built for the exchange sort.

To code a bubble sort:

1 Add a command button with the caption **&Bubble** and the name **cmdBubble**.

2 Enter the code for the bubble sort. Enter lines to clear the textboxes:

```
lstUnSorted.Clear
lstSorted.Clear
```

3 The array used to store the unsorted numbers may have already been sorted. Enter the line that calls the routine to generate a new set of random numbers:

```
cmdGenerate_Click
```

4 Enter the lines to declare local variables:

```
'—Declare pointers into the array
Dim j As Integer
Dim i As Integer
'—Declare space for swapping
Dim Temp As Single
'—Variable to keep track if there's been a swap
Dim Swapped As Integer
```

5 A bubble sort works with an indefinite loop. It stops when there are no more swaps. Enter the sort algorithm.

```
'—The indefinite loop stops when list is sorted
i = MAXITEM     ' LARGEST item ends up in spot i
Do
    Swapped = False
    For j = 1 To i - 1
        '—Compare adjacent elements
```

```
        If A(j) > A(j + 1) Then
            '—Swap
            Temp = A(j)
            A(j) = A(j + 1)
            A(j + 1) = Temp
            '—Swap did occur
            Swapped = True
        End If
    Next j
    '—Largest item is already in position
    i = i - 1
Loop Until Not Swapped
```

6 Once the items in the *A* array are sorted, enter the lines to put them into the List box for display:

```
'—Put sorted values into List box
Dim x As Integer
For x = 1 To MAXITEM
    lstSorted.AddItem Str$(A(x))
Next x
```

7 In step three above, you entered the statement cmdGenerate_Click in the subroutine for cmdBubble. The effect is equivalent to a user clicking on the Generate button on the form. Insert this same statement into cmdSort and delete the Generate button from the form. The code from the button will appear in the general section where it can still be called. In cmdSort, after the lines clearing the listboxes, enter the line:

```
cmdGenerate_Click
```

8 Change the caption of the form to **Exchange and Bubble**.

9 Save the form and project files.

10 Run the program. Click on Sort. Click on Bubble. Time each procedure.

The Comb Sort

The April 1991 issue of *Byte* magazine introduced the comb sort. This sort is an improvement in design over the bubble sort, executing in far less time. Instead of comparing adjacent elements, the comb sort compares elements that are separated by a *gap*. If the values are out of order, they are swapped. This approach to swapping moves values to their final positions much more rapidly. Instead of comparing and swapping elements that are next to each other, the comb sort compares and swaps values that are farther apart.

The sort works by reducing the gap between the elements compared each time through the list, until the gap is reduced to 1. From this point on, the sort is the bubble sort. Because most of the elements are very close to their final positions by this point, the bubble sort makes short work of finishing the job.

HOW THE COMB SORT WORKS

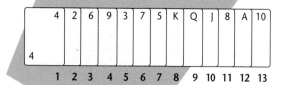

Figure 10-10

Hand of cards

To learn the comb sort, start with the same hand of cards (see Figure 10-10).

The gap is initialized to *MAXITEM*, the number of elements in the array. Before the first pass, the gap is reduced by a shrink factor. Experience and experimentation with this algorithm has demonstrated that a shrink factor of 1.3 yields the best performance. After each pass, the gap will be reduced by the same shrink factor.

```
'—Shrink factor is 1.3
Gap = Int(Gap / 1.3)
```

For the card example, *MAXITEM* is 13, so *Gap* is Int(13/1.3), or 10. The first time through the loop, the comb sort compares elements 10 spaces apart. The card in position 1 is compared with the card in position 11. The card in position 2 is compared with the card in position 12. The card in position 3 is compared with the card in position 13.

After the first pass, there are no swaps. After each pass, the gap is reduced.

```
Gap = Int(Gap / 1.3)
```

The new value of *Gap* is Int(10/1.3), or 7. During this pass, the card in position 1 is compared with the card in position 8, the card in position 2 with the card in position 9, and so forth. See Figure 10-11.

Figure 10-11

Comb sort

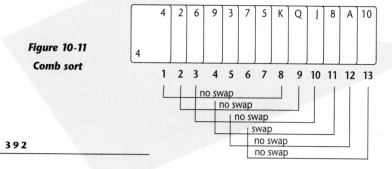

The result is shown in Figure 10-12.

The next value of *Gap* is Int(7/1.3), or 5. Figure 10-13 displays the next four passes, with gaps of 5, 3, 2, and 1.

The code for the comb sort is very similar to that for the bubble sort. The bubble sort compares elements next to each other:

```
If A(j) > A(j + 1) Then
```

The comb sort compares elements that are a gap apart:

```
If A(j) > A(j + Gap) Then
```

The name of the sort refers to the shrinking gap. Each time through the list, the distance between the compared values is reduced, just like using combs with finer and finer teeth on your hair.

Figure 10-12
Swapped cards

Figure 10-13
Passes through the cards with a comb sort

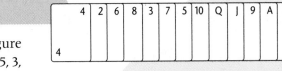

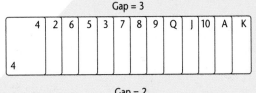

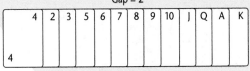

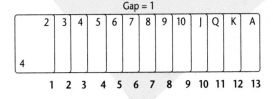

ADDING THE COMB SORT TO THE SORTING EXAMPLE

To add the comb sort to the sorting demo, follow these steps.

1   Add a command button to the form. Change its caption to **&Comb** and its name to **cmdComb**.

2   Change the form's caption to **Three Sorts**. See Figure 10-14.

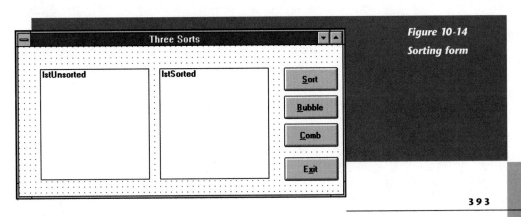

Figure 10-14
Sorting form

3 Add the comb sort code to the procedure for **cmdComb**. The program is over when there are no swaps and the gap is 1.

```
lstUnSorted.Clear
lstSorted.Clear
cmdGenerate_Click
'—Declare pointer into the array
Dim j As Integer
'—Declare the shrink factor as a constant
Const SHRINK = 1.3
'—Declare Gap
Dim Gap As Single
'—Declare space for swapping
Dim temp As Single
'—Variable to keep track if there's been a swap
Dim Swapped As Integer
'—The indefinite loop stops when list is sorted
Gap = MAXITEM
Do
    Gap = Int(Gap / SHRINK)
    '—The gap must not be less than 1
    If Gap < 1 Then Gap = 1
        Swapped = False
    For j = 1 To MAXITEM - Gap
        'Compare elements, Gap apart
        If A(j) > A(j + Gap) Then
            '—Swap
            temp = A(j)
            A(j) = A(j + Gap)
            A(j + Gap) = temp
            '—Swap did occur
            Swapped = True
        End If
    Next j
Loop Until Not Swapped And Gap = 1
'—Put sorted values into listbox
Dim x As Integer
For x = 1 To MAXITEM
    lstSorted.AddItem Str$(A(x))
Next x
```

4 Run the program. Click on each of the sorts and time each one.

5   Save the form and project files.

THE COMB SORT IS FAST

The amazing thing about the comb sort is its speed. It doesn't look very different from the bubble sort, but it is much faster. Try increasing the size of the unsorted array. The difference in times to execute between the comb sort and the other sorts becomes more dramatic as the arrays become larger.

QUESTIONS AND ACTIVITIES

1. Add a fourth command button to the form. Give it the caption **Built&In** and the name **cmdBuiltIn**. Add a third List box to the form. Call the List box **lstBuiltIn**. Set the Sorted property of the box to **True**. The code for the button should clear the List boxes and call cmdGenerate_Click. Copy the entries from lstUnSorted to lstBuiltIn. Run the program and time the results.

2. Modify the comb sort to try different shrink factors. Time the routine before and after each change. Try values of 5, 3, 2, 1.3, 1.1.

3. Write the lines of the simple exchange sort to sort an array, *dognames(30)*, an array of thirty strings.

4. One way to improve the simple exchange sort is to turn it into a selection sort. The selection sort works like the simple exchange sort, but instead of swapping any two values that are out of order, it only swaps at the end of the end of the inner loop. Instead of swapping, the **If** statement sets a pointer to the smallest element of the list. At the end of the inner loop, the smallest element is swapped with the top of the list. The selection sort makes the same number of comparisons, but it makes fewer exchanges. Modify the simple exchange sort to swap just once at the end of the inner loop.

5. Assume information about a list of cars was stored in three arrays, *Make(), Model(),* and *Year()*. Write the statements that would exchange the *Front* entry of each array with the *Back* entry.

Section 2

Creating a General-Purpose Sorting Procedure

The comb sort command handler you created in the previous program is fast, but it is closely tied to that program. The command handler implements the comb sort, but also takes care of tasks that have nothing to do with sorting. The first two lines clear List boxes. The last lines fill a List box with the sorted array. Reusing this code in the future to sort an array would require much editing of the code once you cut and paste it. To save yourself work in the future, you need a general-purpose, or generic, comb sort procedure that you can use in any program.

As you know from Chapter 6, you can create modules of code that you can reuse in any form or any project. In this section, then, you will create a procedure in a code module. The procedure declares a dynamic array to hold the items to be sorted and uses a comb sort to arrange the elements of the array. Whenever you need a sorting mechanism in a project, you can then simply add this code module to the project.

Dynamic arrays are a feature of Visual Basic that you have not yet explored. In the programs you have written so far that used an array, you had to declare the exact amount of memory to be used by the array. **Dim A(20) As Integer**, for example, reserves exactly enough memory for 20 whole numbers.

You declare a dynamic array without specifying a size. This is perfect for a sorting procedure in a code module that you expect to reuse. After all, you are likely to want to sort arrays of many different sizes. The size of a dynamic array is fixed with a **ReDim** statement at the procedure level. By using the **ReDim** statement, you can change the size of the array to be sorted in the middle of the procedure. "Dynamic" refers to the fact that the size of the array changes at run-time. The **ReDim** statement refers to redimensioning, or changing the size of, an array.

You can define dynamic arrays with **Dim** or **Global** statements. In the code module you are about to build, you will declare the array as a global variable in the general declarations section of the module. Clicking on the Numbers command button on the form redimensions the *Numbers()* array to a particular size, fills the array with random numbers, then calls CombSort from the code module. The *Numbers()* array is sent as a parameter to CombSort. The contents of *Numbers()* are transferred to the *A()* array and sorted. See Figure 10-15.

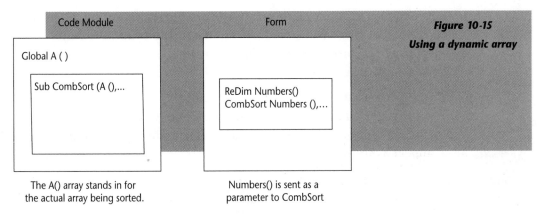

Code Module

Form

Figure 10-15

Using a dynamic array

Global A ( )

Sub CombSort (A (),...

ReDim Numbers()
CombSort Numbers (),...

The A() array stands in for
the actual array being sorted.

Numbers() is sent as a
parameter to CombSort

Setting up the Code Module: Stage 1

The code for the CombSort procedure is borrowed from the last section's project. In these steps you will add a code module to a new project and paste code written for the comb sort. This is the basis for the new code.

Follow these steps to start creating the code module:

1   Start Visual Basic.

2   Load the Three Sorts project, saved in the last section.

3   Select the form in the Project window and click on View Code.

4   Open the cmdCombSort procedure.

5   Select all the code, including the first and last lines of the procedure.

6   Press Ctrl+C to copy the code to the Clipboard.

7   From the File menu, select New Project.

8   Add a code module to the project. It has the default name **module1.bas**.

9   Select the code module in the Project window and click on View Code.

10   Paste the CombSort code into the general declarations section of the code module.

11   Delete the lines that are specific to the program in the last section. Delete the lines that clear the List boxes. Delete the lines from the end of the procedure that write the contents of the *A* array into a List box.

Setting up the Code Module: Stage 2

In this second stage, you declare the dynamic array *A* and create a generic version of the comb sort from the code pasted in stage 1. The generic comb sort is passed the array and an integer indicating the maximum number of items as parameters. When the routine is done, the sorted array is returned to the calling program.

To complete this stage:

1 Add two parameters to the first line of the sort—**A(), MaxItem As Integer**—between the parentheses on the first line. After specific references to the List boxes are deleted, the code should appear as shown here:

```
Sub CombSort (A(), MaxItem As Integer)
'—Entries in the array A() are assumed to start at subscript 1
'—Declare pointer into the array
Dim j As Integer
'—Declare the shrink factor as a constant
Const SHRINK = 1.3
'—Declare Gap
Dim Gap As Single
'—Declare space for swapping
Dim temp As Variant
'—Variable to keep track if there's been a swap
Dim Swapped As Integer
'—The indefinite loop stops when list is sorted
Gap = MaxItem
Do
    Gap = Int(Gap / SHRINK)
    '—The gap must not be less than one
    If Gap < 1 Then Gap = 1
        Swapped = False
    For j = 1 To MaxItem - Gap
        '—Compare elements, Gap apart
        If A(j) > A(j + Gap) Then
            '—Swap
            temp = A(j)
            A(j) = A(j + Gap)
            A(j + Gap) = temp
            '—Swap did occur
            Swapped = True
        End If
    Next j
Loop Until Not Swapped And Gap = 1
End Sub
```

2   Add the declaration of the global dynamic array to the general declarations section of the code module under Option Explicit:

```
Global A()
```

3   Return to the form by selecting the form name from the Project window. Change the caption of the form to **Using Dynamic Arrays**. Change the name of the form to **frmDynamic**.

4   Place a List box on the form. Change the name of the box to lstSorted.

5   Put three command buttons on the form. The caption of the first is **&Numbers**. Change the name to **cmdNumbers**. Change the caption of the second button to **&Strings**. Change the name to **cmdStringSort**. Change the caption of the third button to **E&xit**. Change the name to **cmdExit**. See Figure 10-16.

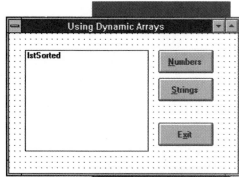

6   Double-click on the Numbers button to open the Code window. Enter the following code to resize the array to a specific size as determined by *MAXITEMS*. The array is filled with random numbers. CombSort is called to sort the array. Once the array is sorted, it is displayed in the List box.

Figure 10-16
Form design in progress

```
'—Declare number of items as constant
Const MAXITEMS = 200
'—Use ReDim to fix the size of the Numbers array
ReDim Numbers(MAXITEMS)
'—Generate random numbers and fill the array
Dim x As Integer
For x = 1 To MAXITEMS
    Numbers(x) = Rnd
Next x
'—Call CombSort with the array Numbers and MAXITEMS as parameters
CombSort Numbers(), MAXITEMS
'—Display sorted array in a List box.
For x = 1 To MAXITEMS
    lstSorted.AddItem Str$(Numbers(x))
Next x
```

7   Run the program. Click on the Numbers button. Scroll through the results in the List box.

8   Save the form, code module, and project files.

Adding the String Sort Driver

A generic implementation of the comb sort will sort any type of array. The declarations used in the code module never specify a data type for the array. When a data type is not specified, Visual Basic uses the Variant type. This type can represent any of the built-in data types. Given this flexibility, you can use the CombSort procedure for whole numbers, singles, strings, currency, or any of the other built-in types.

Follow the steps below to alter the previous demonstration to sort random alphabetic characters. The same generic comb sort routine used to sort numbers is used to sort characters.

1 Copy the code for the Numbers button and paste it into the procedure for the Strings button. Instead of random numbers, you will be modifying the program to generate random characters.

2 Change every instance of *Numbers* to *Letters*.

3 Remove the **Str$( )** function you used in the **AddItem** method for the List box. Because this part of the program sorts characters, you do not need to convert the data to a string before putting it into the List box.

4 Change the assignment statement that inserts values into the array:

```
Letters(x) = Chr$(Int(26 * Rnd + 65))
```

This statement generates a random integer between 65 and 90. These are the ASCII codes of the capital letters. It then converts the integer to a character and puts it into the array.

5 Run the program and click on Strings. Wait a moment, then scroll through the List box checking to see if the code worked.

6 Save the module, the form, and project files.

The code module you created in this program is ready for new tasks. You can add the module to any project you build so that you can sort lists.

LIMITATIONS

Limitations of this approach to code reusability are the problems of arrays of user-defined types and information stored in more than one array. The CombSort routine, as saved, will sort one-dimensional arrays. The only flexibility you gain with this approach is the size of the array is variable and the array may be any built-in data type.

This procedure cannot sort arrays of user-defined types. For example, it cannot be used to sort an array of Person records in alphabetical order (last name, then first name).

It cannot be used to sort multiple arrays in parallel. For example, if you stored people's names in two arrays, one for last names and another for first names, then sorting the collection of names would require that swaps be performed on the elements in the same positions in both arrays.

EXERCISE

Turn the simple exchange sort and the bubble sort into generic sorts. Put them into the code module with the comb sort.

Searching

Section

Searching procedures let you find the information you want within a large expanse of data (arrays and files). When you want to look up information in a book, you don't want to have to read that book from the beginning just to find the passage you seek. Instead, you use the book's index if it has one. Fortunately, most books that can be used as references are organized in a way that speeds up searching. The topics in an encyclopedia are sorted alphabetically, so that you can quickly zero in on the volume and page containing the topic you seek. Other less-structured books have indexes, which can be thought of as tables that speed up searching. In the worst case, though, you would have to scan the book from front to back.

Searching for information among the data maintained by programs is no different. The kind of information you want to search for can suggest a way of organizing and sorting the data so that searches can be performed very quickly. Unless you have only very small amounts of data, you (and the users of your programs) will find it very slow to search by examining every record in an array or a file.

Searching procedures have become more important as storage mechanisms have improved. A CD-ROM, for example, holds 550 megabytes of data. That's enough for a multimedia encyclopedia, with images, sounds, and videos. How do you find any information on a CD-ROM that packed with data? The answer is linear and binary searches, which are covered in this section.

The Linear Search

Figure 10-17

A linear search

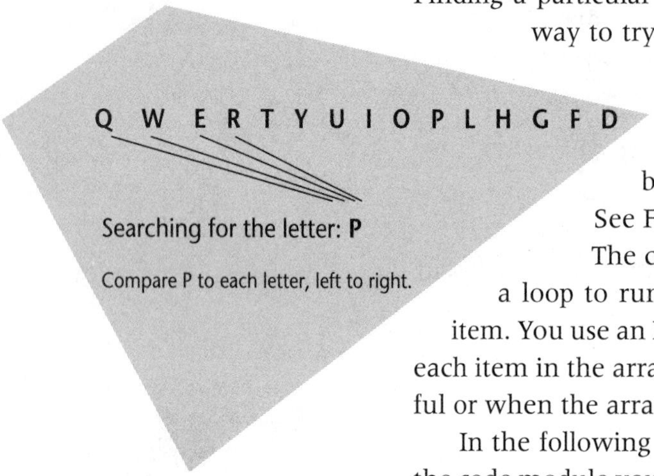

Imagine a phone book in which the entries are not in alphabetical order. Finding a particular phone number would be extremely difficult. One way to try to find that number would be to perform a linear search. This type of search compares the search item with every entry in the array. When a match is found, or when every array entry has been examined unsuccessfully, the search is over. See Figure 10-17.

Q W E R T Y U I O P L H G F D

Searching for the letter: **P**

Compare P to each letter, left to right.

The code you need for a linear search is easy. You set up a loop to run through the array from the first item to the last item. You use an **If-Then** statement to compare the search item with each item in the array. The loop ends either when the search is successful or when the array has been thoroughly checked.

In the following exercise, you will add a linear search procedure to the code module you created for the comb sort. If you did not create that code module, create a new code module for this exercise.

CREATING A LINEAR SEARCH PROCEDURE

In this section, you create a general-purpose linear search procedure. Like the general-purpose comb sort procedure of the previous sections, the linear search subroutine you create will work only with arrays of built-in types, and not with arrays of user-defined types.

You will be sending the following parameters to LinearSearch:

- Dynamic array, *A()*

- Search item, *SearchItem*

- Maximum number of items in the array, *MaxItems*

- Position found—a whole number, *Position*. The linear search procedure passes the result of the search back to its caller by setting the value of this parameter. If *SearchItem* is found, then *Position* is set to its array subscript. If it is not found, *Position* is set to 0. (Entries in the array are assumed to start at subscript 1.)

Follow these steps to add the LinearSearch procedure to the code module.

1   Open the code module.

2   Select New Procedure from the View menu.

3   Enter the name **LinearSearch** and click on Sub.

4   Enter these lines:

```
Sub LinearSearch (A(), SearchItem, MaxItems As Integer, Position As Integer)
'—Parameters:
'—A() — Dynamic array of the variant type
'—SearchItem — Item to be found - variant type
'—MaxItems — Number of items in the array
'—Position — 0 if item not found,
'equal to subscript of item; otherwise
'assume item will not be found
Position = 0
Dim x As Integer
'—Loop traverses entire list
For x = 1 To MaxItems
    If SearchItem = A(x) Then
        ' —If the item is found, record the position in the
        'array and leave the For loop.
        Position = x
        Exit For
    End If
Next x
End Sub
```

ADDING A DRIVER TO THE FORM

Once the routine is in the code module, you can call it from a program. A routine that calls the LinearSearch procedure for testing purposes is called a driver. Follow these steps to add a driver to the form:

1   Open the Using Dynamic Arrays project, if it is not already open.

2   Add a command button to the form. Change the caption to **S&tring Search**. Change the name to **cmdStringSearch**. Change the Enabled property to **False**. The button should not be clicked until the Strings button has been clicked.

3   Open the Code window for the form.

4   In the general declarations section of the form, enter:

```
Dim Letters()
```

This turns the *Letters* array into an array available to all the event procedures of the form, not just cmdStringSort_Click.

5 Open the cmdStringSort_Click procedure. Add this line as the last line of the procedure:

```
cmdStringSearch.Enabled = True
```

6 Open the cmdStringSearch_Click procedure and add the following code:

```
'—Char represents character to search for
Dim Char As String
Const MAXITEMS = 200
'—Position is the subscript at which the character is found
Dim Position As Integer
'—Collect search item from user
Char = InputBox$("Enter character for which to search ")
'—Call the LinearSearch procedure
LinearSearch Letters(), Char, MAXITEMS, Position
If Position = 0 Then
    MsgBox "Character not found."
Else
    MsgBox "Character found at position: " & Str$(Position)
End If
```

7 Save the form, module, and project files.

8 Run the program. Note the String Search button is dimmed. Click on Strings. Click on String Search.

9 Enter a character that occurs in the list (a capital letter).

10 Enter a character that doesn't occur in the list (a lowercase letter).

SEARCHING AN UNORDERED LIST

The only way to search an unordered list is to examine every element of the list. The linear search examines every element.

If the list is ordered, a search that examines every element is wasteful. It doesn't take into account the order of the list.

There are many applications in which lists grow to extreme lengths. When the list is very long, as in the telephone directory of a large metropolitan area, searching an ordered list in a way that takes advantage of its order is far more efficient than searching an unordered list.

The Binary Search

When searching a long ordered list, people take advantage of the fact that the list is sorted. For example, when you look up a person's name in the phonebook, you don't start reading the phone book from the beginning; instead, you first get close to the name you seek by repeatedly subdividing the pages of the book into two ranges: one which the name cannot fall within, and another which does contain the name.

Similarly, computer programs can implement this same idea when searching a long ordered list. The search algorithm that embodies this strategy of repeated subdivision is called the binary search. To get an idea of how efficient the binary search is, find a partner and play the dictionary game.

THE DICTIONARY GAME

To play this game:

1   Get a fairly large dictionary.

2   Determine the number of entries in the dictionary. A typical desk-size volume will have fewer than 60,000 entries.

3   Ask your partner to select a word from the dictionary. Have your partner write the word on a piece of paper, but don't look at the word.

4   Tell your partner you will guess the word in 16 guesses, so long as you can have some help.

5   Make a note of the number of pages in the dictionary. Turn to the middle page. Pick a word off one of the pages, say the word to your partner, then ask whether the word written on the paper comes before or after your word.

6   If your partner says "before," discard the last half of the dictionary and repeat step 5. Use page one as the beginning and the middle page as the end.

7   If your partner says "after," the middle page becomes your starting point and the last page your ending point. Repeat step 5.

Each time you make a guess, you eliminate half the remaining words in the dictionary. See Figure 10-18.

Figure 10-18
Playing the dictionary game

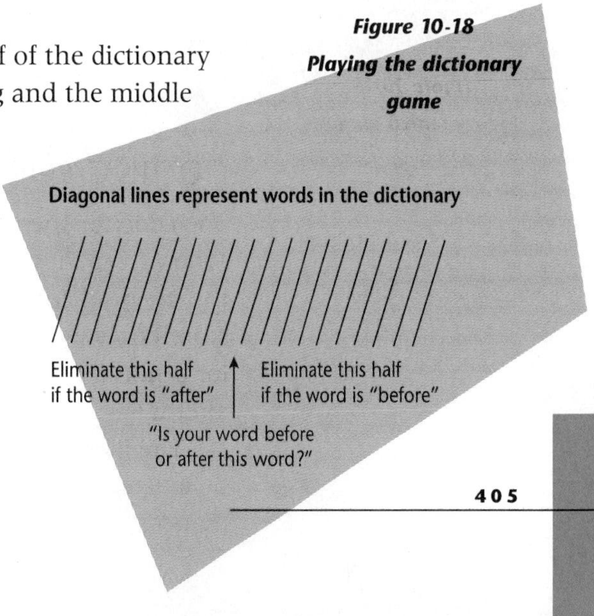

Diagonal lines represent words in the dictionary

Eliminate this half
if the word is "after"

Eliminate this half
if the word is "before"

"Is your word before
or after this word?"

If you start with 60,000 words, the number of words remaining after each guess is shown in the following table. In practice, you can often spot the word before you get to the sixteenth guess.

Guess Number	Words Remaining
1	30,000
2	15,000
3	7,500
4	3,750
5	1,875
6	938
7	469
8	235
9	118
10	59
11	30
12	15
13	8
14	4
15	2
16	1

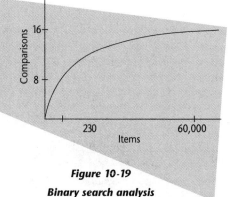

Figure 10-19
Binary search analysis

You have just used the binary search algorithm to find the word. If you look at a graph of this function you'll see it flattens out quite rapidly. Even a large change in the number of elements to search adds very few comparisons. See Figure 10-19.

In contrast, because the linear search examines each element of the array, on the average, it must examine half the elements to find the search item. In an array of 40,000 elements, instead of 16 comparisons—the maximum used by the binary search—an average of 20,000 comparisons are made by the linear search.

CODING FOR THE BINARY SEARCH

The code for the binary search routine is not difficult, but often subtle errors creep in, preventing the search from being successful. First of all, the array of information to be searched must be sorted. The binary search only works when you can ask the question, "If the item searched for is not here in the middle, does it come before the middle element or after it?"

The idea behind the code is easy:

- Find the middle element of the array being searched.
- Compare the item you are trying to find with the middle element. If they match, the search is over.
- If the item you are trying to find is smaller than the middle element, restrict your search to the first half of the list.
- If the item you are trying to find is larger than the middle element, restrict your search to the last half of the list.

The dictionary game is an illustration of the algorithm described here.

As before, you add the code to the code module developed in the last section and added to in this section. The procedure for adding a binary search module to the Dynamic Arrays program is the same as for the linear search. The parameters sent to the binary search are identical to the ones used in the linear search.

Follow these steps to add a binary search procedure to the code module and a driver to the Dynamic Arrays form:

1   Enter the code module.

2   Select New Procedure from the View menu.

3   Enter the name **BinarySearch**, and click on Sub.

4   Enter these lines:

```
Sub BinarySearch (A(), SearchItem, MaxItems As Integer, position As Integer)
    '—Parameters:
    '—A() — Dynamic array of the variant type
    '—SearchItem — Item to be found - variant type
    '—MaxItems — Number of items in the array
    '—Position — 0 if item not found,
    'equal to subscript of item, otherwise
    'assume item will not be found
    position = 0
    Dim x As Integer
    '—Low and High point to the first and last
    'elements of a range of elements
    Dim Low As Integer, High As Integer, Md As Integer
    Dim Rslt As Integer    ' result of string compare
    '—Start with entire range of array values
    Low = 1
    High = MaxItems
    Do While Low <= High
        Md = (Low + High) \ 2    ' an integer division
        Rslt = StrComp(SearchItem, A(Md))
```

continued

```
Select Case Rslt
    Case 0
        position = Md
        Exit Do   ' search is over
    Case -1    ' Search item is in first half of list
        High = Md - 1
    Case 1     ' Search item is in last half of list
        Low = Md + 1
End Select
    Loop
End Sub
```

ADDING A DRIVER FOR THE BINARY SEARCH MODULE

The steps for adding a driver to call the Binary Search module is identical to steps followed on pages 403 and 404 to add a driver for the Linear Search module. Use those steps as a model to add a command button and the code to call the Binary Search routine.

Figure 10-20

Sorted list of numbers

234	333	412	444	490	499	501	505	509	550	560	566
1	2	3	4	5	6	7	8	9	10	11	12
Low				Mid							High

Figure 10-21

Working with the binary search

234	333	412	444	490	499	501	505	509	550	560	566
1	2	3	4	5	6	7	8	9	10	11	12
						Low		Mid			High

Figure 10-22

Continuing to work with the binary search

234	333	412	444	490	499	501	505	509	550	560	566
1	2	3	4	5	6	7	8	9	10	11	12
									Low	Mid	High

HOW A BINARY SEARCH WORKS

To see how the binary search works, start with a sorted list of numbers, such as in Figure 10-20. Assume the search item is 560.

At the start, *Low* is 1 and *High* is 12.

$$Md = \frac{(Low + High)}{2} = \frac{(1 + 12)}{2} = \frac{13}{2} = 6$$

If *Md* is 6, then *A(6)* is 499. If 560 is greater than 499, then bring the lower bound up to the middle plus 1. *Low* becomes 7. *High* is still 12. *Md* becomes 9. See Figure 10-21.

Is 560 equal to 509? If 560 is greater than 509, bring *Low* up to *Md* + 1. See Figure 10-22.

Md points to the search item. The program ends when *Md* is assigned to *Position* and the **Exit Do** leaves the loop.

QUESTIONS AND ACTIVITIES

1. There are times when a search should display all the occurrences of a value. The **Exit For** statement of the LinearSearch procedure prevents this. Rewrite LinearSearch to return two positions: the first occurrence and the last occurrence of the search item.

2. Play the dictionary game. With what other lists could you play this game?

3. Imagine that you are playing the dictionary game and the number of words in the dictionary is doubled. Why does it only take one additional question to find the chosen word?

4. In the binary search algorithm, write the lines it would take to replace the **StrComp()** function and the **Select Case** statement with a series of **If-Then** statements.

5. In the binary search algorithm, replace:

```
Md = (low + high) \ 2    ' an integer division
```

with:

```
Md = (low + high) \ 3
```

Describe the effect of this change.

Searching Files and Arrays

4

Section

In this section you develop a program to gather, display, search, and store information. The CD Database program stores the name of a CD, the artist, and the shelf location.

File management, arrays, user-defined types, sorting, and searching are all a part of this project. The methods used here can be applied to any collection or database of information.

Starting Out

The start-up form displays a menu and a List box. The List box displays the CD list. The List box displays the results of searches. A dialog box is used to gather data from the user.

The menu offers the user a number of choices. The menu structure with explanation follows:

- File
  - New: Clears the List box and sets current number of entries to 0.
  - Open: Opens an existing file of CDs.
  - Save As: Saves a file of CDs using a path and file name entered through an InputBox.
  - Exit: Halts the program.

- Data
  - Enter: Calls the dialog box to enter new data.
  - Delete: Deletes entry whose index number is entered.

- Listing
  - By Artist: Displays entries with artist name on the first line.
  - By Name: Displays entries with name of CD on the first line.

- Search
  - By Artist: Collects artist name from user and lists CDs by that artist in the List box.
  - By Name: Collects name from user and lists CDs by that name in the List box.

- Sort: Sorts items by CD name.

Creating the Menu

Figure 10-23
Menu Design window
with menu completed

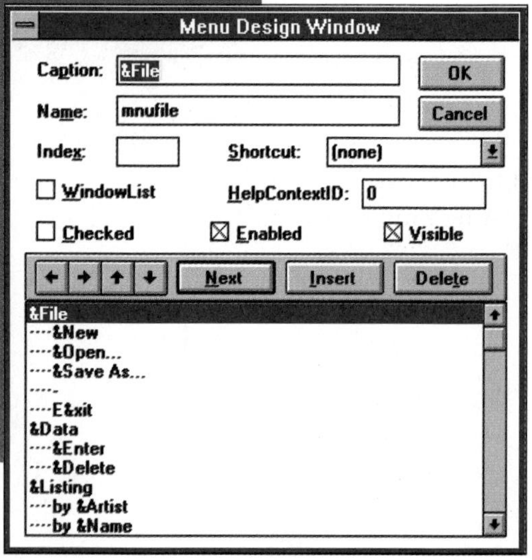

Follow these steps to set up the project and create the menu.

1 Start Visual Basic. If Visual Basic is running, choose New Project from the File menu.

2 Add the file with the CombSort routine to the project. Choose Add File and add the code module with the CombSort procedure. The code will be borrowed later in the project.

3 Select the default form. Change the name of the form to **frmMain**. Change the caption to **CD Database**.

4 Select the form and open the Menu Design window.

5 Enter the menu items in Table 10-1, using the arrows to make submenus. When you are done, your Menu Design window should look like that shown in Figure 10-23.

Table 10-1   Menu Items

Caption	Name	Index	Enabled
&File	mnuFile		
&New	mnuNew		
&Open	mnuOpen		
&Save As	mnuSave		No
E&xit	mnuExit		
&Data	mnuData		
&Enter	mnuEnter		
&Delete	mnuDelete		
&Listing	mnuList		No
By &Artist	mnuListHandler	1	
By &Name	mnuListHandler	2	
&Search	mnuSearch		No
By &Artist	mnuSearchBy	1	
By &Name	mnuSearchBy	2	
So&rt	mnuSort		No

Creating the Code Module

The code module contains the definition of CDType. CDType is a data type with three fields:

- Name, a 30-character field for the name of the CD

- Artist, a 20-character field for the artist

- Location, a 15-character field used to specify the location of the CD in the collection

A global array is declared to hold the entries. The values of the array are of the CDType defined above. A global integer variable, *Current*, is used to keep track of the current number of entries in the array.

Follow these steps to set up the code module:

1 From the File menu, choose New Module.

2 In the general declarations section, enter the following code:

```
Option Explicit
Type CDType
'—Record length is 30+20+15 = 65
    Name As String * 30
    Artist As String * 20
```

continued

```
        Location As String * 15
End Type
Global CDList(1 To 100) As CDType
Global Current As Integer
```

3 Save the file.

Declarations made in the code module with **Global** are available to all procedures in all forms throughout the project.

Creating the Dialog Box

The dialog box is a form used to collect the name, artist, and location of the CD. The dialog form contains three textboxes, three labels, and a command button. The command button reads the information from the textboxes, and transfers the information into the array.

Follow these instructions to set up the dialog box.

1 Choose New Form from the File menu.

2 Select the form. Change the name of the form to **frmData**. Change the caption of the form to **Enter CD Data**.

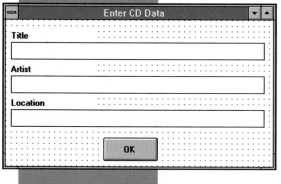

3 Figure 10-24 above shows the layout of the form. Put three textboxes on the form. Name them **txtName**, **txtArtist**, and **txtLocation**. Delete the text from all three.

4 Put three labels on the form, one above each textbox. Change the captions to **Title**, **Artist**, and **Location**.

5 Place a command button on the form. Change the name of the button to **cmdOK**. Change the caption of the button to **OK**.

Figure 10-24
Enter CD Data form

6 Double-click on the command button to open the Code window.

7 Enter the following code for cmdOK:

```
'—Declare temporary storage place for form's data.
Dim Transfer As CDType
'—Check to see if the name of the CD has been
'entered. If it has, collect the rest of the
'information from the form.
If Trim$(txtName) <> "" Then
   Transfer.Name = txtName
   Transfer.Artist = txtArtist
   Transfer.Location = txtLocation
```

```
'—Update Current and load information into the array.
Current = Current + 1
CDList(Current) = Transfer
Else
   '—If the name of the CD has not been entered,
   'display an error message and return to the
   'calling program.
   MsgBox "Error: Enter complete information!"
End If
Unload Me
```

Unload Me not only hides the form from view, it also unloads the form from memory. When the form is displayed again in response to a **Show** statement, the form is loaded in memory. This ensures the Form_Load procedure is executed.

8   Enter the following code into the Form_Load procedure of frmData:

```
txtName = ""
txtArtist = ""
txtLocation = ""
```

9   Save the form.

Adding Code: Stage 1

In this first stage, after the main form is set up, you enter the code to turn on the dialog box. The dialog box prompts the user to enter information about the CD.

The main form displays entries in a List box. The user interface has already been created. Follow these steps to add a List box to the start-up form and enter the code. Refer to Figure 10-25.

Figure 10-25
Form for the project

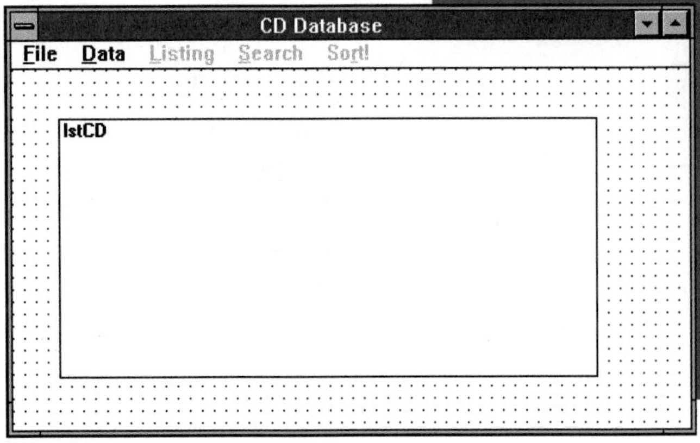

1   Select frmMain from the Project window.

2   Put a List box on the form. Change the name to **lstCD**.

3   Select the form in the Project window and click on View Code. In the general declarations section make sure the following line appears.

```
Option Explicit
```

413

4 Enter the **End** command in the procedure for mnuExit.

5 Enter this code in the mnuEnter_Click() procedure.

```
'—Load and show the data collection dialog box.
frmData.Show
'—Switch on the disabled menu items.
mnuSave.Enabled = True
mnuList.Enabled = True
mnuSearch.Enabled = True
mnuSort.Enabled = True
```

6 Run the program. Click on Data. Click on Enter. The dialog box should appear.

7 Stop the program by selecting File, then Exit.

8 Enter the following lines in the mnuListHandler_Click routine.

```
'—Clear the display ListBox.
lstCD.Clear
'—List all entries
'—List each field on a separate line. If index = 1
'list the artist first. If index = 2, list the name
'of the CD first. Prepare each line and add to the
'listbox.
Dim x As Integer
For x = 1 To Current
    If index = 1 Then    ' by Artist
        lstCD.AddItem Str$(x) & ": " & CDList(x).Artist
        lstCD.AddItem "    " & CDList(x).Name
        lstCD.AddItem "    " & CDList(x).Location
    Else
        lstCD.AddItem Str$(x) & ": " & CDList(x).Name
        lstCD.AddItem "    " & CDList(x).Artist
        lstCD.AddItem "    " & CDList(x).Location
    End If
Next x
```

9 Run the program. Click on Data. Click on Enter. Enter data into the dialog box and click OK.

10 Repeat step 9.

11 Click on Listing. Click on By Artist. The List box should display items just entered. Click on Listing. Click on By Name.

12 Halt the program.

Adding Code: Stage 2

The code you add in this second stage enables the Delete command in the menu. This command deletes the current entry in the CD list. At this point, even though a number of commands, particularly the File commands, have not been entered, it is possible to run the program and test it.

This stage also covers the addition of code to create a new file, open an existing file, and save the current file.

To enter the stage 2 code:

1 Enter the following lines in mnuDelete_Click.

```
'—Variable to hold index number of item to delete
Dim ItemNumber As Integer
Dim x As Integer
'—If Current isn't greater than 0, there is no list
If Current > 0 Then
    '—Set up error checking.
    On Error GoTo DelError
    '—Collect item number from the user
    ItemNumber = Val(InputBox("Enter number of CD to delete:"))
    '—The ItemNumber could be too big, go to the error handler.
    If ItemNumber > Current Then GoTo DelError
    '—Delete ItemNumber by moving all the items below it up
    For x = ItemNumber To Current
        CDList(x) = CDList(x + 1)
    Next x
    '—Reset Current to reflect the loss of an item
    Current = Current - 1
End If
'—Exit procedure before blundering into error handler code
Exit Sub
'—Error handler
DelError:
    MsgBox "A bad value has been entered"
Exit Sub
```

2 Run the program. Add a couple of entries. Choose Data, then Delete. Enter the number of the first item.

3 Choose Listing to see if item has been removed.

4 Halt the program.

5 Enter the following lines in mnuNew_Click.

```
'—Choosing New clears the ListBox and resets
'—Current to 0. This effectively clears the array.
Current = 0
mnuSave.Enabled = True
1stCD.Clear
```

6 Enter the following lines in the mnuOpen_Click routine:

```
Dim FName As String
'—Get file name from user
On Error GoTo ErrorHandler2
FName = InputBox("Enter path and file name:")
'—Random access file is used.
Open FName For Random Access Read As #1 Len = 65
Dim x As Integer
'—Opening the file, Current starts at 0
Current = 0
Do
    '—Current is incremented.
    Current = Current + 1
    '—Data is collected from the file.
    Get #1, , CDList(Current)
    '—Loop executes until the file is empty.
Loop Until EOF(1)
'—EOF lets code go until Get fails to collect data
'—At that point, Current is one too many
Current = Current - 1
Close #1
'—Turn on menu items. Now that a file is open, the
'data can be saved, listed, searched, and sorted.
mnuSave.Enabled = True
mnuList.Enabled = True
mnuSearch.Enabled = True
mnuSort.Enabled = True
Exit Sub
'—Error handler
'—Label names like ErrorHandler cannot recur in the form.
ErrorHandler2:
    MsgBox "Illegal File or Path Name. Error #: " & Str$(Err)
    Exit Sub
```

7   Enter the following lines in mnuSave_Click:

```
Dim FName As String
'—Get file name from user
'—Set up On Error statement
On Error GoTo ErrorHandler
FName = InputBox("Enter path and file name:")
'—Open file for random access.
Open FName For Random Access Write As #1 Len = 65
Dim x As Integer
'—Write (Put) each record into the file.
For x = 1 To Current
    Put #1, , CDList(x)
Next x
Close #1
Exit Sub
'—Error Handler code
ErrorHandler:
    MsgBox "Illegal File or Path Name. Error #: " & Str$(Err)
    Exit Sub
```

Adding Code: Stage 3

The third stage adds code to sort and search the list of CDs. The search routine is the linear search, and the sorting routine is the comb sort from the beginning of the chapter. You can copy the code from earlier programs and paste it into the routines here, or enter the code directly from the listing.

A linear search is used to find items by particular artists or by names. The search is used to display each of the items that match the search string. A match of the first five characters is sufficient to display the item. Actual lines to display items in the List box can be copied and pasted from the Listing routine.

1   Enter these lines in mnuSearchBy_Click.

```
'—Can't use the generic search because of the
'array of user—defined type
'—Declare variable for search item
Dim SearchItem As String
Dim x As Integer
'—Clear the List box
lstCD.Clear
```

continued

```
'—The value of index reflects which menu item has been
'chosen, by artist or by name
If index = 1 Then     ' search by artist
    '—Enter the name of the artist, the loop will print
    'each entire entry whose artist name matches SearchItem
    SearchItem = InputBox("Enter the name of the Artist:")
    For x = 1 To Current
        '—Compare just the first 5 characters of each string
        '—Display each entry where the first 5 character match
        If Left$(SearchItem, 5) = Left$(CDList(x).Artist, 5) Then
            '—Add items to listbox
            lstCD.AddItem Str$(x) & ":" & CDList(x).Artist
            lstCD.AddItem "    " & CDList(x).Name
            lstCD.AddItem "    " & CDList(x).Location
        End If
    Next x
End If
If index = 2 Then     ' search by name
    '—Repeat the whole procedure with search by name
    SearchItem = InputBox("Enter the name of the CD:")
    For x = 1 To Current
        If Left$(SearchItem, 5) = Left$(CDList(x).Name, 5) Then
            lstCD.AddItem Str$(x) & ":" & CDList(x).Name
            lstCD.AddItem "    " & CDList(x).Artist
            lstCD.AddItem "    " & CDList(x).Location
        End If
    Next x
End If
```

2 Copy the code from the CombSort routine. Paste the code into mnuSort_Click. Change the references as follows:

MaxItems → Current

A() → CDList()

Temp is declared as type CDType, instead of Variant type. The **If** statement that performs the comparison is altered to compare the *Name* field of the array.

```
Sub mnuSort_Click ()
    '—Declare pointer into the array
    Dim j As Integer
    '—Declare the shrink factor as a constant
    Const SHRINK = 1.3
```

```
    '—Declare Gap
  Dim Gap As Single
    '—Declare space for swapping
  Dim temp As CDType
    '—Variable to keep track if there's been a swap
  Dim Swapped As Integer
    '—The indefinite loop stops when list is sorted
  Gap = Current
  Do
      Gap = Int(Gap / SHRINK)
      '—The gap must not be  less than one
      If Gap < 1 Then Gap = 1
         Swapped = False
      For j = 1 To Current - Gap
         '—Compare elements, Gap apart
         If CDList(j).Name > CDList(j + Gap).Name Then
               ' —Swap
               temp = CDList(j)
               CDList(j) = CDList(j + Gap)
               CDList(j + Gap) = temp
               '—Swap did occur
               Swapped = True
         End If
      Next j
   Loop Until Not Swapped And Gap = 1
 End Sub
```

3 Run the program. Enter several items. Save the file. Provide an entire pathname, for example, **c:\temp\cdlist.cdl**.

4 List by artist and by name.

5 Sort the list.

6 Search for an entry by name and by artist.

7 Save the file.

8 Halt the program. Start the program again and open the data file.

9 List the file.

10 Halt the program.

11 Remove the CombSort file from the project. Save the project. Save two forms, one code module, and the project files.

QUESTIONS AND ACTIVITIES

1. After a file has been opened, the file name provided should be the default name for subsequent file activities. Modify the CD Database project to save the name of the file from the beginning to the end of the program.

2. The CD Database project sorts only by the name of the CD. Modify the program to give the user the option to sort by artist.

3. In the search routine, what would be the effect of changing:

```
If Left$(SearchItem, 5) = Left$(CDList(x).Artist, 5) Then
```

to:

```
If SearchItem = Artist Then
```

Make the change and test the program. Change the program back to its original form.

4. Disabling menu items is a kind of error handling. If an item is not appropriate, it cannot be chosen. On the other hand, menu items that are disabled cannot be viewed by someone browsing the program. Remove the statements that enable and disable the menu items.

5. In the procedure that deletes an entry the following code is used:

```
For x = ItemNumber To Current
    CDList(x) = CDList(x + 1)
Next x
```

What would be the effect of substituting the following code:

```
For x = Current To ItemNumber Step -1
    CDList(x - 1) = CDList(x)
Next x
```

Make the replacement and check the results. Restore the original code.

The simple exchange sort is about three lines long: if the array to sort is *A()*, containing *MaxItems* items, the following lines will sort the array:

```
For Front = 1 To MaxItems - 1
   For Back = Front + 1 To MaxItems
   If a(Front) > a(Back) Then
         ' swap the items
   Next Back
Next Front
```

The bubble sort works by comparing adjacent items in the list and swapping out-of-order entries. An advantage of the bubble sort is that it will stop when the items are in order.

The comb sort is a modification of the bubble sort. Instead of comparing adjacent elements, it compares elements that are a certain gap apart. The gap between the compared elements is reduced until finally, the comb sort becomes the bubble sort. It is a very fast sort.

This **Open** statement:

```
Open "c:\temp\cdfile.dat" For Random Access Read As #1
```

opens the file **c:\temp\cdfile.dat** as a random access file for read-only access as file number 1.

The **Put** statement writes information to a random access file:
Put #*<file number>*, *<record number>*, *<variable name>*

The **Get** statement reads information from a random access file:
Get #*<file number>*, *<record number>*, *<variable name>*

The **EOF()** function is **True** when the program tries to get from a file that is empty (because all the data has been read).

The **On Error Go To "label"** statement shifts program flow to an error-handling routine when a run-time error occurs.

A linear search checks every item of an array looking for the occurrence of a string or value. A simple loop is used to cycle through the items of the array.

A binary search tests the middle element of a sorted array. If the search item is the middle element, the search is over. If the item sought is less than the middle element, search the first half of the list. If the item is greater than the middle element, search the last half of the list.

The **Left$()** function:
Left$(*string, number of characters*)

takes the first number of characters from the string and returns the result as a string.

Problems

1. Searching for a Random Number Problem
Write a program to generate 100 random integers between 100 and 1000. Store the numbers in an array. Search the array for an occurrence of 750 and display its position (if it occurs) in the array.

2. Searching Through an Ordered List Problem
Write a program to generate 100 random integers between 100 and 1000. Store the numbers in an array. Use the comb sort to put the numbers in ascending order. Use a binary search to look for a number entered from the keyboard using an InputBox and display its position (if it occurs) in the array. Stop the program when the number 0 is entered from the keyboard.

3. Reversing the Characters Problem
Write a program to enter the user's name from the keyboard using an **InputBox$**. With a **For-Next** loop and a **Mid$** function, display the letters of the name in reverse order.

4. Alphabetizing the Characters Problem
Write a program to enter a line from the keyboard using an **InputBox$**. Use a sorting routine (your choice) along with the **Mid$** function to put the characters in order and display the results. The **Mid$** function will return a character of a string as its value. Look up its syntax in Help. Enter the line: "The quick brown fox jumps over the lazy dog." to test your program.

5. The Car Database
Using the following user-defined type:

```
Type Car
    make as string*20
    model as string*20
    year as integer
    cost as currency
End Type
```

Write a program to set up an array with a capacity of 20 of the Car type. Allow the user to enter data into the array (keeping track of how many elements of the array are full), and then save the array in a file named **c:\...\car.dat**.

6.   Displaying the Car Database

Write a program to open the file created above and display the information, sorted by make, in a List box. To put the car information in a List box, you'll need to concatenate the information into a single string or use a new line for each field of the record.

7.   Searching the Car Database

Write a program to open the file created in problem 5 and search for all the cars of a particular make. The make should be entered in a textbox. The results should be displayed in a List box.

```
Function Pop ( ) As
                      Integer
        If TOS > 0 Then
            TOS = TOS - 1
        Pop = Stack(TOS)
                      Else
```

End End

End Function

The Stack

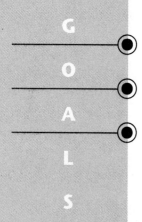
After working through this chapter, you will be able to:

Implement and use a stack data structure.

Understand, use, and evaluate expressions in infix and postfix notations.

O V E R V I E W

After arrays, the stack is one of the most fundamental data structures in computer science. A stack is a restricted kind of list. A general list represented by an array lets you add and remove elements at the top and bottom of the list, as well as anywhere in between. You can access any element of the list by using array subscripts, and can replace any element using an assignment statement. A stack is like a list in that it contains an ordered sequence of elements. However, the operations that you can perform on a stack are fewer and less powerful than those supported by general lists. With a stack, you can only add and remove elements at one end (called the top of the stack). The only element of a stack you can access is the element at the top, and then you can only do so after you have removed it from the stack.

A close relative of the stack is a data structure called the queue. The word "queue" means a line in which people or things wait for some kind of service or processing. A checkout line at a supermarket is a perfect example of a queue. Queues differ from stacks in only one respect: elements are added to a queue at one end (the back), and are removed from the other end (the front). For example, when you get in line at the supermarket, you add yourself to the line at the end. You have to be at the front of the line before you can pay and leave.

You might be wondering what possible advantage there could be in giving up the power of arrays for the limited capabilities of a stack. The answer is that sometimes a stack provides all the power and flexibility you need. The stack is an abstraction, a pattern that arises again and again in the way programs store and operate on data. The stack proves to be the correct tool for the solution of many different kinds of problems. Programmers use stacks extensively when writing interpreters for computer languages such as Visual Basic itself. In this chapter, you will be learn to use a stack to interpret a very small language of simple arithmetic expressions.

Section

The Stack Data Structure

A stack is list with a difference. A stack is a list from which your program can only access a single element at the top. New elements are pushed onto the top of the stack. At any time, the only element that can be removed—or popped—from the stack is the element at the top. See Figure 11-1.

The rack of trays in a cafeteria line is often designed as a spring-loaded stack. The clean trays are pushed onto the top of the stack. The spring in the bottom of the stack compresses to allow the more trays to be added. People going through the line take a tray from the top of the stack. The first trays pushed onto the stack are the last trays removed from the stack. The last trays pushed on top of the stack are the first trays removed.

If the number of trays exceeds the capacity of the rack, the cafeteria staff has stack overflow. You may have seen a message about the same kind of problem when a program goes awry, or a game program overloads the operating system of the computer. Such error messages reveal a hidden truth of computers: underneath the surface of the computer are stacks of information.

A stack can be represented as an array with a pointer pointing to the top of the stack. Access to the elements of the stack is entirely through this pointer. The pointer is in fact just an array subscript. Random access to the elements of the stack, although possible, is not consistent with the concept of a stack.

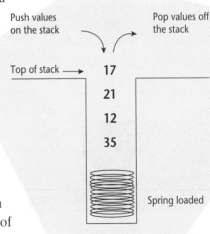

Figure 11-1
Pushing and popping
values from a stack

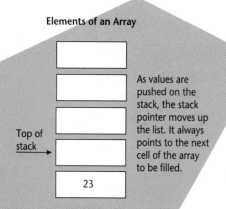

Elements of an Array

As values are pushed on the stack, the stack pointer moves up the list. It always points to the next cell of the array to be filled.

Top of stack →

23

Figure 11-2
Identifying the top of the stack with a pointer

Implementing a stack is easy. You start with an array. Add an integer variable that points to a place in the array called the top of the stack. The top of the stack changes as the number of elements in the stack increases and decreases. See Figure 11-2.

In this section you will write a simple stack program. Values are pushed and popped. This program shows how to implement a stack. Later in the chapter you will use a stack to evaluate expressions.

Setting Up the Form

To experiment with a stack, you need to set up the array, then you need to decide how to display the top entry in the stack. As you know, you use labels to display information calculated during the program. So, you'll need one label to display information, and another label to identify what that information is.

Next, you want users to enter information to be added to the stack. For that purpose, you need a textbox and a label to prompt data entry. After a user has entered data into the textbox, something must happen. What do you want to happen to the user input?

You can add command buttons (or menu commands, for that matter) to perform actions with the user input. Clicking on Push will push the input onto the stack. Clicking on Pop will display the top value in the stack. And, of course, you need an Exit button for the user to close the program. See Figure 11-3.

To run the program, a user enters a whole number in the Data box and clicks Push. The label marked Top of Stack shows the value at the top of the stack. In the figure, the value 41 has just been popped from the stack. The new top of the stack, 33, is displayed.

Follow these steps to set up the form shown in Figure 11-3.

Figure 11-3
Form for the stack experiment

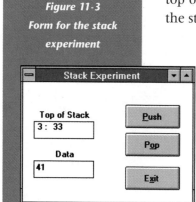

1 Start Visual Basic. If Visual Basic is running, choose New Project from the File menu.

2 Change the caption of the file to **Stack Experiment**.

3 Place three command buttons on the form. Change the names and captions as shown.

Caption	Name
&Push	cmdPush
P&op	cmdPop
E&xit	cmdExit

4   Place three labels and one text box on the form. Alter the properties of the labels according to the following table.

Name	Caption	Other Properties
label1	Top of Stack	AutoSize = True
label2	Data	AutoSize = True
lblTOS	*none*	BorderStyle = 1-single
txtData	*none*	

5   Save the form and project files.

Adding Code to the General Declarations

To make the stack available to all the event procedures, you need to declare it in the general declarations section of the form. A stack is composed of an array and a top-of-stack pointer. You declare both.

Enter the following lines in the general declarations section of the form:

```
Option Explicit
Dim Stack(0 To 20) As Integer
Dim TOS As Integer
```

For this implementation, you will use a stack of integers. In a real application, you are just as likely to use a stack of characters or real numbers. The range of subscripts in this example is 0 to 20. The variable *TOS* points to the top of the stack. The value of TOS is initialized to 0.

You will create general functions of the main form that implement the **Push** and **Pop** procedures. This separates the general logic of pushing and popping items from the specific details of how this program obtains values and displays them.

Coding the Pop Function

The **Pop** function is not an event procedure of a control. You put the function's code in the general section of the form. The routine pops an item from the top of the stack and returns that item as the value of the function. A function value can be assigned to a variable, displayed in textbox, or stand in wherever a value is used in an expression.

TOS normally points at the next empty space in the array. To pop a value from the array, subtract 1 from *TOS* to point it at the top value in the stack. When a program tries to pop a value from an empty stack, the error condition is called stack underflow.

In the **Pop** function, the statement **Pop = Stack(TOS)** assigns the stack value to the function name, providing the function with the value it returns to the calling program. See Figure 11-4.

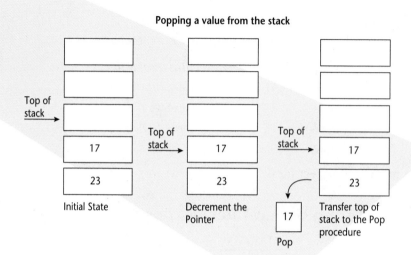

Figure 11-4
Popping a value from the stack

Popping a value from the stack

Top of stack

Initial State

Top of stack

Decrement the Pointer

Top of stack

Transfer top of stack to the Pop procedure

Pop

Follow these steps to enter the code for the **Pop** function.

1 Open the Code window for the default form.

2 Select New Procedure from the View menu.

3 Enter the name of the function, **Pop**. Click on the Function option button, then click OK. Visual Basic puts you into the skeleton routine for **Pop**.

4 Enter the following code to implement the **Pop** function:

```
Function Pop () As Integer
    '—Error message for stack underflow condition.
    Const strUnderflow = "Stack underflow"
    '—Legal stack value is tested, if less than or equal
    'to 0, the stack is empty, a value cannot be popped
    If TOS > 0 Then
        '—Decrement the top-of-stack pointer
        TOS = TOS - 1
        '—Transfer data to the function name
        Pop = Stack(TOS)
    Else
        MsgBox strUnderflow
    End If
End Function
```

The **Pop** function is not yet connected to the command button, Pop. The code in cmdPop_Click calls the function **Pop** to collect a value from the stack.

Coding the Push Subroutine

The overall structure of the **Push** subroutine is very similar to that of the **Pop** function. Convention dictates the use of a subroutine for pushing and a function for popping. It need not be so, but it does make sense. **Pop** returns a value from the stack to the calling program. It is the job of a function to return values. See Figure 11-5.

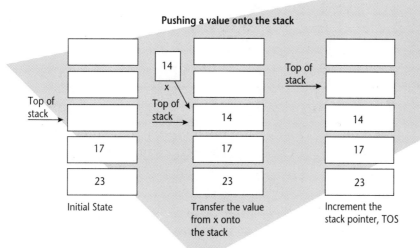

Pushing a value onto the stack

Figure 11-5
Pushing a value on the stack

Push has a single parameter, *x*, the value to be pushed on the stack. It returns no value at all. Using a function for this routine makes little sense.

Push checks for an error condition called stack overflow. This occurs when a program tries to push a value onto a stack that's full. Often this happens when a program using a stack has "run amok"—repeatedly pushing values onto a stack without ever removing those values. This is an error condition that usually crashes the computer.

Follow these steps to enter the **Push** procedure:

1 Open the Code window for the default form.

2 Select New Procedure from the View menu.

3 Enter the name of the procedure, **Push**, and click the Sub option. Visual Basic puts you into the skeleton routine for **Push**.

4 Enter the following code to implement the **Push** function:

```
Sub Push (x As Integer)
    '—Error message for stack overflow condition
    Const strOverflow = "Stack overflow"
```

continued

```
    '—If TOS is less than 20, there is still room
    'in the stack for more values
    If TOS < 20 Then
        '—Use TOS, then add one to point it to the next
        'empty space in the array
        Stack(TOS) = x
        TOS = TOS + 1
    Else
        MsgBox strOverflow
    End If
End Sub
```

Connecting It All

The **Pop** function and the **Push** procedure need drivers to call them from the main program. In addition to those procedures, connected to the two command buttons, cmdPop and cmdPush, the procedure DisplayStack displays the top of the stack.

To enter the code:

1 Open the Code window for cmdPop. Enter these lines:

```
txtData = Pop()      ' read value from stack
DisplayStack     ' show top-of-stack on form
txtData.SetFocus      ' ready for more data
```

2 Open the Code window for cmdPush. Enter these lines:

```
'—Check for problem with value in textbox.
On Error GoTo ErrorHandler
Dim x As Integer
x = Val(txtData)
'—Call Push to put value on stack.
Push (x)
DisplayStack
'—Clear item and set focus to pick up more.
txtData = ""
txtData.SetFocus
Exit Sub
ErrorHandler:
    MsgBox "Problem with the data. Error #: " & Err
    Exit Sub
```

3   Enter the code to display the top of the stack. Remember, *TOS* points to the *next* open space. Either choose New Procedure from the View menu, or enter these lines directly in the general section. Visual Basic automatically gives you a procedure skeleton.

```
Sub DisplayStack ()
    On Error GoTo TOSOutOfRange
    lblTOS = Str$(TOS - 1) & " : " & Str$(Stack(TOS - 1))
    Exit Sub
    TOSOutOfRange:
        MsgBox "Subscript is out of range: empty stack? Error #: " & Err
        Exit Sub
End Sub
```

4   Enter the **End** statement in the procedure for cmdExit.

5   Run the program. Enter a series of values by entering an integer in the Data box and clicking on Push. Pop values by clicking on the Pop button. Test the error checking by pushing too many values and popping too many values. Type a string into the Data box and click on Push.

6   Exit the program. Save the form and project files.

QUESTIONS AND ACTIVITIES

1.   Random access to the contents of memory cells means a program may get a value from any area of an array. What characteristic of a stack deliberately ignores random access?

2.   You may have bought candy in a PEZ dispenser. How is this candy dispenser like a stack?

3.   A southbound train wants to head back north. The cars of the train will remain oriented in the same direction, but the engine needs to be turned around and reattached at the other end. Assuming you can detach the engine from the train and still move the cars of the train with a spare engine, sketch a track that would allow the main engine to be repositioned at the other end of the train.

4.   What is stack overflow? Stack underflow? Remove the error handlers in the **Pop** routine and run the Stack Experiment project. Push three values, then pop four. What error message is displayed?

5.   Sketch the setup for a stack. Label the stack pointer and show where the next element of the stack will be put.

6. Some implementations of stacks use a stack pointer that actually points to the item at the top of the stack, *not* the next open position of the stack. Rewrite both the **Push** subroutine and the **Pop** function using this convention.

7. In the **Push** subroutine you wrote above, under what condition can a stack overflow not occur? In the **Pop** routine you wrote above, under what condition can a stack underflow not occur?

8. Why is it appropriate to use a function subprogram for popping the stack and a subroutine to push a value on the stack?

9. In the Stack Experiment project, change the Enabled property of the cmdPop to **False**. Add code to change the property to **True** when the stack is not empty. Change the property to **False** when the last value is popped from the stack. Add code to change the Enabled property of cmdPush to **False**, when the stack is full.

10. Add a command button and a multiline textbox to the Stack Experiment project. Change the caption of the button to **&Display**. When the button is pushed, display the contents of the stack horizontally in the textbox. The top of the stack should be to the right.

Section

Infix and Postfix Notation

In this section, you use a stack to evaluate the value of an arithmetic expression. The elements of the stack are constantly displayed. The evaluation of expressions with stacks is an important part of computer science.

You will also see that the way we write arithmetic expressions is not the only possible one, nor is it the easiest for a computer to understand. We use what is known as infix notation, so called because the operators (the signs for addition, multiplication, and so on) appear in between their operands (the subexpressions to which operators are applied). One alternative notation is postfix notation. In this notation, operators always appear after their operands. In postfix notation, no parentheses are ever needed to indicate how subexpressions should be grouped. Infix notation is easier for humans to read, write, and understand, probably because it more closely resembles the languages we speak. However, postfix notation is much easier for computers to evaluate.

Although you won't learn how to do it in this course, it is certainly possible to write a program that converts infix expressions to equivalent postfix expressions. Not surprisingly, any program that performed this conversion would use a stack.

Infix Notation

Infix notation is the common notation used to express arithmetic operations. In this notation, the operators, +,-,*,/,^, ..., stand between the operands:

$a + b$

$r - t$

$s * y \char94 2$

A whole set of rules govern the evaluation of such expressions. The operands are the values being manipulated in the expression, and an operator is the operation performed on the operands. Operators that manipulate two values, such as addition or multiplication, are called binary operators. An operator that works on a single operand is called an unary operator. A minus sign in front of a number, such as -5, is a unary operator.

Postfix Notation

In postfix notation the operator follows the operands:

$a \, b +$ means: $a + b$

$b \, b * 4 \, a * c * -$ means: $b*b - 4*a*c$

The use of postfix notation simplifies some important processes. For instance, evaluating expressions in postfix is easier for a computer than evaluating an expression in infix. The rules governing the order of operations for infix expressions are hard for a computer. "Please Excuse My Dear Aunt Sally" is fine for humans, but computers, by their nature, evaluate an expression by scanning its operands and operators sequentially, from one end of the expression to the other.

Postfix comes to the rescue: there is only one rule for the order of operations in postfix expressions: left to right. This rule makes postfix notation ideal for computers.

EVALUATING A POSTFIX EXPRESSION

To evaluate a postfix expression, you use a stack to hold values of subexpressions. Follow these rules:

1. Move from the left to the right.

2. If you encounter an operand, push it on the stack.

3. If you encounter a unary operator:
    ◎ Pop the top of the stack: this is the operand for the operator.
    ◎ Apply the operator to the operand.
    ◎ Push the result on the stack.

4. If you encounter a binary operator:
    ◎ Pop the top of the stack: this is the second operand.
    ◎ Pop the top of the stack again: this is the first operand.
    ◎ Apply the operator to the operands.
    ◎ Push the result on the stack.

In a properly formed postfix expression, when the entire expression is completely evaluated from left to right, the value on top of the stack is the value of the expression.

AN EXAMPLE

Here is an example of using postfix notation. For the sake of simplicity, use single-digit operands. Look at the step-by-step process for evaluating the expression 5 6 * 4 2 / 3 * -. Process the characters one at a time from left to right.

1. The first character is an operand, 5, push it on the stack. Top of Stack: 5

2. The next character is an operand, 6, push it on the stack. Top of Stack: 6   5

3. The next character is an operator, *:
    a) Pop the top of the stack into operand2. op2 = 6; Top of Stack: 5
    b) Pop the top of the stack into operand1. op1 = 5 op2 = 6; Top of Stack: empty
    c) Apply the operator; op1 * op2 = 30
    d) Push result onto the stack; Top of Stack: 30

4. The next character is an operand, 4. Push it on the stack. Top of Stack: 4   30

5. The next character is an operand, 2. Push it on the stack. Top of Stack: 2   4   30

6. The next character is an operator, /. Pop twice, apply the operator, and push the result. 4 / 2 = 2, push; Top of Stack: 2   30

7. The next character is an operand, 3. Push it on the stack. Top of Stack: 3   2   30

8. The next character is an operator, *. Pop twice, apply the operator, and push the result. 2 * 3 = 6, push; Top of Stack: 6   30

9. The last character is an operator, -. Pop twice, apply the operator, and push the result. 30 - 6 = 24, push; Top of Stack: 24

The evaluation of the expression is complete. The value of the expression is 24. In the next section, you write a program using these rules to evaluate postfix expressions.

QUESTIONS AND ACTIVITIES

1. Express the following phrases in both infix and postfix notation.
    a) The sum of x and y
    b) The product of a and (b plus c)
    c) The difference between what you owe and what you have
    d) The product of *mass1*, *mass2*, and a constant G, all divided by the distance r, squared
    e) The average of F and G

2. Translate the following into infix notation.
    a) *a b c * -*
    b) *a b c - **
    c) *a b * c d - /*
    d) *a b * c / d - f e + **

3. What is the difference between operands and operators? List five common operators.

4. What is a unary operator?

5. What is the order of operations for postfix expressions?

6. Evaluate this expression (by hand) using a stack:
    5 6 * 7 - 2 3 + * /

    What error message do you generate?

The Visual Stack

3

Section

This program evaluates a postfix expression using a stack, and shows what's happening each step of the way. The contents of the stack, the position of the stack pointer, the values of the operands, the value of the result, and the characters being processed are all visible through each step of the program. See Figure 11-6.

The goal of this program is to use a stack to evaluate a postfix expression. In addition, the program

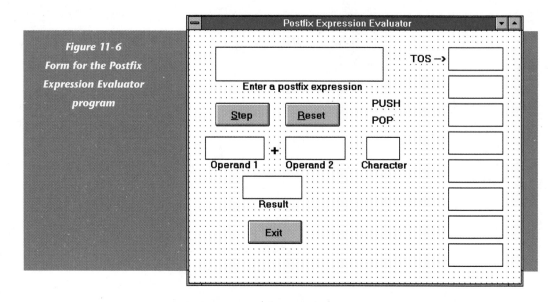

Figure 11-6
Form for the Postfix
Expression Evaluator
program

- ● Displays the entire stack
- ● Shows operands being popped
- ● Shows operators applied to operands
- ● Shows results pushed onto the stack

Starting Out

Think through the form shown in Figure 11-7. A user enters a postfix expression in the textbox at the top of the form. The labels at the right side of the form are used to display the contents of the stack and the position of the top of stack pointer, *TOS*. Two command buttons have been provided for users to step through the processing of the postfix expression.

The label boxes below the command buttons display the first and second operands, and below those there is a label that displays the result of the operation. The operation itself is displayed in a label between the operands which is updated to show the actual operation being performed.

Alongside the command buttons, the labels POP and PUSH are visible when the stack is accessed. A label marked Character shows the character of the input string that is being processed. Clicking on an Exit button at the bottom of the form ends the program.

Figure 11-7 shows the form you are going to build during the processing of a postfix expression. This is the same expression used in the last section.

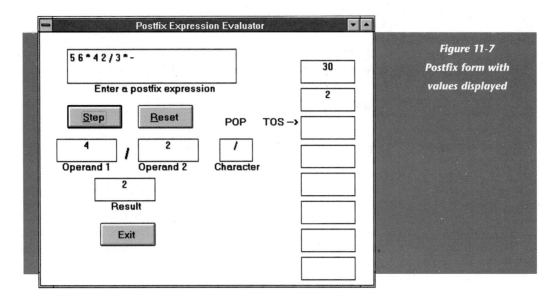

Figure 11-7
Postfix form with
values displayed

As shown in the figure, 5*6 has been calculated and the result pushed on the stack. The quotient of 4 and 2 has been pushed on the stack. You can see the values still displayed in the operand and result textboxes.

Designing the Form: Stage 1

Using Figure 11-6 as a guide, set up a form for the Postfix Expression Evaluation project. Set the FontSize property of every label and box to 9.75. In this first stage, you'll build the part of the form involving the command buttons, the textbox used to enter the postfix expression, and a couple of labels.

1 Start Visual Basic. If Visual Basic is running, choose New Project from the File menu.

2 Rename the default form to **frmStackDemo**. Change the caption of the form to **Postfix Expression Evaluator**.

3 Create a textbox to enter the postfix expression. Delete the text. Change the name to **txtPostfix**.

4 Create a label below the box. Change the caption to **Enter a post-fix expression**.

5 Create two command buttons. Change their captions to **&Step** and **&Reset**. Change their names to **cmdStep** and **cmdReset**.

6 Next to the command button, create two labels. These labels are made visible and invisible depending upon the operation, push or pop. Change the captions to **PUSH** and **POP**, and the names to **lblPush** and **lblPop**.

Designing the Form: Stage 2

In this stage, you set up the labels used to show the operands, the current operation, and the stack itself. The stack is always visible on the form. The contents of the stack are displayed in labels all bearing the same name. Labels with the same name form a control array.

To complete the second stage:

1 Assemble the part of the form that shows the operands and the operator between them. Create a label. Set the Alignment property to Center. Change the name to **lblOp1**. Delete the caption.

2 Select the label you just created. Copy it with Ctrl+C. Paste it with Ctrl+V. Respond No to creating a control array. Creating a label in this way preserves all the properties. Name the box **lblOp2**.

3 Between lblOp1 and lblOp2, insert a label with the name **lblOperator**. Delete the caption.

4 Again select and copy lblOp1. Paste it with Ctrl+V. Respond No to the control array. Change the name of the label to **lblChar**.

5 Place labels below the operand and character boxes. Change the captions to **Operand 1**, **Operand 2**, and **Character**.

6 Select and copy lblOp1. Paste it, respond No to the control array, and change the name to **lblResult**.

7 Label the result with a label with caption **Result**.

8 Create a new label for the top of the stack along the right side of the form. Change the name to **lblStack**. Change the BorderStyle to Single, Alignment to Center, and delete the caption.

9 Select the label just created. Copy and paste. Respond Yes to creating a control array. A control array is like a menu control array. Each of the labels has the same name. Each is accessed as if it is a member of an array. Each has a subscript appended to the name to distinguish it from the other elements of the control array. All elements of the control array share the same event procedures.

10 Paste (Ctrl+V) again and again until there are eight labels equally spaced along the right side of the form.

11 Create a TOS label as shown. Change the name of the label to **lblTOS**. Set the Alignment to Right Justify.

12 Save the form and project files.

Entering the Declarations

Declarations include the stack, the top-of-stack pointer, a pointer to the character being processed in the input string, and a variable, set in Form_Load used to determine the position of the moving *TOS* label.

Enter these lines in the general declarations section of the form:

```
Option Explicit
'—The stack
Dim Stack(0 To 7) As Integer
'—The top-of-stack pointer
Dim TOS As Integer
'—Pointer into the input string
Dim P1 As Integer
'—Number of twips to move and position the TOS label
Dim TOSTwips As Integer
```

Most postfix expressions don't require a stack with a lot of elements. This stack has a capacity of eight values. The values of the stack, the stack pointer, *TOS, p1,* and *TOSTwips* are available to every event procedure in the form.

Entering the Code

Now, enter the code:

1   Enter **End** in the procedure for cmdExit.

2   Enter the following lines in cmdReset_Click:

```
'—Declare local variable as loop index
Dim x As Integer
'—Reposition the top-of-stack label to the top
'of the stack, TOSTwips many twips from the top of the form
'_TOSTwips is initialized in the Form_Load procedure.
lblTOS.Top = TOSTwips
'—Clear the 8 visible stack entries
For x = 0 To 7
    lblStack(x) = ""
Next x
'—Clear several textboxes
lblChar = ""
lblOp1 = ""
lblOp2 = ""
lblResult = ""
txtPostfix = ""
TOS = 0
P1 = 1
```

The screen stack, comprised of the lblStack labels, is something new. Each of the labels is given the same name. Whenever you give controls the same name, Visual Basic creates a control array. This allows you to refer to each box with their common name and a number designating a particular box.

3 Enter the following lines in the Form_Load procedure:

```
lblpop.Visible = False
lblpush.Visible = False
'—Set to first character in input string
P1 = 1
'—Initialize top-of-stack variable
TOS = 0
'—Reposition the top-of-stack label to the top
'of the stack, TOSTwips twips from the top of the form
TOSTwips = ScaleHeight / 9
lblTOS.Top = TOSTwips
'—The loop that follows positions the 8 labels showing
'the contents of the stack evenly down the right edge of the form
Dim x As Integer
For x = 0 To 7
    lblStack(x).Top = (x + 1) * TOSTwips
Next x
```

4 Enter the **Pop** function in the general section of the form. Copy the top and bottom lines:

```
Function Pop () As Integer
    '—If the stack is not empty, decrement pointer,
    'copy value from array, and return as the function's value
    If TOS > 0 Then
        TOS = TOS - 1
        Pop = Stack(TOS)
    Else
        MsgBox "Stack underflow"
    End If
End Function
```

5 Enter the **Push** procedure in the general section of the form. Copy the top and bottom lines:

```
Sub Push (R As Integer)
    '—If the stack is not full, put value, R
    'into the top of the stack, and increment
    'the stack pointer
```

```
    If TOS < 20 Then
        Stack(TOS) = R
        TOS = TOS + 1
    Else
        MsgBox "Stack overflow"
    End If
End Sub
```

6   Enter the following code for cmdStep. This code automates the processing of the postfix expression. Start with local variable declarations. Declare a string for the postfix expression, a single-character
string for the character being processed, and integer variables for
the operands and the result of the operations.

```
'—String used to hold entered postfix expression
Dim Postfix As String     ' input string
'—Declare variables for the operands and the result
Dim Op1 As Integer, Op2 As Integer, Result As Integer
'—Declare variable for characters taken from input string
Dim Ch As String * 1
```

7   Enter the section of code that pulls a character out of the input
string. *P1* points to the next character to be processed. It is checked
against the length of the input string. If there are more characters
left to process, the procedure continues.
The **Mid$**(*string, starting char, number of chars*) function creates a
new string that is a copy of a segment of an existing string. The
source string, the starting point, and the number of characters to
copy are passed as parameters.

```
'—Pick up expression from textbox
Postfix = txtPostfix
'—p1 is a pointer into the input string. It picks out
'the character to work on.
If P1 <= Len(Postfix) Then
    Ch = Mid$(Postfix, P1, 1)
    '—Assign the character to a label for display
    lblChar = Ch
EndIf
```

8   The direction the program takes from here depends on the value
of the character being processed. If it is a digit "0" through "9",
it is an operand and it is pushed on the stack. If it is an operator,
(+ - * /), pop two values from the stack, store them in the
variables *op1* and *op2*, apply the operator, and push the result.

The **Select Case** statement controls which branch of the program executes.

Reposition the *TOS* pointer by resetting its Top property. Its initial position is recorded in twips in the Top property of the control.

The **Select Case** statement branches based on a single value, an aggregate of values separated by commas, or a range of values. To specify a range of values, use the keyword **To** between the low end of the range and the high end of the range: "0" to "9" is the range of characters, 0 through 9.

Enter these lines.

```
Select Case Ch
    '—If the character is a digit, push on the stack
    Case "0" To "9"
        lblpush.Visible = True
        lblpop.Visible = False
        '—Display character in on-screen stack
        lblStack(TOS) = Ch
        '—Push the character on the internal stack
        Push (Val(Ch))
        '—Move the top-of-stack pointer TOSTwips twips down the form
        lblTOS.Top = lblTOS.Top + TOSTwips
        '—Advance to next character
        P1 = P1 + 1
        '—Skip spaces
    Case " "
        P1 = P1 + 1
        '—Operators, Pop, Pop, apply operator, Push result
    Case "+", "-", "*", "/", "\"
        lblpop.Visible = True     ' pop label on
        lblpush.Visible = False   ' push label off
        lblTOS.Top = lblTOS.Top - TOSTwips     ' move TOS label
        Op2 = Pop()      ' second operand
        lblStack(TOS) = ""      ' clear stack value
        lblOp2 = Op2      ' fill op2 box
        lblTOS.Top = lblTOS.Top - TOSTwips     ' move TOS label
        Op1 = Pop()      ' first operand
        lblStack(TOS) = ""      ' clear stack value
        lblOp1 = Op1      ' fill op1 box
        '—Apply operator
        Select Case Ch
            Case "+"
```

```
                  Result = Op1 + Op2
                  lbloperator.Caption = "+"
            Case "-"
                  Result = Op1 - Op2
                  lbloperator.Caption = "-"
            Case "*"
                  Result = Op1 * Op2
                  lbloperator.Caption = "*"
            Case "/", "\"
                  Result = Op1 \ Op2
                  lbloperator.Caption = "/"
         End Select
      '—Display result and push onto stack
      lblResult = Result
      lblStack(TOS) = Result
      Push (Result)
      '—Move TOS label
      lblTOS.Top = lblTOS.Top + TOSTwips
      '—Move pointer to next character
      P1 = P1 + 1
   End Select
End Select
End Sub
```

9 Save the form and project files.

10 Run the program. Enter the following postfix expressions and step
     through the evaluation of each. Use only single digit numbers!
     a) 5 6 7 8 9 + - + *
     b) 5 6 + 7 - 8 + 9 *
     c) 3 3 * 4 1 * 5 * -
     d) 2 3 1 * 4 2 / 5 * - 3 2 + +

QUESTIONS AND ACTIVITIES

1. How deep a stack is needed to evaluate the following expression?
    0 3 - 3 3 * 4 2 * 5 * - + 2 2 * /

2. The labels in the Postfix Evaluation program form a control array.
    The values from a postfix expression are not only pushed onto a
    stack, they are also displayed in the control array of labels used to
    display the stack contents on the form. Could the program have
    been written substituting the control array of labels on the form for
    the stack of values used by **Push** and **Pop**?

3. Use the Help system to look up the entry for the keyword **Static**. How does **Static** work? How is it unlike **Dim**?

4. Assume the string *A$* has the value "George Washington". Write a program segment that would display the following in a textbox named txtStars:

   G*e*o*r*g*e* *W*a*s*h*i*n*g*t*o*n*

   Use the **Mid$()** function in a **For-Next** loop to separate individual letters of *A$*.

5. How would you specify a range of values from top to bottom in a **Select Case** statement? How would you specify the range of characters from "q" through "s"?

Summary

A stack is a list of items for which access is restricted to the top item of the list. You can create a stack by using an array and a variable that acts as a pointer to the top element of the stack. Stacks are accessed by two subprograms: The **Pop** function pops a value from the top of the stack, and the **Push** subroutine puts a value onto the top of the stack. Each procedure leaves the stack pointer pointing to the next open space of the stack.

Infix notation puts the operator between the operands (*a+b*). Postfix notation puts the operator after the operands (*a b +*). Postfix notation is particularly well suited for computers because its rule for order of operations is to process expressions in order left to right.

You can make labels, as well as several other screen controls, into control arrays by giving each the same name. The labels are accessed with the common name and a numerical index.

The Form_Load procedure is used for initializing variables and taking care of other housekeeping chores. This procedure executes whenever a form is loaded into memory.

The **Select Case** statement can use a range of values to choose a branch using the following syntax:

Case *low item* **To** *high item*

1.   Rewriting the Stack Project

Rewrite the stack project to display the entire stack in a list box. Use Visual Basic Help to find out how to use the **RemoveItem** method to remove lines from the list box.

2.   The Unary Minus Modification

Using the tilde, ~, as the unary minus symbol, rewrite the Postfix Evaluator program to process this operation. When the tilde is encountered, the top of the stack should be negated. The unary minus works like this: 5~ 2 + , would add negative 5 to 2.

3.   The Stripped Down Evaluator

Write a program that enters a postfix expression and displays either the value of the expression, or an error message. Leave out all the screen display stuff in the original program.

4.   Reversing Characters with a Stack

Write a program to enter a name using an InputBox. With the **Mid$** function, peel the individual characters off the name, and push the characters onto a character stack. When the last character has been processed, pop and display the characters in a textbox. The characters should be in reverse order.

5.   Multiple Digit Values

Rewrite the Postfix Evaluator program to allow the user to use multiple digit integers separated by spaces. Your program should allow the user to enter the Postfix expression in a textbox, process that expression using a stack, and display the resulting value of the expression.

```
Sub Subtract (X

As Fraction, Y As

Add A,

Fraction, Rslt As

Rslt

Fraction)

Dim Temp As

End Sub

Fraction

Negate Y,

Temp
```

User-Defined Types and File System Controls

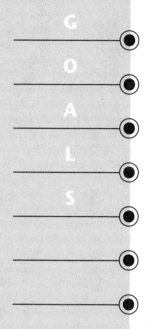

After working through this chapter, you will be able to:

Design and implement a plan for a data structure to represent fractions.

Encode those algorithms in procedures suitable for inclusion in a code module.

Plan and execute a program that will allow the user to interact with information stored in a file.

Implement code for maintaining arrays when information is added, deleted, and modified in the array.

Work with complex user-defined types.

Integrate the drive, directory, and file boxes into programs that use files.

O V E R V I E W

Visual Basic provides a rich variety of data types built into the language. You have already worked with a number of these data types, such as Variant and String. There is a common type of numerical data, however, that is not covered by the built-in data types. Can you think of a data type that is suitable for fractions?

To supply this missing data type, you need to define a user-defined type. Using this data type, you can then create a code module that contains arithmetic functions which operate on fractions represented by the new type. You can then include this code module in any program in which it is more appropriate to work with fractions such as $5/12$ instead of rounded-off floating point numbers such as 0.416666667.

The chapter also looks at the development of a fairly large program. The Multiple Choice Test program is used to create, update, and give multiple choice tests. Along the way, you will see some new statements and use the file management tools included in Visual Basic.

The Arithmetic of Fractions

Section

Dealing with English measurements often requires the use of fractions. Finding the distance between each of four equally spaced shelves in a space 5'8" tall requires fractions. If the answer is provided in decimal form, the tape measure, which divides an inch into fourths, eighths, and sixteenths, will be useless.

In this section, you develop the techniques you need to handle fractions in Visual Basic. You can then use routines built with these expressions in any program in which you need a fraction-handling routine. To reuse the routines, you put them into a code module. Then all you do to use the routines is add the code module to the project.

You will represent fractions with a user-defined type—called Fraction—which stores the numerator and denominator of the fraction separately as integers. This representation makes it simple to write procedures that implement the standard arithmetic operations on fractions.

To work with fractions in a Visual Basic program, you need to be comfortable adding, subtracting, multiplying, and dividing them. You also need to be able to reduce fractions to their lowest terms, finding multiplicative and additive inverses. If you need the review, read this section before you move on to address the issues of coding fraction-handling routines.

Addition

To add fractions, you must first rewrite them so that they have the same denominator. The sum of the fractions is the sum of the resulting numerators, divided by the common denominator. For example, to add $\frac{1}{3}$ and $\frac{1}{2}$, rewrite each with the denominator 2 x 3 = 6. You get $\frac{1}{3} = (2 \times 1) / (2 \times 3) = \frac{2}{6}$, and $\frac{1}{2} = (3 \times 1) / (3 \times 2) = \frac{3}{6}$. Thus, $\frac{1}{3} + \frac{1}{2} = \frac{2}{6} + \frac{3}{6} = (2 + 3) / 6 = \frac{5}{6}$.

In general, if one fractional operand is a/b and the second operand is c/d, the sum of the fractions is $(ad + cb) / (bd)$. To rewrite the fractions so that they have a common denominator, bd, you multiply the first fraction by d/d, then multiply the second by b/b. Then you add the numerators, and divide by the common denominator bd.

The Fraction data type stores the numerator and denominator of the fraction separately as integers. From the result above, the numerator of the sum is $a*d + c*b$, and the denominator is $b*d$. These formulas are used in the addition routine.

Multiplication

You multiply two fractions (such as *a/b* times *c/d*) by multiplying their numerators together, then multiplying the denominators together. The result of multiplying *a/b* and *c/d* is *(ac) / (bd)*. For example, ⅖ times ⅜ is (2 x 3)/(5 x 6), or ⁶⁄₃₀.

Inverses

There are two kinds of inverses—the multiplicative inverse, also known as the reciprocal, and the additive inverse, sometimes called "the opposite" of a number. For example, for the number 7, the multiplicative inverse is ⅐ and the additive inverse is -7.

You calculate the multiplicative inverse of a whole number or fraction by interchanging the numerator and the denominator. Note that you may run into difficulty with a fraction that has a numerator of 0. This type of fraction is perfectly acceptable; but its reciprocal, with 0 as the denominator, is "undefined."

To form the additive inverse of a number, change the sign of the numerator. If the current numerator is positive, make it negative. If the current numerator is negative, make it positive.

Subtraction and Division

After you have defined inverses, you can define subtraction as addition, and division as multiplication. Imagine that you have two fractions, *x* and *y*. To subtract *y* from *x*, you would add the additive inverse of *y* to *x*. In other words:

$x - y$ provides the same result as $x + -y$

Likewise, multiplying *x* by the reciprocal of *y* yields the same result as dividing *x* by *y*. To divide fractions, then, invert the second fraction and multiply:

$x / y = (x)(1/y)$

Why do you need to rewrite subtraction as addition, or division as multiplication? If you do, you will need to create only two routines instead of four. Your addition routine can perform both addition and subtraction, and your multiplication routine can perform both multiplication and division.

Lowest Terms

To build your routines, you also need to know how to reduce fractions to their lowest terms. To do this, find the greatest common factor (gcf) of the numerator and the denominator. The greatest common factor is the largest number that divides into both numbers evenly. For instance, consider the fraction $^{12}/_{16}$.

A common factor is 2, but the *greatest* common factor is 4. Try dividing the top and bottom of the fraction by 4. Do you get $^{3}/_{4}$? Can the fraction be reduced any further?

Greatest Common Factor

The package of fraction-handling routines you are going to build in this chapter includes a routine to reduce fractions to their lowest terms. This routine uses the Euclidean algorithm to find the greatest common factor. (This is the same Euclid who developed the axioms and theorems that have evolved into the high school geometry course.) This algorithm is based on the definition of division. For nonnegative integers x and y, dividing x by y means finding two numbers, q (the *quotient*) and r (the *remainder*), such that:

$x = q*y + r$, and $0 \le r < y$

The terminology used to describe the elements of these equations is:

*dividend = quotient * divisor + remainder*

For example, let $x = 10$ and $y = 27$. Because $27 = 2 * 10 + 7$, and $0 \le 7 < 10$, we see that the quotient is 2, and the remainder is 7.

In this definition, q is the whole number quotient, and r is the remainder. Here's how the Euclidean algorithm can be used to find the greatest common factor of 45 and 105:

$$45 \ = 0 * 105 \ + \ 45 \quad (^{45}/_{105} \ = 0 \text{ rem. } 45)$$
$$105 = 2 * \ 45 \ + \ 15 \quad (^{105}/_{45} = 2 \text{ rem. } 15)$$
$$45 \ = 3 * \ 15 \ + \ \ 0 \quad (^{45}/_{15} = 3 \text{ rem. } 0)$$

When the remainder is 0, the algorithm is complete: 15 is the gcf of 45 and 105. In the first line, 105 and 45 changed places.

To move from one line to the next, the divisor of one line becomes the dividend of the next line, and the remainder of the line becomes the divisor of the new line. When the remainder is 0, the divisor of that line is the greatest common factor.

This algorithm is efficient because it finds the greatest common factor of pairs of large or small numbers very quickly.

QUESTIONS AND ACTIVITIES

1. List three common factors of 30 and 45. What is the *greatest* common factor of 30 and 45?

2. If we add the fractions *a/b* and *c/d* we get the result *(ad + bc) / (bd)*. What is the result if the fractions are subtracted instead of added?

3. Why is a fraction with a 0 denominator "undefined"? What happens to the value of the fraction $1/x$ when x becomes very small?

4. Use the Euclidean algorithm to find the greatest common factor of the following pairs of numbers:
    a) 17 and 23
    b) 85 and 204
    c) 312 and 910

Section 2

Code Modules and User-Defined Types

In this section of the chapter, you create a code module, then within that module, declare a user-defined data type and define a number of routines to handle fractions. Because you will use the data type to declare fractions, you should give it the obvious name: Fraction. You will define the Fraction type as composed of two integers, one for the numerator of the fraction and one for the denominator.

Creating a Code Module

To create a code module, follow these steps:

1 Start Visual Basic. If Visual Basic is running, select New Project from the File menu.

2 Select New Module from the File menu.

3 Open the Code window for the code module. If you have already created the module, open the window by choosing the name of the module from the Project window. Click on the name of the code module, as shown in Figure 12-1.

> **NOTE:**
>
> **A user-defined type declaration can only be made in a code module.**

Double-click to open the general declarations section. You can also open the Code window by clicking on the View Code button in the top-right corner of the Project window.

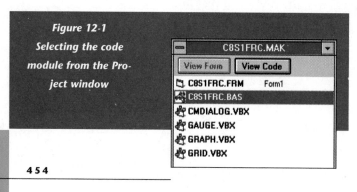

Figure 12-1
Selecting the code module from the Project window

4   Add the **Option Explicit** statement, if it is not already displayed in the general declarations section.

5   Below **Option Explicit**, define the Fraction type by using a **Type** statement:

```
Type Fraction
    Num As Integer
    Den As Integer
End Type
```

Creating a Procedure

Now you are ready to define some procedures for handling fractions; you will include these procedures in the code module. There are two ways to define a new procedure in the code module. The first is to use the Code window:

1   If you have closed the Code window for the code module, reopen it and select the general declarations section.

2   Type **Sub** to indicate a routine, then **NewOne** as the name of the procedure. Press Enter.

3   Visual Basic creates a skeleton for the new procedure. The parentheses after the routine's name are added automatically, along with the last line (**End Sub**). See Figure 12-2. You will enter the names and types of the parameters that will be passed to the procedure within the parentheses.

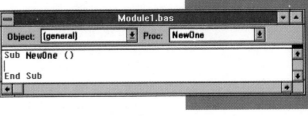

Figure 12-2
A new routine

The other way to create a new procedure in a code or form module is to select the New Procedure command from the View menu. The active window must be a module; otherwise, the New Procedure command is disabled. A dialog box prompts you to enter a procedure name and indicate whether you are creating a function or a subroutine (Figure 12-3). Visual Basic creates a skeleton procedure in the active module. The procedure's parameter list, enclosed within parentheses, is empty; you must enter any parameter declarations yourself.

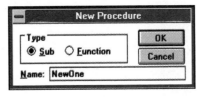

Figure 12-3
Choosing whether to create a function or a subroutine

FUNCTIONS AND SUBROUTINES

A function returns a value, which you assign to the name of the function in the body of the function procedure. A subroutine may perform actions, and/or return values to the calling program via its parameters, but the name of the subroutine is not used to transfer values.

Adding Parameters to the Procedure

After you have created the skeleton of a procedure, you can add parameters inside the parentheses following the name of the procedure. Visual Basic recognizes two kinds of parameters that may be passed to or from procedures and functions: value parameters and reference parameters.

VALUE PARAMETERS

Value parameters are passed as values to a procedure. The value of a variable or expression that you pass to a value parameter is transferred by Visual Basic to temporary storage local to the procedure. The value parameter names, or refers to, that storage. The value parameter may be altered—for instance by assigning it a new value—but the original value of the variable passed to it by the calling program is not altered.

A value parameter is the perfect way to send a value that should be protected from changing. For instance, a procedure might take a person's full name as a parameter and process just the last name. The original value, including the entire name, should not be affected.

To declare a value parameter in the parameter list of a procedure or function use the keyword **ByVal** in the parameter list before the parameter name. For example, after you have the skeleton of the procedure, add the parameter:

```
Sub NewOne(ByVal x As Integer) ' x is passed by value
```

The value of x may be altered within the procedure. For example:

```
x = x + 1,  or,  if x were a string,  x = Left$(x, 5)
```

The value of the argument in the calling program corresponding to x, however, is not affected.

REFERENCE PARAMETERS

Variables that are allowed or intended to change as a result of the action of the procedure or function are said to be passed by reference. This means the actual address of the variable is made available to the procedure or function, allowing the procedure to alter the value of the argument in the calling program corresponding to the parameter. In this case, no copy of the argument's value is made; rather, the parameter refers to the storage occupied by the argument to the procedure call.

Variables passed by reference don't require a special keyword. You define them like this:

```
Sub NewOne(x as integer) ' x is passed by reference and can be changed
'_from within the procedure
```

CAUTION

Generally, if you are sending a value of a variable to a subroutine or function, and you don't intend the value of the variable to change, it should be passed by value. If you pass the variable by reference, you run the risk that the procedure will alter the value in a way you don't expect. These unwanted side effects are difficult to track down when the program is not behaving as you intend.

Unfortunately, you cannot send a variable of a user-defined type as a value parameter to a procedure or function. If you try to put the **ByVal** keyword in the parameter list of a subprogram using user-defined types, Visual Basic displays the error message in Figure 12-4. Parameters of user-defined types must be passed by reference.

Figure 12-4
Error message displayed when you send a variable of user-defined type as a value parameter

Finishing the Fraction-Handling Routines

Now that you know how to start a routine, you can create as many routines as you need in the code module. You will need routines for adding, negating, subtracting, multiplying, finding reciprocals, dividing, and finding the greatest common factor. Each of these routines is quite short.

THE ADD ROUTINE

To create an add routine in the code module:

1   Open the general declarations section of the code module.

2 Add this code:

```
Sub Add (X As Fraction, Y As Fraction, Rslt As Fraction)
    Rslt.Num = X.Num * Y.Den + Y.Num * X.Den
    Rslt.Den = X.Den * Y.Den
End Sub
```

3 Select Save File from the File menu to save the code module with the name **frac.bas**.

As you can see in this code, you send three parameters to the Add routine. The first two are the fractions to be added. The third is the result of the addition process. The code for this procedure is developed from the equations shown in the last section.

Sending the fraction X as a parameter means you are sending both a numerator, $X.Num$, and a denominator, $X.Den$. The result of the procedure is returned in the fraction variable $Rslt$. The numerator is in $Rslt.Num$ and the denominator of the answer is in $Rslt.Den$.

THE NEGATE PROCEDURE

This procedure has two parameters. The first is the fraction to be negated and the second is the negated fraction. The procedure works by changing the sign of the numerator of the fraction. This job could be handled directly in the calling program, but it should not be. The calling program should never have to manipulate the values inside a variable of the fraction type.

In the general declarations section of the code module, enter these lines:

```
Sub Negate (X As Fraction, Rslt As Fraction)
    Rslt.Num = -X.Num
    Rslt.Den = X.Den
End Sub
```

THE SUBTRACT ROUTINE

This subroutine works by negating the second operand and then passing the original first operand and the negated second operand to the Add procedure. It implements subtraction in terms of addition and the additive inverse, using the fact that $x - y = x + (-y)$. You declare a local fraction variable $Temp$, to hold the value of the negated second parameter.

Enter the general declarations section of the code module and enter these lines:

```
Sub Subtract (X As Fraction, Y As Fraction, Rslt As Fraction)
Dim Temp As Fraction
    Negate Y, Temp
    Add x, Temp, Rslt
End Sub
```

THE MULTIPLY ROUTINE

This routine sends the two fractions to be multiplied, *X* and *Y*, as parameters and expects the product to be returned in the parameter, *Rslt*.

Enter the general declarations section of the code module and enter these lines:

```
Sub Multiply (X As Fraction, Y As Fraction, Rslt As Fraction)
    Rslt.Num = X.Num * Y.Num
    Rslt.Den = X.Den * Y.Den
End Sub
```

THE RECIPROCAL ROUTINE

This routine returns the multiplicative inverse of a fraction sent as the first parameter. If the numerator of the fraction sent is 0, the reciprocal doesn't exist and the user is sent an appropriate message. An alternative to displaying a message would be to send a **True/False** variable as a parameter. If the reciprocal is successfully calculated, you set the flag to true. If the reciprocal doesn't exist, set the flag to false. Upon return to the calling program, the flag can be checked and appropriate action taken.

Enter the general declarations section of the code module and enter these lines:

```
Sub Recip (X As Fraction, Rslt As Fraction)
    If X.Num = 0 Then
        MsgBox "The program attempted to take the reciprocal of 0."
    Else
        Rslt.Num = X.Den
        Rslt.Den = X.Num
    End If
End Sub
```

THE DIVISION ROUTINE

Now that you have written a multiplicative inverse routine, you can easily write a division routine. To do so, declare a temporary local variable to hold the reciprocal of the second operand. Then send it along with the first operand to the Multiply routine.

In this routine, you call the necessary subroutines with a second method. In the Subtract routine, you called Negate and Add by stating their names and listing the parameters. In this routine, you call the necessary routines with the **Call** statement. This statement requires that the parameters be enclosed in parentheses. The statement is included here to familiarize you with an older convention that you will see if you look at other Basic programs.

Enter the general declarations section of the code module and enter these lines:

```
Sub Divide (X As Fraction, Y As Fraction, Rslt As Fraction)
    Dim Temp As Fraction
    Call Recip(Y, Temp)
    Call Multiply(X, Temp, Rslt)
End Sub
```

GREATEST COMMON FACTOR ROUTINE

Now you need to write the code to reduce fractions to their lowest terms. To accomplish this, you need the greatest common factor of the numerator and the denominator. The next routine, **Function gcf()**, calculates this value using the Euclidean algorithm.

The parameters are normal integer types, as is the value of the function itself. Therefore, you can use the **ByVal** keyword in the parameter list to send the parameters as value types. The math of the algorithm is described in the previous section.

If you take the variable *a* as the dividend (the number being divided), and *b* as the divisor, the algorithm is finished when the value of *b* is 0. The greatest common factor is the value of *a*. Pairs of numbers that don't have any other divisors have a common divisor of 1, so the function always returns a value. (Two integers whose greatest common divisor is 1 are said to be relatively prime.)

Enter the general declarations section of the code module and enter these lines:

```
Function gcf (ByVal a As Integer, ByVal b As
Integer) As Integer
    Dim Temp As Integer
    Do While b <> 0
        Temp = a Mod b
        a = b
```

```
        b = Abs(Temp)
    Loop
    gcf = a
End Function
```

THE REDUCE ROUTINE

After the greatest common factor of the numerator and divisor is calculated, reducing the fraction requires just a couple of integer division statements.

Enter the general declarations section of the code module and enter these lines:

```
Sub Reduce (Rslt As Fraction)
    Dim Temp As Integer
    Temp = gcf(Rslt.Num, Rslt.Den)
    Rslt.Num = Rslt.Num \ Temp
    Rslt.Den = Rslt.Den \ Temp
End Sub
```

Fraction Handler Program

With the code module built, you are now ready to explore how to use these routines in a program. To do so, you start a new project, then create a form that prompts users to enter values for two fractions. Users can then add, subtract, multiply, or divide the fractions they have entered and display the results (see Figure 12-5). This is the Fraction Handler project.

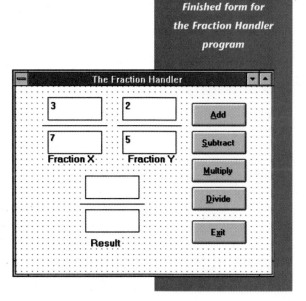

Figure 12-5
Finished form for
the Fraction Handler
program

GETTING STARTED

As you can see from Figure 12-5, you need four textboxes on the form for the user to enter the numerators and denominators of the fractions. You only need to label two of these, though you should place a line between each pair to indicate that the pair is a fraction. Then, you let users perform actions with the fractions by placing command buttons to the right. You display the result of any of these operations in the two labels at the bottom labeled Result.

As you have done in other programs, you should preload the fraction textboxes with reasonable values instead of just clearing their Text properties. When you do so, the user only needs to click one of the command buttons to see the program work.

BUILDING THE FORM

To build the form for the Fraction Handler project, follow these steps.

1 Select the default form in the Project window.

2 In the Properties window, change the caption of the form to **The Fraction Handler**.

3 Place four textboxes on the form. Change the FontSize property of each to 9.75. Change their names to **txtXNum**, **txtXDen**, **txtYNum**, and **txtYDen**. Arrange the textboxes on the form so that the names of the boxes for the numerators are over the appropriately named boxes for the denominators. Label the fractions.

4 Place two labels on the form to display the result of an operation. One way to save some work is to create a single box, give it all the attributes you want, such as BorderStyle: Single, FontSize: 9.75, Caption: deleted. Make it the size you want for both labels. Select the label with a click of the mouse, copy it with Ctrl+C, and paste it with Ctrl+V. Respond No to the inquiry about creating a control array.

5 Name the labels you just created **lblRsltNum** and **lblRsltDen**.

6 Place lines from the toolbox between the numerator and denominator of each fraction.

7 Place four command buttons on the form. Create a control array by creating a single button. Give the button the name **cmdOp**. Copy the button with Ctrl+C and paste with Ctrl+V. This time, when you are prompted to create a control array, respond Yes. Change the captions of the four buttons to **&Add**, **&Subtract**, **&Multiply**, and **&Divide**. Change their Index properties to 0, 1, 2, and 3, respectively.

8 Create a fifth command button. Change the name of the button to **cmdExit**. Change the caption of the button to **E&xit**.

9 Save the form, project, and code module files.

DECLARING THE VARIABLES

In the general declarations section of the code, you need to declare two variables to represent the fractions. You use the Fraction type you defined in the code module in the declaration (*x* and *y* are of the Fraction type).

To declare the variables:

1 Select the form.

2   In the general declarations section of the form, enter the following code.

```
Option Explicit
Dim x As Fraction, y As Fraction
```

CODING THE COMMAND BUTTONS

Because you gave the command buttons the same name (cmdOp), they all call the same event procedures. To differentiate between one command button and another, you assigned a different index value to each one. The Add button has an index value of 0, Subtract is 1, Multiply is 2, and Divide is 3. The Exit button has a unique name and so calls its own event procedure.

Use a **Select Case** statement in the cmdOp_Click routine to process the statements appropriate for each different command button. This approach works very well in this program. No matter which button is pushed, all the operations start by reading the values of the fractions from the upper textboxes, and finish by displaying the result of the operation in the lower textboxes. Using a control array means you can share the code common to all four operations.

As you write the procedure, you need to consider how the code will handle a negative result. What happens, for example, when you divide a positive fraction by a negative one? Where will the form display the negative sign? That sign should *not* appear in the denominator, as in this example:

$$\tfrac{3}{5} \; / \; {}^{-2}\!/_{7} \; = \; {}^{21}\!/_{-10}$$

You will need to be sure the program checks the sign of the denominator before displaying any results. If it is negative, the program should change the signs of both the numerator and the denominator of the result (why both?).

Another fraction issue you need to consider is a denominator with the value of 0. This is an undefined fraction and should display no answer at all. In the code for cmdOp, you will need to add a simple **If-Then** statement to check for and handle this possibility.

To code the command buttons:

1   Enter these lines in the cmdOp_Click() event procedure:

```
Dim Rslt As Fraction
X.Num = Val(txtXNum.Text)
X.Den = Val(txtXDen.Text)
Y.Num = Val(txtYNum.Text)
Y.Den = Val(txtYDen.Text)
```

```
Select Case index
   Case 0      ' Add the operands
      Add X, Y, Rslt
   Case 1      ' Subtract
      Subtract X, Y, Rslt
   Case 2      ' Multiply
      Multiply X, Y, Rslt
   Case 3      ' Divide
      Divide X, Y, Rslt
   End Select
'—Check for negative sign in the denominator
If Rslt.Den < 0 Then
   Rslt.Num = -Rslt.Num
   Rslt.Den = -Rslt.Den
End If
'—Check for denominator equal to 0
If Rslt.Den = 0 Then
   MsgBox "The fraction does not exist."
Else
   Reduce Rslt
   lblRsltNum = Str$(Rslt.Num)
   lblRsltDen = Str$(Rslt.Den)
End If
```

2 Add **End** to the procedure for cmdExit.

3 Save the form, project, and code module files.

4 Run the program. Click on each of the command buttons.

5 Enter new values for the numerators and denominators of the fractions. Note the results.

QUESTIONS AND ACTIVITIES

1. What is the significance of code modules? Why are they necessary?

2. Look at the Project window for the Fraction Handler project. What does each line displayed in Figure 12-6 mean?

NOTE:

Although the Fraction Handler program does not offer a command button to reduce fractions, you can still use the program for this purpose. Enter the fraction that you want to reduce as the first fraction, and enter 0/1 as the second. When you add these fractions, the result displayed is the first fraction in lowest terms.

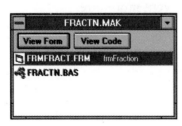

Figure 12-6
Project window for the
Fraction Handler project

3. Create a user-defined type named Lumber. Have it include fields for the following information:

tree	a string
dimensions	three numbers such as 5'x 2"x 4"
quantity on hand	an integer
cost	a currency type

4. Write a routine that will take as parameters *a* and *b* of type Lumber and display in a message box the name of the tree for which the cost is lower.

5. Describe two ways to begin a new procedure in a code module.

6. What is the difference between a Sub procedure and a Function procedure?

7. What are value and reference parameters? When is it appropriate to use each? Put the **ByVal** keyword in front of the first parameter in the Add procedure. Run the program and note the results.

8. In the general declarations section of the form, put the following declaration:

    ```
    Dim Z As Integer
    ```

    In each of the four procedures for adding, subtracting, multiplying and dividing, put the following line:

    ```
    Z = Z + 1
    ```

    Into the Add procedure, put in a line to display the value of *Z* in a message box. Run the program, click several buttons and note the change in the value of *Z*.
    Although not unwanted, the value of *Z* shows a side effect. Its value changes even though it was not passed as a parameter to the procedures that changed its value. When this happens accidentally, it is difficult to fix.

9. Write a subtract procedure that does not use the Add procedure to do the work.

10. Rewrite the Recip routine with the following first line:

    ```
    Sub Recip (X As Fraction, Rslt As Fraction, Succ As
    Integer)
    ```

    The last parameter, *Succ*, should be set to **True** if the result of taking the reciprocal is valid, and to **False** if the reciprocal does not exist. Don't print a message.

11. In the **gcf()** function, the values of *a* and *b* are completely changed within the function. What keeps these changed values from being sent back to the calling program?

12. Write a procedure that will accept a fraction and a positive integer as parameters and return a fraction equal to the original fraction raised to the power represented by the integer. Use the following first line:

```
Sub Power(X As Fraction, Power As Integer, Rslt As Fraction)
```

13. Add to the code module for the Fraction program a procedure with the following heading:

```
Sub Normalize( fract as Fraction )
```

The routine should "normalize" the fraction sent as a parameter by
◎ Calling Reduce
◎ Changing the signs of the numerator and the denominator if the denominator is negative
◎ Making the numerator and the denominator positive if both are negative

Add a call to the Normalize procedure to the end of each math procedure defined in the code module.

3

Section

A Database Program with User-Defined Types

In this program, you'll create a form that lets the user enter, edit, delete, and display a multiple-choice quiz, take the quiz, and display the score. You might want to use the program to create practice quizzes for yourself. Or you and a classmate could create quizzes to exchange.

Building this program covers two sections of this chapter. The first section covers building the forms and defining the user-defined types. The second section covers the code that ties the forms and files together.

Over the course of the program, we will introduce a number of new features of the language and learn something about building a fairly large program. You will declare and use a user-defined type that is more complex than the ones you have used so far; in one of its fields is an array of records of another user-defined type. Nesting user-defined types in this way gives you considerable expressive power. In this program, an entire test is defined by a single user-defined type.

Later in this chapter, you will learn how to use the File System controls, and you will refine the program to use them. These controls let you spare the user from having to type in complete file names whenever your program must interact with the file system. Instead of remembering and typing in long paths and filenames, users of your programs can click with the mouse to choose drives, directories, and files. Your programs become much easier to use.

Starting Out

What data structure do you need to represent a multiple-choice test of 25 questions? A data structure is a framework that stores and organizes data. It is a theoretical structure that is built using user-defined types and arrays. You'll need fields for the body of each question, the five possible answers, and a character for the correct answer. You'll need an array to hold 25 records. The overall data structure should also record information about the title of the test, and how many questions there are.

The algorithms (the step-by-step processes for solving the problems) are mainly bookkeeping procedures: keeping track of where you are in the question array, filling the empty space after a question is deleted, keeping track of correct answers so an overall score can be reported, managing the data files and appearance (and disappearance) of the two forms.

USING MENU COMMANDS AND FORMS AS AN ORGANIZER

You need to determine how many and what kind of forms you will need for the project. In most of the projects to this point, you have used only single forms. This project splits naturally into at least two parts: entering, editing, and deleting questions; and taking the test and keeping score. As a result, you will create one form called the Edit form and another called the Test form.

In your plans for a program like this, you may have thought there should be three forms, or maybe you can envision a single form that will handle the problem. Any of these solutions might work very well. There is no one right answer to any programming problem.

THE EDIT FUNCTIONS

Entering new questions, editing or deleting old ones, and displaying the questions of a test are the kinds of tasks the program will perform. In addition, you will want to save files, open new files, or load existing files. When you load a file, you'll transfer information from the file to a variable that represents your user-defined test type in the program.

Start the program by looking over the Edit form in Figure 12-7. Do you agree with the design decisions made here? If not, what can you improve, and why? The form contains:

- A label to indicate the test name

- A line for "other" information

- A textbox for the body of the question

- Five textboxes for the test choices

- A box for the correct answer

- Labels on the form indicating the current question number, the total number of questions and the filename of the test file

- Two command buttons: one for moving to the next question in the list and one for moving to the previous question

When a user clicks on one of the two command buttons, a different question is displayed. An edited question is added to the array only if the user selects Add from the Questions submenu.

What you can't see from Figure 12-7 is the structure of the menus on the Edit form. That structure is:

Figure 12-7

Edit form for the quiz program

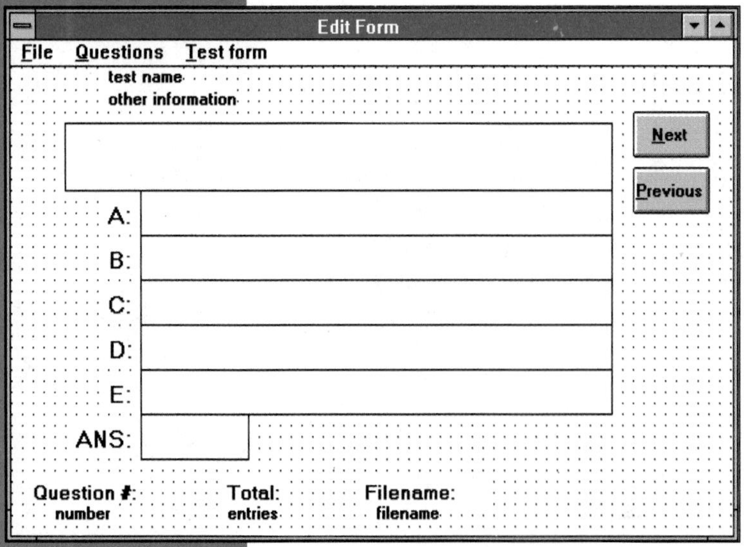

- File
  - New
  - Open
  - Save
  - Exit

- Questions
  - Enter
  - Add
  - Delete
  - Display

- Test form

THE TEST FORM

The Test form is similar to the Edit form (see Figure 12-8). The user clicks Next for the next question. Labels on the form keep track of:

⦿ Name of the test

⦿ "Other" test information

⦿ Record number of the current question

⦿ How many questions are in the test

⦿ Filename of the test file chosen

When finished with the test, the user chooses the Score menu item to see the score. After viewing the score, the user returns to the Edit form or exits the program.

In this form the menu structure is:

⦿ Tests
  ◎ Take a Test
  ◎ Score

⦿ Edit Form

⦿ Exit

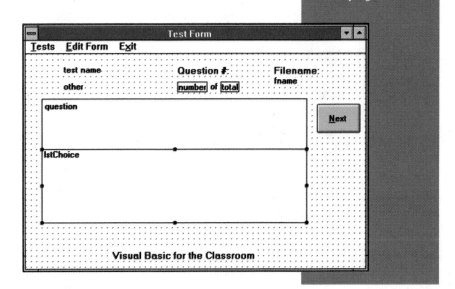

Figure 12-8
Test form for the quiz program

Choosing the Take a Test command lets the user enter the filename of the test to take. The program opens the file, loads the information into the Test data structure, and displays the first question. After an answer is entered, it is compared to the correct answer recorded with the question and a score is kept.

Creating the Edit Form

Follow these steps to create the Edit form:

1 Select the default form.

2 Change the name of the form to **frmEdit**. Change the caption of the form to **Edit Form**.

3 Select the form. Open the Menu Design window.

4 Using Figure 12-9 and the information below, create the menu for the Edit form.

Caption	Name	Index
&File	mnuF	
&New	mnuFile	1
&Open	mnuFile	2
&Save	mnuFile	3
-	mnuFile	4
E&xit	mnuExit	
&Questions	mnuQuestions	
&Enter Question	mnuQuest	
&Add Question to Test	mnuAddTo	
&Delete Question	mnuDelete	
Dis&play First Question	mnuDisplay	
&Test Form	mnuTest	

Figure 12-9
Menu Design window for the Edit form menu

5 At the top-left of the form, place two labels. Change the names to **lblTestName** and **lblOther**. Change the captions to **test name** and **other information**. These labels are intended to display a title for the test, such as "VB File Test," and other information such as "July 4, 1996."

6 Place a textbox across the top of the form to hold the question. Change the name of the box to **txtQuestion**. In the Properties window, change Multi Line to **True**, and TabIndex to 0. Delete the text.

7 Place five textboxes for the responses to the question. Change the names of the boxes to **txtResp1**, **txtResp2**, and so on. Delete the captions. Set MultiLine to **True** for each.

8 Put labels in front of each box representing the letter of the choice. Change the captions to **A:, B:,** and so on, and place them as shown in Figure 12-7. The labels should retain their default names. Change the FontSize to 12 and AutoSize to **True** for all of them.

9 Place a textbox on the form below the five response boxes, for the answer to the problem. Name the box **txtAns**. Delete the text.

10 Place a label on the box just created. Set the FontSize to 12 and the caption to *ANS:.*

11 Below the response boxes and across the bottom of the form, place six labels in pairs, one above the other.

12 Change the captions of the top boxes to **Question #1**, **Total:**, and **Filename**.

13 Change the names of the lower boxes to **lblNum**, **lblTotal**, and **lblFileName**. Change the captions of those boxes to **number**, **entries**, and **filename**.

14 Place two command buttons on the form. Change the captions to **&Next** and **&Previous**. Change both the names to **cmdNextQ**. Set the Index property of the Next button to 0. Set the Index property of the Previous button to 1.

15 Save the form and project files in a directory named mchoice.

Creating the Test Form

Follow these steps to create the Test form:

1 Choose New Form from the File menu.

2 Change the name of the form to **frmTest**. Change the caption of the form to **Test Form**.

3 Select the form. Open the Menu Design window.

4 Using Figure 12-10 and the chart below, create the menu for the Test form.

Caption	Name
&Tests	mnuTests
&Take a Test	mnuTake
&Score	mnuScore
&Edit Form	mnuEditForm
E&xit	mnuExit

Figure 12-10
Menu Design window for the Test form

5 Create two labels in the upper-left corner of the form. Change the captions to **test name** and **other**. Change the names to **lblTestName** and **lblOther**.

6 Near the top center of the form, create a label with the caption **Question #**. Set the FontSize to 9.75. This label heads three labels, two of which are set to reflect the current question number and the total number of questions in the test.

7 Put three labels in a row below the Question # label. Change the captions to **number**, **of**, and **total**. Change the name of the first to

lblQNum and the last to **lblTotal**. Change the BorderStyle of the first and last to Single.

8 Put two labels near the top right of the form. Change the captions to **Filename:** and **FName**. Change the FontSize of the first to 9.75. Change the name of the second to **lblFileName**.

9 Put a large multiline textbox in the center of the form. Change the name of the box to **txtQuestion**. Change the Text property to **question**.

10 Put a large listbox below. Change the name to **lstChoice**.

11 Put a command button on the right side of the form. Change the caption of the button to **&Next**. Change the name of the button to **cmdNext**.

12 Save the form and project files.

Setting Up the Data Structures

You must place declarations for global data types, which are types available to all forms and modules, in the declarations section of a code module. To do so:

1 Add a code module to the project. Choose New Module from the File menu.

2 Enter the following lines to define the special data types for the project:

```
Option Explicit
Type Quest
    N As Integer
    Body As String * 250
    Res1 As String * 100
    Res2 As String * 100
    Res3 As String * 100
    Res4 As String * 100
    Res5 As String * 100
    Ans As String * 1
End Type
Type Test     '26487 is record length
    Title As String * 80
    Other As String * 80
    Current As Integer
    Question(0 To 25) As Quest
End Type
```

Two new types are defined. The first is used as a component of the second. The Quest type represents a single question. It starts with a 250-character string for the question itself. The fields *Res1* through *Res5* are 100-character strings holding the answer choices for each question. The letter of the answer itself goes into a 1-character string with the variable name *Ans*.

The entire test is stored as a single data item. A single record in Visual Basic has a maximum of 32767 characters, more than enough for a multiple choice test of 25 questions. Because each test is organized as a single data item, it is possible to put more than one test into a file. The program as currently implemented stores only a single test per file.

The Test type starts with two fields to store information about the test: the first field, Title, for the name of the test and the second, called Other, for the teacher's name and the date the test was written. The variable *Current* contains the current number of questions in the test, and the array, *Question(0 to 25)* contains the actual questions, choices, and answers for each question on the test.

QUESTIONS AND ACTIVITIES

1. You have probably heard the advice that you should never be afraid to start a project over from the beginning. What is the reason for such a statement?

2. What is the record length for a record of the following type?

```
Type day
    name As String*15
    date As Integer   ' integers are two bytes
End Type
Type month
    name As String*15
    days(30) As day
End Type
```

3. Write out in words (not code) a plan for a program to store information for a pet store. The program should store information about animals the store sells. The animal information should include the breed, the birth date, the price, the quantity, and the place obtained. What kind of data structure would you use? What kinds of jobs should the program handle? What kinds of displays might be generated?

4. If you were writing a program to store information that would be useful in filling out a questionnaire or a petition (pick one), what kind of information would you store?

4

Section

Writing Code for the Quiz Program

You have created two forms and the data structure for the quiz program. This section addresses the code that ties them all together. You will add most of the code to the menu commands and command buttons of the Edit form. Code to be shared by both forms is put into a code module (see Figure 12-11). (In contrast, if you want a procedure to be available only to different event procedures of a single form, you define it in the general declarations section of that form.)

Code Module

General declarations
Procedures defined here are visible to all the forms of a project

form 1   form 2   form 3

General declarations

Procedure
definition

Other procedures of the form
(including event procedures)

Procedures defined within the form are visible
to all the other procedures within the form

Figure 12-11
Determining where to
place procedures

The Edit Form

You now add code to the Edit form that implements its menu commands and command buttons. The menu commands consist of commands in the File and Questions submenus, together with the Test Form command. The commands in the File menu create a new test, load an existing test, and save the current test. The commands in the Questions menu let you or the user add, delete, and edit questions in the current test. The Next and Previous command buttons navigate between the questions.

COLLECTING THE FILENAME

The routine to collect the filename of the test from the user is called in both the Edit form and the Test form. The code for the Filename procedure appears in the code module you have already defined.

This routine, a programmer-defined function, starts with the keyword **Function** in the first line, followed by the name of the function, any parameters sent to the function, and the data type of the information returned by the function to the calling program. In this program, no parameters are sent and the name of the file returned is a string.

In the code, you need to prompt the user to enter the name of the file to be opened. Use string concatenation to build a complete filename that includes the path. Display the filename in lblFileName of both the Edit and Test forms. Assign the string constructed to the name of the function, FileName, so that it can be returned to the calling program.

To enter the code:

1 Select the code module from the Project window.

2   Click on View Code and open the general declarations section.

3   Enter these lines:

```
Function FileName () As String
   Dim Msg As String
   Dim F As String
   Msg = "enter the file name"
   '—InputBox provides default filename
   '—The mchoice directory holds test data
   F = "c:\mchoice\" & InputBox$(Msg, , "test1") & ".dat"
   frmEdit.lblFileName = F
   frmTest.lblFileName = F
   FileName = F
End Function
```

DECLARING VARIABLES

Now you declare the variables that the procedures and event handlers of the Edit form operate on mutually. You need a global variable of Test type to hold the edited test itself, an integer to hold the current question number, and a string to hold the filename of the test. To declare these variables for the Edit form:

1   Open the Code window for the Edit form.

2   Enter the variable declarations you need in the general declarations section:

```
Option Explicit
Dim T As Test
Dim QNum As Integer
Dim FName As String
```

The variable *T* represents the entire Test data structure. *FName* represents the name of the file accessed for loading and storing the test, and *QNum* represents the subscript of the question currently being processed.

DISPLAYING THE FIRST QUESTION OF THE TEST

The routine to display the current question of the test on the Edit form is called from a number of event procedures: it's called from cmdDisplay_Click(), the procedure associated with the Display first question command in the Questions menu. It is also called from cmdDelete_Click(), a procedure that deletes the currently displayed question and replaces it with a display of the previous question. Finally, it's called from the two command buttons, Next and Previous.

The routine receives from the calling program a single parameter, *QNum*, designating the array subscript of the element to be displayed. It transfers values from the Test data type to the textboxes and label on the form.

To write the routine that displays the current question on the Edit form:

1 If you do not have the Code window for the Edit form open, then open it.

2 Open the general declarations section of the form.

3 Add the following lines to the Display procedure:

```
Sub Display (QNum As Integer)
    '—T.Question(QNum) is one question of the test
    '—Body accesses the question itself
    '—Res x accesses the possible RESponses to the question
    txtQuestion = T.Question(QNum).Body
    txtResp1 = T.Question(QNum).Res1
    txtResp2 = T.Question(QNum).Res2
    txtResp3 = T.Question(QNum).Res3
    txtResp4 = T.Question(QNum).Res4
    txtResp5 = T.Question(QNum).Res5
    '—The real answer is designated by a single character
    txtAns = T.Question(QNum).ANS
    '—Display the current total number of questions.
    lblTotal = T.Current
    '—Display this question's number.
    lblNum = QNum
End Sub
```

ACCESSING ELEMENTS OF THE QUESTION ARRAY

To access the elements of the *Question* array, you start with the name of the Test, *T*. Dots separate each level of access to the fields of the record. The dot is followed by the array name, *Question*. The subscript *QNum* is next, followed by the field in the array to be displayed: *Body*, for the actual question, *Res1..Res5* for the choices, and *Ans* for the proper answer.

T	Represents the entire test.
T.Question	Represents the question array.
T.Question(QNum)	Represents a single question.

T.Question(QNum).Body	Represents the actual question for entry *QNum*.
T. Question(QNum).Res1	Represents the first choice for the answer.

DELETING QUESTIONS

One of the edit functions of the program is to delete a question from the test. A question must be displayed, to be deleted.

To code this procedure:

1 Select the Edit form, frmEdit, from the Project window.

2 Enter these lines of code between the first and last lines in the mnuDelete_Click procedure:

```
'—This routine deletes question QNum from the test.
'—Local declarations.
Dim Msg As String
Dim Ys As String
Dim MaxValue As Integer, x As Integer
'—Prompt for InputBox.
Msg = "Are you sure?<y,n>:"
'—Get confirmation for delete.
Ys = InputBox$(Msg, , "Y")
'—Check for yes and whether the question can be deleted.
If (Ys = "y" Or Ys = "Y") And (QNum >= 1) And (QNum <= T.Current) Then
    '—MaxValue is the number of the last question.
    MaxValue = T.Current
    For x = QNum To MaxValue - 1
        T.Question(x) = T.Question(x + 1)
    Next x
    T.Current = T.Current - 1
    QNum = QNum - 1
    Display (QNum)
End If
```

The trick in this routine is to delete a question by filling its place with the question that follows. Once the question is deleted, you reset *T.Current* by setting it equal to *T.Current - 1*. If you delete the last question of the test, there is no subsequent question to replace it. This is not a problem: once *T.Current* is decremented, the last question is effectively cut out.

Your only real problem is what to do if there is only one question in the test. When it is deleted, what will be displayed? The code above allows the first question to be deleted and displays the question at *QNum - 1*. There is no real question at this spot, but it is a spot in the *Question* array. You will recall the declaration for the *Question* array was from 0 to

25. Visual Basic automatically fills this first space in the array (subscript = 0) with blanks, so a blank question is displayed.

DISPLAYING QUESTIONS

The procedure you create in this section displays the first question of the test, provided the test contains any questions at all. Assuming that *T.Current* is greater than or equal to 1, this procedure sets *QNum* to 1 and calls the **Display***(QNum)* routine, which displays question *QNum*. If *Current* is 0, no action is taken.

To display the first question:

1 Select frmEdit from the Project window.

2 Click on View Code.

3 Open the code procedure for mnuDisplay_Click. Enter this code between the first and last lines of the procedure:

```
If T.Current <> 0 Then
    QNum = 1
    Display (QNum)
End If
```

4 Save the form, project, and code module files.

CODING THE FILE ITEMS

Now you need to write the procedure that implements the commands on the Edit form's File menu. This procedure creates new tests, opens and loads existing tests, and saves tests to disk. Enter the code for the file-managing routines by following these steps:

1 Select the Edit form.

2 Select New from the File menu of the Edit form to open the Code window.

3 Enter the following lines of code for mnuFile.

```
Dim Msg As String
'—Read the filename from the form.
FName = lblFileName
'—If file name is blank or New is clicked, collect filename from user
If (FName = "") Or Index = 1 Then
    FName = FileName()
    lblFileName = FName
End If
```

```
'—Process menu items with Select Case statement
Select Case Index
'—New test chosen
   Case 1
       Msg = "Enter the NAME of test:"   ' not the filename
       lblTestName = InputBox$(Msg)      ' get the name
       T.Title = lblTestName.Caption     ' display the name
       '—Collect and display the "other" information.
       Msg = "Enter other information (date or description):"
       lblOther = InputBox$(Msg)
       T.Other = lblOther.Caption
       '—Set current number of questions to 0
       T.Current = 0
       '—Display blank question to clear display
       Display (0)
       '—Set record number to 1
       QNum = 1
       '—Prepare to enter text in question
       txtQuestion.SetFocus
       '—Open saved test from disk
   Case 2
       Open FName For Random Access Read As #1 Len = 30000
       Get #1, , T
       Close
       '—Load test information onto form
       lblTestName = T.Title
       lblOther = T.Other
       lblTotal = T.Current
       lblFileName = FName
       '—Save the current test
   Case 3
       Open FName For Random Access Write As #1 Len = 30000
       Put #1, , T
       Close
End Select
```

The **Open** and **Save** statements open and save a test file. The test file itself is 30,000 bytes long. Although using a single **Get** or **Put** statement to read and write the file is convenient, it wastes disk space.

CODING THE NEXT AND PREVIOUS COMMAND BUTTONS

These two buttons are a control array, meaning they share the same name. The index value for the first button is 0 and for the second, 1. The code controls the display of the next or previous question. If neither of these questions exists, the display is left unchanged.

Follow these steps to code the buttons:

1 If necessary, select the Edit form.

2 Double-click on either the Next or the Previous button to open the Code window.

3 Enter the following lines of code:

```
Sub cmdNextQ_Click (Index As Integer)
    '—Index = 0 is the Next button
    '—Index = 1 is the Previous button
    If Index = 0 Then
        '—QNum is followed by a question it is OK to
        'display the next question.
        If QNum < T.Current And QNum < 25 Then
            QNum = QNum + 1
            '—The Display routine is called to update the display
            Display (QNum)
        End If
    Else
        If QNum > 1 Then
            QNum = QNum - 1
            Display (QNum)
        End If
    End If
End Sub
```

ENTERING THE QUESTION HANDLERS

The Enter Question command in the Questions menu clears the edit space to prepare for a new question. Follow these steps to write the code for this command:

1 If necessary, select the Edit form.

2 Select Enter Question from the Questions menu. In the cmdQuest_Click routine, enter the following code:

```
'—Clear the display.
txtQuestion = ""
txtResp1 = ""
txtResp2 = ""
txtResp3 = ""
txtResp4 = ""
txtResp5 = ""
txtAns = ""
txtQuestion.SetFocus
```

ADDING A QUESTION

A user selects the Add Question to Test menu command when the question displayed on the screen is ready to be added to the test. In the code, you first need to make sure that there is a file currently being edited. The value of *Current* is incremented, showing another question has been added to the test. The information about the question is then read from the textboxes on the form and transferred to the array.

To write this code:

1   If necessary, select the Edit form.

2   Select Add Question to Test from the Questions menu.

3   Enter the following code into the mnuAddTo_Click () subroutine:

```
If txtQuestion.Text <> "" Then
    QNum = T.Current + 1
    T.Question(QNum).Body = txtQuestion
    T.Question(QNum).Res1 = "A) " & txtResp1
    T.Question(QNum).Res2 = "B) " & txtResp2
    T.Question(QNum).Res3 = "C) " & txtResp3
    T.Question(QNum).Res4 = "D) " & txtResp4
    T.Question(QNum).Res5 = "E) " & txtResp5
    T.Question(QNum).Ans = txtAns
    T.Current = QNum
    lblNum = QNum
    lblTotal = T.Current
End If
```

4   Save the form and project files.

SHIFTING FOCUS

The Test Form command shifts the focus of the program to the test form. To write the code that shifts focus:

1 Click on the Test Form menu item in the Edit form menu bar.

2 In the Code window, enter the following code for mnuTest_Click():

```
'—Unload Me unloads the Edit form from memory
Unload Me
'—Show loads a form into memory and shifts the
'focus to that form
frmTest.Show
```

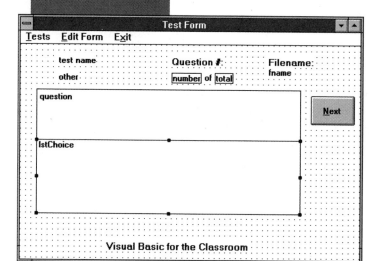

The Test Form

Compared to the Edit form, the Test form is quite straightforward to code. Its purpose is to display the questions one by one for the user to answer. It keeps score and displays the score when the user clicks on the Score command. See Figure 12-12.

DECLARING THE VARIABLES

The Test form requires a few global variables. *T* represents the test. *Scr* is the current score, a whole number. *QNum* is the subscript for the question, just as in the Edit form.

To declare the variables:

1 Select the Test form.

2 Double-click on the form to open the Code window.

3 In the general declarations section of the form, insert the following lines.

```
Option Explicit
Dim T As Test
Dim Scr As Integer
Dim QNum As Integer
```

WRITING THE DISPLAY2 PROCEDURE

The arrangement of the question and answers in this form is different from the arrangement in the Edit form. Part of the difference is in the method of displaying the choices for the answer. The box in the middle of the form is a listbox, not a textbox. You use the **AddItem** method to display the answer choices.

Using the listbox for the answer choices allows the user to select the correct answer by clicking on it in the box. When an answer is clicked, it is highlighted. When the user clicks Next, the answer is processed by reading the index of the item clicked in the listbox, and the score is updated. If the user chooses the wrong answer, a message box displays the correct choice.

To code the procedure:

1   Select the Test form.

2   Open the general declarations section of the form.

3   Enter the following code.

```
Sub Display2 (QNum As Integer)
    If QNum <= T.Current Then
        lblQNum = QNum
        txtQuestion = T.Question(QNum).Body
        lstChoice.Clear
        lstChoice.AddItem T.Question(QNum).Res1
        lstChoice.AddItem T.Question(QNum).Res2
        lstChoice.AddItem T.Question(QNum).Res3
        lstChoice.AddItem T.Question(QNum).Res4
        lstChoice.AddItem T.Question(QNum).Res5
        QNum = QNum + 1
    End If
End Sub
```

The **Display2** routine checks to see that the parameter passed, *QNum*, represents a valid question in the test. If it does, the label on the form indicating the question number is updated, the *Body* of the question is displayed in the upper textbox, and the answer choices are added to the listbox. The procedure ends by incrementing *QNum* to point at the next question in the test (if it exists).

CODING THE TAKE A TEST COMMAND

The cmdTake_Click() procedure, called by the Take a Test command, opens up the test file, transfers data from the file into the variable *T*, initializes the score to 0, sets *QNum* to 1, sets various labels, and displays the first question. The code that actually keeps the score is in the Next button.

To write the code for the command:

1   Select the Test form.

2   Click on Tests, then click on Take a Test.

3 Enter the following lines in the subroutine for this command:

```
Sub mnuTake_Click ()
    '—Local variable for filename
    Dim FName As String
    '—Read filename from form
    FName = lblFileName.Caption
    '—If there is no filename, go back to the Edit form
    If FName = "" Then
        MsgBox ("Choose a filename")
        Unload Me
        frmEdit.Show
        Exit Sub
    Else
        FName = lblFileName
        Open FName For Random Access Read As #1 Len = 30000
        Get #1, , T
        Close
        '—If Current is 0, there are no questions
        If T.Current = 0 Then
            MsgBox "The test has no questions."
        Else
            '—Initialize score to 0
            Scr = 0     ' current score on test
            lblTotal = T.Current
            lblTestName = T.Title
            lblOther = T.Other
            QNum = 1
            Display2 (QNum)
        End If
    End If
End Sub
```

CODING THE NEXT COMMAND BUTTON

In this procedure, the program reads a choice made by the user from the listbox, using the ListIndex property. This property contains a number corresponding to the choice highlighted in the box. The first choice in the box corresponds with ListIndex = 0.

After this index is read, it is converted to an uppercase character using the **Chr$()** function. The ASCII code of "A" is calculated using the **Asc()** function, the value of the ListIndex is added to that code, and the result is converted back into a character.

```
choice = Chr$(Asc("A") + txtChoice.ListIndex)
```

For instance, if choice *b)* is chosen as the correct answer from the listbox, the ListIndex will be set to 1. The ASCII code for "A" is 65. Then 1 is added to 65, giving 66. This value is converted back into a character by the **Chr$()** function. This character is the answer entered by the user, which must be compared with the real answer recorded along with the question as a part of the test.

The value of *choice*, which is the answer entered by the user, and the real answer from the test are compared. The **UCase$()** function is used so that case does not determine whether an answer is correct; either upper- or lowercase answers will result in the same value.

If the answer is correct, the score, *Scr*, is incremented. If not, the correct answer is displayed. *QNum* is incremented to point at the next question of the test. For a correct answer, 1 is added to the total of correct answers.

If *QNum* points to a valid question of the test, that question is displayed. When all the questions have been answered, the user receives the message: "the test is complete".

To enter this code:

1   Select the Test form.

2   Double-click the Next button to open the Code window. Enter the following code in the cmdNext_Click() subroutine:.

```
Dim Choice As String
'—Choice is built from the ASCII code for "A" and
'the ListIndex value of the answer chosen
Choice = Chr$(Asc("A") + lstChoice.ListIndex)
If Choice = UCase$(T.Question(QNum).Ans) Then
    Scr = Scr + 1
Else
    MsgBox "The answer was: " & T.Question(QNum).Ans
End If
'—Set QNum to the next question
QNum = QNum + 1
If QNum <= T.Current Then
    '—Display the next question
    Display2 (QNum)
Else
    MsgBox "the test is complete"
End If
```

CONCLUSION

A balance must be maintained in presenting a project such as this one. Should the program be presented as a "perfect" piece, with all the little problems fixed up, all glitches anticipated and trapped? When a complete work is presented, it is easy to get lost in the details. The details obscure the main ideas of the program and the logic that knits it together.

The approach taken here is that an unpolished program that works and is short enough to be understood is better than a program that is incomprehensible, but perfect.

You'll know you are really starting to become a programmer when you can see places where the code could be a little better, or you figure out how to write code to cover a possibility the program does not handle.

QUESTIONS AND ACTIVITIES

1. Assume the string variable *Name* has the value of "John", and *crlf* has the value *Chr$(13)* & *Chr$(10)*. Write the statements you would need to produce the following :

   "Dear John,

   It's over between us.

   Sincerely, Mary"

2. In an earlier program, you saw how to create a control array of textboxes on a form. If a control array were used for the textboxes txtresp1..txtresp5 representing the answers to a question, how could the code be modified in the **Display***(QNum As Integer)* procedure in the Edit form? Assume the textboxes in the control array have the name txtResp(). Write the code. (Hint: If you are not using a **For-Next** statement, you should rethink your solution.)

3. In the code for cmdDelete_Click (), what would happen if the line:

   ```
   For x = QNum To MaxValue - 1
   ```

   was replaced with:

   ```
   For x = MaxValue - 1 to QNum step -1
   ```

4. Explain each part of the condition that is tested in the **If-Then** statement in the cmdDelete_Click () routine:

   ```
   If (Ys = "y" Or Ys = "Y") And (QNum >= 1) And (QNum <= T.Current) Then
   ```

5. What do you think would be the effect of executing **Display(0)**? Would this be a way to simplify the code used to blank the textboxes on the screen?

6. When the last question of a test is deleted, no questions are actually moved. *Current* is decremented. Why doesn't it matter that the question deleted is still in its spot of the array?

7. How is it possible to store a 25-question test using a single **Put** command?

8. Suppose an incorrect question is present in the test. How would you make sure the corrected question got into the test?

9. Rewrite the cmdNextQ_Click (index As Integer) routine using a **Select Case** statement.

10. As currently coded, the cmdAddTo_Click routine appends a letter to the beginning of each answer as it writes it to the array: *A), B), ..., E)*. If you are trying to add a corrected version of a question to the test, you wind up with two layers of letters: *A) A)*. Fix the code to take care of the problem.

Using File System Controls

Section

Until now, pathnames have been entered by the user in bits and pieces from the keyboard and joined into a single string. In this section you'll see how to use the controls provided by Visual Basic to accomplish these same actions with the mouse instead of with the keyboard. Using the file system controls in your programs lets the user navigate around the file system to choose files and directories. The user does not have to remember and type in long path and filenames. Because nobody likes to type complete filenames, your programs will be perceived as much more friendly and easy to use.

Types of File System Controls

There are three file system controls: the Drive Box, the Directory Listbox, and the File Listbox. The Drive Box displays a combobox of existing drives from which the user can choose. The Directory Listbox contains a list displaying directories in a tree-like form. This list has the same appearance as the Directories list in the standard Windows Open and Save As dialog boxes. The File Listbox displays all files in a directory.

THE DRIVE BOX

If you add a Drive Box control to a form, the user of your program will be able to choose a disk drive from a combobox of available drives from which the user can choose a drive. The name of the selected drive becomes the value of the Drive property of the control. The value of the Drive property can only be modified at run-time; therefore, you will not see this property listed in the Properties window of the control.

Double-clicking on the drive box icon in the Toolbox places a drive box on the active form. You can change the length, but not the height, of this control. When the program is run, the value of the Drive property is set to the default drive. See Figure 12-13.

When a user runs one of your programs that contains a drive box, a click on the arrow in the right-hand box displays a list of available drives. When the user selects a drive from that list, the control's Change event is executed. At that point, your Change event handler should set the path of the directory listbox to the name of the newly selected drive. (See the following section for more on the directory listbox control.) The directory listbox will respond by listing the root directory of the chosen drive.

Figure 12-13
Value of the property set to the default drive

Assuming the drive box has its default name, drive1, and the directory box has its default name, dir1, the code to write the drive name is:

```
Sub Drive1_Change ()
    Dir1.Path = Drive1.Drive
    Dir1.SetFocus
End Sub
```

THE DIRECTORY LISTBOX

Double-clicking on the directory icon in the Toolbox places a resizable directory listbox on the active form. This control lists the directory of the drive written into its Path property. Like the Drive property of the drive box, the Path property of the directory box is available only at run-time. A change to the Path property results in a change in the directory listing. To select a directory from those listed, double-click on the directory name.

When a user clicks on a directory name, it is selected. When a user double clicks, the Path property is updated to include the selected directory. The display in the directory listing window is updated accordingly. See Figure 12-14.

Figure 12-14
Display in the directory listing window

The new path information should be written to the Path property of the file box. The box updates its file listing to reflect the contents of the new directory.

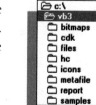

THE FILE LISTBOX

The file box lists the files contained in the directory written into its Path property, a property available only at run-time. Double-clicking on the file box icon in the Toolbox places a resizable file box on the active form. See Figure 12-15.

Figure 12-15

Placing a resizable file box on the active form

This box displays a scrollable listing of the files contained in the path written into the Path property. You set the Path property in the Change routine of the directory listbox. If an item in the file list is double-clicked, that filename is appended to the path information already contained in the Path property of the file box. See Figure 12-16.

Drive box: Select a Drive from the box, the Drive property is set

File box: When a directory is selected in the Directory box, write that path to the Path property of the File box.

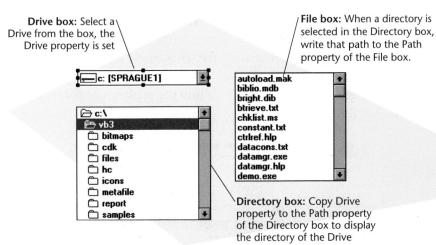

Directory box: Copy Drive property to the Path property of the Directory box to display the directory of the Drive

Figure 12-16

Working with the File listbox

Adding a Form to the Quiz Program

The Quiz program used an InputBox to prompt the user for the filename of the test file. This information was joined with other path information to build a complete pathname. The pathname was used to save and open files containing test data.

Adding the controls described above to a form allows the user to select a file by pointing and clicking existing paths and files. You should now enhance the Quiz program by adding a form to handle file and path names.

STARTING OUT

On this third form, you will be adding drive, directory, and file boxes, as shown in Figure 12-17. The form needs some additional objects as well:

- A number of labels
- A textbox
- A command button

Think about what the user needs to use this form effectively. You should place a label above the file listing containing an instruction for the user, such as "Choose file from list". If you do so, the user will understand the contents of that box. Above that label, you should place a second label with the caption Pathname. When a user selects a directory from the directory box, the Change event will update that label to show what path has been transferred to the file box. Of course, the file box updates its display and reflects the contents of the new directory.

At times, users will want to enter filenames from the keyboard rather than clicking on a selection from a list. To cover this requirement, you need to place a textbox below the file listing. Then place two more labels below that textbox. Use one of the labels to provide an explanation of the information provided in the other label. The program will display the complete pathname of the chosen or selected file in the lower of these two labels. Then, when the user clicks on the Return button, the program writes this pathname into the appropriate places in the Edit and Test forms of the Quiz project.

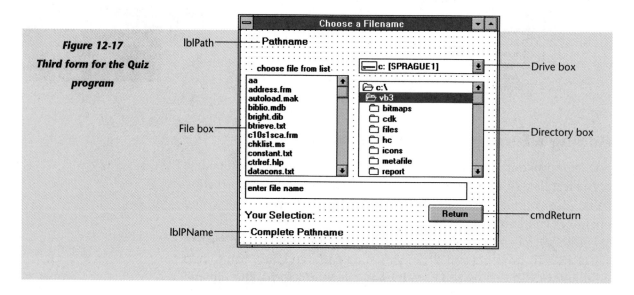

Figure 12-17

Third form for the Quiz program

BUILDING THE FORM

Follow these steps to build the third form for the Quiz project:

1 Open the Quiz project.

2 Choose New Form from the File menu.

3 Change the name of the form to frmFile. Change the caption of the form to **Choose a Filename**.

4 Double-click on the drive box icon. Position the drive box as shown in Figure 12-17.

5 Double-click on the directory box. Position the object.

6 Double-click on the file box. Position the object.

7 Create a long textbox for the file and pathname. Change the name of the box to **txtFName**. Change the text to **Enter the filename**.

8 Create a label for the top of the form. Change the name of the label to **lblPath**. Change the FontSize to 9.75. Change the AutoSize property to True.

9 Create a label for the bottom of the form. Change the name of the label to **lblPName**. Change the FontSize to 9.75. Change the Auto-Size property to True.

10 Create a label for the bottom label. Change the caption to **Your selection:**

11 Create a label for above the file box. Change the caption to **choose file from list**.

12 Add a command button to the form. Change the caption to **&Return**. Change the name to **cmdReturn**.

CODING THE FILE FORM

Follow these steps to add code to the file form.

1 Select the File form from the Project window.

2 Click on View Code to open the Code window.

3 In the general declarations section of the form, enter the following lines.

```
Option Explicit
Dim FName As String
```

4 The path label at the top of the form is initialized to the default drive when the form is activated. Enter these lines in the Form_Load procedure:

```
Sub Form_Load ()
    lblPath = Dir1.Path
End Sub
```

5 When a new drive is selected, a Change event occurs. The Change event procedure writes the new drive name into the Path property of the directory box. Enter these lines in the Drive1_Change event procedure:

```
Sub Drive1_Change ()
    Dir1.Path = Drive1.Drive
    Dir1.SetFocus
End Sub
```

6 When a new directory is selected from the directory box, a Change event occurs. Code in this event writes the new pathname to the file box. Enter these lines in Dir1_Change:

```
Sub Dir1_Change ()
    File1.Path = Dir1.Path
    lblPath = "Path: " & Dir1.Path
    File1.SetFocus
End Sub
```

7 When a file in the file box is clicked, it is selected, then the path and file name are joined and displayed in the txtFName box on the form. The selected filename is available through the file box's File-Name property. Enter these lines in the File1_Click procedure:

```
Sub File1_Click ()
    txtFName.Text = Dir1.Path & "\" & UCase(File1.FileName)
End Sub
```

8 When an entry in the file box is double-clicked, the complete path-name is joined with the filename and displayed in labels. Enter these lines in the File1_DblClick procedure:

```
Sub File1_DblClick ()
    '—Display the selected file name when DblClicked.
    lblPName.Caption = Dir1.Path & "\" & UCase(File1.FileName)
    txtFName.Text = Dir1.Path & "\" & UCase(File1.FileName)
    cmdReturn.SetFocus
End Sub
```

9 When the pathname changes, lblPath at the top of the form is updated to reflect the change. Enter these lines in File1_PathChange:

```
Sub File1_PathChange ()
    lblPath.Caption = "Path: " & Dir1.Path
End Sub
```

10 The textbox is used to enter the filename from the keyboard. When a name is entered and the Enter key is pressed, the path and file names are joined and displayed in the upper label. Focus is shifted to the Return button. Enter these lines in txtFName_KeyPress:

```
Sub txtFName_KeyPress (keyascii As Integer)
   If KeyAscii = 13 Then
       lblPName = Dir1.Path & "\" & txtFName.Text
       cmdReturn.SetFocus
   End If
End Sub
```

11 The Return command button writes the filename to the two other forms, the Edit and the Test forms. Enter these lines in the cmdReturn_Click procedure:

```
Sub cmdReturn_Click ()
   frmEdit.lblFileName = lblPName.Caption
   frmTest.lblFileName = lblPName.Caption
   frmFile.Hide
   frmEdit.Show
End Sub
```

12 Save the form and project files.

13 Integrate the new form into the Quiz Project by inserting two lines of code in the mnuFile_Click procedure. Below are a few lines from that procedure. Two old lines are commented out and two new lines are added. Make the changes:

```
Sub mnuFile_Click (Index As Integer)
   Dim Msg As String
   '—Read the filename from the form
   FName = lblFileName
   '—If file name is blank, collect from user
   If (FName = "") Or Index = 1 Then
      '—FName = FileName()
      '—lblFileName = FName
      frmFile.Show    ' New line.
      Exit Sub        ' New line.
   End If
```

14 Run the program. Test the code by selecting New or Open.

15 Save the form, project, and code module files.

QUESTIONS AND ACTIVITIES

1. For a drive box, why does it make sense that the Drive property is only available at run-time?

2. The Path property of a directory box can be assigned string values and string values can be read from the Path property. What directory box event causes the contents of the Path property to change?

3. What happens when a new path is assigned to the Path property of a file box?

4. Add some file error handling to the mnuFile_Click event of the Edit form. If a bad file name is entered, the program crashes. Trap this error with an **On Error Go To** statement. The handler should call frmFile to get a filename from the user.

5. Add a Save As command to the File menu in the Edit form. This choice should always call frmFile to get a file and pathname from the user.

6. Add a separate menu item to the File menu in the Edit form just to collect a file and pathname.

7. The Test form opens files when the user wants to take a test. Add a file menu command to the menu in the Test form. Provide a single command to collect the file and pathname from the user.

Summary

The greatest common factor (gcf) is the largest number that divides evenly into two given numbers. The gcf of 12 and 16 is 4. You can find the gcf of very large numbers quickly with the Euclidean algorithm.

The code module is a collection of type definitions, variable declarations, and procedure definitions (both sub and function procedures) that are available to every form in a project.

Value parameters are values sent to subprograms without reference to the actual address of the value being sent. The values can be changed within the subprogram without affecting the value of the variable in the calling program.

When parameters are sent by reference to a subprogram, the subprogram is given the address of the value being sent. Because the subprogram knows the real location of the variable in memory, it can make changes to the value of the variable.

Parameters sent by value to a Visual Basic subprogram must be of the built-in Visual Basic types. A user-defined type may not be sent as a value parameter.

There are two ways to call a procedure:

- Subtract *a, b, Rslt*

- Call subtract(*a, b, Rslt*)

When command buttons are given the same name, they form a control array. The first button is assigned an index value of 0 and the second a value of 1. Subsequent buttons added to the array receive successive index values.

The **Hide** and **Show** methods deactivate and activate forms in your project.

A listbox uses ListIndex property indicating a selected entry in a listbox.

The **Asc()** function and the **Chr$()** functions are inverse functions. The first converts a character to its ASCII code. The second converts an ASCII code to its corresponding character.

The drive box allows the user to choose from a listing of active drives. The drive name is available at run-time in the Drive property.

The Change event is often used to transfer drive information from the Drive property of the drive box to the Path property of the directory box.

The directory box lists the directories of the drive specified in its run-time only Path property. The value of the Path property is changed by double-clicking an entry in the window. This path information is often written using a Change event procedure to the Path property of a file box.

The file box displays the files listed in the directory written into the Path property of the box.

Problems

1. The Mixed Numerals Problem

Rewrite the routines to display and read the fractions from the Fraction Handler program to accept and display numbers expressed as mixed numerals. Instead of entering $\frac{5}{3}$rds, allow the user to enter $1\frac{2}{3}$rds. Instead of displaying the answer $\frac{31}{30}$ths, display the mixed numeral $1\frac{1}{30}$th. You'll need extra textboxes, but you should be able to use the same fraction arithmetic routines.

2. Plotting 1/x Problem

Write a program that will plot the function **f(x) = 1/x** for values of x between 0 and 10. Use an **On Error Resume Next** statement to avoid any run time errors. Use a user-defined coordinate system in a picture box. Pick a large maximum value for the y axis.

3. The Two Correct Answers Program

Make a plan to modify the code of the Quiz program to allow two correct answers for each question. Your plan should mention all the areas of code and forms that change, giving specific examples of how you would change the code.

4. The Creating a True/False Test Program

Write a program to create and store a 20-question true/false test. Don't worry about any editing functions (such as deleting or updating); just accept questions and answers from a form, store in an array, and transfer to a file.

5. The Reading a Test Program

Write a program to read the file created in problem 4 and give the test to the user. At the end of the test, print the raw score and the percent correct.

6. The Tutorial Program

Pick one of your favorite activities and write a program that will display a tutorial for that activity. The program should allow the user to create a list of instructions guiding the user through the various parts of the activity. For each instruction, store an additional line with further explanation.

The program should also handle displaying the tutorial. The user should be prompted for a filename. The activities should appear one by one on the screen advancing one frame each time a button is clicked. An additional button should display the extra explanation.

Write the program so that, by assigning different file names, you can record instructions for any number of activities.

7.   The Store Inventory Program

Write a program to maintain a store's inventory file. Each item in the file should have a name, a quantity, and a cost. The edit functions of the program should include the ability to add items, delete items, and update the quantity of items. The display portion of the program should display a listing of all the items in inventory along with all the information recorded about each item.

8.   The Substitution Code Program

Using the **Asc()** and the **Chr$()** functions create a simple substitution code. Enter a string in a textbox, use **Mid$()** to peel it apart, and store the individual characters in an array (the array is really unnecessary). Convert each character to its ASCII code, add two (or three or whatever you like) and, using **Chr$()**, convert the code back into a character. Be sure the last letters of the alphabet are converted to the first letters (hint: you might want to use the Mod operator). Replace the original message entered in a textbox with the modified message.

```
For x = 0 To
ScaleWidth Step 500
every 500 twips
For y = 0 To
ScaleHeight Step
500
PSet
PSet (x, y)
Next y
Next x
```

Chapter 13

Multiple Document Interface and Advanced Graphics

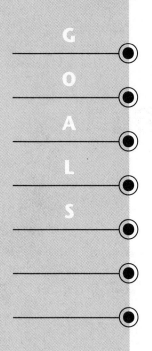

After working through this chapter, you will be able to:

Use option buttons and check boxes in programs.

Implement the Multiple Document Interface in programs that call for such an approach.

Program graphing algorithms for various functions.

Use the MouseDown, MouseUp, and MouseMove events.

Use the **PSet**, **Line**, and **Circle** methods to draw various shapes and figures.

Use static and global variables as flags and indicators.

O V E R V I E W

This chapter looks at three types of tools:
- *Controls*
  - *Option button*
  - *Check box*
- *Mouse events*
- *Multiple Document Interface*
  - *Parent forms*
  - *Child forms*

The Truth in Lending program in the first section lets the user calculate the annual percentage rate of a loan given the monthly payment, the original principle of the loan, and the number of years over which the loan is to be repaid. As you build the program, you will use option buttons to indicate the format of the display and the number of payments made per year.

The Multiple Document Interface (MDI) is described in the second section. MDI creates a parent form as a container for all the child forms of a project. When a child form becomes active, its menu bar replaces that of the parent form. This Multiple Document Interface is used in many Windows applications. You can use it to make your programs have the same "look and feel" as other Windows programs.

The Drawing project described in the third section lets the user customize a drawing utility. In this program you let the user express preferences, by giving him or her more choices than in any program you have written so far. You will learn how to provide those choices and write code that accommodates them. The program also illustrates the Mouse events recognized by forms and picture boxes. Mouse events occur when a mouse button is pressed or released or when the mouse is moved. Each of these events generates an event. Finally, the Drawing project provides a framework for additional work with graphics commands (fourth section).

Option Buttons, Check Boxes, and Frames

Section

Figure 13-1 shows the positions of the frame control, check box, and option button in the Toolbox. You can use these controls to simplify the user interface, making it easier to use and understand. A frame groups related controls. With check and option boxes, you can let the user interact with a program with clicks instead of by adding text.

You will add option buttons to the Truth in Lending program. This program calculates the annual percentage rate of a loan, given information about the payments and duration of the loan. Whether you are thinking of a car loan or a college loan, you can see what the loan costs using this program. Knowing the true cost of a loan (including interest) helps you choose the right loan. In this program, a user chooses the number of payments per year and the format of the output by clicking on option buttons.

Figure 13-1

Position of controls in Toolbox

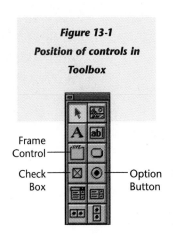

Looking at the Objects

Typically, you group options buttons and check boxes with frames. The frame serves to group the controls together, so the user will understand they stand as a group.

OPTION BUTTONS AND CHECK BOXES

Figure 13-2 shows two frames, each containing two option buttons. The two payments option buttons are related to each other, as are the two format option buttons. Related option buttons must appear in the same frame or on the same form.

Figure 13-2

Two sets of related option buttons

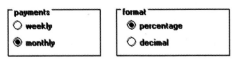

Using the payments group, a user determines the number of payments made in a year. Using the format group, a user selects the display format of the program's output. The output of the Truth in Lending program is a percentage. The user may choose to view the percentage as a decimal with four decimal places, or as a percentage with two decimal places.

To select an option button, a user clicks on it. As you can see from the example, option buttons represent nonoverlapping choices. Payments are made either weekly or monthly, not both. Output is displayed as a percentage or decimal, not both. Users can select only a single option button from a group of related option buttons. If a user clicks on one button, then on another, the first button is turned off. This is an excellent reason to group option buttons with frames, so that it's clear which buttons are related to each other. You will sometimes find it convenient to make a control array out of all the option buttons in a group.

Option buttons within the same frame are grouped together. Clicking an option button in the payments group will not affect the buttons in the format group. When a button is clicked, the value of its Value property becomes **True**, and the values of all related buttons (buttons within the same frame), become **False**.

Option buttons are also known as radio buttons. This name is easy to remember because there is a similarity between option buttons and the buttons on your car radio. You can only select a single station on your radio. When you press a button to select a station, the previously pressed button is unpressed.

Check boxes are also set up in related groups, with related check boxes appearing in the same frame or on the same form. You use check boxes to provide a list of parameters, more than one of which can be set on at the same time. For instance, you may have a frame with check boxes designating the style for the text in a document. A user may select any number of style elements, or none at all. The text may be bold and underlined, one or the other, or neither. See Figure 13-3. When a user clicks on a check box, any other selected check boxes remain selected.

PUTTING THE CONTROLS IN A FRAME

To put option buttons into a frame, you must first place the frame on the form. Do not start by double-clicking on the option button icon or the check box icon. After one of these controls is placed directly on a form, you cannot move it into a frame.

Click on the frame icon, move the mouse pointer to where you want the upper-left corner of the frame, then press and drag to the frame's lower-right corner. As soon as you release the mouse button, the frame appears.

To change the heading, edit the Caption property of the frame. To place option buttons in the frame, click the option button icon in the Toolbox. Click and drag to position the option button within the frame. As soon as you release the mouse button, the option button appears.

Change the label for the option button by changing the Caption property of the control. Using the Name property, give the option button an appropriate name that begins with an "opt" prefix, such as optWeekly or optMonthly.

An important property of option buttons and check boxes is the Value property. This property is a toggle with two possible values: True or False. A value of True indicates that the button or check box is selected. In code, you can refer to the option button or check box by name, then set values within the procedures on the basis of whether the Value property of the control is set to **True** or **False**.

Option button values are read by the program to determine the user's preferences. In addition, the option button controls themselves generate event procedures. In the Truth in Lending program, for example, whenever any of the options is changed, the cmdCalc_Click() event is executed. Clicking the option button sets its Value to **True**. This event is attached to a command button that calculates all the output of the program.

```
Sub optDecimal_Click ()
    Call cmdCalc_Click
End Sub
```

Truth in Lending Program

The goal of the program is to calculate the annual percentage rate of a loan along with the total finance charge that would be paid by the time the loan is paid off. To make these calculations, the program must prompt the user for three pieces of necessary information: the size of the monthly payment, the original amount of the loan, and the duration of the loan.

Figure 13-3
Selecting check boxes

As you have done in other programs, you use labeled textboxes for this purpose (Figure 13-4). Also as you have done in other programs, you should provide default values in these textboxes. In addition, default values should be entered for the option buttons. Then, the user only needs to click on the Calculate button to see the program work.

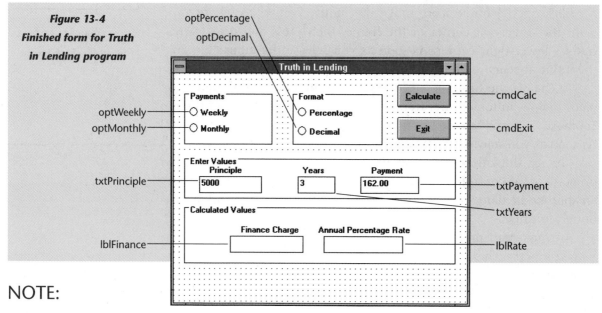

Figure 13-4
Finished form for Truth in Lending program

optPercentage
optDecimal

optWeekly
optMonthly

txtPrinciple

lblFinance

cmdCalc
cmdExit

txtPayment
txtYears

lblRate

Another piece of the puzzle is the number of payments made on the loan. The duration of the loan in years is part of the answer, but you also need another piece of information:

 # Payments = number of years * payments per year

What are the advantages of using a set of option buttons to find out the number of payments per year? You could use a textbox, but users will appreciate just having to click on a choice. Also, with option buttons, you know exactly what the possible responses are as the program runs. You do not have to be concerned with having the program interpret responses such as "4x/mo" from a textbox.

The second set of option buttons on the form cover the format of the final output. This user input is not necessary to perform the program's calculations; instead, the program uses it to provide the data in the desired format.

If the user clicks any of the option buttons, the option button Click event handler will call the cmdCalc_Click routine, which calculates new values for the finance charge and the annual percentage rate (APR).

This formula is used to calculate the total finance charge:

Finance charge = monthly payment* # payments - principal

SETTING UP THE FORM

Set up the Truth in Lending form using Figure 13-4 as a guide.

CODING THE CALCULATE BUTTON

The cmdCalc_click() routine starts by collecting values from the three textboxes: textPrincipal, txtYears, and txtPayment. To determine the number of payments per year, the program reads the Value property assigned to one of the option buttons from the Payments frame. You can use either button to set up the **If-Then** statement: if one is true, the other must be false.

The condition portion of the **If-Then** statement may seem strange to you:

```
If optWeekly Then
    PayPerYear = 52
```

The program treats the name of the button (optWeekly) as either a **True** or **False** value. If the button is selected, optWeekly is **True**; if it is not selected, optWeekly is **False**. The name of the button, then, represents the button's Value property at the time the Calculate button is clicked.

After the number of payments has been determined, the appropriate value, 12 or 52, is assigned to the *PayPerYear* variable. This program uses this value to calculate the total finance charge and the annual percentage rate (APR). You will be using this statement to calculate the APR:

```
APR = 2 * PayPerYear * Finance / (Principal * (NumberPay + 1))
```

This statement is based on the following formula.
APR = 2 * # of payments per yr. * total finance charge / loan amount * (# of payments + 1)

As a final step after the annual percentage has been calculated, the option buttons in the Format frame are read to determine the display format.

To write this code:

1 Double-click on the Calculate button to open the Code window and enter this code between the first and last lines of the subroutine:

```
'—Local declarations
Dim NumberPay, Years, Principal
Dim PayPerYear, Payment, Finance, APR
```

continued

```
'—Read the textboxes
Principal = Val(txtPrincipal.Text)
Years = Val(txtYears.Text)
Payment = Val(txtPayment.Text)
'—Check the option button
If optWeekly Then    'equivalent to: If optWeekly = True
    PayPerYear = 52
Else
    PayPerYear = 12
End If
'—Calculate the number of payments
NumberPay = PayPerYear * Years
'—Calculate and display the total finance charge
Finance = Payment * NumberPay - Principal
lblFinance = Format(Finance, "currency")
'—Calculate annual percentage rate, APR
APR = 2 * PayPerYear * Finance / (Principal * (NumberPay + 1))
'—Check the Format frame buttons
If optDecimal Then
    lblRate = Format(APR, "0.00###")
Else
    lblRate = Format(APR, "Percent")
End If
```

2 Save the form and project files.

3 Run the program. Click on the Calculate button and note the results.

4 Click on the Weekly option button. Click on Calculate and note the results.

5 Experiment with different values for the principle, the years, and the payment.

QUESTIONS AND ACTIVITIES

1. Set up the frame and option buttons necessary to let a user choose between temperature measured in Fahrenheit and Celsius. Set the Caption, Name, and Value properties.

2. What happens to an option button in a frame when an option button on the form is clicked? To find out, put a third option button onto the form created for problem 1 above. Use a message box to display the values of the all three option buttons (Fahrenheit, Celsius, and the third button) when the value of the third button changes.

3. Create a frame with properly labeled check boxes for choosing type style. Provide choices of bold, underline, italic, strikethrough, superscript, and subscript. Give appropriate names to the check boxes. Use the Value properties to set Bold and Underline to **True**.

4. Modify the program code and the form of the Truth in Lending program to include a display label for the total amount paid back over the life of the loan. To calculate this amount, multiply the total number of payments by the payment entered by the user. Display the result, in currency format.

5. What are the differences and similarities between option buttons and check boxes?

6. What is the significance of placing two or more option buttons within a frame?

7. Option buttons and check boxes have properties and generate events. What are two significant properties of these controls and why are they significant? What is one significant event of each, and why is it significant?

8. Given a monthly payment of $401.24, a four-year loan, and an initial loan amount of $14,560, use the Truth in Lending program to calculate the total finance charge for the loan.

Multiple Forms Within a Form

Section

In the Truth in Lending program, you used frames to group option buttons. In the exercises following the program, you used frames to group related check boxes. In both cases, frames worked well as containers for controls. Sometimes, however, you need a container that is bigger than a frame. You need a container that can contain forms. In these cases, you can use a special kind of a form called an MDI form as a container for other forms.

In Microsoft Word or another word processing application, you have probably opened more than one file at a time. By using the Window menu, you can move between one file and another. You can also move material from one file to another by cutting and pasting. Each of the documents is held in its own form. See Figure 13-5.

When you open Microsoft Word, a document is already loaded called **doc1.doc**. You can use this document to create a file, or you can open a previously saved file. Have you noticed that the Word menu bar

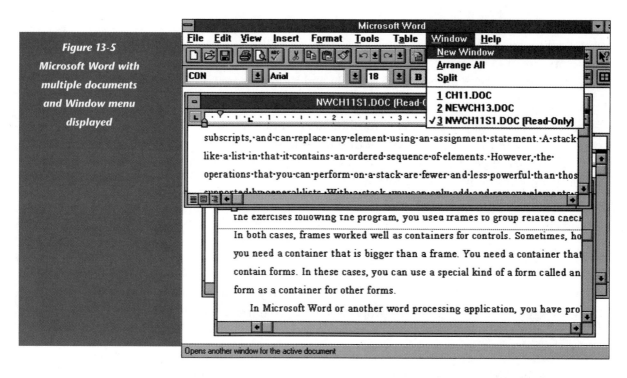

Figure 13-5
Microsoft Word with
multiple documents
and Window menu
displayed

looks different when one or more documents is open, compared to when all documents are closed? Figure 13-6 shows the menu bar with a document open. Figure 13-7 shows the menu bar with all active documents closed.

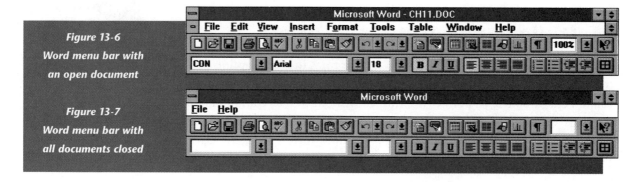

Figure 13-6
Word menu bar with
an open document

Figure 13-7
Word menu bar with
all documents closed

Each of these Word documents exists in its own form.

When you have closed all the documents, there is still a form open. This is the parent form. Any document you open is placed in a child form. The child forms are identical copies of each other (except, of course, that the documents placed in them are probably different).

When a child form is created and loaded, its menu bar replaces the menu bar of the parent form. When that document is closed, the child form is unloaded and the menu bar of the parent form becomes active again. Typically, choices in the menu bar of the parent form activate various child forms. A child form may include a menu command that executes the code to *unload* the child and return control to the parent form. Several child forms may be open at one time within a parent form.

Working with MDI: Stage 1

In this first stage, you create an MDI parent form and experiment with what kinds of controls can be placed on the form. You will find a number of restrictions that don't apply to normal forms. In addition, you turn the default form into a child form and experiment with maximizing and minimizing the child form within the parent while the program is running.

Experiment with the Multiple Document Interface by following these steps:

1   Start Visual Basic. If Visual Basic is running, select New Project from the File menu.

2   Choose New MDI Form from the File menu to open a form on the screen. The default name and caption of this form is MDIform1. See Figure 13-8. This is a parent form.

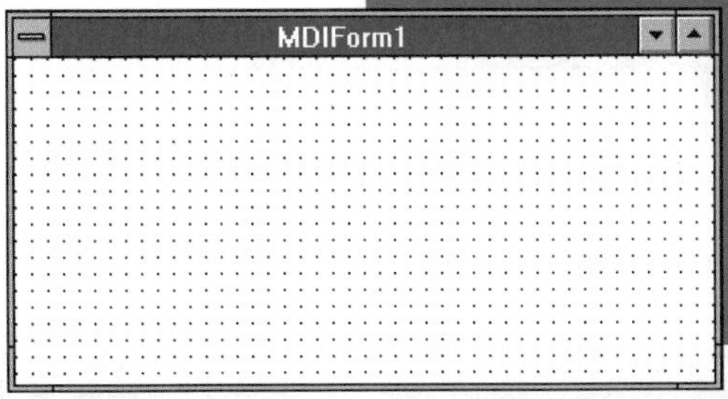

3   Open the Project window from the Window menu. See Figure 13-9. Notice that both the icon and the name of the MDI form is different from that of a non-MDI form.

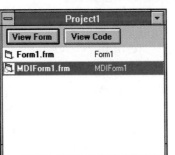

Figure 13-8
Newly created MDI form

Figure 13-9
Project window displaying new MDI form

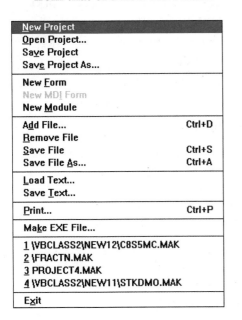

4   Open the File menu again. As you can see, the command New MDI form is dimmed. An application can have only a single MDI parent form, although it may have many child forms. See Figure 13-10.

Figure 13-10
File menu with command dimmed

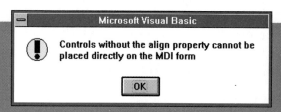

Figure 13-11
Experimenting with
adding controls to the
parent form

5 Select the MDI parent form, then double-click on the textbox icon in the Toolbox. What happens? See Figure 13-11.

As you can see, you cannot place any control that lacks the Align property on a MDI form. That includes, for example, textboxes, labels, and command buttons (though you can create menus for these forms).

6 Double-click on the picture box icon in the Toolbox to place a picture box on the form. See Figure 13-12.

The only control that you can place on a MDI form is a picture box. The toolbars you see in many Windows applications are actually picture boxes that stretch from one side of the form to the other.

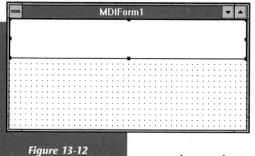

Figure 13-12
Placing a picture box
on a MDI form

7 Try to resize the picture box by selecting the box and dragging the handles. You can adjust the box's height, but not its width. The box is always the same width as the parent form. The part of the parent form not covered by a picture box is called the client area. All child forms you create will be scaled to fit in this area.

8 Turn the default form (form1.frm) into a child form. Make that form active, open its Properties window, and toggle the MDIChild property of the form to **True**. During design time, you will not notice any change resulting from the toggle.

Figure 13-13
MDI parent and child
form in run mode

9 Change the BackColor property of Form1.

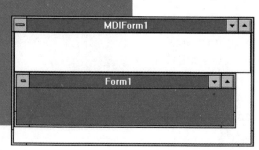

10 Run the program from the toolbar and note the results. See Figure 13-13. What happened? You design each child form independently of the parent form. Both parent and child forms can have menus, and child forms may have menus that are different from each other. Whenever a child form is loaded, its menu bar, if it has one, replaces the menu bar of the parent form.

11 Click on the maximize button in the upper-right corner of the child form.

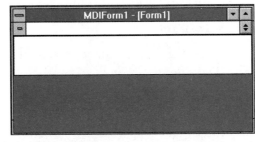

Figure 13-14

Maximized child form

12 When a child form is max-imized, its name is added to the name of the MDI parent in the caption. See Figure 13-14.
Note that the area occu-pied by the picture box has not been covered by the child form.

13 Restore the child form by clicking on the restore box in the upper-right corner of the form.

14 Minimize the child form by clicking the minimize button.

15 Note the results. The icon representing the form is contained in the parent form. See Figure 13-15.

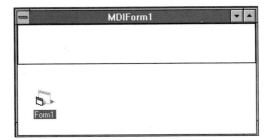

Figure 13-15

Minimized child form represented by an icon in the parent form

Working with MDI: Stage 2

In this stage, you create additional child forms, giving each a distinctive caption. With the program running you'll activate one form after another and experiment with minimizing and maximizing the forms.

To continue your work with MDI:

1 Change the name of the MDI parent form to **USA**.

2 Change the name of form1 to **Illinois**.

3 Add another form to the project. Set the MDIChild property to **True**. Change the caption to **Texas**.

4 Add another form to the project. Set the MDIChild property to **True**. Change the caption to **California**.

5 Add another form to the project. Set the MDIChild property to **True**. Change the caption to **New York**.

6 Select the parent form. Delete the picture box.

7 Double-click on the Illinois form to open the Code window. Enter the form_Click procedure and enter the following line of code:

```
form2.Show
```

8 Double-click on the Texas form to enter its Code window. Enter the form_Click procedure and enter the following line of code:

```
form3.Show
```

9 Alter the California form similarly.

10 Run the program. Click on the Illinois form. Click on the Texas form. Click on the California form. See Figure 13-16.

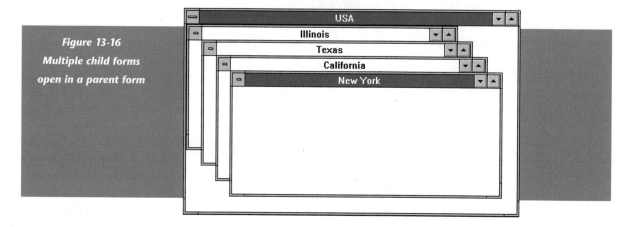

Figure 13-16
Multiple child forms
open in a parent form

11 Minimize each of the forms. See Figure 13-17.

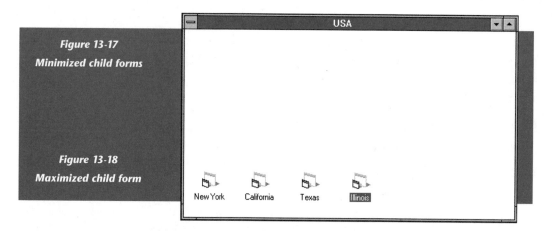

Figure 13-17
Minimized child forms

Figure 13-18
Maximized child form

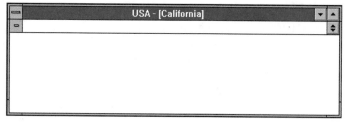

12 Click on the California form and maximize the form. The caption of the child form joins the caption of the parent. See Figure 13-18.

13 Close the project without saving.

QUESTIONS

1. Describe the relationship between the parent form and the child forms in the Multiple Document Interface.

2. What are some of the significant differences between a MDI parent form and a regular form?

3. How are picture boxes used in conjunction with a MDI form?

4. What is the client area in a parent form?

The Drawing Project

Section

Visual Basic is a very rich language. There are so many features it's hard to know where to stop. This section looks again at mouse events. A drawing application that allows the user to draw lines, rectangles, triangles, and circles on a form using mouse events and graphics methods is presented in this section; the finished form is shown in Figure 13-19.

If you've used the Paintbrush program, you may have noted some of its limitations. It's hard to accurately position circles in a drawing, for example. There is no freestyle drawing mode. To create triangles, you have to carefully align the third side to connect to the other two sides. You don't have the option of using a grid to place objects accurately. The drawing application you create in this section addresses several of these deficiencies. In addition, you can add or alter features to meet your particular needs.

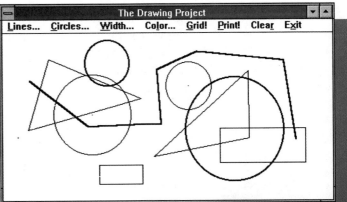

Figure 13-19
Finished form for the drawing project

While writing the program, you'll be reviewing a number of events generated by the mouse. You'll use the **Line** and **Circle** methods introduced in a previous chapter. And, you'll use variables as flags indicating the current state of the drawing. As a result, you'll be better able to use mouse events and graphics routines in your programs.

More on Mouse Events

Forms respond to many events. The Form_Load event, for example, is executed whenever the form is activated. As a result, it is a good place to put start-up code for an application. For this Drawing program, four events generated by mouse clicks are particularly important. These are:

- ◉ MouseDown
- ◉ MouseUp
- ◉ MouseMove
- ◉ Click

Think about how you work in other drawing programs. Often, for example, you select a shape, such as a rectangle, with a mouse, then click and drag in the window to draw the rectangle. In that process, you generated all four of the events listed above. These events control the drawing on the form.

For example, in many drawing programs, you see dotted lines outlining shapes you are drawing; when you release the mouse, the shapes appear. What makes a shape appear at that point? It appears because the designer of the program wrote the appropriate code for the MouseUp event.

MOUSEDOWN EVENT

The MouseDown event is generated when a user depresses the mouse button. Clicking the mouse button is the rapid depression and release of the button. The first part of a click, when the button is pressed, is called pressing or depressing the mouse button. The event procedure has four parameters:

```
Sub Form_MouseDown (Button As Integer, Shift As
Integer, x As Single, y As Single)
```

The *Button* parameter indicates which mouse button is pressed (your mouse may have two or three buttons). The *Shift* parameter indicates whether the user pressed the Alt, Control, or Shift keys in combination with pressing the mouse button.

The *X* and *Y* parameters represent the coordinates of the mouse pointer at the time the user pressed the mouse button. The units in which these coordinates are reported depend on which coordinate system has been selected. In this Drawing program, you will leave the default coordinate system, the twip system, unchanged. The Scale-Height and ScaleWidth properties of the form hold the dimensions of the form in twips.

CLICK EVENT

In addition to the MouseDown and MouseUp events, depressing and then releasing a mouse button with the pointer over the same control or form generates another event: a Click event. The MouseDown and MouseUp events correspond to individual physical actions. By contrast, the Click event is a higher-level abstraction, a logical event that Visual Basic detects and informs your program about by calling a click handler. The Click event of a form or control occurs when the user presses a mouse button with the cursor over that object, and then releases the same button with the cursor over that same object. In between the button press and release, the user may move the mouse outside the object; a Click event will still occur.

When the mouse button is clicked, the status of the Alt, Control, and Shift keys, and the position of the mouse pointer, are not available with the Click or the DblClick procedures. If you need to know the location where the mouse button is released when you process a Click event, you should handle the MouseUp event by saving the coordinates of the mouse cursor, and then use these values in the Click or DblClick event, which will occur *after* the MouseUp event.

MOUSEUP AND MOUSEMOVE EVENTS

The MouseUp event and the MouseMove event are both sent the same parameters as the MouseDown event: *Button*, *Shift*, *X*, and *Y*. The MouseUp event is generated when the mouse button is released. A MouseMove event is generated when the coordinates of the mouse pointer change.

Starting Out

You may have experimented with drawing programs before. If so, what did you think of them? Could you do everything you wanted to do? Chances are, you found something that didn't seem quite right to you. It is almost impossible to design a drawing tool that everyone will think is perfect. This section explains how to create the rudiments of a new drawing tool. You will then have the opportunity to customize and enhance the tool to fit your specific preferences.

Like many of the programs covered in this book, the Drawing project is deliberately left unfinished. It runs and it is useful as it stands; yet it suffers from the same serious limitation of other drawing programs you may have tried. It has not been customized for your purposes.

Before you start customizing, start with the basics. Which shapes will the user be able to draw with this program? Start with the obvious ones:

- Single lines, drawn from point to point

- Continuous lines, drawn from point to point to point

- Freestyle lines, lines drawn to follow the mouse movement as long as the button is depressed

- Triangles, drawn between three points

- Rectangles, sides parallel to the form, drawn from one corner to another

- Circles, drawn by clicking the center and a point on the circle

- Circles, drawn by clicking the endpoints of a diameter of the circle

Besides drawing shapes, users will want to perform functions such as modifying their drawings and so forth. What functionality are you going to provide? There is much you could add; for now, stay with these:

- Changing the line width

- Changing the color of the line drawn

- Printing the form

- Providing a grid on the form to aid alignment

- Clearing the form

Program development starts with setting goals for the program. In this case, the goals listed above were designed to remedy some of the limitations of other drawing programs, specifically Paintbrush. Once the goals are set, think through the techniques you'll use to actually write the program: the variables needed, the graphic methods used, how you'll handle differentiating between the three points of a triangle.

Much of the program development is determined by the user interface you design. Once the menu structure is determined, a lot of other program elements fall into place. You will develop the program in this order:

- Define the user interface (the menu)

- Declare and initialize the variables

- Code the routines that control the drawing of circles

- Code the line drawing routines

- Code the grid, colors, and line widths

- Code the mouse event routines

Creating the Menu

The program needs only a single form, so most of the work on the look-and-feel of the program goes into the menu.

The menu itself is arranged to meet the goals for the program discussed above. You may have goals of your own for the project. If so, this is a good place to decide how you will implement those goals. The first step in designing the menu structure is to identify components that go together. There are two kinds of circles—they should share a single menu. There are three types of lines, as well as two shapes made of lines: the triangle and the rectangle. They could all share the same menu or they could be split into two menus: a line menu and a shape menu.

Another decision to make concerns building menu control arrays. Can two or more menu items be grouped together in the same event procedure? Only closely related actions should share the same procedure.

As you look over the menu structure given below, see if you agree with the design decisions that have been made. Change any items that seem wrong. Add new items to make the program more useful.

To create the menu for the Drawing project:

1 Create a new directory for the Drawing project.

2 Start Visual Basic. If Visual Basic is running, click New Project from the File menu.

3 Change the name of the default form to **frmDrawing**. Change the caption of the form to **The Drawing Project**.

4 Open the Menu Design window (Figure 13-20), then use the chart below to create the menu for the Drawing project.

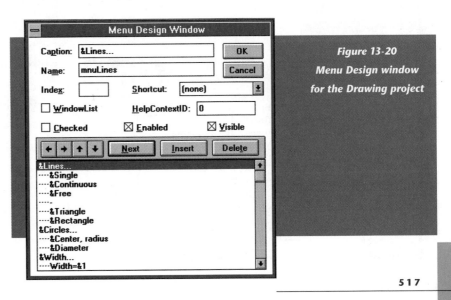

Figure 13-20
Menu Design window
for the Drawing project

Menu Item	Event Name	Description
&Lines...	mnuLines	initializes True/False variables
&Single	cmdLines()	sets True/False
&Continuous	cmdLines()	sets True/False
&Free	cmdLines()	sets True/False
&Triangle	cmdTriangle	sets True/False
&Rectangle	cmdRectangle	sets True/False
&Circles...	mnuCircle	initializes True/False variables
&Center, radius	cmdCircle()	sets True/False
&Diameter	cmdCircle()	sets True/False
&Width...	mnuWidth	no function
Width=&1	cmdWidth()	set DrawWidth to 1
Width=&2	cmdWidth()	set DrawWidth to 2
Width=&3	cmdWidth()	set DrawWidth to 3
Width=&5	cmdWidth()	set DrawWidth to 5
&Choice	cmdWidth()	user enters DrawWidth
Co&lor	mnuColor	no function
&Black	cmdColor()	sets Colr=QBColor(0)
B&lue	cmdColor()	Colr=QBColor(1)
&Red	cmdColor()	Colr=QBColor(4)
&Green	cmdColor()	Colr=QBColor(2)
&Yellow	cmdColor()	Colr=QBColor(14)
&Choice	cmdColor()	user enters color number
&Grid!	cmdGrid	sets grid of points
&Print!	cmdPrint	prints form
Clea&r	cmdClear	clears form
E&xit	cmdExit	exits program

Figure 13-25
Color menu for the
Drawing project

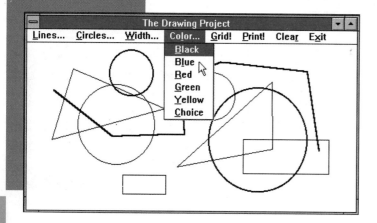

5 When the menu is complete, close the Menu Design window. The Color menu is shown in Figure 13-21.

Visual Basic lets you reposition and resize the form to accommodate the size of your drawing.

Working with the Global Variables

Before you start writing code for the project, you should determine the variables you are going to need. If any of those variables are going to be used by more than one event procedure, you should make them global variables by declaring them in the general declarations section of the form.

Table 13-1 suggests which variables you should declare as global and briefly explains their use. Except for the variable *Colr*, each one is used as a **True/False** (or Boolean) variable indicating the status of some aspect of the program. Some of these variables indicate whether the user has chosen a particular option such as the continuous line style. The rest are used by the program to keep track of when the user is in the process of drawing a figure using the mouse. The *Colr* variable is used to represent the value returned by the **QBColor()** function in the routine that sets the drawing color.

Table 13-1. Variables for the Drawing Project

Name	Use
Sing	Set to True when the "single" line option is selected.
Cntin	Set to True when the "continuous" line option is selected.
Fre	Set to True when the "freestyle" line drawing tool is selected.
Drwing	Set to True when a Figure is being drawn.
Center	Set to True when a circle specified by clicking the center and a point on the circle is being drawn.
Diameter	Set to True when a circle specified by clicking the endpoints of a diameter is being drawn.
Triangle	Set to True when the triangle option is selected.
Rectangle	Set to True when the rectangle option is selected.
Colr	Set to the color number.

Declare these variables in the general declarations section of the form:

```
Option Explicit
Dim Sing As Integer, Cntin As Integer, Fre As Integer
Dim Colr As Long, Drwing As Integer
Dim Center As Integer, Diameter As Integer
Dim Triangle As Integer, Rectangle As Integer
```

Setting the Boolean Variables

When the user clicks on Lines or Circles on the menu bar, a drop-down menu appears. The Lines menu contains various lines and polygons supported by the program. The Circles menu contains choices for the two circles drawn by the program.

Each of the event procedures called by these menu choices sets one or more of the global variables to True, indicating that, for instance, a single line is to be drawn. The drawing actually occurs in the Mouse-Down event handler.

Each command of the Lines and Circles submenus sets one of these **True/False** variables. The main menu command itself—&Lines, &Circles—also generates a Click event when that item is clicked. In previous programs, this event has been ignored for menu commands that have submenus. In this program, it is used to initialize the **True/False** variables to **False**.

To set the Boolean variables:

1 Select frmDrawing from the Project window.

2 Click on View Code.

3 Enter these lines in the mnuCircle() procedure:

```
'—Turn off each kind of circle
Center = False
Diameter = False
mnuLines_Click   ' Turn off all the lines
```

4 Enter these lines in the mnuLines() procedure:

```
'—An itemized list of all the True/False variables
Drwing = False     ' not drawing
Sing = False     ' single lines
Cntin = False     ' continuous lines
Fre = False     ' freestyle lines
Triangle = False     ' triangles
Rectangle = False     ' rectangles
Center = False     ' circles from center and point
Diameter = False     ' circles from diameters
```

Coding the Circles Menu

Selecting Circles from the menu bar lets the user draw circles by choosing a center and a point on the circle's circumference, or by selecting two endpoints of the circle's diameter. Both commands on the menu call the same event procedures, making them part of a menu control array. The first command generates an index of 1 and the second, an index of 2. You use the **Select Case** statement to choose between the two. If a user selects the "center" type circle, the Circle variable is set to **True**. If a user chooses a "diameter" type circle instead, the Diameter variable is set to **True**. These values control the drawing of each figure.

To write the necessary code:

1   Select frmDrawing from the Project window.

2   Click on View Code.

3   Enter these lines in the cmdCircle_Click() procedure.

```
Select Case index
    Case 1     ' center to radius type circle
        center = True
    Case 2     ' diameter type circle
        diameter = True
End Select
```

Coding the Lines Menu

By selecting Lines from the menu bar, a user is presented with a choice between single lines, continuous lines, freestyle lines, triangles, and rectangles. Each of these call the same event procedures.

To code the menu:

1   Select frmDrawing from the Project window.

2   Click on View Code.

3   Enter these lines in the cmdLines_Click() procedure.

```
Select Case index
    Case 1     ' single lines
        Sing = True
    Case 2     ' continuous
        Cntin = True
    Case 3     ' free form
        Fre = True
End Select
```

Adding the Miscellaneous Routines

Follow these steps to code some miscellaneous routines.

1 Select frmDrawing from the Project window.

2 Click on View Code.

3 Type **End** in the cmdExit_Click() procedure.

4 Type **Cls** to clear the screen in the cmdClear_Click() procedure.

5 Type **PrintForm**, a command to print the active form, in cmdPrint_Click().

6 Enter the following line in cmdTriangle_Click().

```
Triangle = True
```

7 Enter the following line in cmdRectangle_Click().

```
Rectangle = True
```

Adding the Grid Routine

This routine has nothing to do with the grid control in the Visual Basic toolbox. This item calls a procedure to plot a grid of fine dots on the drawing area to help the user line up graphic elements. Using nested loops controlled by the values of the ScaleHeight and ScaleWidth properties of the form, it spaces small points every 500 twips from top to bottom and from side to side.

A MEMORY JOG

A twip is the measure used in the default coordinates system to measure graphic elements. A twip is 1/20th of a printer's point. It is the standard of all Windows graphics routines.

ScaleHeight is the height of the form expressed in twips. ScaleWidth is the width of the form expressed in twips.

The only challenge in the Grid procedure is saving the value of the DrawWidth property. The current value of the DrawWidth property is read and saved in a local variable, *d*. The DrawWidth is set to 1, to plot an inconspicuous point. When the loops have finished, the original value of DrawWidth is restored.

To code this routine:

1 Select frmDrawing from the Project window.

2   Click on View Code.

3   Enter these lines in cmdGrid_Click.

```
Dim x, y, d     ' local variables for the loops
d = DrawWidth     ' current value of DrawWidth
DrawWidth = 1     ' tiny point
For x = 0 To ScaleWidth Step 500 ' every 500 twips
   For y = 0 To ScaleHeight Step 500
      PSet (x, y), 0  ' color is black
   Next y
Next x
DrawWidth = d     ' restore the DrawWidth
```

Adding the Color Routine

When users select Color from the menu bar, they see a small selection of colors. The event procedure called by these menu items uses **QBColor()** to provide color information for the *Colr* variable. You will use this variable every time you use the **Line**, **PSet,** and **Circle** method to set the color of the lines and dots drawn.

Users can choose a new color at any point while they are drawing. The color may be changed in the middle of a "freestyle" line session or a "continuous" line sequence. The last item in the menu lets the user choose a color with which to draw, still using the **QBColor** function.

To add this routine:

1   Select frmDrawing from the Project window.

2   Click on View Code.

3   Enter these lines in cmdColor_Click.

```
Select Case Index
   Case 1
      Colr = QBColor(0)     ' black
   Case 2
      Colr = QBColor(1)     ' blue
   Case 3
      Colr = QBColor(4)     ' red
   Case 4
      Colr = QBColor(2)     ' green
   Case 5
      Colr = QBColor(14)     ' yellow
   Case 6
      Colr = QBColor(Val(InputBox("Enter color #<0-15>:", , "1")))
End Select
```

Adding the Line Width Routine

This routine lets the user choose a DrawWidth of 1,2,3, or 5 with a click of the mouse. A fifth item lets the user enter a value for the DrawWidth property of the form from the keyboard.

To add the routine:

1 Select frmDrawing from the Project window.

2 Click on View Code.

3 Enter these lines in cmdWidth_Click.

```
Select Case Index
   Case 1
      DrawWidth = 1
   Case 2
      DrawWidth = 2
   Case 3
      DrawWidth = 3
   Case 4
      DrawWidth = 5
   Case 5
      DrawWidth = Val(InputBox("Enter the width:", , "1"))
End Select
```

Drawing a Single Line

The purpose of this interlude is to try out the drawing program. As you go through the steps required to draw a line, the text describes what is going on "under the hood". The use of the Boolean variables is traced to show how the program knows what to do each step of the way.

To draw a single line on the form:

1 Click on the Lines menu command. Result: All **True/False** variables are set to false. This means no figure has yet been selected and drawing has not yet begun.

2 Click on the Single command. Result: the **True/False** variable *Sing* is set to **True**. A line is being drawn.

3 Click the mouse on the form. Result: The *Drwing* variable is checked. It is **False** (set in step 1), so the line drawing has just begun. *Drwing* is set to **True** and the first point of the line is PSet.

4 Click the mouse a second time. Result: *Drwing* is **True** (set in step three), so this is the second click. A line is drawn from the first point to the current position of the mouse pointer. Because single lines are being drawn, *Drwing* is reset to **False**.

Coding the MouseDown Event Procedure

The menu command handlers that have already been defined set Boolean variables which indicate what kind of figure is being drawn. The MouseDown event procedure actually handles drawing dots on the screen. The procedure uses the Boolean variables to determine what graphics methods to use to draw the figure.

1   Select frmDrawing from the Project window.

2   Click on View Code.

3   Enter these lines in the Form_MouseDown() procedure of the drawing form. These lines declare local variables. Static variables retain their values from call to call. x1 and y1 keep track of previously clicked positions.

```
Static x1 As Single, y1 As Single
'-P keeps track of point number
Static p
```

4   Enter the lines to handle single-line drawing as described above. Continue after the lines entered in step 3.

```
'-Single line handler
If Sing Then      ' single lines
   If Not Drwing Then
      Drwing = True     ' beginning of line
      PSet (x, y), Colr     ' initial point
   Else    ' second point of line
      Line -(x, y), Colr    ' draw to clicked spot
      Drwing = False    ' end of line
   End If
End If
```

5   Continuous lines are much like single lines. *Drwing* is not reset to **False** when the second point of the line is clicked. This allows line after line to be drawn. Enter these lines in the MouseDown event.

```
If Cntin Then     ' continuous lines
   If Not Drwing Then
      Drwing = True     ' start a set of lines
      PSet (x, y), Colr     ' at the clicked point
   Else
      Line -(x, y), Colr     ' draw to clicked spot
   End If
End If
```

6 Freestyle lines are drawn with the right mouse button. Hold the button and drag the mouse around the form. At the first mouse click, the first point is plotted and the *Drwing* variable is set to **True**. The rest of the drawing takes place in the MouseMove event to be presented later. Enter these lines in the MouseDown event.

```
'—Freestyle lines, use the right mouse button
If Fre And Button = 2 Then
    Drwing = True
    PSet (x, y), Colr
End If
```

7 To draw a triangle on the form, you need to differentiate between each of three clicks—one for each vertex of the triangle. In addition you need to store the coordinates of the first point clicked. You need those coordinates to draw the third side of the triangle. Enter these lines in the MouseDown event:

```
'—Triangle
If Triangle Then
    '—P keeps track of what point is being drawn
    If p = 0 Then     ' first point of triangle
        PSet (x, y), Colr
        x1 = x: y1 = y     ' save coordinates to close triangle
        p = 1              ' set p to next point
    ElseIf p = 1 Then     ' if second point,
        Line -(x, y), Colr     ' draw line from first to second
        p = 2     ' set p to next point
    ElseIf p = 2 Then     ' if third point
        Line -(x, y), Colr      ' draw line from second to third
        Line -(x1, y1), Colr     ' draw line from third to first
        p = 0                 ' reset p to first point
    End If
End If
```

8 Rectangles drawn by this program are specified by clicking on two opposite corners of the rectangle. Rectangles drawn from these points have sides parallel to the sides of the form. The coordinates of the first point are saved in the variables *x1* and *y1*. The *x* and *y* values of this coordinate are used to generate the appropriate **Line** methods. The diagram below shows how the coordinates of the first click, saved in *x1* and *y1*, are used along with the coordinates of the second mouse click to draw the sides of the rectangle. See Figure 13-22.

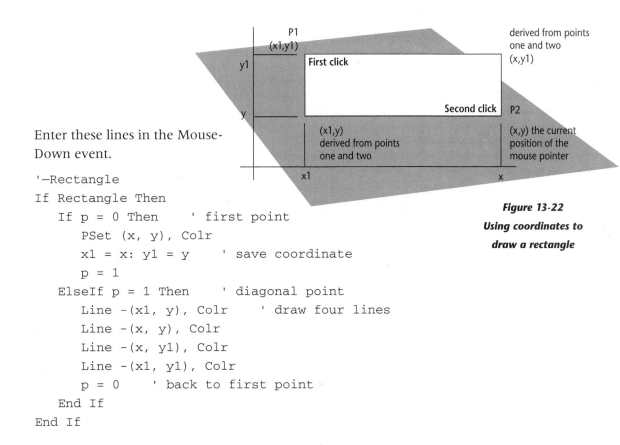

Figure 13-22

Using coordinates to draw a rectangle

Enter these lines in the Mouse-Down event.

```
'—Rectangle
If Rectangle Then
    If p = 0 Then     ' first point
        PSet (x, y), Colr
        x1 = x: y1 = y    ' save coordinate
        p = 1
    ElseIf p = 1 Then    ' diagonal point
        Line -(x1, y), Colr    ' draw four lines
        Line -(x, y), Colr
        Line -(x, y1), Colr
        Line -(x1, y1), Colr
        p = 0     ' back to first point
    End If
End If
```

THE CIRCLE METHOD

The **Circle** method has the syntax:

Circle *(x, y), r, color*

Where *(x,y)* is the center of the circle, *r* is the radius, and *color* is the color.

To draw a circle, use the first mouse click to determine the center of the circle, and the second to determine the radius. Plot a point at the center of the circle and save the coordinates in the variables *x1* and *y1*. Use the value of *p* to determine which point is being clicked: the center, or a point on the circle.

Once the second point is clicked, calculate the radius. The coordinates of the first point are *(x1,y1)*. The coordinates of the second point are the current values of the position of the mouse pointer, given by *X* and *Y*. A distance function is added to the general section of the form, to take care of the calculation. The length of the radius is calculated by using the distance formula and the coordinates of the two points.

9 For details on the **Circle** method, see the textbox. To code the method, enter these lines in the MouseDown event.

```
'—Circle with click on center and radius
If Center Then
    If p = 0 Then      ' first point is center
        PSet (x, y), Colr     ' plot center point
        x1 = x: y1 = y     ' save coordinates
        p = 1
    ElseIf p = 1 Then      ' second point is at the end of a radius
        '—Calculate the distance (the radius) and draw the circle.
        Circle (x1, y1), distance(x, y, x1, y1), Colr
        p = 0
    End If
End If
```

10 The second kind of circle is drawn by specifying the endpoints of the diameter of the circle. From these coordinates, the midpoint is found. The midpoint of the diameter is the center of the circle. The distance formula is called to find the radius.
Enter these final lines in the MouseDown event.

```
'—Draw circle with diameter
If diameter Then
    If p = 0 Then
        PSet (x, y), Colr   ' plot first point
        x1 = x: y1 = y      ' save coordinate
        p = 1
    ElseIf p = 1 Then
        '—Calculate midpoint of diameter, which is the center
        '—Calculate distance from the midpoint to the edge; the radius
        Circle ((x1 + x) / 2, (y1 + y) / 2), distance(x, y, x1, y1) / 2, Colr
        p = 0
    End If
End If
```

Coding the MouseMove and MouseUp Event Procedures

The MouseMove event continuously reports the position of the mouse pointer as the pointer is moved. This continuous reporting makes it the perfect routine to draw the "freestyle" or continuous lines. While the mouse is moving the MouseMove events updates the position of the pointer. The update occurs so frequently, and the lines drawn are so short, the result appears to be a continuous line that follows the position of the mouse pointer.

The MouseUp event terminates most drawing events. When the mouse button is released, the MouseUp event is fired. This resets the *Drwing* variable to **False**, which stops the drawing of any figure.

1   Enter these lines in the MouseMove event procedure:

```
'—If freestyle lines are being drawn, and
'Drwing is True, continue to draw lines from
'the last point plotted to the current position
'of the mouse pointer.
If Fre And Drwing Then
    Line -(x, y), Colr
End If
```

2   Enter this line in the MouseUp event procedure:

```
If Fre Then Drwing = False
```

Finishing Up

You are almost finished. Take these final steps:

1   The distance function is used to calculate the radius for use with the **Circle** method. Enter these lines in the general section of the form.

```
Function Distance (x1 As Single, y1 As Single, x2 As Single, y2 As
Single) As Single
    '—The distance function returns a single value,
    'the calculated distance between (x1,y1) and (x2,y2).
    Distance = Sqr((x1 - x2) ^ 2 + (y1 - y2) ^ 2)
End Function
```

2   Save the form and project files in the directory created for the project.

3   Run the program and try out each feature. See Figure 13-23.

Figure 13-23
Drawing with the
Drawing program

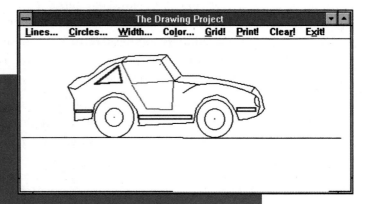

QUESTIONS AND ACTIVITIES

1. What are the four parameters sent to a MouseDown event? What is the purpose of each one?

2. Using the Visual Basic Help system, look up the Form object. What are the names and functions of two Form events that are not mentioned in this section?

3. Describe the differences and similarities of the Form_Click and the Form_MouseDown event procedures.

4. To explore the differences and similarities between the Form_Click event and the Form_MouseUp events, follow these steps:
   a) Create a new project. Add the following code to the project's form:
      Form_Click event: `MsgBox "Click!"`
      Form_MouseUp event: `MsgBox "MouseUp!"`
   b) Press the mouse button while the cursor is on the form (notice: there is no Click event), drag the mouse outside the form, and release the button. Again notice: the MouseUp event fired, but no Click event occurred.
   c) Press the mouse button while the cursor is outside the form, drag the cursor onto the form, and release. A MouseUp event occurred, but no Click event.
   d) Press the mouse button inside the form, drag the mouse outside the form, then back inside it. Release the button. A MouseUp event occurred (press Enter to close the message box), then a Click event.

5. Rewrite the Color event procedure to use the **RGB** function instead of the **QBColor** function.

6. Write the statements to add an additional case to the Color event procedure so that a user could choose a random color. To generate a random color, generate a random integer in the range 0 to 15 and use that value in the **QBColor** function. Remember, the **Rnd** function in Visual Basic returns a random number in the range from 0 to 1. Multiply by 15 and use the **Int()** function to convert the number to an integer.

7. The **Line** method can be used to draw a rectangle. Replace the four **Line** statements in the rectangle section of the MouseDown event with a single **Line** statement. The *B* parameter draws a box.

8. Add a command to the Lines menu that draws a filled box of the current color. (Hint: add the *BF* parameter to the **Line** method.)

9. Add an erase function. Use the **Line** method, with the *BF* parameter and a color read from the BackColor property to draw a small, fixed size rectangle.

The frame is used to group logically related collections of option buttons or check boxes. In a group of option buttons, only one can be selected at a time. In contrast, more than one check box in a logically related group can be checked at one time.

You can gain access to the contents of these controls through their Value property. This property is **True** if the control is selected.

The Multiple Document Interface is characterized by the presence of a single parent form that becomes the container for one or more child forms. The menu bar of the child form replaces the menu bar of the parent form when the child form becomes active.

An MDI parent form is created by selecting New MDI Form from the File menu. A MDI child form is created by changing the MDIChild property of a normal form to **True**.

You cannot place any control on a MDI form that does not have the Align property. Controls you cannot use include textboxes, labels, and command buttons. The picture box does have the Align property; therefore, you use it to contain the graphic toolbar of programs such as Visual Basic.

Problems

1. The Car Option Program

Write a program that allows a car buyer to specify options and features to be included in a car. Start by sketching a form including frames with option buttons and check boxes to choose features. When all the options and features are chosen, use a multiline textbox to display a summary of the choices made.

Provide a form that gives the following choices (you decide whether to use option buttons or check boxes):

◎ Four door
◎ Two door
◎ Station wagon
◎ Sport utility
◎ Colors: bold blue, sea green, hot pink
◎ Wheel size: 14″ or 15″
◎ Interior: bucket seats, bench seats, leather, vinyl, AM-FM, AM-FM CD player, short wave, trip computer, satellite positioning system, built-in phone, fax
◎ Engine: 6 cylinder, 8 cylinder, 12 cylinder

2. Versatile Grapher Display of Coefficients

Modify the graph procedure of one or more of the forms in the Versatile Grapher to display the values of *a, b, c,* and *d,* in marked labels near the bottom of the graph.

3. Change the Scale

Modify the graph procedure of one or more of the forms in the Versatile Grapher to allow the user to set the scale by entering the coordinates of the upper-left-hand corner and of the lower-right-hand corner. For an extra challenge, put the following new choices into the menu of each child form: Zoom Out, Zoom In. These choices will automatically change the scale, the **For-Next** statement, and redisplay the graph.

4. Determining the Features of a Computer System

Write a program using option buttons to let a computer buyer choose features to include on a computer. Do some research and find prices and descriptions for alternate choices for monitors, hard drives, CD ROMs, sound cards, processors, memory, and so forth. Put together a form allowing the user to choose what options to include. When the choices have been made, display a list showing the options chosen and the final cost of the machine.

5. The Stock Chart

Write a program with a picture box and an array that allows the user to plot the performance of stock over a period of time. Prompt the user to enter ten closing values for a stock. Display a graph reflecting those closing prices. Choose the scale so the daily differences show up well. How does the scale chosen affect the possible interpretation of the fluctuations of the graph?

6. Tic-Tac-Toe

Write a program that will allow two players to play a game of tic-tac-toe. Use a picture box with some lines to display the playing field. Use the MouseDown event to determine in which box the mouse was clicked, then fill that box with an X or an O, depending on whose turn it is.

7. The Mouse Trail Program

Use the MouseDown event along with the **PSet** command to make a simple drawing program. When the mouse is down, the mouse leaves a trail. When the mouse is up, no mark is left.

8. Saving the Drawings

Modify the graph program to save and recall the drawing. The **Point(x,y)** method returns the RGB color of the coordinate *(x,y)*. Use the ScaleWidth and ScaleHeight properties to determine the dimensions of the form. Save the dimensions of the form, the ScaleWidth and ScaleHeight, and each of the RGB values read from the form.

```
If Index = 7 Then
Data1.RecordSource
= "SELECT * FROM
Animals ORDER BY
CommonName"
Data1.Refresh
```

OLE and the Data Control

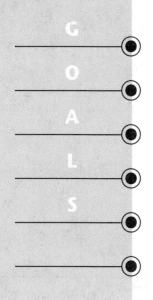

After working through this chapter, you will be able to:

Use Visual Basic to create containers for objects created in other applications.

Understand the differences and similarities between linked and embedded objects.

Use the Data Manager program, supplied with Visual Basic, to create databases compatible with Microsoft Access.

Use Visual Basic applications to display and manipulate database information.

Use the Structured Query Language to initiate searches in the Animal Species database.

O V E R V I E W

Object linking and embedding, or OLE (oh-lay), is a powerful and exciting option you can use to enhance your Visual Basic programs. With OLE, you can use applications such as Excel as custom controls. You click and drag the Visual Basic OLE control to place it on a Visual Basic form, just as you would for any other control. Then, you choose which file to display in the control, or which application to associate with the control.

Choosing Excel or a specific Excel spreadsheet, for example, gives you access to that application from within the form. You couldn't ask for a better spreadsheet control than Excel. OLE lets you use the full functionality of Excel while you are in a Visual Basic program.

This ability to open one application within the other is an example of an extraordinary level of connectivity between applications. You can see the results of this enhanced communication as you work in many of the popular programs that may be loaded on your computer. Today, for example, you can paste a spreadsheet into a word processing document, next to a graph or table from a database program. As a result, you bring to bear the strengths of different programs on the same topic (the subject of the document).

Another dimension of OLE is OLE Automation. Windows applications that support OLE Automation are said to "expose" objects and their func-

tionality to other programs. Using OLE Automation is similar to borrowing application programs from the library or video store.

While on loan, the applications, or parts of the applications, are available for your use. When you are done using the programs, you return them. The parts of the applications available for your use are called "objects." For instance, if your Visual Basic application "borrows" an Excel spreadsheet object, the full power of the Excel program is available ("exposed") to your program.

OLE Automation is supported by Versions 3 and 4 of Visual Basic. It is not covered in this text, but you can find details and samples in the Visual Basic manuals and on line help.

The second half of the chapter explores Visual Basic's role as a front end to a database. This term—a front end to a database—means that Visual Basic provides the user interface that lets people access the data stored in the database. Imagine, for example, that you want to look up information on a particular musical artist in a database. You need a way of asking, or querying, for that information. Visual Basic forms are often used to provide that "face" to the database, so that users can request specific information from the database or add information to it.

Visual Basic reads and writes databases; in fact, one of the most common tasks for which programmers use Visual Basic is to develop databases or applications that interact with databases. In this chapter, you will use the Data Manager program, which comes with Visual Basic, to create a database. This database will be compatible with Microsoft Access, which is a powerful and sophisticated program for creating databases, editing their data, and refining their design. Your program will use Visual Basic's Data control to give users access to the data in this database.

Object Linking and Embedding

In some ways, OLE is as simple as cutting or copying and then pasting material. You are familiar with the process of marking a portion of text, cutting it, and pasting it to another part of the document. You have used a similar method to copy code from one procedure to another. A logical extension of this process is copying and pasting between different applications, not just between documents from the same application.

Section

Think about the possibilities available when you copy a graphic from one application to another. In a simple paste, you would end up with a copy of the graphic in your document. That copy would no longer be connected in any way to the original; if you edited the original graphic, for example, none of those changes would appear in the pasted image.

Object linking and embedding takes this process of sharing material another step. Instead of merely pasting an image, you can create a "live" linked object. The data contained in a "linked" object remains in the application that created the object. The object itself may be pasted in any number of other applications. If a user changes the object in any of its host applications, the changes affect all the "instances" of the object. (An "instance" is an occurrence of the object in another application.)

In an "embedded" object, the data that makes up the object is contained in the application in which it is pasted. Any change made to the object within a particular application stays in that application. In addition, if you double-click on an embedded (or linked) object, you can actually run the application in which it was created in order to edit the data.

Before working with OLE in Visual Basic, let's experiment with these different concepts of pasting, linking, and embedding. OLE is not unique to Visual Basic; as you will see, other applications also give you access to its power.

To create a live Paintbrush object in a Write program:

1 From the Program Manager in Windows, run Paintbrush (the icon is often found in the Accessories program group).

2 Sketch a picture. Save the picture with the name: **p1.bmp** in the **c:\vbfiles** directory or on your disk. You will use the figure in a future demonstration. See Figure 14-1.

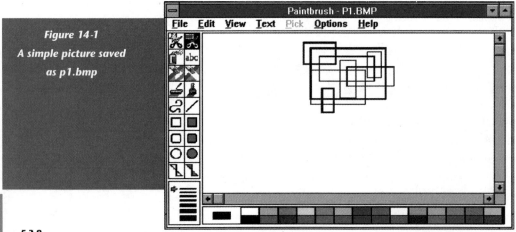

Figure 14-1
A simple picture saved
as p1.bmp

3   Use the Scissors tool to select the drawing. See Figure 14-2.

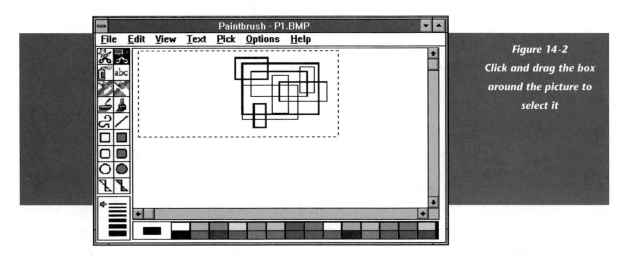

Figure 14-2
Click and drag the box
around the picture to
select it

4   Select Copy from the Edit menu.

5   Return to the Program Manager.

6   Double-click on the icon for the Write program to start it (this icon is also usually in the Accessories program group).

Write

7   Select Paste from the Edit menu. The drawing appears in the Write document, as an embedded object. See Figure 14-3.
If you wanted to link to the drawing, you would choose Paste Link from Write's Edit menu. Applications that support OLE, such as Paintbrush and Write, use object linking and embedding in ordinary cut and pastes. As you will see, this allows you to edit the object in the original application that created the object. Save the file as **p1.wri**.

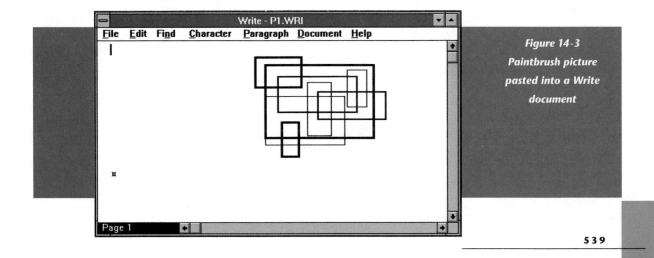

Figure 14-3
Paintbrush picture
pasted into a Write
document

8 Double-click on the drawing in the Write document. This object is live: it retains its identity as a Paintbrush object. This property of being "live" is a consequence of OLE. The Paintbrush program opens so that you can edit the picture.

9 Close Paintbrush. Note the special Exit command in the menu: Exit and Return to **p1.wri** (Figure 14-4). You have opened a copy of Paintbrush to edit the picture while you are working in Write. The original picture is still open in another copy of Paintbrush.

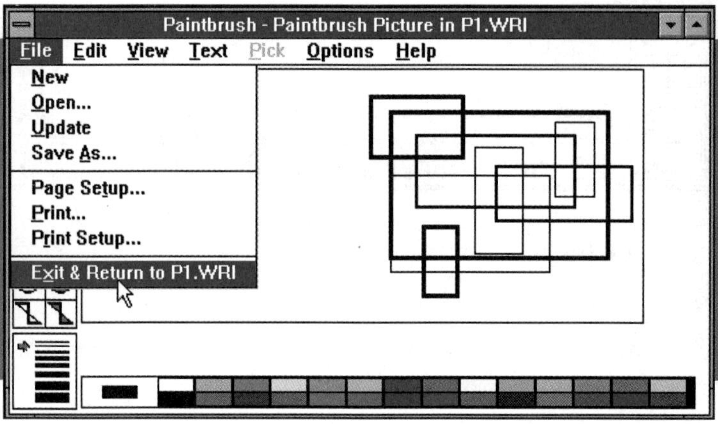

Figure 14-4
Exiting out of the copy
of Paintbrush

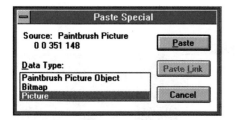

10 Return to the original picture by pressing Alt+Tab.

11 Select the picture again, select Copy from the Edit menu, then press Alt+Tab to return to Write.

Figure 14-5
Message box for Paste
Special

12 Position the cursor at the end of the document and select Paste Special from the Edit menu. The message box in Figure 14-5 opens.

13 Select Picture from the Data Type list, then click on Paste. A second copy of your picture is pasted into the Write document.

14 Double-click on the second drawing. As you can see from the message box that opens (Figure 14-6), this second copy of your graphic is not an OLE object; it is not a Paintbrush object. You cannot edit it.

Figure 14-6
Message box explaining
that the pasted object is
not live

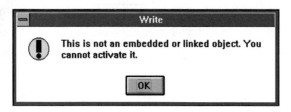

Creating a Linked Object

1   Switch back to the Paintbrush program, select the drawing with the scissors tools, and copy the image with Ctrl+C or with the Copy command from the Edit menu.

2   Return to the Write document, **p1.wri**.

3   Move the cursor to the end of the document and choose Paste Link from the Edit menu. A third copy of the drawing appears. The data making up this object is still in the Paintbrush program. The Write document merely contains a "link" pointing to the picture. You can see this by altering the drawing in Paintbrush.

4   Return to Paintbrush and add an additional shape to the drawing.

5   Return to Write and notice the third drawing changes but the other two do not. Only the linked object is sensitive to changes in the original.

Loading the OLE Control

The OLE control is a custom Visual Basic control. In versions 2 and 3 of Visual Basic, the OLE controls are found in the Windows **\System** directory with a **.vbx** extension. Before using one of these controls, you may have to take steps to add it to your project. In version 4 of Visual Basic, the OLE control is always included in the toolbox.

The OLE icons for versions 2 and 3 are shown in Figure 14-7.

The Project window shows the filenames of all the custom controls included in the toolbox. The Project window shown in Figure 14-8, for example, includes the objects shown in the toolbox in Figure 14-7.

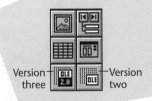

Figure 14-7
Visual Basic v2 and
v3 icons

The file named **msole2.vbx** is the version of the OLE control that comes with version 3 of Visual Basic. **ole-clien.vbx** is the version that comes with version 2 of Visual Basic. There are significant differences in the ways the two controls work. The text that follows, for the most part, applies to the version 3 control, **msole2.vbx**.

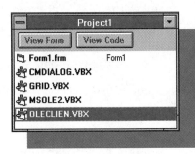

Figure 14-8
Project window showing custom controls available from the Toolbox

The OLE control is, by default, included in new projects. When you create a new project in VB3, the controls that appear in the Toolbox are the usual controls (such as label and editbox) together with those controls that have been added to a special project named **autoload.mak**.

This project contains all the defaults that are used when you create a new project; these controls are loaded into the toolbox, together with the options you can set using the Project command from the Options menu.

When you install Visual Basic, an **autoload.mak** project is created in the Visual Basic directory. It must be located there in order for Visual Basic to apply its settings to your new projects. The **autoload.mak** project that is automatically created includes **msole2.vbx** (as well as the grid control).

When you choose Add File from the File menu, the VBX you select is added to the current project. If you load the **autoload.mak** project, choose Add File to add VBX controls to the project, and save it, then all the controls added to this project will automatically be included in the toolbox for each new project.

To use the OLE control in programs, you must make the control available in the toolbox by adding the **.vbx** file to projects. Note that this may already have been done by someone else using Visual Basic on your computer. In addition, you may need to load a file called **share.exe**, which lets data be transferred from one program to another. If you are running Windows for Workgroups or Windows 95, then you do not need to load **share.exe**. If you are running Windows 3.1, however, then you should ensure that you load that program whenever you start your computer. The **share.exe** program is located in the DOS directory of your computer. Make sure that your **autoexec.bat** file contains the following line:

```
C:\DOS\SHARE.EXE /L:500
```

For more information about **share.exe**, type the following command at the MS-DOS Prompt:

```
HELP SHARE
```

To add the OLE object to the toolbox:

1 Open Visual Basic. If Visual Basic is already open, select New Project from the File menu.

2 Add the OLE icon to the toolbox by selecting Add File from the File menu. Look for **msole2.vbx** in the Windows **\System** directory. The control in the VBX is now added to the current project.

Placing an OLE Control on a Form

An OLE control is a window, or a container, in which you can display a portion of an application created in a different program. The OLE control can show a portion of a spreadsheet, a graph, a document, or a piece of clip art. The difference between pasting and object linking and embedding is that the data in a live object can be modified using the original application.

In the previous Paintbrush and Write example, you implemented OLE by embedding a Paintbrush object in a Write document. The data making up the object is maintained within the Write document: it is saved with the document as part of the Write file. When you pasted using the normal Paste command, Write (which is OLE-aware, as is Paintbrush) created an embedded object. OLE-aware applications do not implement a "naive" paste (naive pastes are not OLE-aware unless that option is specifically chosen). In the previous exercise, the Paste Special command was used to paste a copy of the Paintbrush picture that could not be edited by the Paintbrush program.

The Paste Link command created an object whose data remains in Paintbrush. The Write document maintains a "link" to the original object in Paintbrush, where it may be edited. The object itself is saved by the Paintbrush application.

To place an OLE control:

1 Start Visual Basic. If Visual Basic is running, choose New Project from the File menu.

2 Change the caption of the default form to **OLE Demo**.

3 Double-click on the OLE icon to place the object on the form. Alternatively, single-click on the icon and place the object by clicking and dragging. As soon as you have placed the object on the form, a dialog box opens.

After you have placed an OLE control on a form, you are given a choice between two option buttons: open an application in the OLE control or open a specific file in the control. To create the OLE object from scratch, you would open the application, such as Word, then create the new file. By double-clicking on the control, you can open the application from Visual Basic. Alternatively, you can insert an existing file into the control. The file must be one that can be edited by an OLE-aware application. Your choice of option button determines which of two sets of choices appear in the dialog box.

Creating Another Linked Object

You have placed an OLE object on the form (see previous steps). By default, the Insert Object dialog box opens with the Create New option button selected. See Figure 14-9.

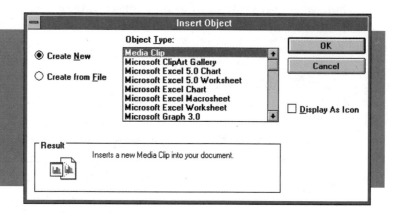

The Object Type drop-down list displays programs you can select to create OLE objects.

To place a linked object:

1 Click on the Create from File option button to display the alternative Insert Object dialog box. The choices that now appear are the ones you use to choose an *existing* file containing an object to insert into your Visual Basic form.

2 Click on the Browse button to look through different directories for a file to connect to the OLE object. The extension of the file tells the OLE control what kind of application is being imported.

The Link check box allows the data in the object to be dynamically linked to the original source of the data. In this demonstration, you will create an embedded object from the drawing used above. Don't click on the Link check box.

3 Select the name of the Paintbrush drawing you saved (**p1.bmp**). The filename now appears in the Insert Object window (Figure 14-10). Click the Link check box to create a linked object.

4 Click OK to display the Paintbrush file in the OLE object on your Visual Basic form.
Notice that the name of the file is now the value of the SourceDoc property of the OLE control (Figure 14-11).

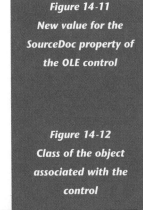

Figure 14-11
New value for the
SourceDoc property of
the OLE control

5 Look at the other properties of the OLE control. The default name for the first OLE control you place on a form is OLE1. The control has a "type" of object associated with it: the Class property shows the OLE object is a Paintbrush object. See Figure 14-12.

Figure 14-12
Class of the object
associated with the
control

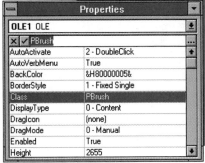

6 Look at the AutoActivate property. When this property has the value of **True**, a user can start the underlying application by double-clicking on the OLE control. Test this: run the program, then double-click on the drawing to open Paintbrush. Make changes to the drawing.

7 Save the altered drawing and close Paintbrush. Do you see the changes in the drawing on your form?

Creating an Embedded Object

For an embedded object, you place the OLE control on the form in exactly the same way as you did for a linked object (see previous steps). With a second OLE object placed on the form, you are ready for these steps:

1 In the Insert Object dialog box, check that the Create New option is checked. Also make sure the Link check box is not checked.

2 Select Microsoft Excel Worksheet and click OK.

3 When Excel opens, enter the data shown here:

Computer Component	Prices
540MB hard drive	$165
Mini tower case	67
486 motherboard	175
Monitor	247
Keyboard	89
Mouse	59

continued   **545**

Computer Component	Prices
Modem	179
Sound card	100
Video card	139
Disk drive	40
I/O card	40
Memory	300
Misc.	400
Total	**2000**

4   In the row *total*, where the amount *2000* appears, enter a formula to add the values above. For instance:

`+Sum(D3:D15)`

5   Select Update from the File menu, then close Excel. The spreadsheet is visible in the OLE control.

6   Change the SizeMode property of the OLE control to Stretch. Note the results. The metafile image of the spreadsheet cells is stretched to fill the OLE control on the form.

7   Change the SizeMode property of the OLE control to AutoSize. The OLE window assumes the shape of the displayed spreadsheet.

Figure 14-13
Changing an entry in
an embedded Excel
spreadsheet

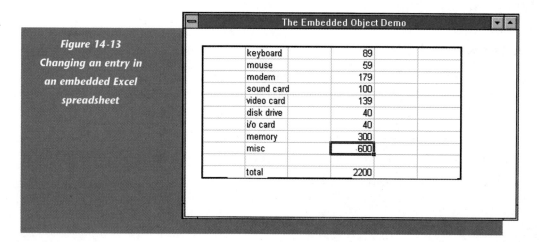

8   Run the program. Double-click on the OLE control. Change the entry in Misc from 400 to 600. Note the results. See Figure 14-13.

9   Save the project and form files.

Working with OLE Objects

If you place the mouse pointer on the OLE control, then click on the *right* mouse button, a pop-up menu opens (Figure 14-14). Try this now.

The commands that are available from this pop-up menu vary. For example, try placing an OLE control on the form, but do not associate an application or file with it (click Cancel in the Insert Object dialog box). What commands are available from the pop-up menu, if you right-click on this OLE control?

Experiment with the options in the pop-up menu using your three OLE controls. What happens when you delete an embedded object? You may wonder what the Paste Special command lets you do. This command is available if you have cut or copied something from another application onto the Clipboard. By choosing this command, you can paste a "live" display into the OLE control, retaining a link to the original application and the original source of data being displayed.

Now, let's look at some of the properties of OLE controls. If you have deleted your embedded object, select another file, then embed it. (In the Insert Object dialog box, select the file, leaving the Linked check box unchecked, then click OK.) What happens when you do that? Why does the application associated with the file open? The reason is the setting of the AutoActivate property. When that property has the value of 2-Dblclick, the application opens when you double-click on the control at run-time. As a result, you (or the user of your program) can modify the contents contained in the OLE control using all the features of the original application.

If you double-click on the SourceDoc property of an OLE object, you find yourself in the Browse dialog box. This box lets you choose a file to associate with an object and decide, using the Link check box, whether the object is embedded or linked. Double-click on the SourceDoc property now and find a bitmap file (**.bmp**), a spreadsheet file (**.xls**) or a document file (**.doc**) and insert the file into your OLE object on the form. The data from that file appears in the OLE object.

The SourceItem property, if it is used, will specify the subrange of the object copied from the SourceDoc. In the case of a spreadsheet, the SourceItem property indicates a named range of the spreadsheet, or it can explicitly specify a range. If a SourceItem property is defined, it will be added to the SourceDoc property, separated with an exclamation point:

```
SourceDoc:    C:\vbfiles\Mustang.xls
SourceItem:   R1C1:R8C7
```

After the SourceItem has been defined, the SourceDoc becomes:

```
C:\vbfiles\Mustang.xls!R1C1:R8C7
```

Creating Objects at Run-Time

You don't have to create or associate an object with an OLE control during design time. You can also decide to have that happen under program control while the program is running. To do so, you use a property that is not available at design time and, therefore, is not displayed in the Properties window of the OLE control. The Action property is used after the Class, SourceDoc, and SourceItem (if used) properties are set. The integer value assigned to the Action property determines what action will take place. When the Action property is assigned the value 0, an embedded object will be created, using the information provided in the Class, SourceDoc, and SourceItem (if used) properties.

When the Action property is assigned the value 1, a linked object is created within the OLE control.

A number of actions are available through this property. For a complete list, check the Visual Basic Help file under the topic Action (OLE). You will find commands to paste from the Clipboard, save to a file, collect from a file, and delete, among a number of others.

Constant symbols for the permissible Action values can be found in the file **constant.txt**, located in the Visual Basic directory. For example, OLE_CREATE_LINK is defined as 1. You can use these constants in your code instead of numerals by adding them to a code module of your project. To do so, choose the Load Text command from the File menu, then select the file **constant.txt**.

QUESTIONS AND ACTIVITIES

1. Describe the process of cutting (or copying) and pasting within a document. If you were going to use the keyboard of the mouse to perform these commands, what keyboard combinations would you use?

   a) Marking text

   b) Cutting text

   c) Copying text

   d) Pasting text

2. Where is the data held in a linked OLE object?

3. What is the difference between a linked and an embedded object?

4. Describe the following design-time properties of the OLE object:

   a) AutoActivate

   b) Class

   c) OLETypeAllowed

   d) SizeMode

   e) SourceDoc

   f) SourceItem

5. Give a good reason to include the Stretch option in the SizeMode property.

6. How can you associate an application object to an OLE object after the OLE object has been created?

7. What action is performed when 0 is assigned to the Action property of an OLE object? What action is performed when 1 is assigned to that property?

The Mustang Data Container Program

2

Section

The first step in OLE mastery begins with using an OLE control to display data under program control. A program that uses OLE to display another program's data is called a container application. In this section, you will use the OLE control to create a Visual Basic OLE container application that displays an Excel spreadsheet.

The application is a simple one: a Visual Basic program that displays a spreadsheet containing information with production figures, original prices, and current prices for 1964 to 1966 Mustangs from one of two years. See Figure 14-15.

Mustang Data

1964.5 - 1966 Ford Mustang Models, Original Prices, Production, Current Prices						
Year	**Body**	**Wght**	**Price**	**Prod**	**Good**	**Excellent**
64.5-65	htp cpe	2583	2372	501965	5500	10000
	conv cpe	2789	2614	101945	7700	14500
	fstbk cpe	2633	2589	77079	6800	12000
Year	**Body**	**Wght**	**Price**	**Prod**	**Good**	**Excellent**
1966	htp cpe	2488	2416	499751	5500	10000
	conv cpe	2519	2607	35698	7700	14500
	fstbk cpe	2650	2653	72119	6800	12000

[64.5-65 Data]   [1966 Data]   [Complete Data]   [Exit]

Figure 14-15
Data on Ford Mustangs

Starting Out

In this project, you are going to place an OLE object on the form, then select an Excel spreadsheet file to associate with it. The object will be linked, meaning that the data displayed in the OLE object is maintained in Excel rather than in the Visual Basic program.

The Mustang Data program displays information about the 1964.5 through 1966 Ford Mustang. The information covers the first two and a half years of production. Included in the information is the year, the body style, the weight, the original list price, the number of units produced, the current price for a used vehicle in good condition, and the current price of a vehicle in excellent condition.

Building a Spreadsheet

In Microsoft Excel, you can build a spreadsheet with multiple layers, called worksheets. For this program, you build a single worksheet from data provided to you on the disk accompanying this textbook. The command buttons display the 1964-1965 information, the 1966 information, or the entire spreadsheet. For the first command button, the range displayed is determined using the row and column notation familiar to spreadsheet users. For the second command button, the range displayed is named within the Excel application.

You can use the file **mustang.xls** from the Template disk or create your own. To create the spreadsheet:

1 Start Excel.

2 Place information from the Mustang Data table shown in Figure 14-15 into the worksheet.

3 Once the data is entered, select the rectangular area starting in row 6 column 1 and ending in row 9, column 7. This frames the data for 1966.

4 Click on the Insert menu, then click on Name and Define. Name the selected area **sixtysix**. This named range will be displayed when the 1966 Data command button is clicked.

5 Save the file in the **vbfiles** directory with the name **mustang.xls**.

Using Visual Basic as a container provides direct access from within a Visual Basic program to data created in programs such as Excel. With a Visual Basic container, the user doesn't need to explicitly open Excel in order to view and edit data that the Visual Basic program uses; instead, the data is accessed directly within the Visual Basic application.

Setting up the Form

Follow these steps to set up the form.

1 Create a new directory for the Mustang Data project.

2   Start Visual Basic. If Visual Basic is running, choose New Project from the File menu.

3   Change the caption of the form to **Mustang Data**.

4   If the OLE control is not available in the toolbox, add it to the project, by adding the file **msole2.vbx** from the Windows **\System** directory.

5   Click on the OLE icon and drag to put an OLE window on the form. The Insert Object dialog box opens.

6   Use the Browse command button to find the **mustang.xls** file in the **vbfiles** directory. If the file is available on the disk that comes with the text, move it into the **vbfiles** directory.

7   Click the Link check box to create a linked object. Leave the dialog box by clicking OK. The spreadsheet should appear within the OLE control.
The result of this dialog box is that the SourceDoc property of the OLE control is set to **C:\vbfiles\mustang.xls**. If the SourceItem property is not set, the entire spreadsheet is selected and displayed in the OLE control.

8   Place four command buttons on the form. Change their captions and names as shown in Figure 14-15.

9   Select the OLE control. In the Property window, confirm the OLE-TypeAllowed property is set to 2 (Either), its default value.

10   Change the SizeMode property to AutoSize.

11   Save the form and project files.

Writing the Code

The command buttons display portions of the entire spreadsheet. The first displays just the data for 1964-1965. The second displays data for 1966. The third displays the entire sheet.

Follow these steps to write the code:

1   Select the default form in the Project window. Click on the View Code button to open the Code window. Select cmdEarly from the Object drop-down list. Enter the code to display the first year and a half of data. The phrase "R2C1:R5C7" causes the part of the spreadsheet from row 2 to row 5 and from column 1 to column 7 to be displayed in the OLE control on the form. Setting the Action property to 1 reestablishes the link between the OLE control and the spreadsheet.

> **NOTE:**
>
> The Visual Basic version 4 OLE control is backward compatible with the version 3 control, allowing the program to use the Action property as described above. In version 4, though, most of these actions have become methods that apply to the OLE control. The Visual Basic version 2 implementation of the OLE control is quite different.

```
Ole1.SourceItem = "R2C1:R5C7"
Ole1.Action = 1
```

2 Enter the Click event handler for cmdLater. The code in this command button takes advantage of the named range in the Mustang data spreadsheet. Set the SourceItem property of the OLE object to the range name, sixtysix. Once the SourceItem property is set, it is appended to the SourceDoc property, set when the form was designed, and a link is established between the OLE container and the spreadsheet.

```
Ole1.SourceItem = "sixtysix"
Ole1.Action = 1
```

3 Enter the Click event handler for cmdAllData. The code in this button deletes the contents of the SourceItem property of the OLE control. The SourceDoc property, still set to the file **mustang.xls**, becomes the default and the entire spreadsheet is again selected. Enter the code for cmdAllData:

```
Ole1.SourceItem = ""
Ole1.Action = 1
```

4 Enter **End** in the Click event handler for cmdExit.

5 Save the form and project files.

6 Run the program. Click each command button and note the results.

Looking at Some Issues

Figuring out how to set the SourceItem property is not always easy. The Visual Basic Programmer's Guide makes it clear that a spreadsheet range is to be specified by row and column.

The row and column method of specifying a ranges marks each row with an "R" followed by a row number. Each column is marked with a "C" followed by a column number. For instance, the upper-left corner of the spreadsheet is designated r1c1, or row 1, column 1. The cell at the fifth row, third column is designated r5c3. This notation is called R1C1 notation, or sometimes RC (Row, Column) notation.

When using this system to designate a range, specify the upper-left corner and the lower-right corner of the range separated by a colon: *r1c1:r3c5*. This is the system used with a Visual Basic application to specify a range of an Excel spreadsheet. The only modification of the system is the ability to specify a particular *sheet* of the spreadsheet. To specify the range as a part of the first sheet, you add the name of a sheet, such as *sheet1*, as a prefix to the range specification: *sheet1!r1c1:r3c5*. The sheet designation is separated from the rest of the range string with an exclamation point.

Excel spreadsheets use the notation used by Lotus 1-2-3, in which the columns are labeled with letters and the rows with numbers. The top-left corner cell in this notation is *A1*. The range above, *sheet1!r1c1:r3c5*, in the alternate Excel notation is *sheet1!a1:e3*. *A* is the first column and *e* is the fifth column. *1* is the first row, and *3* is the third row. This notation is often called A1 notation.

Although Excel lets you use either notation to designate ranges when working within the program, Visual Basic requires you to use R1C1 notation when referring to a range of cells.

Often cells are specified in positions relative to other cells. To "nail down" a reference to specific cells so the relative references will not change when the formula is copied, put a dollar sign ($) in front of the column letter and/or the row number. The cell designation, *a5* is nailed down like this: *a5*. When you see the dollar sign in a range specification, it always means the cells so marked are not to be changed when formulas are copied.

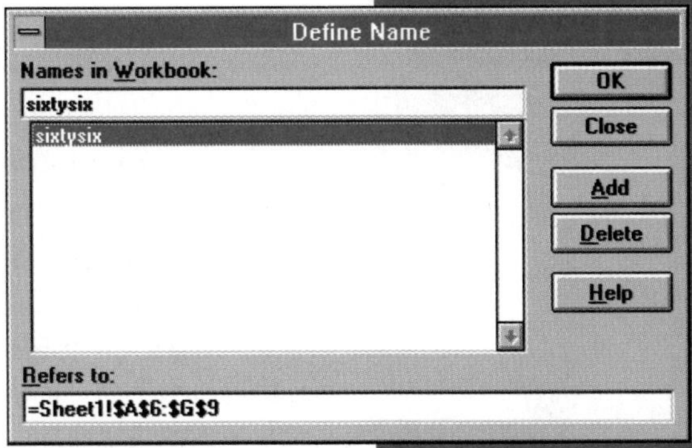

Figure 14-16
The Define Name dialog box from Excel

In the Mustang Data program, the information for 1966 was named *sixtysix*. The Define Name dialog box shown in Figure 14-16 shows the Excel range of cells used in the definition:

   Sheet1!$A$6:$G$9

In R1 notation the range would look like:

   Sheet1!$R6$C1:$R9$C7

This range was named when the spreadsheet was created. Naming a range of cells lets you refer to the range of cells symbolically, rather than using the normal, rather cryptic, range specifications.

If you try to set the SourceItem property using A1 notation, Visual Basic generates an error message.

QUESTIONS AND ACTIVITIES

1.   What are the multiple layers of an Excel spreadsheet called?

2.   What are the two ways to associate an object with an OLE control?

3.   A well-designed menu is a way of organizing a programming project. Design a menu that would be appropriate for a program that figures out the amount of a payroll check. Commands should include the number of regular hours worked, the number of overtime hours, and the hourly wage. The display should include both

a facsimile of a check and an itemized listing of the deductions. Don't write the code for this program, just design the menu.

4. Describe the following OLE properties:
   a) Class property
   b) SourceDoc property
   c) SourceItem property
   d) Action property

5. Use the row-and-column method of expressing a spreadsheet range to encode these areas:
   a) a7:e20
   b) a1:z26
   c) c4:g12

6. What do you do to designate a range in sheet 2 of a spreadsheet?

7. Explain the significance of the dollar sign in spreadsheet ranges.

8. If, in the last lines of the code, the Action property were set to 0 instead of 1, what changes would occur in the application?

Section

Exchanging Data with Databases

Information is the substance and product of computing. A collection of related information is called a database. Schools use databases to record course, student, teacher, and financial information. Businesses use databases to record transactions, inventories, personnel files, and customer files. A home computer user might use a database to record information about financial transactions, to keep track of a checkbook, or to trace stock prices. Museums and historical societies use databases to catalog collections or to record genealogies. Users find new and creative ways to use databases all the time.

Database files are created and maintained by database programs. The Microsoft products Access and FoxPro as well as Borland's Paradox and dBASE are examples of database programs.

Database programs have a number of distinct tasks, no matter which program you are using. Creating a database means designing the layout and format of the information contained in the database. A database program lets a user add, edit, and delete information from a database file. A database file is the file that actually holds the information in the database.

A database program also lets the user display the information contained in the database in a variety of ways. Early database programs could do little more than display tables of data. Today's programs can do much more, attaching pictures and sounds to information and displaying tables and graphs. A user can select the graphs from a huge selection of available types.

A database engine is a group of routines that allow programs to perform the functions listed above with database files of a particular format. These routines allow you to write programs that query and manipulate database files in a high-level way, without your having to know the physical layout of data within the files. The Access database engine is part of Visual Basic as well as being a part of the Access database application. As a result, Visual Basic can manipulate database files with the same format as Access files. This ability to perform database functions under program control makes Visual Basic an extremely powerful tool. Automating database functions under program control makes it easy for users uncomfortable with computers to interact with database files.

Many, and perhaps most, professional Visual Basic programmers use Visual Basic to develop database or database-aware applications. This is one of Visual Basic's most frequently used features.

In these sections, you use Visual Basic to display, add, edit, search for, and delete information from a database.

The Student Schedule Project

The Student Schedule project uses the Data Manager program to create a simple database. Before going through the actual steps needed to create the database, you are introduced to terms and concepts you'll need to understand databases.

STARTING OUT

Imagine a database application that keeps track of a student's daily schedule. The information necessary to create and maintain this schedule might be stored in a number of separate, though related, tables of information.

Take a look at a sample student schedule. The information for Erin Sprague might be stored in a table named Schedule.

Period	Course	Teacher	Room
1	cs101	johnson	203
2	math102	shenk	104
4	lit101	dwyer	204
6	chem101	peterson	211
8	bus104	minor	155

More detailed information about each course might be stored in a table named Courses:

Course #	Dept.	Name	Instructor
cs101	cs	intro to computers	johnson
math102	math	foundations of math	shenk
lit101	english	introduction to lit	dwyer
chem101	science	intro to chemistry	peterson
bus104	business	business math	minor

Information about the teachers can be stored in another table. All in all, a complete software package to manage the affairs of even a small school district is a formidable piece of programming.

Use the Data Manager program to create a database in Access format; start by naming the tables. A simple database may have only a single table; nevertheless, it must be named.

Once the information is arranged in tables, you must design the format of each table. The categories of information contained in a table are called fields. A field has both a name and a datatype associated with it. The datatype of a field will remind of you of the datatypes available to variables in Visual Basic—the list of available datatypes is very similar.

After you name the tables and determine the fields of each table, you must add information to the database. Each discrete piece of related information is called a record. For instance, in the student schedule database described above, the description of each period's class is a record. The fields are the period, the course title, the teacher's name, and the room number.

Each piece of information stored about each class in the schedule goes into its own field. Separating the data into fields lets us search for records that meet specific criteria. You might want to list all the classes that meet in a particular room, or all the classes taught by a certain teacher. Because these pieces of information are stored in separate fields, you can search for records based on these criteria.

INSERTING DATA

After you have designed the database, it's time to insert data. Visual Basic is capable of adding new information to the database. Right now, though, to gain familiarity with the other functions of the Data Manager program, you will use it to insert data.

To insert data:

1 Close the Fields and Indexes window by double-clicking on the close box in the upper-left corner of the window. Closing this window returns you to the table window.

2   In the table window, click on the Open button to add information to the database. In the window that opens, you will see a list of the fields defined as a part of the database. Notice that you have the options of adding, finding, or refreshing, records of the database. See Figure 14-17.

Figure 14-17

Options for working with records in the database

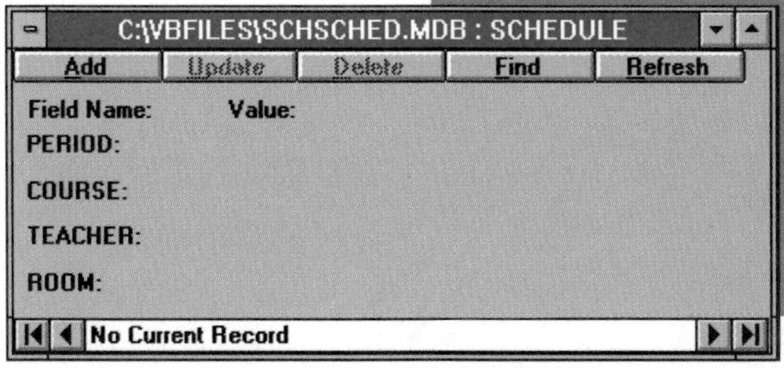

Refreshing the database means getting new copies of the records from the database. This allows any recent changes in the data to be reflected in Data Manager windows. At the bottom of the window is a new kind of scroll bar. This is the Data control. The ends of the control look like the buttons on a compact disc player. The caption in the middle of the bar reflects the current status of the database—there are no records in the file.

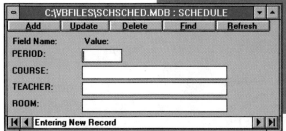

3   Click on the Add button and notice that the caption changes. See Figure 14-18.

Figure 14-18

Effect of clicking on the Add button

Now each of the command buttons at the top of the form have been enabled. From this window, you can add new data, update data stored in the file, delete records, find records with certain values in particular fields, and refresh the listing of the data held in memory. Textboxes to enter data for the file are included, along with labels indicating the names of the fields. The top caption of the window shows the path and filename along with the table name.

4   Make up and enter data for a couple of entries. Close the Data Manager program.

QUESTIONS AND ACTIVITIES

1.   Define the term "database." Be sure to describe some of the jobs a database program performs.

2.   What kind of database applications would store pictures? Name and write a sentence about at least two.

3.   What is a database engine?

4.   What job does the Data Manager program perform?

5.   Why is Data Manager not a replacement for Access?

6.   Explain the relationship between database tables and fields.

7. Write the field names and a few sample entries for a database that would save information about the stuff around your house. Assume the database will be used to help make claims against the insurance company if your possessions are stolen.

8. Every field of a database has at least two properties. What are they?

9. If you were to add a field to the Student Schedule database, what would it be?

10. What is an index to a database?

11. In Portugal almost everyone has about five names. In addition, many people in a classroom may have the same first name. To differentiate between one student and another, often two names are used. Usually the first name is used along with one of the middle names. Design the fields of a database to handle names of Portuguese students.

12. What does refreshing the database mean?

Section 4

Using the Data Control

The Data control gives versions 3 and 4 of Visual Basic access to database files created with Access or with the Data Manager program. In addition to Access databases, Visual Basic can process data stored in a number of other database formats in widespread use. However, Visual Basic lets you create and manipulate Access databases with the greatest ease. In this section, you go step by step through the procedures necessary to use the data control to display and process the information in an Access-format database of information about animal species.

The Data control connects a database to other controls on a form in which you display record fields. As you will see, the Data control lets you create a powerful and easy-to-use database front end with very little code.

You could easily use these same procedures in many different classes. The same programming techniques apply whether you are creating a database of video tapes, classifying species, or storing vocabulary words for a foreign language course.

Creating the Database

The information stored in the Animal Species database is a summary of some important characteristics of particular animal species. Figure 14-19

NOTE:

If you are using Visual Basic version 2, you will not be able to create this database or work with the Data control.

shows the database definition as it is displayed in the Fields and Indexes window of the Data Manager program. A number of fields contained in the database do not appear in the figure.

The Fields and Indexes window shows the fields that make up the Animals table of the database:

◉ The species name of the animal, called here the ScientificName

◉ The order to which the animal belongs

◉ The animal's common name

◉ The animal's habitat

◉ The animal's family name

◉ The animal's height and weight

◉ The animal's lifespan

◉ Whether the animal is warm or cold blooded

◉ Whether the animal lays eggs or bears live young

◉ Whether the animal is domesticated

◉ Whether the animal is on the endangered species list and, if so, what date the animal was put on the list

◉ Whether the animal is nocturnal

◉ A description of the animal

For instance, Figure 14-19 shows a portion of a typical entry. It is a screen shot of the Data Manager program's listing of an entry in the Animal Species database.

The choices you make about the organization of the database determine how the database will be used. To build a database about animals,

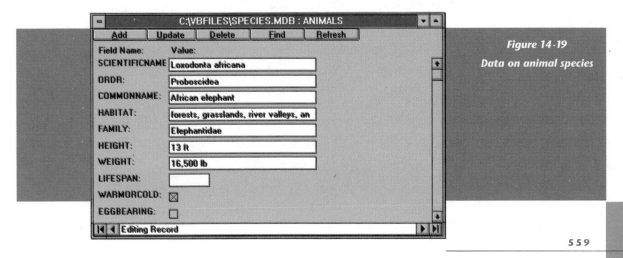

Figure 14-19

Data on animal species

you need to know what facts about the animals are important. If your database is to have an ecological slant and will contain information about whether an animal is on the endangered species list, certainly information related to that topic must be included.

As you investigate what kind of information is available concerning your subject, you must make decisions about what to include and what to exclude. When you decide to include a particular topic, you then must decide what form that information will take. Should the lifespan be represented by an integer, allowing a single number representing the number of years the animal lives, or should the lifespan be represented with a string, so that ranges of lifespans, such as 15 to 20 years, can appear? The importance you assign to a topic will partially determine how long that particular field is. How detailed a description is necessary? If your database deals with endangered species, a lengthy description of the habitat, or a separate field for changes in the habitat, may be necessary.

After you have organized the database, it can be searched. For example, you could create a list of all animals whose weight exceeds a certain value or that are cold-blooded. You could produce lists using any single field or any combination of fields.

Follow these steps to design the Animal Species database. If you are using the **species.mdb** file included on the Template disk, there is no need to enter the information. If you are not using the disk, follow these steps. Enough information is supplied for two entries in the database. You should use an encyclopedia to look up information for several more entries.

1 Start the Data Manager program.

2 Name the file **species.mdb**. Place the file in the **c:\vbfiles** directory.

3 Name the table **Animals**.

4 Enter the fields shown here. The field called ScientificName represents the name of the species. The order is represented by the field named Ordr. If you spell out this term, it conflicts with a reserved word used later in the section.

Name	Type	Length
ScientificName	Text	50
Ordr	Text	30
CommonName	Text	40
Habitat	Text	50
Family	Text	40
Height	Text	10

Name	Type	Length
Weight	Text	10
Lifespan	Integer	
WarmOrCold	Boolean	
EggBearing	Boolean	
Domestic	Boolean	
Endangered	Boolean	
DateEndangered	Date/Time	
Nocturnal	Boolean	
Description	Text	80

The Boolean data type sets up the field as a check box. Either the box is checked or it is not. No indexes are defined.

5 Use the Data Manager to enter some of the data shown in Figure 14-20. The program automatically saves the information without you having to choose Save from the File menu.

ScientificName: Giraffa camelopardalis
Order: Artiodactyla
CommonName: giraffe
Habitat: grasslands of the Saraha
Family: Giraffidae
Height: 18 ft
Weight: 3,000 lb
Lifespan: 18
☒ WarmOrCold
☐ EggBearing
☐ Domestic
☐ Endangered
DateEndangered:
☐ Nocturnal
Description:
　long neck, three horns, dark patches on a tawny coat

ScientificName: Loxodonta africana
Order: Proboscidea
CommonName: African elephant
Habitat: forests, grasslands, river valleys, and deserts
Family: Elephantidae
Height: 13 ft
Weight: 16,500 lb
Lifespan:
☒ WarmOrCold
☐ EggBearing
☐ Domestic
☐ Endangered
DateEndangered:
☐ Nocturnal
Description:
　largest living land animals

Figure 14-20
Two sample records for the Species database

Working with the Data Control

Look at the Data control. On a form, the Data control may appear as shown in Figure 14-21. The control is resizable to allow more or less room for the caption, but the icons on the end remain the same.

　You use the Data control to establish a link from Visual Basic to a set of records of the database—for instance, an entire table. The Data control opens an imaginary window into the table, then selects a single record from it. Clicking on the left arrow button fetches the previous record, if one exists. Clicking on the left-most button fetches the

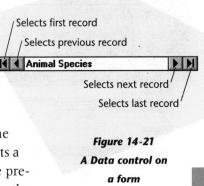

Selects first record
Selects previous record
Selects next record
Selects last record

Figure 14-21
A Data control on a form

first entry of the table. In a similar fashion, clicking on the right arrow button fetches the next record, if one exists. Clicking on the right-most button fetches the last record of the table.

The Data control itself does not display the contents of the database. As you can see in Figure 14-22, the Data control is the source of information about each record, but this information is displayed in other controls from the Visual Basic toolbox. The Data control, then, is the conduit through which the records of the database are accessed, one by one. You use other controls to let the user view and edit the fields of these records. This two-tiered architecture gives you great flexibility when designing forms.

For other controls to display information from a database, they must be (a) data-aware, which means they are able to display information from a database, and (b) linked to a Data control. The textbox, the check box, the picture box, the image control, and the label are some of the data-aware controls from the toolbox. A textbox, for instance, can be linked to display a particular field of the database linked to the Data control.

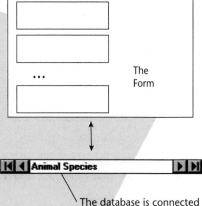

Each data-aware control is connected to a field of the database through the data control. It is a two-way connection.

The Form

The database is connected to the data control

Figure 14-22

Data-aware controls

linked to a database

Setting up the Form

Now you need to set up a form to display information from the database. This form acts as a container for the database information.

To set up the form:

1 Run Visual Basic. If Visual Basic is running, choose New Project from the File menu.

2 Change the caption of the default form to **Animal Species**.

3 Put a Data control on the form. Double-click on the icon and resize the control to stretch the area for the control's caption.

4 Select the Data control, Data1. In the Properties window, link the Data control to a particular database by setting the DatabaseName property to **c:\vbfiles\species.mdb**. See Figure 14-23.

5 Set the Caption property of the control to **Animal Species**.

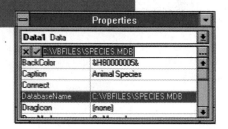

Figure 14-23

Linking the Data control to a database

6   Set the RecordSource property of the data control to
the table name of the database. See Figure 14-24.
This property, when selected for editing, displays a
menu of the table names of the database. The database
has only one table defined. As soon as the
DatabaseName property was set, the data control
establishes a link to the database.

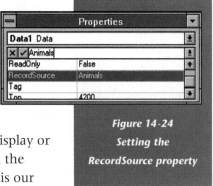

Figure 14-24

Setting the

RecordSource property

7   Determine what information of the database you wish to display or
edit. In most cases, you want to put at least one textbox on the
form to display or edit text from the database. The textbox is our
primary vehicle for interaction with the database. The Animal
Species project displays all the fields of the database.

8   Use the information in Figure 14-25 to put textboxes and check
boxes (with the proper labels) on the form.

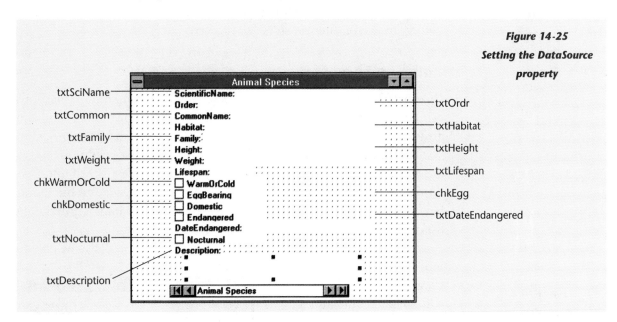

Figure 14-25

Setting the DataSource

property

9   Link each textbox you placed on the form with a field from the
database. This is a two-step process:
◎ Set the DataSource property of the textbox to indicate the
source of the data (Data1, the default name of the Data control).
Double-clicking on the DataSource property sets up the link.
◎ Set the DataField property of the textbox, to indicate which field
of the DataSource is to be displayed. This edit field provides a
list of all the possible choices for the fields of the database to be
linked to this textbox.

10 Repeat steps 8 and 9, putting textboxes on the form, binding them to the Data control *Data1* through the DataSource property, and linking them to particular fields of the database through the DataField property. The txtDescription textbox accommodates the longest text field. This textbox's MultiLine property is set to **True** to allow the data to spread to the second or third line if necessary.

11 Save the form and project files in the **c:\vbfiles** directory.

If you ran this program now, the Data control would bind itself to the proper database. The Data control would latch on to the first record of the database, giving Visual Basic access to the information. The textboxes, through their DataField property, would each grab a piece of data from the record and display that information.

If all you want to do is establish a link between data-aware controls and the information stored in the database, you are done. There is no code to write. If you want to process that information and do something with it, however, there is still a ways to go.

Building the Menu

How will you use the Animal Species database? What kind of questions can be answered with the Animal Species information? When you can answer these questions, you are ready to design a menu for the program.

Two basic uses for any database are display and searching. The two are usually interrelated. Often you will want to display lists of information that meet specific criteria: all the endangered species, all the members of a particular order or family. A search of the database provides a list of all the entries that meet those criteria.

A program that displays records of a database should also be able to modify those records. The program should be able to edit, delete, and add new records to the database.

Figure 14-26

Menu structure

The kind of searches and displays you choose are determined by your needs. A program that tries to meet every need can be confusing, so you need to organize your menus carefully.

See Figure 14-26 for the structure of the menu.

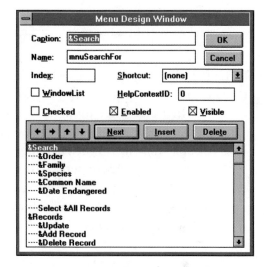

To build the menu:

1 Select the form in the Project window.

2 Open the Menu Design window.

3 Construct the menu using Figure 14-26 and the table below.

Caption	Name	Index
&Search	mnuSearchFor	
&Order	mnuSearch	1
&Family	mnuSearch	2
&Species	mnuSearch	3
&Common Name	mnuSearch	4
&Date Endangered	mnuSearch	5
-	mnuSearch	6
Select &All Records	mnuSearch	7
&Records	mnuRecords	
&Update	mnuUpdate	
&Add Record	mnuAdd	
&Delete Record	mnuDelete	
E&xit!	mnuExit	

4 Save the form and project files.

The code contained in the event procedures for these menu commands allows the user to search the database, choosing the records that meet certain criteria based on the content of the fields. The program selects and displays each record of an animal belonging to a particular order, family, or species, as well as displaying the record of an animal with a particular common name.

SQL, the Structured Query Language, is the reason the form you have created can act as a "face" to a database. This is a marvelously rich language that allows a multitude of different operations. Besides search operations, the SQL language lets us join sets of records together, delete large numbers of records, or find the first or last occurrence of a particular piece of data.

Don't look in the Visual Basic *User's Manual* for a discussion of SQL. Most of the information about SQL can be found in the Visual Basic Help files. In addition, any bookstore with a computer section will probably have books that describe this language. SQL was not designed by Microsoft. It was designed to generate search criteria independent of the details of internal file structures or specific computer architectures. SQL is device- and software-independent. Many programs use it as a query language, which is a language in which users can ask questions of a database.

Editing Current Entries of the Database

Users can interact with database information through the form you have just created. They can do far more than read the information displayed in the textboxes; they can also change that information. Textboxes, in fact, were designed for editing string information. If a user alters text from the currently displayed record within the textbox, that change can be made permanent. That is, the contents of the database file can be altered to reflect the change. The Data control is capable of sending changes in the contents of the record back to the database file for storage. The new data overwrites the old.

There are two ways to make changes permanent:

1. If a user changes information displayed in a textbox, then uses the Data control to move to another record, the altered record is written back to the database file. The changes are saved. You don't have to write any code for your program to have this behavior: the Data control gives it to you "for free."

   You could try this out now with Animal Species database. Even though the menu items have yet to be coded, you can run the program and edit a field's textbox. Advancing to the next record, or returning to a previous element, makes your change permanent. Try closing the file, reopening it, and checking for your change.

2. You can execute the **Update** method on the Data control by adding code to the event procedure of the appropriate menu command (Update, in the Records menu).

   The syntax for the **Update** method is:

   ```
   Data1.RecordSet.Update
   ```

RecordSet refers to the collection of records currently linked to the Data control. This collection can be an entire table from the database, a subset of a table, or even a set of records composed of fields from several tables. Using SQL, you can define a set of records chosen by specific criteria. These records, once chosen, are separated from the other records of the database and are treated as a unit. Examples of how to use SQL are presented later in the chapter.

The **Update** method forces the contents of the copy buffer to be copied back into the database file. This replaces the record in the database on disk with the edited contents of the Data control's current record. The copy buffer is the area of memory used to hold the current record—the one being edited.

For the Animal Species application, you can think of the copy buffer as being the textboxes and check boxes in which the fields of the record are displayed. The real copy buffer may be larger. It is not required that every field of the record be displayed in a bound control. (A bound control is a data-aware control, like a textbox, connected to a database through its DataSource property.) Nevertheless, all the fields of the current record, even those not displayed, are present in the copy buffer.

The Records menu contains three commands in its submenu. See Figure 14-27. The first allows the user to force the database to be updated with the information contained in the bound controls, when that information has been edited. For instance, if there were a spelling error in one of the records, the user could use the Data control's arrows to make that record the current record, so that its fields appear in the textboxes. Once the record is displayed in the textboxes, the user could edit the text of its fields. The version of the record in the copy buffer will then differ from the record stored in the database.

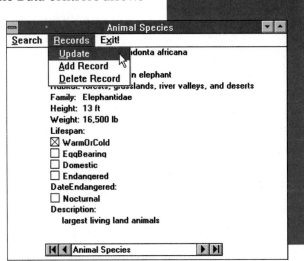

Figure 14-27

Records menu

After a record has been edited, the user can write the changes back to the database by choosing the Update command from the Records menu. This command forces an update of the current record in the database file with the contents of the copy buffer. The user can also update the database simply by moving to a different entry using the arrows on the data control.

Enter this line in the mnuUpdate_Click event:

```
Data1.RecordSet.Update
```

Adding a Record

Users may want to add information to the database, as well as editing or updating it. For this purpose, you included an Add Record command in the Records menu. Writing the code for this command involves adding a single line to its event procedure.

To add a record to the database, the copy buffer must be cleared. When this buffer is cleared, the user can enter information directly into the textboxes connected to the fields of the database. When the fields are filled, the **Update** method is executed to write the contents of the new record to the database file.

You use the **AddNew** method to clear the copy buffer and the textboxes connected to the database file. The syntax of this method is the same as that of the **Update** method:

```
Data1.RecordSet.AddNew
```

Add this line of code to the mnuAdd_Click routine. Note that you could have used a command button (captioned Add) instead of a menu command for this purpose.

Deleting a Record

Another way in which users will want to interact with the database is to delete information from it. For this purpose, they will select the Delete Record command from the Records menu. Coding this menu command to delete database information is as easy as coding the Update and Add Record commands: you need to add a single line to the routine for the command.

A deleted record doesn't disappear from the textboxes immediately, but it is removed from the database file. Once a user moves to another record, the deleted record is no longer available.

The syntax for the Delete method is the same as that for the **Update** and the **AddNew** methods. Add this line to the mnuDelete_Click routine:

```
Data1.RecordSet.Delete
```

Writing the Code for the Search For Command

You have written only three lines of code so far for this program. Updating, deleting, and adding records are quite simple operations. Searching the database, however, is a more complex operation. It is one of the principal means by which data is transformed into information. We store data in databases to unburden ourselves from remembering vast amounts of detail. The ability to search a database justifies this approach: it lets us reliably and rapidly find the needle in the haystack. By searching, we can sift through tons of data to isolate the small amount of material we seek. Searching lets us discover patterns and structure in large amounts of data that we would not be able to detect without the aid of a computer.

For all but one of the menu items in the Search For submenu, a search string is collected from the user with an **InputBox** function. The overall structure of the routine is as follows.

If Select All Records is clicked **Then**
    choose all the records from the database
    and display them ordered by their CommonName field
Else
Collect search string, *Target*, from user
    If "Order" is chosen
        choose records whose "Ordr" matches the *Target*
    If "Family" is chosen
        choose records whose "Family" matches the *Target*
    If "Species" is chosen
        choose records whose "Species" matches the *Target*
    If "Common Name" is chosen
        choose records whose "CommonName" field matches
the *Target*
    If "Date Endangered" is chosen
        choose records whose "Date Endangered" field matches
the *Target*
Finally, refresh the record set from the database.

Last things first. The **Refresh** method goes to the database file and selects the records that match the search criteria expressed in the SQL query. This is always the last step in an SQL search.

Coding the SQL Search

To initiate an SQL search, load the RecordSource property of the Data control with an SQL query string. Take a look at such a string:

SELECT * FROM Animals ORDER BY CommonName

The first part of the phrase, *SELECT *,* tells Visual Basic to select all the fields of all the records that match the search criteria.

The next part of the string designates the table from which the records are to come. In this case, the records come from the Animals table. Recall that this is the only table defined in the database. It is possible to fetch records containing fields from more than one table using the *FROM* clause of the *SELECT* statement.

The last part of the statement displays the records in *ORDER BY* the values in the *CommonName* field. This shows the Animal Species database in alphabetical order by the common name of the animal. Regardless of the order in which records have been entered into the database, this command lets the Data control move through the records in the order of their *CommonName* field.

In some ways this is not a typical SQL search string. There is no *WHERE* clause. The *WHERE* clause puts restrictions on what records are chosen. The way this SQL string is written, all the records of the database are chosen. This string is used in the code that selects all the records from the database.

Now you will enter the code for the commands in the Search menu:

1 Select the form from the Project window.

2 Enter these lines in the mnuSearch_Click procedure.

```
Dim Target
'—Select All is different from the others.
If Index = 7 Then
    Data1.RecordSource = "SELECT * FROM Animals ORDER BY CommonName"
    Data1.Refresh
Else
```

From this code you can see how to use the SQL string. It is enclosed in quotes and assigned to the RecordSource property of the Data control. The **Refresh** method is applied to the Data control to reselect the appropriate records from the database. The next section of code collects the target string from the user. By this point of the procedure, the user has chosen one of the submenu choices that requires the entry of a search string.

3 Enter these lines:

```
Const Msg = "Enter search string"
Const Msg2 = "Searching For..."
'—Collect search information from user
Target = InputBox(Msg, Msg2)
```

4 The section of code that deals with finding records that have a certain date has an interesting twist. Unlike the other SQL statements in this section, the date string isn't really a string at all. The date is a special kind of value, neither string nor whole number nor decimal. To signal Visual Basic you are dealing with this special kind of data, enclose the date string within number signs: #.
Enter these lines:

```
Select Case Index
    Case 5
        Data1.RecordSource = "SELECT * FROM Animals WHERE DateEndangered=
#" & Target & "#"
```

The SQL string is joined together from standard pieces like "SELECT *" and "FROM Animals" along with the *WHERE* clause and the actual target string. Notice the number signs bracketing the date string collected through the **InputBox** function.

The *WHERE* clause puts a restriction on the records collected from the Animals table of the database. In this clause the DateEndangered field is restricted to those values that match the date in the *Target* string. No other records are chosen from the database file.

The remaining cases all assign to *Data1.RecordSource* an SQL string with a *WHERE* clause of the following form: WHERE *fieldname* = "Target". This clause will restrict the records fetched to those that match this selection criterion.

5   Enter these lines:

```
    Case 1
        Data1.RecordSource = "SELECT * FROM Animals WHERE
    Ordr= '" & Target & "' ORDER BY Family"
    Case 2
        Data1.RecordSource = "SELECT * FROM Animals WHERE
    Family= '" & Target & "' ORDER BY ScientificName"
    Case 3
        Data1.RecordSource = "SELECT * FROM Animals WHERE
    ScientificName= '" & Target & "'"
    Case 4
        Data1.RecordSource = "SELECT * FROM Animals WHERE
    CommonName= '" & Target & "'"
    End Select
    Data1.Refresh
End If
```

Look at the "Ordr" and "Family" branches. The *SELECT* statements in those branches have a *WHERE* clause and an *ORDER BY* clause at the end. These statements pick all the records whose Ordr field or Family field matches the target string. In addition, the records are displayed in order. If select by Ordr is chosen, the records are displayed in order by their Family. If select by Family is chosen, the records are displayed in order by their scientific names.

QUESTIONS AND ACTIVITIES

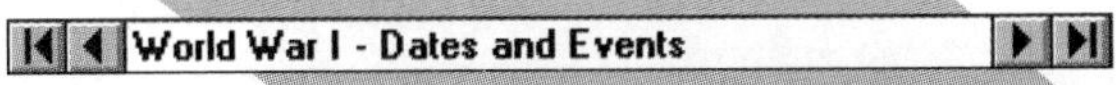

Figure 14-28
Functions of arrows on
Data control

1. If you were redesigning the Animal Species database, what new fields would you include? Which, if any, would you drop? Justify your answers.

2. Explain the functions of the arrows on the Data control. See Figure 14-28.

3. Is the Data control more like a linked or an embedded object? Why?

4. What does it mean when we say the Data control is the "conduit through which the records of the database are accessed"?

5. What properties do data-aware controls have that nondata-aware controls do not have? Which controls are data-aware?

6. Summarize the steps necessary to set up a Data control on a form to link to a database file.

7. Summarize the steps necessary to link data-aware textboxes to the database through the Data control to display fields of the database.

8. Explain the syntax and action of the following methods: **Update**, **AddNew**, and **Delete**.

9. What is the RecordSet?

10. What does SQL stand for?

11. Describe the copy buffer.

12. What does the **Refresh** method do?

13. Explain and give an example of each of the following SQL terms:
    a) "SELECT *"   c) "WHERE ..."
    b) "FROM ..."   d) "ORDER BY ..."

14. What special action needs to be taken to indicate that a string in an SQL string represents a date or time?

15. Use the Help system to look up WHERE. Write an SQL string that will choose all the records in the Animal Species database where the Weight is more than 80 lb.

Summary

OLE, or object linking and embedding, and the Data control are two of the ways Visual Basic can manage data from other applications.

OLE permits sophisticated cutting and pasting of data from one place to another. The Class property of an OLE object determines the type of data that may be represented by the object. An example of an entry in the Class property is "ExcelWorksheet", indicating the object represents an Excel spreadsheet.

The SourceDoc property links the OLE control with a file that contains the data for the object. The SourceItem property links the OLE control with a subset of the information contained in the SourceDoc file.

The OLETypeAllowed property determines whether the object displayed on the form is linked or embedded. A linked object maintains a connection from the data displayed in the OLE object to the original data in the original application. The displayed data is stored in and maintained by the original application that created the data. An embedded object contains the data displayed in the OLE object and maintains a link to the application that created the object.

If the AutoActivate property is set to **True**, double-clicking on the OLE object on the form starts up the application that created the data displayed in the OLE object. This allows the user to modify the information contained in the OLE object.

The SizeMode property of the OLE object determines the relationship between the size of the data represented by the object and the size of the window given to the object in which to display the data. The SourceItem property represents spreadsheet ranges with the Row, Column format. For instance, R1C1:R3C10 indicates the rectangular range in a spreadsheet from row 1, column 1, to row 3, column 10. The Action property of the OLE object can create the linked or embedded object at run-time once all the other properties just discussed are set.

The Microsoft Access database engine, which is the name for the routines that perform much of the work on Access database files, is a part of Visual Basic. As a result, Visual Basic has the ability to manipulate these database files.

The Data Manager program lets the user create database files in the format of an Access database. A database is made up of tables of related information. Each table in turn is made of fields. Each field has a data type and a name. The information of the database is stored in the fields. A record is a complete entry of information in a database.

The Data control, which is included in versions 3 and 4 of Visual Basic, gives a Visual Basic program access to the information contained in database files. Data-aware controls, such as the textbox or picture box, link to the Data control and display information from the file to which the Data control is linked. The DatabaseName property of the Data control links the control with a file containing a database.

The RecordSource property of the Data control links the control to the records of a particular table within the database. It is used to select particular records specified by an SQL search string. The DataSource property of a data-aware control links the control with a Data control. This is the source of the data displayed by the data-aware control. The DataField property of the data-aware control links the control with a particular field of the database. This field is then displayed and can be modified through the data-aware control.

The **Update**, **AddNew,** and **Delete** methods let you control the contents of the database through the copy buffer. The contents of the copy buffer are displayed through the data-aware controls such as the text or picture boxes. When the **Update** method is executed, any changes made to the copy of the currently displayed record in the copy buffer are written back to the database file. The **AddNew** method clears the copy buffer and the textboxes of the form and allows the user to enter a new record into the database file. Using the **Delete** method, a user can remove the currently displayed record from the database file.

Visual Basic supports Structured Query Language, which is a language designed for searching in a database file. Some commonly used parts of the SQL language are the SELECT, FROM, WHERE, and ORDER BY clauses.

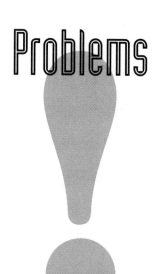

Problems

1. The Excel CD Program

Use Excel to create a simple list of CDs. Use categories such as the following:
- ◎ Title
- ◎ Artist
- ◎ Performance date
- ◎ Number of songs
- ◎ Total playing time
- ◎ Guest Artists

Once the spreadsheet has been created, write a Visual Basic program that uses an OLE control to display the spreadsheet. First, link the spreadsheet to the Visual Basic program. Then try embedding the spreadsheet. What differences do you find in the way the application behaves?

2. The Personal Inventory Program

Create a database of personal items. Use categories like those below, but add, adapt, or omit categories to meet your needs:
- ◎ Description
- ◎ Quantity
- ◎ Date last used
- ◎ Location
- ◎ Value

Create an Access format database using Access or the Data Manager program. Each of the categories will become field names in the *Inventory* table. Each record of the database will represent a different item. Once the database has been designed, write a Visual Basic program to access the fields of the database. Your program should let you display each record of the database. It should also let you edit, delete, and add new records.

3. The Word Processor Project

Create three word processing documents, using Microsoft Word, Write, or any other application that supports object linking and embedding. In the first document, include a short summary of events from your home life that have been significant; in the second, a list of interesting classroom events; and in the third, a summary of events you have enjoyed in your work or extracurricular activities.

After these documents are created, create a Visual Basic program using the Multiple Document Interface (or just four forms if you skipped that chapter). The first form should contain a menu to load each of the other three. The second form should contain an OLE control linked to your first document, displaying a paragraph of that document. The third form should be linked to the second document, and the fourth form should be linked to the third document. Size the windows and open the word processor and the Visual Basic program so you can see both at once. Make changes to the word processing document and see if the changes are reflected in the Visual Basic OLE control on the appropriate form.

4. The Database Project

Pick a subject that interests you, find a source of information about that subject, and design a database structure to represent information about that subject. For instance, if you were interested in Historic Route 66, you could find a book about it in your library and create a database of famous or historic businesses and tourist sites along the route. Once the database is designed, write a Visual Basic program that will let you display, edit, delete, and search the database for records that meet specific search criteria. Use the SQL search strings to find information in the database.

5. The Baseball Card Project

Write a program to display, maintain, and search the baseball card database.

6. Home Possessions Project

Design a database to hold information about the possessions of your home, with information about their purchase price, their current market value, the date bought, a description of the item and a location of the item. This kind of data is invaluable should your home be burglarized. Write a Visual Basic program to display and maintain that database.

```
Dim Row As Integer
Dim CellAddr As
String
For Sheet = 2 To 7
ShAddr = "g" &
Trim$(Str$(Row))
Sheets("Sheet2")
.Select
```

Programming in Word and Excel

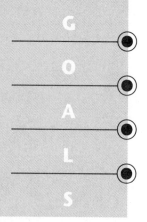

After working through this chapter, you will be able to:

Recognize some of the differences between WordBasic and Visual Basic.

Record macros in WordBasic and add programming statements to turn them into applications.

Record macros in Excel and add Visual Basic for Applications (VBA) procedures to build a worksheet application.

O V E R V I E W

Microsoft Office is completely programmable. Every part and feature can be programmed with languages that look very much like Visual Basic.

*You may already have some experience with applications programming in Office because when you record a macro, that produces code. In addition to the macro code, you can add program statements such as **For-Next** and **Do-While** loops to automate repetitive processes. Every time you find yourself cutting and pasting over and over again, or reformatting file after file, you are performing tasks that probably could be automated by writing a program. Using programs to link different parts of Microsoft Office together allows you to build custom tailored applications for your specific needs.*

The difficult part of programming Office is interacting with objects in the different applications. Using macros to learn how to interact with the application is the key to learning how to program the application. Recording a macro and then examining the code produced, teaches you how to program exactly what you want.

The first section in this chapter presents an overview of programming with Microsoft Office as well as examining some of the differences between Visual Basic and Office's versions of Basic. The second section guides you through recording macros in Word and Excel, examining the code produced, and then enhancing the macro code. The third section guides you through a Word application to learn how to automate the process of converting file formats. Finally, the fourth section shows you how to program an application using macros and programming techniques to automate a car dealership's customer and vehicle database.

Application Programming Overview

Microsoft Office Professional is comprised of four applications, or programs: Word, Excel, PowerPoint, and Access. Software, like most things, grows in fits and starts. For example, most software, including each of the Microsoft Office applications, evolves and changes from one revision to the next. Usually, revisions to a program range from fixing bugs to the addition of new features. At other times, a revision can mean a complete overhaul. Of the four applications in Microsoft Office, Word and Excel are quite mature, PowerPoint is newer, and Access, the database program, has been extensively revised and updated. Because of these different evolutionary stages, there are three versions of Basic to be used with the three main applications of Office.

Section 1 presents an overview of programming in Word and a little about Excel. You will learn the major differences between Visual Basic and Office's versions of Basic; a few reasons for programming Word and Excel; and you will record a Word macro and study its code.

WordBasic Programming

Because Word is the oldest application in Microsoft Office, WordBasic, its version of Basic, is the least sophisticated. With the release of Office 97, the old WordBasic language is being replaced with Visual Basic for Applications (VBA), a language much more like Visual Basic. However, thousands of companies still use Word with WordBasic, so the emphasis here will be on programming in WordBasic.

Why would you want to program your word processor? Word is a very rich program already. It has hundreds of features such as templates, wizards, and mail merge to help you create documents and perform tasks productively. However, even with all these tools there will be times when Word alone can't perform the tasks you need it to do. For example, suppose your company is switching from a different word processing program to Word, and you need to convert all of the company's documents to Word format. Also, newer versions of Word are integrated with the Internet. So a world of incompatible documents may be waiting to be processed. With a knowledge of WordBasic, you can be ready to do it.

If you're using Word now to create documents, you may be wondering where to put the program code. The answer is that WordBasic code is added to Word macros. When you record a macro, the keystrokes are converted into WordBasic commands and saved in a file. Originally, a macro was just a way to prerecord keystrokes, and that's still part of what a macro is. However, today, you can extend that code by adding WordBasic commands.

Next, you will record a macro and look at the code it produces. Later in this chapter you will learn how to add your own code to macros.

Recording the email Macro

The world has not yet decided how to spell e-mail. Various authorities use the hyphenated spelling; others omit it. As an introduction to Word-Basic, you will record a macro to convert E-mail or e-mail to email for a single document.

1 Start Word and open a document. It doesn't matter if the document contains the word e-mail or not. You cannot record or run a macro unless a document is open.

2 Click on the Tools menu and select Macro. The Macro dialog box appears.

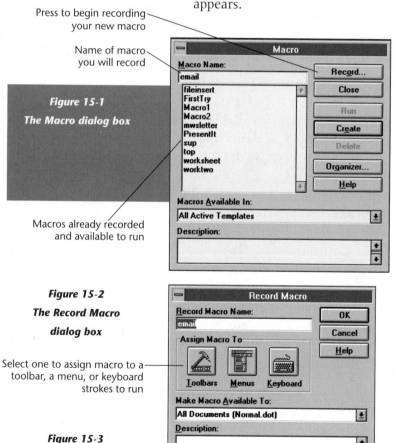

Press to begin recording your new macro

Name of macro you will record

Figure 15-1
The Macro dialog box

Macros already recorded and available to run

Figure 15-2
The Record Macro dialog box

Select one to assign macro to a toolbar, a menu, or keyboard strokes to run

Figure 15-3
The Macro toolbar

3 Enter **email** as the name of the macro as shown in Figure 15-1.

4 Click on Record. The Record Macro dialog box appears. This dialog box lets you insert the macro command you are recording into a menu or toolbar, or assign keyboard strokes to run it. You won't do that now, but remember this for later.

5 Click OK in the Record Macro dialog box to begin recording your keystrokes. You are returned to your document, and the Macro toolbar appears as shown in Figure 15-3. It contains buttons to Stop and Pause recording.

Stop — Pause

6 Press Ctrl+Home to move the cursor to the top of the document. Be sure to do this even if you are already at the top of the document.

7 Click on Edit and select Replace. The Replace dialog box appears as shown in Figure 15-4.

Figure 15-4

The Replace dialog box

8 Enter **E-mail** in the Find What box and **email** in the Replace With box. The options Match Case, Find Whole Words Only, Use Pattern Matching, and Sounds Like, should not be checked. If they are checked, you must uncheck them.

9 Press the Replace All button.

10 Word searches the document for the word *E-mail* or *e-mail* and when either is found, Word replaces it with the word *email*, and reports the result in a message box. Click OK and Close.

11 Click the Stop button on the Macro toolbar to stop recording.

Once the macro is recorded, it can be executed from the Macro dialog box, which is displayed by first selecting the Tools menu, then Macro.

Next, you will examine the code generated by the macro.

1 Click Tools and select Macro. Enter the name **email** in the Macro Name box or click on *email* in the macro list. Do not double-click on the name because that will execute the macro.

2 Click on Edit. A window appears with the code that was generated when you recorded the email macro. The code you see should be similar to that shown below:

```
Sub MAIN
StartOfDocument
EditReplace .Find = "E-mail", .Replace = "email", .Direction = 0,
.MatchCase = 0, .WholeWord = 0, .PatternMatch = 0, .SoundsLike =
0, .ReplaceAll, .Format = 0, .Wrap = 1
End Sub
```

Here, the only lines of code that look like Visual Basic language are the first and last lines. The rest of the commands generated by the macro are commands that execute Word actions. **StartOfDocument** is the command generated by Ctrl+Home, the command that moved the cursor to the top of the document.

EditReplace is equivalent to clicking the Edit menu and selecting Replace. **.Find**, **.Replace**, and the rest, correspond to actions chosen in the Replace dialog box. They are *named parameters*. WordBasic uses named parameters because most commands have many, many parameters.

In Section 3 you will learn how to adapt this macro to work with multiple files.

Some Differences Between WordBasic and Visual Basic

There are only two data types in WordBasic: Number and String. The Number type can represent either whole or decimal numbers. Variables of the String type must end in a dollar sign. The data types of the variables are implicit in the variables' names and are not stated in the program.

True and *False* are not predefined constants in WordBasic. A program that uses *True* and *False* must declare and initialize these variables.

WordBasic's **InputBox$** function is much the same as it is in Visual Basic, but it requires the dollar sign to indicate that the function returns a String value. In Visual Basic, omitting the dollar sign means the function returns a Variant type—a type that doesn't exist in WordBasic.

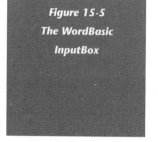
Figure 15-5
The WordBasic
InputBox

The **InputBox$** function in WordBasic opens a dialog box that looks quite different from the Input dialog box generated by Visual Basic.

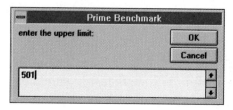

The **For-Next** and **Assignment** statements are the same as Visual Basic's; however, WordBasic uses a more primitive form of the indefinite loop:

> **While** condition is *True*
> ... body of loop
> **Wend**

This is similar to the Visual Basic command for the **Do-While** loop, but the syntax is not as versatile as it is in Visual Basic. Visual Basic (VB) allows the following variations of the Do-Loop:

> **Do**
> ... body
> **Loop While** condition is *True*

This version tests the condition at the end of the loop, thus ensuring that the body of the loop will execute at least once.

> **Do**
> ... body
> **Loop Until** condition is *True*

In this variation, the loop continues while the condition is false, in other words it continues until the condition is *True*.

Finally,

> **Do Until** condition is *True*
> ... body
> **Loop**

This version tests the condition at the top of the loop and continues executing the loop until the condition is *True*.

In contrast, WordBasic's **While-Wend** statement tests the condition at the top of the loop and continues while the condition is *True*.

The **If-Then-Else-End If** is the same in WordBasic as it is in Visual Basic.

The **Chr$()** function, which converts an ASCII code to a character, requires the dollar sign.

To join two strings, WordBasic uses the plus sign. The ampersand used in Visual Basic doesn't work in WordBasic.

The **Insert** command inserts text into a document. There will be more about this in the next section.

You *cannot* cut and paste a Visual Basic program into WordBasic, but you *can* cut and paste a WordBasic program into Visual Basic with only minor modifications.

All in all, there are more similarities than there are differences, but those differences can cause long frustrating minutes of debugging when you are writing programs.

Suggestions for How to Learn More

The best way to learn more about WordBasic is to experiment with it. Record a macro. Edit its code. We will do that later in this chapter. Put the cursor on a menu command and press F1, and WordBasic Help will provide an article on that command. Reading the article will probably raise further questions and provide links to other articles. Follow the links. Many of the articles have sample code. Study the code. Copy the code and paste it into your experimental macros. This kind of interactive learning is the best way to learn about WordBasic.

In addition, Office comes with extensive printed documentation that explains each command. Microsoft will provide a Developer's Handbook. Books are available in bookstores, and sample code is available on the Internet.

There are many sources of information. Find an experienced programmer and ask questions. Post questions on an electronic bulletin board or the Usenet. Posted questions usually receive helpful answers.

VBA for Excel Programming

The Basic built into Excel is called Visual Basic for Applications (VBA). It is much more like Visual Basic than WordBasic. In fact, it has some of the most up-to-date features found in recent versions of Visual Basic. Because of the strong similarity between Visual Basic and VBA, writing code in VBA is much easier than it is in WordBasic. In addition, VBA's programming environment (the way you enter programs) is much more like the Visual Basic you already know.

You can use VBA for simple tasks such as formatting worksheets or changing the report heading in many worksheets. However, an entire complex financial analysis program can also be written with VBA. For example, you could write a VBA program that imports data from an Access database, and using Excel, rework that data into tabular or chart form. Then it can be formatted as a report or exported into a Word document.

Once you start programming in Office, you'll see that everything you do gives you ideas for new programs. In Sections 2 and 4 of this chapter you will find out how to record Excel macros, analyze their code, and extend them with VBA statements into true applications.

QUESTIONS

1. Give two reasons why programs are revised.

2. What is a macro?

3. In the email macro, you typed E-mail in the Find What box and email in the Replace With box. Why doesn't the case of the letter *e* matter in the search and replace operation that is performed?

4. Edit the email macro and delete all the named parameters except **.Find** and **.Replace**. Run the macro. What happens?

5. Why are named parameters used in WordBasic?

6. What are the two WordBasic data types? Are two types enough? How do Visual Basic's many data types make programming easier?

7. The earliest versions of Basic did not have any kind of indefinite loop. **While-Wend**, although an older statement than **Do-While-Loop**, did not appear in the original versions of Basic. Look up the **While-Wend** statement in Visual Basic Help. Can it be used in Visual Basic programs? Write a summary of the **While-Wend** syntax.

8. In Visual Basic, the **Chr()** function returns a Variant type. Because the Variant type is compatible with the String type, there is no problem when you use the result of the function in the place of String. Why won't **Chr()** work in WordBasic?

9. What symbol do you use in WordBasic to join two strings? Does it work in Visual Basic?

10. Describe two ways you can find out more about WordBasic.

11. Describe a situation in which you would use VBA to program an Excel application.

Programming Macros

Section

In Section 2 you will record another macro in Word, examine the code produced, and add a shortcut button to a toolbar to run the macro. Then you will record an Excel macro, examine its code, and add Visual Basic statements to enhance its functionality.

As you saw earlier, recording a macro translates the keystrokes and mouse clicks into commands. In Word, the commands are in WordBasic. In Excel, the commands are in VBA. In Access, the commands are translated into Access Basic.

By studying the commands created and run by macros, you are studying the language that underlies each of the applications: Word, Excel, and Access.

Programming Word Macros

The macro you will record does not have a valid function. The keystrokes have been chosen just to learn how typical Word formatting commands are translated into WordBasic, a technique you will use frequently.

When you have completed all the steps, your document should look like Figure 15-6 (although your default fonts may be different):

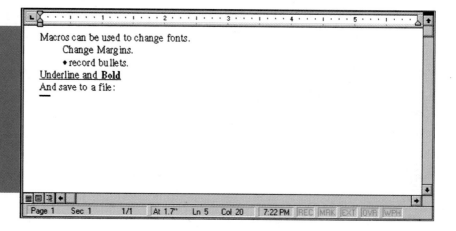

Now you will record the macro and examine the code generated.

1 Start Word, and, if necessary, click on the New document button in the toolbar or pull down the File menu and click on New. Accept the document based on the Normal template.

2 Click on Tools and select Macro to open the Macro dialog box.

3 Enter **FirstTry** as the name of the macro.

4 Click on Record to open the Record Macro dialog box.

The Record Macro dialog box allows you to insert your new macro into a menu or toolbar, or define keystrokes that will execute your command when pressed.

5 Click on the Menus icon to add your new macro to a menu. The Customize dialog box appears with the Menus tab chosen as shown in Figure 15-7.

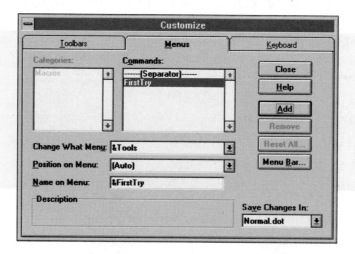

As a default, the command is added to the Tools menu, below a separator bar, with the macro's name as its menu entry.

6 Accept these defaults by clicking on Add and then Close. You are returned to your original document with the Macro toolbar present, and each keystroke you make will be recorded.

7 Click on the New document button in the toolbar or pull down the File menu and click on New. Accept the document based on the Normal template.

8 Click on the Font window in the toolbar and choose Times New Roman even if it is the default. If this font is not installed in your system, pick another font.

9 Set the Font Size to 12.

10 Enter the text **Macros can be used to change fonts**. Press Enter at the end of the line.

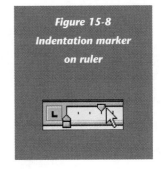

11 On the left edge of the ruler, pull the top indentation marker to the third unit from the left edge. (Click View and select Ruler if needed.) This changes the first line indentation of a paragraph as shown in Figure 15-8.

12 Enter the text **Change Margins**. Press Enter at the end of the line.

13 Click the Bullet icon on the toolbar and press the spacebar. Enter the text: **record bullets**. Press Enter, then click the Bullet icon to turn bullets off.

14 Press the Underline button to turn on underlining and enter the following text: **Underline and** followed by a space.

15 Press the Bold button to turn on bold face and enter the word **Bold**.

16 Press the Bold button to turn bold face off. Press the Underline button to turn underlining off. Press Enter.

17 Enter the text **And Save to a file:**

18 Click File and select Save As. Enter the file and pathname **c:\temp\firsttry.doc** and click on OK or Save. Your new document is saved. This does not save the macro itself—the macro is saved as a part of the Normal template.

19 Click the Stop button on the Macro toolbar.

20 Close the document.

Before examining the code generated by the macro, execute the macro.

1 Click the Tools menu and select FirstTry, the macro you just recorded.

2 A new document is created and saved that should resemble Figure 15-6.

That's it. You've recorded and run your macro from a menu. Now let's look at the code.

1 Click the Tools menu and select Macro. The Macro dialog box opens again.

2 Click on the name FirstTry or enter it into the Macro Name box.

3 Choose Edit.

4 Your code should be similar to the following:

```
Sub MAIN
FileNewDefault
Font "Times New Roman"
FontSize 12
Insert "Macros can be used to change fonts."
InsertPara
FormatParagraph .FirstIndent = "0.38" + Chr$(34)
Insert "Change Margins"
InsertPara
FormatBulletDefault
Insert " record bullets"
InsertPara
FormatBulletDefault
Underline
Insert "Underline and "
Bold
Insert "Bold"
Bold
Underline
InsertPara
Insert "And Save to a file:"
FileSaveAs .Name = "C:\TEMP\FIRSTTRY.DOC", .Format = 0,
.LockAnnot = 0, .Password = "", .AddToMru = 1, .WritePassword =
"", .RecommendReadOnly = 0, .EmbedFonts = 0,
.NativePictureFormat = 0, .FormsData = 0
End Sub
```

All of these WordBasic commands have something to do with manipulating documents. Many of the commands in the code above are self-explanatory, like: **Font "Times New Roman"** or **FontSize 12**. Some of the commands toggle features on and off like **FormatBullet-Default**, **Underline** and **Bold**. The first toggle turns the feature on, the second turns it off.

The **Insert** command inserts the text that follows into the document at the current cursor position. The text may be enclosed in double quotes as shown or may come from a string function or a variable. Strings can be joined together with a plus sign. Text longer than a single line wraps around to the next line. The **InsertPara** command appears wherever you press the Enter key when recording the macro.

Some commands, like **FormatParagraph** and **FileSaveAs**, have several optional subparts called arguments. Each argument, also called a *named parameter*, starts with a period.

As you would expect with any Microsoft product, the WordBasic Help system holds a large amount of information about each command. Many commands even have samples that can be copied and pasted into your own code. The only obstacle to using WordBasic Help is that you may not have installed it when you first installed Microsoft Office. One of the options when installing Office is to omit WordBasic Help. Luckily, however, it's easy to install just the Help system part of Office from the original disks.

Is there anyone on Earth who knows all these commands? Maybe, but the usual way to learn commands that you don't know is to record them in a separate macro, and then cut and paste them into the macro on which you're working.

Adding *FirstTry* to a Toolbar

In the exercise above you learned how to add a macro to a menu, now you will add a shortcut button for the FirstTry macro on the Formatting toolbar.

1 Start Word. Open a document or click on the New document icon.

2 Click Tools and select Customize. The Customize dialog box appears.

3 Choose the Toolbars tab as shown in Figure 15-9.

4 In the Categories list, scroll down and select Macros.

5 In the Macros list, click and hold on FirstTry. When you click and hold on a macro name in this list, the mouse cursor becomes a square the size of a toolbar button. Drag the mouse to the Formatting toolbar and release the mouse button to the right of the Font Size control. A blank button appears in the toolbar.

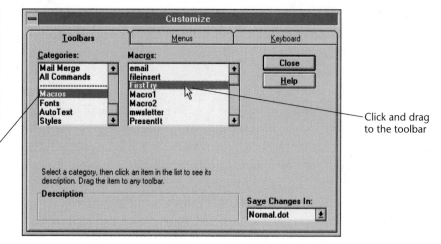

Select Macros from
the Categories list

Click and drag
to the toolbar

6 The Custom Button dialog box appears, giving you a selection of buttons with icons or a Text Button. Click on Assign. The macro becomes a part of your toolbar with the name of the macro on the Text Button. With this button you can execute FirstTry with a single mouse click.

If you don't want the FirstTry macro as a permanent part of your toolbar, click and drag it off the bar. If you have closed the Customize dialog box, you will have to reopen it to remove the button.

Programming Excel Macros

In WordBasic, the canvas you use to record macros is the document. In Excel, you draw directly onto a worksheet to record macros. The resulting VBA programs are stored in module sheets that become part of the workbook. The module sheet can be moved from workbook to workbook as needed.

VBA allows you to vary the "look and feel" of your programs with many of the same features you used in Visual Basic: input boxes, text boxes, labels, command buttons, list boxes, and so on. These can help turn an Excel worksheet into something that looks and works like a custom application, and is easy for even a nontechnical user to run.

Now, you will record an Excel macro and examine the code generated. This macro builds a worksheet to determine the cost of an auto loan. Later you will enhance the code by adding input boxes.

1 Start Excel.

2 Click Tools and select Record Macro (in Win95, click Record New Macro). The Record New Macro dialog box appears as shown in Figure 15-10. Enter the name **AutoWorksheet** and click OK to

begin recording your keystrokes. You are returned to the
worksheet, and the Macro Stop button appears.

3 Move to or click on
each cell (including
A1) listed below
and enter the text,
formulas, and
further actions
shown. Figure 15-
11 shows the com-
pleted worksheet.

Figure 15-10
Record New Macro
dialog box

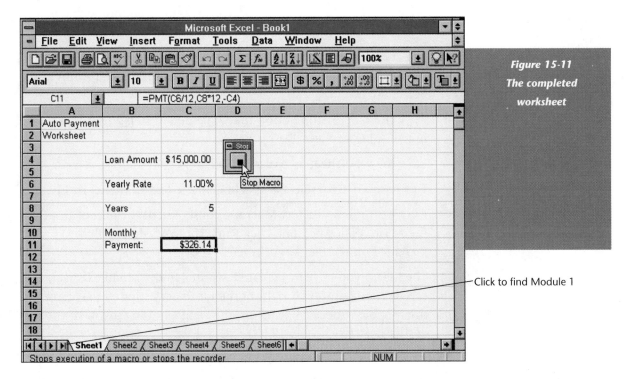

Figure 15-11
The completed
worksheet

Click to find Module 1

Cell	Text	*Further Action*
A1	Auto Payment	
A2	Worksheet	
B4	Loan Amount	
B6	Yearly Rate	
B8	Years	
B10	Monthly	
B11	Payment:	

Cell	Text	Further Action
C4	15000	Select cell C4 and click the currency style button on the toolbar.
C6	0.11	Select cell C6 and click the percent style button on the toolbar. Click the Increase Decimal button on the toolbar twice.
C8	5	
C11	=PMT(C6/12,C8*12,-C4)	Select C11 and click the currency style button even though it is already formatted.

4 Select columns A through C, using the mouse to select the column letters. Click the Format menu and select Columns and AutoFit Selection.

5 Click the Macro Stop button that appeared in step 2 to stop recording your keystrokes.

6 Save the worksheet as **AutoWrk.xls**.

7 To run the macro, select and delete all the text in the worksheet.

8 Click on Tools and select Macro. Choose **AutoWorksheet** from the Macro dialog box and click Run. The worksheet will be recreated on the blank worksheet.

The Macro you have just created is stored in the Module1 sheet, and can be found at the far right of the tab sheet listing. If you can't see the Module1 sheet tab, click on the right-pointing arrow at the left of the sheet tabs.

9 Click on the Module1 sheet tab. Your code should be similar to the code below. If you altered the order of keystrokes in the steps above, the commands will be in a different sequence, but that probably won't affect the results.

```
Sub AutoWorksheet()
    Range("A1").Select
    ActiveCell.FormulaR1C1 = "Auto Payment"
    Range("A2").Select
    ActiveCell.FormulaR1C1 = "Worksheet"
    Range("B4").Select
```

```
    ActiveCell.FormulaR1C1 = "Loan Amount"
    Range("B6").Select
    ActiveCell.FormulaR1C1 = "Yearly Rate"
    Range("B8").Select
    ActiveCell.FormulaR1C1 = "Years"
    Range("B10").Select
    ActiveCell.FormulaR1C1 = "Monthly"
    Range("B11").Select
    ActiveCell.FormulaR1C1 = "Payment:"
    Range("C4").Select
    ActiveCell.FormulaR1C1 = "15000"
    Range("C4").Select
    Selection.Style = "Currency"
    Range("C6").Select
    ActiveCell.FormulaR1C1 = "0.11"
    Range("C6").Select
    Selection.Style = "Percent"
    Selection.NumberFormat = "0.0%"
    Selection.NumberFormat = "0.00%"
    Range("C8").Select
    ActiveCell.FormulaR1C1 = "5"
    Range("C11").Select
    ActiveCell.FormulaR1C1 = "=PMT(R[-5]C/12,R[-3]C*12,-R[-7]C)"
    Range("C11").Select
    Selection.Style = "Currency"
    Columns("A:C").Select
    Selection.Columns.AutoFit
    Range("C11").Select
End Sub
```

Selecting a cell by clicking, generates the command **Range("A1")**. The string included inside the quotes is the name of the cell or a range of cells. Once a cell is selected, text can be entered. Labels, numbers, and formulas are all considered text when entered. When calculations are made, numbers are interpreted as values and formulas as mathematical instructions, but when the values are entered, they are all considered text.

The command generated when inserting a label is similar to:

```
ActiveCell.FormulaR1C1 = "Auto Payment"
```

ActiveCell is the name of the currently selected cell. **FormulaR1C1** is the property that reads or sets the text contained in the cell. **R1C1** refers to the naming method used. **R2C12** is interpreted as row 2 and column 12 in this scheme. The label itself is enclosed inside double quotes.

The line:

```
Selection.Style = "Currency"
```

sets the style of the currently selected cell to the Currency format. The styles available are quite similar to the format strings available in the **Format$()** function.

Most of the other lines are self-explanatory. One that isn't is:

```
ActiveCell.FormulaR1C1 = "=PMT(R[-5]C/12,R[-3]C*12,-R[-7]C)"
```

This line enters the payment function, which is a built-in function that calculates the payment required to pay off a loan, given the parameters of interest rate per period, the number of periods, and the value of the loan. The formula looks a little like the one entered in step 3 above: **"=PMT(C6/12,C8*12,-C4)"**. The formula you entered contained references to cells like C6, C8, and C4. The formula generated for the macro uses relative addressing of cells. The cell containing the yearly interest rate, C6, is 5 cells above the cell where the formula is being entered. It is referred to as R[-5]C, meaning, the current row minus 5, same column. Each of the cell references in the formula is named using this scheme.

The loan amount is entered as a negative number. This returns a positive value for the monthly payment.

Enhancing the Auto Loan Macro

Once the macro is recorded, Visual Basic statements can be added to enhance its functionality. In the following steps, you'll add commands to query the user for the loan information using input boxes, and a command button to execute the macro.

1 Open **AutoWrk.xls**, and select Module1 (if it is not already open).

2 Move the cursor just above the lines:

```
Range("C4").Select
ActiveCell.FormulaR1C1 = "15000"
```

This is the code that sets the initial value of the auto loan.

3 Insert the following lines:

```
Dim Principal
Principal = InputBox("Enter the Loan Amount:", "Auto Loan")
```

and change **ActiveCell.FormulaR1C1 = "15000"** to

```
ActiveCell.FormulaR1C1 = Principal
```

You might be tempted to declare *Principal* as a Currency type, but this would require a **Val()** function to convert the text returned by the **InputBox** function to a value before it could be assigned to *Principal*. It is not necessary to do this since the value is converted back to a string when it is assigned to the cell. It is better to enter the value as a string and assign it directly to the cell.

4 Return to the worksheet Sheet1, delete the contents and run the revised macro. As the macro is building the worksheet, it will display an input box and ask you to enter the loan amount. Enter any number, and the macro will finish running.

5 Add code necessary to prompt the user to enter the yearly interest rate as a decimal and the number of years. Run the macro to make sure it works properly.

Now, you will add a command button to the worksheet to run the macro.

1 Select Sheet1. Click on the Drawing tool icon.

2 The Drawing toolbar appears. Click the Create Button icon on the toolbar.

3 Using the click and drag technique, draw a command button on the worksheet.

4 Once the button is drawn, the Assign Macro dialog box appears. This dialog box lets you associate a macro with a command button. Choose AutoWorksheet and click OK.

5 Click on the button text, Button1, and edit it. Replace the text with **Enter Data**.

6 Click the worksheet to leave the edit mode.

7 Click the command button and enter the loan amount, yearly rate, and number of years.

8 Save the program.

Command buttons and input boxes make the user interface clear. This is one way to turn a worksheet into an application.

QUESTIONS

1. In what way is an Office macro more than just a record of keystrokes?

2. What are three of the ways a macro may be executed?

3. What does the Customize dialog box allow you to do?

4. What is a bulleted list?

5. Where are Word macros saved?

6. The commands **FormatBulletDefault**, **Underline**, and **Bold**, are called toggles. What does that mean? And how does a toggle switch work?

7. What command is recorded in a Word macro when the Enter key is pressed?

8. Describe how you would find the WordBasic commands that perform an action such as setting the line spacing in a document to 2.

9. Where are Excel macros saved?

10. How might you use a command button and an **InputBox$** in an Excel program?

11. While recording a macro in Excel, what VBA command is generated when the cell "C3" is clicked?

12. What is an **ActiveCell**?

13. How does the **R1C1** naming convention work? How is it different from the **A1** naming convention?

14. What does this cell reference mean: **R[-5]C**?

15. What VBA statement would query the user to enter his/her first name and assign the result to *Fname*?

Section

Programming in WordBasic

Computer software is continually updated. Occasionally a piece of software is discontinued altogether. If this happens to your word processing program, you could be stuck with hundreds of documents saved in an old file format. Or you could find that you want to exchange documents with someone (or some company) that uses a different word processing program. In either of these situations, you need to convert many documents from one file format to another. You can automate this tedious process using WordBasic.

In Section 3 you'll develop a macro to convert any number of files from one file format to another. The program will be developed in incremental steps, each step adding another feature or level of complexity. When you're done, you'll have a useful file format conversion utility, and you'll know a lot more about WordBasic.

Converting from Write to Word

As the first step, you'll record a macro to convert a document created in Write for Windows 3.1 to the Word file format. To do this, the document conversion utilities must be installed (these are usually installed as a normal part of Office installation). Just opening the Write file in Word calls the conversion utility. If the conversion utilities are not installed, you will have to install them.

If you are running Windows 3.1, you will find Write in the Accessories program group. Use Write to create several test files and put them in a temporary directory. Then follow these directions to create a simple macro to open the file in the Write file format and save it in the Word file format.

1   Open Word.

2   If necessary, click on the New document icon in the toolbar, or click File, New, and create a new document using the Normal template.

3   Double-click the dimmed REC button in Word's status bar to open the Record Macro dialog box as shown in Figure 15-12. Enter **WriteToWord** as the Record Macro Name, and click OK.

4   The Macro toolbar appears indicating that your keystrokes will be recorded.

Figure 15-12
The Record Macro dialog box

5   Click File menu and select Open. Find and select the .WRI file you want to convert; in this example, c:\windows\readme.wri. The file is opened. As the file is being loaded, a message in the status bar across the bottom of the screen announces that readme.wri is being converted.

6   The file appears in a window in Word.

7   Click File and select Save As. The Save As dialog box appears. Click the Save File as Type down arrow and a drop-down list appears at the bottom of the dialog box, giving you a choice of file formats in which to save, as shown in Figure 15-13. The Word file format is usually the first in the list. Choose the Word file format, and observe that the extension of the file automatically changes from .WRI to .DOC. Click OK to save the file.

8   The file is saved. Close the window displaying the file.

9   Click on the Stop button to stop recording the macro.

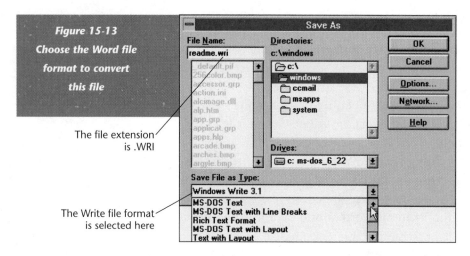

Figure 15-13
Choose the Word file
format to convert
this file

The file extension
is .WRI

The Write file format
is selected here

10 Click Tools and select Macro. Choose WriteToWord, the name of the macro just recorded. Click on Edit. Your code should be similar to the following:

```
Sub MAIN
ChDefaultDir "C:\WINDOWS\", 0
FileOpen .Name = "README.WRI", .ConfirmConversions = 0, .ReadOnly = 0,
.AddToMru = 0, .PasswordDoc = "", .PasswordDot = "", .Revert = 0,
.WritePasswordDoc = "", .WritePasswordDot = ""
FileSaveAs .Name = "README.DOC", .Format = 0, .LockAnnot = 0, .Password =
"", .AddToMru = 1, .WritePassword = "", .RecommendReadOnly = 0,
.EmbedFonts = 0, .NativePictureFormat = 0, .FormsData = 0
FileClose
End Sub
```

The macro will be discussed in four parts: (1) setting the default directory; (2) opening (and automatically converting) the file; (3) saving the converted file; and (4) closing the file and its window.

The line:

```
ChDefaultDir "C:\WINDOWS\", 0
```

changes the default directory to c:\windows\. In this macro, the directory is hard-coded to the location of your test file. However, you could replace the specific string, c:\windows\, with a variable whose value is loaded from an input box or dialog box.

The second part of the macro performs a number of different jobs.

```
FileOpen .Name = "README.WRI", .ConfirmConversions = 0, .ReadOnly = 0,
.AddToMru = 0, .PasswordDoc = "", .PasswordDot = "", .Revert = 0,
.WritePasswordDoc = "", .WritePasswordDot = ""
```

The **FileOpen** statement is self-explanatory. The **.Name** property provides the name of the file to open. Later you will replace this specific string with a string variable that allows you to process many files at the same time.

The **.ConfirmConversions** property is set to 0. This prevents Word from asking the user to confirm the conversion of the incoming file to Word file format. **.ReadOnly** is set to 1 if the file is not to be edited. In this case the file can be edited, so **.ReadOnly** is set to 0. In general, if a property is set to 0, it is disabled. If a property is set to 1, it is enabled. If the **.AddToMru** property is set to 1, it adds the incoming file to the Most Recently Used list of files at the bottom of the File menu. The **.Revert** property determines what happens if the file to be opened is already open. The rest of the properties deal with passwords associated with the document and with the document template. In this example, these properties are not set.

In the third part of the macro, the newly converted file is saved.

```
FileSaveAs .Name = "README.DOC", .Format = 0, .LockAnnot = 0, .Password =
"", .AddToMru = 1, .WritePassword = "", .RecommendReadOnly = 0,
.EmbedFonts = 0, .NativePictureFormat = 0, .FormsData = 0
```

The only properties that concern you are the **.Name** and **.Format** properties. The **.Name** property provides the name of the file to be saved. Notice that the file's extension has been changed. When you chose to save the file as a Word document, the extension was automatically changed to .DOC.

The **.Format** property is used to specify the file type of the document being saved. By changing the value assigned to this property, you can change the file type of the saved document.

Lastly, **FileClose** closes the file window, but it unnecessarily resaves the open document. Saving is part of the **FileClose** command. It should be replaced with **DocClose 2**. This command closes the document window without resaving the document.

Extending the Macro's Usefulness

As it stands, this macro is fairly useless. There is no good reason to record a macro to convert a single file to a different file format unless that particular file is constantly being imported (from a disk or a network) and needs to be converted each time.

So the next step is to extend your macro to read a number of files in a particular file format from one or more directories. Before you can convert the files, you have to find the files. To do this, you'll use the

FileFind statement. Pretend you do not know this and follow along to prepare for extending your macro.

1 Look in WordBasic Help for **FileOpen**. You know about this statement because it was generated by the macro you recorded. There are two ways to find an article about a particular statement: Move the cursor to the word for which you need help and press the F1 function key, or start WordBasic Help and search for **FileOpen**. At the end of many help articles there are references and links to related commands. At the end of **FileOpen**, there is a link to **FileFind**.

2 Click on the **FileFind** link to open its article. When you get there, you will find not only a description of all the **FileFind** options (there are many), but you will also find a link to some sample code. Click the link to open the sample code window.

The importance of these snippets of code cannot be overemphasized. These samples are the way you get things done in WordBasic. Microsoft's programmers have used WordBasic for years in every kind of way. Many of their programs are found in the code samples attached to help topics.

Figure 15-14 shows part of the code sample found in the **FileFind** article. It shows how to use **FileFind** to find all the files with a particular extension, and how to load the file names into an array of strings.

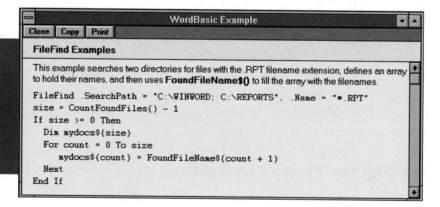

Figure 15-14
The FileFind
code sample

When examining the sample, you'll see a number of other Word-Basic statements that you'll want to look at in WordBasic Help.

3 Click on the Copy button in the WordBasic Example window. Another window (in a different font) appears. This window allows you to select and copy code. Copy the following portion of code.

```
FileFind .SearchPath = "C:\WINWORD; C:\REPORTS", .Name = "*.RPT"
size = CountFoundFiles() - 1
If size >= 0 Then
    Dim mydocs$(size)
    For count = 0 To size
        mydocs$(count) = FoundFileName$(count + 1)
    Next
End If
```

4   Paste it into the macro just below the first line.

The **FileFind** code sample shows how to use the **FileFind** command along with other commands to create a list of files that meet the search criteria. In the search shown, files with the .RPT extension in either of two paths are found. Note in the **.SearchPath** parameter that pathnames are surrounded by quotes. If two or more paths are to be searched, their pathnames must be separated by semicolons.

As always, any string in quotes can be replaced with a string variable. This allows the user to set the pathname interactively through an input box or a dialog box.

The **.Name** parameter lists the file name in quotes. The asterisk stands in for any file name. This search string finds files with the .RPT extension and any first name.

The context makes it clear that **CountFoundFiles** is the number of files found in the search. What is not clear is that when the search is complete, an internal list of files will have been assembled. This list can be accessed using **FoundFileName$**.

CountFoundFiles minus one is used to initialize the *size* variable. The **FoundFileName$** list assembled by WordBasic is numbered from 1 to **CountFoundFiles**. The sample code numbers and stores the files with subscripts that start at 0. Thus, **size = CountFoundFiles - 1**. If no files are found, *size* will be -1. If one file is found, *size* will be 0.

The **Dim mydocs$(size)** statement reserves space for the list of file names. The loop that follows transfers file names from the internal list, **FoundFileName$()**, to **mydocs$()**. The subscript for the former is one more than the subscript for the latter.

Now you will modify this code to apply to the conversion process:

1   Change the **FileFind** statement as follows:

```
FileFind .SearchPath = "C:\temp", .Name = "*.wri"
```

> **NOTE:**
>
> **If you don't have WordBasic Help installed, it is worth the time it takes to install it. But to keep going right now, type the code shown above in the WriteToWord macro right after the first line.**

This uses a single search path, "C:\temp", and selects all files with the .WRI extension. Be sure before you begin that you have a few .WRI files in the c:\temp directory.

2 To see the file selection code actually work, insert the following statements after the line: **mydocs$(count) = FoundFileName$(count + 1).**

```
Insert mydocs$(count)
InsertPara
```

This code displays each file name as it is transferred to **mydocs$()**.

3 End the macro editing session by clicking File, Close. Answer Yes to the Save query. The macro is not finished, but it is time to run it to see how the file selection code works.

4 Run the macro from a blank document. Each file with a .WRI extension should be displayed in the document.

5 As the macro continues to run, it opens the file that has already been converted to Word format and converts it again. The macro may be interrupted with the Esc key at any time. After the macro has displayed the file names, stop execution by pressing Esc.

Converting Multiple Files

Now you'll wrap some code around the rest of the macro to make it open, convert, and save each of the files found in the file search.

1 Click Tools, select Macro, choose WriteToWord, and click on Edit.

When you finish, the macro will have two sections: the first part finds all the file names with the .WRI extension. The second part opens a particular file, converts it to the Word file format, and saves it as a .DOC file. The modifications in this section are made to the second part of the macro.

2 Insert the following line between the first and second section of the macro following the **End If** and preceding the **ChDefaultDir** command.

```
For count = 0 To size
```

This sets up a loop to process each file in the file list constructed in the first part of the macro.

3 Change the directory in the **ChDefaultDir** command to match the directory you've chosen.

```
ChDefaultDir "C:\temp\", 0
```

Word keeps track of a number of different default directories such as document, picture, user templates, and so forth. The 0 following the pathname specifies the default directory for documents.

4   Change the **.Name** parameter of the **FileOpen** command:

```
FileOpen .Name = mydocs$(count), ...
```

This replaces the file name recorded by the original macro with a reference to the list of file names contained in **mydocs$()**. The variable *count* controls access to this list. The rest of the **FileOpen** command remains the same.

5   If you want to change the destination path of the converted files, this is the time to do it. For instance, if you want the newly converted .DOC files to go into the (preexisting) directory c:\windoc\, insert the following line immediately preceding the **FileSaveAs** command:

```
ChDefaultDir "C:\windoc\", 0
```

6   The next change is more complex. You need to save the file with the same first name, but with a new extension, the .DOC extension. To do this you'll use the **FileNameInfo$** function. This function takes the full pathname of the file saved in **mydocs$()** and strips away all but the first name of the file. Other options are available. Replace the **.Name** parameter of the **FileSaveAs** statement with the following:

```
FileSaveAs .Name = FileNameInfo$(FileName$(), 4) + ".DOC", ...
```

The **4** following **FileName$()**, specifies that just the first name of the file is to be returned. **FileName$()** returns the path and file name of the active document. The active document is the one just opened (and converted) in the **FileOpen** statement above. The extension .DOC is joined to the first name of the file. The rest of the path is supplied by the **ChDefaultDir** command. The rest of the **FileSaveAs** command remains unchanged.

7   Remember to change **FileClose** to **DocClose 2**.

8   To finish, put the command **Next count** just above the **End Sub** statement. WordBasic allows you to just put in **Next** without reference to the control variable, *Count*. The entire macro appears below:

```
Sub MAIN
' Part One -- Find files with a .wri extension and save in mydocs$().
FileFind .SearchPath = "C:\temp", .Name = "*.wri"
size = CountFoundFiles() - 1
If size >= 0 Then
    Dim mydocs$(size)
    For count = 0 To size
        mydocs$(count) = FoundFileName$(count + 1)
        Insert mydocs$(count)
        InsertPara
    Next
End If
' Part Two -- Open, convert, and save files in Word format.
For count = 0 To size
    ChDefaultDir "C:\temp\", 0
    FileOpen .Name = mydocs$(count), .ConfirmConversions = 0, .ReadOnly =
0, .AddToMru = 0, .PasswordDoc = "", .PasswordDot = "", .Revert = 0,
.WritePasswordDoc = "", .WritePasswordDot = ""
    FileSaveAs .Name = FileNameInfo$(FileName$(), 4) + ".DOC", .Format =
0, .LockAnnot = 0, .Password = "", .AddToMru = 1, .WritePassword = "",
.RecommendReadOnly = 0, .EmbedFonts = 0, .NativePictureFormat = 0,
.FormsData = 0
    DocClose 2
Next count
End Sub
```

9 Click File, select Close, and choose Yes to save the macro to the Normal template.

10 Run the macro from a blank document. Depending on the speed of your computer and the size of the files opened and closed, you should see the first screenful of each document as it is opened, converted, and closed. When the macro is finished, the .WRI files are unchanged, and a set of matching .DOC files has been created.

This exercise has shown you how to generate a list of files using the **FileFind** command and how to use the list to process a number of files. The same programming techniques can be added to other macros.

QUESTIONS

1. Why might you need to convert a document from one file format to another?

2. Describe two ways to begin recording a Word macro.

3. How would you replace a hard-coded file name in a macro?

4. In the **.AddToMru** property, what does **Mru** stand for?

5. What is the difference between the **FileClose** command and the **DocClose** command?

6. How do you use Word to convert a document in the Write file format to a document in the Word file format?

7. What character is used to separate multiple pathnames in the **.SearchPath** parameter of the **FileFind** statement?

8. What does the **ChDefaultDir** command do? What is the meaning of the number that follows the parameter string?

9. Look up **FileNameInfo$** in WordBasic Help. Describe three of the options available in this function.

10. What does the **.Format** parameter of the **FileSaveAs** do? What does a value of 0 mean?

Programming in Excel

Section

Your next program is a multipart project in Excel. You'll find that the programming statements and environment are much more like what you're used to in Visual Basic, but there's still plenty to learn about interacting with worksheets.

The workbook you create is a database for a car dealership. One sheet contains information on prospective customers: names, income, family members, and so on. Another sheet contains information on used autos in the lot. A final worksheet is a form letter to send to a customer about suitable cars on the lot.

Your program calculates a typical monthly payment for each vehicle and a reasonable payment affordable by the customer. The data is compared and a list of cars that meet the customer's needs is generated. The list is printed along with a letter urging the customer to come in and look over the stock.

Building the Worksheets

Parts of the worksheets are entered by hand and parts are calculated by the program.

1 Start by opening Excel and entering the following customer information on Sheet2. For now, reproduce the table as shown, paying careful attention to row and column numbers. The first line, including the column heads, are part of row 1. The last name, *Sprague*, starts in row 2 and so on. The first column starts in column A.

Columns

Row	A	B	C	D	E	F
1	Last Name	First Name	Title	Income	Family Members	First or Second
2	Sprague	Joel	Mr. & Mrs.	32000	4	1
3	Blaine	Briana	Ms.	28500	1	1
4	Laurent	Erin	Miss	12500	1	1
5	Sue	Cathy	Ms.	62000	2	1
6	Weston	Byron	Mr.	41000	1	1
7	Dorant	Jack	Mr. & Mrs.	49500	5	2

2 Format the Income as currency.

3 Select Sheet3 and enter the following information about the used cars on the lot. The labels *Yearly Rate:* and *Years:* are in the top row (row 1). Row 2 is blank. The label, *Make*, is in row 3, column A. The label, *Dodge*, in row 4, column A.

Columns

Row	A	B	C	D	E	F	G	H
1		Yearly Rate:	8%		Years:	4		
2								
3	Make	Model	Year	List Price	Wholesale Price	Passengers	Body Style	Color
4	Dodge	Caravan	1991	7500	5200	7	van	white
5	Ford	F150	1992	4500	3800	2	pickup	red
6	Mazda	626	1994	8200	6800	5	sedan	red
7	Renault	Encore	1984	2400	1800	4	sedan	silver
8	Ford	Thunderbird	1989	7200	4800	4	sedan	tan
9	Ford	Mustang	1995	16450	12500	4	sedan	white
10	Olds	Roadmaster	1994	14000	11500	7	wagon	brown
11	Olds	Park Avenue	1996	28000	24000	6	sedan	pale green

4 Save the worksheet with the name **AutoDlr.xls**.

At the top of the worksheet are fields for the yearly interest rate and the number of years to pay off the loan. These figures are used to calculate the monthly payment for each vehicle. If the interest rate or number of years is changed, then the monthly payments also change.

5   Select Sheet1 and create the form letter.

6   Enter the following in row 3, starting in the first column. Put each word in an adjacent column. *Dear* should be in A3, *Laurent* should be in D3.

Dear Miss Erin Laurent,

These, except for *Dear*, are just placeholders. Each will be replaced with specific data for each customer.

7   The next element in Sheet1 is a textbox. Add a textbox to the worksheet by clicking the Textbox button on the Standard toolbar. Draw the box on the screen by clicking in the left corner and dragging to the right corner. The textbox should span the sheet from about column A through column H, and from about row 4 to row 11.

Once the textbox is drawn on the screen, add text by clicking in the box. While the I-beam cursor is visible, a click on the right mouse button allows you to change the font. When the arrow cursor is pointing to the edge of the box, a click of the right mouse button brings up a dialog box that allows you to format the textbox. Figure 15-15 shows the Patterns folder with the borders of the textbox turned off.

Figure 15-15

The Format dialog box for the textbox object

8   Enter the following paragraph into the Text Box.

```
We would like to draw your
attention to the following
automobile(s). We've matched
your needs against our stock
and we know you'll find some-
thing you like and can afford
in the following list. Please
come to the showroom and talk
to one of our friendly sales-
persons to find out how you
can drive one of these subur-
ban driven used cars home tonight!
```

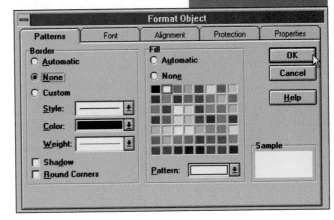

9   Below the textbox, starting in column D, row 12, enter the following three rows of information as shown in Figure 15-16. The actual entries below the column headings are cleared and replaced before the worksheet is printed.

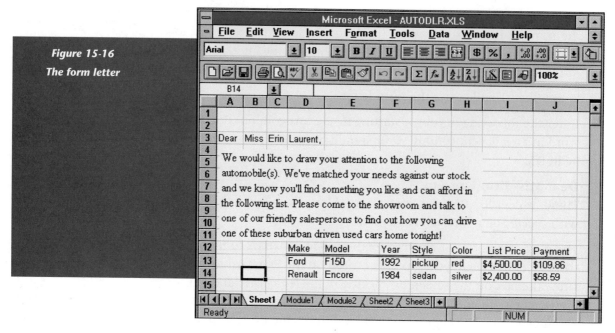

Figure 15-16
The form letter

10 Set up a header and footer for the printed document by clicking on File and selecting Page Setup. Select Header/Footer and enter a header and footer similar to the ones visible in Figure 15-17. Separating the parts of the header with commas left-justifies, centers, and right-justifies three short messages across the top of the page, as shown in Figure 15-17.

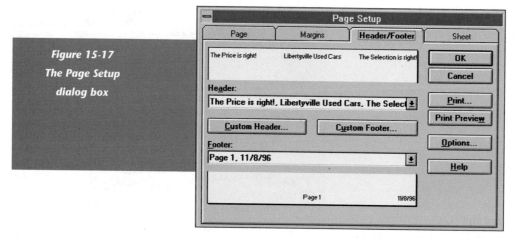

Figure 15-17
The Page Setup
dialog box

Generating Possible Payments

The first program calculates the approximate monthly payment that the prospective customer can afford and the typical monthly payment for each car. An additional column is added to each of the tables you entered above for those values.

There are several ways to access the cells of the worksheet, two of these ways are represented in the code below. Of the two, the latter method, using the Cells method, is the preferred technique.

Recall that when a macro is recorded in Excel, a module sheet is created where the code is saved. Modules are part of the workbook for which they are created. A module can also be added using the Insert menu item.

Follow these instructions to write code that adds columns for the payments:

1   Click Insert, select Macro, and choose Module, to add a module to the worksheet.

2   Add the following code to the module. Parts of the code are commented out. The two lines that are commented out below "Next Row" call a macro that you haven't entered yet. The three lines below "For Row = 4 To 11" show the alternate way to address a cell. Later, you'll delete the comment markers from the calls to the **borderline()** macro.

```
Sub GenPossible()
Sheets("Sheet2").Select
Dim Row As Integer
Dim CellAddr As String
For Row = 2 To 7
    CellAddr = "g" & LTrim$(Str$(Row))
    Range(CellAddr).Select
    ActiveCell.FormulaR1C1 = "=(RC[-3]*.72)/12/3/2"
    Selection.Style = "Currency"
Next Row
'borderline ("G1")
' process payments
Sheets("Sheet3").Select
For Row = 4 To 11
    'CellAddr = "i" & LTrim$(Str$(Row))
    'Range(CellAddr).Select
    'ActiveCell.FormulaR1C1 = "=pmt(Yearly_Rate/12,Years*12,-rc[-5])"
    Cells(Row, 9).Formula = "=pmt(Yearly_Rate/12,Years*12,-rc[-5])"
    Selection.Style = "Currency"
Next Row
'borderline ("I3")
End Sub
```

3 Select Sheet2 from the tabs along the left-hand bottom part of the screen.

4 Run the macro by clicking Tools, Macro, the name of the macro GenPossible, and clicking Run.

5 Watch as the macro creates a new column for each of the tables.

6 Save the worksheet, the module will automatically be saved as part of the worksheet.

The **Sheets("Sheet2").Select** command makes sure the macro is working with the right worksheet. Later in the program the Sheets command is executed with "Sheet3" to switch to the worksheet with the list of used cars.

The first section of the program addresses cells with the **A1** addressing method, which assigns a letter to each column and a number to each row. The second section uses the **R1C1** method, which assigns numbers to both rows and columns. In the "A1" method, a string representing the cell's address is built:

```
CellAddr = "g" & LTrim$(Str$(Row))
```

The **LTrim$()** function trims blank characters from the front of a string. This is useful when building a pathname or cell address from a value by joining strings together. This address is used to select the cell with the **Range** command:

```
Range(CellAddr).Select
```

Once the cell is selected, it is filled with an estimate of the family's affordable monthly payment. The algorithm uses the gross yearly income, subtracts 28% for taxes, divides by 12 to scale the amount to the monthly income, divides by 3, using the assumption that housing should cost one third of the family income, and finally divides by 2, assuming a car payment should be no more than half a house payment. This value is assigned to the selected cell:

```
ActiveCell.FormulaR1C1 = "=(RC[-3]*.72)/12/3/2"
```

The formula uses relative addressing. **RC[-3]** refers to the cell three columns to the left of the selected cell. In Sheet2, this is the family's yearly income.

Finally, the entry is formatted in the currency style:

```
Selection.Style = "Currency"
```

The **borderline("G1")** command, which is commented out following the loop, calls a macro recorded separately to insert a column heading.

1   Add the following macro definition to the current module, create a new module, or record a macro with the name *borderline* to insert the column heading Payments. If you record a macro, modify your macro to match the code below:

```
Sub borderline(CellAddr As String)
    Range(CellAddr).Select
    Selection.Borders(xlLeft).LineStyle = xlNone
    Selection.Borders(xlRight).LineStyle = xlNone
    Selection.Borders(xlTop).LineStyle = xlNone
    With Selection.Borders(xlBottom)
        .LineStyle = xlDouble
        .ColorIndex = xlAutomatic
    End With
    Selection.BorderAround LineStyle:=xlNone
    ActiveCell.FormulaR1C1 = "Payment:"
    Range(CellAddr).Select
    With Selection
        .HorizontalAlignment = xlGeneral
        .VerticalAlignment = xlCenter
        .WrapText = False
        .Orientation = xlHorizontal
    End With
End Sub
```

This routine was recorded as a macro and modified to apply to the cell whose address is sent as a parameter.

2   Return to the **GenPossible** procedure and remove the comment marking in front of both occurrences of **borderline()**.

3   Return to Sheet2 and delete the Payments column. Return to Sheet3 and delete the Payments column.

4   Run GenPossible.

5   Save the worksheet.

Creating the Main Routine

To run the main routine, the user selects the last name of the customer to whom he or she wants to send a letter, and then executes the macro. **Main()** starts by saving the original location of the name selected. This is necessary because various cells on various sheets are selected in turn—the location of the original cell is lost. **ActiveCell** returns the location of the currently selected cell. It is important that the last name of the customer be selected when the macro is run. Other cells are accessed with relative addressing in relation to the cell containing the last name.

1 Enter this code:

```
Sub Main()
    ' -- Save the original selected cell - it's the
    '     customer's last name.
    Dim NameCell
    Set NameCell = ActiveCell
```

2 The next bit of code calls the **GenPossible** routine to generate the Payment columns.

```
    ' -- Generate the possible monthly payments for
    '     the customers and for each vehicle.
    GenPossible
```

3 The next section of code declares variables for the customer information. The location of the customer's last name was saved in *NameCell* above. The commented out **MsgBox** statement was used to debug the code as it was being developed. The **Offset** method is used to address cells relative to the position of a given cell. The parameters indicate a row and column offset. For instance, **NameCell.Offset(0,1)** is the cell to the right of *NameCell*. The 0 indicates to leave the current row number unchanged, while the 1 indicates to add 1 to the current column number.

```
    Dim LastName As String, FirstName As String
    Dim Title As String, Members As Integer
    Dim CarNumber As Integer, Payment As Currency
    ' -- Transfer data from worksheet to variables.
    LastName = NameCell
    'MsgBox "Last name is: " & LastName
    FirstName = NameCell.Offset(0, 1)
    Title = NameCell.Offset(0, 2)
    Members = NameCell.Offset(0, 4)
    CarNumber = NameCell.Offset(0, 5)
    Payment = NameCell.Offset(0, 6)
```

4   Enter the next section of code. It selects Sheet1 and sets the salutation of the letter. The last line uses the **AutoFit** method to size the columns to fit the names and salutation. The textbox, located at the top of the worksheet, is not affected.

```
Sheets("Sheet1").Select
Range("b3").Select
ActiveCell.FormulaR1C1 = Title
Range("C3").Select
ActiveCell.FormulaR1C1 = FirstName
Range("D3").Select
ActiveCell.FormulaR1C1 = LastName & ","
Columns("a:d").Select
Selection.Columns.AutoFit
```

5   Enter the next section of code. It begins by declaring variables to store the information about each vehicle. The **Sheet1Row** variable is used to select the row on sheet1 on which to print vehicle information. Every time a line of information is inserted in Sheet1, the **Sheet1Row** variable is incremented. The monthly payment for the car, *MonthlyPay,* is read and compared to the amount of monthly payment the family can afford. If the car is big enough for the family (**Passengers >= Members**) the information for the vehicle is written to Sheet1.

```
' -- Find appropriate vehicles and list on Sheet1.
Dim Make As String, Model As String, Year As Integer
Dim ListPrice As Currency, Passengers As Integer
Dim BodyStyle As String, BodyColor As String
    Dim MonthlyPay As Currency
Dim Sheet1Row As Integer
Sheet1Row = 13
ClearTable
For Row = 4 To 11
    Sheets("Sheet3").Select
    MonthlyPay = Cells(Row, 9)
    Passengers = Cells(Row, 6)
    If MonthlyPay <= Payment And CarNumber = 1 And Passengers >= Members Then
        MsgBox Str$(Passengers) & " " & Str$(Members)
        Make = Cells(Row, 1)
        Model = Cells(Row, 2)
        Year = Cells(Row, 3)
        ListPrice = Cells(Row, 4)
```

```
                    BodyStyle = Cells(Row, 7)
                    BodyColor = Cells(Row, 8)
                    'MsgBox BodyStyle
                    Sheets("Sheet1").Select
                    Cells(Sheet1Row, 4) = Make
                    Cells(Sheet1Row, 5) = Model
                    Cells(Sheet1Row, 6) = Year
                    Cells(Sheet1Row, 7) = BodyStyle
                    Cells(Sheet1Row, 8) = BodyColor
                    Cells(Sheet1Row, 9) = ListPrice
                    Cells(Sheet1Row, 10) = MonthlyPay
                    Sheet1Row = Sheet1Row + 1
                End If
            Next Row
    End Sub
```

6 The call to the ClearTable macro is not valid until you enter the following code. Its purpose is to clear the table of vehicles so the next letter can start over.

```
Sub ClearTable()
    Sheets("Sheet1").Select
    Range("D13:J31").Select
    Selection.ClearContents
End Sub
```

7 The last step is to put a Command button on the worksheet to run the macro. It should go on Sheet2 so the user can select the last name and click the macro. Activate the Drawing toolbar and click on the Command button icon.

8 Draw a Command button on the worksheet. The Assign Macro dialog box appears. Associate the button with Main.

9 Change Button1 to **Build Letter** by clicking on the button's text and typing. Click outside the button to end the editing session. Sheet2 should look like Figure 15-18.

10 Select a last name and click on the Command button.

11 Check the worksheet in Print Preview mode. Make any changes you need to polish the look of the display.

12 Print the worksheet.

13 Save the worksheet.

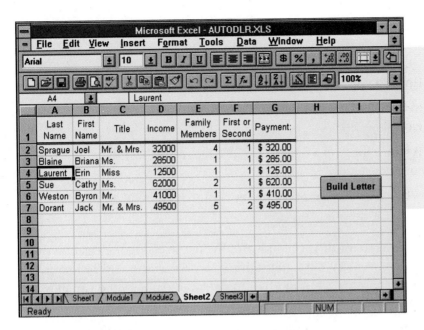

Figure 15-18

Sheet2 with the

Command button

There is still a long way to go to make this into a really sharp application.

⦿ Nothing has been done with the information about whether the customer is looking for a second car or a first car.

⦿ Adding customer or vehicle information could be automated.

⦿ Different letters can be defined.

This program, however, does illustrate getting information into and out of a multiple worksheet workbook. Excel is an application rich in features, each of which is available to the VBA programmer. Volumes could be written about those features, but now you have enough information to start writing your own applications.

QUESTIONS

1. How is a textbox added to a worksheet?

2. How do you change the font and formatting of a textbox?

3. In Excel, where can you find a button to put a textbox on a worksheet?

4. When setting up a header for an Excel worksheet, what do commas signify?

5. What does the **Sheets().Select** command do?

6. What is relative addressing?

7. The macro for this section is run by first selecting the customer's last name. Why is it important to have the customer's last name selected? Why is it important to save that name in the variable *NameCell?*

8. How does the Offset method work? Give an example.

9. How are the widths of the columns of worksheet 1 adjusted to accommodate the customer's name?

Summary

Software is revised to add new features, fix bugs, or to completely change the way the program works.

WordBasic is used when you want to automate actions for many files or to customize a document.

When a Word macro is recorded, WordBasic commands are generated and saved in the default template, Normal.

Once a macro is recorded, it can be added to a menu or a toolbar.

The **Do While** and **Do Until** loops are the versatile indefinite loop structures of Visual Basic and VBA. Unfortunately, they are not available in WordBasic. The **While <condition is true> ... Wend** loop is the indefinite loop structure of WordBasic, a throwback to earlier versions of Basic.

There are two data types in WordBasic, String and Numeric. String variables are suffixed with a dollar sign. Numeric variables represent either whole numbers or decimals.

The **InputBox$** and **MsgBox$** functions work the same in Word-Basic as they do in Visual Basic, as do the **For-Next**, the assignment statement, and the **If-Then-Else-End If**.

WordBasic uses the plus sign to join strings.

The **Insert** command inserts text into a document. The **InsertPara** command is equivalent to pressing the Enter key.

Visual Basic for Applications, or VBA, is the future of programming for Office. It is the language used to program Excel. It will be the language for all of Office and will be indistinguishable from Visual Basic.

A macro is a way to record a sequence of keystrokes. Using Basic commands, macros can be enhanced to become entire application programs.

Macros are used to explore Basic code generated by events and commands within an application. To find out what code is generated when a file is saved, start recording a macro, save the file, and stop recording. Edit the macro to see what code has been produced. Every event and command has corresponding Basic code.

Macros in Word are saved in templates. Macros saved in the Normal template are global, available to every document created with that template.

In Excel, macros and Basic code are entered into modules. Each module is saved along with its workbook.

There are three ways to access cells in an Excel worksheet: **A1**, **R1C1**, and relative addressing. The **A1** method is most familiar to Excel users. It assigns each column a letter (starting with *A*) and each row a number. The **R1C1** method of addressing cells is used with some worksheets and facilitates automating repetitive actions with loops. Relative addressing is used when accessing a number of cells with a fixed relation to a known cell.

When designing documents where the alignment of elements is critical, use a nonproportionally spaced font, such as Courier New.

"Incremental programming" is a programming technique that starts with a minimal running program, and, as sections of code are added, makes sure the program still runs. This isolates problem areas in the code.

Named Arguments are parameters sent to WordBasic commands.

The **LTrim$()** function trims blank characters from the front of a string. This is useful when building a pathname or cell address from a value by joining strings together.

ActiveCell returns the location of the cell that's currently selected.

Application programs in both WordBasic and Excel are a combination of recorded macros and the programming that connect the pieces of the application together.

Problems

1. Favorite Fonts

   Record a series of macros for your favorite fonts and font sizes. Install the macros as buttons on the toolbar.

2. Inserting a File

   Record a macro that inserts a .DOC file into another .DOC file. Edit the macro and insert a statement with an **InputBox$** function to collect the name of the inserted file from the user.

3. Spellcheck From Top

   Record a macro that spell-checks a document starting from the top of the document. Put the macro into the Edit menu.

4. Modified Auto Loan

   Modify the Auto Loan Worksheet to display the total amount paid back (the monthly payment times the number of pay periods), and the total finance charge (the total amount paid back minus the loan amount).

5. Generalized WriteToWord

   Rewrite the WriteToWord macro to use InputBoxes to collect the path names for both the original files and the converted files.

6. Generalized Email

   Add code to the email macro to let the user enter pathnames and extensions for source files and destination files. When the macro is run, it should prompt the user to enter a path and extension for the source files and a path for the destination files.

7. File Printer

   Write a macro to print all the .DOC files in a directory entered by the user. Use an **InputBox$** to enter the user's directory.

8. Home Budget

   Write an Excel application that helps the user build a home budget worksheet. The program should prompt the user to enter dollar amounts for set categories as well as allow the user to add his or her own. The worksheet should not only list each line item and total them, but also display summary values. For instance, include: all housing expenditures, all charitable contributions, all utilities, and all credit cards.

   The program should guide the user through the construction of the worksheet and format a copy for a printed report.

Technology and Issues

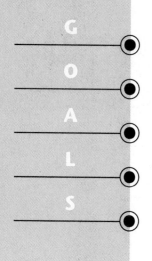

After working through this chapter, you will be able to:

Work with Windows 95 desktop elements and windows, and manage your files and folders.

Understand the two major storage technologies in use today, and be able to select the appropriate media for your needs.

Understand what is dangerous to your computer, and know the preventive maintenance you should supply.

Recognize the legal and ethical issues about computing and information systems and be sufficiently knowledgeable to make your own informed ethical decisions.

O V E R V I E W

There are two versions of Visual Basic in use today, versions 3 and 4. If you have version 4, you will need to use Windows 95 rather than Windows 3.1. Before you can program in Visual Basic version 4, you must be able to create, move, copy, rename, and delete files and folders using Windows 95. This appendix covers these procedures and other basics of working with Windows 95. If you own a computer or one day will purchase one, you also need to know how to choose the appropriate storage, and how to take care of your computer. This appendix describes the major types of storage and proper care. And, lastly, a computer user should be aware of the legal and ethical issues surrounding computing, because you will encounter them early on, and have to learn to deal with them. So, some of those major issues are discussed here.

The Basics of Working in Windows 95

Section

Windows 95 is Microsoft's upgrade to Windows 3.1, a graphical user interface (GUI) used to make communicating with the computer easier. Windows 95 represents a major step forward in computer design because it is now a 32-bit operating system as well as the graphical interface. If you are interested in comparing the two programs, review Chapter 1, Section 3.

In this section you will learn how to start a Windows 95 computer, understand the purpose of the desktop elements, use and control program and document windows, view and manage your information stored on the computer—folders and files—and run an application program.

Starting Windows 95 and Using the Desktop

When you start a Windows 95 computer, a title screen displays for a few moments and then Windows 95 is active on your screen and should resemble Figure A-1.

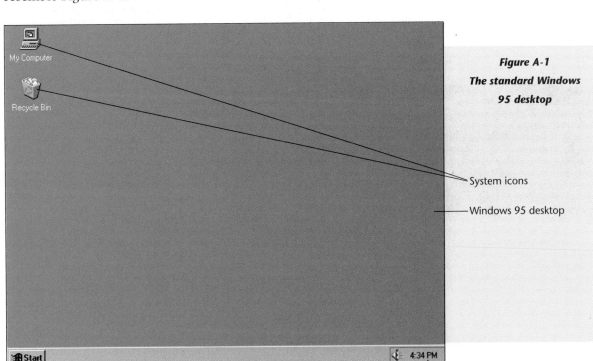

Figure A-1
The standard Windows 95 desktop

System icons

Windows 95 desktop

Start button   taskbar   status area

This screen is called the Windows 95 desktop, and is the background for all your computer work. Figure A-1 shows the standard Windows 95 setup with the taskbar at the bottom of the screen displaying the Start button on the far left and the status area on the far right. Two icons, graphical representations of objects that can be selected and opened, labeled My Computer and Recycle Bin are at the top left of the desktop. In general, you communicate with the computer using the mouse pointer to either click on icons such as these, or to make selections from menus and interact with dialog boxes.

Clicking the mouse means pressing and releasing the left mouse button. Double-clicking means rapidly pressing the left mouse button twice. Dragging the mouse means pressing and holding the left button and moving the mouse.

THE TASKBAR AND START MENU

The Start button on the left side of the taskbar is for displaying the selection of programs you can run. The status area on the right of the taskbar displays the current time, and can be used to change Date and Time values. When you click on the Start button, the pop-up Start menu appears as shown in Figure A-2.

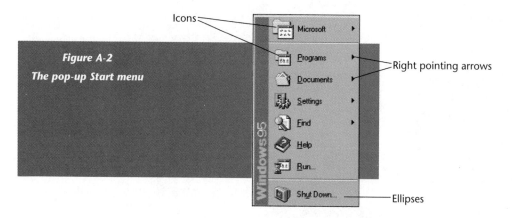

Figure A-2
The pop-up Start menu

The Start menu displays menu options showing their icons on the left, and the option name, followed by other symbols when applicable. For example, the menu option Shut Down is followed by ellipses (...) indicating that, if selected, a dialog box will display requesting more information concerning your selection. Also, the menu options Programs, Documents, Settings, and Find are followed by right pointing arrows indicating that, if selected, they will expand to show additional choices. Figure A-3 shows the series of menus and submenus that display when Programs, Accessories, and Notepad have been selected.

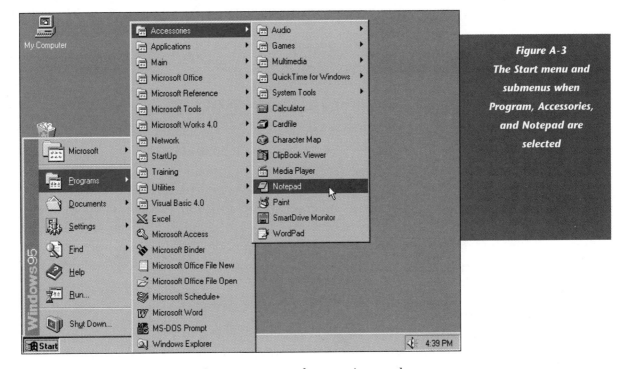

Figure A-3
The Start menu and submenus when Program, Accessories, and Notepad are selected

With Windows 95, several programs can be running at the same time, but only one can be active at a time. When programs are running, a button with their icon and name is displayed in the blank space on the taskbar as shown in Figure A-4.

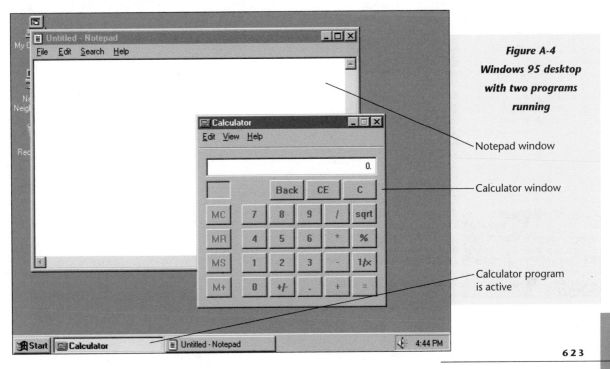

Figure A-4
Windows 95 desktop with two programs running

Notepad window

Calculator window

Calculator program is active

Calculator and Notepad are both running, and you know that Calculator is the active program because its button on the toolbar is depressed. You can switch between the programs by clicking on the buttons. Try doing that now.

DESKTOP ICONS—MY COMPUTER AND THE RECYCLE BIN

My Computer is a set of programs that allows you to view and manage your private, local system. The My Computer icon is a shortcut or quick way to activate the programs or tasks associated with it. The Recycle Bin lets you delete and later recover information. It also has a shortcut icon for fast access. Because My Computer and the Recycle Bin help you manage your computer, their icons are called system icons. You will learn more about the Recycle Bin later in this section.

Windows and Windows Controls

All the work you do in Windows 95 and other GUIs takes place inside of windows. For example, when you run a program, its windows are open, when you write a letter the document window is open, and when you write a Visual Basic program, various windows are open. Because windows are your interface with the computer, you must be familiar with their standard elements, and know how to use them. Windows are not static on your monitor's screen. You can make them bigger and smaller, and drag them around on your desktop, so you will learn how to do that too.

ELEMENTS OF WINDOWS

Double-clicking the My Computer icon opens its window, so you can have access to its contents as shown in Figure A-5.

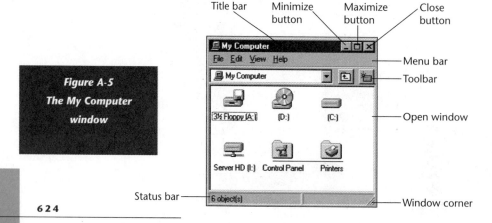

Figure A-5
The My Computer window

At the top of the window is the title bar showing the name of the program or document that is open, in this case, My Computer. Windows are like programs, in that several can be open at the same time, but only one window can be active at any given time. A window is active—ready to accept your input from the mouse or keyboard—when its title bar is dark. Any other open windows on the desktop will have dimmed title bars, indicating that they are inactive—temporarily out of use. You make an inactive window active by clicking anywhere in the window.

On the right side of the title bar are buttons that allow you to minimize, maximize, and close the window. You use these buttons to accomplish the following tasks:

- To keep the program running, but reduce its window to a button on the taskbar, click the Minimize button.

- To expand the window to fill the entire screen, click the Maximize button.

- To stop running the program and remove it from the desktop, click the Close button.

The menu bar is immediately below the title bar. Clicking a menu name displays a drop-down menu giving you access to commands that will execute a particular process or action, such as those in the Edit menu in Figure A-6.

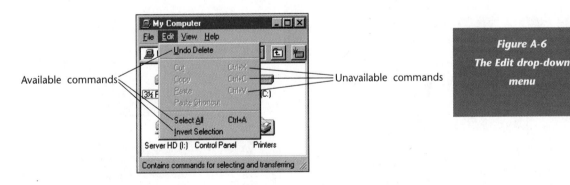

Available commands

Unavailable commands

Figure A-6
The Edit drop-down menu

Menu commands are not all available in every context. When they are available, the commands are dark, like the Undo Delete, Select All and Invert Selection commands in Figure A-6, and unavailable menu commands are dimmed, like the Cut, Copy, Paste, and Paste Special commands.

The toolbar is located just below the menu bar. It is composed of shortcut icons or buttons to activate many of the commands found on the drop-down menus. To use the toolbar buttons, just double-click on their icons.

The large, white background area just below the toolbar is the actual open window where your work is done. On the window in Figure A-5, four Drive icons are displayed as well as two folders.

The bottom frame of the window is the status bar. Messages such as the number of objects displayed, as shown in Figure A-5, or the meaning of a command, appear on the status bar. This information can be very helpful in understanding how Windows 95 works, so remember to check it as you do your work. The right side of the status bar is called the window corner, and is a convenient place to size the window.

SIZING AND MOVING WINDOWS

To resize a window, position the mouse pointer over an edge or window corner. When the pointer changes into a horizontal, double-headed arrow as in Figure A-7, press and hold down the left mouse button, and drag the window's outer line as shown in Figure A-8 until it is the size you want; then release the mouse button.

Figure A-7
Window ready to
be sized

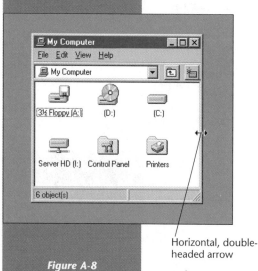

Horizontal, double-headed arrow

Figure A-8
Dragging the border of
a window

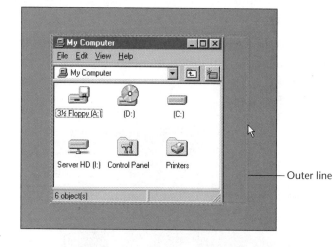

Outer line

Figure A-9
Dragging the corner
of a window

Dragging a corner rather than an edge allows you to change the height and width of the window at the same time as shown in Figure A-9; dragging an edge changes only one dimension or the other.

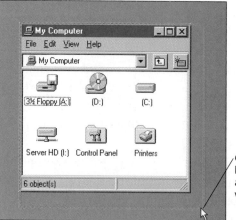

Changes
height
and
width

Often you will need to move a window out of the way in order to see your work. To move a window, just click on and drag the title bar of the window to the desired location.

There will be occasions when you need to see information from several windows at the same time. You can position and size individual windows using the techniques you just learned, but it is faster to use the arrangement commands built into Windows 95: cascade, tile horizontal, and tile vertical. To use these commands, point to an empty part of the desktop taskbar and click the right mouse button. The taskbar shortcut menu as shown in Figure A-10 is displayed.

Then select Cascade, Tile Horizontally, or Tile Vertically to show the different arrangements. Go ahead and open the Control Panel, and try the three arrangements now.

Figure A-10
The taskbar shortcut menu

Exploring Folders and Files

Information is the computer's most important product. As you use programs to do your work, you create information that must be saved and managed so you can find it later when you need it. For example, you create documents with word processing programs and you create programs with Visual Basic, and most likely you will use them again and again. Windows 95 provides a tool, the Windows Explorer, for you to use to view and manage this information.

WINDOWS EXPLORER

To start the Windows Explorer, click the Start button, click Programs, then click on Windows Explorer. The program opens and displays its Exploring window as shown in Figure A-11 on the next page.

Like the other windows you've seen, the Exploring window has the standard title, menu, toolbar, and status bars. However, to facilitate viewing both the storage structure and the actual units of information, this window is divided into two panes called All Folders and Contents.

Folders are the computer's containers that store other folders and documents of various types. You use folders to organize the information, so it is easier to find. The left pane of the Exploring window, All Folders, shows a tree or outline of icons and folders that represent the hierarchical organization of storage media, such as hard and floppy disks. A plus sign (+) next to a folder or icon indicates that it contains more folders (subfolders) and it can be expanded to show them. A minus sign (−) indicates that it is already expanded and it can be collapsed to hide the subfolders that are currently visible in this pane. For example, in Figure A-11, the C: drive is expanded, all its subfolders are

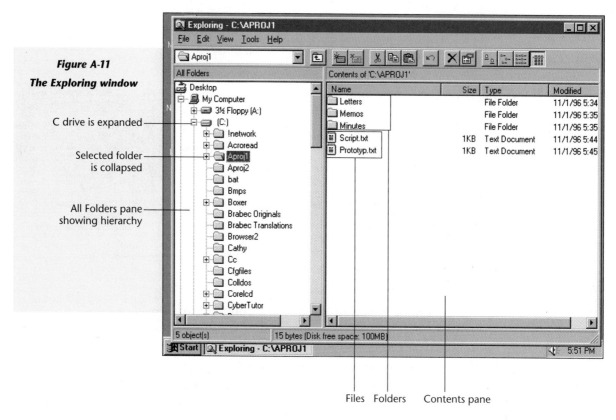

Figure A-11

The Exploring window

C drive is expanded

Selected folder is collapsed

All Folders pane showing hierarchy

Files Folders Contents pane

visible, and the Aproj1 folder is collapsed. Just click the plus or minus symbols to expand or collapse the structure.

Files are the computer's name for the individual units of information that you will create, such as programs and documents. The right pane of the Exploring window, Contents, shows the subfolders and files of the object selected in the All Folders pane. For example, in Figure A-11, the selected folder Aproj1 contains three folders, Letters, Memos, and Minutes and two files, Script.txt and Prototyp.txt.

The Contents pane is currently displayed in Detail mode, but you can customize the mode with the View menu commands: Large icons, Small icons, List, and Detail. Go ahead and experiment with that now.

WORKING WITH FOLDERS

A newly formatted disk does not contain any folders. Without folders for organization, finding the files you want would be hard to do. To create a new folder, you must:

⦿ Identify the location desired for the new folder, for example the desktop, the C: drive, the $3\frac{1}{2}$ Floppy A: drive, or another folder.

⦿ Select New then Folder from the File menu.

⦿ Give the new folder a name.

The folders and files used for this exercise are on your Template Disk, so to do this exercise, insert the disk and click on its drive designator A: or B:.

To create a new folder within the Aproj1 folder,

1 Open the Windows Explorer if it is not already open.

2 Click the Aproj1 folder in the All Folders pane to identify where you want the new folder to be placed.

3 From the File menu select the New command and the Folder option as shown in Figure A-12.

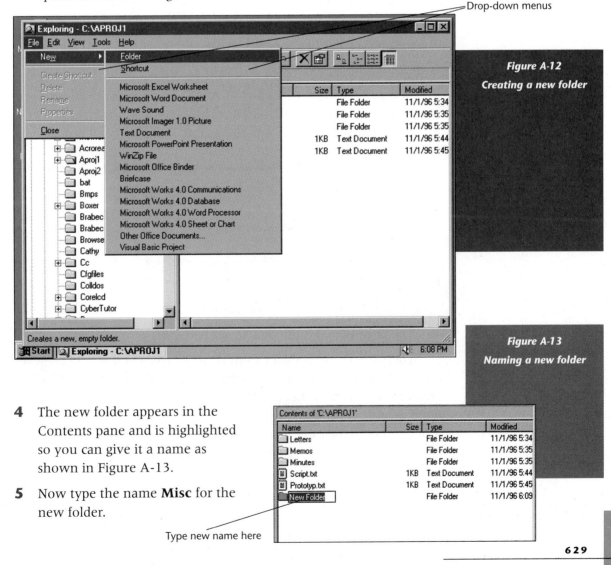

Drop-down menus

Figure A-12
Creating a new folder

Figure A-13
Naming a new folder

4 The new folder appears in the Contents pane and is highlighted so you can give it a name as shown in Figure A-13.

5 Now type the name **Misc** for the new folder.

Type new name here

After creating folders, you can move, copy, rename, or delete, them. Folder manipulation commands affect not only the folder itself, but also all the files and subfolders it contains.

To move the subfolder called Letters in the Aproj1 folder to the Aproj2 folder,

1 Click on the Aproj1 folder in the All Folders pane.

2 Click and drag the Letters folder from the Contents pane to the Aproj2 folder in the All Folders pane. When the Aproj2 folder is selected, release the mouse button. Check to verify that the Letters folder is no longer in the Aproj1 folder.

3 Click on the Aproj2 folder in the All Folders pane to see that the Letters folder was moved.

To copy, rather than move, the subfolder called Letters that is now in the Aproj2 folder to the Aproj1 folder,

1 Click on the Aproj2 folder in the All Folders pane.

2 Press and hold Ctrl while you drag the Letters folder from the Contents pane to the Aproj1 folder in the All Folders pane. As you drag, the pointer develops a plus sign to indicate that it is in copy mode. When the Aproj1 folder is selected, release the mouse button. Check to see that the Letters folder is still in the Aproj2 folder.

3 Click on the Aproj1 folder in the All Folders pane to see that a copy of the Letters folder is in this folder too.

To rename the Misc folder,

1 Click on the Misc folder.

2 Select Rename from the File menu.

3 Type **Otherdoc** for the new folder name.

When you delete a folder from the C: drive, Windows 95 removes the folder and its files from its original location and places the files in a holding area called the Recycle Bin on the desktop. At this point you can remove objects permanently from storage or change your mind and restore them to their original locations.

To delete the Memos folder that holds one file, ToStaff.txt, from the Aproj1 folder,

1 Click on the Aproj1 folder in the All Folders pane.

2 Click on the Memos folder in the Contents pane.

3   Press Delete and answer Yes to the dialog box query "Are you sure you want to remove the folder 'Memos' and move all its contents to the Recycle Bin?"

4   Double-click on the Recycle Bin icon on the desktop to verify that the file ToStaff.txt has been placed there as is shown in Figure A-14.

Now you can erase the file permanently or restore the file and folder to their original location. To do so, click on the file, ToStaff.txt. Then open the File menu and make your selection. Then close the Recycle Bin.

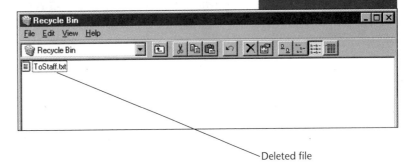

Figure A-14
Recycle Bin window

Deleted file

WORKING WITH FILES

You move, copy, rename, and delete files in much the same way that you do with folders. But first you must create a file, and you do that with application programs.

Running an Application

Running a program from Windows 95 is easy. To experiment, you will work with Notepad, a small program provided with Windows 95 that allows you to create and edit unformatted text. Program code is unformatted text similar to what you will enter here, and Notepad's editing commands are similar to those you will use when you are entering or editing text in Visual Basic.

To start Notepad,

1   Click on the taskbar's Start button.

2   Click on Programs then Accessories from the submenu.

3   Click on Notepad.

The Notepad window opens as shown in Figure A-15.

The Notepad window has title, menu, and status bars, like the other windows you

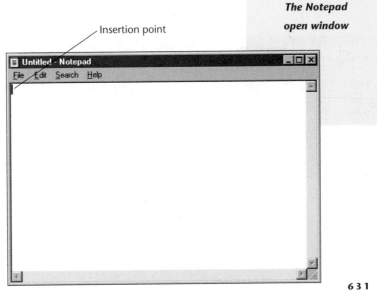

Figure A-15
The Notepad
open window

Insertion point

have seen, but because it is such a small program it does not provide the toolbar feature.

NAVIGATING IN A TEXT FILE

The insertion point (blinking vertical line) in the document window shows where the next text you type will appear.

1 Enter the following paragraph.

```
    The Notepad is a simple text editor. One major dif-
ference between a text editor and word processor is "word
wrap." In a word processor, when the typist reaches the
end of a line, the words automatically appear on the next
line. To switch to the next line in a text editor, the
Enter key must be pressed.
```

2 Select Word Wrap from the Edit menu and observe what happens.

Editing text works exactly the same as it does with Notepad in Windows 3.1. So if you need to review how to do it, follow the directions on pages 20–23 down to the heading "Saving a File." Then return here to finish. The Clipboard in Windows 95 is viewed by selecting the Start button, then Accessories, then Clipboard Viewer.

SAVING A FILE

To keep the text you have typed in the Notepad window, you must save it as a file. To save the information,

1 Select Save As from the File menu.

The Save As dialog box opens, as shown in Figure A-16.

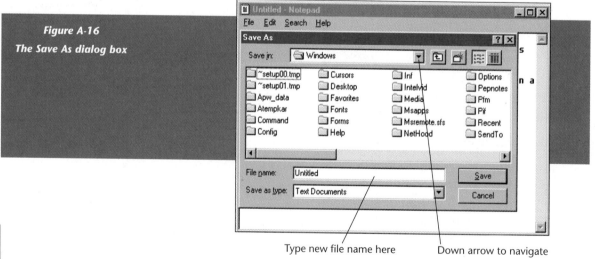

Figure A-16
The Save As dialog box

Type new file name here   Down arrow to navigate

2   Navigate to the Aproj1 folder by clicking the Save in: down arrow and scrolling up or down until you find it. Then double-click on Aproj1.

3   Double-click in the File name: text box and type the name **Sample**, then press Save.

MOVING, COPYING, RENAMING, AND DELETING A FILE

Open Windows Explorer again and experiment with moving, copying, renaming, and deleting the Sample file you just created. Follow the same instructions as you used for folders.

Move file	Drag file to a new folder
Copy file	Hold Ctrl and drag file to a new folder
Rename file	Click on file and select File, Rename, and type the new name
Delete file	Click and press Delete

QUESTIONS

1. Describe how you switch between programs that are running.

2. What is the tool that Windows 95 provides for managing files? What are its various parts and their uses?

3. Describe the purpose of the Minimize, Maximize, and Close buttons on the window's Title bar.

4. How do you make a new folder, and how do you move, copy, rename, and delete folders and files?

5. Describe how to resize and move windows on the desktop.

Section

Types of Storage Media and Storage Methods

Two main technologies are used to store data today: magnetic and optical storage. The primary types of magnetic storage are floppy disks, hard disks, magnetic tape, and cartridge drives. The primary types of optical storage are CD-ROM and CD-ROM Recordable. In this section, we will review these major types of storage and their uses.

Magnetic Disks-Floppy Drives

Most microcomputers of the early 1970s stored programs and data on tapes in cassette tape recorders. Every computer had one, and the circuitry to transform the 0s and 1s of computer data into sounds suitable for recording was simple and inexpensive.

Unfortunately, loading and storing information took a long time, and was prone to failure. Those who could afford it added a floppy drive to their systems. A floppy disk, the storage media of a floppy drive, is a plastic disk coated with the same magnetically sensitive material found on a cassette tape. Data is stored by aligning magnetic fields on the material in different directions. One direction represents 1s, and the other direction, 0s.

Disks are more efficient than tapes because they are direct-access devices. That is, the computer can directly access any part of the disk immediately to read or write information, rather than having to run past previous material (see Tape Drives below) before arriving at the desired information. Disks store information in a set of concentric ring patterns, called tracks, which are divided like pie wedges into sectors. As the disk spins in the drive, the drive's read/write head can move directly to any sector to read or write data.

The standard floppy drive today is 3.5" in diameter and holds 1.44 megabytes (MB) of data or programs. It still uses the same magnetic principles of data storage used by the first floppy drives. Now, virtually every computer comes with one of these drives.

Hard Drives

In addition to the floppy drive, every computer sold today comes with a hard drive. A hard drive uses a rigid magnetic disk to store data and programs in the same way that a floppy disk does, with concentric tracks divided into sectors. A rigid disk can store much more data than a floppy disk can because its magnetic material is much denser.

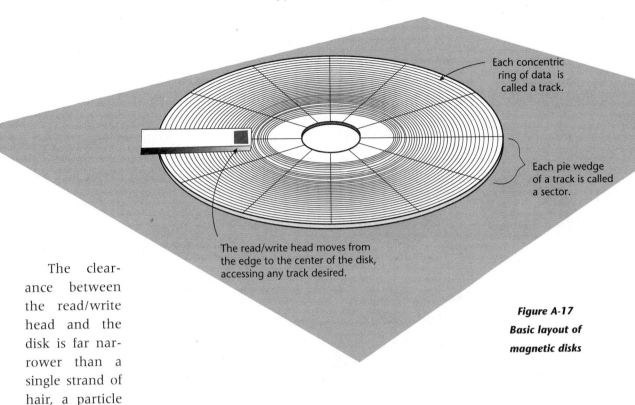

Each concentric ring of data is called a track.

Each pie wedge of a track is called a sector.

The read/write head moves from the edge to the center of the disk, accessing any track desired.

Figure A-17
Basic layout of
magnetic disks

The clearance between the read/write head and the disk is far narrower than a single strand of hair, a particle of dust, or even a fingerprint. Hard drives are assembled in rooms far cleaner than hospital operating rooms. If it was exposed to a normal atmosphere, the disk assembly would be contaminated with dust and other air particles.

Today, typical hard drives hold 1 to 4 gigabytes (GB) of programs and data. A drive of this size could store all the information contained in a set of encyclopedias, including text, pictures, and sounds, several times over.

Cartridge Drives

Cartridge drives attempt to combine the speed and capacity of a hard disk with the portability of a floppy disk. There are many different types of devices in this category. Currently, the most common are SyQuest and Zip drives. Most work similarly to a floppy disk, with a disk in a plastic case that is inserted into and removed from the drive. Typical storage capacities range all the way from 44 MB to 1 GB of data.

Tape Drives

Tape was one of the first widely used media for mass storage. The media itself is a long strip of plastic coated with magnetic material, so the tape drive has to write data on it sequentially—one character after another.

This means that when you want to access a specific set of information on a tape, the drive has to scan through all the data from the beginning of the tape to reach the data you need. Needless to say, this is a much slower process than direct access provided by media such as disks. Despite the longer access times, however, tape drives are well suited for certain purposes, especially for backing up your system's entire hard disk.

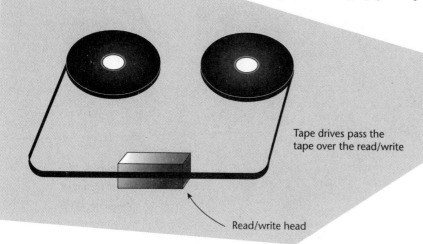

Figure A-18

Basic layout of magnetic tapes

Tape drives pass the tape over the read/write

Read/write head

Today, most tapes are housed in cassettes that contain two reels for transporting the tape, and look similar to an audio cassette. The tapes come in various sizes and capacities ranging from 40 MB to 40 GB. There are three common formats used in tape drives for personal computers: quarter-inch cartridge (QIC), which uses tape one-quarter-inch wide and stores anywhere from 40 MB to 8 GB, depending on the cartridge; 8mm digital audio tape (DAT), which stores anywhere from 1 GB to 8 GB; and half-inch digital linear tape (DLT), which stores up to 40 GB.

Optical Disks–CD-ROM

CD stands for compact disk. ROM stands for read-only memory. Today, a CD-ROM is a common piece of computer equipment. It holds a great deal of data (650 MB) and the storage media, the disk, is removable, portable, and inexpensive.

Like your compact disk player, a CD-ROM uses a laser to read the data from a CD. Data is recorded as a series of 0s and 1s by burning pits into the reflective surface of the disk. The data is stored in a long spiral, as on a vinyl record, in a series of pits (nonreflective spots) and lands (reflective spots). When the laser shines on a pit, the light is scattered. When the laser shines on the land, the light is reflected to a sensor. The pattern of pits and lands thus makes a flashing pattern of reflected laser light that duplicates the pattern of 1s and 0s in the original data.

CD-ROMs can store music, pictures, videos, and text. Once a master is made, copies can be manufactured for about one dollar each. This large storage capacity and low duplication cost, makes the CD-ROM an excellent choice for distributing programs and data. An additional advantage is that the disks last a very long time, with minimal care, making it easy to restore programs if needed. Today, therefore, many computers come with software on CD-ROM.

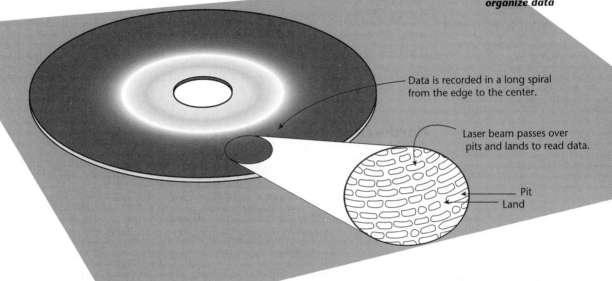

Figure A-19

How CD-ROMs organize data

Data is recorded in a long spiral from the edge to the center.

Laser beam passes over pits and lands to read data.

Pit
Land

CD-ROM Recordable (CD-ROM-R) is a newer technology that allows users to create their own CDs. This is a dream come true for users who need to *archive* (store for long-term access) large amounts of data. For example, NASA uses CD-ROM-R to store images and data from space missions. CD-ROM-R uses a laser to burn away a dye on the surface of the disk, revealing a reflective layer of gold beneath the dye. CD-ROM-R disks can be read in any CD-ROM drive.

QUESTIONS

1. Describe how a removable hard disk offers the benefits of both diskettes and hard disks.

2. Describe the functions of lands and pits on the surface of a CD-ROM.

3. Name and describe briefly the two main storage technologies in use today.

4. For what purpose would you choose to use a magnetic tape and why?

5. What is the biggest advantage of the CD-ROM over other storage devices?

3

Section

Proper Care of Hardware and Software

Although prices of computers have gone down significantly, they are still a sizable investment. Just like your automobile or any other sizable investment, computers need proper maintenance and care. In this section we will investigate the main concerns of hardware and software maintenance.

Hardware Concerns—Heat

Is it true that you can pop microwavable popcorn on a Pentium processor? Probably not, but don't touch a microchip while the computer is on—it's hot enough to hurt.

Heat is the enemy of electronic circuits. When a circuit gets hot, it runs slower or stops running altogether. As processors have become larger and faster, heat has become an increasing problem in personal computers. To make processors faster, their components are made smaller and smaller, and they are placed closer together. Since all the components give off heat, and since there are more of them packed closer together, the more powerful microprocessors become, the more heat they generate.

Heat is removed from computers with air vents, fans, and heat sinks that dissipate heat by exposing it to a lot of air. Since the movement of air to remove heat is so important, never install a computer where it cannot "breathe," and make sure the air vents in the case are free of obstruction and clean.

You may need to add a fan (or a second fan) to your computer. Fans that fit directly on the processor are available, as are fans that are built into a board that you insert into an expansion slot.

Hardware Concerns—Dust

Excess heat can be caused by too much dust in a computer. Computers run on and on, sometimes for years. All that time, fans are moving air through the case. Along with all that air comes a lot of dust. It packs in around the components of circuit boards like a blanket, making it impossible for excess heat to dissipate.

Dust also damages the electrical contacts that make a keyboard work. Keyboards are also susceptible to damage from hair or spilled drinks.

The preventive maintenance for these types of problems is to vacuum the inside and outside of your computer periodically. Pay special

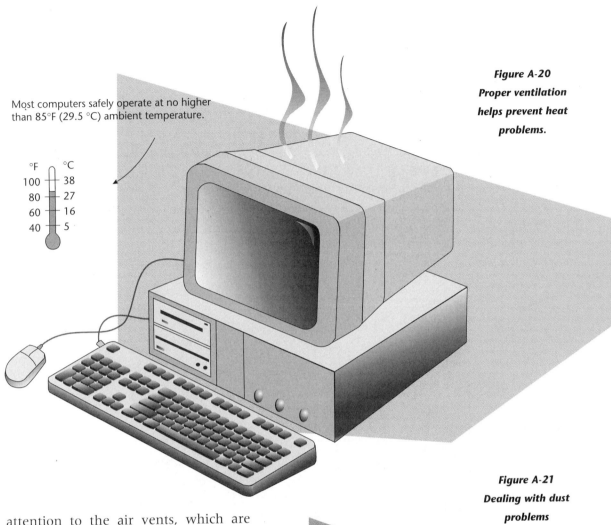

Most computers safely operate at no higher
than 85°F (29.5 °C) ambient temperature.

°F		°C
100		38
80		27
60		16
40		5

Figure A-20
Proper ventilation
helps prevent heat
problems.

Figure A-21
Dealing with dust
problems

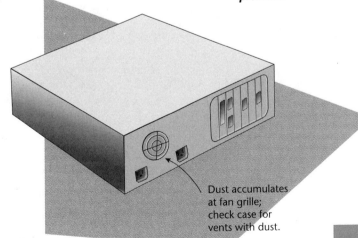

Dust accumulates
at fan grille;
check case for
vents with dust.

attention to the air vents, which are
often clogged with dust. Your computer
store can sell you a vacuum designed for
computers, but a normal vacuum with a
dusting attachment works fine. Be very
careful when vacuuming around components; any impact can damage the circuits. If you're at all unsure of how to
vacuum it, or if your computer's war-
ranty would be voided by opening the
case, bring your computer to a service
center to have the inside cleaned.

Hardware Concerns—Voltage

Voltage spikes, where the line voltage coming into your house jumps to several hundred volts, are real and happen often enough to be a serious concern. When lightning hits a transformer on a telephone pole, a momentary surge of power can come into your house, and can destroy unprotected equipment. A good precaution is to unplug electronic equipment during electrical storms and when you go away on a vacation.

Protecting your computer from a voltage surge is easy. Just buy a surge protector from a hardware or computer store, and plug your computer into it. Although surge protectors look like normal power strips or plugs, they have circuitry built into them that breaks the circuit if a surge comes down the line. Some surge protectors burn out on the first spike, however; so if yours is that type, you'll need to replace it. Circuit-breaker types work better and don't need replacing.

Figure A-22
A surge protector protects your computer from voltage spikes.

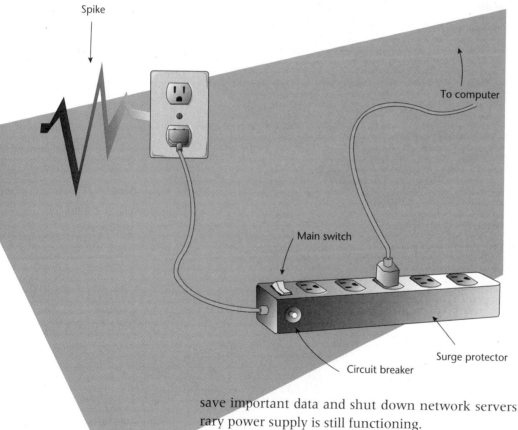

An Uninterruptable Power Supply (UPS) protects a computer from voltage surges and voltage drops. Additionally, it can provide temporary power if the main power supply goes out. Because network servers that are shut down unexpectedly can lose important data, many network installations are protected with a UPS. Some UPSs automatically save important data and shut down network servers while the temporary power supply is still functioning.

Hardware Concerns—Physical Damage

Since an ordinary pencil stuck into a drive might cost you $100 to fix, your computer should be protected from children, animals, and yourself. For example, don't balance your computer on a makeshift table or on the very edge of a desk. Most computers probably wouldn't survive a three-foot drop.

A laptop is not a briefcase, so don't toss it in the back seat of a car or under a chair. These types of jolts can cause mechanical parts to be knocked out of alignment or circuits to break.

For the same reason, computers should not be transported upside down or subjected to sharp bumps. Both boards and chips can be knocked loose from their connections.

Here are a few other practical precautions: don't roll your mouse through crumbs or liquids, keep your screen clean, and place the power cord where no one can trip over it.

Because loose connections are so commonplace, if something isn't working, the first thing to do is to check the connections. Check cable connections, and check to see that add-on boards are properly seated in their slots. Don't force anything, however, and don't run your computer with the cover off.

Protecting Software

Do you like to sharpen pencils with an electric pencil sharpener? Pencil sharpeners are likely to be found on or near desks. They have electric motors and like any electric motor, they work by creating a magnetic field. Magnetic fields can erase data on disks or tapes stored next to them.

For this reason, don't store your floppy disks where they might be exposed to a magnetic field. Besides pencil sharpeners, fans and speakers also produce magnetic fields. Speakers produced for computer use are shielded, but regular audio speakers can produce a magnetic field strong enough to damage data on disks. Television sets also generate strong magnetic fields.

Floppy disks, especially those containing your application software, should be stored in boxes away from any equipment that uses electricity or magnetism.

Backing up Software

"The dog ate my homework" has never been a believable excuse for not having finished homework. Far more likely today is: "My computer lost the file." Too many computer users assume that computer disasters happen only to others. In fact, all computer data is in peril.

Backing up your data is one important line of defense. "Backing up" means to make an additional copy of important files and store those copies in a safe place. Most computers have hundreds of megabytes of programs and files on a single hard drive. If the drive fails, all the data and programs may be lost.

You can use any file-copying utility to back up files. For example, just copying important data files to floppy disks and storing the disks in a safe place ensures you will not lose important work. Special backup utility programs, however, compress the data as it is being stored. Compression has the advantage of reducing the amount of disk space required to store the data. MS-DOS and Windows both have backup utility programs. More sophisticated backup programs also store the structure of files and folders on your disk and even the computer's system settings, allowing you to completely restore the state of the machine before the drive failed.

The best media to back up your data on are tape drives or cartridge drives. Tape drives are inexpensive and easy to use, but they are slow compared to hard drives. When making a backup, however, speed is usually not very important. The other good choice for backup is a cartridge drive. Depending on the type of cartridge drive you use, you can back up your entire hard disk quickly using a few cartridges or even only one. Trying to back up your hard drive to floppy disk, in contrast, is a test of patience and endurance. How many 1.44 MB floppies does it take to back up a 1.3 GB hard drive?

No matter what media you choose for backup, remember to check your results. One company made daily and weekly backups for years. When the data on their hard drive was accidentally lost, they didn't worry. But when they went to restore their system from tape, they found all the tapes were empty. They hadn't recorded a thing for all those years.

Hard Drive Maintenance

After some use, the files on a hard drive become fragmented. This means that one part of a file is in one location while another part of the file is in another place on the drive. This slows the computer down when you are saving or loading files, because it must constantly shift its position to read or write parts of the file.

Modern operating systems and third-party software vendors provide utilities for "defragmenting" your hard drive. Defragmentation analyzes the hard disk to find all the pieces of data files, then rearranges them so all the pieces of each file are stored together in sequence. This means the drive mechanism no longer has to skip around the surface of the disk to find all the pieces of a file and performance therefore improves. The MS-DOS program DEFRAG is a simple utility for optimizing your hard disk's performance. Norton Utilities' SpeedDisk is the best-known third-party utility.

QUESTIONS

1. List three preventive maintenance actions you should take to increase the life of your computer, and discuss why.

2. List three precautions you should take to safeguard your software, and discuss why.

3. Describe how defragmentation slows down your computer.

4. What solutions are available for defragmenting your hard drive, and how do they work?

Issues and Ethics

Section

The computer and data communications field offers opportunity, to be sure. But it also poses certain threats—piracy to software manufacturers, data security to businesses, and privacy to individuals. In this section we will look at the issues of computer crime, privacy, responsible use, etiquette and netiquette, and ergonomics.

Computer Crime

Computer security starts at home with keeping your machine and your data physically secure. Don't leave your laptop unattended, and don't leave data disks unsecured. It's a good idea at home or work to have your PC and all its major components secured with locks and/or security cables.

Everyone understands that stealing a computer is a crime, but not everyone understands that copying a program or data can also be a crime. There is a mindset prevalent among computer criminals that since the targets of their crimes are large institutions, such as corporations and the government, those institutions can absorb any damage; and that much of the theft does no real harm anyway. The fallacy of this kind of thinking is that large organizations are made up of individuals and they serve the needs of individuals. Breaking into and/or damaging a large organization's computers or stealing software often affects individuals, whether the computer criminal intends that or not. Following are some of the more common types of computer crime.

HACKERS

Computers are fascinating all by themselves, but when they are connected to other computers through a network or phone line, they become even more interesting. Just as some people will open a medicine cabinet or diary that they shouldn't, some want to see into every file, run every program, and explore every network. These people are called hackers.

The term *hacker* applies to a wide range of people. Those who talk of the "hacker ethic"—the principle of examining everything and damaging nothing—are fairly harmless. They like to pry into every corner of a system or network, and examine files and run programs. They try to penetrate networks and systems by bypassing security systems or stealing (or guessing) passwords.

The purpose of their activity is to satisfy curiosity and to prove their superiority to those who would deny them access. Hackers in this group seldom damage or delete programs or data, but they often leave calling cards that announce their penetration.

MALICIOUS MISCHIEF

Some hackers go one step farther. They don't talk much about the "hacker ethic," and they have little respect for others' property. If they penetrate your system, they won't hesitate to destroy data and erase files. One hacker of this type penetrated a company's computer and noticed that they backed up their files at the same time every month. He waited until just before the backup was due to be performed and then destroyed the company's data files. It took weeks for the company to rebuild its files from source documents.

These hackers often trick computer systems into giving them privileges they shouldn't have. Many systems welcome guests, but limit their access. Clever hackers can often find a way around the limitations and make themselves into "supervisors" or "superusers." This allows them to access every file on the computer. For example, they can authorize new accounts or destroy existing ones. This kind of hacker is a nightmare to system administrators.

HACKER CRIMINALS

There are those who call themselves hackers, but their real objective is to rip off the systems they penetrate. Many have specific objectives that they relentlessly pursue. Credit card numbers and phone access codes are favorite targets because they are easily converted into goods and services.

COMPUTER ESPIONAGE

One major purpose of computer networks is to give people access to information. For example, computer networks are indispensable to researchers who need to keep up with the latest work in their field, or who want to communicate with colleagues throughout the world. Because of easy access, computers from both universities and military installations attract hackers looking for classified or otherwise sensitive information. Furthermore, it's difficult to facilitate access to systems for researchers and to restrict access for hackers.

Corporate espionage is also conducted through computer networks. Also, companies that give employees access to information through the Internet or other networks potentially are also giving access to hackers or to corporate spies.

HOW SYSTEMS ARE PENETRATED

There are a variety of ways that security systems are defeated. Some people have a hard time remembering their passwords, so they write their password on the computer or on another easily accessible place on their desk. Some system administrators naively assign a user's first name as a password. Some err in the other direction by making a password a random series of characters. A random password is usually so hard to remember that the user almost always writes it down. Some users change their passwords to the names of their children or pets, and those passwords are usually easy to guess.

If it isn't that easy, hackers are frequently willing to work hard to find out the information that can help them penetrate a system. They may call an employer posing as someone who needs information about users, pass out questionnaires to users pretending to take a survey or do a study, or even go through a person's garbage to get the desired information.

Sometimes the computer system itself allows a hacker in. Many systems are built with a "back door," a secret way of accessing the system. These are similar to the "back doors" familiar to video game players: secret parts of the program that provide extra weapons or unlimited health to some of the characters in the game. Some systems have passwords used by field technicians for servicing the computer. Almost all systems come with predefined passwords for the system administrator, and some administrators never change these generic passwords. The system's operating system may even contain flaws that allow unauthorized users access. Even when the flaws are highly publicized and easily fixed, some systems are never updated.

VIRUSES

A virus that affects human health inserts its DNA into human cells and takes over the cells' biochemical production. Then the cells start producing virus cells that, in turn, infect more human cells. A computer virus is a program that infects a computer system. It enters the system in a number of different ways. The user can intentionally, but unwittingly, bring the virus program into his or her system, thinking it is something else. Viruses can masquerade as utility programs or get-rich-quick messages. Viruses can enter a system as e-mail or as part of a document template or spreadsheet, and viruses can send themselves to your computer through a network or over a modem connection.

Once the virus is active in your system, it will attempt to do one or more of the following:

1. It will let you know you are infected. It may print a message on your screen. Or the characters on the screen might start falling to the bottom of the screen like letters falling off a sign. One virus sends an ambulance across the bottom of the screen. Another fills the screen with bouncing balls. Viruses with these kinds of effects as their primary goal are fairly harmless, but they are certainly annoying because they must be cleaned from every disk.

2. A malicious virus will try to destroy your system software. One virus fills the hard drive with nonsense characters. Many viruses run the format program to clean everything off the hard drive. Some viruses damage the boot sector and keep the drive from booting when the computer is reset. Others just lock up your system.

3. Replication is another primary goal of most viruses. Most viruses try to infect as many disks and machines as possible. Some copy themselves to every disk when a disk access is performed. A network virus tries to send itself to network machines. One Internet virus once brought thousands of machines all over the country to a halt, because it sent itself through the network over and over until the network traffic slowed to a grinding halt.

No present-day cure can permanently solve the problem, because virus authors constantly become more inventive as they try to bring systems down and leave their mark on the world.

GETTING RID OF VIRUSES

Viruses are a serious problem because as many as 50 percent of all corporate computer users have become infected, and it costs thousands of dollars to clean viruses from company computers. Every system should be protected by an up-to-date antivirus program such as the one in Figure A-23, because as fast as creative vandals make new viruses, computer scientists create cures. A good antivirus company is constantly issuing new releases with the latest cures. For a licensed user, updates cost little or nothing. Some antivirus programs are available on the World Wide Web and can be downloaded on a trial basis.

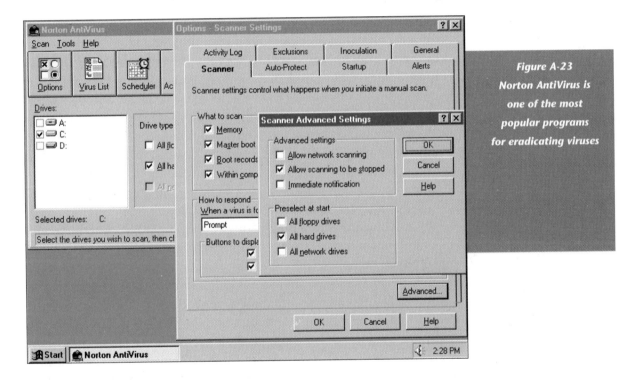

Figure A-23
Norton AntiVirus is one of the most popular programs for eradicating viruses

It's easy to download a virus without being aware of it, so your antivirus program should run automatically as part of your start up procedure. The program can be installed in the Autoexec.bat file to run whenever the computer is turned on. Unfortunately, there is a price to pay for this protection. The time it takes to check your memory and files is relatively brief, but it is annoying. This causes many to turn off virus protection with predictable results—infection.

SOFTWARE PIRACY

In 1995, in China alone, it is estimated that one to two billion dollars was lost to software piracy. Software piracy is stealing programs. Sometimes it involves direct copying of software, right down to the manuals and the packaging box. Other times, programs are reversed engineered; their code is reconstituted like frozen orange juice from executable files. Either way, software piracy costs billions of dollars a year. On a smaller scale, people make illegal copies of programs and share them with friends or post them on bulletin boards. Some companies and even schools (both of whom should know better) depend on cloning illegal copies of software to reduce their software costs.

One way to eliminate piracy is to make it impossible to copy a program. Schemes to make disks uncopyable proliferated in the 1980s, but there was great hue and cry throughout the computing community because users couldn't make legitimate backups of their software.

Some programs require a dongle to run. This is an uncopyable (in theory) hardware device that plugs into the computer's parallel port or keyboard port. The dongle has a corresponding port so you can attach your printer or keyboard to the computer through it. It contains a code the program needs to run. Without the dongle the program won't run.

Some companies hoped users would buy legitimate copies of programs just to get the manuals. Online help systems, however, have gone a long way toward eliminating manuals. And, if you want written documentation, you can always go to the bookstore and buy a book about the product.

It appears there is no fail-safe way for a software company to protect its product, so companies are largely dependent on users making the ethical and morally correct decisions. Software companies do, however, vigorously pursue other companies (largely offshore) that clone software and sell it in place of the real thing. They also prosecute blatant cases of program copying in businesses and schools. Bulletin boards that specialize in pirated programs are shut down and machines are often confiscated.

The only solution is to choose to pay for the programs you use. With legal copies, you get manuals, updates, and the right to purchase technical support.

Privacy

We have a right to privacy. Right?

That all depends on what you mean.

Well, at least my e-mail and documents are private, aren't they?

In many businesses, e-mail and documents are not private. If your documents are stored on the corporate system's network servers, the corporation may feel they have the right to examine them. In some states, telephone conversations are also subject to monitoring.

Cell phones and computers that communicate with cellular modems are not secure. For very little money, a cellular scanner can be purchased or built. This allows the user to monitor cellular phone calls. Security codes, passwords, credit card numbers—anything transferred with a cellular phone or modem is potentially accessible.

Information on computer networks may be accessible to people outside the network. If the network has an Internet connection, your data is vulnerable to anyone who can penetrate the system's firewall—a software program that is supposed to keep outsiders out of your system. Unfortunately, even the best firewalls can be breached.

Sometimes, it is the users themselves who break security. A user might establish an Internet connection that bypasses network security, or unwittingly download a browser plug-in that transmits sensitive data outside the network.

As information bounces through the Internet from computer to computer, it can be intercepted and read by anyone who tries hard enough. So, as you can see, whether or not we have a right to privacy, there is no (or very little) privacy on the Internet or in corporate computers.

ENCRYPTION

One way to ensure some privacy is to encrypt your data. Pretty Good Privacy (PGP) is a program available on the Internet that encodes data so it cannot be read except by those who have the key. Many other encryption programs are available but as this is written, none are built into any Web browser.

COMPUTER RECORDS

Your name and information about you and your family are on dozens of lists, and some of these lists are for sale. Some are meant to be secure, but, as we have seen, they are not. Computers that provide credit data to companies doing credit checks on customers are on-line. That means they are vulnerable to attack.

There's no good way to ensure that personal information about you and your family will not be available to someone who really wants to access it.

Responsible Use

It may be hard to resist looking at someone's files, or reading someone's e-mail, but it just isn't right to do it. Every human being has a right to be treated with dignity and respect, in cyberspace and out. Everyone should be treated the way you would wish to be treated. This means respecting other people's privacy.

Even without having to make an effort to defeat security measures, information on many systems is accessible. Those who use computers depend on other users to make ethical decisions, good decisions about what's right and what's wrong.

It may seem fun and harmless to read someone else's files, but it can potentially put both of you in a difficult situation. Even if reading someone's files is merely sport, you still need to choose not to do it.

COMPANY TIME

Solitaire on the company computer? Is it OK to play games while you're being paid for your time? It's easy to rationalize. One person spends 20 minutes reading the newspaper, why shouldn't you spend a few minutes playing a computer game? You may need to use the Internet daily to keep current in your field or to communicate with a colleague; why not spend some time doing some recreational cruising? Doesn't the company expect it?

Even if the company does turn a blind eye to occasional recreational use of its computers, it does steal time and resources from the company, and your time is worth something to the firm. You are paid to provide a service, not to cruise the Web. In addition, cruising the Web can be addictive. You may find yourself spending more and more time doing it, so your productivity suffers.

There's no question that it's wrong to bring home 100 plastic bags from the janitor's closet to use in your garbage cans at home, so why is it any different to download your employer's software to use at home? If you work at home, your employer should provide you with a legal copy of the software for home use. Or you should know up front that acquiring a legal copy of a particular piece of software is a job requirement. You should not download software from a company computer to use at home.

Etiquette and Netiquette

Networks are for communication. Often the communication is from file to human, or human to file. Sometimes the communication is from human to human. Whenever communication is from human to human, questions of etiquette come into focus. Etiquette is how you treat other people. It is concerned with courtesy.

USENET

One part of the Internet is the Usenet. It is thousands of bulletin boards, called *newsgroups*, where users post and read notes. Each newsgroup has a topic, and notes are posted pertaining to each topic.

Before a user posts a note, however, he or she is expected to do some *lurking*. Lurking is reading without posting. Lurking helps ensure that when you do post, your posting will not incur the wrath of the readers of that newsgroup. By reading some of the typical postings, you can get a sense of what kind of information is expected to be posted.

One of the first things a user should read is the FAQ file. *FAQ* stands for frequently asked questions. Most well-run newsgroups have a FAQ regularly posted. With thousands of readers, the same questions occur frequently, so the frequently asked questions are collected in FAQ files. New users are supposed to read these files before they post. You can search the newsgroup with your browser's news reader to find the FAQ and read it.

If a posted message is perceived as stupid or frivolous, the user may be *flamed* and possibly *spammed* if the offense is seen as particularly gross. Flaming is sending angry or abusive e-mail. Spamming is arranging for dozens or even hundreds of messages to be e-mailed to a user just so they have to spend time deleting or reading them.

CHAT ROOMS AND ANONYMITY

Chat rooms are where people gather electronically to exchange talk in *real time*. Real time means the messages are not posted to be read later, but are sent to everyone in the chat room as they are entered. Your identity is shielded by using a *handle*, which is the name you go by but is not necessarily your name. If you see pdp1134, the name of an old Digital minicomputer, in a chat room, it is probably me. But, you probably won't see me; I find most chat rooms pretty boring.

Anonymity does give a user a chance to break every rule of etiquette. Some chat rooms are monitored but for the most part anything goes. Far more disturbing is the hatred and racism that swirls through the Usenet. Under the protection of free speech and the cloak of anonymity, people get away with saying appalling things. The Internet is about the free exchange of ideas. Some things, though, should not be said.

ADVERTISING

When the Internet was funded by grants from the National Science Foundation, there were rules against advertising. Today the Net is expected to pay its own way in the world. Advertising has become an unavoidable part of the Net.

Some Net companies give free services in exchange for sending advertising. More than one place will let you set up an e-mail account just as long as you let them send you their advertising.

Some companies foolishly offend Internet users by sending bulk e-mail—advertising that is not directed to interested customers, but to everyone. These companies should know that such practices just incite anger. A much better way to advertise on the Net is to make information available only to those who are interested in receiving it. Classified ads and job ads are collected in a number of places. People looking for work, or to find a worker, can visit Internet sites dedicated to helping employers get together with prospective employees.

Ergonomics

Ergonomics is the study of the "fit" between people and machines. For us, it is specifically concerned with the comfort and health of computer users.

HEALTH ISSUES

One controversial issue is that of electromagnetic radiation, EMF. The monitor of your desktop computer works by spraying electrons at a phosphor-coated piece of glass. Unfortunately, your monitor may not be doing a very good job of screening that radiation from your body.

Studies in Europe have shown the increased incidence of certain diseases that could result from EMF. Not all accept these findings. Still, it cannot be a bad idea to limit the amount of radiation to which you are subjected. If you sit in front of a monitor for eight or more hours a day, you want to err on the conservative side.

Repetitive stress injuries are another issue. Repetitive stress injuries occur in workers, athletes, and anyone else who repeats the same action over and over again with little variation. Some repetitive stress injuries are quite debilitating. Preventing these injuries depends on arranging your work environment to reduce the stress as shown in Figure A-24. The kinds of things to address are: height of the desk, height and angle of the viewing screen, the keyboard, the chair in which you sit.

Carpal tunnel syndrome affects the nerves where they pass through a tunnel in your wrist. If you hold your hand cocked at an angle to type, these nerves can become irritated. At first you experience numbness, then pain radiating up through the arm. Eventually, the numbness does not go away, because the nerves become permanently damaged.

To fix the problem, you must deal with the cause. That means changing your position or your work routine. Ergonomic keyboards

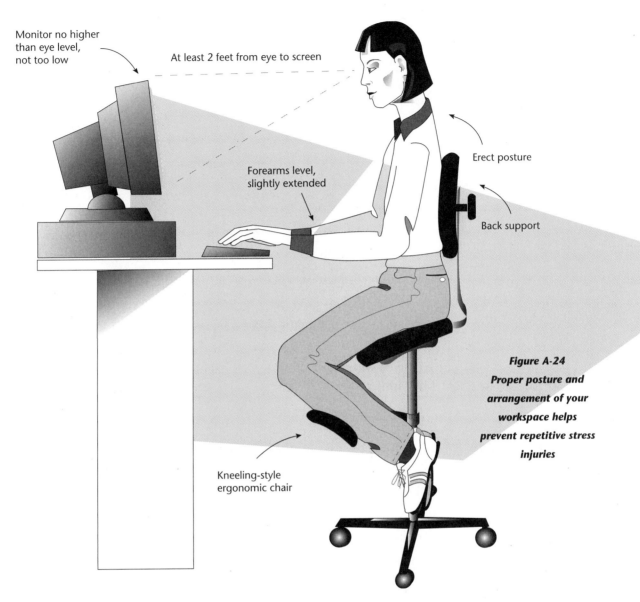

Monitor no higher than eye level, not too low

At least 2 feet from eye to screen

Forearms level, slightly extended

Erect posture

Back support

Figure A-24
Proper posture and arrangement of your workspace helps prevent repetitive stress injuries

Kneeling-style ergonomic chair

with keys at a more comfortable and logical angle are available. Workstation desks can be adjusted so the heights and angles of keyboards and monitors are optimized. Proper posture and a good chair may be more important than all the rest.

NOTEBOOK ERGONOMICS

The whole idea of a notebook computer is its portability. In the early days of computing, a "portable" computer was one designed to be carried from place to place. They usually had full-sized keyboards, small, hard-to-read monitors, and weighed 20 or more pounds. The only bright spot in this picture was the full-sized keyboards.

Modern laptop computers are lighter and have better displays, but a number of other ergonomic concerns are still relevant. Today, computing is largely mouse-dependent. Laptop manufacturers have tried a number of different mouse substitutes. Track-balls, tiny joysticks, and touchpads have all been used with varying degrees of success.

The smallness of the computer necessitated a smaller keyboard, which was a disaster for many. IBM's butterfly keyboard, which opens into a full sized keyboard, is one solution.

A more fundamental problem is inherent in the very nature of the laptop—some find it impossible to type on a machine sitting in one's lap.

QUESTIONS

1. What should you do to protect your computer from getting a virus?

2. What do companies do to protect their information from theft or misuse?

3. Write a short statement about what you think about copying software illegally.

4. Discuss with others your feelings about the privacy of your computer files.

5. Plan a proper workstation for your new computer.

Summary

With a graphical user interface such as Windows 95, you communicate with the computer using the mouse pointer to either click on icons, or make selections from menus. Almost all the work you do is in windows, either program windows or document windows, and with modern-day systems more than one window or program can be open at the same time, but only one can be active at one time. You can move, size, minimize, maximize, close, or switch between windows with the click of a mouse.

Information is the computer's most important product. As you use programs to do your work, you create information that needs to be saved and managed so you can find it when you need it. For example, you create documents with word processing programs and you create programs with Visual Basic, and most likely you will use them again and again. Windows 95 provides a tool, the Windows Explorer, for you to use to view and manage this information.

Using the Windows Explorer, you can create, move, copy, rename, and delete folders for organizing your files, and you can move, copy, rename, and delete files.

Two main technologies are used to store data today: magnetic and optical storage. The primary types of magnetic storage are floppy disks, hard disks, magnetic tape, and cartridge drives. The primary types of optical storage are CD-ROM and CD-ROM Recordable.

Today, almost all computers come with floppy disk drives and hard disk drives. Both of these organize information in concentric circles making it quick and easy to retrieve any of the data. The hard disk is used to store your programs and files. The floppy disk is removable, so it is used to transport information from one computer to another. The floppy disk's capacity, however, is small, only 1.4 MB. For this reason the greater capacity cartridge drives, Syquest and Zip drives, are very popular.

Tape drives store information in a sequential manner, so they are slower to retrieve information at the end of a tape. For this reason they are mostly used for backup purposes.

CD-ROMs organize information in a long spiral from the edge to the center, and laser beams read the data. CD-ROMs have longer shelf life and are inexpensive to duplicate in large quantities; therefore, they are very popular with software manufacturers for distributing their software.

Just like your automobile or any other sizable investment, computers need proper maintenance and care. Besides physical damage, dangers to your hardware are heat, dust, and voltage spikes. So, provide proper ventilation, keep your computer clean, and plug your computer into a surge protector.

Backing up your programs and data is an important defense against losing your software and data if your computer experiences a power outage.

Along with the benefits computers provide to society, they also pose certain threats—piracy to software manufacturers, data security to businesses, and privacy to the individual.

Computer crime ranges from malicious mischief to computer espionage and theft. A computer virus is a program that infects a computer system. A virus can also range from being just a nuisance to completely erasing all the data from your hard drive. Every system should be protected by an up-to-date antivirus program.

Information on computer networks—intranet and Internet—may not be very secure, and there is no good way to ensure its privacy. Those who use computers depend on other users to make ethical, good decisions about what is right and what is wrong.

Repetitive stress injuries occur in workers and others who repeat the same action over and over again. Preventing these injuries depends on arranging your work environment to reduce the stress. Your monitor should be no higher than eye level, you should sit at least two feet from the screen, you should sit erect with proper back support, and your forearms should be level and slightly extended.

Index